Corporate Strategy for Irish Companies

3rd Edition

Gerry Gallagher

CHARTERED
ACCOUNTANTS
IRELAND

Published by
Chartered Accountants Ireland
Chartered Accountants House
47–49 Pearse Street
Dublin 2
www.charteredaccountants.ie

ISBN: 978-1-912350-32-2

Typeset by Compuscript
Printed and bound by CPI Group (UK) Ltd, Croydon, CR0 4YY

To
Fiona, Cormac and Ciara

Education is not the filling of a pail, but the lighting of a fire.

William Butler Yeats.

Table of Contents

Chapter

Chapter

Chapter

Part Two: Strategic Analysis

Chapter

Chapter

Chapter

Chapter

Chapter

Chapter

Chapter

Lists of Illustrations, Figures and Tables

Illustrations

Figures

Tables

Introduction

The 1st and 2nd editions of this textbook were published during the worst recession the Irish economy had suffered in many decades. The enormous prosperity enjoyed by so many Irish people in the late 1990s and the early part of this century vanished like early morning mist being burned off by the summer sun. It was the result of so many factors, from greed to hubris. It was, above all, a failure of leadership.

It is, however, very easy to focus on the negative news and information that often flows from the media. While the recession had a devastating impact on so many Irish companies, it is important to recognise that there are also good-news stories for both existing companies and start-ups. Despite the difficulties, many Irish companies are succeeding. In any discussion about the economy or the recession it must be remembered that there is no such entity as "Ireland Inc." There is the Irish State, of which the economy plays a central part, along with the institutions of State, and most importantly, its people. As a nation, we have no choice but to galvanise all our resources into continuing to rebuild the country. We must also learn from experience to ensure such a debacle never happens again.

Revision

This 3rd edition of *Corporate Strategy for Irish Companies* covers the entire spectrum of managing organisations at a strategic level. The 3rd edition has been updated to reflect recent developments in Ireland, and around the world, and the entire textbook has also been extensively revised. In particular, the chapter on leadership and corporate culture has been considerably expanded. The 3rd edition also contains a selection of detailed case studies (more case studies are also available online). The beginning of each case briefly summarises the main topics covered. These cases will help the reader develop their understanding of the various elements of strategy outlined and will also develop critical thinking skills.

This textbook is divided into four distinct parts. Part One lays the foundation for strategy within the organisation. Given all that has happened in Ireland over the last decade, this part must be seen as a vital element of the process of developing strategy in organisations. When things go wrong, the implications for all stakeholders are far too great. The social cost to this country as a result of the recession has been enormous.

Parts Two, Three and Four then explain the strategic process that is required in formulating and implementing strategy: analysing the business environment and the internal capability of the organisation; examining different strategic options; picking the optimum course of action; and finally, implementing the chosen strategy and dealing with changing circumstances.

Though the book is divided into four parts, it must be remembered that these parts are not separate entities – they are all interlinked. The Introduction to each part provides an overall perspective on the chapters within that part. The textbook is aimed primarily at students preparing for exams. It will also be useful for those working in business who wish to develop a more strategic approach to running their company.

An Irish Textbook

While there are numerous textbooks on strategy available, this textbook presents the concepts of corporate strategy in an Irish context. There are many examples included to illustrate the theory being discussed. Some of these examples are developed in greater detail and presented in separate illustration boxes. The examples cover large multinational companies that operate on a global basis, and also focus attention on the Irish economy and Irish companies. In some cases, such as with Kerry Group Plc, the 'local' example is also a 'global' one. Such examples are important as they reflect what is happening in the business world in Ireland and demonstrate that strategic management is not an abstract science but is directly relevant to every manager. By reflecting on these examples, it is hoped that the reader will appreciate the importance of corporate strategy in successfully guiding an organisation within a competitive environment. The case studies provided at the end of the book, and also as extra online resources, will provide a greater opportunity for the student to understand the theoretical concepts explored in the textbook.

While there are differences in meaning between terms such as 'organisation', 'company', 'corporation' and 'firm', for the purpose of this book, the terms are used interchangeably.

Research

The material contained in this 3rd edition comes from an extensive literature review of what leading international experts say about different aspects of corporate strategy. This review has been extensively updated. Some of the studies referred to have taken teams of researchers years to gather and interpret the relevant data. Such research provides valuable insights into corporate strategy. There are perhaps thousands of books and journal articles covering strategy in general, as well as more specific areas of research. The research referred to in this book is intended to give the reader the breadth and depth required to equip them with good, rounded knowledge of the subject matter. It is brought together in a comprehensive way and applied in a critical analysis to the business environment in Ireland.

Referencing

In discussing the academic literature in this area, the original source of material is given and is referenced using the Harvard system. This gives the author's name, the date of publication and, where a specific page is referenced, this is also included after the date. The full reference to the book, journal article or other source can then be found in the References section at the end of the textbook. This will allow readers to develop their knowledge in greater detail if desired or required. In many cases, additional recommended reading on the subject matter is provided.

There are numerous quotes throughout the book that are drawn from English literature and many other different disciplines. These are intended to demystify corporate strategy and help the reader to realise that underpinning the subject is a lot of common sense, and that we can draw inspiration from all around us. William Shakespeare, in particular, demonstrated remarkable insight into human behaviour, especially in his commentary on different types of leadership. It will be seen throughout the textbook that people play a central role in the success of organisations. While many aspects of leadership and management have evolved over time, there are many other aspects that are immutable and are the same today as they were 400 years ago when Shakespeare was writing his plays.

Principles of Strategic Management

Regrettably, some of the Irish companies mentioned in the 2nd edition have now ceased trading – casualties of the very difficult times that we have been through. There remain enormous challenges ahead, and, unfortunately, there will be many more companies that go out of business over the next few years. Such is the nature of business, which only serves to highlight the importance of good governance and strategy.

Gandhi once said: "It's not that Christianity has failed; it's just that it has never been tried." While the examples themselves may lose their significance, the principles and theories outlined in this textbook remain valid despite the turmoil and, indeed, will assume even greater importance. It is relatively easy to make profits in business during a boom period. In a recession, it is a lot more difficult. The challenge for those managing companies will be to step back from the day-to-day issues in their organisations and think strategically. In many situations, it is a case of getting back to the basics of strategy.

Each chapter begins by setting learning objectives, which are intended to assist the reader to focus on the material contained therein. For example, the learning objectives for Chapter 2 are as follows:

LEARNING OBJECTIVES

On completion of this chapter, you will be able to:

■ Distinguish between the different types of leadership
■ Evaluate the effectiveness of different leadership styles
■ Assess the relationship between leadership and corporate culture
■ Critically examine the role of leadership in the formulation and implementation of strategy

While the material is grouped into parts and chapters as much as possible, it should be remembered that there is a strong link between all the various elements running through the entire textbook. At the end of each chapter, there is a summary of the main points. Discussion questions are also provided, which are designed so that the reader can reflect on the material contained in that chapter.

Definitions

There are a number of definitions and terms that are used throughout this book. These are standard terms used in the world of strategic management. They are defined and explained the first time they appear in the textbook and are highlighted for the reader, as in the following example:

 Corporate strategy is charting the future direction of a company by developing long-term goals that reflect stakeholders' interests and achieve sustainable competitive advantage.

A glossary of these terms is also included at the end of the textbook to facilitate understanding.

Acknowledgements

Once again, I am deeply indebted to a great number of people who have helped in the writing of the third edition of this textbook.

To Michael Diviney and the team at Chartered Accountants Ireland for all your help and support and for making this, and the previous editions, a success.

To the Band of Brothers – a big note of thanks to all my former Army colleagues who have helped both directly and indirectly, and most of all for the tremendous friendship over the last forty years.

To my colleagues in the Institute of Technology, Tralee, and in particular to my colleagues in the Department of Business. A special word of thanks is due to all the library staff, who assisted in the search for books and journal articles.

To the numerous people in the various organisations who provided information and advice. In particular, I would like to thank all those who contributed directly and indirectly to the writing of the case studies and chapter examples.

Finally, I would like to thank Fiona, Cormac and Ciara for all their support throughout the process. Writing a textbook such as this demands endless hours of work, and it would not have been possible without such support.

Tralee, August 2019

Understanding Strategy

LEARNING OBJECTIVES

On completion of this chapter, you will be able to:

- ■ Evaluate corporate strategy and its various elements
- ■ Distinguish between the different levels of corporate strategy
- ■ Critically examine the four core areas of corporate strategy
- ■ Analyse the various ways in which strategy is developed

INTRODUCTION

'Strategy' is a term used to describe the actions of a company. In essence, it is about the long-term direction of an organisation. It takes into account its vision and mission, its interaction with the world around it; it looks at the company's current situation, deciding where it needs to go from its present position, and how it is going to get there. Ultimately, the chosen strategy should result in better company performance and a sustainable competitive advantage.

Chapter 1 begins with defining strategy and examines the nature of corporate strategy. It then examines some of the challenges involved in developing a strategy for an organisation and how strategy applies to all types and sizes of organisations. There are various levels of strategy within organisations and these are discussed. It then examines in detail the various elements of the process of formulating and implementing strategy.

There are four core areas of strategy:
- the foundation;
- strategic analysis;
- strategy development; and
- strategy implementation.

These are introduced to the reader in this chapter and will be developed in greater detail throughout the textbook. The final section of this chapter examines the variety of different ways in which strategy is actually developed within organisations.

DEFINITION OF STRATEGY

There are many terms used for strategy and strategic management. These include 'corporate strategy', 'business policy' and 'competitive strategy'. While each has its own nuance, they are essentially synonyms; so, for consistency, the term used here is corporate strategy.

 Corporate strategy is charting the future direction of a company by developing long-term goals that reflect stakeholders' interests and achieve sustainable competitive advantage.

The Nature of Corporate Strategy

Adopting a strategic focus is of vital concern for all organisations. When markets are in turmoil some managers may focus on the immediate issues that are pressing on the organisation. Without doubt these matters must be attended to, but so too must the long-term strategic issues. They are not mutually exclusive. What is important is that the day-to-day issues are examined in the context of the overall strategic direction of the company and that they support the attainment of its strategic goals. Adopting a strategic focus, therefore, requires senior managers to step back from the organisation and examine it in a holistic manner with an eye to long-term sustainability. The challenges facing organisations today make it far more difficult to adopt such a strategic focus, yet it is vital that managers meet that challenge. In good times, a company will find it relatively easy to succeed. When times get tough, sound strategic decisions will make the difference between survival and oblivion.

According to McCarthy *et al.* (2010), a lack of business skills is one of the main reasons behind Ireland's loss of competitiveness. Drawing on research from both the London School of Economics and McKinsey, the Irish Management Institute (IMI) in its report, *Closing the Gap*, found that underperformance in management skills leaves the country uncompetitive in relation to other European states and could be costing Ireland in the region of €2 billion a year (McKinsey & Co., 2009). In particular, small to medium-sized enterprises (SMEs) are lacking the necessary management skills to compete internationally. These observations are just as valid today. The Government has directed its efforts to improving skills among employees, which is of course a necessary step in improving competitiveness. However, the report also highlights the necessity to concentrate on improving skills among managers as there is a direct correlation between management skills and company performance. One of its recommendations is that managers in all companies, but particularly SMEs, focus specifically on long-term strategy. This textbook will help underpin the academic knowledge required to develop those strategy skills.

Definitions can be useful to help focus attention on a particular subject. There are many characteristics of strategic decisions that are implicit in the definition of corporate strategy given above. These characteristics can be summed up as:

Complex In general, strategic decisions are complex in nature: they demand rigorous analysis and, in looking to the future, there will inevitably be significant uncertainty as to the best course of action. There are a number of analytical tools available to assist executives in deciphering the information available to them in order to make decisions that are appropriate to their company.

Tailor-made strategies In developing options for the future, it is essential that those options are tailored for each individual organisation. What is right for one company may not be right for another. Therefore, while much can be learned from observing other companies in operation, care must be exercised in applying those lessons to each individual company. There are many examples and company illustrations to explain the concepts in this textbook. The strategy of a company can be identified in a number of ways, such as observing its action in the market place, noting what the company says about itself in its annual reports, marketing material, press releases, etc. (Such analysis forms an integral part of environmental analysis in **Chapter 5**, which discusses how companies analyse the competitive environments in which they operate.) While it may be difficult to acquire some relevant information on competing companies, a considerable amount of it is readily accessible and just requires constant environmental scanning (the process of collecting information about the forces at play in the organisation's environment) and analysis.

Subjectivity In using analytical tools, one may get the impression that strategy is an exact science. While it is important to analyse the data, particularly financial data, there is still a large element of subjective judgement required by the executive. This is true for all industries as companies grapple with uncertain and fast-changing markets. By being well-informed and having a good grasp of the use of strategic tools, executives can be more objective in their deliberations.

Holistic view In thinking strategically, senior executives require an holistic view of the organisation rather than focusing on just one specific area. It must be remembered that there are strong links between all parts of the organisation, and decisions made in one area will impact other parts.

Resources Usually, large resources will be needed to implement these decisions, and such resources will have to be identified and allocated. These resources are often tied up for a considerable period of time, so there is often an opportunity cost involved, i.e. by using resources to support one particular strategy they are then not available for others. Strategic decisions, therefore, require careful consideration before committing to them. These resources should be seen as an investment rather than a cost; Huff *et al.* (2009) observe that strategy should generate more resources than it uses in terms of revenue, reputation and commitment.

Change Factors such as Ireland's membership of the European Union, and increasing globalisation in many markets mean that the environment within which the organisation is operating is constantly changing. At the time of writing, the United Kingdom is about to leave the European Union, and this is going to generate enormous change for many Irish companies. Change is not always obvious, and so the organisation must recognise any changes that are taking place and be able to spot opportunities when they arise. In response to the changing environment, organisations themselves must change (see **Chapter 14**).

Competitive environment All organisations, even not-for-profit ones, operate in a competitive environment; so whatever business the organisation is in, it is about doing it better than its rivals and at lower costs. Strategic decisions, therefore, require a thorough understanding of the capability (the resources and competences) of the organisation, as well as using that capability in the most effective manner possible to achieve its goals. Competition must be increasingly seen in global terms, particularly in such an open economy as Ireland. The internet has radically altered the nature of competition not just in terms of the source of competition, but also the speed at which the competitive environment can change.

Sustainability Whatever course of action an organisation is following it must be sustainable over the long-term and not focused merely on immediate gain at the expense of its continuing viability. A company must obviously respond to the competitive threats that it faces. However, in the search for opportunities it has to strike a balance between managing for today, while simultaneously positioning itself strongly for the future. The implosion in the banking industry in Ireland in 2008 highlights this need very clearly. Outside of the banking industry, private sector companies do not fall under the mantle of 'systemic importance' and do not qualify for state assistance. All strategy decisions must, therefore, be made with the long-term sustainability of the company in mind.

Defining the organisation and industry Strategic decisions, through the goals that are generated by the organisation, will generally define the organisation under consideration. Defining the organisation refers to whether it is a single business operation or a conglomerate (a collection of different businesses within a group); which products and markets the company is involved with; and, just as importantly, those products and markets that they are *not* involved in. It also defines the boundaries of the industry. Some industries are clearly defined in terms of what they do and fall within set parameters, e.g. the cement manufacturing industry. Others are more difficult to define, such as the tourism industry. Tourism crosses over many other industries, such as the airline industry and the restaurant business. However, each of these elements of the tourism industry also provides a service to people who are local to the area and clearly could not be described as tourists.

Long-term Strategic decisions are generally long-term in nature, rather than about day-to-day operational issues, though such operational decisions will ultimately derive from strategic decisions that have been taken in the organisation. The timeframe involved in developing and implementing strategy will differ from one industry to another. For example, in the software industry a year will see many changes. In the oil exploration industry, 20-year planning periods are not unusual. Given the turmoil in international markets and the level of disruption caused by technology, such timeframes are getting shorter, though on average the timeframe for strategic decisions can be taken to mean a three-to-five-year period. However, for all organisations, flexibility is required as timeframes can change quite considerably depending on the level of turmoil in the environment within which it is operating. It should also be noted that different strategies will necessarily have different timeframes, depending on the nature of the course of action being undertaken. Therefore some strategies will be effected within a one-year period, while other strategies might be rolled out over a three-to five-year timeframe. (This point will be developed further in **Chapter 3** in discussing Balanced Scorecards.) One very important aspect of the timing of different strategies is that the nature of the strategy must be clearly communicated to employees at all levels in the organisation. In most instances, strategies will have different elements and employees must understand what element the organisation is currently focused on and what part they play in that process.

Inclusive approach An important aspect of the above definition of corporate strategy is the inclusion of 'stakeholders'. Freeman (2010:46) defines a stakeholder as:

Definition "Any group or individual who can affect or is affected by the achievements of the organisation's objectives."

Many companies focus on their obligations to shareholders, often to the exclusion of other stakeholders. The interests of an organisation's stakeholders will differ, and these should be balanced in driving the organisation forward. The values of an organisation should also inform its strategy, and these values need to reflect those of its stakeholders. (This point will be developed further in **Chapter 4** when discussing corporate governance.)

A Changing Workforce

Corporate strategy has become more complex in recent years due to various forces impacting on organisations, including globalisation and technological change. Individually and collectively, these forces have radically changed the manner in which many businesses operate. Globalisation is having a major impact on competition, not just in terms of more competitors but in the dynamic pace at which competition can change in just a short period of time. There is now much greater mobility of people internationally, particularly within the European Union. The Central Statistics Office (CSO) in 2019 estimated that there were 535,475 foreign nationals from over 200 different countries working in Ireland. This represented 11.6% of the total population, with Polish nationals the largest group at 23%. These people have brought much-needed skills and experience, but this also presents challenges in terms of cultural integration. Overall, the Irish workforce is now quite diverse, with Galway being the most multicultural city in Ireland with 18.6% of its population recorded as being foreign nationals.

Technology in Business

In all areas of strategy, technology is assuming greater importance in business in every sector. From data analytics to artificial intelligence, technology is rapidly changing how companies design, manufacture and deliver their products and services to customers. Such use of technology varies according to the specific needs of different industries. The rate of change in technology is having a very disruptive effect on business. It is a game-changer and will impact greatly on not just the type of decisions that companies make, but also on how they make those decisions.

According to a 2017 PwC report, artificial intelligence (AI) is a collective term for computer systems that can sense their environment, think, learn and take action in response to what they are sensing. AI includes digital assistants, chatbots (computer programmes designed to stimulate a conversation with a human user over the internet) and machine learning. Technology has become increasingly digitised and is moving from the first wave of digital, including the internet and mobile technology, known as the 'internet of people' (IoP), to data generated from the 'internet of things' (IoT). This increased data will lead to automation and the personalisation of products and services, and finding new ways of doing things that heretofore have not been imagined.

AI systems can be hardwired/specific systems or adaptive systems. **Hardwired systems** are those that do not learn from their interactions, such as those that assist humans in making decisions or taking action, or else systems that provide for the automation of manual and cognitive tasks. **Adaptive systems**, on the other hand, augment human decision-making *and* continuously learn from their interactions with humans and the environment, or else are ones that can adapt to different situations and can act autonomously without human assistance. It is estimated that AI will contribute up to $15.7 trillion to the global economy by 2030, including $6.6 trillion coming from increased productivity and $9.1 trillion from consumption-related effects. The main industries expecting to benefit from AI are: retail, technology and communications, transportation, financial services, energy, and healthcare (PwC, 2017).

This textbook will make reference throughout to the use of technology, with one important caveat. In most cases, technology is an enabler rather than an end in itself. This is an important distinction as executives must still understand that, while the power of technology has changed exponentially in recent years, the fundamental principles of corporate strategy, as discussed in this textbook, must still be understood. How these principles are implemented is a different matter, and technology can certainly improve the effectiveness of strategy formulation and implementation. There are also serious ethical and legal considerations relating to AI, specifically regarding its impact on people and their jobs, and also in relation to the use of 'big data' and the requirements of privacy and data protection legislation (specifically the General Data Protection Regulation (Regulation (EU) 2016/679) ('GDPR')). We have already seen enormous fines imposed on companies for breaches of the GDPR. For major multinational companies, such fines are perhaps small relative to their turnover (maximum fines under GDPR are €20 million or 4% of global turnover, whichever is the greater). However, privacy and data protection issues can have a bigger reputational impact on companies, which in turn can lead to tighter State regulations – both of which could have very significant negative impacts on their business model. Business ethics, which will be discussed in **Chapter 4**, must be considered an integral part of doing business.

The big question for each organisation is how AI will impact on their business model. The need to understand fundamental principles of strategy is particularly acute when it comes to making investment decisions in relation to technology infrastructure. There are many examples of enormous sums of money being spent on IT systems that simply do not deliver on their promise. The Health Service Executive (HSE), for example, spent €150 million on the development of its PPARS programme (personnel, payroll and related systems) before the project was finally abandoned in 2007.

When started in 1995, it was originally estimated to cost €10 million. The PPARS debacle received a great deal of publicity as the HSE is a state body and its spending is open to public scrutiny. There can be no doubt that there are many similar examples in private companies, where such investments are quietly written off the balance sheet. Whether such systems are funded by public money or private resources, executives must ensure that the system is fit for purpose and its cost can be justified by significant savings in efficiency for the organisation.

The challenge in writing about technology in a general textbook on strategy, is that such technology is often industry specific, and will also be rapidly changing, becoming dated in the process. The main emphasis in this textbook is on the core principles of strategy. In some cases, this will incorporate technology as a core element of the strategy, and in other instances, it will be merely supporting the strategy. **Salaso**, as featured in **Illustration 5.3** in **Chapter 5** is an example of a leading-edge company that is using technology to deliver its core business model to its customers.

While AI is still at an early stage of development and it will be a few years yet before the full impact on business will truly be known, it is expected that AI will, nevertheless, completely alter the nature of business over the next 10 to 15 years in many different ways. Where relevant, technology will be discussed in different chapters in the context of changes that are likely to take place and its impact on corporate strategy.

Climate Change

One of the biggest challenges facing companies in the next number of years is the issue of climate change and environmental sustainability. These issues have been discussed for many years, with little concrete action. Action on climate change can no longer be seen as an optional extra but must become an integral part of how companies are run. As the world is slowly waking up to the disastrous impact of the effects of climate change, failure to respond will have serious consequences for companies ignoring their responsibilities. Corporate social responsibility (CSR) is discussed in detail in **Chapter 4**, and is also discussed throughout the textbook and case studies.

Strategic Drift

In making strategic decisions it is becoming more difficult to keep up to date with changes in the complex environment of contemporary business, and to understand the implications at individual company level. This often leads to what Johnson *et al.* (2018:180) call **strategic drift**, where "the strategy of the organisation gradually drifts away from the realities of its environment and towards an internally determined view of the world. This can lead to significant performance downturn, and potentially the demise of the organisation."

This textbook is designed to provide you with strategic tools to assist in the formulation and implementation of strategy. Kaplan and Norton (2008) believe that most companies' underperformance is due to a breakdown between strategy and operations. They stress the importance of understanding the management cycle that links strategy and operations, and knowing what tools to apply at each stage of the cycle.

Illustration 1.1: The Garda PULSE System

Management information systems (MIS) are a vital element in the running of any large organisation, in both the public and private sectors. Such systems must be able to supply senior management with accurate information to make informed decisions in a timely manner. While all organisations accept the principle of the need for effective information systems, not all systems meet their requirements.

PULSE ('Police Using Leading Systems Effectively') is a database system used by An Garda Síochána for the recording of crime. The contract for developing the system was awarded in 1996 to what was then Andersen Consulting at a projected cost of €23.6 million. The system was introduced in November 1999 at a cost of €61 million. A further €13 million was spent between 2001 and 2006 in upgrading the system. In 2006, the Garda Information Services Centre (GISC) was established in Castlebar, County Mayo, as a contact centre for operational members of An Garda Síochána, to send and receive information to and from Gardaí on duty.

Over the years, the PULSE system has been the subject of complaints by the courts, the Garda Representative Association and the Association of Garda Sergeants and Inspectors on the basis that the system is unreliable. This view has been echoed by the Garda Inspectorate. Statistics on homicides and drink-driving offences were called into question by Garda whistle-blower Maurice McCabe in the O'Higgins Commission of Inquiry. These were also subject to review by the Garda Inspectorate. In September 2017, for a second time, the Central Statistics Office (CSO) suspended the publication of any further crime statistics until a Garda review into homicide case statistics was completed.

Many of the issues in regard to PULSE relate to the classification of crimes by the investigating officers. However, the system itself has a number of drawbacks. One significant factor is that the PULSE system terminals are available to Gardaí in just under half of Garda stations across the country. The system was very slow to activate and the logging-off process was also slow. It became common practice for a number of different Gardaí to input information while a colleague Garda was still logged on. As a result, it became very difficult to determine which Garda actually recorded a specific incident. With staff shortages, backlogs arose in the inputting of data and, according to the Garda Inspectorate, incidents were frequently not recorded on the database until a number of months later, which had follow-on implications for progressing cases through the criminal justice system.

In 2015, the Garda Inspectorate called for the PULSE system, which is based on 1990s technology, to be retired. In 2018, the Assistant Garda Commissioner, Michael Finn, stated at an Oireachtas Justice Committee hearing that the system was "not fit for purpose", and that Garda management were examining whether to replace the system with one built around current policing needs.

It should be noted that while this example is from the public sector, there are also many examples in the private sector of poor MIS projects and systems. The main difference is that with state bodies the information about the system is in the public domain, while in the private sector, such information will be deemed commercially sensitive and kept under wraps. Either way, the lessons for managers are the same: MIS are a vital component for running any organisation, but such systems must be tailored to meet the current needs of each organisation as well as future developments, and must be properly resourced.

Sources: Garda Inspectorate and
Oireachtas Reports (2018) at www.oireachtas.ie.

Every company will face its own challenges in implementing strategy. In their book, *The Strategy Focused Organisation*, Kaplan and Norton (2001) articulate five principles that are common to each organisation when meeting that challenge:

- Translate the strategy into operational terms to which people in the company can relate and understand.
- Align the organisation to the strategy – individual strategies must be linked and integrated and the organisation must support the implementation of these strategies.
- Make strategy part of everyone's everyday job. It needs to be moved from the boardroom to the backroom. All employees must understand the company's overall strategy and conduct their day-to-day business in a manner that supports it.
- Make strategy a continual process. It should be an ongoing process with constant reviews that involves everyone in the organisation. It should also be an opportunity for learning.
- Mobilise change through executive leadership. The single most important condition for success is the active involvement and sense of ownership of the executive team. Strategy involves change in the organisation and this change must be led from the top. Leading change is also a central theme of Kotter (1996, 2002).

STRATEGY APPLIES TO ALL ORGANISATIONS

When one thinks of strategy, large multinational companies come to mind. However, strategy is relevant to *all* organisations. The examples in this textbook are drawn from a wide variety of industries and different-sized companies. It must be remembered that such companies would not have grown to be multinationals unless they made the right decisions along the way.

The Tralee-based company, Kerry Group Plc, is now one of the largest and most successful food ingredients companies in the world. The company was founded in Listowel, County Kerry, in 1972 and grew steadily throughout the 1970s. In 1986 it became a public limited company, listing on the Dublin and London stock exchanges. Since then it has continued to grow by internal development and acquisitions. The Group now employs 24,000 people throughout its manufacturing, sales and technical centres around the world and is regarded as a leader in its chosen markets. This success did not happen by accident. It needed sound strategic decisions from its beginnings as a small company, and right through each stage of development.

Equally, strategy is just as relevant in service organisations as it is in manufacturing. It is axiomatic that, as economies develop, a greater percentage of GDP will be derived from service industries. It is estimated that €58 billion in Irish exports in 2007 represent service exports, accounting for 40% of total exports. Increasingly, there is much greater focus on public sector bodies to ensure that they are delivering value-for-money to the taxpayer. Such bodies also need a clear understanding of strategy. The same can be said for aid agencies and other not-for-profit bodies. According to the Charities Regulator, there were 9,632 charities registered in Ireland in 2019. A report by Indecon Consultants, commissioned by the regulator, concluded that the charity sector directly employed 189,000 people in 2018 and has a turnover of €14.5 billion (Charities Regulator, 2019). The sector employs 63,000 people and accounts for 8% of GDP (McKay, 2009). The purpose of these organisations differs from commercial bodies, yet they too operate in a competitive environment, competing for resources, and this requires effective strategies. While the circumstances of all of these organisations may differ, the basic principles of strategic management are common to all.

LEVELS OF STRATEGY WITHIN THE ORGANISATION

Strategy exists at three main levels in the organisation: corporate-level, business-level and operational strategies, forming the following hierarchy:

- Corporate-level strategy
- Business-level strategy
- Operational strategy

These three levels are set against a background of functional strategies. These levels of strategy are shown graphically in **Figure 1.1**.

Corporate-level Strategy

Corporate-level strategy refers to the decisions that are taken at the corporate headquarters and which impact on the entire organisation. They are concerned with deciding whether a company will operate as a single business entity, in which case corporate-level and business-level strategies are the same; or in a number of different industries, in which case strategy governs the relationship between the headquarters and the various strategic business units (SBUs) of the organisation. A **strategic business unit** is a unit within the organisation that has its own distinct market for its goods or services, and is distinct from other SBUs. While a large company may have many SBUs operating in different markets, the actions of these SBUs will have to be co-ordinated at the corporate level. The corporate headquarters does not, in general, deal directly with customers, and thus does not generate revenue directly. It must, therefore, concern itself with adding value to the different elements of the organisation.

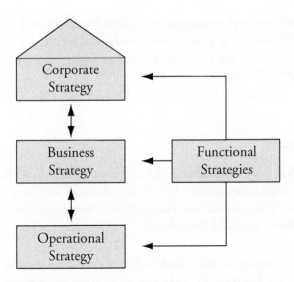

Figure 1.1 *The Levels of Strategy*

Corporate governance is an important element of strategy at this level and has come in for considerable attention in recent times in Ireland. The board of directors of the company will give its imprimatur to the strategies that are proposed by senior management. Decisions taken at this level will also have to accommodate the expectations of the different stakeholders, and these expectations should be reflected in the strategy. (This point will be developed further in **Chapter 4**.)

Business-level Strategy

In the case of a single business operation, or a strategic business unit, business-level strategy involves competing successfully in different markets. It concerns decisions about the markets in which the company operates and what goods and services to offer in those markets. Competitive strategy is a core element as this will distinguish market leaders from followers. For commercial organisations profitability will also be important, though there may be some circumstances where a particular SBU might be subsidised by other SBUs within the organisation for other strategic reasons (see **Chapter 10**). Such cross-subsidy would need the approval of senior management. Strategies at the business-level should be consistent with corporate-level strategies, as ultimately this is how the overall organisation will achieve its desired results.

Operational Strategies

Strategy is meaningless until it is reflected in the everyday operations of the company. Lynch (2018) considers strategy as existing only at corporate-level and business-level and does not include operational-level strategy. Other writers, such as Johnson *et al.* (2017) and Thompson *et al.* (2018), include operational strategies directly in the overall hierarchy of strategy. Operational strategies are concerned with how front-line managers in different parts of an organisation translate the corporate- and business-level strategies into delivering goals and objectives. Operational strategies require the effective use of people and resources, as well as control and other processes. While on the one hand operational strategies do not fit neatly into the definition of corporate strategy, which is essentially long-term in nature, they are still part of the process of how organisations achieve their goals. In that regard they can be considered part of the overall hierarchy of strategy.

Functional Strategies

Some writers such as Thompson *et al.* (2018), Hill and Jones (2011), and Huff *et al.* (2009) refer to functional strategies as either being another layer in the hierarchy, or else as an alternative name for operational strategies. In reality, functional strategies form an integral part of all levels of strategy, i.e. corporate-level, business-level and operational.

Consequently, functional strategy forms a backdrop that runs from corporate-level strategy down through the hierarchy (see **Figure 1.1**). Take the accounting function in a large company, for example. The group financial controller will set financial policy for the entire group in terms of the financial structure of the company – master budgets, consolidation of accounts and the accounting policy to which the entire organisation will adhere. Each SBU will develop its own financial policy in line with the overall directives of the organisation. It will formulate budgets for the SBU and adapt its accounting procedures to comply with the laws of the jurisdiction within which it is operating. In turn, each part of the SBU will develop its own budgets and accounting procedures relevant to its section. While conforming to the agreed policies for the SBU, the budget and other accounting functions needed in the production department will obviously differ from those for the marketing department.

It should be noted that all three levels of strategy (corporate, business and operational) should be aligned both horizontally (across the organisation) and vertically (from corporate to operational) and, if such alignment is not achieved, then problems will occur in the organisation's strategy.

CORE AREAS OF STRATEGY

In broad terms, strategy can be divided into four core areas:

- the foundation;
- strategic analysis;
- developing strategy; and
- strategy implementation.

These four core areas are not separate, sequential stages but are very much integrated and concurrent processes. An organisation might be in the process of implementing a particular strategy when changes in the environment cause it to modify or even abandon that strategy. These four core areas, forming the strategic planning model, are represented graphically in **Figure 1.2** below.

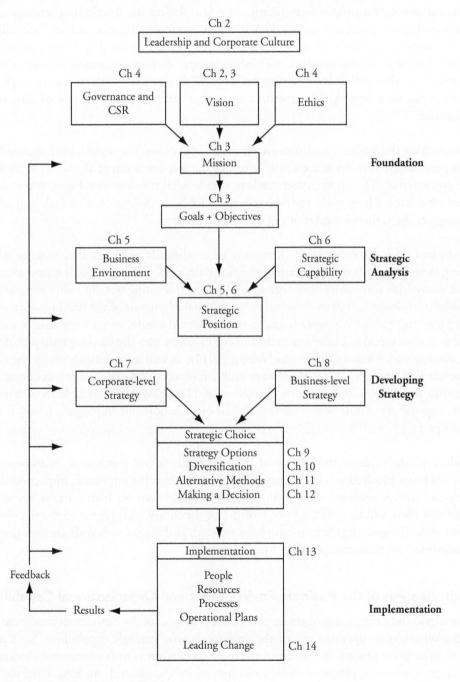

Figure 1.2 *The Strategic Planning Model*

13

The Foundation

An essential part of the process of developing and implementing strategy for any organisation is the laying down of a proper foundation. The foundation for developing strategy consists of understanding the processes involved within that particular organisation and establishing a vision and mission. Leadership is an essential element of the process that drives and underpins all aspects of strategy. It also involves establishing proper corporate governance procedures and ethical structures that will guide decision-making. With these foundation stones in place, the organisation can then develop a competitive enterprise that will stand the test of time and also moral scrutiny.

Before examining the business environment in which it operates, the organisation should be clear about its purpose and mission as these will influence the interpretation of all further analysis, both internal and external. The organisation needs to decide what it wants to achieve, and to set clear goals and objectives. These goals and objectives should be both legal and ethical, and reflect to varying degrees the various expectations of all its stakeholders.

Warren Buffett once famously said: "It is only when the tide goes out that you see who was swimming in the nude". In the aftermath of the global financial crisis of 2008, it is now abundantly clear that many Irish companies have been caught by the tide going out. So many companies, not least of all the banks and property developers, went in naked pursuit of the maximisation of profit but had failed to establish a proper foundation that would create, or in some cases continue, a sustainable business model. There were a number of inquiries into the banking collapse: Honohan (2010), Regling and Watson (2010) and Nyberg (2011), as well as investigations by the Director of Corporate Enforcement. While there were only a few successful criminal prosecutions arising, it is clear that for many companies their business model had provided incredible short-term gains, but at the expense of the long-term viability of their organisation and employees. It was, for many, a Faustian pact.

In addition, whatever about the legality of the way business was conducted, in some cases the behaviour of those involved was highly unethical at best. Given the enormous impact on the Irish economy and its international reputation, as well as the impact on Irish citizens, there can be no doubt that there will be much greater scrutiny in the future with regard to the decisions that executives make. Tougher regulations have been enacted, and higher standards are now demanded from companies and those charged with running them.

Strategic Analysis of the Business Environment and Organisational Capability

The next step in the strategic management process is an analysis of the business environment within which the organisation operates and of the company's own strategic capabilities. Such analysis should be an ongoing process, as change in the business environment is continuous. Indeed, such small changes can, over a period of time, constitute major change and can have a serious impact on performance.

Organisations are open systems that interact with their environment; strategic analysis consists of the development of a detailed understanding of that environment. While there are a number of strategic tools available, it is a difficult process that involves making assumptions about the future and understanding the environment, something that inevitably entails uncertainty. The organisation needs to anticipate any changes but, at the very least, it must be able to react when such changes occur.

Environmental analysis examines the **macro environment**: all the wider political, economic, socio-cultural and technological factors that impact on the organisation's industry or industries. It also looks at the **micro environment**: the level of competition within the organisation's particular market or industry, and how the organisation is positioned within this competitive environment. It also examines the changes taking place – the driving forces and the key success factors required to operate in the industry. The purpose of carrying out environmental analysis is to develop a fuller understanding of the opportunities and threats that exist. (Environmental analysis is discussed in detail in **Chapter 5**.)

Internal analysis of the organisation follows on from the examination of the external environment. (This is examined in **Chapter 6**.) Its purpose is to understand the strategic capability of the organisation. Such analysis highlights the organisation's strengths and weaknesses and, combined with opportunities and threats, will enable it to complete a detailed Strengths, Weaknesses, Opportunities and Threats (SWOT) analysis. SWOT analysis can provide the basis for strategic options that the organisation could develop further.

Developing Strategy

The third core area of strategic management is the development of strategies for both corporate and business unit levels. As described above, companies must first decide on their corporate-level strategy, as this will impact on business-level strategy. Issues such as what businesses it will include in its portfolio, what range of products it will manufacture and what markets, both at home and internationally, it will operate in must be decided. Such decisions will depend on the level of resources at its disposal, along with the skill and competences that are needed to support such decisions.

Business-level strategies are formulated in line with corporate-level strategies and are translated into specific strategies for each individual SBU. Porter (1985) defined three generic business-level strategies: cost leadership, differentiation and focus. These generic business strategies have been further developed by other writers and are discussed in detail in **Chapter 8**.

Once business-level strategies have been chosen, the company can then set about generating possible strategic options. It is important that managers generate as many options as possible before making a decision on the future direction of a company. Often there is a tendency to pick the most obvious choice, but this may not necessarily be the best option. Possible options here include:

- **Market penetration** – building up market share
- **Product development** – developing new products for existing markets
- **Market development** – developing new markets for existing products

- **Diversification** – moving away from existing businesses into new parts of the industry or, indeed, new and different industries

All of these options must be underpinned by the necessary capability to pursue a specific course of action. This will vary considerably from one organisation to another (see **Chapter 6**). As competition becomes more intense and diverse it will also need to be underpinned by a culture of innovation.

For each of these possible directions, there are different methods by which such strategies can be pursued. For most organisations, growth by **internal development** will form an important part of their future plans. **Mergers and acquisitions** provide a quick method for expansion or, alternatively, they may consider various forms of **strategic alliances** with other organisations. (**Chapters 9**, **10**, **11** and **12** examine these factors along with methods of analysing the various options.)

Strategy Implementation

The fourth stage of strategy is its implementation. Without successful implementation the chosen strategy remains merely a plan or aspiration. Implementation requires putting an appropriate strategic architecture in place, along with ensuring that all the necessary resources (human, financial, physical and technological) are made available when needed. In most instances, implementing the chosen strategy will involve change for the organisation, and this process has to be carefully led.

While implementing the strategy, it is also necessary to monitor its suitability as well as monitoring the process of implementation itself. In that regard, the entire process of developing and implementing strategy is an iterative process whereby executives should be constantly referring back to all stages of the process to ensure that the strategy being implemented remains the best course of action. A number of questions should be asked to test the suitability of the strategy that has been chosen:

1. Is the strategy consistent with the vision and mission of the organisation?
2. How well does the strategy fit the company's situation? (The company must have the resources and competences to deliver on the strategy.)
3. Is the strategy different from what competitors are doing, and will it help the company develop a competitive advantage that is sustainable in the long-term?
4. As the strategy is being implemented, is it achieving the intended results? (This should include a balance between financial and strategic goals.)
5. What corrective measures need to be taken?

DEVELOPMENT PROCESSES

The division of strategy into the four core areas that have been discussed above (the foundation, strategic analysis, developing strategy options and strategy implementation) implies that strategy is developed in an organised and sequential manner. The reality for most organisations is different and, in most instances, the strategy that an organisation is actually pursuing is constructed in a combination of different ways. It is useful to examine these various processes as it is important for executives to understand all of the various influences that impact on the strategy-making process. It will be seen that it is not a case of senior executives deciding on a course of action and then giving directions to ensure its implementation. The planning of such a course of action by those at the top of the company is, of course, a very important part of the overall process, but it does not paint the full picture. According to Mintzberg (1985), the strategy development process can be divided into two broad categories:

- intended strategy development; and
- emergent strategy development.

This is depicted in **Figure 1.3** below. It is only by understanding all of the processes involved, and the mixture of those constituent parts, that executives can play a truly effective role in formulating and implementing strategy in their organisation.

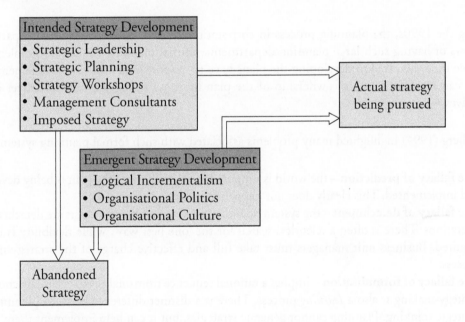

Figure 1.3 *Strategy Development Processes*

Intended Strategy Development

Strategic Leadership For any organisation, leadership plays a central role in its success. In the context of strategy formulation, leadership fulfils two important functions. First, leaders provide a clear vision for the future of the company. Secondly, they create an environment within the organisation in which all members can develop to their full potential and work together towards achieving the strategic goals that have been agreed. In this regard, leadership also provides the environment in which all the other processes of both intended strategy development and emergent strategy development take place. (The role that leadership plays in formulating strategy will be further developed in **Chapter 2**.)

Strategic Planning The development of a strategic plan is an essential element of the overall process of strategy development. Strategic planning provides a structured means for the organisation to take a longer-term view of strategy and to evaluate both its environment and its capabilities. The plan can be used to formulate goals and objectives and move the organisation in the desired direction. The plan, and its resulting budgets, also help co-ordinate the various divisions within the organisation and help them work in unison.

In the 1960s and 1970s, most multinational corporations had large planning departments staffed with specialists whose job it was to produce a series of plans for the approval of senior management. It was very much a top-down process based on the intentions of senior management and backed up by the appropriate resources. This process would have had its antecedents in the military, in that armies would have been the precursors of large corporations in the organisational sense.

During the 1990s, the planning process in corporations became much less formal. Apart from the costs of having such large planning departments, formal planning can create problems, for example those involved in developing the plans have no responsibility for their implementation, which can result in a lack of ownership of the plan by those whose job it is to deliver on the objectives.

Mintzberg (1994) highlighted many problems associated with such formal planning systems:

- **The fallacy of prediction** – the world is supposed to stay still while the plan is being developed and implemented. This clearly does not happen in reality.
- **The fallacy of detachment** – the system does the thinking and the strategists are detached from operations. There is often a relentless search for the 'one best way', while flexibility is usually required. Business unit managers must take full and effective charge of the strategy-making process.
- **The fallacy of formulisation** – implies a rational sequence from analysis to eventual action, but strategy-making is also a *learning* process. There is a distinct difference between planning and strategic thinking. Planning cannot generate strategies, but it can help implement them.

Planners do, however, have a very important role in the process in terms of general analysis and as catalysts. There also needs to be a balance between analytical thinking – bringing order to the organisation – as well as creative, intuitive thinking to open up the process.

Strategy Workshops Most organisations now involve managers at all levels in the development of strategy, giving people a meaningful input into the process. This is often done using strategy workshops where people meet (often off-site) and discuss the issues facing the company and how they might be addressed. It still feeds into a formal strategic plan, but it is as much a bottom-up process as a top-down approach, and it enables those responsible for the execution of the plan to participate meaningfully.

Having started off with a very autocratic style, Jack Welch, former CEO of General Electric, gradually switched to a much more inclusive one, involving his managers in strategy 'workout sessions'. These were sessions where managers at many levels would debate the issues facing the company and how best to tackle them, debates which would be facilitated by outside people, such as university professors, who had 'no axe to grind'. Managers were taught how to identify the root cause of any problem and to quickly find a solution so that the company could move forward (Welch, 2001).

Illustration 1.2: Strategy Formulation – Dublin Docklands Development Authority

---

The **Dublin Docklands Development Authority (DDDA)** is one Irish organisation that used workshops involving multiple stakeholders to help formulate strategy. The DDDA was established in 1997 with a remit covering the social and economic redevelopment of the 520-hectare docklands area in Dublin. To enable it to achieve this, the DDDA developed a five-year strategic 'master plan'. This was subsequently updated in 2003 and a new master plan was developed. These plans covered all aspects of the development of the docklands area. The establishment of the International Financial Services Centre (IFSC) in Dublin was the initial part of the physical regeneration of the area. This progress continued year after year and there are now many stunning contemporary buildings north and south of the River Liffey, including the National Conference Centre, which was opened in 2010.

These magnificent buildings are only one element of the regeneration. An integral part of the overall development is the social regeneration of the area, which was home to long-established communities that had worked for generations in the labour-intensive docks. As shipping companies moved to containerisation in the second half of the last century, unemployment became endemic in the area. An extra challenge for the DDDA was how to integrate the new residents who came to work and live in the area with the established residents, and to develop a vibrant community in the docklands.

To be successful, any development has to be community-led rather than adopting a top-down approach. The DDDA has been very successful in working hand-in-hand with all of the community stakeholders: young people, senior citizens, community groups, educational establishments, sports clubs, Gardaí, business groups, and many more, to discuss issues of mutual concern. For many years, the DDDA hosted a Social Regeneration Conference and invited over 200 delegates, representing a complete cross-section of the community. The conferences were addressed by international speakers, and these talks were followed by workshops for the delegates where the main issues facing the community were discussed and action points developed.

At the beginning of each annual conference, there was an update on all of the action points from the previous year. In so doing, the DDDA demonstrated its commitment, as the vast majority of objectives that had been adopted the previous year were completed, with an update given on the progress of the others. In addition to these conferences, the DDDA held regular meetings throughout the year with different groups of stakeholders. The purpose of these consultations was to feed into the master plan and develop goals and objectives that would have real meaning in the development of communities and not just the physical infrastructure.

With its work largely completed, the functions of the Dublin Docklands Development Authority were subsumed into Dublin City Council in 2016, but the legacy lives on.

Source: Docklands Master Plan and interview with former CEO Paul Maloney

The concept of strategy workshops does not just involve managers; it includes a much wider group of stakeholders working on the premise that good ideas can come from anywhere, not just from those at the top. By including various stakeholders, a workshop is likely to create much greater acceptance of the outcome.

Management Consultants On occasion, outside consultants may be brought in to assist the strategy development process, to provide expertise and experience not available in-house. This may apply to every size of organisation, from the small family-owned business to international corporations seeking advice on major strategic initiatives such as mergers and acquisitions or perhaps a flotation on the stock market.

There are a number of advantages in bringing in outside consultants. It can give the management a new perspective, one they couldn't see before because they were too close to the problems at hand. In other cases, the management may lack the specific skills needed at crucial times, such as the development of an integrated information technology system. Yet, on other occasions, consultants may be brought in to justify cost-cutting measures and redundancies. What is important from the management's point of view, regardless of the advice obtained, is that they take ownership of the strategy that is being proposed.

Imposed Strategy There are occasions where organisations may have strategic plans imposed upon them. This has happened with semi-state companies where the Government had a political imperative that took precedence over the commercial imperative. An example is the postal service (An Post), which for many years continued to operate small rural post offices that were not commercially viable but which provided a very valuable social service in isolated communities.

Another example of imposed strategy in the public sector in Ireland is the provision of electricity. In 1927, the Electricity Supply Board (ESB) was established as a semi-state company for the purpose of supplying the country with the electricity it needs for commercial and domestic use. For most of its life the ESB was in a monopolistic position. The market is now opened up to competitors and the ESB has been split into two organisations, one generating electricity and the other ESB Networks, responsible for operating the national grid. The grid operator must accept electricity from all suppliers in the country. Ireland does not have nuclear power and the ESB has traditionally used coal-, peat- and gas-burning stations as well as hydroelectric power. Apart from water and wind, the other sources of electricity generation are contributing to greenhouse gases and they are finite in terms of supply. As part of the Government's 'green' strategy, it has directed that by 2020 the

ESB must be generating one-third of its electricity from renewable sources. It will generate 1,400 megawatts of electricity from wind generators and will also exploit the potential of wave, tidal and biomass resources. As a semi-state company, managers are obliged to accept this imposed strategy. The ESB board has approved a strategic framework, with a €22 billion investment programme to 2020, to halve carbon emissions by 2020 and have zero emissions by 2035 (ESB, 2019).

Imposed strategy also happens in commercial organisations where the corporate headquarters may impose a strategy on a SBU or subsidiary company when a certain balance is required in its corporate portfolio. (This is discussed in detail in **Chapter 10**.)

In addition, for companies quoted on a stock exchange, the capital markets are in a powerful position to impose a particular strategic direction on a company. Senior managers in such companies regularly meet their large institutional shareholders to brief them on their company's plans. If such large shareholders were to express strong views about a strategy, it would, in many cases, be adjusted to take account of those views. The net result is that strategies are often imposed on the company by these large shareholders and bond-holders as the threat of withdrawal of funds is enough to steer the company in a direction that reflects their views. (The Corrib Gas Project (see **Chapter 4**, **Illustration 4.3**) demonstrates how powerful stakeholders can impose strategy on an organisation.)

Emergent Strategy Development

Logical Incrementalism Von Moltke, the famous Prussian general, once remarked that "no plan survives contact with the enemy". In commerce as well as in combat, circumstances can often change rapidly, rendering the original plan useless. Companies often develop strategies that result in success not thanks to a detailed strategic plan, but as a result of choices made between alternatives, and decisions taken that evolved the strategy in one particular direction over a period of time. Robert Frost in his poem "The Road Not Taken" describes travelling on a road, coming to a junction and having to make a choice about which direction to proceed, knowing that whichever road chosen would take on a momentum of its own, to the exclusion of other options:

> "Two roads diverged in a yellow wood,
> And sorry I could not travel both…
>
> Oh, I kept the first for another day!
> Yet knowing how way leads on to way,
> I doubted if I should ever come back. …"

Quinn (1980:58) describes this process as "**logical incrementalism**" — the development of strategy by experimentation and learning from partial commitment rather than through global formulations of total strategies.

There are a number of underlying reasons for the logical incrementalism approach, including the lack of a long-term understanding of where the organisation is heading, uncertainty of the environment in which they are operating, keeping objectives broad, and the need to retain complete flexibility to be able to take advantage of opportunities when they arise. Social processes play a major part in the development of such strategy.

Pascale (1984) describes the entry of Honda to the US motorcycle market in the 1960s and how they had to adjust rapidly to circumstances different to those which they had expected. A Northern Irish example of a company that has had to react quickly to rapidly changing circumstances is the cloud computing company, Anaeko – see **Illustration 1.3**.

Illustration 1.3: Anaeko and Emergent Strategy

Belfast-based software firm, Anaeko, was founded in 2004. Anaeko has pioneered innovations in mobile messaging, mobile internet and the internet of things. The company is a cloud integrator for multi-cloud enterprises that emphasises quality, speed and innovation across a number of different product offerings:

- **Integrated Analytics Services** to accelerate decision-making by providing business leaders with timely insights.
- **Hybrid Cloud Integration Services** optimise workflows between applications, appliance and devices to perform at scale.
- **Storage Optimisation** enables "best fit" cloud strategies by allowing applications and stored data to migrate independently between clouds.
- **Multi-Cloud DevOps Services** accelerate innovation by delivering business services faster across complex cloud environments.

In 2016, with the assistance of Invest Northern Ireland, Anaeko beat off stiff competition to win a major multi-million pound contract for a huge cloud provider in the United States, which allowed it to create an additional 15 jobs. In 2017, the company achieved the internationally recognised ISO 9001 certification for its software consultancy practice, underlining its commitment to customers and its focus on quality, ultimately giving the company a competitive advantage.

Anaeko is rapidly expanding and experiencing strong growth in the software-defined storage, disruptive cloud applications and business operating reporting parts of its business. The company recently opened a new office in Enniskillen, County Fermanagh. Unlike many traditional industries, the software industry is rapidly changing and, inevitably, strategy development is largely 'emergent'.

Source: interview with Anaeko CEO, Denis Murphy.

A vital element in the concept of logical incrementalism is the people working in the organisation. The success of a strategy, particularly one that requires a great deal of flexibility, requires having the right people on board. Jim Collins in his book *Good to Great* cites the example of the American bank, Wells Fargo:

"Wells Fargo began its 15-year stint of spectacular performance in 1983, but the foundation for the shift dates back to the early 1970s, when then-CEO Dick Cooley began building one of the most talented management teams in the industry. Cooley foresaw that the banking industry would eventually undergo wrenching change, but he did not pretend to know what form that change would take. So instead of mapping out a strategy for change, he and chairman Ernie Arbuckle focused on 'injecting an endless stream of talent' directly into the veins of the company. They hired outstanding people whenever and wherever they found them, often without a specific job in mind. 'That's how you build the future', he said. 'If I'm not smart enough to see the changes that are coming, they will. And they will be flexible enough to deal with them'."

Collins (2001:42)

The allocation of resources can also play a major role in emergent strategy. The organisation will have made strategic decisions in the past that will have directed it along a certain route. Resources will have been allocated to support that strategy and, inevitably, this will create further momentum. Bower and Gilbert (2007) believe that the cumulative impact of the allocation of resources by an organisation's managers at all levels ultimately has a significant impact on strategy development.

Spotting an opportunity when it arises and knowing when to move on a 'window of opportunity' is an essential element of leadership. Timing is of the essence. Shakespeare summed it up thus:

"There is a tide in the affairs of men, which taken at the flood leads on to fortune. Omitted, all the voyage of their life is bound in shallows and in miseries. On such a sea we are now afloat and we must take the current where it serves or lose our ventures."

Julius Caesar, Act IV, Sc. 3

Organisational Politics Aristotle believed that humans are, by nature, political animals. Business organisations are social constructs. They are designed by people to work together towards achieving certain goals. It is inevitable that, in many instances, different stakeholders will have different views about what those goals should be, and how best to achieve them. Shareholders will want a good return on their investment, and workers will want the best working conditions. While this dichotomy is not necessarily mutually exclusive, it does point to differences in personal aims. If these aims are deemed to be mutually exclusive, who wins? In all companies, a certain amount of negotiation and bargaining will take place, and this brings much greater subjectivity into the more objective planning process. Such battles can also take place in family-run businesses. Collins (2007) describes many sibling battles that made their way into the public domain in Irish family-run companies, such as Dunnes Stores.

Different people having very different views of what direction a company should take can have a big impact on the strategy that is eventually chosen. According to Johnson *et al.* (2017),

stakeholder mapping can be used to ascertain people's support or opposition to a particular strategy, depending on their level of interest in a particular course of action being taken and the level of power they possess to either implement or block a certain strategy. Those with a high level of interest and power are in a key position to influence strategy one way or another (see **Chapter 4**).

Baggage handlers in Ryanair went on strike in 1998 seeking union recognition, but had to abandon their strike after a couple of weeks when the airline made alternative arrangements (Creaton, 2004). It was only in December 2017 that Ryanair was finally compelled to recognise trade unions. On the other hand, the unions in Aer Lingus have traditionally wielded a lot of power, although this power has gradually been eroded over the last number of years.

When embarking on a particular course of strategic action, it may be the case that not everyone in the organisation will agree with the direction being taken. However, it is vital that the CEO has the support of senior managers for the chosen course of action. Without their support, the proposed strategy would surely flounder. Before deciding to invade France, Henry V sent for the Archbishop of Canterbury to ascertain his legal right to claim France, and then discussed the expedition with his nobles. He knew he had their support when Westmoreland replied:

> "Never King of England had nobles richer and more loyal subjects, whose hearts have left their bodies here in England and lie pavilion'd in the fields of France."
>
> *Henry V*, Act 1, Sc. 2

The flow of information plays a major part in organisational politics. There are ethical issues to be considered here. By filtering certain information and feeding it into the decision-making process, or alternatively, by withholding vital information, decisions may be swung one way or the other. Even the choice of words used in an argument can have an emotive impact and this can channel thinking in a particular direction.

The bargaining involved in organisational politics can, in some instances, have a positive effect. It can challenge staid thinking and result in innovative approaches by the company. A CEO should be confident about a chosen course of action and be able to defend it to managers within the organisation. If, on the other hand, it cannot be justified, then it is time to go back to the drawing board.

Organisational Culture The culture of an organisation will also have an impact on its strategy. Culture is often described simply as 'the way things are done around here'. Just as an individual person has their own personality, an organisation has its own culture:

> **Definition**

Culture can be defined as: "a set of beliefs, values and learned ways of managing – and this is reflected in its structures, systems, and approach to the development of corporate strategy. Its culture derives from its past, its present, its current people, technology and physical resources and from the aims, objectives and values of those who work in the organisation" (Lynch 2008:608).

The culture of an organisation can be a very powerful force in either blocking or supporting a strategy. The problem for managers is that, in addition to being powerful, culture is also a difficult phenomenon to observe and understand. Johnson *et al.* (2017:172) refer to the paradigm in an organisation as: "the set of basic assumptions held in common and taken for granted in an organisation".

The paradigm guides how people in the organisation view that organisation and its environment. Faced with uncertainty, managers try to define the environment in ways that are familiar and in light of past experience. Such cultural influence can be a strong force supporting a particular strategy, but it can also have a major negative impact when change is required. Trying to understand the underlying assumptions of an organisation can be difficult and Johnson *et al.* recommend the use of a 'Cultural Web' to analyse the different elements of an organisation's paradigm. This consists of the organisational structures; control systems; rituals and routines; stories; symbols; and power structures. Through an awareness of these elements, an understanding can be gained of the organisation's culture and how it will impact on strategy.

Abandoned Strategy

Organisations may have spent a considerable time developing a particular strategy, whether it be a deliberate strategy or one that has gradually emerged over a period of time, and then find that the circumstances in which they are operating have changed dramatically, thus calling that strategy into question. It might be that the strategy no longer makes sense, and a decision may have to be made to abandon that course of action. This can be a very difficult decision to make as a large amount of money may have already been spent in the process, and this investment would have to be regarded as a sunk cost (where resources have already been committed and these costs cannot be recouped if the project is abandoned).

With the major cost increases in the building of the National Children's Hospital in Dublin, a number of other large capital projects in the health sector will most probably have to be either postponed or abandoned as a result.

CONCLUSION

Strategy is developed using a variety of the methods described above. Organisations will differ in how they mix these elements together. In all cases, some elements of each will be detected, despite the predominance of any one particular type. There are certain occasions when detailed planning is vitally important. Even when the environment is changing rapidly, mergers and acquisitions still require meticulous planning. However, on its own, strategic planning will never be the only process used in the formulation and implementation of strategy. In general, company statements and reports give the indication that all moves by the organisation are carefully orchestrated by senior managers as part of a carefully thought-out plan. However, close observation of the actual strategies being pursued by various companies will reveal a lot more about the strategy-forming processes involved than that articulated by the management in official communiqués.

SUMMARY

Chapter 1 has introduced you to strategic management. Strategy applies to every type of organisation: big and small, commercial and non-profit. Understanding how strategy is developed will assist when examining more specific areas of developing and implementing strategy.

There are three broad levels of strategy in an organisation:

- At the top, there is **corporate-level strategy** dealing with the type of decisions taken at the corporate headquarters concerning the portfolio of businesses and markets in which the company operates.
- The next layer is **business-level strategy** dealing with how a single business operates in a competitive environment.
- Both the corporate-level and the business-level strategies have to be **operationalised** in the day-to-day routines of the company.
- **Functional strategies**, covering areas such as finance and marketing, form a backdrop to all three levels.

The crafting and implementation of strategy can be divided into four distinct elements. The first part is laying **the foundation** for the organisation and the type of strategy it will pursue. This involves establishing a vision for the organisation and proper corporate governance structures based on sound ethical principles and leadership. **Strategic analysis** is concerned with making sense of the environment within which an organisation is operating, along with understanding its own capabilities. **Strategy development** examines all of the possible options open to the company as a means of achieving its objectives. Choices will have to be made as resources are limited, and so it includes a decision-making framework. Once that decision has been made, it must be **implemented** by the organisation. This involves putting the correct structures and processes in place and supporting the strategy with the necessary resources. It also requires the organisation to deal with changing circumstances.

The final section of this chapter examined the different process by which strategy is developed. There are two broad divisions. First, **intended strategy development** includes the formal strategic planning process underpinning much of this textbook. It also includes strategy workshops, which is a more inclusive process involving managers at different levels of the organisation. The section on intended strategy also examined how management consultants may be brought in to advise the company on the way forward. On other occasions, strategy may be imposed on an organisation, either by the government, as in the case of public sector bodies, or on a strategic business unit by its corporate parent.

The second broad division includes **emergent strategies**. This covers logical incrementalism, where strategy is developed by experimentation and learning from partial commitment, rather than through global formulations of total strategies. It requires strategic flexibility, and an essential element is having the right people involved. Emergent strategies also look at the impact of organisational politics and culture. It has to be remembered that organisations consist of many different stakeholders, each with their own view of how strategy might suit their needs.

Finally, there are occasions where strategy has to be abandoned because changed circumstances would make it non-viable.

DISCUSSION QUESTIONS

1. Taking an organisation of your choice, critically analyse the major strategic challenges facing that organisation.
2. In reference to question 1 above, what opportunities present themselves to Irish companies?
3. Distinguish between the different levels of strategy in an organisation.
4. With regard to the four cores areas of strategy, discuss the importance of laying a solid foundation for strategic decisions.
5. Choose an Irish public limited company and evaluate the strategy-making processes that you can identify that form part of its chosen strategy.
6. Analyse each of the strategy development processes described, and state the different circumstances in which one method might be more suitable than others.

PART ONE

The Foundation

Introduction to the Foundation

Part One of this textbook deals with the philosophical foundation of strategy. It comprises three chapters: leadership and organisational culture; vision, mission, goals and objectives; and corporate governance, business ethics and corporate social responsibility. The business environment in Ireland has emerged from one of the worst recessions since the foundation of the State, but it is now facing

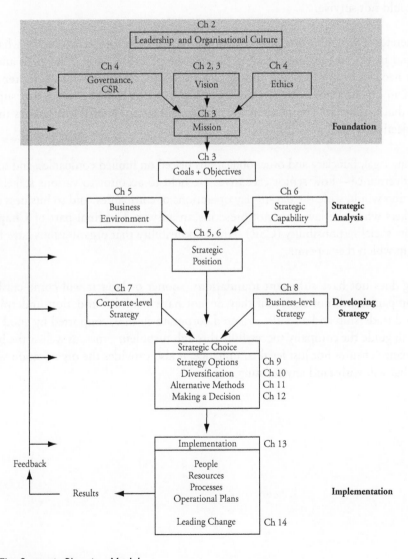

Figure 1.2 *The Strategic Planning Model*

the enormous uncertainty of the United Kingdom leaving the European Union. This will have serious implications for many Irish companies and they will require a solid foundation in order to survive. The elements outlined in the Foundation (**Figure 1.2**) play an essential role in the long-term sustainability of organisations.

Part One begins with a chapter on leadership and organisational culture (**Chapter 2**). One of the biggest failures across Irish corporate life was one of leadership. Prior to the financial collapse in 2008, the economy was awash with money and many companies were making substantial profits despite having no clear leadership or vision. Many companies, like the economy itself, were on autopilot. When the downturn came, the lack of proper leadership meant that many of these companies could not survive.

It is vital, therefore, that those running companies have a clear understanding of what their core business is and to whom they are targeting their products and services. The goals and objectives that they set need to be aligned with the organisation's vision and mission. **Chapter 3** examines the nature of an organisation's vision – the leadership that drives it, the values that support it and the purpose that justifies it. The mission stems from the vision, and in turn guides the setting of goals and objectives.

There are many legal, fiduciary and other obligations placed on limited companies, and so **Chapter 4** deals with governance – how senior executives are held to account to various stakeholders. Too much legislation would stifle the day-to-day operations of companies, and so business ethics guide decision-makers when the law does not prescribe an answer. The final part of **Chapter 4** deals with corporate social responsibility (CSR) – the responsibility that organisations have to the wider community in which they operate.

If a building does not have sufficient foundations, sooner or later it will come crashing down. Likewise, companies will not survive if they do not have a solid foundation underpinning their strategy. Good leadership and a results-oriented corporate culture, supported by good governance structures, will guide the company successfully through turbulent times, as well as the boom times. Good governance ensures not just legal compliance; it also provides the organisation with a moral framework that will withstand any scrutiny.

CHAPTER 2

Leadership and Organisational Culture

LEARNING OBJECTIVES

On completion of this chapter, you will be able to:

- Distinguish between the different types of leadership
- Evaluate the effectiveness of different leadership styles
- Assess the relationship between leadership and corporate culture
- Critically examine the role of leadership in the formulation and implementation of strategy

"The great leader is he who the people say 'we did it ourselves'."

Lao Tsu

INTRODUCTION

Leading an organisation to achieve its goals is central to its success. Leadership exists at many levels: the directors on the board, the chief executive and other senior executives and those heading up the different divisions and sections throughout the organisation, right down to supervisor level. Leadership should underpin the values and expectations of the company and is the catalyst behind the energy and commitment of its employees. As such, it is an essential element in laying the foundation of strategy, as well as the other phases of strategy formulation and implementation.

This chapter looks at leadership from a number of different perspectives. Having defined leadership, it then draws a distinction between management and leadership. While many theorists suggest that leadership is a function of management, there is an important distinction between the two. These theories include examining traits, behaviour, situations and charismatic leadership.

The functions that leaders perform in organisations are also explored:

- Creating a vision
- Building teams
- Motivation

- Development – individual and organisational
- Creating a high-performance organisation
- Succession planning
- Leading change
- Decision-maker.

The chapter refers to a wide range of contemporary authors and theories on leadership. William Shakespeare, in particular, showed a tremendous understanding of human nature and how it applies to leadership. Four hundred years later, his insights hold true.

The final section of the chapter deals with organisational culture, how it is established and maintained and the different types of culture in an organisation. Leaders play an important role in developing and maintaining organisational culture. In turn, culture plays an important role in supporting those leaders in the organisation in achieving results.

LEADERSHIP

Leadership can be defined thus:

 Leadership is the ability to inspire and motivate others to work willingly towards achieving organisational goals.

Inspiration

Strategic goals are achieved by senior management working with the employees of the organisation. This implies being able to motivate and inspire people so that the collective effort can enable the organisation to achieve goals that individuals on their own could never achieve. There are many ways in which people can be influenced. There has been much research over the years on influence tactics. Yukl *et al.* (1993) propose generic influence tactics, ranging from rational persuasion (using logic and reason) to legitimating tactics (using one's authority and organisational rules). Ultimately, rational persuasion and inspirational appeals that build on employees' values and ideals are much more effective than having to exert authority.

Power

Leadership also implies power. There are two dimensions of power in organisations. The first is *socialised power*, which is aimed at helping people to achieve their goals. The second is *personalised power*, which is directed at helping oneself. When discussing organisational leadership, it is socialised power that enables people and organisations to achieve their goals.

History shows many examples of people who amassed personal power. In some cases, personalised power was used in an autocratic manner but for what the leader presumed was the good of the people. When the Duke of Wellington became Prime Minister of Britain in 1828, he obviously had some trouble making the transition from the army to political life (he was a strong opponent of parliamentary reform). In describing his first cabinet meeting, he is quoted as saying: "An extraordinary affair. I gave them their orders and they wanted to stay and discuss them!"

In other cases, power has been greatly misused, with devastating consequences. In modern business, many of the major ethical scandals were due to people amassing personal power and wealth (for example, Kenneth Lay, former chair of the US company Enron at the time of its collapse in 2001). In the business context, it is important that power is used for the benefit of the organisation rather than the individual. In that respect, it is important that leaders and managers reflect on the source of their power and realise that it is organisational and positional, rather than personal.

In addition to the dimensions of power, there are different **bases for power**. The most widely used classification is that devised by French and Raven (1959), who argued that there are five bases for power:

- Reward power – obtaining compliance by granting rewards
- Coercive power – threat of punishment or actual punishment
- Legitimate power – derived from one's position in the organisation
- Expert power – having expert knowledge or information
- Referent power – using one's personality or charisma to influence people.

CEOs of an organisation will, by virtue of their position, have legitimate power. To be effective, they should be able to rely on expert power and, to a lesser extent, on some referent power. Power underpins so many of our interactions. It must be carefully used, not abused. It must be remembered that leadership implies 'followership'. People must be willing to respond and come on board. An educated workforce is unlikely to do this unless they see the leader has a clear vision based on sound, ethical values (Duff, 2014).

Leaders and Managers

The above section reminds us that simply holding a management position at the top of an organisation does not make one a leader. There is an important distinction between leadership and management. While 'management' and 'leadership' overlap as activities, they each have their own distinct characteristics. The word 'management' derives from the Latin word '*manus*', meaning a 'hand'. Management literally means 'handling' the organisation, whereas leadership involves showing the way. A succinct summary of the difference between leadership and management was that provided by Bennis and Nanus (1985):

"Managers do things right. Leaders do the right thing."

Managers

Mintzberg (1973) studied a variety of organisations and observed that managers performed 10 different roles (of which leadership was one). The managerial functions identified by Mintzberg are integral to the running of any organisation. Many earlier writers looked on leadership as a function of management, but more recent writers, such as John Adair and John Kotter, regard leadership, while still being linked with management, as being an essential role in its own right.

Leaders

Leadership is a much broader concept than just a function of management. Leadership is concerned primarily with inspiring and motivating others in the organisation. Leaders develop a vision of the future and how the organisation will get there. In **Chapter 3** we will see that this vision encompasses a moral element, which underpins the notion that 'leaders do the right thing'. There is a strong inter-personal element to the role of leaders and how they relate to people both inside and outside the organisation.

Not every manager will be a leader, even those who make it to the top of their respective companies. When corporate strategy is being developed and implemented, the emphasis is much more on leadership than on management. In discussing leadership here, the main focus will be on those running the organisation. However, it must be stressed that leadership takes place at many different levels in an organisation. Each divisional or functional head should also lead those within their own unit. This should happen at every level, right down to front-line management (Katbzenback and Santamaria, 1999; Duff, 2014). The need for leadership at front-line level was very evident in the University of Bath studies conducted by Purcell (2004) on people and performance. Front-line managers were seen as particularly important for translating organisational policy and making it relevant to employees (Gunnigle *et al.*, 2017). Also, leadership is not exclusive to positions of authority and there are often situations where leadership is demonstrated by individuals who 'rise to the occasion'. (A study of the Antarctic exploration by Scott and Shackleton shows that Tom Crean from County Kerry displayed great leadership qualities, despite the fact he was not in a position of formal authority (Smith, 2000; Nugent, 2003) – see **Illustration 2.1** below.)

In recent years, many failures of corporate governance have been exposed across a broad spectrum of organisations and sectors, resulting in resignations and, in some cases, criminal convictions. What is clear, however, is that there has been widespread abuse of power in organisations that demanded respect. This raises serious questions on how organisations develop leadership qualities in their people (as opposed to developing management skills). Part of their leadership training should be teaching people how to handle power properly and to behave in an ethical manner.

These problems have developed over a long period of time, and are partly caused by a societal deference in Ireland to people at the top of their organisations, whether they are church, state, professional or commercial. What is required, therefore, is a more open approach internally and externally to leadership and governance. The Report into the Catholic Archdiocese of Dublin, known as the 'Murphy' report (Murphy *et al.*, 2009:23), states:

> "Institutions and individuals, no matter how august, should never be considered to be immune from criticism or from external oversight of their actions. In particular, no institution or individual should be allowed such pre-eminent status that the State, in effect, is stymied in taking action against it or them should there be breaches of the State's laws."

Across the board in Irish business and society there have been failures in leadership, and there has been enormous collateral damage – the implications go far beyond the organisation itself. In future there will have to be far greater openness and accountability by business leaders for their stewardship of the company with which they have been entrusted. It will require a more inclusive approach, recognising that the actions of executives have far-reaching consequences on a wide group of stakeholders.

LEADERSHIP THEORIES

Different theories have evolved over time to understand the nature of leadership, and these can be classified as follows:

- Trait Theories
- Behavioural Theories
- Situational Theories
- Theories of Charismatic Leadership
- The 'Level 5' Theory of Leadership.

Trait Theories of Leadership

Historically it was believed that leaders were born, not made. This belief underpinned the concept of hereditary monarchs and, with the advent of the Industrial Revolution, expanded to include 'captains of industry'. It was assumed that such people possessed certain innate traits or personal characteristics that set them apart as leaders.

Studies on leadership early in the last century focused on innate traits, which included qualities such as intelligence, vision, self-confidence, initiative, lateral thinking, the need for power and achievement, being goal-driven, etc. This view of leadership continued until the 1950s. For example, Stogdill (1948) identified five common traits that differentiate leaders from their followers: intelligence, dominance, self-confidence, level of energy, and task-relevant knowledge. However, Stogdill's study, and a later one by Richard Mann in 1959, showed that, while leaders possess many of these traits, the concept of leadership was much more complex than just identifying certain individual traits.

Perhaps the greatest limitation to the traits theory is its inability as a predictor of leadership – by identifying these traits in an individual, can one identify a leader? It is also difficult to measure these traits in an individual, and leadership is also dependent on an employee's perception of what constitutes effective leadership. According to Buelens *et al.* (2011:47) a '**leadership prototype**' is a mental representation of the traits and behaviours that a person believes is displayed by a leader. Thus, a person is regarded as a leader if their behaviour is consistent with the people's leadership prototype. The task of predicting leaders is made more difficult by the fact that this concept of leadership prototype is culturally bound with differences between English-speaking and non-English speaking countries and between different clusters of countries in Europe. In other words, it is "influenced by national cultural values".

While the presence of leadership traits in a person is not necessarily a predictor of leadership qualities *per se*, such traits are usually present in leaders. Research is once again looking at traits. Kouzes and Posner (1995) sought to examine the qualities that people admire in their bosses. Results from around the world indicate that leaders should be "honest, forward-looking, inspiring and competent". Jack Welch, the former CEO of General Electric, refers to the four Es: "energy; ability to energise others; the edge to make tough decisions; and execution..." (Stewart, 1999).

Perhaps an important distinction to make is between the redundant concept that people are born with these traits, and recognition that nurturing plays an important role in developing the necessary traits required to lead an organisation. Writers such as Kotter (1996), Goleman (2002) and Duff (2014) firmly believe that leadership can be taught. Armies around the world, for example, place a strong emphasis on developing leaders, and such development takes place throughout the person's career using a mixture of theoretical concepts learned in military academies and command experience with troops. Many commercial organisations now recognise the importance of leadership development, either in their own in-house training centres (such as GE's Crotonville Management Development Centre), or externally as part of MBA programmes.

Emotional Intelligence Goleman (1995 and 2002) linked the concept of emotional intelligence to leadership. Emotional intelligence is the extent to which people can understand their emotions. He argues that such traits are not innate but can be learned. Goleman believes that emotional intelligence increases with age, but it does require a sincere desire and concerted effort on behalf of the individual. Quoting Ralph Waldo Emerson: "Nothing great was ever achieved without enthusiasm."

According to Goleman (1995), there are five components of emotional intelligence at work:

- **Self-awareness** – how we can recognise and understand our moods, emotions and what drives us, as well as recognise their effect on others. The hallmarks of self-awareness include self-confidence, and a self-deprecating sense of humour. It gives leaders a strong sense of who they are and helps them align their personal values with work values.
- **Self-regulation** – how we control our impulses and moods and the ability to think before acting. Our emotions are driven by biological impulses, but these impulses can be controlled. Self-regulation is characterised by trustworthiness and integrity, openness to change and being comfortable with ambiguity, all of which are very necessary attributes for a leader. Self-regulation is important for a number of reasons. First, it creates an environment of trust and fairness. Secondly, it enables people to cope with change. Finally, it helps build lasting relationships with stakeholders.
- **Motivation** – intrinsic motivation goes well beyond financial rewards or status. Along with the energy and persistence to pursue goals, it manifests itself as a strong desire to achieve,

optimism even in difficult circumstances and a commitment to the organisation. Motivation creates a passion for work and an eagerness to explore new ways of doing things. People who are motivated are forever raising the performance bar.

- **Empathy** – the ability to understand and respond to the emotional make-up of other people. It requires cross-cultural sensitivity, service to both clients and customers, and an expertise in building and retaining talent. It is important to recognise that empathy does not mean adopting other people's emotions or trying to please everybody. It does, however, mean considering employees' feelings, in conjunction with other factors, when making decisions.

- **Social skill** – a proficiency in managing relationships and building networks and an ability to build a rapport with people. These attributes are important in working with and through people and team-building, and social skill is a particularly important attribute in leading change. Organisations are social constructs – designed by people to enable people to work together towards the attainment of agreed goals. Social skill entails finding common ground with employees and motivating them towards those end goals. In essence, it is the combination of the other four dimensions of emotional intelligence.

As leadership is primarily about relating to people, emotional intelligence plays an integral part in successful leadership (Duff, 2014). While emotional intelligence is undoubtedly an important attribute in leaders, there is debate in the literature about its validity. This is based primarily on the difficulty of measuring it and its predictive ability. Yet, it is difficult to dismiss it. Shakespeare's plays on leadership show a deep understanding of human emotions. Before the battle of Agincourt, King Henry recognised the fear in his men (being totally outnumbered by the French) yet he was able to appeal to their emotions:

> "If we are marked to die, we are enough to do our country loss; and if to live, the fewer men, the greater share of honour…
> We few, we happy few, we band of brothers.
> For he today that sheds his blood with me shall be my brother…".

Henry V, Act 4, Sc. 2

On the other hand, Shakespeare's Coriolanus, while a brilliant general, lacked any emotional connection with his troops.

Cultural Intelligence According to Earley and Mosakowski (2004), cultural intelligence is similar to emotional intelligence but picks up where emotional intelligence leaves off. Those with emotional intelligence are able to distinguish between what makes us human and, at the same time, individual. Cultural intelligence enables us to identify features that are common to all groups of people: those peculiar to a particular person, and those that are common to specific ethnic groups.

In leading a multicultural group, cultural intelligence is particularly important in understanding the behaviour of people in that group. It allows the leader to suspend judgement – to think before acting. By understanding cultural patterns, one can read body language and anticipate how people will react in a certain situation. Earley and Mosakowski believe that, while some cultural intelligence is innate, much of it can be learned. They believe that there are three components to cultural intelligence: cognitive; physical; and emotional/motivational.

The cognitive element concerns learning about different cultures, such as that provided by corporate training programmes. However, while one can learn much about the beliefs and customs of foreign cultures, one cannot be prepared for every situation. The physical element concerns itself with how well a person adopts the habits and mannerisms of a culture, e.g. the amount of personal space that should be allowed when in conversation with another person. Finally, the emotional element relates to how willing a person is to relate to and embrace other cultures.

At a basic level, having such cultural intelligence can prevent leaders from insulting employees or customers through cultural ignorance. When it is cultivated, it can enable leaders to understand people from different cultures and so relate to them more effectively. In the past 25 years, the demographics of the workforce in Ireland has changed dramatically, with many companies having employees from a wide variety of countries. In addition, Irish companies are now dealing in markets all over the world. As a result, cultural intelligence is a vital trait for leaders to have.

Behavioural Theories of Leadership

The limitations of the trait theories prompted a wider study of leadership (particularly in the United States) during the Second World War when there was a strong imperative to develop effective leaders for the army. The emphasis shifted from the possible traits that leaders might possess to their behaviour. Two major, and somewhat overlapping, studies on leadership behaviour emerged – the Ohio State University study and the University of Michigan studies.

The **Ohio** research was extremely extensive, but was eventually narrowed down to just two independent variables, based on a manager's focus on the employees' needs, known as **considerate style**, and the manager's focus on getting the job done, referred to as **initiating structure**. The combination of these two factors resulted in four types of leadership behaviour, with a high initiating structure/high consideration style being regarded as the best (Stogdill and Coons, 1957).

The **Michigan** studies investigated the behavioural relationship between effective and ineffective leaders. Like the Ohio study, they came up with two similar variables centred on employees (employee-oriented), and on achieving results (production-oriented). Results indicated that effective leaders balance a supportive, employee-centred approach with a focus on setting and achieving high performance goals (Likert, 1961). Blake and Mouton (1962) developed the '**managerial grid**' to determine the one best style of leadership. Again, they use two dimensions (each divided into nine units): concern for people and concern for production.

Behavioural research was an important development in the study of leadership as it explored different leadership styles. It was also seen that the effectiveness of leadership style depended on the particular context, a realisation which gave rise to the development of situational theories of leadership.

Illustration 2.1: Behavioural Theories – Antarctic Expeditions

Accounts of the early Antarctic expeditions by the Norwegian explorer Roald Amundsen, the British explorer Robert Falcon Scott, and Irish explorer Ernest Shackleton provide a fascinating study of contrasting leadership styles and their effectiveness.

Scott, a strong disciplinarian in the Royal Navy tradition, sought to be the first man to reach the South Pole. However, he lacked focus in his vision. Scott had included a large team of scientists to explore conditions on the continent. While such exploration had perfect validity in its own right, in terms of the race to be the first to reach the South Pole, it detracted from his primary mission. Scott also had inadequate resources, and had failed to master the use of one vital resource – teams of dogs to pull the heavy provisions. He regarded the use of dogs as "not the right thing to do". But by man-handling sledges (in four-man teams) weighing approximately 360kgs, they were operating at a much slower rate, and it was exhausting work in what are the most severe conditions on the planet (temperatures as low as minus 40° centigrade and 80 km/h winds).

Behind his strong authoritarian approach, Scott had poor leadership skills. In particular, he was indecisive. During the expedition, he waited until the last minute to decide on picking the team that would make the final push to the South Pole. This had major implications for the men concerned. The team picked to reach the South Pole should have been relieved of heavy pulling work at an early stage in the trek in order to conserve their energy for the final push. Instead, they were physically exhausted by the time they got to the Pole. This undoubtedly contributed to their death on the return leg.

Scott also made a poor decision in leaving Tom Crean behind (the strongest and probably the most capable member in the entire group), and did not have the courage to be direct with him in telling him he was not included. On hearing the Irishman cough, Scott used that as an excuse not to include Crean in the final team. He said: "You have a bad cold there Crean". The ever-loyal Crean understood he was not being included but was not about to let such a poor excuse pass by. He retorted: "I understand a half-sung song, Sir!"

In addition, Scott picked a *five*-man team including himself, Bowers, Wilson, Oates and Taff Evans, while all along, the training and division of supplies had been based on a four-man team. They reached the South Pole on 17 January 1912, only to find that they had been beaten by the Norwegian team led by Roald Amundsen. On the way back to the main group, Scott and his colleagues perished (Alexandre, 1998; Smith, 2000).

Roald Amundsen by contrast, was completely focused on his mission to be the first to reach the South Pole, which he achieved on 14 December 1911, a month before Scott. A team leader to the end, he insisted that all five members simultaneously plant the Norwegian flag at the South Pole. This was his vision, and for years he had prepared for it, acclimatising himself to the severe cold, mastering the use of skis and the use of dog-teams for pulling sledges, as well as learning all of the survival skills needed to operate in such harsh conditions from native Norwegians living in the far north of the country. Amundsen and his team made far greater progress than Scott, averaging 36 km a day compared to Scott's 24 km a day. By the time Scott had reached the South Pole, Amundsen was already safely back at his Franheim base having covered the round trip of over 3,000 km in just 99 days (Smith, 2000).

Ernest Shackleton's 1914 expedition to cross the Antarctic went terribly wrong when his ship *The Endurance* was crushed by ice in the Weddell Sea, and turned into one of the greatest survival epics ever known. It is an incredible story of leadership and change management. (Shackleton's leadership ability is explored in a case study at the end of this textbook.)

Situational Theories of Leadership

The study of leadership traits and behaviours showed that leadership is a great deal more complex than previously thought and that there was still a general lack of understanding about the effectiveness of leadership styles. It was seen that context was also an important element. Different situations require different leadership styles, and as the situation changes, so too must the style. This effectively contradicted the notion that there is one best leadership style. This section will examine two situational theories: Fielder's Contingency Model and House's Path–Goal Theory.

Fielder's Contingency Model examines leadership in different work situations. There are two interconnected elements: leadership style and the situation context. The leadership styles examined by Fielder were similar to previous studies in that he isolated two styles:

- **Relationship-motivated style**, which focuses on developing relations between the leader and followers.
- **Task-motivated style** where the focus is on accomplishing the particular task.

Fielder then developed a measurement instrument called the '**least-preferred co-worker**' to ascertain a person's leadership style, whether it is relationship-motivated or task-motivated. He believed that leaders had a particular style of leadership (a dominant style) and they were reluctant to change or modify that style.

House's Path–Goal Theory has strong links with Vroom's 'expectancy theory' of motivation (1964), where the effort put into work is linked to performance and, in turn, impacts on the outcome.

People are motivated by the value that they receive from the outcome. According to House (1971), leaders should focus their attention on identifying goals and helping employees achieve them. The attainment of those goals is linked to rewards. The leader should clarify the path to achieving the goals and help remove any obstacles along the way (hence the name path–goal). House identified four different leadership styles:

- **Directive leadership** – a prescriptive approach to how employees should carry out the task
- **Supportive leadership** – being friendly, approachable and supportive
- **Participative leadership** – taking on board the ideas of employees when making decisions
- **Achievement-oriented leadership** – enabling employees to perform at their best to achieve goals.

In contrast to Fielder, House believed that leaders can exhibit more than one style, and their ability to help employees achieve their goals is dependent on how well they can adapt the style to the situation. In turn, this is linked to two situational variables: employee characteristics (locus of control, task ability experience, need for achievement and need for clarity) and environmental factors, including the employee's task, the work system in place and the work team to which they belong.

In reality, most individual CEOs are probably slow to change their leadership style. Organisational needs will vary from time to time, and so the appropriate leadership style is dependent on the strategic issues facing the organisation at that particular time. As a result, it may well be that the existing leader does not have the appropriate style to bring the organisation through its current difficulty. In such situations, the organisation may require a different leader with a different set of skills. An example being a company in a crisis situation where strong, directive leadership may be more appropriate than a more inclusive style. On the other hand, this directive style would be inappropriate for organisational learning.

Charismatic Leadership

The types of leadership discussed above (trait, behavioural and situational) are generally referred to as **transactional** leadership, where leaders use a mixture of rewards and sanctions to achieve organisational goals.

Charismatic leadership, by contrast, is **transformational**. It has a profound effect on employees and is responsible for appealing to their values and beliefs, and gives them a sense of direction. As a result of its ability to get to the heart of employees, it plays a significant role in bringing about organisational change (see **Chapter 14**).

One of the primary functions of charismatic leadership is providing a vision for the organisation and creating a belief that such a vision can be achieved. According to Bass (1990), transformational leaders are charismatic role models for their organisation: they inspire and motivate, provide intellectual stimulation, and coach and advise staff.

Illustration 2.2: Charismatic Military Leaders

Admiral Nelson was a charismatic leader who had a profound effect on the morale of his officers and men. As he arrived at the Royal Navy fleet anchored at Cadiz just before the battle of Trafalgar in 1805, "the mood of the fleet changed as its seventeen thousand men realised that Nelson was amongst them" (Pocock, 1987:318). Despite the British fleet being outnumbered by the combined French and Spanish fleets, the 'Nelson Touch' is believed to have had a major impact on the outcome of the battle.

Napoleon too had a similar effect on the French nation and its army. His great nemesis, Wellington, recognised the impact that Napoleon had on the Grande Armée when he said:

"I used to say of him that his presence on the field made the difference of forty thousand men."

Unfortunately for Napoleon, when it came to the Battle of Waterloo the Prussian general, Marshal Blücher, made up the numbers for the coalition side, led by Wellington, before the day was done.

While there is evidence to support the concept of charismatic leadership, and good examples in politicians like Nelson Mandela and John F. Kennedy, and business people like Anita Roddick (founder of the Body Shop) and Richard Branson (Virgin Group), charismatic leadership seems to be somewhat elusive in reality. Manfred Kets de Vries, who lectures at INSEAD in France, is particularly critical of the concept of charismatic leaders. He believes that there is a negative or 'shadow side' of leadership that can have a detrimental impact on the whole organisation. This is mainly because these people surround themselves with subordinates who will not challenge, nor will they seek advice, believing that they know best (Kets de Vries, 2001). This criticism of charismatic leadership is also shared by Collins (2001) who argues that the most successful type of leadership is 'Level 5' leadership.

'Level 5' Leadership

In sharp contrast to the concept of charismatic leadership is what is termed 'Level 5' leadership. In his book *Good to Great*, Jim Collins (2001) examined the factors that underpin companies that constantly achieve greatness. His research team contributed 15,000 hours of work to the project and initially examined 1,435 'Fortune 500' companies, involving both qualitative and quantitative research. They picked a 15-year period for the study in order to show sustained long-term results, rather than companies that achieve good short-term, but unsustained, results. They selected companies with results that were three times the market average. Next, they chose comparison companies and sought to ascertain what the good-to-great companies shared in common, defining what distinguished them from these comparison companies. The comparison companies were divided into two groups: similar companies in the same industry, and other companies that showed short-term good results, but failed to maintain them.

The results covered a range of topics from strategy to the use of technology. One result that surprised the team was the style of leadership in the highly successful companies:

"We were surprised, shocked really, to discover the type of leadership required for turning a good company into a great one. Compared to high-profile leaders with big personalities who make the headlines and become celebrities, the good-to-great leaders seem to have come from Mars. Self-effacing, quiet, even shy – these leaders are a paradoxical blend of personal humility and professional will."

He refers to these leaders as 'Level 5' leaders – the highest level in a hierarchy of executive capabilities. They are ambitious people, but their ambition is directed for the benefit of the company, not for themselves. The five levels are:

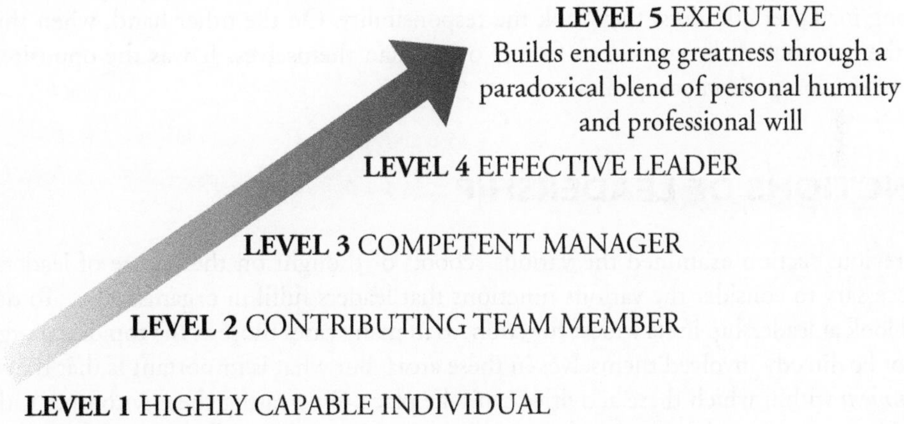

LEVEL 5 EXECUTIVE
Builds enduring greatness through a
paradoxical blend of personal humility
and professional will

LEVEL 4 EFFECTIVE LEADER

LEVEL 3 COMPETENT MANAGER

LEVEL 2 CONTRIBUTING TEAM MEMBER

LEVEL 1 HIGHLY CAPABLE INDIVIDUAL

Adapted from Collins, J., 2001, *Good to Great*, London, Random House Business Books.

Figure 2.1 *Level 5 Leadership*

Interestingly, the team did not set out to investigate the role of leadership; rather, Collins had initially told the team to downplay the role of top executives. As the study continued:

"The research team kept pushing back, 'No! There is something consistently unusual about them. We can't ignore them'. When they examined the evidence, they found that all of the good-to-great companies had Level 5 leadership at the time of transition."

(Collins, 2001:22)

A number of interesting and important observations about these leaders emerged from the research. 'Celebrity' CEOs who come in from the outside were negatively correlated with going from good to great. In practically all cases, the good-to-great CEOs came from inside the organisation, whereas comparison companies chose outside CEOs six times more often. There are, however, some exceptions. There has been much criticism of Irish banks in promoting insiders. When the chief executives of Bank of Ireland and Allied Irish Bank were forced to resign as a result of the financial crisis, they were replaced by insiders. Many people considered that the banks should have recruited from outside, as it was believed that appointing senior executives who were also board members at the time of the crisis would not inject the fresh thinking that was required to lead the banks out of the mess and, in particular, change banking culture. Despite these exceptions, the evidence still suggests that promoting from within produces better results for the organisation (see case study on the Four Seasons Hotel).

According to Collins, the style of work of Level 5 leaders was more reflective of a "plough horse rather than a show horse". They were fanatically driven towards achieving sustainable results and would make whatever decisions were necessary. They displayed a compelling modesty, were self-effacing and understated, whereas the comparison companies usually had leaders with enormous egos who contributed to the continued mediocrity or the demise of the company. When things did go wrong for Level 5 leaders, they took the responsibility. On the other hand, when things went right, they attributed the success to factors other than themselves. It was the opposite with the CEOs of the comparison companies.

FUNCTIONS OF LEADERSHIP

The previous section examined the various schools of thought on the nature of leadership. It is also necessary to consider the various functions that leaders fulfil in organisations. To do this, we should look at leadership in its widest function, as in many cases those at the top of the organisation may not be directly involved themselves in these areas, but what is important is that they *create the environment* within which these activities can take place. By creating the environment, the people within the organisation become empowered and can achieve their full potential. When employees fulfil their potential, the organisation will achieve competitive advantage. Lao Tsu, the Chinese philosopher (b. 604 BC) who inspired Confucius, identified the type of leader who would enable an organisation to achieve that competitive advantage:

"The great leader is he who the people say 'we did it ourselves'."

These leadership functions are many and varied, and are important in making everything happen within an organisation. There are a number of functions that leaders perform:

- Creating a vision
- Building teams
- Motivation
- Development: individual and organisational
- Creating a high-performance organisation
- Succession planning
- Bringing about change
- Decision-making.

Creating a Vision

A vision plays a vital part in giving direction to an organisation and, as will be seen in **Chapter 3**, goals and objectives are then chosen to reach the desired end-state for that organisation. Leaders play a vital role in creating that vision and this, in turn, helps motivate people to work toward achieving success. It will also be seen in **Chapter 3** that organisational values are an integral part of creating a vision. Yaragadda *et al.* (2017:11) suggest that leaders must have a "strong sense of moral self" and take an ethical approach to leadership that encompasses stakeholders.

People are often attracted to organisations that display values similar to their own (see **Chapter 4**). For senior executives, the values of the organisation and their own values are likely to be strongly linked. They are the people who make the strategic decisions and, inevitably, their own values will be reflected in the type of decisions that are made. Likewise with ethics: those at the top of an organisation must be able to stand over their decisions from an ethical standpoint.

Chapter 4 offers a cogent case for strong organisational values. Prahalad (2010) argues that managers are the custodians of society's most powerful institutions and must hold themselves accountable to a higher standard. In short, leaders must achieve success with responsibility. He reminds us that, over a long career, leaders will experience high points and low points and "humility in success and courage in failure are hallmarks of a good leader". Achievement must be balanced with compassion for others, and learning with understanding. It must be remembered that leaders should lead by example. If they do not display strong values in their own actions, it cannot be expected of others. An essential element in all of this is how leaders communicate their vision. Hamm (2006) believes that, all too often, people leading organisations fail to communicate what they are thinking, and talk to employees in a manner that is unclear and vague. It is imperative that all members of the organisation know exactly what is required of them in terms of their contribution to achieving organisational goals. In turn, strong values will assist in the generation of trust. It is vital that leaders create a climate of trust within the organisation: people will not follow a leader whom they do not trust (Houghton, 2016). (The importance of trust will be developed in greater detail later in this chapter when discussing organisational culture.)

Building Teams

Many influential writers, such as Peter Drucker and Manfred Kets de Vries, believe that teams are playing an ever-increasing role in business organisations. Being able to pick the right team is a valuable competence required to implement a chosen strategy. Different people have different skills, and being able to recognise those skills and then motivate people to use them to the best of their ability is an essential element in achieving organisational success.

> "All the world's a stage, and all the men and women mere players: they have their exits and their entrances, and one man in his time plays many parts, his act being seven ages."
>
> *As You Like It*, Act 2, Sc. 7

According to Adair (1983), leadership is about teamwork and the creation of teams. Teams tend to have leaders and leaders tend to create teams. Teams do not happen by accident. First it requires finding the right people and then getting the mix right. Nowhere is this more evident than in Irish rugby. The panel that is chosen to represent Ireland consists of many very talented individuals. One of the greatest challenges for the Irish rugby coach and fellow coaches is picking the optimum team based on individual skill, performance, motivation and, most importantly, an ability to work together towards a common goal. The same principles also apply to every company.

One must distinguish between groups and teams. Teams have been defined as "a small number of people with complementary skills who are committed to a common purpose, performance goals and approach for which they hold themselves mutually accountable" (Katzenback and Smith, 1993: 45). The concept of the team is also central to Adair's **Action-Centred Leadership** model, which was developed while he was lecturing at the Royal Military Academy, Sandhurst. In this model are three overlapping elements for which the leader is responsible:

- **Task** – creating a vision and purpose for the group, developing a plan to achieve the task, providing resources and monitoring progress.
- **Team** – establishing and agreeing standards of behaviour, culture, ethics, building team spirit and resolving conflict, developing roles within the group, changing team members as necessary, establishing open communication and giving feedback to the group, and gradually developing greater autonomy for the group.
- **Individuals** – understanding each individual's needs, skills, hopes and aspirations, training and developing the individuals to undertake the necessary tasks both individually and as members of a team, assigning responsibility and giving recognition to people for work well done.

Each of these elements is mutually dependent on the other two and failure in one can affect the others. Leadership is common to them all.

According to Buelens *et al.* (2011), for work teams to be effective, they must achieve a level of performance that meets users' expectations. They must also be viable, meaning that members must be satisfied and willing to continue contributing. Work teams must be supported by the organisation if they are to be successful. Factors here include strategy, organisational structure, technology, culture, the reward system and administrative support and training. They also list five important factors of the internal processes of work teams: member composition, interpersonal dynamics, purpose, resources, and co-ordination with other work groups. Leaders play an important role in creating the environment in which teams can operate effectively. When work teams fail, it is often the result of a hostile environment where there is poor staffing of the teams, poor communication and a lack of trust (Hope-Hailey and Gustaffsson, 2014). Team members themselves can also be responsible for failure in taking on too much and having poor interpersonal skills.

In every team there will be those who are effective and those who are not. Performance evaluation is another important function of leaders in aligning the efforts of individuals to the goals of the organisation. There are many reasons why people may not achieve goals that were assigned to them, from the goals being too difficult in the first instance, to a lack of necessary training, or simply a case of the person underperforming due to a lack of effort. Performance evaluation, when carried out objectively, should discover the underlying reason so that it can be rectified. In many cases, various incentives, such as bonus payments, are linked to performance. To be motivational, it is imperative that employees view the system as being fair and impartial. At times, leaders will have to make tough decisions, not just on whether incentives should be paid, but also on who should be promoted, and whether an individual actually belongs in the team.

Motivation

People working in an organisation will only 'go the extra mile' when they are motivated. This applies equally to people at every level of the organisation, not just those at the top. In turn, leaders at each level must energise those working in their section, which has a cascading effect as managers motivate those with whom they work directly. Motivation is a complex process and it is necessary that leaders have a proper understanding of what works for different individuals.

There is a variety of different theories of motivation. In broad terms, theories of motivation can be divided into two groups. First, content theories, which identify people's needs and the goals they want to achieve to attain those needs, e.g. Maslow's Hierarchy of Needs. Secondly, process theories explain the actual process of motivation and acknowledge people's personal decisions, e.g. Adam's Equity Theory and Vroom's Expectancy Model. Financial rewards are one aspect of motivation, but research shows that it actually has little effect on improving executive performance (O'Higgins, 2012).

The main objective of motivation from an organisational perspective is to improve work performance. Clear communication is an essential element of motivation. People must understand clearly what is expected from them. There is also an onus on leaders to ensure that staff members have the ability to do the job that is being asked of them and that they also have the opportunity to perform the job in terms of organisational support and time. It must also be remembered that people model the behaviour of managers who, in turn, must constantly demonstrate good behaviour and reinforce it. Buelens *et al.* (2011) suggest that the link between motivation and improved productivity is also dependent on three factors: direction, intensity and persistence. 'Direction' is whether people prefer intrinsic rewards (personal growth) or extrinsic rewards (bonuses). 'Intensity' refers to the intensity of the response once the person makes the choice. Finally, 'persistence' refers to how long a person will channel their energy and effort to attain a goal.

As Ireland moves more and more towards a high-knowledge economy, organisations will require people who have achieved a much higher level of educational attainment. In turn, this will place a greater onus on executives to provide leadership and to motivate team members. In most situations a prescriptive form of management will not suffice. When a directive approach is applied to staff with experience and knowledge, a lack of consultation will undermine engagement and cause frustration (Zheltoukhova, 2014).

Development

Individual Development Coaching and mentoring are important elements of leadership. There are different aspects to coaching. In order to develop individuals to their full potential, their strengths and weaknesses need to be identified. It is only then that the weaknesses can be lessened or eliminated and the strengths built upon. It is a good deal easier for another person to identify these points in us than we can do ourselves. It is the exact same with organisations. Leaders need to be developed and encouraged in order to achieve their potential (Yarlagadda *et al.*, 2017) and this development must include specific leadership training, in addition to broader training. Stewart and Rigg (2011) identify such development as being an essential element in a high-performance culture.

The development process is continuous. To quote Darwin Smith, former CEO of Kimberly-Clark (one of the good-to-great companies identified above): "I never stop trying to become qualified for the job," Collins (2001:20). Development also involves reflective practice – getting the individual to reflect on how he or she handled a particular situation. This is not to be confused with performance evaluation (which is also necessary), but rather facilitating the person in a non-confrontational way to learn from the process that they have been through. Mentoring involves taking an individual and helping to develop their career by being there to guide them when required. It is ensuring that the person gets the right work experience in terms of different markets and skills, and once that has been attained, moving on to the next appointment. In Shakespeare's *King Henry IV, Parts 1 and 2*, the young Prince Hal enjoyed a wild lifestyle, but all the time he was getting to know and understand his future subjects. He does so in preparation for the time that he will accept the crown from his dying father:

> "My gracious liege, you won it, wore it, kept it, gave it me; then plain and right must my possession be; which I with more than common pain 'Gainst all the world will rightfully maintain."
>
> *Henry IV Part 2*, Act 4, Sc. 5

Martin and Schmidt (2010) highlight a number of potential pitfalls when identifying talented individuals who are potential future leaders. It should not be assumed that just because employees are talented, that they are engaged. Talented employees need to be given stimulating assignments and need to be recognised in a variety of ways, not just pay. It should also be remembered that those who are performing well in current roles do not always have the potential to progress to higher levels. Employees being considered for promotion need to be tested for three critical attributes: ability, engagement and aspiration. These employees must be placed in assignments where new capabilities can be acquired and they must be involved in the development of future strategies. The development of future leaders should be managed primarily at corporate level; line managers may try to hoard high-performing individuals for the benefit of their strategic business unit, rather than do what is best for the overall company – or the individual.

Organisational Development Organisational development occurs at both individual and organisational levels and the two are interwoven. At present, the Irish economy is becoming knowledge-based. This implies a greater move by organisations to what Garratt (1987) referred to as "the learning organisation", a concept later made popular by Senge (1990). A learning organisation is one that has a culture that supports challenging assumptions around a common vision and one that is capable of regeneration through continuous learning by its members. Inherent in organisational development is a focus on innovation. There is a growing need for organisations to be constantly innovating. In dealing with intelligent and highly trained staff, a different type of leadership is required. A number of writers have discussed the importance of organisational learning, and leadership is an essential element in promoting such organisational development.

High-performance Organisation

Perhaps one of the biggest challenges for any leader is creating a high-performance organisation. There are a number of different aspects to this. It begins with laying the foundation for strategy development in terms of the values and governance of the organisation. The type of values that the organisation has will impact on many of the decisions that it takes, and the organisation and all its members will take its cue from the values displayed by those at the top.

Strategic analysis, in the form of analysing the business environment and, more importantly, understanding and building the strategic capability of the organisation, is also an integral part of the development process. The paradigm that is created will influence the type of strategy that the organisation develops. However, there is no 'acid test' to prove that any one strategy is the best one. Yet, the chosen strategy will have a profound impact on the organisation and its performance in the marketplace. Implementing the chosen strategy is the final element in creating a high-performance organisation. Up to this point the strategy is merely a blueprint; the implementation process must be led properly for it to be successful. It involves putting constant, constructive pressure on the organisation to achieve results, and adapting the strategic plan to meet changing circumstances.

A high-performance organisation is underpinned by that organisation having a high-performance culture. It will be seen in the section on culture below that there is a strong link between leadership and culture.

Succession Planning

Good leadership plays a very important role in the success of any organisation. Leaders come and go but there must be continuity in the leadership process. A very important role of leadership is planning the succession of leaders at every level, from the top down. This involves identifying people who display leadership potential and developing their skills and experience. Vacancies in critical areas may come about unexpectedly due to a person leaving, illness or death. For that reason, it is important to prepare and groom future leaders at every level. Without proper planning, a vacuum will occur and the wrong person could be appointed to the position.

Kerry Group Plc is an example of a company that has made a very successful transition from Denis Brosnan, its first CEO, to Hugh Friel, then Stan McCarthy and now to Edmond Scanlon. Each leader has successfully grown the company in a sustainable manner during their tenure, while maintaining the company's vision. King Lear planned his succession on a more spurious basis. Addressing his three daughters, he asked:

> "Since now we will divest us both of rule, interest of territory, cares of state — Which of you shall we say doth love us most? That we our largest bounty may extend where nature doth with merit challenge."
>
> *King Lear*, Act 1, Sc. 1

Bringing about Change

Every organisation undergoes change in its environment (see **Chapter 5**). As Charles Darwin discovered in terms of evolution, it is only those species that can adapt to a changing environment that can survive. The subject of change will be discussed in detail in **Chapter 14** but, in the context of leadership, it is important to stress the role that the leader plays in bringing the organisation through the change process. One of the most notable experts on change, John Kotter, stresses that change must be led rather than managed (Kotter, 1996). Similarly, Brown (1994) argues that effective leaders are those who understand the nature of the change affecting their organisation and can transform their organisation to create competitive advantage.

Coping with change is something most employees find very difficult, and so being able to motivate them is an integral part of the change process. Motivation also plays a much wider role in the attainment of organisational goals. Change involves taking tough decisions and being able to stand over them. This is particularly so when the organisation has to downsize and people are made redundant. While decision-making is an integral part of management, leaders will often take decisions that require great courage and can have a profound impact on the organisation. One major difficulty in leading change is balancing the necessity to create stability in the organisation, while anticipating and implementing the change that must take place to secure its future. Leaders also play an essential role in how they interpret and deal with uncertainty.

The nature of the challenges that change will bring about will also place many pressures on the leader of the organisation. Perhaps one of the biggest challenges on a human level is how to counter adversity with resilience. Resilience is the capacity to respond quickly and constructively to crises. According to Margolis and Stoltz (2010), dealing with a crisis needs a shift from cause-oriented thinking to response-oriented thinking. It requires leaders to: turn their attention to what they can control; focus on identifying positive effects that action may bring about; assume the crisis is specific and can be contained; and, finally, take action on addressing the problem immediately.

Prahalad (2010) reminds us that "leadership is about self-awareness". The importance of coaching in developing the potential of leaders was discussed above. While this is important in all aspects of the leader's job, it is particularly so in helping the leader to cope with change. If on a personal basis the leader is having difficulty in coming to terms with a new reality, there is little hope of them leading the organisation through the crisis. To facilitate this process, O'Donovan (2009) provides a framework known as CRAIC (Control, Responsibility, Awareness, Impetus and Confidence), which demonstrates how coaching can unlock the potential in individuals and help them maximise their performance. The leader must first focus on 'control', which refers to the feeling of control over one's environment and its importance in terms of self-esteem, motivation and self-efficacy. He or she must then take 'responsibility' for change and exercise control and self-discipline in terms of committing to action. Successful action is dependent on the leader's level of 'awareness' of his or her thinking patterns – a vital element in creativity and developing workable solutions. In turn, this requires the 'impetus' to begin and sustain effort towards achieving goals. Finally, it requires the 'confidence' to take the necessary action. Napoleon once described leaders as "dealers in hope". To be able to inspire hope in others, leaders must first be masters of themselves.

Decision-making

Underpinning all of the above functions is the ability of the leader to make decisions. According to Brousseau *et al.* (2006), a manager's decision-making style should change as the manager advances within the organisation. This is due to changes in the nature of the work being done and the demands on the individual. Making strategic decisions that will have a major impact on the organisation brings enormous responsibly to bear on the chief executive. Such hard decisions must not be avoided:

> "Upon the King, let us our lives, our souls, Our debts, our careful wives, Our children, and our sins, lay on the King: We must bear all."
>
> *Henry V*, Act 4, Sc. 1

Lower down the organisational chain, action is at a premium and managers are required to be more directive and focused on specific tasks. At senior executive level, managers are required to make decisions that involve multiple courses of action that may evolve as circumstances change. In general, for senior executives the emphasis should be on a more participative style of leadership and decision-making. (Decision-making is discussed in detail in **Chapter 12**.)

Leadership Constraints

Leaders at different levels in organisations face a number of possible constraints that may prevent them from exercising effective leadership, including a lack of support from the board or senior management. This support is particularly important when a change of culture is required. Other constraints include a lack of time and resources, and also cost pressures. However, while certain constraints might make leadership more difficult, there are also situations where there are simply failures in leadership.

Failures in Leadership

The last few years have laid bare many unedifying examples of poor leadership across the globe. Ireland has been no exception, and the consequences have been extremely serious for all concerned. It is essential to acknowledge and examine such failures and, most importantly, learn from the mistakes that were made. To paraphrase Karl Marx: history has happened, first as tragedy; it must not be allowed repeat itself as farce.

Many international factors contributed to the deep recession in Ireland after 2008. However, despite the initial widespread denial by many politicians and those at the top of many organisations (banks in particular), there can be no doubt that Ireland is responsible for a large portion of the problems that caused the crisis. In particular, a failure of leadership played a major part in creating that problem. As a leader article in the *Economist* put it: "hubris was followed by nemesis" (*Economist*, 2011). Inevitably, the collapse of the banking industry in Ireland had a major consequential effect on the rest of the economy and, as Regling and Watson (2010:5) state: "Ireland's banking crisis bears the clear imprint of global influences, yet it was in crucial ways 'home-made'." The report into the Irish banking crisis by the Governor of the Central Bank (Honohan, 2010:6–10) was even more unequivocal about the causes of the financial crisis in Ireland, blaming a number of factors: domestic macroeconomic imbalances (Government pro-cyclical policies), and a systemic failure in regulation both in terms of having reliable information and a lack of "intrusiveness and assertiveness on the part of regulators in challenging the banks". He also laid the blame firmly with "the directors and senior managements of the banks that got into trouble".

In any country, there is a strong overlap between politics and business. In Ireland, this overlap is clearly illustrated by a number of writers, including: Cooper (2009), Leahy (2009), O'Toole (2009), Ross (2009), Ross and Webb (2010), O'Toole (2010), Lyons and Carey (2011) and Byrne (2012). For those who have been observers of political and business affairs over the last 30 years or more, these writers provide a useful summary of events that have unravelled so many of the enormous gains made by the Irish economy since the early 1990s. Criticism of these blunders is not restricted to what some termed the "four angry men" (four journalists/authors who wrote polemics on the corruption in Irish business and politics: Matt Cooper, Pat Leahy, Fintan O'Toole and Shane Ross). A trawl of the international press, from the *Financial Times* to the *Washington Post*, over the last number of years does not present the country in a very flattering way. As far back as April 2005, Brian Lavery and Timothy O'Brien of *The New York Times* controversially branded Ireland as "the wild west of European Finance" (Lavery and O'Brien, 2005). While many in Ireland took offence at this comment, our "light touch" regulation clearly failed. However, regulation – particularly in the Financial Services Industry – has been greatly tightened in recent years. Also, companies are now having to place far greater emphasis on corporate governance.

International commentary by respected journals and rating agencies is important as it will inevitably impact on the decision by foreign companies whether or not to invest in Ireland (as well as the rate of interest charged on Irish sovereign bonds). It has also impacted negatively on other sectors such as tourism. The number of overseas visitors to Ireland declined from 7.7 million in 2006 to 6.9 millon in 2009, before rising slowly to 8.25 million in 2017 (Fáilte Ireland, 2018). The period also saw significant emigration from Ireland. In 2012 alone, 83,000 people left Ireland, over 50,000 of whom were Irish – the highest gross figure of emigration in over a century. It took until 2018 until this figure was reversed (CSO, 2018). While there are many reasons for the decline, including lack of competitiveness, the perception by potential visitors of the economic problems in Ireland also played a part. The country had to receive an €85 billion bailout loan from the EU/IMF in November 2010. Many of the banks are in state ownership. During this time, the unemployment rate peaked at 15.9% in 2012, at the height of the crash. Since then, it has dropped steadily to 5.2% at the end of 2018 – back to pre-crisis levels (CSO, 2018).

The failure of leadership has been across the spectrum of organisations in Ireland. The "Murphy Report" by Yvonne Murphy into the Archdiocese of Dublin (Murphy, 2009:4) is a dreadful indictment of those at the top who were preoccupied with "the maintenance of secrecy, the avoidance of scandal, the protection of the reputation of the Church, and the preservation of its assets. All other considerations…were subordinated to these priorities." While all churches usually operate at a remove from the business world, they can also be involved in running key services, such as many of the country's hospitals. On a broader level, they have traditionally played an important part in framing societal values which, in turn, inform how people in business conduct their affairs. It can be argued that investigations such as the Murphy Report, the Ryan Report (2009) and the 2019 inquiry into the Mother and Baby Homes (Tuam Babies scandal) clearly undermine the central message that should underpin such societal values.

The above examples do not reflect well on many of those who were entrusted with leadership positions in this country, and hubris has played a large part in causing such a depth of problems. In moving on, we first of all need to learn from the mistakes and to recognise the importance of true leadership in successfully guiding organisations of every type.

Fr Harry Bohan, founder of the Céifin Centre in Ennis, ran an annual conference over many years that attracted leading commentators from the world of broadcasting, business, religious groups, the health sector, academia, etc., to examine the changes taking place in our society. Fr Bohan believes that leadership is one of the critical challenges facing Irish society in the 21st Century. He calls for a redefinition of leadership at every level and in every sphere:

> "The 20th Century was very much the era of the institution. Our lives were shaped by institutions – whether financial (banks), spiritual (church), corporate (big business) or political (parties). Problems arose when those institutions that were central to our lives became ends in themselves and lost the notion of service upon which they had been founded. Trust has been broken in many instances and broken trust is not easily mended. Many institutions have to return to first principles and ask themselves some basic questions. What are banks for? What is the church for? Is politics about parties or people? How can business and community connect?" (Bohan, 2009)

Bohan goes on to criticise top-down leadership – the command and control model – and what he terms the disconnect between those at the top of the organisation and those at the bottom. Instead, he calls for a new kind of leadership – "a leadership of service" (Bohan, 2009).

ORGANISATIONAL CULTURE

Every type of society has its own culture or set of cultures. Societal culture is a product of many different factors, such as ethnic background, politics, economic conditions, religion and language. In larger countries, there may be differences between regions in terms of culture, e.g. the northern part of Germany has quite a different culture compared to the south. Our culture impacts on our assumptions about how we perceive things, how we think, act and feel. It is an integral part of who we are and, hence, it is inevitable that we bring our societal culture to work with us in the form of our values, customs and language. Societal culture impacts directly on our personal values and assumptions, and societal culture also impacts on organisational culture. When we join an organisation, its culture will also impact on our values. The combined effect of societal culture and organisational culture on the individual will ultimately direct people's behaviour in organisations (Buelens *et al.*, 2011). In the context of strategy, it is, therefore, important that we understand organisational culture and how it impacts on the decisions made by individual organisations.

Understanding Culture in Organisations

Just as each society has a culture of its own, an organisation likewise has a particular culture that defines its own separate identity. Charles Handy (1999:180) sums it up thus:

> "Anyone who has spent time with any variety of organisations, or worked in more than two or three, will have been struck by the differing atmospheres, the differing ways of doing things, the differing levels of energy, of individual freedom, of kinds of personality. For organisations are as different and varied as the nations and societies of the world."

Organisational culture is extremely difficult to observe and understand. It has so many levels, it has been described by Trompenaars and Hampden-Turner (1998) as being like the layers of an onion. A number of writers have proposed various frameworks that can be used for the purpose of understanding culture. Though there are no truly common themes running through these frameworks, it is worth reviewing a selection of theories for a better understanding of organisational culture.

One of the most cited researchers in the area of organisational culture is Edgar Schein, former Sloan Fellows Professor of Management Emeritus at the Sloan School of Management at MIT, who defines organisational culture as:

> "A pattern of shared basic assumptions learned by a group as it solved its problems of external adaptation and internal integration, which has worked well enough to be considered valid and, therefore, to be taught to new members as the correct way to perceive, think, and feel in relation to those problems."

Schein (2010:18)

According to Schein, organisational culture can be observed at three different levels, which can best be described by drawing an analogy to an iceberg. The **artefacts** are above the waterline and are easy to see, but difficult to decipher. The **espoused beliefs and shared values** are below the waterline and are not as easily seen. The **basic assumptions** are deep down and are barely discernible.

ARTEFACTS
The tangible factors of
the culture

BELIEFS and VALUES
The principles by which
it operates

BASIC ASSUMPTIONS
The unconscious and taken-
for-granted way of operating

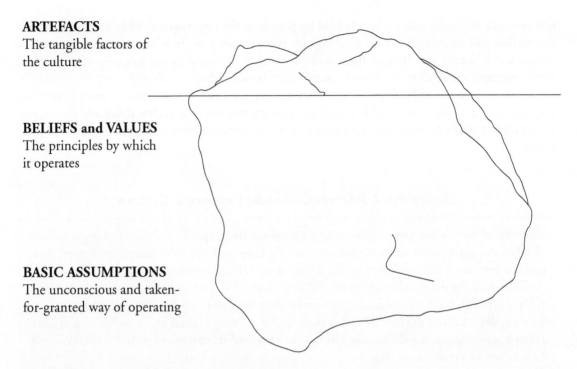

Figure 2.2 *Model of Organisational Culture (Schein)*

Artefacts Artefacts are the visible, tangible phenomena that represent an organisation's culture. They include: the stories and legends that are told about the organisation by its staff and outsiders; the rituals and ceremonies that define organisational life; the language used by its staff; the physical manifestations such as buildings and office layout, logos and branding style; and organisational dress code (see **Illustration 2.3**). Schein believes that it is dangerous to try to infer deeper assumptions from artefacts alone as a person's interpretation of those artefacts is a projection of that person's own feelings and reaction.

Espoused Beliefs and Values In solving problems, a group will develop a shared understanding of what will work for that particular group and will thus be validated by them. The shared values of an organisation (see **Chapter 3**) are the principles by which people in it operate. They define what the organisation considers important and guide decision-making. They provide meaning and comfort for group members. These beliefs remain conscious and are explicitly articulated as they guide the group in tackling situations and train new members in how to behave. In some cases, these beliefs and values may not be congruent with employee behaviour and other artefacts. Espoused beliefs and values often do not present a full understanding of an organisation's behaviour and so, to get a fuller understanding, one must examine the basic assumptions of that organisation.

Basic Assumptions When basic beliefs and values are applied in an organisation over time, and they are seen to constantly work, they gradually evolve into shared assumptions. These are the unconscious, taken-for-granted beliefs held by people in the organisation. They are deep beneath the surface and cannot be readily observed by those looking in. It is how the group perceives reality, and it means that there is little variation within the social group in terms of its actions. Basic assumptions tend to be non-debatable and because they are shared, they are mutually reinforced and, hence, difficult to change. They are implicit (rather than explicit) assumptions and they are very powerful, as they guide people as to the correct way to perceive, think and feel. When events do not conform to people's assumptions, group members often resort to defensiveness and denial.

Illustration 2.3: Dress Code and Corporate Culture

The style of clothes worn by employees says a lot about the corporate culture of an organisation. While companies in the software industry usually have no fixed rules about employees' dress code, things are a little different in the Swiss bank, UBS. According to a report in *The Wall Street Journal*, the dress code consists of a 40-page illustrated book, which gives very prescriptive rules for staff on what is considered appropriate dress for work. The book is designed to inform new employees about the culture in the bank and it is being piloted in a number of branches. It has been designed to differentiate UBS in the minds of its customers and, if successful, may be adopted as a code for all staff.

The book contains some general sections, and in terms of the colour of clothes, it says that suits should be dark grey, navy-blue or black, since these colours "symbolise competence, formalism and sobriety". Suits should also be stored on large, rounded hangers to preserve their shape. Furthermore, the code includes pointers about eating and smoking. Staff members are encouraged not to smoke and should not spend time in smoke-filled rooms. Garlic and onion-based dishes are also to be avoided.

There are also separate sections for male and female staff. Men are not allowed to wear short-sleeved shirts and stubble or excessive facial hair is to be avoided. They should have their hair cut every four weeks. Socks should be black and high enough to prevent skin from showing when legs are crossed. They must use tie-knots that match the bone structure in their face. Shoes must be black and highly polished. Men should not dye their hair, and their finger nails should not be any longer than 1.5 millimetres. Men are not allowed to wear jewellery but are encouraged to wear a wrist watch as it suggests "reliability and great care for punctuality".

For women, the guide recommends wearing pearls and illustrates details on stitching. Trendy glasses should not be worn. Hair should be well-cared for and cut by a stylist. Women must wear flesh-coloured underwear and must ensure that they do not get foundation on their collars. Makeup should consist of foundation, mascara and discreet lipstick which will "enhance your personality". The hemline of skirts should hit the middle of the knee. Scarves, if they are worn, must be tied in a certain manner. Fragrances should be applied as soon as one gets out of the shower (Berton, 2010).

Time are changing, however. In March 2019, Goldman Sachs chief executive, David Solomon, sent a memo to staff telling them that formal business attire would no longer be an everyday requirement. He acknowledged that people now dress formally in fewer and fewer businesses. The memo told staff they should "dress in a manner that is consistent with your clients' expectations" (Armstrong, 2019). One Irish company that traditionally had a very strict code for dress was Aer Lingus. However, as part of the re-branding of the airline in 2019, the company now permits female cabin crew to wear trousers instead of skirts, and make-up is optional (Aer Lingus, 2019).

CLASSIFICATION OF ORGANISATIONAL CULTURE

A trawl of the literature will reveal that there is no universally accepted way of classifying organisational culture, and many writers approach such typologies in very different ways. This is probably due, in no small way, to the nature of organisational culture and how difficult it is to observe, let alone understand, the culture of a particular company. To gain a fuller appreciation of organisational culture, it is perhaps useful to examine a number of the different typologies that are applied, including:

- Handy's Four Types of Organisational Culture
- Miles and Snow Typology
- Peters and Waterman Excellence Model
- Thompson *et al.* Cultural Strength
- Management Philosophy.

Handy's Four Types of Organisational Culture

Charles Handy (1999) built on early work by Harrison (1972) and drew together the structures of organisations (see **Chapter 7**) and the types of culture associated with them. He describes four manifestations of organisational culture:

1. **Power culture** – normally small or family-run companies where one person is the sole authority and everything revolves around them in regard to decision-making.
2. **Role culture** – bureaucratic, centralised and highly structured organisations where everyone has a clear role to play.
3. **Task culture** – best suited to volatile markets, this type of culture focuses on getting the task done, often with a project management approach.
4. **Person culture** – where people's expert knowledge is emphasised, e.g. professional firms.

Miles and Snow Typology

Miles and Snow (1978) developed a typology linking different types of organisational culture and strategy. Based on different sets of values, each organisation will develop strategic goals in line with its values, as depicted in **Table 2.1** below.

Table 2.1: *Miles and Snow Typology*

Type	Characteristics	Emphasis	Examples
Defender	A conservative company that sets low-risk strategies that will secure its current markets and customers. Slow steady growth.	Long-term planning. Efficiency.	Marks & Spencer Dunnes Stores
Prospector	Concerned with innovation and growth. Always searching for new opportunities. Willing to take risks and can handle uncertainty.	Visionary company. Change.	3M Kerry Group Plc
Analyser	Maintains its current markets while searching for new markets. A mid-way point between Defenders and Prospectors.	Planning. Moderate innovation.	IBM Ryanair
Reactor	No clear strategy. Reacting slowly to changes in the environment.	Delayed reaction.	Some educational and professional organisations

Peters and Waterman Excellence Model

In their book, *In Search of Excellence*, Peters and Waterman (1982) attempted to identify one best form of organisational culture for American organisations. Their research was conducted using data from client companies of McKinsey, a large American consulting company. They concluded that the best run companies operated on the basis of eight cultural tenets that underpinned their success:

1. **A bias for action** – a quick reaction, make-things-happen approach.
2. **Stay close to the customer** – listen to your customers and understand their needs.
3. **Autonomy and entrepreneurship** – empower employees and encourage innovation.
4. **Productivity through people** – employees are the most important resource, and it is through employees that productivity is delivered.
5. **Hands on, value driven** – the organisation must have clear values and managers must demonstrate their commitment to work and organisational values.
6. **Stick to the knitting** – reduce risk by sticking to what the organisation does best, and not be distracted by diversifying into areas where the company lacks expertise.
7. **Simple form, lean staff** – creating a flat organisation that is flexible in its response.
8. **Simultaneous loose-tight control** – striking a balance between the controls and values that are necessary but giving staff autonomy to take action.

There has been much criticism of the work by Peters and Waterman, particularly around their methodology, and the fact that many of the companies identified subsequently failed (Martin,

2005:496; Tiernan *et al.*, 2006:38). However, the eight cultural tenets they identified still provide a useful insight into organisational culture and performance. It must be remembered that, in many cases, companies lose sight of the fundamentals of their business and no longer practise the basic principles that helped them achieve success in the first instance. Irish banks are a perfect example of this.

Thompson et *al.* Cultural Strength

Thompson *et al.* (2018) classify organisational culture according to its strength and influence, and divide culture into five categories:

1. **Strong culture** – deeply rooted values that strictly regulate conduct and are practiced by all within the company, with its underlying values set by strong leaders. Strong culture can provide continuity and be integral to the company's success, but may lead to group-think that clouds judgement (see **Chapter 12**).
2. **Weak culture** – lack of values and principles that are widely shared, with no dominant culture to guide staff or assist in developing a coherent strategy or creating a sense of attachment to the organisation.
3. **Unhealthy culture** – impacts in a negative way on company performance and often results from internal politics at play, which results in unethical behaviour and also a resistance to change.
4. **High-performance culture** – a 'can-do' spirit prevails, which is results-oriented. Staff are accountable for their actions and are open to development and change. High-performance culture inspires loyalty, dedication and a commitment to excellence.
5. **Adaptive culture** – a culture that reacts quickly to environmental change and all the challenges it can bring; it is particularly important in industries where such change is the norm.

Management Philosophy

Press (1990) argues that culture is related to one or more management philosophies based on the company's relationship with its stakeholders:

- **Market focus** – importance of satisfying customer needs.
- **People focus** – building on the expertise of its people and meeting their expectations.
- **Shareholder focus** – maximising shareholder return.
- **Resource focus** – minimising costs and achieving efficiencies.

Companies need to take all of these philosophies into account, but each company will prioritise one or two above the others. For example, Ryanair's primary focus is on cost reduction and then on maximising shareholder return.

Different Approaches

Each of the five methods of classifying culture examined above are very different in terms of their approach and insight into organisational culture. When examining the culture of any organisation, there will be traces of each of these classifications to some extent or another, which will help us in understanding the uniqueness of that culture.

CHAPTER 2

Subcultures

The discussion on culture in this chapter is primarily centred on the dominant culture of an organisation – the culture that is widely shared throughout the organisation. It is also quite common to have different subcultures within organisations, particularly if an organisation is large and/or diversified. The values and beliefs in these subcultures can vary quite considerably depending on factors such as the type of business unit, geographical location or functional division involved. These differences can manifest themselves in various ways. According to McShane and Von Glinow (2009), some subcultures can support the dominant culture with parallel values and assumptions, while other subcultures act as countercultures in that they work against the dominant values of the organisation. This raises the issue of how much standardisation is required throughout the organisation. People do not want to be over-engineered into fitting into the head office mould. While there are certain non-negotiable things that head office is right to expect, such as commitment to organisational values, quality, customer care, etc., beyond that, there can be certain differences so long as it works for the people in each region (CIPD, 2014).

Countercultures can create many problems for the company by creating unnecessary conflict and can be disruptive in terms of developing and implementing strategy. They often have their own objectives which run counter to organisational objectives. Elton Mayo identified this in the early 1920s in the Hawthorn experiments in the Western Electric Company. In the last of the experiments, known as the 'Bank Wiring Observation Room experiments', Mayo and his team observed the existence of informal groups that created their own rules of behaviour separate to the 'official' culture of the company (Tiernan *et al.*, 2013). In cases where subcultures clash within an organisation, managers must act to resolve the problem. This is particularly so when a company merges with another or, more commonly, when it makes an acquisition. In general, a high percentage of mergers and acquisitions fail and irreconcilable cultural differences play a substantial part in such failures where, according to Buelens *et al.* (2006:603), it "multiplies the chance of failure".

A changing aspect of the workplace that will have a large impact on the creation of a culture that is both unified and desirable is the fact that many organisations no longer employ workers on a full-time basis but on short-term or zero-hour contracts. Such arrangements provide flexibility from the employer's perspective, but it makes it a lot more difficult to create a strong, unified culture (FRC, 2016). Given the importance of a healthy culture to the success of the organisation, as well as building trust, such flexibility needs to be carefully balanced (see below).

On the other hand, McShane and Von Glinow believe that countercultures can also serve a number of useful functions by challenging a dominant culture and generating useful ideas. In turn, this can help an organisation to align with the needs of the market in which they are operating. Finally, countercultures can also be of benefit in not tolerating illegal or unethical behaviour (**Chapter 4** will deal with the issue of whistleblowing).

When the culture of a society changes over a period of time, problems can arise if the internal culture of particular organisations does not change in tandem with it. This can manifest itself in different ways. Johnson *et al.* (2017:180) refer to **strategic drift** where there "is the tendency for strategies to develop incrementally on the basis of historical and cultural influences, but fail to keep pace with a changing environment". Martin (2005:500) refers to it as "cultural fragmentation", which can create particular challenges for public services. Irish society has changed enormously in the last number of years with large ethnic groups living and working in the country. Organisations such as the Health Service Executive and the Gardaí face cultural diversity in the workplace in a way that would have been considered unimaginable even 20 years ago. Policing ethnic groups in Ireland, for example, requires more than the ability to speak their language; it requires police men and women from those ethnic groups who fully understand all of the cultural issues at play. In turn, this creates a challenge for police organisations to ensure full cultural integration of their members.

THE NATURE OF CULTURE

The Importance of Organisational Culture

Culture serves a number of valuable functions in an organisation, according to Smircich (1983). First, it gives people working in the organisation a sense of identity and belonging, and a sense of pride in what they do. Armies throughout the world, for example, have long recognised the importance of the sense of identity which soldiers have for their own particular unit. *Esprit de Corps*, or morale, is an essential attribute in the fighting soldier. The same positive effect can be experienced by commercial organisations in galvanising their workforce behind a chosen strategy. Just as staff members identify with the organisation, it must be remembered that organisations are also social constructs, and so providing a stable social system for employees is important. This point was illustrated by Elton Mayo in the 1920s during the Hawthorne experiments, which first identified the impact of the social structure of employees in an organisation on their productivity (Tiernan *et al.*, 2013). Organisational culture can help employees make sense of their environment and what the organisation stands for. With aid agencies, for example, the culture of the organisation and the values of the individual volunteers working for it are usually aligned in a powerful synergy.

Trust

The G20/Organization for Economic Cooperation and Development (OECD) *Principles of Corporate Governance* (2015) stresses the importance of stakeholder relations for good governance. This is echoed in a report by the Financial Reporting Council, *Corporate Culture and the Role of Boards* (FRC, 2016), which suggests that companies should build and maintain successful relationships with a wide variety of stakeholders in order to be successful. Human capital, as well as intangible assets, including intellectual property, brands and customer bases, now account for over 80% of the total value of an organisation, and these are inextricably linked with reputation. Organisational culture is complex and is one of the hardest attributes of an organisation to measure, but it is also one of the most important and valuable at its disposal (CIPD, 2016). It is critically important for the delivery of sustainable long-term performance and is a key source of competitive advantage.

Culture is much more about people than it is about regulations. It is about beliefs and not rulebooks. Culture also forms a very important part of the company's risk appetite and evaluation of strategic options (see **Chapters 7** and **12**).

It is the role of the board and the CEO to ensure there is an alignment between the values and purpose of the organisation and its business model. They set the 'tone at the top'. The board should be clear on what values it wants, which should include institutional standards of respect, fairness, honesty and integrity (Central Bank of Ireland, 2018). In reality, there are a variety of different interpretations of the importance of ethical values. Yarlagadda *et al.* (2017) suggest there is a spectrum representing the ethical context of organisations, ranging from:

- **Values driven** – where ethics forms a critical component of the organisation and is embedded in its culture.
- **Values implicit** – a widely accepted culture of ethical behaviour, but not explicitly supported by an organisational narrative on ethics.
- **Aspirational values** – where the narrative around ethical behaviour is limited to the organisation's vision, but is absent from day-to-day behaviour.
- **Transactional** – ethics is absent from the organisation's vision and from employees' behaviour.

In each of the above scenarios, leaders have an important role in either developing or changing organisational (ethical) values depending on where on the spectrum the organisation sits. Those charged with running the company must embody the desired culture and embed it at every level across the entire organisation. These standards must be communicated clearly and often. Such communication is important in building trust and encouraging the desired behaviours, but that trust must be earned. According to Hope-Hailey and Gustafsson (2014), trustworthy leadership has four pillars:

- **Ability** – demonstrable competence at doing their job
- **Benevolence** – a concern for others beyond their own needs and having benign motives
- **Integrity** – adherence to a set of principles acceptable to others, encompassing fairness and honesty
- **Predictability** – a regularity of behaviour over time.

While trust is a necessary condition for employee engagement, the two are not the same. Engagement relates to the giving of one's energy to the organisation cognitively, emotionally or physically, but it is generally on a reciprocal basis. Trust, on the other hand, is about facing uncertainty and a willingness to take risks and go into the unknown: you trust that the other party will act in a positive way toward you. As discussed in **Chapter 14**, trust is an essential element of leading organisational change, particularly in helping to secure the benefits of learning and co-operation (Scott and Brown, 2012).

With a strong culture in place, every member of the organisation should be clear about what is expected of them and the consequences if they do not measure up to those standards. Individual accountability is central to such standards. Codes of ethics and conduct can be a useful way to translate values into more specific policies to guide people when making decisions and taking action. Such codes must be available to, and understood by, all in the organisation.

Culture is not something that has its own separate status; it must be intrinsic in everything the organisation does. Openness and accountability are essential for good governance and should be demonstrated in the way the company conducts its business with all its stakeholders and in every aspect of its business (OECD, 2010). In turn, these values should be reflected in the performance management and reward system. The organisation should have the appropriate indicators and measures to confirm that an appropriate culture is in place that balances risk and reward (CIPD, 2016). In particular, the company must make sure that it does not have perverse incentives in place (whereby the wrong behaviour is rewarded). Building a culture of engagement, and a strong employee voice, will improve the performance of human capital in the organisation that, in turn, will support a healthy culture.

Establishing and Maintaining Organisational Culture

The initial culture of a company is normally established by its founders, who impose their philosophies and beliefs on the organisation. This will happen to a greater or lesser extent depending on the individuals concerned. Some will give it a great deal of consideration and set very clear standards for others to follow. The establishment of organisational values can be seen in **Illustration 2.4** below.

Illustration 2.4: Whole Foods Market

Founded in Austin, Texas in 1980, Whole Foods Market is the world's largest retail chain of natural and organic food. It is an example of an organisation that has established a corporate culture based on very clear principles that reflect the values of its founder, John Mackey. Whole Foods Market has expanded constantly and now has 497 stores across the US, Canada and the UK, employing 91,000 people. According to the company's website, the values that underpin its culture are practised daily in every aspect of the company's dealings with its customers and employees. The organisation describes its values as being constant – not changing from time to time, or person to person. Each employee is part of the company culture, and employees are the soul of the company. Whole Foods Market's values centre around the quality of natural ingredients and organics foods; delighting customers with their produce and highly-trained staff; supporting staff in their personal development; caring about local communities and the environment; and educating customers on healthy eating.

Whole Foods Market was acquired by Amazon in 2017 for $13.7 billion. While the company pays great attention to animal welfare and protecting the environment, it has been criticised in the media for a number of reasons. The company promotes its own-label products at the expense of local products and the founder John Mackey has also built a reputation for being vehemently anti-union despite calls by many employees for union recognition. Staff have also voiced concern about many aspects of the company's employment policies. At the same time, the company has been listed in *Fortune's* "Best Companies to Work For" on a number of occasions. In recent years, the number of customers has begun to decline – down 3% per cent in 2017. Since 2017, the company has also closed nine stores.

In his 2014 book, *Conscious Capitalism: Liberating the Heroic Spirit of Business*, co-authored with Raj Sisodia, Mackey espouses the importance of stakeholder integration and, in particular, "passionate, inspired team members". In addition, he discusses the importance of both leadership and corporate culture in how organisations are run (Mackey and Sisodia, 2014). Companies around the globe are coming under increasing scrutiny in relation to their values. Corporate values must hold up to such scrutiny.

Sources: Whole Foods Markets, 2019; Mackey and Sisodia (2014); Aschoff (2017)

How leaders embed culture is important for an organisation's success. Schein (2010:236) proposes a number of primary and secondary measures to help establish and embed culture. The primary embedding mechanisms include:

- The issues that leaders pay attention to, measure and control
- How leaders react to critical incidents
- How resources are allocated within the organisation
- Criteria for allocating rewards
- Recruitment and selection, as well as retention
- Role modelling and coaching.

According to Schein, the secondary articulation and reinforcement mechanisms include:

- Organisational structure
- Building design and layout
- Systems and procedures
- Organisational rituals and ceremonies
- Formal statements by the organisation concerning its philosophy
- Stories about important people and events that have happened within the organisation.

Just as the actions of the founders of an organisation are important in establishing organisational culture, the behaviour of senior managers also plays a vital role in maintaining the culture. Employees will reflect the values they see practised by those running the organisation, rather than whatever values are being espoused. The culture of the company, and what it stands for, will have to be communicated clearly to all new staff members. This is achieved through a socialisation process, and it plays a major role in maintaining the culture over time. It will require staff to learn and to adjust to their new surroundings. A three-phase model of socialisation was proposed by Feldman (1981):

1. **Pre-employment socialisation** – where people research the company in terms of the type of employment conditions they can expect and the compatibility of their values with those of the organisation. The organisation should be open about itself and paint a realistic picture of what

it is like to work there. Recruitment and selection processes are time-consuming and expensive, and it does not serve anyone's purpose to create unrealistic expectations about the organisation. By clearly defining its culture, the company can more effectively select potential new employees that will be compatible with that culture and the values embedded in it. As a consequence, the employees that it selects are more likely to stay longer, thus reducing recruitment costs.

2. **Encounter** – the person has now signed the contract and started in the organisation. They have to start making the necessary adjustments to fit in with the work demands placed upon them. They will have to reconcile differences with regard to what they previously expected and the reality they now face. Many will encounter what is known as reality shock – stress associated with reconciling preconceived notions about the company and the realisation of the day-to-day routine they are now experiencing. Some people may decide to leave at this point.

3. **Adaptation** – once they have gotten over the initial stages, the process of adaptation to the company will have to continue, and new employees must learn to fit into the work practices that exist within the organisation. They learn to internalise the values and the norms of the organisation and, over time, become "insiders". In addition, they will have to understand the social hierarchy of their new colleagues and resolve workplace conflicts.

Clear communication is essential to help employees clarify what is expected of them. This will include formal briefings about the company, its vision and the values that underpin its culture. Some organisations will provide mentors to help new employees make the transition into their new role and to ensure they understand the company's philosophy. Explanation about the rewards' system operating in the company will also be important. While a company's official induction programme is very important, it must be remembered that an informal process will also take place, especially in the absence of a proper company programme. Managers must, therefore, take the initiative and ensure the induction process is comprehensive.

Identifying an Organisation's Culture

A number of different ways of classifying organisational culture were discussed above. Similarly, there are different ways of identifying which type of culture is dominant within an organisation. Identifying the culture of an organisation is by no means an exact science, however, given the rather nebulous nature of culture. Despite the difficulties involved, it is important for managers to develop an understanding of their organisation's culture as this culture will either help or impede the development of certain strategies. This is probably one of the most difficult aspects of leading change in an organisation (see **Chapter 14**).

Perhaps the most comprehensive framework for understanding the culture of an organisation is that by Johnson *et al.* (2017:175) who suggest using a **cultural web** to "show the behavioural, physical and symbolic manifestations of a culture". They place the organisational "paradigm" or basic assumptions at the centre of a web which includes the following overlapping elements, all of which impact on the central paradigm:

- **Routines and rituals** – the daily routines that show how things are done in the organisation, as well as the rituals that are emphasised.
- **Symbols** – "the objects, events, acts or people that convey, maintain or create meaning over and above their functional purpose".
- **Power** – how people in the organisation use their influence over others to achieve certain outcomes.
- **Organisational structures** – the structure of the organisation and its reporting lines.
- **Control systems** – not just the formal control systems but also the informal systems that support people.

Johnson *et al.* believe that understanding the central paradigm or basic assumptions is central to understanding the organisation's approach to strategy. The central paradigm is the managers' judgement on what they consider to be important. However, the difficulty lies in developing an awareness of the paradigm, particularly as an outsider. By observing the different elements above, a greater understanding of an organisation's culture can be developed. In isolation, no one element will present a full picture, but examined together, a cultural web will convey a reasonably comprehensive understanding of the culture that exists in that organisation. In reality, it takes a lot of time and questioning before that understanding emerges clearly. For example, statements made in a company's annual reports about its values may not truly reflect the way it operates away from the glare of the media.

Organisational Culture and Performance

Of critical importance to leaders is the relationship between organisational culture and an organisation's performance. Peters and Waterman's study (above) has been criticised and, while many of their recommendations remain valid, no direct correlation can be drawn between the culture they advocated and organisational success. McShane and Von Glinow (2009:280) looked at the relationship between strong organisational culture and performance. They suggest "that only a modestly positive relationship exists between culture strength and success". There are a few reasons for this. First, once the external environment shifts, strong organisational cultures can impede success, in that the company may no longer be responding to the needs of its customers. Secondly, very strong cultures can restrict decision-makers when searching for solutions to problems or for new opportunities. Finally, strong cultures can suppress dissenting voices within an organisation and also suppress diversity.

Barney (1986) concluded that superior financial performance is dependent on sustained competitive advantage. In turn, organisational culture plays an important part in building competitive advantage, providing that: the culture is valuable and facilitates high performance; it is rare; and it is not easily copied by competitors. Ryanair is perhaps a good example. It is a highly profitable airline, and its approach to low costs is deeply embedded in its culture and facilitates high performance. It is rare, in the sense that Ryanair has perfected this culture and, thus, it is very difficult for any rival airline to copy it. With other companies, particularly those following differentiation strategies (see **Chapter 8**), staff will need considerable autonomous decision-making. Weick (1987) argues that both organisational culture and standard operating procedures can impose order, but only culture can add latitude for interpretation of unique circumstances where there is no precedence.

Intercultural Differences

At the beginning of this chapter, the influence of national culture was examined in relation to organisational culture. For many Irish companies understanding national culture is a relatively straightforward affair, as they are subject to similar national cultural forces. For multinational companies, be they foreign or Irish, different national cultures will impact on internal organisational culture in a number of different ways, including: language, both verbal and non-verbal; religion; values; customs and manners; and social institutions such as clubs and societies. These are all factors that need to be considered when expanding abroad, whether by foreign direct investment or by acquisition. According to Hofstede (1985), some of the main considerations include:

- **Individualism v. collectivism** Societies differ in terms of whether their focus is on the individual (US and Britain), where people pursue their own self-interest and expect to be rewarded accordingly, or on the extended family and wider community (France, Germany and most Eastern countries, such as China, etc.).
- **Power distance** refers to how much inequality people expect to find in their dealings with organisational and governmental bodies. The higher the power distance score (Philippines, Mexico and India) the greater the distance between those at the top and the bottom. A low score implies closer links (Sweden and Denmark).
- **Uncertainty avoidance** refers to how people deal with uncertainty. People in societies with high uncertainty avoidance require strong institutional procedures and control to help them cope (Greece, Portugal and Japan). Societies with low uncertainty avoidance are better at coping with risk and will accept a variety of different views (US, Sweden and the UK).
- **Masculinity v. femininity** Masculine societies place emphasis on achievement and making money, and jobs tend to be gender-based (Japan and Australia). Feminine societies place greater emphasis on people and quality of life (Sweden, Denmark and Finland).

What Hofstede's study and similar investigations show is that there is no one correct way to lead people from across different cultures. The earlier discussion in this chapter on cultural intelligence highlights the importance of leaders having a strong sense of cultural awareness and sensitivity. Cultural differences can have very practical implications for an organisation in terms of people's perception of time (punctuality), personal space, communication, socialising and, in general, how people adapt to foreign assignments, as well as the level of company support that might be needed to help the employee adjust. Recognising the existence of intercultural differences is a useful starting point.

CONCLUSIONS

Leadership plays a vital role within organisations in giving them direction and in establishing strong values that will form the bedrock of organisational culture. Leadership is about inspiring and motivating others to work towards achieving organisational goals; it is quite separate from management. Leadership is about doing the right thing. Unfortunately, in Ireland, as indeed across the globe, those who are entrusted with leadership do not always live up to the mark. Jim Collins's "Level 5 Leader" provides a useful framework for aspiring leaders. Central to all the functions of the leader is the ability to get the best from people. Trust is a vital element in achieving that. While there are many different types of organisational culture, the leader of an organisation must understand the nature of the dominant culture that exists in their company, and they must also ensure that the prevailing culture supports the company in achieving its goals.

SUMMARY

Leadership plays a vital role in the success of organisations. It is the catalyst for the entire strategy process from development through to implementation.

Leadership involves giving direction to organisations. There is an important distinction between **leadership** and **management**: managers do things right; leaders do the right thing. Leadership is concerned primarily with inspiring and motivating others at every level in the organisation.

Early studies on leadership focused on traits, which generally included qualities such as intelligence, vision, self-confidence, initiative, lateral thinking, the need for power and achievement, and being goal-directed. Behavioural theories looked at the way leaders act.

Later studies saw that **context** was also an important element in leadership – different situations require different styles. Fielder's model looked at the leadership style and the situation context to come up with the most effective style. House's theory examined the role that goals play in **motivation**, and how leaders can help employees achieve organisational goals.

Charismatic leadership has a profound effect on employees by appealing to their values and beliefs, and giving them a sense of direction. In reality, examples are rare and there is conflicting evidence as to the effectiveness of this style. In contrast, Level 5 leaders are self-effacing and shy, with a paradoxical blend of personal humility and professional will.

There are a number of **functions** that leaders can perform in organisations. Effective leaders are those who understand the nature of the change affecting their organisation and can transform it in such a way as to create competitive advantage.

Those leading the organisation should do so ethically and instil sound values that guide employees in the decisions that they make.

Being able to pick the right **team** is a valuable competence required to implement a chosen strategy. Teams have to be built and maintained, and different people will each have their own contribution to make to the team. **Development** occurs at both individual and organisational levels, and the two are interwoven.

A **learning organisation** is one that has a culture that supports challenging assumptions around a common vision and one that is capable of regeneration through continuous learning by its members.

Leadership is also a catalyst for establishing and maintaining the **culture** of the organisation. Good strategy must be supported by an appropriate culture as it underpins all aspects of the process and guides people in the decisions that are made.

Organisational culture is defined by Schein as "a pattern of shared basic assumptions learned by a group as it solved its problems of external adaptation and internal integration, which has worked well enough to be considered valid, and therefore to be taught to new members as the correct way to perceive, think and feel in relation to those problems".

It can be observed in organisations at three different levels:

- **Artefacts** – aspects of the culture that are visible to outsiders
- **Espoused beliefs** – the values that members hold and use to guide their decisions
- **Basic assumptions** – the unconscious, taken-for-granted beliefs held by people in the organisation.

There is no universally accepted way of classifying organisational culture and a number of different approaches were examined in this chapter.

While most studies on culture focus on the organisation as a whole, it is also quite common to have **subcultures** within an organisation that represent different groups and geographical divisions.

Culture serves a number of important **functions** in organisations. It gives people a sense of identity and belonging. It also provides a stable social structure for people to work together, and it can help them make sense of the environment within which they are working.

The culture of an organisation is established initially by its founder, and there are a number of primary and secondary embedding mechanisms that can be used to perpetuate the culture. The example given by managers is of vital importance. So too is the **socialisation** process by which the culture of an organisation is passed on to new members. There are three phases: pre-employment socialisation, the encounter, and adaptation. Clear communication plays a pivotal role in this process.

Identifying an organisation's culture can be a very difficult process, but Johnson *et al.* suggest using a **cultural web** to show the "behavioural, physical and symbolic manifestations of a culture". It involves examining the routines and rituals; the symbols; power; organisational structures; and the control systems.

Intercultural differences can pose many difficulties for managers in dealing with staff members from different national and ethnic groups. It requires a much greater awareness of such differences and an ability to bring people together to achieve common goals.

For those who wish to read more on different topics discussed in this chapter, the following is a list of suggested readings.

CHAPTER 2

For a contemporary exploration of the wide-ranging debates surrounding the relationships between business and society in 21st Century Ireland, read:

Hogan, J. et al.	2010	*Irish Business and Society: Governing, participating and transforming in the 21st Century*	Dublin	Gill & Macmillan

For enduring insights on leadership from the Drucker Foundation:

Hesselbein, F. and Cohen, P	1999	*Leader to Leader*	New York	Jossey-Bass

For a practical and accessible guide for talent development in organisations:

Stewart, J. and Rigg, C.	2011	*Learning and Talent Development*	London	CIPD
Duff, D.	2014	*Managing Professionals and Other Smart People*	Dublin	Chartered Accountants Ireland
Willink, J. and Babin, L.	2015	*Extreme Ownership. How U.S. Navy SEALS Lead and Win*	New York	St. Martin's Press

For a comprehensive view of organisational culture and leadership:

Schein, E.	2010	*Organisational Culture and Leadership* 4th ed.	San Francisco	Jossey-Bass
Barret, R.	2017	*Building a Values-Driven Organization. A Whole System Approach to Cultural Transformation*	London	Routledge

There is a wide selection of books that will provide the reader with an understanding of the business and political events that led both directly and indirectly to the 2008 recession:

Carswell, S.	2006	*Something Rotten: Irish Banking Scandals.*	Dublin	Gill & Macmillan
Cooper, M.	2009	*Who really runs Ireland: The story of the elite who led Ireland from bust to boom... and back again*	Dublin	Penguin Ireland
Creaton, S. and O'Cleary, C.	2002	*Panic at the Bank: How John Rusnak lost AIB $691,000,000*	Dublin	Gill & Macmillan

Leahy, P.	2009	*Showtime: The inside story of Fianna Fáil in power*	Dublin	Penguin Ireland
Lyons, T. and Carey, B.	2011	*The Fitzpatrick Tapes: The rise and fall of one man, one bank and one country*	Dublin	Penguin Ireland
Murphy, D. and Devlin, M.	2009	*Banksters: How a powerful elite squandered Ireland's wealth*	Dublin	Hatchette Books
O'Toole, F.	2009	*Ship of Fools: How stupidity and corruption sank the Celtic Tiger*	London	Faber & Faber
O'Toole, F.	2010	*Enough is enough: How to build a new Republic*	London	Faber & Faber
Ross, S.	2009	*The Bankers: How the banks brought Ireland to its knees*	Dublin	Penguin Ireland
Ross, S. and Webb, N.	2010	*Wasters: The people who squander your taxes on white-elephant projects, international junkets and favours for their mates – and how they get away with it*	Dublin	Penguin Ireland
Byrne, E.	2012	*Political Corruption in Ireland 1922–2010*	Manchester	Manchester University Press

DISCUSSION QUESTIONS

1. Discuss the role that power plays in leadership.
2. Distinguish between leadership and management.
3. Critically analyse the relevance of emotional intelligence as a necessary trait in leaders.
4. Discuss the nature of leadership in organisations and state whether you think leadership exists only at the top of the organisation or if it is reflected at all levels.
5. Explore the role that leaders play in supporting organisational culture.

CHAPTER 3

Vision, Mission, Goals and Objectives

LEARNING OBJECTIVES

On completion of this chapter, you will be able to:

- Analyse the different elements of a company's vision
- Differentiate between a company's vision and its mission
- Assess the importance of goals and objectives for an organisation and be able to distinguish between them
- Using the Balanced Scorecard, identify suitable goals and objectives for an organisation

"Nurture your mind with great thoughts, for you will never go any higher than what you think."

Benjamin Disraeli

INTRODUCTION

Leadership plays a vital role in organisations. It is the leader who sets the scene within which all those in the organisation work together to achieve their purpose. But what is that purpose and how is it shared throughout the organisation?

In *Alice's Adventures in Wonderland*, when Alice asks the Cheshire Cat in which direction she should go, the Cat advises her:

"That depends a great deal on where you want to get to."

Every organisation needs direction and if you don't know where you are going, any road will take you there. This chapter distinguishes between the vision and mission of an organisation and how goals and objectives are set. This is a vital part of strategy formulation. If the organisation is not clear about these essential elements of its foundation, it will not succeed for very long in a competitive environment. Yet it would appear that there is a lack of clarity among many organisations about the concepts that are examined in this chapter.

A company's vision concerns its long-term future direction. What company would it like to be in, say, 10 years' time? This vision will guide the company through difficult times and keep it focused. The vision consists of the values and purpose of the organisation, and it is driven by leadership at the top. They are all interlinked.

The mission works hand-in-hand with the vision. The essential difference is that the mission is more concerned with the here and now. What type of company is it currently and what does it do? Every organisation will have resources to support its strategies. These resources are scarce and expensive, and they must be used to maximum effect. Goals and objectives are not set in isolation, but are formulated to help the process of using those resources to fulfil the mission in the most efficient manner possible. Goals are broad, general statements of intent in line with the mission, and are usually qualitative in nature. Objectives are also statements of intent but are much more specific in terms of the desired outcomes.

Illustration 3.1: Differentiating Vision, Mission, Goals and Objectives

Vision
A vision is the desired end-state of an organisation, which consists of its values and purpose, underpinned by leadership and expressed in motivating terms to inspire its members. Achieving the vision is a long-term process that will stretch the capabilities of the organisation.

Mission
A mission guides the members of an organisation in making decisions that will achieve strategic goals and objectives.

Goals
Goals are a broad, general statement of intent in line with the mission; they are focused on achieving a certain outcome and are usually *qualitative* in nature. A goal may have a number of objectives emanating from it.

Objectives
Objectives are also statements of intent but are much more specific in terms of the desired outcomes to be achieved. They are, generally speaking, *quantitative* in nature.

VISION

Jonathan Swift described vision as:

"The art of seeing what is invisible to others."

Companies should differentiate between the need for a constant focus on what the company is trying to achieve, while retaining flexibility to respond as circumstances change. **Chapter 1** examined the concept of emergent strategies and the difficulty in strategic planning because of rapidly changing circumstances. What links that long-term focus and the challenges that currently exist is vision. According to Kotter (1996), developing a vision plays a major part in leading change (see also **Chapter 14**).

Collins and Porras (1996) found that companies that have taken the time to craft a proper vision have outperformed the general stock market by a factor of 12 since 1925: "Companies that enjoy enduring success have core values and a core purpose that remain fixed, while their business strategies and practices endlessly adapt to a changing world."

Collins and Porras regard a well-conceived vision as consisting of two major components:

- A **Core Ideology** consisting of core values and core purpose – what the company stands for and why it exists.
- An **Envisioned Future** – what the company aspires to become, where long-term objectives are set (what they refer to as "Bhags" – "Big Hairy Audacious Goals") and how these objectives are communicated to all concerned. This is, in effect, a vision statement.

Thompson *et al.* (2018:22) outline the characteristics of an effectively worded strategic vision. It should be:

- **Graphic** – paint a picture of the kind of company management want it to be.
- **Directional** – forward-looking; charting the strategic course.
- **Focused** – specific enough to guide actions without being prescriptive.
- **Feasible** – the company should be able to achieve it within the time frame.
- **Desirable** – in the interest of stakeholders.
- **Easy to communicate** – preferably summed up in a simple statement.

The environment for many industries is changing at an ever-increasing rate, making long-term planning, in particular, extremely difficult. As a result, companies have to be flexible and adaptable when opportunities arise. Without vision, companies could take the wrong direction. Vision enables organisations to spot opportunities as they arise and provides the end-goal to work towards. There are many ways of achieving that end-goal, and those methods will change as circumstances unfold. Essentially, however, vision is about creating an environment in which managers at every level can work in harmony towards agreed objectives, rather than about the nuts and bolts of every decision.

Illustration 3.2: PulseLearning

An example of a successful technology company, PulseLearning, was one of the Ernst & Young 'Entrepreneur of the Year' finalists in 2006. It was also voted Deloitte Fastest Growing Technology Company in 2007. The company continues to gain numerous awards, including the Top eLearning Content Providers in 2017. It was also a 2018 Gold winner at the LearnX Impact Awards. Jim Breen, Executive Chair of PulseLearning, is very clear about the importance of having a vision. "The vision of PulseLearning is to be the number one eLearning technology company in the world in its chosen markets." For a company in the south-west of Ireland, operating in a global market may seem an unrealistic aspiration. Yet, when one examines the meteoric rise of companies like Microsoft and Apple, people could have said the same about them. As the winner of numerous awards in its sector, PulseLearning is well on the way to achieving its vision. As G.B. Shaw said:

"You see things; you say. 'Why?' But I dream of things that never were; and I say 'Why not?'"

PulseLearning believes its vision should be shared by all the employees of the company throughout the world, and it is through this shared vision that the company will achieve the level of growth required to become the number one eLearning company in its chosen market.

Source: Interview with CEO Jim Breen

One of the most famous quotations (indeed, it is usually mis-quoted) regarding vision statements was made in 1993 by Louis Gerstner, the then newly appointed CEO of the computing giant, IBM:

"There's been a lot of speculation as to when I'm going to deliver a vision for IBM, and what I'd like to say to all of you is that the last thing IBM needs right now is a vision."

Gerstner's statement made great copy in the business press. However, he claims he was quoted out of context. In his autobiography he states:

"A lot of reporters dropped the words 'right now' from my vision statement when they reported my stories. And so they had me saying that 'the last thing IBM needs is a vision'. That was inaccurate … I said we didn't need a vision right now because I discovered in my first ninety days on the job that IBM had file drawers full of vision statements."

While Gerstner had a drawer full of vision statements when he took over the company in 1993, there were many critical operational challenges facing IBM that had to be dealt with as a matter of urgency. By March 1996, having turned his attention to the most pressing issues, he was then in a position to look to where the company was heading in the future. The emphasis could now shift from urgent, pressing issues to a more long-term focus. As with all companies, IBM's long-term effort needed clear direction: "what IBM needs most right now is a vision" (Gerstner, 2002). Gerstner realised that an important aspect of vision is consistency. People become rapidly disillusioned by frequent changes to an organisation's vision, how it is applied in practice and how it is communicated to all concerned (Yarlagadda, *et al.*, 2017). In such circumstances, the existence of a vision ceases to have any meaningful impact on employees.

Benefits of a Vision

Vision plays a very important role in business. First and foremost, having a vision for a company provides its senior executives with a clear and shared understanding of where the organisation is going over the long term. This will inevitably impact on the decisions that are made, which correspond with achieving that vision. Vision also serves as a guiding light for the entire organisation, both in terms of lower-level managers setting departmental objectives, and in terms of employees buying into the process. Finally, vision will guide the organisation through inevitable periods of change and uncertainty.

Components of an Organisation's Vision

Collins and Porras (1996) spoke of the core ideology consisting of values and purpose. One essential element of a vision that they did not discuss is the driving force behind it – the leadership required to give the process energy and direction. Therefore, building on the framework provided by Collins and Porras, it can be argued that there are three essential components of an organisation's vision:

- leadership;
- values; and
- purpose.

Leadership

Leadership, values and purpose together constitute the organisation's vision. **Chapter 2** examined leadership in detail. In particular, it examined the role of leadership in creating and promoting values. It can be seen from **Figure 3.1** below that leadership, values and purpose are all integral components of vision. Leadership is discussed in this context in regard to how it drives and supports the other two elements of a company's vision – values and purpose. Values and purpose do not exist in isolation. Leadership plays a very important part in the process of building and sustaining the values and purpose of the organisation. **Illustration 3.4** (see below) examines the Johnson & Johnson 'Credo' – the stated values of the Johnson & Johnson company. It will be seen that the Credo was developed by

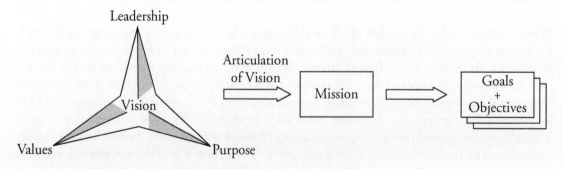

Figure 3.1 *Components of Vision and Relationship to Goals and Objectives*

Robert Johnson, the then-CEO of the company, who was setting out his stall as chief executive with regard to the type of corporate values that he thought were important for the company to practise in its dealings with all its stakeholders. Other functions of leadership that were discussed in **Chapter 2** are also relevant here, namely, building teams of people that are culturally compatible with the values and purpose of the organisation, as well as developing individuals as future leaders who will ensure the continuity of the values and purpose of the organisation.

Building and sustaining a vision is, by its nature, a long-term process. Therefore, an important function of leadership is to maintain the level of motivation and commitment within the organisation, while simultaneously achieving the mission and objectives. In 1942, Winston Churchill was quick to recognise the importance of the victory at the battle of El Alamein, while at the same time keeping in sight the long struggle that the Allies still faced: "Now this is not the end. It is not even the beginning of the end. But it is, perhaps, the end of the beginning."

Perhaps the most important function that binds leadership and vision is the necessity to bring that vision to fruition. All of the other elements – values and purpose – can be present, but without leadership, the vision will not be realised:

"Leadership is the capacity to translate vision into reality."
Warren Bennis

However, in driving the purpose and values of the organisation, leaders must have a moral compass that embraces an ethical approach to dealing with all stakeholders.

Values

 Dose (1997) defined **values** as: "standards or criteria for choosing goals or guiding actions, and they are relatively enduring and stable over time".

While societal values are relatively enduring and stable, it is natural that they will evolve over time. The fact that values can evolve is important. Rokeach (1973) argues that social change would not take place if values were absolutely stable. On the other hand, if there were a lack of stability with regard to values then there would be no continuity in society. Each set of values ultimately reflects the society in which it exists.

Buelens *et al.* (2011) distinguish between 'content' and 'intensity' when considering values. The content aspect relates to what people find important, while the intensity aspect deals with how those values are ranked according to their intensity — a value system that can be described as "an enduring organisation of beliefs concerning preferable modes of conduct or end-states of existence along a continuum of relative importance". It is generally accepted that people are not born with an internal set of values, but that they are acquired through a process of socialisation during their lifetime from a variety of sources, including family, peers, school, work and national culture. Initially, values are learnt in isolation from each other in an absolute, all-or-nothing sense. As people mature, they learn to integrate these isolated values into a hierarchy of importance.

CHAPTER 3

Schwartz and Sagie (2000) consider that there are a number of value types that are common to most societies. This has obvious implications for global companies in terms of creating common values throughout their organisations.

Business organisations are social constructs. They are designed by people to enable them to work together to achieve collective goals. When the strategy of an organisation is being discussed, it must be remembered that it is the people in that organisation who develop its strategy. Consequently, when looking at values, it is important to recognise that there is a link between organisational values and individual values.

Ross *et al.* (1999) state that work values are expressions of basic values in the work setting and are ordered by their importance as guiding principles for evaluating work outcomes and settings, and for choosing among different work alternatives. Thus, corporate values ultimately reflect the personal values of those running the company. Ireland has become a multicultural country, and this can present challenges for organisations. Various cultures may differ in their values, but there will still be shared core values to which they can all aspire.

In turn, the values of an organisation will often attract people whose personal values reflect those of the organisation (Yarlargadda *et al.*, 2017). Examples of organisational values attracting like-minded people are aid agencies such as Goal or Concern. Each year, such organisations attract a wide variety of volunteer doctors, nurses, engineers and others, who often give up the opportunity to earn good salaries at home, operating in hostile physical conditions to alleviate the plight of their fellow human beings in the developing world. **Illustration 8.2** (see **Chapter 8**) gives the example of Isadore Sharp, CEO of Four Seasons Hotels and Resorts, using a promotional video on the recruitment section of the company's website. In the clip, he describes the culture and values of the organisation. For any potential new employee it sends out a clear message about the personal values that they are required to have: "It's not something they train for. This is the way they are brought up."

Values guide an organisation in its dealings with all its stakeholders. While values might be explicitly stated, they are ultimately of intrinsic value to the organisation and do not require any justification to outsiders. Each company will generate its own values. There is no right answer *per se*; what is important is that they have core values. Collins and Porras (1996) recommend having only a few – perhaps three or four – as only a few values can be truly core and define what is central to company beliefs.

Illustration 3.3: Diageo and its Stated Values

Diageo, the parent company of Guinness, defines its values thus:

"Our culture is rooted in a deep sense of our purpose as a company – celebrating life, every day, everywhere. This culture is built and maintained by the values that underpin our business and guide how we work. We are passionate about our customers and consumers and want to be the best. We give each other the freedom to succeed and value each and every person's contribution. We work hard so we can be proud of what we do and how we do it.

- We're **passionate about customers and consumers** – our curiosity and customer and consumer insights drive our growth. We care for our brands. We're courageous in pursuing their full potential. We're innovative, constantly searching for new ideas that drive growth and developing them across our business.
- We give ourselves and each other the **freedom to succeed** because this fosters an entrepreneurial spirit. We trust each other; we're open and challenging. We always behave as a team – when we're together and when we're apart.
- We're **proud of what we do** – we act sensitively with the highest standards of integrity and social responsibility. We celebrate and benefit from diversity.
- We will strive to **be the best** – we are restless, always learning, always improving. We constantly set high standards and then try hard to exceed them. We deliver results, win where we compete and celebrate our success.
- We **value each other** – we seek and benefit from diverse people and perspectives. We strive to create mutually fulfilling relationships and partnerships."

Source: www.diageo.com

As guiding principles, values should be largely independent of the environment in which they operate. The acid test of a core value is if it would still be applied even if this meant that the company would be put at a competitive disadvantage. Perhaps one of the most famous examples of stated values being used to guide an organisation's actions is the Johnson & Johnson 'Credo'.

Illustration 3.4: The Johnson & Johnson 'Tylenol' Crisis

Established in 1884, Johnson & Johnson is a multinational manufacturer of pharmaceuticals and diagnostic, therapeutic and personal hygiene products, and a household name for many products, such as talcum powder and sticking plasters.

It also makes the pain reliever Tylenol®. It was with this product that the company showed the importance of the values embodied in its 'Credo' in guiding daily action. In 1982, the product was indirectly responsible for the death of seven people when some bottles containing the tablets were interfered with in a Chicago drugstore and poison was inserted. At a cost of over $100 million, the company withdrew the product from the shelves until it was sure of the cause of the problem. In the process, it also developed the first tamper-proof containers for medicines. The action by Johnson &

Johnson is still used as a case study on how a company should respond to a crisis. Over time, public confidence was restored and the company more than made up for lost revenues.

First written in 1943 by Robert Wood Johnson, the Johnson & Johnson 'Credo' has been updated slightly from time to time. The company has used this Credo for over 60 years to guide its daily decision-making. It describes the Credo as:

> "A set of values that we live by, we work by. It is the North Star, the guiding light, the foundation of Johnson & Johnson and everything we stand for and everything we are."

The Credo identifies four types of stakeholders:

- The company's first responsibility is to "the patients, doctors and nurses, to mothers and fathers and all others who use our products and services…
- "We are responsible to our employees who work with us throughout the world. We must provide an inclusive work environment where each person must be considered as an individual. We must respect their dignity and recognise their merit…
- "We are responsible to the communities in which we live and work and to the world community as well. We must be good citizens…"
- The company believes the final responsibility is to their stockholders. Business must make a sound profit, invest in new equipment and facilities, launch new products and create reserves and by operating to these principles, stockholders should realise a fair return.

Source: www.jnj.com

Rosabeth Moss Kanter believes that values are truly a primary consideration which help companies find business opportunities and motivate employees and partners. They require "the serious nurturing of hearts and minds." Once people are in agreement as to what their collective values are, they can then make decisions independently. Kanter believes that there are many benefits for companies with embedded values:

- It helps integration, which in turn permits collaboration among diverse people
- It enables the transfer of knowledge and technical innovation
- It assists in post-merger integration
- Values allow people to make consistent decisions, even under pressure.

Values can be a strong motivational tool that provide people with a basis of engagement with their work, a sense of membership in their organisation and stability during change.

Sam Palmisano, the former CEO of IBM, considered values to be of absolute importance to an organisation: "Management is temporary; returns are cyclical. But if we use these values as connective tissue, that has longevity. If people can get emotionally connected and have pride in the entity's success, they will do what is important to IBM" (Kanter, 2008).

Many organisations will have espoused values. Stating values is one thing, but practising them is another. Enron had espoused corporate values, including respect, integrity, communication and excellence, yet displayed very different values in its actions. (Enacted values reflect the actual values that employees demonstrate in the workplace.) In the case of Enron, greed took over and a number of senior executives were involved in 'creative accounting', which gave investors and staff alike the impression that the company was doing extremely well. However, huge debts were allowed to mount up, and the company was eventually put under Federal investigation and declared bankrupt in Autumn 2001. Many of the senior executives were found guilty of fraud and were given jail sentences. The chair and former CEO, Kenneth Lay, was found guilty, but died of a heart attack in prison while awaiting sentencing. He had taken over $300 million from Enron. The accounting firm Arthur Andersen was the firm's auditors and were found to be complicit in the cover-up of Enron's accounting procedures. Tons of paper documents were shredded by Andersen to hide its role in the affair from investigators. The firm collapsed in 2002.

Values in themselves are morally neutral. It is vital that a company's values are based on a strong ethical foundation that embodies honesty and fairness (Yarlargadda *et al.*, 2017), and this ethical foundation must be reinforced by training and development, and performance management appraisals. Creating an internal alignment in such values can have a strong positive impact on employees' experience and behaviour in the organisation.

In conclusion, the values of a company should underpin the actions of all members of the organisation and be exemplified by its leaders.

Purpose

The third element of a vision is purpose. The Irish playwright, George Bernard Shaw, wrote in *Man and Superman*:

> "This is the true joy in life: being used for a purpose recognised by yourself as a mighty one; being a true force of Nature instead of a feverish little clod of ailments and grievances complaining that the world will not devote itself to making you happy. I am of the opinion that my life belongs to the whole community, and as long as I live, it is my privilege to do for it whatever I can. I want to be thoroughly used up when I die. For the harder I work, the more I live. I rejoice in life for its own sake. Life is no brief candle to me; it's a sort of splendid torch which I've got to hold up for the moment and I want to make it burn as brightly as possible before handing it on to future generations."

It might seem a little incongruous quoting Shaw in a textbook about corporate strategy. However, organisations as well as individuals need a sense of purpose. Purpose is the organisation's *raison d'être*. While business objectives will change, Collins and Porras (1996) suggest that you cannot fulfil the organisation's purpose; it is like a guiding light on the horizon, forever pursued but never reached. While the purpose itself does not change, it inspires change.

Many companies describe their mission statement as their purpose. However, the purpose *precedes* the mission. The mission statement may embody the purpose (as we shall see later), but there is a fundamental difference between discovering the organisation's purpose and its public manifestation in a mission statement. The importance of purpose in an organisation is illustrated in Collins and Porras's (1996) quote from David Packard in a speech to employees in Hewlett Packard in 1960:

> "I want to discuss why a company exists in the first place. In other words, why are we here? I think many people assume, wrongly that a company exists to make money. While this is an important result of a company's existence, we have to go deeper and find the real reasons for our being. As we investigate this, we inevitably come to the conclusion that a group of people get together and exist as an institution that we call a company so that they are able to accomplish something collectively that they could not accomplish separately – they make a contribution to society…"

This is as relevant today as it was 60 years ago. According to Mourkogiannis (2006), purpose both drives a company forward and helps build sustainable advantage. Purpose becomes "the engine of the company". Collins and Porras (1996) believe that a purpose should not be descriptive in terms of its current product lines. For the Sony Corporation it is not about televisions or PlayStations, it is "to experience the joy of advancing and applying technology for the benefits of the public". For the American company 3M it is: "to solve unsolved problems innovatively". The best way of developing purpose is the '**five whys**'. Start with the descriptive statement: we make X products or we deliver X services, and then ask, 'Why is that important?' Then repeat the process five times. After a few whys, you will get down to the fundamental purpose of the organisation.

Core purpose is not about the maximisation of shareholder wealth. As Peter Drucker pointed out in his 1954 book, *The Practice of Management*: "The purpose of a business is to create and keep a customer". If the focus is only on the creation of wealth, the customer will not be looked after and business will decline, taking wealth along with it. The collapse of the Irish banking industry is raw proof of this. In the absolute pursuit of profit maximisation, Irish banks lost focus of their purpose and their customers, and were ultimately the architects of their own downfall. A primary function of core purpose is to inspire, and not many people in the organisation will be inspired by a purpose based on maximisation of shareholder wealth. Many people in business are wealthy beyond their dreams and still remain passionate about their work. For others, wealth does not come into it. As Peter Drucker pointed out, the best and most dedicated people are ultimately volunteers, for they have the opportunity to do something else with their lives.

From Vision to Strategic Intent

The vision of the company consists of its values and purpose and is driven by those leading the organisation. In order to achieve this envisioned future, the company must translate the vision into a more tangible form. Collins and Porras (1996) refer to the second component of the vision framework as being the **envisioned future**, consisting of a 10- to 30-year audacious goal and a

vivid description of what it would be like to achieve that goal. In many ways, however, these are just the articulation of the organisation's vision rather than being an integral part of it. There is a saying that every journey of a thousand miles begins with the first step. In reaching for this envisioned future there will be many steps to be taken along the way. It is the function of those leading the company to decide on what the priorities should be and to galvanise the entire organisation behind the process. The process of striving towards the envisioned future is often referred to as 'strategic intent'.

Definition	According to Hamel and Prahalad (2005): "**Strategic Intent** envisions a desired leadership position and establishes the criterion the organisation will use to chart its progress".

They first coined the phrase in 1989 when they compared how Western and Japanese companies attained their long-term goals. Japanese companies, they argued, developed among their employees the desire to succeed, and maintained it by spreading the vision of global leadership. Rather than setting goals to fit their resources, Japanese companies developed 'stretch targets' that forced them to innovate, and so succeed on world markets. They cite a number of Japanese examples, such as Komatsu taking on Caterpillar and Canon taking on Xerox, and succeeding to become world players. One of the big differences was that Western companies tailored their ambitions to fit their resources, while Japanese companies had leveraged their resources to achieve seemingly impossible goals. They invested heavily in core competences (see **Chapter 6**) as well as in product-market units.

With these Japanese companies, their strategic intent is stable over time and so, in terms of formulating strategy, it lengthens the organisation's attention span rather than just focusing on the here and now. It also sets a target that deserves personal effort and commitment, not in direct terms of contribution to shareholder wealth, but indirectly towards global leadership. The latter has a much greater motivational impact on employees. In essence, strategic intent is more like a marathon than a 200-metre sprint. To be effective, management and staff must understand it and see the implications for their own jobs. Hamel and Prahalad (2005:153) suggest management face a number of challenges:

- Creating a sense of urgency throughout the organisation
- Developing a competitor focus at every level of the company through widespread use of competitive intelligence (hard information about what approach other companies are taking in the marketplace)
- Providing employees with the skills they need to work effectively. This should be an ongoing process
- Giving the organisation time to digest one challenge before launching another
- Establishing clear milestones and review mechanisms (discussed later in this chapter).

The process of developing strategic intent involves a different approach, with an emphasis on engaging employees emotionally and intellectually in the development of new skills and in reciprocal responsibility for competitiveness. They believe that cost reductions are achieved not through lower wages but from better working methods developed by employees. A winning strategy is achieved by creating tomorrow's competitive advantages quicker than competitors can copy the ones your company possesses today. This requires a constant focus on innovation, building layers of competitive advantage over time, exploiting areas that competitors are not immediately concerned with. It also means changing the terms of engagement (here Hamel and Prahalad cite how Kodak and IBM tried to take on Xerox, but it was Canon who changed the rules of engagement by standardising machines and components to reduce costs and selling through office product dealers rather than trying to match Xerox's huge sales force) and the use of licensing, outsourcing agreements and joint ventures (see also **Chapter 11**).

Thompson *et al.* (2018:28) describe strategic intent thus:

"A company exhibits strategic intent when it relentlessly pursues an ambitious strategy objective, concentrating the full force of its resources and competitive actions on achieving that objective."

Ambitious companies that establish exceptionally bold strategic objectives, and have an unshakable commitment to achieving them, almost invariably begin with strategic intents that are out of proportion to their current capabilities. Starbucks' strategic intent is to make the Starbucks brand the world's most recognised and respected brand. In 1987, the company had nine stores in Seattle; it has grown each year since, and currently has over 29,000 stores worldwide.

John Lonergan (2006), a former Governor of Mountjoy Prison in Dublin, once stated that: "Vision without action is a daydream. Action without vision is a nightmare." An integral part of the process of developing a vision for every type of organisation is developing long-term goals that will translate the vision into reality. This process of creating 'audacious goals' (goals that will stretch the organisation) is about giving practical reality to strategic intent.

These long-term goals can be a narrative description of the general long-term direction – articulating the vision of the company. There is also a need for management to spell out precisely the short-, medium- and long-term strategies to realise the vision, so that employees can play a meaningful part in helping the organisation achieve its goals. This cannot be done if people do not understand the strategy. The Balanced Scorecard (see below) helps achieve this by explaining precisely what is required.

Illustration 3.5: Long-term Goals – The Apollo Programme

The American Apollo space programme had an audacious goal. President Kennedy, in his address to Congress on 25 May 1961, stated that the US would land a man on the Moon before the decade was out. This caught everyone (including NASA!) by surprise. However, it has to be seen in the context of the time. The Russians had beaten the US in the space race by launching the first spacecraft to orbit the earth when the cosmonaut Yuri Gagarin circled the earth on 21 April 1961. This was happening at the height of the Cold War and the defence of the West was predicated on technological superiority, and missile technology in particular. The US had to increase spending dramatically (estimated at the time to be $40 billion (Daller, 2003)). It resulted in an intense focus on the space programme, and one that caught the popular imagination. There is an anecdotal story told of President Kennedy visiting NASA some time later. During his tour of the space centre, he asked one elderly gentleman (whose job it was to keep the toilets clean) what his role was in the centre. Straightening his back, he said proudly: "Mr President, I am helping put a man on the Moon". A number of years later on 21 July 1969, Apollo 11 landed on the Moon and Neil Armstrong uttered the famous words: "One small step for man, one giant leap for mankind".

When Jack Welch became CEO of General Electric (GE), he set the objective for the company to "become number one or number two in every market we serve and revolutionise this company to have the strengths of a big company combined with the leanness and agility of a small company" (Welch, 2001). In 1984, Michael Dell started his computer company with $1,000, and the company rapidly grew. By 1990, he set a long-range objective for the company to become one of the top three PC companies in the world. By 1998, he had achieved his target and by 2005, Dell was the number one seller of PCs worldwide.

Sharing the Vision

A vital part of the process of achieving a vision is getting others to buy into the process – getting them to picture what the organisation will look like when vision has been achieved. Covey (1994:97) suggests that we "begin with the end in mind – and work backwards to where we are currently at". This involves describing that vision and then deciding what needs to be done to achieve it. That vision has to be shared with everyone in the organisation and their support for the process galvanised. President Kennedy's inauguration speech in January 1961 – "…The torch has been passed to a new generation of Americans… tempered by war, disciplined by a hard and bitter peace" – was an exhortation that appealed to Americans' sense of patriotism and duty: "And so my fellow Americans: ask not what your country can do for you – ask what you can do for your country."

Two years later, the civil rights leader, Martin Luther King Jr, delivered perhaps one of the most famous vision statements of all time in his "I have a dream" speech. Repetition is a powerful oratorical tool, and in his speech King used the word 'dream' 10 times. His speech is a very powerful vision of society without racial prejudice and conflict. It is a speech with vision, which he relates back to the dream of freedom in the Declaration of Independence: "They were signing a promissory note to which every American was to fall heir. This note was a promise that all men, yes black men as well as white men, would be guaranteed the unalienable rights of life, liberty and the pursuit of happiness…".

It is a speech with values, with encouragement, with urgency. It is a speech that recognises the problem of racial inequality, and the enormity of the struggle. It is a vision laced with hope for a better future: "I have a dream that one day this nation will rise up and live out the true meaning of its creed: we hold these truths to be self-evident that all men are created equal. I have a dream…"

America has come a long way, and while further progress needs to be made, who would have thought that a black senator from Illinois would be inaugurated President of the United States in January 2009?

Other vision statements are much shorter, such as Henry Ford's vision of a car for every family. The Model T Ford was the first mass-produced car in the US that was affordable to wage-earning people. A century later, Ryanair is achieving a similar vision in making air travel available to the ordinary person. For Nike it is: "To bring innovation and inspiration to every athlete in the world."

MISSION

There is a clear distinction between a strategic vision and a mission statement. In essence, a vision concerns the company's future business – where it is heading in the long term – and is therefore aspirational. A mission, on the other hand, defines the company's current business: "who we are, what we do and why we are here". In essence, the vision guides the mission; and the values and purpose described in the vision will often be reflected in the mission statement. It is important that the company gives a great deal of consideration to defining the mission because, in turn, the mission guides the selection of goals and objectives. The mission, therefore, gives all employees a shared sense of direction that points them towards opportunities. A mission can be defined in the following terms:

Definition A **mission** guides the members of an organisation in making decisions that will achieve strategic goals and objectives.

Kotler (2017) describes a mission as an "invisible hand" within the organisation. The company's mission is derived from the vision and describes the current position of the company in terms of what it does. According to Dibb *et al.* (2006:42), creating a mission statement is very difficult because there are a number of complex variables involved. However, the process is an important one because the mission statement can benefit the organisation in five ways:

1. It gives the organisation clear direction, keeping it on track.
2. It helps differentiate the organisation and sets it apart from competitors.
3. It keeps the organisation focused on customer needs.
4. It guides managers in making decisions about what opportunities to pursue.
5. It acts like a glue in holding the organisation together, particularly in the case of large multinationals operating across the globe.

Ideally, mission statements should be brief, allowing them to be remembered easily by employees and customers. Mission statements take a long-term view, but they do evolve over time. Therefore, they should also be phrased in a manner that allows flexibility. Product lines and technologies come and go, but the mission statement should be reasonably broad and flexible enough to cater for such changes without the need for redrafting. While vision statements are by their nature more aspirational, mission statements should be realistic regarding what the company is capable of doing given its current capabilities. Most of all, mission statements should motivate employees, and appeal to outsiders. It must be remembered that statements like "maximising shareholder wealth" is not a great motivator for staff unless they all have large share options. In reality, mission statements vary considerably in length as well as content.

As stated in **Chapter 1**, strategic management applies to all types of organisations, from big to small, public sector and private sector, entrepreneurial start-ups to long-established corporations. The following is a selection of mission statements that reflect such variety of organisations. (Some organisations embrace the principles of constructing mission statements better than others.)

Illustration 3.6: Mission Statements

The following examples of mission statements represents a variety of commercial and not-for-profit organisations across a wide range of industries and sectors.

The Health Service Executive (HSE) (The state body charged with providing healthcare):
"People in Ireland are supported by health and social care services to achieve their full potential. People in Ireland can access safe, compassionate and quality care when they need it. People in Ireland can be confident that we will deliver the best health outcomes and value through optimising our resources".

Kerry Group Plc (An Irish multinational food and ingredients producer):
"At Kerry, our mission is to help nourish and delight consumers across the globe. Our vision [is] to be the leader in Taste and Nutrition for global food, beverage, and pharmaceutical industries, creating sustainable value for our customers, employees, environment, community and shareholders."

Concern Worldwide (A global charity):
"Our mission is to permanently transform the lives of people living in extreme poverty, tackling its root causes and building resilience ... For the voiceless, we use our voice to bring the human stories of extreme poverty to the tables of world leaders. Our mission doesn't stop until extreme poverty does."

FBD Insurance (An Irish insurance provider):
"In our target markets, to be the leading customer-focused insurance group, delivering long-term sustainable value".

Castleknock College, Dublin (A secondary school run by the Vincentian Order):
"Our mission is to have a college which is concerned with the development of the whole person in a Christian atmosphere which encourages involvement in a balance of religious, intellectual, cultural and sporting activities which promotes the growth of self-worth and respect for others in the spirit of St. Vincent de Paul."

Intel (A leading semiconductor chip manufacturer):
"Delight our customers, employees and shareholders by relentlessly delivering the platform and technology advancements that become essential to the way we work and live."

Facebook (A social media platform):
"Bring the world closer together".

Source: company and organisational websites (2019)

GOALS AND OBJECTIVES

In order to achieve the mission, the company must translate it into more immediate goals and objectives (which will ultimately help the organisation achieve its audacious goals). In textbooks about management and strategy, the terms 'goals' and 'objectives' are often used interchangeably. There is a large overlap between the two terms, but there is a distinction, nonetheless, and both are necessary in linking the mission with achieving results.

Goals are a broad, general statement of intent in line with the mission; they are focused on achieving a certain outcome and are usually *qualitative* in nature. A goal may have a number of objectives emanating from it.

Objectives are also statements of intent but are much more specific in terms of the desired outcomes to be achieved. They are, generally speaking, *quantitative* in nature.

The distinction between goals and objectives can be illustrated as follows. To be successful in business, it is vital that customers have a high level of satisfaction with a company's products or services. Following a review of internal capability, it might be decided that improvements need to be made in the area of customer satisfaction. Improving customer satisfaction then becomes a necessary **goal**. Bill Hewlett of Hewlett Packard once said: "what gets measured gets done".

However, measuring customer satisfaction can be somewhat difficult as it is a broad concept that can mean different things to different people. As a goal, customer satisfaction can be further broken down into specific objectives, along with the appropriate metrics as follows:

Goal: Improve customer satisfaction in ACDB Limited within a three-month period.

Objectives: The following objectives relate to the goal of increasing customer satisfaction:

Objective	Description	Metric	Timeframe for results
1	Introduce staff training in customer care	All staff to complete three days' training in customer care	31 January
2	Reduce waiting time for answering phone calls	All phone calls to be answered within 10 seconds	20 January
3	Reduce customer complaints about staff interactions	No more than one complaint per 500 staff/customer interactions	28 February
4	After-sales follow-up	All customers to be contacted within two weeks of purchasing items	31 January

SETTING ORGANISATIONAL GOALS AND OBJECTIVES – GETTING THE BALANCE RIGHT

In setting goals and objectives for an organisation, it is essential that they reflect all aspects of the organisation. The use of the Balanced Scorecard will assist in this process.

The Balanced Scorecard

Most organisations set goals and objectives based on financial performance. Depending solely on financial measures of performance does not give a balanced view of how well the organisation is performing overall. One of the big problems associated with financial performance is that the measures used are lagging indicators – the focus is largely on what has happened in the past, and these are not necessarily a good indicator of future performance. Moreover, financial reports may indicate areas that need improvement, but without necessarily indicating how these improvements might be made. Leading indicators of the company's future strategic position show whether the company will be in a stronger or weaker position in the marketplace.

For example, by setting ambitious targets for the coming year, and achieving those targets, in all likelihood the end-of-year financial results will be strong. On the other hand, if after a good year the company rests on its laurels, it is unlikely that the results will be anything more than mediocre. The targets that are set for the organisation must reflect a balance between financial and strategic goals. This is achieved by use of a Balanced Scorecard, which combines both qualitative and quantitative measures that reflect different aspects (and stakeholders) of the company. The Balanced Scorecard also ensures a link between the organisation's vision, its mission and the resulting goals and objectives.

Robert Kaplan of the Harvard Business School and his colleague David Norton first developed the **Balanced Scorecard** in 1992, arguing that organisations should monitor both financial and operational metrics simultaneously, and that the perspective should be forward-looking. They draw an analogy to a pilot flying a jet. The pilot does not rely on just one instrument but is simultaneously monitoring various gauges such as airspeed, bearing, altitude, fuel and other indicators, all of which build up an integrated and comprehensive picture of overall performance. In isolation no one instrument would provide all that information. Likewise, executives need an overview of the entire organisation when goals and objectives are being formulated. The Balanced Scorecard is primarily a planning device, but it also serves as a control device in the implementation of strategy. It also plays a very important role in the process of change and helps the organisation keep market-focused.

According to Kaplan and Norton (2005), there are four elements to the Balanced Scorecard:

- The customer perspective
- The internal perspective
- The innovation and learning perspective
- The financial perspective.

Customer perspective – how do our customers see us and do our products/services meet or exceed their expectations? A company must be customer-focused if it is to remain in business. It must be able to supply a range of products that will satisfy customer demand. In particular, when examining customer service, it is essential to look at it from the perspective of the customer and then develop specific measures that the customer considers important.

Internal perspective – knowing what our customers want, we then need a clear understanding of what we have to do internally in order to deliver on those expectations. The organisation must examine all its internal systems and procedures to ensure that it can meet and exceed customers' expectations. The most important factors here are those that have the greatest impact on customer satisfaction. In a service industry, the calibre of people delivering the service is of the utmost importance. Placing a priority on choosing good quality staff and on training will ensure that they meet customers' needs regarding time, service and quality. Appropriate cost control systems and management supervision will reduce any unnecessary cost in running the business.

Innovation and learning perspective – expectations will change over time. What measures are we taking now in order to be able to deliver good results in the future? Can we improve on what we are doing? In a competitive environment, standards keep rising, so it is essential that the company is able to anticipate and satisfy future customer demand. The ability to innovate and develop new products and processes that will meet future customer needs is, therefore, essential. To do that, the organisation must be constantly striving to improve its performance and to learn. It must be able to innovate and launch new products, penetrate new markets and increase revenue and profits. Building a relationship with customers is essential for receiving accurate feedback in current performance and on what customers would like to see improved. Spending quality time with key clients will, therefore, also be essential. Many of the measures here will overlap with others, such as improvement in staff training and performance.

Financial perspective – how is the organisation doing financially, and is it delivering good returns to its investors? Financial control is an essential part of any organisation and is, therefore, an integral part of the Scorecard. The financial measures will examine how the organisation is doing in the various departments and how they are contributing to the bottom line. It must be remembered that it does not always follow that improvements in the other areas of the Balanced Scorecard will automatically result in financial improvements. For example, improving the number of front-line staff will improve service levels and the level of customer satisfaction but, beyond a certain ratio, it will have a negative effect on the bottom line.

All four elements of the Balanced Scorecard are linked together, and what impacts on one will impact on the others. For example, the innovation and learning perspective is dependent on the provisions of adequate finance to support innovation and, in turn, will affect the internal perspective on customer satisfaction. It thus provides a forward-looking and holistic perspective on the performance of the organisation.

A number of goals are listed for each element along with appropriate metrics to gauge performance. **Figure 3.2** illustrates the approach. By limiting the number of measures used, the Balanced Scorecard helps minimise information overload – it forces managers to concentrate on those measures that are of critical importance to the organisation. It brings all the critical information together from different elements in to one report and helps prevent sub-optimisation by showing managers the inter-relationship between those parts. Improvements in one area should not be at the expense of another. While some trade-offs between different measures may have to be made, those trade-offs should not involve key success factors – those areas where the organisation must excel if it is to be successful (see also **Chapter 5**).

The Scorecard for each individual business will be different because of variances in market situations, strategies and competitive environments. Each business unit will, therefore, have to customise the Scorecard to fit in with its own particular circumstances. It will have to be updated

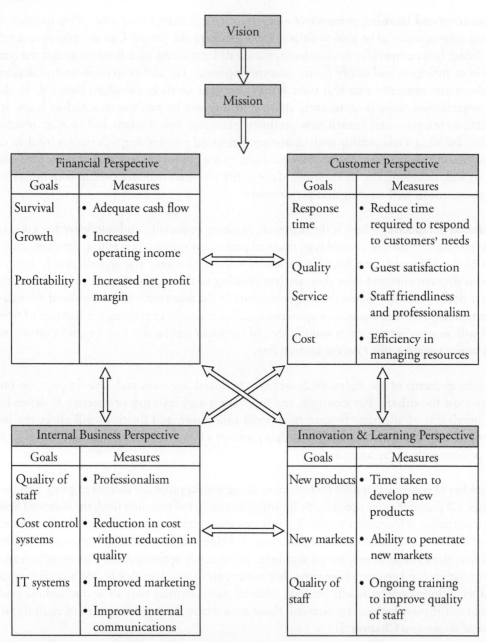

Source: Adapted from Kaplan, R. and Norton, D., "The Balanced Scorecard: Measures that Drive Performance", *Harvard Business Review*, July/August 2005, Vol. 83, Issue 7/8, p.174.

Figure 3.2 *The Balanced Scorecard: A Five-star Hotel*

regularly as circumstances change, while at all times remaining consistent with the company's long-term strategy.

Since the Balance Scorecard was first developed, Kaplan and Norton have worked with many major international corporations using it as a strategic tool. As a result of the feedback they have received, they have consistently developed the concept of the Scorecard and how it might be applied. One major innovation was the use of strategy maps.

Strategy Map

Kaplan and Norton (2008) recommend the development of a **strategy map** as a powerful tool to help all staff members visualise the strategy, and the cause-and-effect relationship between strategic objectives. It begins with the long-term financial objectives, and these are then linked to the other processes:

- The customer perspective
- The process perspective
- The learning and growth perspective.

Larger organisations will have an overall strategic map for the entire company and will then connect it to strategic maps for each operational unit. These are then linked to corresponding measures and targets. The process of developing a strategy map can be simplified somewhat by using just three to five strategic themes. A **strategic theme** is a vertical slice within the map that consists of a set of related strategic issues. These themes have a number of advantages: they all manage to customise the various themes to suit their particular circumstances while, at the same time, help integrate the different objectives with the overall strategy. The themes can also be developed to deliver results over different time periods. This will help executives to manage short-, medium- and long-term value-creating processes simultaneously.

The strategy map is then linked to **performance metrics** for each objective. Such metrics are a vital part of the process in terms of managing and improving the organisation. Another essential element is authorising and allocating the resources necessary for attaining the desired results, along with the strategic initiatives required. Kaplan and Norton believe that achieving results requires an integrated and cumulative impact of the different themes across the organisation. Finally, they recommend that a senior manager is assigned responsibility for each theme, as this allows for much greater co-ordination between different parts of the organisation and provides for greater chances of success. Each of the metrics can be assigned a colour-coded, traffic-light indicator (green, orange and red) that will focus management attention on the most pressing issues that require their attention. This will form a central part in the implementation of strategy which will be discussed in **Chapter 13**.

Strategy Map: Five-star hotel

Figure 3.3 applies the strategy map approach to a five-star hotel, stating three strategic themes: operational excellence, customer service and customer relationship management. These themes can then be superimposed on the four perspectives of the Balanced Scorecard.

Strategy Map for a Five-star Hotel			
Perspective	**Operational Excellence**	**Customer Service**	**Customer Relationship Management**
Financial	Increase margins	Create higher margins	Increase revenue and ROCE
Customer	Increase contribution from customer	Customer-focused service Create a compelling place to visit	Add and retain high-value customers
Internal Processes	Develop efficient internal processes, to include environmental processes and CSR	Create seamless and co-ordinated service between departments Minimise absence New product and service development	Create a comprehensive customer database to include detailed information about likes and dislikes
Innovation and Learning	Develop a capable and efficient workforce Develop a customer-focused competence in staff		

Figure 3.3 *Strategy Map: Five-star Hotel*

In turn, each of the strategic themes is supported by the appropriate metrics, strategies and budgets that will manage performance. **Figure 3.4** elaborates on the strategic theme of customer relationship management.

Customer Relationship Management					
Perspective	**Strategy Map (Figure 3.3)**	**Measure**	**Target**	**Initiative**	**Budget**
Financial	Increase revenue and ROCE ↑	Revenue mix Revenue growth	New: + 10% Existing: + 25%		
Customer	Add and retain high-value customers ↑	New customers Increase in repeat visits Longer stay	15% increase in new customers 10% increase in repeat visits (calendar year) I night extra per guest per visit	Marketing campaign Discount for extra night	€ __
Internal Processes	Create a comprehensive customer database to include detailed information about likes and dislikes ↑	Targeted marketing. Improve process for customer feedback. Develop integrated database	Complete database of all customers c/w personal preferences, interests, etc.	Data mining Social media Email/write to targeted customers	€ __ € __
Innovation and Learning	Develop a capable and efficient workforce Develop customer-focused competence in staff	Staff training Staff development	Certification awards Top rating for customer feedback Staff Incentive scheme	Internal training External training Secondment/ posting to other hotels and resorts Profit sharing	€ — € — € — € —

Figure 3.4 *Customer Relationship Management: Five-star Hotel*

The Balanced Scorecard framework thus provides a clear link between the vision that has been crafted for the organisation, the mission, and the subsequent goals and objectives. The scorecard illustrates the precise targets and the initiatives that are required to deliver the desired results and gives managers a clear understanding of where they need to be focusing their attention. Different timeframes can be applied to the different themes, and so they can tie in with short-, medium- and long-term objectives.

In itself the Balanced Scorecard does not guarantee a winning strategy. What it can do is assist managers to operationalise strategy throughout the organisation in a co-ordinated and market-oriented manner, while helping the organisation make all the necessary changes as the environment around it evolves. It helps managers examine the link between operations and finance and, more importantly, it represents a fundamental change in the assumptions about performance measurement in the organisation.

Translating Strategy into Great Performance

Translating strategy into great performance can be a difficult process at the best of times. Setting clear goals and objectives that reflect all aspects of the organisation is obviously very important. When corporate goals are not achieved, where does the fault lie? Is it because the goals were unrealistic in the first instance or is the problem in the execution of those goals?

According to Mankins and Steele (2005:67), companies realise only 63% of their potential because of defects in planning and in the executing phases of strategy. If senior executives do not fully understand the cause of the failure, the wrong corrective action will be taken. Moreover, when goals are not realised on a regular basis, it will foster a culture of under-performance in the company. They argue that the gap between planning and performance can be closed by focusing on better planning *and* better execution simultaneously. They list seven rules that are applicable to organisations wishing to achieve high performance:

Rule 1 – Keep it simple, make it concrete Often, the organisation's strategy is quite abstract and does not lend itself to translation into plans that can be executed. It should be expressed in clear language to enable people to understand what the strategy does and does not include. Everyone needs to be going in the same direction.

Rule 2 – Debate assumptions, not forecasts Planning in an organisation is often a political process. Forecasts usually understate short-term performance and overstate long-term performance. Financial forecasting is often done in isolation from the marketing or strategy functions. Forecasts should drive the work the company does. Therefore, the assumptions underlying its long-term plans should reflect the actual market realities. Cross-functional teams will help achieve detailed information on the profitability of different markets as well as costs. There should be discussions about the assumptions that would drive each unit's long-term financial performance, not about the actual performance itself.

Rule 3 – Use a rigorous framework, speak a common language It is vital that there is open dialogue between the corporate headquarters and strategic business units (SBUs) in terms of the potential profit available in each market in terms of size and growth. Corporate headquarters can then create the financial projections that will drive the SBU. It is critical that the framework establishes a common language between the centre and the SBU that can be used by all functions.

Rule 4 – Discuss resource deployments early An important part of the process is making an early decision about critical resource requirements. Once agreements are reached, they are then factored into the plan and put in place to support the execution of the strategy.

Rule 5 – Clearly identify priorities Not all tactics are equally important – some steps must be taken at the right time. The priorities that will have the *greatest impact* on performance must be identified and acted upon with clear timetables, budgets and key performance indicators.

Rule 6 – Continually monitor performance Seasoned executives will know instinctively the correct amount of resources to allocate for a project. They also need real-time performance tracking to help the process. They must constantly monitor the use of resources against the plan. These reviews should indicate 'red light' events that require instant action by management.

Rule 7 – Reward and develop execution capabilities Management is key to success and companies must motivate and develop staff. There are huge hidden costs in hiring bad employees. Incentives must be built into the delivery of good results.

Mankins and Steele (2005:72) consider that "the prize for closing the strategy-to-performance gap is huge". Improvement in performance often achieves a cultural multiplier effect as people become more confident about what they can achieve, and they become willing to make stretch goals that both inspire and transform their companies. The Balanced Scorecard can go a long way towards closing the strategy-to-performance gap.

Setting Goals and Objectives – Individual Level

Once the organisation is clear about what it wants to achieve, these corporate goals and objectives must be understood by all concerned within the organisation. The role of the manager at every level is to translate these organisational goals and objectives into goals and objectives for each department. In turn, departmental/unit goals and objectives are further broken down until each individual in the organisation is assigned personal goals and objectives. There must be a straight alignment between corporate goals at the top of the organisation right down to those of the individual. Each person must have a clear understanding of how their personal goals will fit into, and contribute to, the attainment of their departmental goals. As objectives are specific elements of goals, the principles involved in setting goals and objectives overlap. For that reason, the following framework suggested by Buelens *et al.* (2011) can be applied to both goals and objectives:

1. Set Goals Goals and objectives can be set in a number of ways: managers looking at the past performance of employees and then setting targets; the manager and employee participating in the process; or through benchmarking whereby best practice can be the target. There is no best way; it very much depends on circumstances and the personalities of the employees. Some are happy to have the goals set for them; others, particularly those with what McClelland (1961) referred to as a high 'Need for Achievement', will want to have an active involvement in the process. The acronym SMART is often applied to setting objectives. SMART stands for:

- **S**pecific – expressed in precise rather than vague terms and be quantifiable when possible.
- **M**easurable – some form of measurement is needed to confirm when the goal or objective has been achieved.
- **A**ttainable – challenging, but not impossible.
- **R**esults-oriented – corporate goals should focus on the results that are needed by the organisation. In turn, the goals set for each individual should be supporting the objectives of the particular division and the organisation as a whole.
- **T**ime-bound – there should be a date set for the completion of objectives.

2. Promoting goal achievement When employees consider that goals are fair and reasonable, they are much more likely to commit to achieving those goals. Such goal commitment should not be taken for granted, and there are many ways in which managers can develop it. The rationale for the goal should be explained clearly, along with demonstrating how the individual's goals form part of the organisation's goals. It is important that the goals are challenging and, where employees demonstrate a willingness to be part of the goal-setting process, those employees should be included.

3. Provide support and feedback It is important that employees are encouraged to achieve their results and that they are given whatever support is required. Training, for example, may be needed to enable them to accomplish the task, or other resources and supports not currently available. Feedback is also vital. It plays a dual role: instructional and motivational. To be effective, feedback should be timely and specific. In addition, it should be credible, accurate and fair.

Motivational Aspect of Goal-setting

Setting goals and objectives is an integral part of the strategic management of any organisation. Frederick Taylor's concept of 'scientific management' was based on setting goals for each worker. This was developed in much greater detail by Peter Drucker (1954) in his book *The Practice of Management*, in which he coined the term: 'Management by Objectives' (MBO). Management by Objectives is a process where managers and employees participate in decision-making, goal-setting and feedback. According to Buelens *et al.* (2011), research has shown a substantial gain in productivity in organisations that used Management by Objectives, provided top management commitment to the process is high. Setting performance goals increases individual, group and organisational performance.

Csikszentmihalyi (1990) believes that clear goals play a central role in creating '**flow**' in the workplace. In that regard, goal-setting also plays an important role in motivating individuals.

According to Locke and Latham (1990:126), there are four motivational components in goal-setting that are reasonably common across cultures:

- Goals focus one's attention on what is relevant and important.
- The level of effort involved in completing a goal is related to the difficulty of the goal, and consequently motivates people. In general, there is a strong relationship between goal difficulty and performance – the greater the level of difficulty, the greater the performance. However, if the individual perceives the goal to be beyond their reach, then performance drops considerably as many people will adopt the attitude it is not worth the effort trying to achieve their goals.
- Goals develop persistence and, over a period of time, people tend to see obstacles as challenges to be overcome rather than something that would cause them to give up. People are generally committed to achieving goals when they are committed to the goals themselves. Consequently, it is important for managers to get those involved to 'buy into' the process.
- Goals encourage people to develop action plans in order to achieve their goals.

Rewards

Achieving goals and objectives is often linked to monetary rewards, particularly at senior executive level. In some organisations it is considered to be an important part of attracting and motivating senior executives, and it can represent a significant payment for some. Such payments need to be looked at in a more holistic way, however, as research by Bloom (1999) examined the effects of pay dispersion (the pay gap between high-level and low-level employees) and found that the smaller the gap, the better the individual and organisational performance. In motivating those at the top, the motivation of management at levels below, as well as employees, should also be taken into account.

Many large organisations use appraisal systems to rate the performance of their employees. These appraisals would normally be conducted on an annual basis and are used to guide departmental managers in awarding bonus payments to staff. For those whose performance was considered exemplary, the rewards can often be significant. These rewards must be shared throughout the organisation by those who contributed to achieving the organisation's goals. At the other end of the scale, for those who are constantly underperforming, decisions will have to be made concerning the future of that employee. There has been much criticism globally in recent years, however, of enormous salaries and bonuses being paid to top executives, particularly in the banking sector, despite dismal performance. Even where performance has been good, there have been many examples of 'shareholder revolts' in the past couple of years in big-name companies such as BT, WPP, AstraZeneca, and Unilver, where shareholders voted down proposed pay packages for senior executives (Garrahan and Marriage, 2018).

As a result of a High Court ruling in November 2010, AIB had to pay backdated bonuses to approximately 90 employees. The ruling affected employees in the Capital Markets division of AIB (the division comprises Global Treasury, Investment Banking and the Corporate Banking Division) and relates to their performance in 2008. The case was taken by one trader who sued the bank for non-payment of a €161,000 bonus who claimed in court that the non-payment would cause "unjustified hardship" to himself and his family. The bank said it would honour contractual payments for 2008 but that it has no plans to pay any bonuses for 2009 (Lynch, 2010:18). The Minister for Finance subsequently intervened and prevented further payment of bonuses to banking executives in Irish banks, which is still in place (at the time of writing) despite calls from the banks' CEOs to have them restored.

As well as enraging shareholders who have lost a considerable amount of their wealth, the payment of bonuses to top executives who have underperformed also exacerbates the de-motivating impact on lower-level employees of the pay dispersion referred to above.

CONCLUSION

The recession that followed the financial collapse in 2008 has taught us the need for sustainability over the long term. It is relatively easy to make profit when times are good, but when the economy starts to decline the pressure on businesses mount. It is, therefore, imperative that senior managers have a clear vision for their company and understanding of what they want to achieve. The mission statement will derive from the organisation's vision and, in turn, it will guide the setting of strategic goals and objectives. One of the biggest lessons that can be learned from recent business failures is the absence of a sustainable plan for the organisations in question. By developing a balanced approach that puts responsibility on each individual in the organisation, the chances of succeeding are greatly enhanced.

SUMMARY

This chapter has dealt with setting a vision, mission, goals and objectives for an organisation. Such a process is vital in order to ensure the effective and efficient use of resources so that the organisation can survive in a competitive environment.

There is a strong link between visionary companies and success. Leaders must take an holistic view of the organisation and all its stakeholders, and there must be internal alignment that connects the vision, mission, goals and objectives. There are three broad elements to a vision:
- Leadership to drive the process and maintain commitment on a continuous basis.
- Values to guide the decision-making process in the organisation in its dealings with all stakeholders. Such values should also be ethical in nature.
- Purpose – the reason the organisation exists – a reason greater than just making profits. It is often described as 'the engine of the company'.

The **strategic intent**, or long-term goals must be communicated clearly to the entire organisation. The **mission statement** guides the members of an organisation in making decisions that will achieve strategic goals and objectives. Mission statements should be brief and reflect the organisation's competences and capabilities.

Goals are broad statements of intent in line with the mission, and are usually qualitative in nature. A goal may have a number of objectives emanating from it. **Objectives** are more specific and measurable and are usually quantitative in nature.

The **Balanced Scorecard** presents a broader, more balanced perspective of how an organisation should develop and consists of financial, customer, internal processes and learning and growth perspectives. When these four elements are combined, it should ensure the long-term success of the organisation.

All organisational goals must be translated into department goals and ultimately into individual goals for which each employee must be held accountable. Goals, in themselves, can be highly motivational for employees as they rise to the challenge of achieving them. Many companies provide financial incentives which are linked to targets to encourage greater effort. However, there is much evidence to suggest that bonus payments do not provide any incentive to work harder, other than with manual work where extra productivity can be easily measured.

DISCUSSION QUESTIONS

1. Distinguish between an organisation's vision and its mission.
2. Taking a selection of organisations, examine whether a clear vision for their future direction can be identified.
3. Discuss the need for values underpinning corporate strategy.
4. Construct a Balanced Scorecard for an organisation with which you are familiar.
5. Examine the process for developing individual goals and objectives in your organisation. What changes or improvements to the process would you suggest?

CHAPTER 4

Corporate Governance, Business Ethics, and Corporate Social Responsibility

LEARNING OBJECTIVES

On completion of this chapter, you will be able to:

- Critically examine the corporate governance structures of an organisation
- Differentiate between various ethical approaches
- Evaluate actions from an ethical perspective
- Assess the actions of an organisation from a corporate social responsibility perspective

"It is necessary only for the good man to do nothing for evil to triumph."

Edmund Burke

INTRODUCTION

Corporate governance, business ethics and corporate social responsibility (CSR) are the subjects of the final chapter in Part One of this book, which deals with three related, and important, elements concerning the foundation of corporate strategy. This is an important chapter because it lays down an ethical foundation for the entire textbook. It is an approach that should underpin all of the decisions that managers take in the development and implementation of strategy.

The first section of the chapter discusses corporate governance, which is concerned with how the various structures are put in place to ensure that proper control is exercised on the direction an organisation is pursuing and that it is compliant with the law.

The middle section of the chapter examines business ethics. Company and tax law governs much of what an organisation does, laying down specific and prescriptive rules about how it conducts its affairs. Making VAT returns and submitting company accounts are some of the many legal obligations that an organisation must fulfil. There are also a number of other decisions that managers must make that are not so clear-cut. What is the right thing to do when the law does not prescribe an answer? Ethics guide the manager as to what the correct course of action should be. Included in this section is a discussion on whistleblowers. When one sees something wrong being done by a company, does loyalty to the organisation override the obligation to have the practice stopped? It is often the case that the practice will cease when it is brought into the public domain.

The final section of this chapter, on CSR, recognises that the organisation has obligations to groups other than shareholders. The obligation to provide financial returns to shareholders must be balanced with its obligations to all its stakeholders. Companies are slowly beginning to realise that by fulfilling those obligations it is not really costing anything, and in many cases it is actually providing a sound financial return – in addition to doing the right thing.

It will be seen throughout this textbook that strategic decisions are rarely cut and dried in regard to the correct course of action. It is often only after the event that one can see whether or not the correct course of action was chosen. With strategic decisions, there is also the added complication as to whether or not the actions stand up to moral scrutiny. Often, companies make good returns without the actions supporting those returns coming under investigation. On other occasions, it emerges that the company was operating in a manner that was either illegal or unethical, or both. Reputations or companies come crashing down.

CORPORATE GOVERNANCE

Corporate governance is an important factor in how strategic decisions are made. It will vary considerably depending on the type of company and from one country to another.

 Corporate governance is the control mechanism by which board members and senior executives are accountable to stakeholders for the strategic direction of an organisation and for legal and ethical compliance.

There are a number of factors that need to be considered when examining corporate governance, including:

- Company structures
- Chain of governance
- Company directors
- Differing board structures
- Investment information.

Company Structures

Strategy applies to all types of companies, both big and small. In terms of corporate governance, there is a large variation between the different types of ownership. Many people in business are self-employed and answer only to themselves in terms of their decisions; the owner and the manager are one and the same person. Once a limited company is formed, there are more legal and accounting requirements to be observed. The majority of companies in Ireland are small, employing perhaps just a few staff, some of whom may be family members. The law prescribes rules in regard to the appointment of directors and their duties. These duties were codified for the first time in the consolidated Companies Act 2014 (MacDonnell, 2015; Duffy, 2017). If the company is a private limited company, most aspects of corporate governance will be straightforward. Once the company goes public and is listed on a stock exchange, the corporate governance structures change significantly, and the number of people involved in the process grows considerably.

Chain of Governance

A large, listed company could have tens of thousands of shareholders – the people who own the company. In such situations, there is separation of ownership between those who own the company and those who run it on a day-to-day basis. The managers are employees of the organisation. In a public company, the managers are accountable, through the board of directors, to the shareholders for the decisions that are made. This is known as the 'chain of governance' (Tricker, 2015). It describes the different roles that various people have to play in the running of the company and who is answerable to whom. While publically quoted companies will have many individuals as small shareholders, a large proportion of the shares will be held by pension funds and investment managers. When money is paid into pension funds by individuals, it is invested on behalf of the trustees of the fund by professional fund managers. These fund managers will place the money in various public companies according to the level of confidence they have in the management of the company to deliver growth in the value of the shares through dividends and capital growth. The board of directors is the main group in charge of authorising strategy within the organisation, but these fund managers are in a very powerful position, albeit vicariously. While they do not have any formal authority to approve strategy, by moving funds in or out of the company, they show their confidence in the management to achieve results, and thereby influence strategy. The position of power held by fund managers and investment analysts are in a powerful position in how they deal with companies, and this imposes strong moral and ethical obligations on how they perform their work.

Company Directors

Directors are elected by the shareholders at the company's annual general meeting. In exercising their functions as directors, they owe a fiduciary duty to act in good faith on behalf of the company as a whole and for the purpose of the powers invested in the directors. They are free to exercise unfettered discretion in how they vote, which should be in the best interests of the company. They owe a duty to not be in a position where there is a conflict of interest; and to account to the company in regard to benefits obtained by their position as directors. In addition to fiduciary duty, directors also owe a duty of skill, care and diligence in how they exercise their duties as directors. If a director does not exercise such duties, he or she may be held legally liable. The onus is, therefore, on the director to be well acquainted with company law and to ensure that the company is being run in a proper manner (Duffy, 2017).

An important issue here is defining those to whom a duty of care is owed. Is it simply the shareholders, or do company directors have a wider duty of care to balance the interest of all stakeholders (see **Chapter 1**)? The Companies Act 2014 and the Companies Act 2006 in the UK are clear that the duty of directors is to the company (and not to the shareholders, as is commonly thought). The duty to the company reflects the common law judgment of Lord Cullen in the landmark 1902 case of *Percival v. Wright* (Callanan, 2015). However, this textbook takes the view that in order to act in the best interest of the company, it is a natural corollary to consider the interests of all stakeholders, particularly employees (Freeman *et al.*, 2010; Mackey and Sisodia, 2014). Interestingly, section 172 of the UK Companies Act 2006 makes explicit reference to the duty that directors have in regard to the interests of stakeholders – a glaring omission in the Irish Act, which came out 12 years later.

Public companies will have a mixture of executive and non-executive directors on their boards. The executive directors are full-time managers in the company with specific responsibilities for the day-to-day running of the company. Non-executive directors are appointed from outside the company, and their purpose is to provide a balanced and an independent perspective to the board. There should be a majority of independent, non-executive directors to ensure that managers are operating the company according to the rules and in the interest of all interested parties. Being independent means not being in a business relationship with the company, or receiving consultancy payments or share options. In 2003, the Chancellor of the Exchequer in the UK commissioned a report on the role and effectiveness of non-executive directors. Building on the earlier work on corporate governance by Sir Adrian Cadbury, Derek Higgs compiled a very extensive review of these responsibilities. One of the more important recommendations of the 'Higgs Report' (paragraph 5.7) states that a chief executive should not become chair of the same company (Higgs, 2003).

One issue that needs to be addressed regarding the composition of boards is gender balance. The percentage of women members on boards of directors across the globe is low, and in Ireland it is particularly low. Research carried out by Clancy *et al.* (2010) on Irish PLCs and semi-state companies found that women were significantly under-represented on the boards of these leading companies. According to the Public Appointments Service (PAS), by 2018 the situation had improved in the Irish public sector, and 53% of all new appointments to state boards were women, making up for decades of under-representation. The total of female directors in the public sector now stands at 40% overall. The PAS notes, however, that the private sector still lags behind, where only 13% of all directors are women, though the figure is higher for ISEQ-listed companies at 18% (Public Appointments Service, 2018). A number of European countries have introduced a quota system for women on boards of directors, including Austria, Belgium, France, Germany, Greece, Italy, the Netherlands, and Spain. The actual percentage of women directors varies in each of these countries, and also the stipulation in regard to company size and ownership structure (EU Commission, 2016). Such prescriptive approaches are, however, controversial.

In addition to the gender imbalance, Clancy *et al.* (2010:2–14) also state that "all the available evidence shows a lack of diversity across other characteristics, such as social background, occupation and age". Their research has shown that a small number of executives in Ireland held a disproportionately high number of directorships between them. One group of nine directors simultaneously sat on the boards of up to five of the top 40 Irish publically quoted or semi-state companies. Each one of that group was also a member of the boards of up to 17 other companies. These directorships also included a number of cross-directorships (where an individual on the board of company A is offered a seat on the board of company B, and vice versa).

People who hold simultaneous directorships in a large number of companies (multiple directorships), and in particular cross-directorships, have the potential to undermine good corporate governance in a number of areas. First is the independence of board members (in particular where there is a crossover of membership of remuneration committees) where directors on these committees recommend increases in salaries/directors fees on a basis of mutually supporting self-interest rather than any objective performance-related criteria. Second is the lack of diversity of those members. Thirdly, it raises serious questions about the amount of time that those individuals can devote to the complexity of board matters. The Walker Report in the UK was commissioned by the then Prime Minister Gordon Brown in 2009 to review corporate governance in UK banks and other financial entities. It recommended that the overall time commitment of non-executive directors in financial institutions should be greatly increased and should in future be a minimum of 30 to 36 days a year (Walker, 2009:14). In Ireland, the Central Bank has introduced limits on the amount of directorships that directors of financial institutions can hold. These limits are, however, still quite generous: for "high impact designated credit institutions", the limit is up to three financial directorships and up to five non-financial directorships. There are still no restrictions on the number of directorships the directors of non-financial companies can hold (Central Bank of Ireland, 2015).

The main purpose of the board of a company is to scrutinise the actions of executive management and to ask hard and probing questions about the proposals they are making to the board, and also decisions that they have made under delegated authority. The board must make independent judgements about the strategy proposals being made by management, and satisfy themselves that the proposals are in the best interests of the company and have been properly analysed. This should take the form of asking incisive questions about the rationale and methodology behind the proposals and about how management will implement company strategy if given approval. This will include examination of the element of risk involved in the proposals. Assessing risk is a very important aspect of the role of directors, especially non-executive directors. A challenge for non-executive directors in this regard is 'asymmetry of information', i.e. where non-executive directors are dependent on the executive management of the company to provide them with accurate and complete information required for objective assessment. Directors must overcome this limitation by ensuring they ask probing questions of management to ensure they are getting full information on each topic, and that they use independent judgement on the quality and accuracy of that information and its implications for the company (FRC, 2018). (The issue of analysing risk is discussed in **Chapter 7**.)

Proper oversight of the accounting procedures of the company is a very important element of the board's work. They must ensure that all of the proper accounting standards and regulations are being complied with. There will usually be an audit committee, consisting of non-executive directors, whose role is to oversee the financial reporting processes of the company on behalf of the board, as well as act as liaison with the internal audit function and the external auditors.

There is an obvious distinction between economic success and moral probity, and another very important role of the company's board is to test the moral dimension of the strategies being proposed. This is something, however, that is not as clear-cut as, for example, seeing whether the accounts have been properly compiled. It requires much more subjective judgement. That does not lessen its importance in any way and, indeed, with strategy in general, there is a great deal of judgement required. Given the company's obligation to a wide group of stakeholders, ensuring high ethical standards in the actions of the company is an essential part of the remit of the board.

There should be no doubt about this responsibility when one examines the social fallout from the global financial crisis in 2008. Much of the responsibility lies with the strategic decisions taken in boardrooms across the world. To dismiss it as a by-product of the free market for which no one is responsible, or to view it as 'just one of those things', is not just simplistic; it is a total abrogation of moral responsibility. For a market to operate it needs society, and people who have the means to purchase goods and services. The strategic decisions of companies must reflect the needs and well-being of society. The board of directors must show ethical leadership in their own actions and send a strong message to the company as to the high level of standards that are expected by all employees from the chief executive down.

Compliance has not always measured up to the mark, however. As former Financial Regulator, Matthew Elderfield, put it: "The old rules were too generous in their nature and encouraged box ticking as a means of compliance. Most disturbingly, all of the evidence points to some boards that were seriously out of touch with what was happening on the ground in their organisations." (Handcock, 2010:18). Perhaps the most incisive comments about corporate governance, and specifically about the role of directors in banks, was made by Niall Fitzgerald. Mr Fitzgerald is a former CEO of a multinational company, Uniliver, and he is perhaps one of the most successful Irish-born businessmen of his generation. In an interview in *The Irish Times* in March 2010 (O'Toole, 2010), he spoke about being a bank director in Ireland in the 1990s. He said that he had recently posed an awkward question at a dinner party to some friends of his (all of whom acted as bank directors):

"I want to confront you as a friend with a very difficult question. Because unless we all together and individually learn from this, I'm not sure it has been of any great value. The question you have to ask yourselves is: did you know what the institution was doing and the full consequences of what it was doing? Because if you did, you were complicit with the recklessness. Or if the answer is you didn't know, then you cannot have been discharging your responsibility as a director of that company properly."

Fitzgerald also spoke about the importance of the values that he learnt at home, particularly from his mother. Her basic rule was to treat people as you would wish to be treated yourself. Her litmus test was the mirror – if you are unsure if it is the right thing to do, look in the mirror; if you find you are averting your eyes then you have a problem. There are many business leaders who could learn from this advice. And while the interview with Niall Fitzgerald took place in 2010, the principle of directors knowing what is going on in their company, and taking responsibility for it, is timeless.

A number of significant high-profile cases around the world have prompted many governments to bring in regulations governing how companies operate. After the collapse of major companies such as Robert Maxwell's Communications Corp in the early 1990s (owing £440 million to the company's pension fund) and the Bank of Credit and Commerce International (BCCI), the UK Government commissioned Sir Adrian Cadbury in 1992 to chair a committee to investigate corporate governance systems and to make recommendations, many of which we have already discussed. In the US, the Sarbanes–Oxley Act of 2002 was intended to combat fraud, improve the reliability of financial reporting and restore investor confidence. Similarly, this was brought in after the collapse of a number of companies such as WorldCom and Enron. Perhaps the two most important elements of 'Sarbanes–Oxley' are sections 302 and 404:

- **Section 302** – Corporate responsibility for financial reports. The CEO and the CFO must personally certify the accuracy of financial statements and disclosures and that those statements fairly present in all material aspects the results of operations and financial condition of the company. Section 906 deals with white-collar crime penalties, and states that wilful failure by CEOs and CFOs to comply with the regulations can result in fines of up to $5 million and imprisonment for up to 20 years.
- **Section 404** requires companies to have annual evaluations of internal controls and procedures for financial reporting, and to include these in their annual reports.

www.sarbanes-oxley.com

Among other requirements, Sarbanes–Oxley obliges publicly traded companies to have a code of ethics (see the section on Business Ethics below). Rather than considering the Sarbanes–Oxley Act a financial burden, Wagner and Dittmar (2006) believe that it can be turned to a company's advantage, bringing operations under control while driving down compliance costs.

Reaction in Ireland to the many lapses in corporate governance prompted the Companies (Auditing and Accounting) Act 2003, which is similar in purpose to the Sarbanes–Oxley Act. In addition, the Company Law Enforcement Act 2001 established the Office of the Director of Corporate Enforcement (ODCE), which has responsibility for, *inter alia,* ensuring compliance with the Companies Act 2014, the primary piece of legislation covering companies in Ireland. In May 2010, the Financial Reporting Council in the UK introduced the *UK Corporate Governance Code* (this was formally known as the *Combined Code on Corporate Governance* or just the "Combined Code"), which is updated every few years. The *UK Corporate Governance Code* (the most recent version of which was published by the FRC in July 2018) operates on a 'comply or explain' basis, whereby companies must either comply with the regulations, or where they deviate from those regulations, the reason must be explained in their annual report. Euronext Dublin (formally the Irish Stock Exchange) has adopted these provisions for Irish-listed companies. Euronext Dublin is responsible for *inter alia* the listing of securities on the Irish market, the reporting of trading activity by member firms and reporting of potential market abuse to the Central Bank of Ireland for further investigation (Euronext, 2019).

For those who consider that the 'business of business is business', it is important to remember that the cost of non-compliance with ethical standards can be extremely high. Thomas *et al.* (2018) list three levels of cost of ethical failure:

- **Level 1 Costs** – these include government fines where laws have been broken, e.g. the BP Deepwater Horizon environmental disaster in the Gulf of Mexico. Level 1 costs also include penalties arising from any civil law cases. Generally speaking, these will also result in falling share prices.
- **Level 2 Costs** – include all the costs incurred by the company in investigating possible breaches of regulations and also the costs involved in rectifying the situation, e.g. the costs incurred by the banks involved in the DIRT Inquiry (see section on Business Ethics).
- **Level 3 Costs** – these costs are much more intangible, but real nonetheless. They include the loss of customers as a result of the company's actions, the damage to the company's brand (e.g. the reputational damage done to Irish charities such as Rehab, Console, and the Central Remedial Clinic, and the negative impact this has had on their ability to raise much-needed funds from the public) and the impact it has on staff morale, which often results in high staff turnover.

If things go wrong, the process of repairing the company's shattered reputation is both costly and time-consuming. The third part of this chapter deals with corporate social responsibility, which advocates a proactive approach to how companies interact with all of their stakeholders. It will be seen that, in addition to being the 'right thing to do', it also confers significant advantages on the organisation.

Implicit in all of the discussion above is that the board must satisfy themselves as to the calibre of the executives and their ability to do the job. This is particularly so in relation to the chief executive and the leadership he or she exercises. Very often, a significant part of the remuneration package of senior executives is given in the form of a bonus payment, and this is decided by the board (or a subcommittee thereof). Another one of the more important recommendations of the Higgs Report relates to the separation of the role of chair of the board from that of chief executive (paragraph 5.3). This is to ensure the independence of the chair from the day-to-day management responsibility of the company (Higgs, 2003). This separation of roles is considered best practice and is adopted by most Irish public companies. In many situations there may be dissent in the board over certain proposals and the chair must act in a decisive and independent manner to encourage debate, but also to bring the discussion to a conclusive end.

The role of directors has become a great deal more onerous in recent years. The Institute of Directors in Ireland was established in 1980 as an independent, non-political body whose aim is to support and develop the role of directors in Irish business. While most of the discussion in this book will centre on the role of executives in formulating and implementing strategy, the board of directors plays a very important role in the oversight of the company.

Differing Board Structures

There is no standard international structure for boards of directors. Different structures have developed around the world depending on a variety of influences, including different legal frameworks and different national ideological approaches to business. In Ireland, there is a single board whose function is to supervise the management of the company. This is often referred to as the 'Anglo-Saxon model' or the 'shareholder model' and is common to most English-speaking countries, such as the UK, the US, Australia and Canada (Tricker, 2015). Within this structure, there tends to be widespread ownership of shares and these shares trade regularly. The relationship of banks to these companies is largely limited to contractual arrangements with regard to overdrafts and loans. In many European states, a more inclusive corporate governance structure exists. The norm is for two-tier structure boards, which comprise a fixed level of worker representation which enjoys powers of co-determination and veto. As such, it goes much further than consultation and amounts to joint decision-making (Tricker, 2015). In the two-tier structure, the first tier consists of managers who are responsible for the day-to-day supervision of the company. The upper tier is a supervisory board whose role is to oversee the management board. Banks tend to be more involved in what the company is doing and in Japan, for example, banks tend to have a long-term relationship with companies by taking out equity investment. This was one of the reasons why it took Japan so long to emerge from the recession in the 1990s. It took the banks a long time to recover because of their direct involvement in failing businesses and, in turn, the banks were unable to lend money to support recovery in the business sector.

Investment Information

The detail and level of information available to members of the governance chain will vary considerably depending on their position. One of the major strategic benefits of IT is that it can provide managers with accurate and detailed information in a timely manner (and on occasions, in real-time). Such detailed information is necessary for managers to make the correct decisions (Sharda *et al.*, 2018). However, much of this information will be highly confidential and will need to have restricted access within the company. Shareholders will also want information about the performance of the company as they will base their investment decisions largely on this information. However, the information given to shareholders will be largely confined to that issued in the annual accounts. Public companies must publish their results every six months in Ireland, while in the US it is every three months. One of the big drawbacks to such short reporting periods is that it can put undue pressure on executives to come up with short-term gains at the expense of the long-term interests of the company, which is central to corporate strategy.

Stockbrokers and investment managers, while they will not have access to internal management reports, will compile detailed information about industries and companies within those industries, and this will form the basis of their investment decisions. It is common, however, for corporate executives to meet with investment managers to discuss the strategy being pursued and to explain the rationale behind it. When Ryanair bought its 29% shareholding in Aer Lingus in 2006, it caught the investment community by surprise, and Ryanair CEO Michael O'Leary had to meet with the large institutional investors to satisfy them that the move was part of a coherent plan (Cooper, 2018). Without such assurances, fund managers could quickly remove large amounts of money from investment in the company, causing the share price to fall dramatically.

BUSINESS ETHICS

Introduction

In recent years, there has been a much greater focus on how businesses and individuals conduct their affairs. There have been many high-profile cases of serious lapses in ethical standards not just around the world, but also here in Ireland. Ethics, of course, covers all aspects of how we live our lives and each of the various professional bodies has its own code of ethics. Medical ethics is obviously different to ethics in the accountancy profession, but each serves to guide people as to what is right and what is wrong. There are rarely clear-cut answers when it comes to ethics:

> "The business of philosophy is not to give rules, but to analyse the private judgements of common reason."
>
> Immanuel Kant

The Walker Report in the UK made the following observation in relation to regulatory changes:

> "The behavioural changes that may be needed are unlikely to be fostered by regulatory fiat, which in any event risks provoking unintended consequences. Behavioural improvement is more likely to be achieved through clearer identification of best practice and more effective but, in most areas, non-statutory routes to implementation so that boards and their major owners feel 'ownership' of good corporate governance."
>
> (Walker, 2009:9)

By recognising that not every aspect of governance can, or indeed should, be governed by regulation, we see that ethics clearly plays an important role in how companies operate.

The focus of this section relates to how individuals in business make decisions from an ethical perspective, and also on understanding why such situations can be evaluated as either morally right or wrong (Crane and Matten, 2016).

Definition | **Business ethics** can be defined as the ethical conduct of people within organisations and the impact it has on decisions they make at corporate and individual level.

This section will deal with business ethics under a number of headings:

- Historical background
- Ethical theories: teleological ethical systems, deontological ethical systems and ethical relativism
- Code of ethics
- Evidence of unethical behaviour
- Relating ethics to business
- Whistleblowing
- Organisational approaches to ethical behaviour.

Historical Background

While most management theory is relatively new, the study of ethics goes back to the beginnings of philosophy. To understand modern business ethics, it is perhaps useful to understand the development of philosophy over the millennia. The study of ethics is an entire body of knowledge in its own right, and just part of a chapter cannot possibly do it justice. The purpose of this section is merely to highlight its influence rather than catalogue its development over time.

Early philosophy began by trying to understand the world through the use of reason. The three great Greek philosophers, Socrates, Plato and Aristotle, brought it to a new level. Socrates, born in 470 BC, unlike earlier Greek philosophers, was not concerned with the natural world, but believed what mattered most is how we ought to live our lives. Regarded by many as the founder of moral philosophy, much of his work centred on finding the answer to questions such as: 'What is justice?' 'What is right?' 'What is good?' Having the answers to these questions would have a profound effect on our lives. His style was to pose questions: he did not necessarily know the answers himself, but sought to create discussion and debate in order to increase the level of understanding of philosophical questions. He was the first to teach about the importance of personal integrity in its own right rather than in response to the law or deities (Magee, 1998).

Plato, the greatest pupil of Socrates, recorded in writing much of Socrates' teaching and concerned himself with a much broader range of topics, regarding mathematics as key to understanding the natural world. Plato's most famous work, *The Republic,* applies the principles of philosophy to political affairs and covers a whole range of social and moral issues.

In turn, Aristotle was a pupil of Plato's Academy for 20 years. His teachings were very broad, but in the context of this discussion, his development of our understanding of virtue ethics is important. He believed that people want to be virtuous, and that self-indulgence will only bring us into conflict with others. According to Aristotle, 'the golden mean' was a virtue, the midway point between two extremes (vices). Thus, courage was the midway point between rashness (excess) and cowardice (deficiency). Other virtues included temperance, magnificence, magnanimity, proper ambition, patience, truthfulness, righteous indignation, modesty and friendliness (Aristotle, Ed.1976: 104).

His discussions also cover topics such as moral goodness, moral responsibility, justice and the intellectual virtues.

The teachings of Socrates, Plato and Aristotle laid the foundation for generations of philosophers that have influenced ethics over the years. Many regard virtue ethics as being a classification in its own right. Certainly, there are necessary prerequisites for ethical leadership in managers and board members. These virtues are not innate but are developed in the individual over time. The fact that virtues are developed over time is in keeping with the concept of the learning organisation (Senge, 1990), and consequently managers must pay due cognisance to developing a culture of ethical compliance in their organisation.

There are a number of classifications used for ethical theories. The classifications used here are:

- Teleological ethical systems – dealing with consequences
- Deontological ethical systems – dealing with universal principles
- Ethical relativism – allowing for regional variation in standards.

Teleological Ethical Systems

Teleological ethics is based on the concept that the morality of a decision is measured by examining its probable outcome and consequences. It is closely linked with the theory of utilitarianism, which was developed by Jeremy Bentham and John Stewart Mill in the 19th Century. Utilitarianism is very similar to the managerial concept of cost–benefit analysis. It involves examining a decision from the point of view of its costs and its benefits, and that the decision should yield the greatest possible benefit. (In many ways, it underpins the decision-making process described in **Chapter 12**.) It appears a simple concept at first, and easy to apply in theory, but on closer examination, it is not so clear-cut.

To make morally correct decisions requires discussion on the issue and full knowledge of the problem and likely consequences. Inaction must also be considered as well as action (acts of omission and acts of commission). In reality it is often very difficult to foresee all consequences. The question of measurement is another problem. Financial cost and benefits can be measured, but how can happiness be calculated, for example, or goodness? Another version of teleological ethics is **distributive justice**. Developed by Harvard professor John Rawls, the theory is based on a concept of fairness. Distributive justice believes that ethical acts are those that lead to an equitable distribution of goods and services (Hartman, 2002).

Deontological Ethical Systems

Deontological ethical systems are based on universal principles or concepts of what is right and wrong. They are termed 'universal' in that they transcend cultures and societies. The person most credited with developing the theory was the German philosopher Immanuel Kant (1724–1804).

Actions are considered right or wrong regardless of the consequences of the action or its impact on others. The concept of goodwill is central to Kant's philosophy. A person's moral worth is based on their decision to discharge their duty. In deciding what is right, a person is guided by the "categorical imperative" – what a rational person would believe to be universal laws that apply to all humankind (Hartman, 2002).

Deontological ethical systems underpin general principles such as the UN Declaration of Human Rights, which sets out the universal rights of people around the world. It also underpins legislation such as the Employment Equality Acts 1998–2015, which prevents discrimination on nine grounds. It is a prescriptive law – a manager cannot discriminate on age grounds because he or she does not agree with the legislation. Deontological ethics also prescribes that people should perform acts because those actions are the right thing to do, rather than from fear of the consequences, such as being fined or going to jail.

In some respects **virtue ethics** are linked with deontological ethical systems in that virtues such as honesty, truthfulness, and many more are held in esteem by most societies and, in that regard, are universal. Such virtues guide human behaviour in making ethical decisions. There is also a strong overlap between deontological ethics and most of the world's religions. Christianity, Judaism, Islam and Buddhism all share prescriptive rules as to how one should lead one's life – such as the Ten Commandments. Virtue ethics and religion were brought together by St Thomas Aquinas, who divided virtue into two categories. Theological virtues included faith, hope and charity; and intellectual virtues included wisdom, justice, temperance and fortitude. Aquinas considered that virtue was not innate but something that was learned or acquired (Hartman, 2002).

Ethical Relativism

Universal principles cover many aspects of what is right and wrong. According to Thompson *et al.* (2018), ethical relativism believes that different societies and cultures have divergent values and that there are also various political systems. Consequently, there can be no absolute rules guiding business activities. When there are regional differences about what is considered proper behaviour, it is appropriate to allow local standards to prevail and take precedence over ethical standards applicable at home. Common dilemmas faced by multinational corporations are whether or not to pay bribes or use underage labour. Deontological or universal ethics would dictate that the use of child labour is always totally wrong. Ethical relativism would have us examine the issue in a different way. Is it wrong to employ the child if the child's family is dependent on that wage for subsistence living? What are the consequences of not employing the child? What are the alternatives for the individual: starvation, prostitution? It is evident that these decisions are more complex than they first appear. Ethical relativism believes that there are few absolute rules, and one size does not fit all. Therefore, companies must tailor their decisions according to local customs. For a local company operating in just one location, it is an ethical dilemma. For a multinational company operating in over 100 countries worldwide, it would be an administrative nightmare, in addition to being a moral dilemma. Thompson *et al.* (2018:322) argue that such a position is "tantamount to rudderless ethical standards" and "is morally unacceptable".

Integrative Social Contracts Theory

Donaldson and Dunfee (1994) propose a compromise between universalism and relativism. The integrative social contracts theory suggests that a company should, as much as possible, adhere to universal ethical principles that control company action, while also taking into account local customs that further define ethically acceptable behaviour. Where there is a conflict between the two, then universal principles take precedence. The universal rules about right and wrong, to which groups around the world subscribe, form a binding social contract between the company and society. It is essentially a universal system, with some flexibility built in. Ethical relativism might be 'morally unacceptable', but the variations in ethical standards from one country to another make universalism very difficult to operate in a competitive environment. The integrative social contracts theory goes a long way to reconciling the two.

While universal laws are very prescriptive, in reality they often require some interpretation. Measurement of human rights in a country, for example, cannot be calculated in the same precise manner as, for example, measuring temperature. It requires managerial judgement. From that point of view, the integrative social contract theory seems to safeguard universally accepted principles while allowing for managerial judgement. However, when one re-examines the universal system above, it must be recognised that Kant allowed for interpretation: "The business of philosophy is not to give rules, but to analyse the private judgements of common reason."

Code of Ethics

Many organisations have drawn up a code of ethics to guide managers in making difficult judgements. A code of ethics is a written statement of what the organisation considers to be important values and standards of behaviour. It is important that time and effort goes into making this a meaningful document. Enron had a values statement, but it was meaningless. According to Lencioni (2002: 113), "empty value statements create cynical and dispirited employees, alienate customers, and undermine managerial credibility". Lencioni provides a framework for drafting meaningful company values:

- Managers must understand the different types of values and what actually constitutes the company's core values.
- The values statement must be aggressively authentic; something that the company considers integral to the success of the company rather than a slogan more fitting to a greeting card.
- It must be owned by the company and be reflected in how it operates.
- The values must be woven into every aspect of the company.

In addition to guiding ethical decisions, values are also important for the company's vision. It will be remembered from the previous chapter that Collins and Porras (1996) regard values as an integral part of the company's vision. It is important that directors, managers, and employees consider the ethical aspect of all decisions that they make. **Chapter 12** will deal with decision-making. The framework below will help guide all concerned in making both day-to-day and long-term decisions about their work.

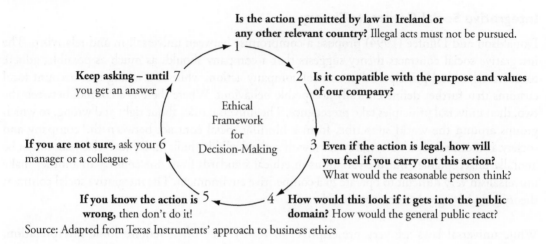

Is the action permitted by law in Ireland or any other relevant country? Illegal acts must not be pursued.

Keep asking – until 7
you get an answer

Ethical
Framework
for
Decision-Making

2 **Is it compatible with the purpose and values of our company?**

If you are not sure, ask your 6
manager or a colleague

3 **Even if the action is legal, how will you feel if you carry out this action?**
What would the reasonable person think?

If you know the action is 5
wrong, then don't do it!

4 **How would this look if it gets into the public domain?** How would the general public react?

Source: Adapted from Texas Instruments' approach to business ethics

Figure 4.1 *Diagram of Ethical Framework for Decision-making*

The aspiration for all employees should be to behave in an ethically sound fashion, dedicated to maintaining the highest standards. Managers should exercise ethical leadership. This entails not only complying with the law on all matters, but ensuring that all aspects of their work reflect high moral standards. That includes ensuring that there are no unintentional acts or ethical breaches as well as deliberate ones.

Evidence of Unethical Behaviour

There are many examples of unethical and illegal behaviour around the world. There are various reasons for such behaviour. If it were to be summed up in two words, they would be: human nature. Despite the ideals expressed by the great philosophers, there have always been those who will act in their own self-interest and believe, to borrow the line from the original 1988 movie *Wall Street*, that "greed is good". It is unfortunate for the majority of people who work in an honest and ethical fashion that they should be affected by such behaviour. With the collapse of the banks in Ireland in the aftermath of the financial crash, it was not only thousands of small investors who lost their money in the destruction of the share price; tens of thousands also saw the value of their pension funds destroyed. In addition, many staff members employed by the banks lost their jobs.

Despite having to be bailed out by the State with €64 billion, however, some of the main retail banks subsequently took customers off tracker mortgages (which were losing money for the banks) and moved them to higher-interest-rate variable mortgages. This was despite the customers having a legal entitlement to the lower tracker rates, and despite objections made by them when they were switched. Many customers subsequently lost their homes as they were unable to pay the higher interest rates and their houses were repossessed. Derville Rowland, Director of General Financial Conduct at the Central Bank conducted an investigation into 39,800 individual cases of wrongful charging of customers. By March 2019, €647 million has been paid by way of redress and compensation. The total cost to the banks is expected to exceed €1 billion. This behaviour has yet again caused immense reputational damage to the banks (Central Bank, 2019). The narrow focus on maximising short-term profits has clearly failed, and therefore a wider stakeholder approach to running organisations is advocated (OECD, 2015; FRC, 2018).

Companies must ensure that there are procedures in place, supported by an ethical culture, to prevent unethical conduct by employees. While a company cannot directly account for an individual's excessive pursuit of personal wealth, there are ways in which it can ensure proper corporate behaviour. In particular, it must ensure that the pressure on staff members to reach financial targets is fair and reasonable. Once the company prioritises the bottom line over ethical behaviour, it starts on a slippery slope. As discussed above, the company's values statement must be woven into every aspect of its work and embedded in its culture.

There are many examples of unethical and illegal behaviour over the years in Irish business, including (Byrne, 2012):
- cases of abuse of various forms of EU funding;
- the Ansbacher Affair, where wealthy business and professional people lodged money in offshore accounts in the Cayman Islands to avoid tax;
- a similar scheme, known as 'Faldor', run by AIB executives investing money in the British Virgin Islands (breaking Irish tax law);
- the 'DIRT scandal', whereby some banks facilitated customers to (knowingly and falsely) declare they were non-resident in Ireland and consequently not be liable to pay deposit interest retention tax;
- insider trading with company shares;
- price fixing in various industries; and
- widespread tax evasion at corporate and individual levels.

In addition to investigations by the Comptroller and Auditor General, there have been a number of official inquiries into such events by the State – at enormous cost to the exchequer. These include, among others, those listed in **Table 4.1** below.

Table 4.1: State Inquiries and Reports

Year	Investigation
1991–94	The Tribunal of Inquiry into the Beef Processing Industry
1997	The Tribunal of Inquiry (Dunes Payments) ('The McCracken Tribunal')
1997–2011	The Tribunal of Inquiry into certain Payments to Politicians and Related Matters ('The Moriarty Tribunal')
1997–2012	The Tribunal of Inquiry Into Certain Planning Matters and Payments ('The Flood / Mahon Tribunal')
1998	Dáil Public Accounts Committee DIRT Inquiry
2011	Nyberg Report of the Commission of Investigation into the Banking Sector

(Source: Byrne, 2012:144)

Dr Diarmuid Martin, Archbishop of Dublin, at the World Economic Forum meeting in Davos, Switzerland in January 2009, spoke about the responsibility that bankers have in "creating a climate of responsibility from within". Bankers have responsibility not just to themselves, their boardrooms and investors, but also to economic and social sustainability. Commenting on the excessive amount of "irresponsible lending and irresponsible management of lending" that had taken place in recent years, the Archbishop said that this will have enormous social consequences for Irish people. Martin believes that "morals and ethics cannot be injected from the outside", and that the business and financial community were part of the problem in the first instance, but they would also have to be part of the solution (Carswell, 2009).

The repercussions of these revelations go far beyond the reputation of the institutions involved. The reputation of the country as a place to do business has been severely damaged as a result. One thing is certain at this point: the approach to corporate governance and regulation had to undergo significant change.

Relating Ethics to Business

The above relates to serious ethical failures in business. Ethics also concerns everyday decisions that managers have to make. Organisations are open systems, meaning they are dealing with a wide variety of stakeholders, and ethics shapes all of these relationships. **Chapter 6** will deal with the value chain and the value system: how organisations deal with their suppliers and distributors. Each person and organisation that the company deals with is entitled to be treated fairly, and to share in the overall profit. The organisation also deals with the wider community, with the government, and other groups. Ethics also concerns internal issues: how does it treat its employees in terms of pay and conditions, does it treat them in a respectful manner, does it provide them with stimulating jobs? How the organisation deals with these stakeholders will be examined in detail in the next section on corporate social responsibility. Another topical ethical issue that requires examination is whistleblowing.

WHISTLEBLOWING

Whistleblowing occurs when a member (or ex-member) of an organisation discloses any action by others in that organisation that is either illegal or unethical. It covers issues such as when a company is causing harm, directly or indirectly, to members of the public, violating human rights, or doing things that are illegal either under statute law or common law. It may also be an action of a serious nature that is contrary to the purpose of the company. All of these situations can be as a result of managerial action or, in other cases, a lack of such action.

Illustration 4.1: The Watergate Scandal

Long before Julian Assange became famous for releasing sensitive, classified information on his controversial Wikileaks website, Mark Felt was one of the first and most famous whistleblowers. Felt, who went by the alias 'Deep Throat', was number 2 to Interim Director L. Patrick Gray of the FBI at the time of the break-in at the Democratic National Committee's Headquarters in the Watergate office complex in Washington D.C. in June 1972. It later emerged that it was members of President Richard Nixon's campaign team that broke into the offices to spy on the Democratic Presidential campaign. Mark Felt was the source that helped reporters Bob Woodward and Carl Bernstein of the *Washington Post* uncover the Watergate scandal. He insisted on remaining anonymous and it was Woodward and Bernstein's editor who came up with the alias. He fed the reporters information on the break-in bit by bit and the reporters eventually cracked the story that ultimately brought down President Nixon. The Nixon Administration did everything in its power at the time to subvert the FBI's investigation into the break-in and the subsequent cover-up of the crime.

The year prior to the scandal, Mark Felt had been passed over for promotion as Director of the FBI after J. Edgar Hoover retired. Was being passed over for promotion his motivation or was it disgust at the abuse of political power? Felt died in 2008 at the age of 95 and, while his identity was only made public three years before his death, his motivation was never made clear.

"Soft you; a word or two before you go. I have done the state some service, and they know't; No more of that."

Othello, Act V, Sc. 2

Regardless of his motivation, Felt's actions changed US history and strengthened democracy.

Whistleblowing raises a number of ethical issues. First, one must examine the motivation of the person making the disclosure. It could be for perfectly laudable reasons or it may be because the employee has a personal grudge against the company, such as not being considered for bonus payments or not being promoted. For the purpose of the discussion here, it will be assumed that there are genuine reasons for any disclosure and that it is of substantial interest to the wider public.

Employees must distinguish between loyalty owed to the organisation on one hand, and the wider public on the other. This can pose a dilemma for the employee in question. Loyalty to an organisation is something that is generally fostered and is seen to be a good thing. Working closely with colleagues further develops this sense of corporate identity and commitment.

In the course of their work, employees will come across information that is commercially sensitive and confidential. For that reason, every employee owes loyalty to that organisation. It is qualified, however, in the sense that each and every individual has to take responsibility for his or her actions, and if those actions by the company are illegal, it is immaterial if the employee was acting under the direction of a manager or not.

Any work being carried out in commercial life has to be within the bounds of what is legal. Where any activity is illegal or morally wrong, the employee has a clear duty to report it. However, this can often have grave consequences for the individual involved. If the organisation is involved in illegal activity, it will not take kindly to those actions being made public. The whistleblower concerned may not be promoted in the future, may find themselves out of a job, and could face difficulties in finding another job as the company may destroy their reputation in the industry. If a person is the breadwinner in a family, such a prospect is quite daunting. On the other hand, doing nothing is not a moral option. In the words attributed to Edmund Burke: "For evil to flourish, all that is necessary is for good men to do nothing."

The consequences of whistleblowing can be very serious for all concerned. There is an onus on the individual to ensure that, in making a public disclosure, they have accurate information. If it is inaccurate, not only will it damage the reputation of the company, but it will also besmirch the reputation of fellow workers – without justification. In many cases, the facts may not be all that clear-cut and there will be a question of judgement involved as to whether or not it should be reported. In many aspects of law, the acid test is what would the reasonable person think? The person concerned will have to take into account the seriousness of the situation, as well as the immediacy of the problem. Where possible, the whistleblower should endeavour to obtain documentary evidence. In making or not making a disclosure, the person involved must take responsibility for their own actions.

In the first instance, the person should seek to have the problem redressed within the company. There are many occasions in which illegal activity is carried out without the knowledge or approval of those at the top, as in the case of 'rogue' traders such as Nick Leeson (Barings Bank). As a result, one's duty to the organisation takes precedence over making such knowledge public. Indeed, it may jeopardise any legal action that the company may wish to take against the individual concerned. Again, this can pose a dilemma. Is the activity being carried out at a lower level or at the very top of the organisation? Unless one has genuine grounds to believe that the activity concerned is being undertaken with the approval of top management, there is an obligation to exhaust all internal channels before bringing it to the attention of those outside the organisation. Going outside the organisation should be the last resort.

From the perspective of good corporate governance, the organisation should be run in such a way that makes whistleblowing something that should never have to happen in the first instance. The organisation has a clear moral duty to its employees to ensure that they are not being asked to do anything illegal or compromising. By having clear corporate goals based on ethical principles, and by ensuring that the organisation is run in a clear and transparent manner, employees should feel free to notify management of any wrong doing without fear of repercussions. This again highlights the need for sound corporate leadership. Just as the organisation should not cause the situation in the first instance, it also has a moral duty to protect employees who highlight illegal practices by the corporation.

Whistleblowers' Charter

Many organisations are now developing a 'whistleblowers' charter', which is designed to enshrine the rights of employees in disclosing any untoward practices. To ensure that such a charter is based on substance rather than rhetoric, some companies will subject themselves to an independent audit to validate the charter. In order to give employees confidence that the company's attitude to whistleblowing is serious, it may set up a separate division to allow employees to bypass the normal chain of command and report directly to a company-nominated investigator, perhaps anonymously. The investigator can than examine the claim and take whatever action is appropriate. Central to the policy of whistleblowing must be the clear expectation by the employee that they will be protected by the organisation and not be victimised in any way. On the other hand, employees must be aware that making false or malicious allegations will be considered a serious disciplinary matter.

While many private organisations have brought in their own charter, it was only in recent years that the State brought in legislation covering whistleblowing with the Protected Disclosures Act 2014 (see below). This is despite the fact that there have been numerous examples in recent years where many organisations stood over wrongdoing, and where numerous people in those organisations were aware of what was going on and yet did nothing. This became quite evident in the Morris Tribunal findings in relation to Garda members in Donegal. There are many reasons, no doubt, why people who are aware of illegal or unethical behaviour do nothing about it, but without proper protection in place, fear must play a part.

In the UK, the Public Interest Disclosure Act 1998 came about as a result of a number of disasters that could have been avoided if employees had been able to voice their concerns without fear of retribution. In their 2008–2009 annual report, the UK's Committee on Standards in Public Life highlighted the importance of such channels: "Whistleblowing, following agreed procedures can be an instrument of good governance and an important safeguard against fraud, malpractice or maladministration" (Committee on Standards in Public Life, 2010:41).

Challenging unethical behaviour is important to maintain an ethical climate in an organisation. Whether or not employees are prepared to challenge the system will depend on a number of factors, including the clarity of policies for tackling unethical behaviour, the individual's role and level within the organisation, and the quality of interpersonal relationships between employees, their peers and their managers (Yarlagadda *et al.*, 2017). A confidential reporting system is important as a mechanism by which employees can raise concerns, as well as support networks that provide them with guidance.

In Ireland, there was a lot of opposition to changing the law on whistleblowing, for example from the Company Law Reform Group, which, in a report in 2007 stated that it had found no evidence to support the inclusion of whistleblowing provisions into company law, and favoured a continuation of the government's 'sectoral approach' rather than a broader regulatory regime that may "hinder entrepreneurship and investment" (CLRG, 2007:89). However, the 2009 *Code of Practice for the Governance of State Bodies* did include a section (section 2.11) dealing with confidential disclosures. The *Code of Practice for the Governance of State Bodies* was updated in 2016 and the old provision was replaced by section 5.9, which states that "section 21 of the Protected Disclosures Act 2014 requires that every public body shall establish and maintain procedures for the making of protected disclosures by workers who are or were employed by the public body and for dealing with such disclosures" (DPER, 2016).

Protected Disclosures Act 2014

It took 16 years after the UK introduced its Public Interest Disclosure Act 1998 for Ireland to follow suit and introduce comprehensive legislation dealing with whistleblowing. The Protected Disclosures Act 2014 removed the sectoral approach and, for the first time, provided a consolidated framework for all public and private sector bodies to provide protection for those seeking to highlight wrongdoing in organisations.

Under the Protected Disclosures Act 2014, a protected disclosure is a disclosure of information that, in the reasonable belief of the person disclosing the information, tends to show a "relevant wrongdoing" in the organisation. "Relevant wrongdoing" is a broad term and includes: criminal offences; failure to comply with legal obligations; miscarriages of justice; serious breaches of health and safety obligations; environmental damage; unlawful or improper use of funds or resources; and an act or omission by or on behalf of a public body that is oppressive, discriminatory, grossly negligent or constitutes gross mismanagement. If information related to these matters is concealed or destroyed, this is also a relevant wrongdoing.

The purpose of the Protected Disclosures Act, which came into effect on 15 July 2015, is to protect people who raise concerns about possible wrongdoings in the workplace. It provides redress for employees who are dismissed or otherwise penalised for having reported possible wrongdoing. The Act's definition of the term 'worker' includes employees or former employees, trainees, people working under a contract for services, independent contractors, agency workers, people on work experience, members of An Garda Síochána and members of the Defence Forces.

Illustration 4.2: Punishing Whistleblowers

The need for legislation to protect whistleblowers is self-evident. There are many examples of people who have spoken up and were victimised or punished for whistleblowing. Eugene McErlean, former Group Auditor for AIB, was wrongly blamed by the bank for not preventing rogue trader John Rusnak losing $691 million in 2002 at AIB's US subsidiary, Allfirst. McErlean was effectively forced to leave the bank in 2002 – the same day that AIB issued a press release on the Rusnak affair, thus creating the (false) impression that McErlean was to blame (Ross, 2009; O'Toole, 2017). McErlean had previously uncovered systematic overcharging of customers at AIB as well as the use of off-shore companies to trade in AIB shares by Goodbody, AIB's stockbroking subsidiary at the time. McErlean reported the matter to his superiors in AIB and also to the Financial Regulator. However, nothing came of it at the time, and it was only after RTÉ ran an investigative programme a few years later that the matter was properly dealt with. Nevertheless, nobody in AIB was disciplined over the affair and it was not until May 2009 before then-CEO of AIB, Eugene Sheehy, finally apologised publicly to McErlean for the way in which he had been treated by the bank.

Since the implementation of the Protected Disclosures Act 2014, perhaps the most infamous public disclosure was that made by Garda Sergeant Maurice McCabe who, in 2012, made the first of a number of internal disclosures to An Garda Síochána (and subsequently a protected disclosure) concerning various wrongdoings relating, *inter alia*, to not properly investigating a number of serious crimes by Gardaí and also to the widespread cancellation by senior Gardaí of penalty points that had been given to members of the public for speeding offences. Sgt McCabe had made complaints internally about these matters, but was dissatisfied with the way they were investigated within the force. He was subsequently victimised by superiors and colleagues for making the allegations. In early 2014, at a televised Oireachtas hearing, the then-Garda Commissioner Martin Callinan referred to Sgt McCabe's actions as "disgusting", a matter which caused considerable public outcry. The commissioner retired early in March 2014 (Charlton, 2018).

In 2015, the Government asked Senior Counsel Sean Guerin to investigate allegations that serious crimes were improperly investigated by An Garda Síochána. Guerin's report was critical of the treatment of Sgt McCabe by the force and recommended the establishment of a comprehensive commission of inquiry. The Government asked Supreme Court Judge, Mr Justice Peter Charleton to set up a statutory tribunal of inquiry. The "Tribunal of Inquiry into protected disclosures made under the Protected Disclosures Act 2014 and certain other matters" – known as the 'Disclosures Tribunal' – was established in February 2017. The Tribunal covered *inter alia*: "The Health Service Executive; The Child and Family Agency (TUSLA); Raidió Teilifís Éireann; Garda Headquarters; and Garda Officers concerning Sergeant Maurice McCabe and related matters". In essence, it investigated the many allegations made by Sgt McCabe of various wrongdoings in An Garda Síochána.

The Tribunal published its report in October 2018. Sgt McCabe was completely vindicated by the Tribunal in his actions in raising concerns under the Protected Disclosures Act 2014. Sgt McCabe retired from the Force three weeks' later, after 30 years of distinguished service. Mr Justice Charlton said Sgt McCabe had done the State a considerable service by bringing policing problems to the attention of the public and that he remained an officer of exemplary character and a person of "admirable fortitude". He also found that there was a campaign of calumny led by former Commissioner Martin Callinan against Sgt McCabe (Charleton, 2018). Sgt McCabe initiated a legal action against the State in relation to the manner in which he had been treated following his protected disclosures. In April 2019, Sgt McCabe settled this action (Bray, 2019). The terms of the settlement are confidential, but he is believed to have received a considerable settlement from the State in compensation.

The Maurice McCabe affair had a very negative impact on the reputation of An Garda Síochána and how it handles wrongdoing within its ranks. The current Garda Commissioner, Drew Harris, who was appointed in September 2018, said the Charleton Report made for difficult reading for the organisation, adding that it was vital that An Garda Síochána take the opportunity to change how it operates in order to provide a professional and ethical service to the public (RTÉ, 2018a). While the whole affair had enormous consequences for a number of people, including the resignations of two Ministers for Justice and a Garda Commissioner, arguably the greatest human impact of the 12-year saga was on Maurice McCabe and his family (as portrayed poignantly in an RTÉ Prime Time investigation by journalist Katie Hannon on the matter (RTÉ, 2018b)).

ORGANISATIONAL APPROACHES TO ETHICAL BEHAVIOUR

Different companies will adopt different ethical stances on how they conduct their affairs. This will largely be a reflection of the culture of the organisation and of the individual managers and their ethical standards. There are various frameworks, usually based on a continuum. Thompson *et al.* (2018) list four organisational approaches to ethics:

- **The unconcerned approach** – where executives believe that the notion of right and wrong is dictated by government in its laws and regulations. Once it keeps within the law, the company is entitled to do what it likes and management's time should not be wasted by concerning itself beyond what it is legally required to do.
- **The damage control approach** – managers are wary of scandal and adverse public comment. They will adopt a code of ethics for the purpose of window dressing, but company personnel are not required to adhere to its contents. It will turn a blind eye to shady practices as long as there is no danger of public exposure.
- **The compliance approach** – where executives will comply with a high ethical standard in their dealings with staff and customers, and it is strictly enforced. However, much of the motivation for this approach is a desire to avoid damage to the company's reputation.
- **The ethical culture approach** – top executives believe in a high ethical approach that becomes ingrained in the corporate culture and governs everything the organisation does.

Every organisation will fit somewhere along the continuum. It is towards the latter end of the continuum that companies will engage in corporate social responsibility, which is discussed in the third section of this chapter.

STAKEHOLDER GOVERNANCE

Introduction

Stakeholder management is a strategic approach embedded in the culture of the organisation and is integrated with governance, strategy and operations. Corporate governance must be based on partnership between stakeholders and mutual responsibility for creating wealth and financially sound enterprises (OECD, 2004). Under stakeholder theory, this element of partnership does not necessarily presume that the organisation's managers are the only locus of corporate control. Viewing corporate governance through the stakeholder lens allows a wider range of issues to be considered, allowing the organisation to focus on what really matters (Mason and Simmons, 2014). The principle of co-determination in Germany, for example, has long recognised the role of employees as stakeholders in how the firm is managed; while Japan has a well-established corporate governance model based on a close connection between various stakeholders (Tricker *et al.*, 2015). The European Commission (2011) also takes in a wide perspective of stakeholders' interest in addition to a company's shareholders, thus giving official recognition within the EU to stakeholder theory, such recognition ultimately forming a central part of its policy on corporate social responsibility (see below).

Definition of 'Stakeholder'

As mentioned in **Chapter 1**, Freeman (2010:46) defines a stakeholder as:

 "Any group or individual who can affect or is affected by the achievement of the organisation's objectives."

While this definition of stakeholder is broad, most authors and commentators include the following constituent elements: owners, customers, employees, suppliers, the community and the environment. Lawrence (2010) also draws a distinction between market stakeholders (primary or economic stakeholders such as employees, customers, etc.) and non-market stakeholders (secondary or societal stakeholders including local communities, NGOs and others), while Simmons (2004) refers to 'silent stakeholders' – those who are affected by decisions made by organisations but often have little input into the process, e.g. local communities. Central to these constituents and their relationship with the organisation is the notion of legitimacy – though they do not all have equal claim (Donaldson and Preston, 1995; Freeman, 2010).

Identifying and Managing Stakeholders

Freeman (2010:54) suggests a stakeholder map as a framework for identifying all of an organisation's different stakeholders, from employees to customer advocate groups. It must be recognised that stakeholders are not one homogenous group with similar aims. Even within each category of stakeholder, there may not be a unanimous approach. Businesses constantly scan the environment to identify issues that are of importance to them in developing strategy, allowing them to be proactive in responding. Johnson *et al.* (2017) also suggest the use of stakeholder mapping in the form of a power/interest matrix, whereby each concerned stakeholder group is plotted according to the level

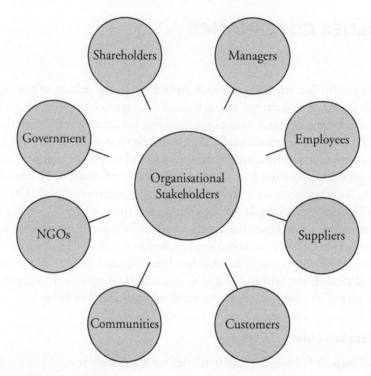

Figure 4.2 *Organisational Stakeholders*

of interest it has in a particular strategy and the level of power it has to influence it, though this can frequently be no more than satisfying its own self-interest. In that respect, the power/interest matrix must be seen as a management tool with which to identify potential blockages to strategy implementation, but without adopting any moral responsibility for the potential impact that a particular strategy may have on certain stakeholders (Jamali, 2008).

Clearly, the company is entitled to pursue courses of action that are in its best interest, but it must balance that self-interest with the interests of its stakeholders. The company must be able to identify its key stakeholders and understand the issues that are of concern to them. It can then prioritise each group of stakeholders and decide on how best to engage with them. An alternative way of mapping stakeholders, therefore, is to examine stakeholder interest and the commercial impact of different issues (ICSA, 2017), as illustrated in **Figure 4.3** below.

As stakeholders will change from time to time, and their interests will also vary from one period to the next, the process of stakeholder mapping should be reviewed on a regular basis. It may also be necessary for companies to prioritise within stakeholder groups as well as between them. Once the various groups have been prioritised, the company should then engage with them. Companies will also need to make decisions on the level of intensity of engagement with each group, and how best to engage with the various groups – either directly or indirectly – as appropriate for each group.

For example, worker directors sit on state boards in Ireland to ensure that the views of workers are taken into consideration. While this would not be common in the private sector in Ireland, it is mandated by law in many EU Member States.

In stakeholder mapping, different stakeholder groups need be assessed in relation to the level of interest each group has for a particular proposed strategy. In addition, the proposed strategy should be considered in regard to the likely commercial impact on each stakeholder group. This will assist senior management in understanding the impact of each strategic proposal and guide management in determining what needs to be done to best support that strategy. As shown in **Figure 4.3** below, there are three main categories of consideration when it comes to stakeholder interest:

- long-term and emerging issues that will be of growing importance to the company;
- current priority decisions; and
- critical considerations that will determine the company's 'licence to operate'.

These three categories must include a strong critical analysis of not just the legal implications of the actions of the company, but also the ethical implications in regard to *all* their stakeholders, not just those who are considered powerful.

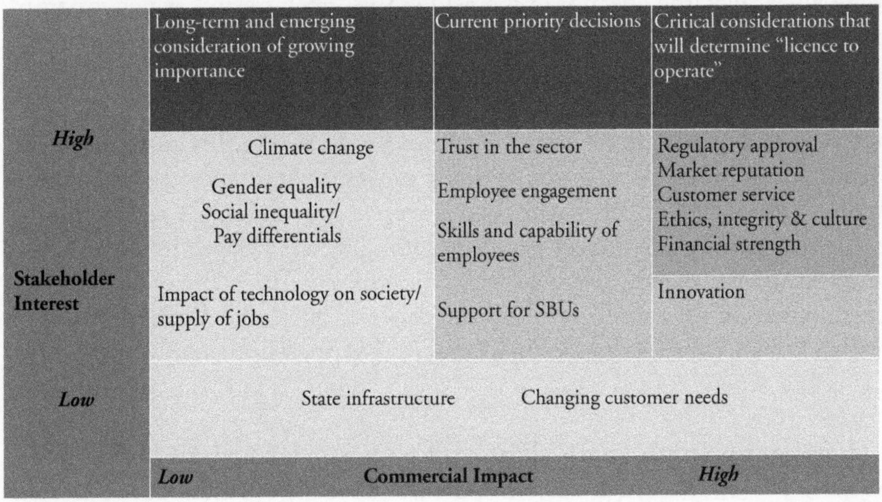

	Long-term and emerging consideration of growing importance	Current priority decisions	Critical considerations that will determine "licence to operate"
High	Climate change	Trust in the sector	Regulatory approval
	Gender equality	Employee engagement	Market reputation
	Social inequality/ Pay differentials		Customer service
		Skills and capability of employees	Ethics, integrity & culture
			Financial strength
Stakeholder Interest	Impact of technology on society/ supply of jobs	Support for SBUs	Innovation
Low	State infrastructure	Changing customer needs	
	Low	**Commercial Impact**	*High*

Source: The Governance Institute: The Stakeholder Voice in Board decision Making (ICSA, 2017).

Figure 4.3 *Stakeholder Mapping*

The process of stakeholder mapping, as illustrated in **Figure 4.3** above, is a holistic approach to strategic management that takes into consideration all short-, medium- and long-term issues facing the organisation. By considering not just the economic factors facing the organisation, but also current and possible future regulation, as well as the ethical implications, it assists in the process of risk analysis and provides a comprehensive governance framework from the point of view of control and future direction. However, corporations don't always take stakeholder interests into account when deciding on their strategic direction, and this can have a negative impact on the outcome. **Illustration 4.3** below is an example of Shell E&P Ireland, a subsidiary of Royal Dutch Shell, who faced major delays to the Corrib gas field as a result of opposition from some of the local community to the development.

Illustration 4.3: Corrib Gas Project

In 1996, natural gas was discovered in the Slyne Trough basin (block 18/20) off the coast of County Mayo. Known as the Corrib gas field, the project involves the development of the Corrib gas field itself, the construction of a natural gas pipeline and a gas-processing plant where the pipeline comes ashore. It is estimated that the field contains some 1,000 billion cubic feet of natural gas, over half of which is recoverable. The gas is 3,000m below the earth's surface, which in turn is in waters 350m deep. The field is of particular importance to Ireland as it is the first find of natural gas off the Irish coast since the Kinsale field was discovered in 1973, and it is hoped that the Corrib field will supply some 60% of the natural gas needs of the country for the foreseeable future. Since 2002, when Enterprise Oil – one of the original developers – was acquired by Royal Dutch Shell, the operator of the field is Shell E&P Ireland, which is part of a consortium consisting of Royal Dutch Shell (45%), Statoil (36.5%) and Vermilion Energy Trust (18.5%).

Shell E&P Ireland proposed to develop the field as a sub-sea production facility and to bring the gas ashore to County Mayo by an 83 km pipeline, before processing it (dry the gas and remove any impurities) some 9 km inland at Bellanaboy. The processed gas would then be fed into the Bord Gáis grid. Development of the project began in 2004, but was delayed in 2005 due to protests from locals in the Bellanaboy area, who had concerns over the safety of the pipeline and its proximity to houses in the area. There were also concerns about the discharge from the processing plant into Broadhaven Bay, an area that contains EU Special Areas of Conservation and Special Areas of Protection.

Shell E&P Ireland contended that all of the facilities involved were in line with best international practice. The project, however, received unwelcome publicity on many occasions due to protests by the "Shell to Sea" campaign. Some of the protestors, known as the "Rossport Five", spent time in jail as a result of these protests, but much of the media coverage of these events was sympathetic to the locals involved. The protestors have, on occasions, damaged property belonging to Shell, and Gardaí have had to intervene to protect Shell workers. In 2005, Mr Peter Cassells was appointed as an independent mediator in the dispute.

In addition to the disruption caused by local protests, the project has not had a smooth run with the various planning authorities, and in 2009 An Bord Pleanála (the statutory authority that deals with planning appeals) directed that Shell E&P Ireland redesign its pipeline to direct it away from residential areas as it constituted an unacceptable risk.

Despite the negative publicity that the project has received, it has many supporters. From the Government's perspective, it will bring much-needed employment to a rural part of County Mayo, both in the construction phase (up to 1,000 jobs) and in ongoing operations (130 permanent jobs), and this is naturally supported by many of the local population (Pro Gas Mayo). Shell E&P Ireland has provided funding for many community projects in Mayo. The company stated that they were committed to employing local people wherever possible. The Department of Communications, Marine and Natural resources commissioned independent safety reports on the project.

In addition to the benefits brought by employment in the area, the Government estimated that the well could be worth up to €1.7 billion in tax over the life of the gas field. In 2007, taxation rates of 25% were imposed, although in some cases, this can increase to 40% for very large finds. In addition to having a strong interest in the project, the Government is also in a very powerful position in terms of granting licences. However, there are many critics of Government policy in regard to the taxation of oil and gas revenues, claiming that exploration companies can write off 100% of costs before declaring a profit and that the terms for the exploration companies are among the most favourable in the world.

As the project developed, it was many years behind schedule and millions of euro over budget, and the dispute with many of the local residents continued. Shell E&P Ireland admitted that the project was initially handled badly by the company and that it should have taken greater interest in the concerns being expressed by various stakeholders from the beginning. In 2008, Mr Andy Pyle, the previous managing director of Shell E&P Ireland Ltd, retired and was replaced by Carlowman, Mr Terry Nolan. Prior to his new appointment, Mr Nolan spent two years living in Mayo building links with the local community. When gas finally came ashore to the processing plant, the project was by that stage 12 years behind schedule. In 2018, Shell E&P Ireland sold its stake in the Corrib gas field to the Canadian Pension Plan Investment Board. The long delay in bringing gas ashore resulted in much lower revenues than originally planned for by the company, as well as significant legal and other costs. It is estimated that when Shell E&P Ireland sold its stake, the company had lost €2 billion on the project. A greater focus on stakeholder engagement may well have resulted in a more profitable outcome for the company.

Source: this illustration was obtained from a variety of sources, including: www.shell.ie/; www.shelltosea.com; www.colmrapple.com; newspapers and television reports.

Many authors and commentators believe that managers are not equipped with the skills to make what they regard as political judgements (Friedman, 1982; Jensen, 2002; and Reich, 2008). Differing aims among diverse stakeholders can sometimes appear mutually exclusive, and so present a considerable challenge for management in terms of the trade-offs that might be required.

Jensen (2002:245) believes that the stakeholder approach is incomplete as a corporate function and that companies should have a single objective of the "enlightened value maximisation proposition", i.e. profit that is capable of being measured. This will clearly satisfy one important stakeholder group: the company's shareholders.

Jensen disregards Kaplan and Norton's Balanced Scorecard which suggests that objectives other than purely financial ones are required to manage a company. In their Balanced Scorecard model (see **Chapter 3**), Kaplan and Norton suggest four perspectives: customer/stakeholder, internal process and innovation and learning, as well as a financial perspective – all pointing to a more plural and longer-term approach, and one that supports a broader stakeholder approach. Inevitably, such an approach places significant restrictions on self-serving managerial behaviour (Donaldson and Preston, 1995). The difficulty for many companies is that through social activism and regulatory activity, the expectations of the role of companies in society has overtaken many managers' ability to comprehend and deal with these issues (Wood, 1991b), though the diversity and complexity of modern firms suggest that executives do, in fact, require these skills. Furthermore, societal expectations of businesses are continuingly evolving (Carroll, 1979), hence the requirement for managers to respond is constantly growing (Picciotto, 2011). Traditionally, the shareholder/stakeholder divide is a contested one, depending on one's ideological perspective on the role of the firm and its place in society. Former CEO of General Electric, Jack Welch, was traditionally one of the strongest proponents of the shareholder value perspective. Over the years, he had a fundamental change of heart on this subject. In an interview in the *Financial Times* (Guerrera, 2009), he is quoted as saying:

> "On the face of it, shareholder value is the dumbest idea in the world. Shareholder value is a result, not a strategy... Your main constituencies are your employees, your customers, and your products."

Welch's quote is a powerful endorsement of the general shift towards the stakeholder perspective and the central importance of both customers and employees in creating value for the organisation (these will be discussed in more detail below). First, the three main elements of stakeholder theory will be examined.

Elements of Stakeholder Theory

Donaldson and Preston (1995) argue that there are three, mutually supportive elements to stakeholder theory, which are nested within each other: the descriptive, the instrumental and the normative.

Descriptive The descriptive element concerns the nature of the company and is a description of how it is actually managed. Donaldson and Preston believe that the vast majority of companies adhere to some form of stakeholder management theory in their day-to-day operations, even if they do not make explicit reference to it.

Instrumental The second element is the instrumental justification of stakeholder theory. Does stakeholder management lead to better financial results for the company? Donaldson and Preston acknowledge that at first glance it is hard to prove a direct connection, but suggest that satisfying multiple stakeholders need not be a zero-sum game. Modern firms have very close relationships with a variety of stakeholders throughout their value chains and networks, with the sole aim of achieving greater efficiency (within the firm). Thus, they conclude that stakeholder management is instrumentally linked to organisational performance, and cite the Johnson & Johnson 'Credo' (see **Chapter 3**, **Illustration 3.4**) as an example of a company considering that the instrumental interests of shareholders are satisfied when the company puts its priority stakeholders first, i.e. its customers, its employees and its community.

Normative The third element is the normative justification of stakeholder theory. Donaldson and Preston consider that all stakeholders have an intrinsic value based on fundamental, normative philosophical concepts. Such value is often reflected in the development of the different laws that impact on business, taking into consideration the rights of various stakeholders. This broader interpretation of property rights forms a counter-argument to the traditional interpretation of such rights underpinning the principal–agency approach to corporate governance as advocated by Friedman (2002). This, Donaldson and Preston argue, places a moral as well as a legal responsibility on mangers to recognise a variety of stakeholders in the business, and also to manage these stakeholders in a manner that reflects Kant's categorical imperative (as discussed in the section on ethics above).

In summary, the objective of maximising shareholder wealth is by no means mutually exclusive to wider stakeholder management. On the contrary, given how societal expectations have changed, it can be argued that listening to and taking on the views of stakeholders is a *sine qua non* for profitable business. In addition, changes to law affecting companies over time have encouraged a broader stakeholder concept of management (FRC, 2018).

Stakeholder Expectations

In order to highlight the importance of stakeholders in the development of a company (and also the link with CSR), it is worth expanding the discussion about two particular groups of stakeholders: customers and employees. In essence, these two groups are very much inter-linked as the quality of customer service is directly dependent on the quality of employees. If the company cannot attract and retain customers, ultimately there will be no need for employees as the company will cease to exist.

Customers Without customers, an organisation would cease to exist. The marketing concept has evolved enormously in recent decades and the emphasis has shifted from being production-oriented to satisfying the customer (Kotler *et al.*, 2018). This, of course, is central to the success of a service industry and is inherently linked with stakeholder theory. Martin (2010) considers the concept of maximising shareholder value to be inherently flawed and that companies do better when they put customers first. This is echoed by Rust *et al.* (2010), who believe that this requires a strategic shift within the organisation, with the customer, rather than the product, placed at the centre. The focus is on 'customer lifetime value' – the potential future profits that come from a satisfied customer. Customers must therefore be considered as key stakeholders, and customers must be put first, particularly in issues of safety. Putting customers' needs at the centre of what the organisation does highlights the link between a company, its culture (and values), the extent to which it complies with regulation, and the role of stakeholders (particularly employees, be they managers or front-line workers) in decision-making.

Employees Employees play a dual role in organisations. First, they are instrumental in achieving organisational results. Secondly, they play an important normative role in stakeholder management and in CSR.

In their instrumental role, employees deal with customers, suppliers, owners, regulators, the community, trade associations and, through their actions, the ecological environment (Porter and Kramer, 2011). In addition, it is people in an organisation, the managers and staff, that make decisions on behalf of the organisation – ethical and otherwise (Tsai, 2012), and such decisions will impact on organisational performance. Employees are also an important normative part of the organisation (i.e. people with legitimate interests in their own right), both in how they treat all stakeholders of the organisation, and in how the organisation treats them as people as opposed to physical assets (Donaldson and Preston, 1995). The relationship between employees and customers is particularly strong in service industries, where front-line employees are critical to a company's success (Park and Levy, 2014).

When employees play such an important part in the success of an organisation, recruitment and selection processes are important to get right (Gunnigle *et al.,* 2017). Monks and Minnow (2001) remind us that a company's balance sheet does not subscribe any value to human resources; yet people are of vital importance to businesses, particularly in the knowledge economy and in the services sector. The culture and values of an organisation determine whether employees become highly engaged and can bring many benefits in terms of high-performance work practices. Yet, in a global employee survey by international consultants Towers Watson (2012:5), only 35% of employees, across a wide range of industries, regarded themselves as highly engaged ('engagement' being defined as "the intensity of employees' connection to their organisation"). The remainder felt unsupported (22%); detached (17%) or disengaged (26%). As employees are probably the most valuable element of most organisations, particularly service-oriented organisations, a company will not be successful unless its employees are appropriately engaged and the programme of engagement is supported by the organisation's culture (Benavides-Valesco *et al.*, 2014).

To enable companies to achieve greater productivity, Pfeffer (1995) has identified a number of best practices in human resources management (HRM). Pfeffer's work is linked to the concept of high-performance work systems (HPWS), which is based on the premise that productivity in organisations can be increased through certain HR practices (Gunnigle, *et al.,* 2017). There is a strong correlation between high-performance HR practices and greater productivity, lower employee turnover and corporate financial performance. According to Barney (1991), the development of employees can create a competitive advantage for the firm that is difficult for other firms to replicate. Employees' skills are particularly relevant for the service sector as the quality of the service delivered to customers is used as a competitive tool. Consequently, the appropriate HR style in many service-oriented organisations is what is termed a 'soft HRM' approach where "employees are seen as proactive, capable of being developed, and worthy of trust and development" (Nickson, 2007:9). This is particularly so where some degree of customisation in the level of service is required.

Organisations often draw a distinction between who they consider to be core employees who are often subject to HPWS, and peripheral employees who are usually part-time, temporary or contract employees and who often have different (and poorer) terms and conditions, the latter indicating a purely instrumental approach. Nevertheless, the thinking has moved on from earlier criticisms of HPWS and there is an overlap with the concept of 'best practice' HRM and CSR as it pertains to an organisation's employees, provided it is approached in a win–win fashion (Zhang *et al.,* 2014). An alternative to best practice HRM is 'best-fit'. According to Boxall and Purcell (2011), the fundamental economic goal in HRM is concerned with developing a cost-effective system of labour management that supports the company's strategic objectives. This approach is often referred to as 'hard HRM' and its emphasis is on managing people as just another resource. In reality, most firms use a mixture of both hard and soft HRM policies, depending on the particular circumstances and the level of heterogeneity in the organisation's staff (Gunnigle *et al.,* 2017).

The Stakeholder Approach

The stakeholder approach thus ranges from a narrow instrumental approach dealing with powerful stakeholders (Johnson *et al.,* 2017) to a broader and more ethical interpretation as advocated by Donaldson and Preston (1995). The normative element suggested by Donaldson and Preston ultimately provides a direct link with CSR. Thus, the relationship between stakeholder management and CSR can be seen as overlapping. Working with stakeholders is an essential element in business success. In particular, employees play a central role in the process, and the company must recognise this and take whatever measures are required to ensure that those employees are fully engaged with the organisation. Employees also play an essential role in the implementation of and compliance with regulation. In both instances, organisational culture underpins this commitment. It is worth reflecting on Louis Gerstner's (2002) understanding of culture: it's what people do when no-one is watching.

Having examined stakeholder management as a form of governance, what then is the relevance of CSR? There is, in reality, a significant overlap between stakeholder management and CSR, and thus, stakeholder management is an essential element in CSR (European Commission, 2011). CSR goes a stage further along the continuum from the shareholder perspective to the acceptance of wider societal involvement in business, and it does so in two main ways:

1. CSR achieves a greater level of regulatory compliance. Stakeholder management involves taking into consideration different stakeholders in the decision-making process within the company, but does not necessarily impose any obligation to go beyond the legal minimum. CSR also takes the interests of various stakeholders into account but goes beyond what it required by law (Davis, 1973), sometimes significantly so, and, in the process, also achieves a greater level of ethical stakeholder involvement.

2. In achieving a greater level of ethical stakeholder involvement, CSR takes into account the 'silent stakeholders', i.e. those stakeholders who do not have a powerful voice, or indeed have no direct voice at all. It recognises that businesses also have a moral imperative in how they operate, not just in relation to people, but also the environment (European Commission, 2011).

The next section will now discuss corporate social responsibility in detail.

CORPORATE SOCIAL RESPONSIBILITY

Introduction

Over 50 years ago, Davis (1960) argued that the social responsibility of business people needs to be commensurate with their considerable social power, not just within the firm, but outside it as well. Carroll (1979) considered that a company's social responsibility had four categories:

- economic responsibilities (in his opinion, the primary responsibility as everything else is dependent on the business being successful);
- legal responsibilities (to obey the law);
- ethical responsibilities (which he considered ill-defined); and
- discretionary responsibilities (philanthropic contributions left to individual judgement).

Carroll regarded these components of social responsibility as not being mutually exclusive or cumulative. It is important to point out that the legal responsibility that Carroll referred to is, in effect, also a primary responsibility (Bowie, 2012), as violations of certain regulations could cause the closure of a business, e.g. under health & safety legislation.

Woods (1991) considers that Carroll's four categories of CSR are not principles in themselves, but domains within which such principles operate. She lists three principles of CSR:

- the principle of legitimacy – society grants businesses permission to exist and have power, but this power must not be abused;
- the principle of public responsibility – businesses are responsible for outcomes related to their primary and secondary areas of involvement in society. This relates to the way the business produces its goods and also how it interacts with its stakeholders, in particular its suppliers and customers;
- the principle of managerial discretion – managers are considered to be moral actors and must exercise the discretion that is available to them to achieve socially responsible outcomes.

The traditional approach to CSR was one based on philanthropy, where companies made charitable donations to worthy causes (although such philanthropy is more common in the US than in Europe) (Bowie, 2012). There are many who disagree with the concept of CSR. Some critics such as Friedman (2002) focus on the role of the company and believe that these company executives are spending other people's money (unless it is from their own personal wealth). Jensen (2002) considers that managers should pursue the single-valued objective of profit maximisation as they do not have the skills required for deciding on trade-offs between conflicting objectives. Reich (2008) takes a broader, macro perspective, suggesting that social issues are properly the role of democratic government, rather than business, as government is better placed in providing such services for society.

In reality, CSR as a concept has now evolved to a level that it can also support the delivery of sound financial results as well as benefits to society (O'Higgins, 2010; Porter and Kramer, 2011). Freeman (2010:40) considers that there is a need to analyse the "complex interconnections between economic and social forces" in an integrated strategic manner. By integrating core business objectives and core competences to create business value, companies can achieve positive social change (McElhaney, 2008). A strategic approach to CSR will improve the competitiveness of the enterprise, bringing benefits in terms of risk management, cost savings, access to capital, customer relationships and HRM. It also "offers a set of values on which to build a more cohesive society" as a base for a sustainable economic system (European Commission, 2011:3). In addition, Mason and Simmons (2014) believe that CSR provides a more holistic approach to governance.

The focus of CSR is, therefore, on the social and environmental returns, as well as the financial returns of the business, known as the 'triple bottom-line effect' (Elkington, 1997), which are leveraged against its core competences. Porter and Kramer (2006) suggest a framework to identify the points of intersection between the company's value chain and the needs of society, and choosing areas that fundamentally underpin the firm's competitiveness. Porter and Kramer (2011:66) build on their earlier work to suggest the move by companies to creating shared value, which they define as "policies and operating practices that enhance the competitiveness of a company while simultaneously advancing the economic and social conditions in the community in which they operate". The result, they believe, is a greater increase in total revenue compared to situations where the emphasis is more on redistribution only.

Definition of Corporate Social Responsibility

The concept of CSR is a contested one and depends to a great deal on what ideological perspective one takes of corporate governance, as discussed earlier in this chapter in relation to the differing board structures (and further discussed below). The neo-liberal approach often focuses on short-term profitability, which many believe is incompatible with CSR. Yet, the *UK Governance Code* (and its associated *Stewardship Code*) clearly focuses on long-term viability: "The purpose of corporate governance is to facilitate effective, entrepreneurial and prudent management that can deliver the long-term success of the company" (FRC, 2018). If a strategic view is taken of CSR, then the long-term success of the company and CSR are, by no means, mutually exclusive. The focus of corporate governance should therefore be on the long-term sustainability of the company.

Gro Harlem Brundtland, a former Norwegian Prime Minster, defined 'sustainability' in a UN report as meeting the "needs of the present without compromising the ability of future generations to meet their own needs" (UN, 1987:37).

Another fundamental question arises in relation to CSR: in order to be effective in meeting society's needs, does CSR need to be underpinned by law or do companies decide for themselves what steps they do or do not take in regard to social and environmental responsibility? Parker (2007) concedes that at the transnational level enforcement would be difficult as there are few international legal mechanisms for holding corporations accountable. In Ireland, the Companies Act 2014, makes no provision for CSR. Thus, even if one accepts the argument that there should be legal underpinning of CSR, it would seem that this is a long way off both internationally and in Irish law.

One of the main problems in the study of CSR is the lack of a commonly accepted definition (Tsai *et al.,* 2012), which makes it hard to measure. In addition, there are also various terms used including: 'corporate social performance', 'corporate responsibility,' and 'corporate social responsiveness' (also known as CSR2). Wood (1991) considers that responsiveness is merely the action phase of, rather than an alternative to, management responsibility in the social sphere. In essence, responsibility and response are inter-linked and cannot properly be separated from each other.

For the purpose of this textbook, the definition of CSR that is used is that provided by the European Commission in its policy document, *A renewed EU strategy 2011–14 for Corporate Social Responsibility* (2011:6): "the responsibility of enterprises for their impacts on society". The Commission adds that:

> "To fully meet their corporate social responsibility, enterprises should have in place a process to integrate social, environmental, ethical, human rights and consumer concerns into their business operations and core strategy in close collaboration with their stakeholders, with the aim of:
> – maximising the creation of shared value for their owners/shareholders and for their other stakeholders, and society at large;
> – identifying, preventing and mitigating their possible adverse impacts."

This definition is also the one used by the Irish Government in its policy document on CSR: *Towards Responsible Business: Ireland's national plan on CSR 2017–2020* (DEI, 2017).

Social cohesion has been at the heart of the European Union since its foundation; it views CSR as working in conjunction with, and not as a substitute for, legislation governing social rights or environmental norms. Corporations are increasingly aware of ethical obligations beyond literal compliance with law, and increasingly feel compelled to behave accordingly. However, the above definition allows for financial as well as social/environmental returns.

The EU definition is a much more comprehensive approach to governance than stakeholder management on its own. Stakeholders are, however, integral to CSR and the Commission exhorts companies to work in close collaboration with stakeholders in the creation of shared value. The final part of *A renewed EU strategy 2011–14 for Corporate Social Responsibility* is concerned with taking a proactive stance to identifying, preventing and mitigating any adverse impact of the business's activities on society or the environment. When taken together, all elements of the EU's definition of CSR constitutes a more strategic and holistic approach to governance than stakeholder management, as there can be no doubt about the normative demands on companies. The voluntary nature of such codes allows significant advantages over rigid laws externally imposed, and they can also give substance to the CSR programme as they can become the mechanism by which organisations are held accountable by their stakeholders (Picciotto, 2011).

A descriptive conceptual framework for CSR is provided by O'Higgins (2010), which is grounded in instrumental and normative stakeholder theory, and consists of four possible orientations: sceptical, pragmatic, engaged and idealistic. The 'engaged' quadrant in O'Higgins's model is normative as well as instrumental, and has an organisational purpose aimed at embracing a broad range of stakeholders with whom it has a mutual interdependency, dealing with them using legitimacy and fairness, and measuring progress using a virtuous cycle of financial performance and corporate social performance. This strategic approach to CSR differs from those such as Porter and Kramer (2006) and McElhaney (2008), whose approach is 'strategic' but largely instrumental.

Arguments in Favour of CSR

There are many compelling arguments in favour of CSR. Friedman (2002:133) considers that companies are free to operate once they play by the 'rules of the game', i.e. that companies operate within the rule of the law, but do not engage in any other environmental or social activities beyond the legal minimum. However, the law by its nature lags behind societal change (Sethi, 1975), and because of their size and power, many large multinational companies have been extremely successful in controlling government legislation through effective lobbying, or operating in jurisdictions with lighter regulation (Reich, 2008). In addition, many of the world's citizens live in countries where the state does not properly protect their interests (Fisher *et al.*, 2013). The law is not a simple list of prescriptive rules dictating corporate behaviour, but a complex web of regulations involving the active participation of a wide variety of societal actors in controlling the business (Parker, 2010). By voluntarily going beyond what is legally required, industries and individual firms can often ameliorate more restrictive legislation being imposed should firms not be proactive (Davis, 1960; Papasolomou-Doukakis *et al.*, 2005). This is the approach of the advertising industry in Ireland regarding its code of conduct for the industry (ASAI, 2019).

Freeman (2010) suggests that a wide variety of stakeholders play a vital role in the success of any business. It must be remembered that there are few effective international legal mechanisms to curtail multinationals in how they might exploit stakeholders (including the environment) in their pursuit of profit. However, there is a moral imperative that they balance their enormous economic power with appropriate voluntary social and environmental measures that will underpin their legitimacy. It must be remembered that limited liability, a central part of the wealth-creating aspect of companies and their shareholders, is a privilege conferred by society. The company benefits from society in the form of protection of property rights, the rule of law, transport infrastructure and an educated workforce (Bowie, 2012). With privilege comes responsibility and therefore the company must consider the wider societal aspects of its actions. Davis, (1973:314) coined the phrase 'the Iron Law of Responsibility', which states that "in the long run, those who do not use power in a manner which society considers responsible will tend to lose it". Without society, and its customers, the company could not exist (Wood, 1991). Green (2009) reminds us of the all-embracing need to accept responsibility of building businesses in ways that sustainably enhance the common good and which must, therefore, be considered an integral part of managerial action.

CSR and Shareholders

In terms of the agent–principal relationship within a company, shareholders clearly expect a return on their investment, and expect the directors (and by extension, the company's managers), to deliver on this expectation. Directors who are perceived not to be performing will not be reappointed at the company's AGM. Shareholders must therefore be convinced by directors and managers that it is in the long-term interest of the company (and ultimately to the shareholders themselves) to engage in CSR. This makes the communication of CSR with all stakeholders a vital part of the process (Ward and Wylie, 2014). More and more, pension funds and other large investors are placing their investments in companies that have strong CSR credentials (Motta and Uchida, 2018; Dyck *et al.,* 2019).

Companies and other types of organisation do not develop policies other than those their directors and executive managers decide upon. CSR will not succeed unless those at the top are totally committed, and they must lead by example. Management are ultimately the engine driving CSR in an organisation and must develop initiatives that will have a positive impact for the beneficiaries as well as a strategic impact on the organisation (O'Higgins, 2010; Porter and Krammer, 2011).

An example of this is where a business can simultaneously achieve its strategic objectives while also engaging in environmental or social development. The use of plastic is having a devastating impact on the environment, particularly on the oceans, where 8 million tons of plastic is dumped each year. In 2019, Kingspan, an Irish building materials and insulation company, launched an initiative to support the 'circular economy' in recycling plastic. The company, partnering with the EcoAlf Foundation, will work with fisherpeople in the Mediterranean to collect and recycle plastic bottles from the water and convert them into building insulation. Initially, the plastic bottles (an estimated one billion) will be recycled at the company's plant in Barcelona and from there will feed into the global Kingspan supply chain (O'Sullivan, 2019).

CSR and the Role of Employees

The EU Commission (2011) considers that socially responsible enterprises should build long-term employee trust – a necessary condition for a sustainable business model (see **Chapter 2**). The link between employees and how business is regulated is an important one from a governance perspective in that employees play a central role in the implementation of regulation in the workplace, particularly in self-regulation (Parker, 2010). Adherence to regulation is only a part of corporate governance, however. Personal standards of honesty, integrity and ethics must also be considered, particularly in regard to issues such as 'aggressive accounting', where actions may be technically legal, but are often unethical (Robins, 2006). Employees are integral to everything an organisation does or does not do in deciding employee behaviour and ethical standards.

It can be argued, however, that concerns with productivity are often viewed only from the perspective of the company and its shareholders (Garay and Font, 2012), and do not take into account broader issues such as 'employment citizenship' (Boxall and Purcell, 2011), or how the company interacts with the environment (Elkington, 1997). Employment citizenship concerns an organisation's standing as an employer and its employment practices. It is an important element of the social legitimacy of organisations. CSR can help achieve these dual objectives of employment citizenship, and the environment, when the organisation places a particular focus on its employees.

Employees and Legal Issues

While regulations are often sector- or industry-specific, a broad range of regulations relating to social and environmental concerns cover all sectors, linking them in consequence directly to CSR, albeit at a minimal level. The organisation has a moral and legal culpability for the action of its employees (and managers) which extends to the culture of the organisation and how it conducts its business (Gibson, 2000). Therefore, regulation and CSR also require an appropriate corporate culture to support compliance and strong governance (Parker, 2009). Hence the importance of employee involvement in the process.

In dealing with a broad range of stakeholders (including employees), regulators are able to engage with companies' capacity for self-governance (Parker, 2010), allowing them to evaluate their own performance and the regulators, in turn, to evaluate the effectiveness and levels of compliance. It is important to note that while non-compliance with the law will incur major costs for a company when detected, compliance on its own will not build brands – and value (Pohle and Hittner, 2008). In 1995, the decision by Royal Dutch Shell to sink the Brent Spar platform in the North Sea was, in fact, complying with all the regulations agreed among the states bordering the North Sea. The action by Greenpeace in highlighting the environmental impact led to a consumer boycott of Shell, resulting in significant financial loss and reputational damage to the company (Picciotto, 2011). Yet Shell was not breaking the law.

For those who demand to see a return on investment for any costs associated with implementing CSR programmes, it must be remembered that many of the benefits of CSR are derived benefits that are often difficult to measure directly, though such benefits are significant nonetheless (Sweeney, 2009). So much depends, therefore, on the overall behaviour and performance of the organisation's managers and employees when making and implementing corporate decisions. This level of performance will now be examined.

CSR and HR Policy in the Firm

For CSR to be effective, it must involve an integration of 'hard' and 'soft' approaches infused into the operations of the business. In regard to HRM, it applies to the formal procedures for employee recruitment, retention, promotion criteria, monetary rewards and the organisation's written code of ethics. The desired HRM outcomes can be incorporated into written competency statements and embedded in company culture to achieve a high level of compliance with societal expectations (Mason and Simmons, 2014; Park and Levy, 2014). The combination of hard HRM and soft HRM can then support both an instrumental and normative foundation for the company to pursue CSR (O'Higgins, 2010). In essence, it becomes seen as the right way to do business and achieve value.

Organisations have a wider responsibility to the environment (see below) and to social issues, including treating their employees with respect and dignity (Melé, 2014). Many organisations take this responsibility seriously, and the number that do so is growing. According to Longo *et al.* (2005), employees have expectations of their employers that can be divided into four value classes:

- health and safety at work;
- development of employees' skills;
- wellbeing and satisfaction of the worker, including the quality of work; and
- social equity.

As companies evolve and become more global, so too do the skills required to manage them. These skills are particularly needed to lead highly educated employees in the process of wealth creation in the knowledge economy. Shareholders may own the residual assets of the company, but they do not own the employees. The creativity and endeavour of employees cannot be restricted to a principle–agent contractual agreement, and instead must constitute a more collegiate arrangement of mutual respect and freedom (Handy, 2002).

Managers play an essential role in passing on values and "building up communities of persons" capable of delivering good service (Grant, 2011:10; McKinsey *et al.*, 2012) and supporting CSR. These values must be shared by all employees in the organisation, and are an important motivator to implement CSR, overcoming many barriers such as budgetary restrictions (Garay and Font, 2012). In the section on organisational culture above, it was discussed how organisational culture has a powerful impact on the effectiveness and willingness of employees to engage. According to Sharp (2009), the Four Seasons Hotel Group has built its success on what it calls the 'Four Pillars': quality, service, culture and brand. Central to how it delivers its promise to its customers are the people who work for the company. Sharp sees employees as being instrumental in the delivery of good service, but there is also a strong normative approach that develops employees as individuals and helps them reach their full potential within the company. The Four Seasons' approach to business is based on its employees, its customers and its product (quality service) – and employees are the common denominator that produce the quality service and deal with customers. When this happens, the shareholder wealth follows (Park and Levy, 2014). Like many other organisations, Four Seasons' approach is driven by its value system (see the case study on Four Seasons at the end of this textbook). Values can help managers overcome the issue of trade-offs between conflicting criteria, thus overcoming Jensen's (2002) criticism of the stakeholder approach. Organisational values also fit into the third element of Donaldson and Preston's (1995) framework: the normative element.

Young and Thyil (2008) remind us that corporate governance failures often occur, not because the governance frameworks themselves are faulty, but because of poor implementation. It is employees who implement governance procedures. Employees are central to CSR in every aspect from implementing CSR-friendly policies in the workplace to volunteering in the community (Cohen, 2010). This is not just an instrumental challenge for the organisation; for CSR to be successful, employees must be normatively engaged in the process. Consequently, the design of CSR policies in an organisation should involve the employees themselves, as well as all relevant stakeholders (Park and Levy, 2014).

Employees are attracted to organisations that engage in CSR, and these employees will be of a higher quality in terms of skills and productivity (Sprinke and Maines, 2010; Glavas and Kelley, 2014). Over half a century ago, Theodore Levitt (1958:49) – himself a strong opponent of CSR – conceded that employee welfare problems "help attract and hold manpower". Stakeholders, including employees, make value judgements about companies, and this can directly influence potential employees' motivation to work in a more attractive environment (Park and Levy, 2014). Internal advertising and word of mouth are common forms of recruitment in many companies and therefore the reputation of the employer is particularly important in attracting staff. It is imperative that the company communicates its CSR values, activities and messages clearly to its employees (Vlachos *et al.*, 2013). Attracting staff is one thing, but reducing absenteeism and staff turnover is another. There is considerable expense involved in high levels of staff turnover (Gunnigle, *et al.*, 2011). CSR has a positive effect on employee motivation and retention, as well as on commitment and performance (Park and Levy, 2014). An important element of retaining staff in an organisation is the thorny issue of work–life balance in a high-performance work setting. Employee-friendly workplaces provide companies with a competitive advantage as it is linked to attracting and retaining talented employees, especially in a tight labour market (Purcell, 2004). In short, CSR helps build a positive brand image.

To achieve excellence, there needs to be investment in an organisation's employees so that they can achieve their full potential. This requires more than just investing in training in order to achieve a high level of productivity and quality, but also a clear ethical concern and respect for the dignity of employees (Melé, 2014). The development of employees to their full potential is particularly important in service industries where there is direct interaction between the customer and the service provider, and quality is not necessarily achieved by standardisation in the production sense, but in customisation to meet clients' particular needs. The quality of this interaction depends on the level of engagement by the employee and their intrinsic motivation, as well as their interpersonal skills (Baum, 2008). All of these factors are critical to the effective implementation of a CSR policy in an organisation and, most importantly, good corporate governance.

CSR and Suppliers

Companies cannot engage in CSR in isolation and must work together with companies in the supply chain (see **Chapter 6**) to ensure the entire production process is meaningful and transparent (European Commission, 2011). The type of issues that arise here are supply chain transparency, ethical purchases/sustainability and environmental concerns (e.g. carbon footprint). Nike was criticised in the early 1990s because of its practice of using poorly paid labour in supplier companies operating in developing countries, resulting in a consumer boycott (Crane and Matten, 2016). There are conflicting demands here: Porter's Five Forces Analysis (see **Chapter 5**) suggests that companies should use their power to bargain the lowest possible price from their suppliers (Porter, 1980); however, this approach disregards the ethical imperative of doing business with suppliers, that they too are entitled to reasonable remuneration for their goods. The Fairtrade mark, for example, ensures that coffee growers receive reasonable price for their products (see the case study on Primark in this textbook, which discusses measures companies can take in regard to supply chain management).

CSR and Customers

The demand for CSR often originates from a company's customers. Customer power is not to be underestimated, and it ranges from positive action in purchasing on the one hand, to boycotting companies, on the other. Many companies have begun to pursue CSR either to develop and enhance their brands or to minimise damage to those brands. For such companies, it is about minimising risk, co-operating with governments, NGOs and communities in order to be more responsible citizens, and also to make their brands more appealing. Brand equity, the value associated with a brand's strength in the market, can represent a sizable investment. According to Forbes (2019), the top five brands in the world are: Apple $182 billion; Google $132 billion; Microsoft $104 billion; Facebook $95 billion; and Amazon $80 billion. With so much value at stake, companies will do all that they can to protect their investment. Ultimately, no company, irrespective of its size, can afford to alienate potential customers. As stated above, companies must communicate their engagement with CSR (Ward and Wylie, 2014), but there must be a substantial basis to their message.

CSR and Communities

When organisations are negligent or are prepared to exploit resources for their own profits, it is often local communities that suffer, and sometimes the consequences can be devastating. In December 1984, for example, an explosion at the Union Carbide pesticide factory in Bhopal, Madhya Pradesh, India, caused 27 tonnes of deadly methyl isocyanate gas to leak, quickly spreading to the nearby city of Bhopal with a population of half a million. It is estimated that some 25,000 people died as a result. The plant was loss-making from the start and managers had allowed the equipment to fall into disrepair; it was inevitable that such an incident would happen. The surrounding area is contaminated to this day and over 150,000 people are still suffering serious effects from the disaster (Bhopal, 2019).

The 2010 BP Deepwater Horizon explosion in the Gulf of Mexico resulted in the deaths of 11 workers and caused enormous environmental damage around the Gulf coast, impacting on wildlife and devastating the fishing industry in the area. Unlike the Bhopal disaster, BP was forced to pay for the clean-up and pay compensation to all affected. According to *The Financial Times* (2018), the total cost to BP was €66 billion.

However, there are also many positive examples of how companies engage in a positive way with local communities. In **Chapter 1**, we saw how the Dublin Docklands Development Authority (**Illustration 1.2**) worked with the local community to create a positive social, physical and economic environment that helped to integrate Dublin's existing dockland community with the new financial services sector that was emerging in the area. Companies must engage directly with the community and they both need to work together to ensure that maximum benefit is obtained from available resources. In some cases, it is the local community that benefits, but with globalisation it can also be distant communities who reap the benefits, such as with Fairtrade products.

CSR and Non-governmental Organisations (NGOs)

The term 'non-governmental organisation (NGO)' covers a wide range of organisations that campaign or operate on a variety of issues, including poverty, the environment and human rights. Initially, it was often NGOs that highlighted unethical and illegal practices by companies around the globe (Fisher *et al.*, 2013). Such interventions often led to heightened antagonism between both groups (such as with Greenpeace and Royal Dutch Shell). However, both sides have much to gain by co-operating and working towards the same goals (Porter and Kramer, 2011): such co-operation can pre-empt difficulties from stricter regulatory regimes being brought in by government due to inaction by companies (see below), and it can lead to a win–win outcome for all concerned.

Governments

To ensure maximum benefit of CSR programmes, it is also necessary to work closely with governments, particularly in developing countries. In Ireland, and indeed throughout the EU, Government is bringing in much tighter regulations covering a broad spectrum of issues, from climate change to health and safety. This blurs the line between CSR and what companies are required to do by law and regulation, and there is a marked difference in this regard between EU Member States and countries outside the EU where such measures are not compulsory and may or may not be followed. While responsible companies may complain about the over-interference of a 'nanny state', the approach does ensure that the damage caused by irresponsible companies is kept to a minimum, and that when breaches occur, companies, their directors and managers are held accountable.

Climate Change

There is now a growing awareness of the responsibility of individual businesses (as well as governments) to take drastic action to prevent further irreparable damage to the planet. The impact of climate change on the planet has been immense and is growing at an exponential rate. The report by the Inter-governmental Panel on Climate Change (IPCC, 2018) spells out in clear and frightening language the irreversible nature of this change and the impact it is having in the form of more heat extremes, storms and floods, acidification of the oceans and rising sea levels. There can be no doubt that collective action is needed – by governments, by companies and by individuals – if we are to prevent truly catastrophic consequences. Greenhouse gas emissions need to be reduced to near zero or below by 2100. The UN has set a target of limiting the average temperature of the earth's surface to 2°C above pre-industrial times (it is already 0.85°C above that level). This will require fundamental change in how businesses operate and the regulations required to achieve this. However, from a governance perspective (both regulation and corporate governance), this is one area of business where compliance is not a minimal requirement but where every organisation, and its employees, must have maximum impact on reversing emissions. The question for organisations seems to be not whether they *should* engage in CSR, but what is the best way *to* engage (Vlachos, et al., 2013).

Again, employees must be considered key. From an instrumental perspective, engaged employees are capable of attaining much greater levels of productivity. From a normative perspective, those employees must also be engaged in the whole organisational philosophy underpinning a policy of CSR. When that happens, it means that employees can contribute in a meaningful way to maximising the organisational impact of CSR measures.

The health of the world's population is another important focus for CSR. There is clearly a strong correlation between the availability of clean drinking water and peoples' health, particularly in developing countries. In addition, many people are suffering from diseases that are either curable or at the very least containable. In poorer countries, people often cannot afford the necessary drugs for basic illnesses. The reputation of several large pharmaceutical companies has been damaged by their refusal to make cheaper drugs available to combat diseases such as AIDS in Africa. That is changing and many of these companies are now making HIV drugs available at cost price.

Education is an essential component in raising the living standards of a nation. Ireland has benefited over many years from the (anonymous) largesse of the Irish-American billionaire, Chuck Feeney, and his foundation Atlantic Philanthropies (O'Cleary, 2013). Other Irish business people have contributed to third-level education, and such contributions have played an important role in the development of college facilities, particularly in light of chronic underfunding by successive governments, as highlighted in the Cassels (2016) report. This raises other ethical issues relating to people becoming tax resident abroad under generous rules regarding foreign domicile. Taxes are not, as the New York hotel millionaire Leona Helmsley one famously said, "only for the little people".

CSR and Small Business

Much of the thinking on CSR is from the perspective of large businesses, and related to manufacturing rather than service industries (Garay and Font, 2012). However, small and medium-sized enterprises (SMEs) constitute the vast majority of businesses worldwide.

In Ireland, some 99.8% of businesses are SMEs, employing 69.1% of the workforce and producing 51.5% of corporate turnover (CSO, 2019). Enterprise Ireland (2019) defines small enterprises as companies with less than 50 employees and with an annual turnover and/or balance sheet not exceeding €10 million, while medium-sized enterprises have between 50 and 249 employees and either an annual turnover not exceeding €50 million or an annual balance sheet not exceeding €43 million.

From a CSR perspective, large businesses and SMEs are different in a number of respects. In SMEs, ownership and management are often not separate (as discussed in the section on corporate governance above). As a result, the management style is very different in the way decisions are made. CSR in SMEs often amounts to a reflection of the personal values of the owner (Tsai *et al.*, 2012), though time and resources can be significant barriers (Sweeney, 2007). For small, owner-managed firms, the issue of how best to run the company is reasonably straightforward as they do not have to seek any outside approval. They also tend to take a long-term perspective. SMEs tend to be more deeply rooted in their communities and there is a particularly strong focus on their employees. The European Commission (2011) is placing specific focus on CSR by SMEs. According to Mandl and Dorr (2007), European SMEs are engaged to a considerable degree in CSR, even though they may not refer to it as such.

Societal expectations of business have changed enormously in the last couple of decades, while many businesses also recognise that there are significant benefits to pursuing a CSR agenda, particularly in relation to human resource management.

CONCLUSION

There have been myriad examples of poor corporate governance in Ireland in the last decade, from the collapse of the banking industry to funding issues in the charity sector. As a result, there has been a considerable tightening of regulations governing how businesses and other organisations operate. This has increased the cost of compliance for Irish companies and has placed a greater burden on company directors. In turn, it will increase the necessity for appropriate professional training for people who sit on company boards. There will also be a greater requirement for openness and transparency and for executives to operate in an ethical manner. The focus on maximising shareholder returns must shift to a more pluralistic stakeholder approach to management, and a recognition of social and environmental responsibilities on companies that must be upheld.

SUMMARY

Corporate governance is an important factor in how strategic decisions are made. It is concerned with the structures and systems of control by which management are held accountable to those who have a legitimate stake in an organisation. There are a number of factors that need to be considered when examining corporate governance, including:

- Company structure – corporate governance will vary with the size and type of company.
- Chain of governance – this is concerned with the company's decision-making process. The board of directors has ultimate responsibility for the actions of the company.
- Company directors – their role and responsibility has increased greatly in recent years. They are responsible for the oversight of the company, and they must be familiar with how the company is operating and that it is complying with all legal requirements. Failure to do so can cause directors to be held liable, and it can severely damage the reputation of the company.
- Differing board structures – the structure of the board of directors will differ from one country to another. In Ireland, the board consists of a single tier to whom management report.
- Investment information – different stakeholders will require, and are entitled to, different amounts of information about the company. Board members will obviously require detailed information about the performance of the company.

Business ethics concerns the application of general ethical principles and standards to the actions and decisions of companies and the conduct of company personnel. While most management theory is relatively new, the study of ethics goes back to antiquity.

There are different classifications used for ethical theories. The classifications used here are:

- **Teleological ethical systems** – based on the concept that the morality of a decision is measured by examining the probable outcome and its consequences. It is closely linked with the theory of utilitarianism and is very similar to the managerial concept of cost–benefit analysis.
- **Deontological ethical systems** – based on universal principles or concepts of what is right and wrong. They are termed universal in that they transcend cultures and societies. The philosopher most credited with developing the theory is Immanuel Kant. Actions are considered right or wrong regardless of the consequences of the action or its impact on others.
- **Ethical relativism** – argues that different societies and cultures have divergent values and different political systems. Consequently, there can be no absolute rules guiding business activities.

Donaldson and Dunfee (1994) propose a compromise between universalism and relativism. The integrative social contracts theory suggests that a company should, as much as possible, adhere to universal ethical principles that control company action while also taking into account local customs that further define ethically acceptable behaviour. A code of ethics is a written statement of what the organisation considers to be important values and high ethical standards.

Whistleblowing is when a member (or ex-member) of an organisation discloses any action by others in that organisation that is either illegal or unethical. It covers issues such as when a company is causing harm directly or indirectly to members of the public, violating human rights or doing things that are illegal.

Different companies adopt different ethical stances in how they conduct their affairs. This is largely a reflection of the values and culture of the organisation, and of its individual managers and their ethical standards. It is towards the upper end of the business ethics and corporate values spectrum that companies will engage in corporate social responsibility (CSR).

CSR is a concept whereby companies integrate social and environmental concerns into their business operations and into their interaction with their stakeholders on a voluntary basis. For those companies that engage in CSR, there is the potential to create even greater shareholder wealth than they otherwise would. CSR is not about how you spend the money you make, it is about how you make the money you spend.

Inherent in the concept of CSR is the view that organisations are open systems dealing with multiple stakeholders. These relationships are ever-present, dynamic and inter-related. It involves discussing with stakeholders the issues that are of common interest and then incorporating them when strategy is being developed. There are many different areas in which companies may become involved in CSR; for example, a pressing issue for many companies is climate change and the environment, with a number of large companies actively moving away from practices that are harmful to the environment. The health of the world's population is another important theme for CSR, as is education.

There are many reasons why organisations engage in CSR or in giving something back to the community. One difficult challenge for leaders is trying to decide which compelling cause the organisation should support. There can be a number of pressing choices. Many companies have begun to pursue CSR to minimise damage to their brands. Other companies see CSR as an opportunity to enhance their brands. The third and most compelling reason is the opportunity to create value, which becomes part of the company's competitive advantage. This is where sound business objectives overlap with CSR. It is this category of CSR practice that separates the leaders from the rest.

If CSR is to benefit an organisation and the community, it must be approached in a strategic manner. It must have a unique value proposition where a company meets the needs of its customers in a way that competitors cannot. It is an approach to business that requires leadership, as well as configuration of the organisation to support the strategy. It is about creating shared values.

DISCUSSION QUESTIONS

1. Corporate governance in Ireland has been the subject of much criticism. Discuss whether such criticism is valid or not.
2. "Ethics cannot be taught." Discuss the role that ethics plays in the education of business students.
3. As chief executive of a large Irish corporation, you wish to put in place a charter for whistleblowers. What are the main elements that should be included in the charter?
4. "The business of business is business." Critically analyse this statement in light of recent corporate scandals.
5. Taking a company of your choice, critically analyse the opportunities for creating value through CSR.

PART TWO

Strategic Analysis

Introduction to Strategic Analysis

There is often a debate as to whether organisations should set goals and objectives *after* they have analysed the organisations's external and internal environment. Certainly, short-term goals and objectives will have to take this analysis into account and adjustments may be made to accommodate the reality facing the organisation. However, there are very strong arguments in favour of developing a vision, along with goals and objectives, as the starting point for the strategic process. First, given the considerable resources that are needed by a company to compete in the market, it is necessary to have a very clear understanding of what the company is trying to achieve so that all activity can be directed towards the achievement of its vision. The strategies that will be chosen are the means of achieving those strategic goals, and there are many possibilities. Secondly, while realism must prevail, companies must also be positive in their outlook. Many companies thrive in a recession, simply because they did not let the constraints of the recession hold back their thinking and their action. While some see crises, others see opportunities and they go after them.

In many ways, the process of internal and external analysis is not so much sequential to setting strategic goals and objectives, but rather, it should be an ongoing process, effectively without a start or finish. Events change in the external environment. These changes can range from very gradual, and almost imperceptible adjustments, to situations where the response by the organisation has to be rapid and determined.

Chapter 5 looks at the external environment. Analysing the external environment is outward-looking in its focus – factors often outside the direct influence of the company. It examines the international and national environment that will ultimately impact on every organisation in some shape or form. It also examines the particular industry within which the company is operating. Such analysis includes examining the competitive situation, as well as examining how the market is segmented. Finally, it identifies what the critical success factors are for operating in that industry.

Evaluating the organisation's strategic capability is the subject of **Chapter 6**. Analysing strategic capability is inward-looking in that it examines the capability of the organisation to pursue a course of action. While resources may be a constraining factor in the short term, that does not mean that those necessary resources cannot be obtained or developed. In all cases, a critical factor is the quality of leadership and the quality of the people in the organisation. If Ireland is to operate in the smart economy, it is critical that there is a substantial investment in people – both at national level and in every organisation.

When the external and internal analysis is complete, the company can then construct a detailed SWOT analysis (strengths, weaknesses, opportunities and threats). Ultimately, the company will endeavour to capitalise on its strengths to pursue whatever opportunities are available. The variety of strategic options open to the company will be considered in Part Three of this textbook.

The strategic options that are chosen will be predicated largely on the results of the SWOT analysis. While such analysis is somewhat subjective, it nevertheless forms a vital layer in the strategy-development process.

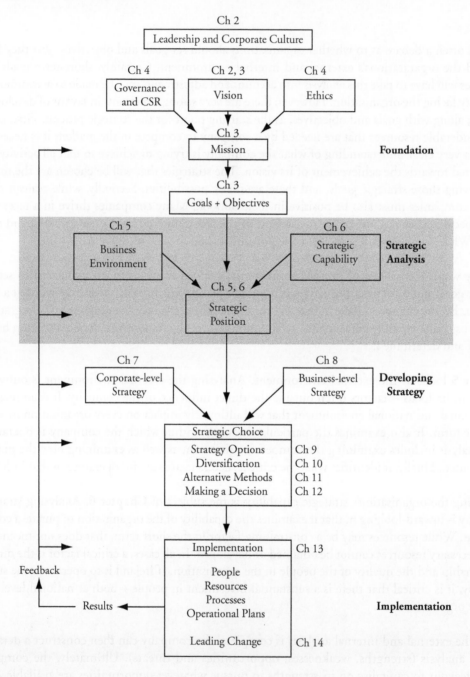

Figure 1.2 *The Strategic Planning Model*

CHAPTER 5

Examining the Business Environment

LEARNING OBJECTIVES

On completion of this chapter, you will be able to:

- Differentiate between the macro and micro environments
- Evaluate the different factors impacting on an organisation
- Assess the competitive forces operating in an industry
- Conduct an analysis of the opportunities and threats facing an organisation

"We must not cease from exploration. And the end of all our exploring will be to arrive where we started and know the place for the first time."

T.S. Eliot

INTRODUCTION

The poet John Donne wrote: "No man is an island". Just as no person can live in isolation, neither can an organisation. Each one is part of a much greater business environment that impacts directly and indirectly on every aspect of its operations. The environment is ever-changing and analysing it is a complex affair. While some of the issues will be obvious, others will be much more subtle and may well impact on an organisation before that organisation is even aware of it. For that reason, environmental analysis is not something that is done once every couple of years; it should be an ongoing appraisal. Environmental analysis involves scanning the business environment to get a better understanding of what is happening in the economy and how it will impact on the company.

 Environmental scanning is the process of collecting information about the forces in the environment.

Environmental scanning involves monitoring newspapers, journals, magazines, radio and television programmes, the internet, government publications and other relevant publications, as well as meeting people working in whatever industry one is operating in. For many executives, the volume of information coming at them can be overwhelming, and they must focus on and analyse those issues that are of real relevance to their company. There are a number of different analytical tools that will be examined in this chapter to assist in such analysis. However, there are no set guidelines for the interpretation of whatever information is available and, consequently, experience plays an important part. Analysing and interpreting the environment can be difficult, as illustrated by the comments of Donald Rumsfeld, US Secretary of Defence (2001–2006), prior to the US-led invasion of Iraq in 2003, when he stated:

> "Reports that say that something hasn't happened are always interesting to me, because as we know, there are known knowns; there are things we know we know. We also know there are known unknowns; that is to say we know there are some things we do not know. But there are also unknown unknowns – the ones we don't know we don't know."

The ultimate aim of environmental scanning and analysis is to be able to spot the opportunities and threats facing the organisation. As the Duke of Wellington put it:

> "All the business of war, and indeed all the business of life, is to endeavour to find out what you don't know by what you do; that's what I called 'guessing what was at the other side of the hill'."

Environmental analysis consists of two main divisions: the macro environment and the micro environment.

The Macro Environment This consists of all of the factors that will impact internationally on all countries and the factors that are more specific to the country the organisation is operating in. A multinational company will obviously have to take into account how these issues differ in each of the countries in which it operates.

In this chapter, examination of the macro environment will include:

1. The global environment
2. Porter's Diamond
3. PESTEL analysis
4. The use of scenarios.

The Micro Environment The micro environment looks at what is happening in the particular industry in which the organisation is operating. These factors will have a more direct, and possibly much greater, impact than any of the macro factors. They include:

1. Understanding the industry's economic structure
2. Five Forces Analysis
3. Industry life cycle
4. Industry driving forces
5. Strategic groups
6. Market segmentation

7. Critical success factors
8. Opportunities and threats.

THE MACRO ENVIRONMENT

The first aspect of the macro environment that needs to be considered is what is happening generally in the global environment as this will ultimately impact on an organisation, however indirect that relationship may be. There is a very large overlap between what is happening in the global environment and in the more immediate macro environment in each country. In some cases, such as multinational companies, the relationship is reasonably seamless. For smaller companies operating in the domestic market here in Ireland, the difference is more pronounced. However, even for these companies, knowledge of what is happening in the global marketplace will help give an understanding of the changes that are taking place at home.

The Global Environment

In examining the global environment, it becomes apparent that there are different types of economies operating around the world. However, many of these can be grouped into different trading blocs. The nearest, and from Ireland's perspective the most important, is the European Union.

The European Union

The European Union has a major influence on every aspect of Irish life, but most especially on our business environment. It is a unique economic and political partnership between 28 democratic countries (at the time of writing the United Kingdom is still a part of the European Union) with the aim of providing peace, prosperity and freedom for its 508 million citizens. If the United Kingdom does leave the EU as planned, then the population of the remaining 27 Member States will drop to 443 million people. There are various bodies to enable the EU to function. These include:

- The European Parliament (representing the people of Europe). Its members are directly elected every five years
- The Council of the European Union (representing the national governments)
- The European Commission (representing the common EU interest).

Background The European Union had its antecedents in the signing on 9 May 1950 of the Schuman Declaration (named after the French Foreign Minister at the time) which established a European Coal and Steel Community. This came into effect a year later with the Treaty of Paris. This put in place a common market in coal and steel between the six founding members: Belgium, the Federal Republic of Germany, France, Italy, Luxembourg and the Netherlands. On 25 March 1957, these six countries signed the Treaty of Rome, which established the European Economic Community. This was a much broader agreement covering a wide range of goods and services. Customs were abolished later and common policies on trade and agriculture were put in place. In 1973, Denmark, Ireland and the United Kingdom joined, and at the same time new social and environmental policies were put in place. The European Regional Development Fund, from which Ireland benefited greatly, was established in 1975. Four years later, in 1979, the first elections to the European Parliament took place.

In 1987, the Single European Act came into force which enshrined the concept of a single market, which was to be achieved by 1993. The Berlin Wall fell in 1989, and this led to the reunification of Germany in October 1990. In December 1991, the Maastricht Treaty was signed (coming into force on 1 November 1993) adding areas of intergovernmental co-operation to existing integrated Community structures, thus creating the European Union (Europa, 2019).

The Single Market The creation of the single market has had important implications for the way in which business is conducted within the EU, and Ireland in particular, as we shall see below. There are four main areas in which barriers have been removed.

1. **Physical Barriers** All border controls on goods and services have been removed, together with customs control on people. Police controls still remain in place for security reasons. The Schengen Agreement, signed in 1985, governs police co-operation and common asylum and immigration policy (Ireland and the UK are not party to this agreement). The enormous growth that took place in the Irish economy up to now would not have been possible without the number of eastern Europeans coming to work here in every area, from construction to the tourism industry. Should Brexit proceed, it will most likely cause significant complications for trade between Ireland and the United Kingdom. The exact nature of any barriers and tariffs are impossible to determine at the time of writing and will depend on the final outcome of negotiations between the EU and the United Kingdom.

2. **Technical Barriers** Throughout the EU any product legally manufactured and sold in one Member State must be allowed to be placed on the market in all others. This has had major positive implications for Ireland in attracting foreign direct investment into this country. For example, the pharmaceutical company Pfizer, with its manufacturing bases here in Ireland, is able to sell its products throughout the EU without any restrictions. One area in which Irish people have benefited enormously is in the deregulation of the airline industry, which allowed companies like Ryanair to be established, resulting in airfares now being a fraction of what they were in the early 1980s. While obstacles remain in the services sector, this too has been freed up considerably.

3. **Tax Barriers** These have been reduced through the partial alignment of national VAT rates. Each Member State still has control over the rates of taxation. Ireland's corporation tax rate of 12.5% has come under much criticism by other member states as they see it as giving Ireland an unfair advantage in attracting foreign direct investment. There is also an integrated market for

financial services, which cuts the cost of borrowing for businesses and consumers and offers savers a wider range of products from which to choose.

4. **Public Contracts** All public contracts awarded by national, regional or local authorities must be open to bidders throughout the EU.

There is much work in progress at the EU level that will also impact on how business operates, such as the recognition of professional qualifications, protection to prevent piracy and counterfeiting of EU goods, further liberalisation in the area of transport (particularly land transport) and liberalisation of services (the Services Directive), which will introduce competition throughout the EU. This will have huge economic implications for Ireland.

Monetary Co-operation In 1971, the United States abolished the link between the US Dollar and the official price of gold, thus putting an end to the system of fixed exchange rates. European countries responded by preventing exchange fluctuations of more than 2.25% between member countries. This led to the development of the European Monetary System in March 1979. Ten years later in 1989 at an EU Council meeting in Madrid, the EU leaders adopted a three-stage process to achieve economic and monetary union. This later became part of the Maastricht Treaty in December 1991.

The first stage of the process to achieve economic and monetary union allowed for the free movement of capital within the EU, and further developed the structural funds to remove inequality between regions and accelerate economic convergence. The second stage in 1994 established the European Monetary Institute (EMI) in Frankfurt. This was made up of the governors of the central banks of the EU countries. It also allowed for the independence of national central banks and rules to apply to curb national budget deficits. The third stage saw the introduction of the euro on 1 January 1999, which was adopted by 11 countries, including Ireland. The European Central Bank took over from the EMI and became responsible for monetary policy. Euro notes and coins followed on 1 January 2002 and are the only form of legal tender for cash and bank transactions in the eurozone.

Under monetary co-operation, there are five convergence criteria that member countries must meet in order to qualify for euro membership, including:

- Price stability in relation to the three member states with the lowest rate of inflation
- Inflation – long-term rate of inflation not greater than 2%
- Budget deficits below 3% of GDP
- Public debt less than 60% of GDP
- Exchange rate stability.

The Stability and Growth Pact was signed in 1997, which provided for a permanent commitment to budgetary stability and allowed for penalties to be imposed on member countries whose budget deficit exceeded 3%. This pact was subsequently reformed in 2005. New Member States are due to adopt the euro when they meet the criteria.

Member States At the time of writing, there are 28 Member States in the European Union, 19 of which are members of the eurozone.

Table 5.1 *European Union Member and Eurozone Countries*

Austria (Eurozone)	Latvia (Eurozone)
Belgium (Eurozone)	Lithuania (Eurozone)
Croatia	Luxembourg (Eurozone)
Bulgaria	Malta (Eurozone)
Cyprus (Greek part) (Eurozone)	Netherlands (Eurozone)
Czech Republic	Poland
Denmark	Portugal (Eurozone)
Estonia (Eurozone)	Romania
Finland (Eurozone)	Slovakia (Eurozone)
France (Eurozone)	Slovenia (Eurozone)
Germany (Eurozone)	Spain (Eurozone)
Greece (Eurozone)	Sweden
Hungary	United Kingdom*
Ireland (Eurozone)	
Italy (Eurozone)	

*At the time of writing, though a Member State, the UK has voted to leave the EU.

The financial turmoil with the euro began with the bailout of Greece in April 2010, followed by Ireland later that year. It highlighted many structural weaknesses in the common currency. The Maastricht Treaty was meant to keep all Member States in line by keeping budget deficits less than 3% of GDP. Including the bank bailout, Ireland's budget deficit was 32% of GDP in 2010,[1] and nearly all the other EU Member States were above the 3% level. As a result of efforts to stabilise the Eurozone area following the financial crisis, there is now much greater supervision by the European Central Bank and the European Commission of fiscal policy in each Member State.

---

1 This figure of 32% of GDP includes the cost of the banking crisis, and was the highest ever recorded by a developed country in peacetime. The US had a deficit of 30% in 1943 due to the massive expansion in the production of war materiel. The net budget deficit figure (discounting the banking crisis) was 11.6%, a figure similar to Sweden in 1992 and Argentina in 2002.

Other Trading Blocs

The North American Free Trade Agreement (NAFTA) which consists of the United States of America, Canada and Mexico, operates as a free-trade zone where tariffs and quotas have been eliminated. As a trading bloc, it is somewhat similar to the EU, but one important distinction is that it does not cover the free movement of labour. In late 2018, it was announced that NAFTA would be replaced by a new treaty: the United States–Mexico–Canada agreement. There are similar arrangements between many of the Caribbean (CARICOM) and South American countries.

Asia has also become a very important trading bloc with powerful economies such as Japan, Singapore, Hong Kong, South Korea, and Taiwan. There are other economies emerging in the region including the Philippines, Vietnam, Thailand and Malaysia. China, with a population of 1.4 billion, is re-emerging as a huge economic powerhouse, not just regionally, but globally. Two centuries ago, China was also a dominant power, accounting for 30% of world GDP (Tian, 2018). It then began to decline because of outdated political, economic and social systems due to domination by feudal overlords and foreign powers. The People's Republic of China was established by Mao Zedong in 1949. After Mao's death in 1976, Deng Xiaoping initiated changes, introducing Western-style market systems and opening up the country to foreign trade. China became a member of the World Trade Organisation (WTO) in November 2001. China's economy has been growing at almost 10% each year for the last couple of decades, and now has a major trade surplus with the United States. The rise of China as a world power has major implications for the West, both in terms of competition with European and American companies, but also in terms of increasing demand for Western goods and services. However, according to *The Economist* (2019), Western demand will not provide the same level of growth in the coming years and the current trade war between the US and China will further stunt future growth in China.

In recent years there has been an enormous increase in foreign direct investment in China, which offers preferential tax treatment to steer investment to desired locations, preferred industries and also to encourage specific investment modes, such as forming strategic alliances. China strongly prefers the formation of strategic alliances between foreign companies and indigenous companies as it provides a means for home industry to gain access to vital Western technology. Traditionally, most investment in the country occurred along the coastal region which had better infrastructure. However, this was leading to a widening economic gap between the various provinces and, since 2005, China has encouraged foreign investment in its interior (Tian, 2018).

Doing business in China is very different from Western countries, not just because of language difficulties, but in terms of the entire business culture. Nowhere is this more pronounced than in the importance of relationships. The Chinese term is *guanxi,* which would best be described as 'close-knit connections'. It also implies obligations for continued exchange of favours. When *guanxi* is present it can open up many doors. The difficulties in operating in China can be overcome, and many Irish companies are succeeding in this vast country (see **Illustration 5.1**).

Illustration 5.1: Sino–Irish Co-operation

Beingmate is a leading infant food producer in China. In 2013, the company set up an Irish subsidiary called Beingmate (Ireland) with the intention of sourcing Irish milk and infant food formula for the Chinese market. In order to further develop its technology and expertise, it formed a 15-year strategic partnership with Irish multinational company Kerry Group Plc. The partnership has allowed Kerry Group to enter the enormous Chinese market and, by the end of 2018, Kerry Group had sold over 10,000 tonnes of its products through established sales network in China (*Irish Times,* 2018).

In recent years, many Chinese companies have set up in Ireland across a variety of different industries. The bilateral relationship between the two countries has also benefited Irish companies and there are now over 400 Irish firms operating in China. Many of these Irish companies have received backing from Enterprise Ireland, particularly in relation to attending major international trade shows in China. In February 2019, four Irish businesses signed deals worth over €50 million with Chinese companies: Irish Breeze, Reagecon Diagnostics, Solvotrin Therapeutics and Novaerus. Given the sheer size of the Chinese market, deals such as these provide enormous potential for Irish companies (Donnolly, 2018).

Organization of the Petroleum Exporting Countries (OPEC)

The Organization of the Petroleum Exporting Countries (OPEC) includes many, but not all, of the oil-exporting nations and sets the price of oil for world markets. The price of oil has emerged as a major factor in the cost of doing business for companies around the globe. At the beginning of this decade, oil was approximately $25 a barrel. By July 2008, oil had reached $147 a barrel, but then fell back considerably. Unrest from time to time in many oil-producing countries ensures volatility in world oil prices. Some industries are hit directly by rising oil prices, such as the airline industry, the haulage industry, the fishing industry and many more. However, in the long run, all industries are hit as input costs soar. While the search for alternative energies continues, it will be a long time before oil can be effectively replaced, and until then the pace of economic development may well be severely curtailed (www.opec.org).

The World Trade Organization

The General Agreement on Tariffs and Trade (GATT) was established in the wake of the Second World War in an effort to promote world trade in a balanced way that would not see the rich countries develop at the expense of poorer ones. On 1 January 1995, the World Trade Organization (WTO) came into being to replace GATT. The WTO is headquartered in Geneva, Switzerland and consists of 150 member countries and accounts for 97% of world trade. Its principal objective is to help trade flow freely, fairly and in a predictable manner. Its main functions include:

- Administering WTO trade agreements
- Providing a forum for trade agreements
- Handling trade disputes between nations
- Monitoring national trade policies
- Providing technical assistance and training for developing countries
- Co-operation with other international organisations.

Negotiations under the WTO are referred to as 'Rounds'. These agreements are made by the entire membership and are then ratified in the member countries' parliaments. The WTO's top level decision-making body is the Ministerial Conference and below this is the General Council (ambassadors and heads of delegation). It has a number of sub-groups including the Goods Council, Services Council and Intellectual Property Council, as well as various specialised committees and working groups. The WTO Secretariat in Geneva has a staff of 673 and is headed by a director-general.

The Uruguay Round began in 1987, lasted until 1994 and ultimately resulted in a wide range of trade liberalisations, in areas such as telecommunications services, information technology products and financial services worldwide. The present round began in Doha, Qatar in November 2001 and has a wide agenda, including agriculture, services, WTO rules on dumping and subsidies, investment, competition, as well as a range of issues faced by developing countries in implementing present WTO agreements (www.wto.org).

Porter's Diamond

Later in this chapter we will examine competition within industries. However, it is also important to look at competition at a macro level. In his book, *The Competitive Advantage of Nations*, Harvard professor Michael Porter argues that some countries are more competitive than others, and why some industries within those countries are also more competitive.

According to Porter (1990 and 1998), countries can create their own prosperity by taking a number of steps which are not dependent on their supply of natural resources. (These steps will be discussed below.) As a result, there are major variations in competitiveness between countries, and no one country will be competitive in all industries. Porter considers that traditional economic theory on competitiveness is no longer relevant. Companies will become competitive through acts of (incremental) innovation in technology and in new ways of doing things and anticipating foreign and domestic needs, e.g. Volvo's reputation for safety. Innovation is the result of sustained effort and must be constantly upgraded and sustained as any advantage can be imitated – Korean companies have successfully copied Japanese electronics companies. Porter suggests there are two prerequisites to achieving competitiveness. First, adopt a global approach, selling the product worldwide under its own name and channels. Secondly, make existing advantages obsolete, even while they are still an advantage. He believes that innovation and change are inextricably linked.

So why then are some nations more competitive than others? The answer, according to Porter, lies in four broad attributes of a nation. These attributes, individually and together as a system, constitute the "diamond of national advantage". They are:

- Factor conditions
- Demand conditions
- Related and supporting industries
- Firm strategy, structure and rivalry.

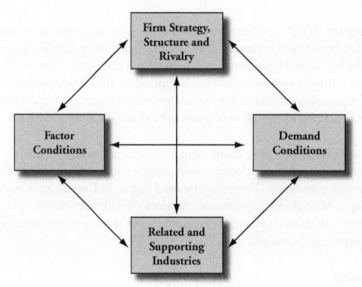

Source: Michael E. Porter, *The Competitive Advantage of Nations*, London, Macmillan, 1998

Figure 5.1 *Porter's Diamond*

Factor Conditions Traditionally, basic factors of production such as land, labour, natural resources and capital dictated the wealth of a nation; e.g. Britain during the Industrial Revolution. In the decades following independence and until the late 1950s, it was assumed that Ireland lacked such factors. Porter argues that in the modern world, countries must create the necessary factors, such as skilled human resources and scientific bases, which can be used to meet the specific needs of different industries. Countries and industries need to create specialised factors and then work continuously to improve them.

Countries that are relatively disadvantaged in the more basic factors of production can encourage businesses to constantly innovate and upgrade. Porter cites how labour shortages in Switzerland after the Second World War forced improvements in productivity. Similarly, high labour costs in Ireland will make productivity increases imperative in order to maintain global competitiveness.

In recent years, there has been a large increase in those attending third-level education (CSO, 2019), and the Government has targeted science and engineering as being particularly important for the future development of the economy. The Hunt Report on Higher Education (2010) stated that priority should be given to areas with the highest potential for economic and social returns. However, both the Hunt Report and the Report of the Expert Group on Higher Education (Cassells, 2016) are particularly critical about the lack of government funding in third-level education.

Another area requiring increased investment in Ireland is research and development (R&D). Under the Lisbon Strategy, Ireland had committed to increasing its spending on R&D to 3% of GDP by 2010, but 10 years later we are still well short of this figure (Europa, 2019). While Ireland has seen enormous growth since the early 1990s, the State will have to invest far greater amounts in training, third-level education and R&D.

One final point that Porter makes in relation to factor conditions: it is not just their presence, but the efficiency with which they are deployed that is important.

Demand Conditions Porter believes that, despite living in a globalised economy, the home market is very important as it can have "a disproportionate effect on how companies perceive, interpret, and respond to buyer needs". As a result, this information puts pressure on firms to innovate. If the home demand conditions are very high in terms of the standards expected, then any company that can survive in that home market can be confident that they can withstand any competitive pressure from elsewhere in the world. While Ireland is still a small country, the size of the home demand is less significant than the character of its demand. The market puts pressure on companies to meet high standards, to improve and to innovate constantly, e.g. small Japanese apartments created a demand for miniature electronics that was not met by American or European manufacturers. If the home market becomes saturated at an early stage it will encourage firms to export. Many Irish companies are now competing very successfully in global markets, e.g. Kerry Group Plc (see **Chapter 1**).

Related and Supporting Industries Suppliers that are located in the home base that are also internationally competitive can achieve a number of advantages in the value system. They can deliver supplies and components in an efficient and cost-effective way. They also provide close working relationships that encourage innovation and upgrading, especially when located near each other, e.g. the Italian footwear cluster (shoe producers, leather manufacturers and fashion houses are mutually advantageous and self-reinforcing). The internationally successful horse-breeding business in Ireland has also led to the development of internationally successful horse feed companies, e.g. Connolly's 'Red Mills' in Kilkenny.

Being located in close proximity to suppliers also means shorter lines of communication, facilitating the sharing of information on customers' needs and also facilitating innovation. Companies achieve most if suppliers are global competitors. It does not benefit companies to create captive suppliers that are dependent on the home producers, as this is likely to impede innovation at supplier level. Innovation in one industry often transfers into related and supporting industries.

Firm Strategy, Structure and Rivalry Countries differ in many ways such as culture, demographics and infrastructure. A number of different national circumstances influence how companies are managed. Porter cites Italy as an example where many companies are privately owned and operated like extended families. This lends itself to creative industries such as the fashion industry. In Germany, companies tend to be more hierarchical in organisation and management practice – suitable for production-type industries such as car manufacturing or chemicals. Despite these differences, no one system is universally appropriate. Ireland, for example, has become famous for its wealth of literary and musical talent, as well as software development. These require an individualistic, artistic approach, and a hierarchical structure would be totally inappropriate in fostering such creativity.

Competitiveness in a specific industry results from a convergence of the management practices and organisational modes favoured in the country. In Germany and Switzerland, where shares are held for a long time (often by banks), companies do well in mature industries. In the US, there is a considerable amount of risk capital available, thus supporting new industries like software development. Competitive advantage is dependent on individual attitudes to work, and improving competences is also important. Local rivals play an important role as they create pressure on companies to innovate and improve, lowering costs and improving service. Geographic concentration magnifies competitive advantage, e.g. Silicon Valley in California. Companies are less likely to be hooked on government aid and will look abroad for markets.

Porter's Diamond as a System Porter suggests that each point on the diamond is self-reinforcing and 'together constitutes a system'. Domestic rivalry is particularly important: it promotes improvement, stimulates development of specialised factors, upgrades domestic demand and promotes related and supporting industries. Working as a system, the Diamond also tends to create 'clusters of competitive industries' linked through supply chain relationships, e.g. Japanese laptops/portable products/LCD display watches. They are often linked geographically as well as in clusters. The obvious example is Silicon Valley in California. In Ireland, there is a large cluster of (competing) pharmaceutical companies operating in Cork.

Governments play an important part in developing national competitiveness, but not in the traditional way by protecting industries through tariffs or barriers. The role of government should not be to prop up industries that are not sustainable; nor should governments preside over an unregulated market. The failure of the 'light touch' approach to financial regulation in Ireland proves the necessity for an appropriate level of regulation.

According to Porter, government's function is to act as a catalyst and challenger: it should focus on specialised factor creation that is advanced, specialised and applied to industry. It was mentioned above that the government here in Ireland is putting resources into developing a greater interest in science. This will be essential in ensuring a future supply of science graduates (including PhD students) for, say, the pharmaceutical industry. In this regard, the lack of funding for third-level education and R&D, as discussed above, must be seen as a major impediment to world-class competitiveness.

Porter suggests that governments should avoid intervening in currency markets in terms of devaluing currency as it works against upgrading industry. Ireland, as a member of the eurozone, no longer has the ability to devalue its currency as it did in the early 1990s. Instead, the focus should be on ensuring strict product safety and environmental standards, which will promote domestic demand. We have witnessed this in recent years with stringent safety measures brought in by Irish law.

In addition to government, individual companies must play their part in developing a competitive advantage. It requires leadership that "harnesses and amplifies the forces to promote upgrading". The CEO should create a pressure of innovation within the company that responds to sophisticated buyers' needs and channels, e.g. the 3M Corporation. Companies should welcome competition rather than trying to be protected from it, as competition will improve performance and deliver a competitive advantage. By working closely with suppliers and distributors, companies can upgrade the entire value chain, thus creating a more competitive product that will satisfy the end consumer, regardless of what part of the globe that consumer is found. Porter's Diamond can be used by both governments and individual companies to understand the nature of the global factors that are affecting competition in different industries and to build a sustainable competitive advantage.

Porter's Diamond provides a very good understanding of competitiveness at a national level. The danger, however, is that it may present a somewhat simplified version of reality. Globalisation has complicated the picture a great deal. For example, an organisation may be headquartered in one country, conduct its R&D in another, source supplies from many different parts of the globe, and manufacture in one or more countries. For many multinational companies (MNCs), this represents their reality. Where, then, does such a business sit in Porter's Diamond? The reality for MNCs is now much more complicated than at first glance. Nevertheless, the majority of companies worldwide are small, centered in one manufacturing base in their home country, and export from there. In such situations, Porter's Diamond provides a useful insight at both company and governmental level.

PESTEL Analysis

Continuing with the analysis of the macro environment, it is necessary to look at other factors in the environment that will impact on the organisation, both directly and indirectly. Johnson *et al.* (2017) suggest the PESTEL framework to examine the list of possible influences. PESTEL stands for:

- Political
- Economic
- Sociological
- Technological
- Environmental
- Legal.

Inevitably there is a big overlap between many of these factors, and what is important when examining them is not which category any one item falls into, but the likely *collective* impact they are going to have on the organisation. For example, a government's annual budget overlaps a number of categories: political – it is the government's budget for running the country; economic – it impacts on the economy; sociological – it impacts on our standard of living; and legal – when passed in the Finance Act it becomes law and will be enforced by the courts.

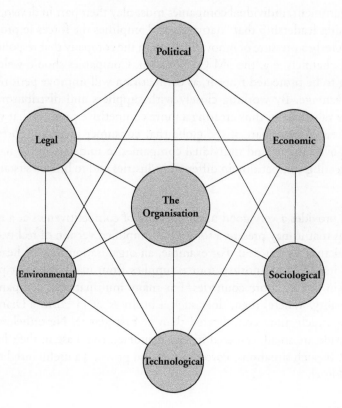

Figure 5.2 *PESTEL Analysis*

When we looked at the definition of strategy in **Chapter 1**, we saw that strategy deals with the long-term direction of a company. It is, therefore, important that when looking at the different factors, we assess their impact not just in the present time, but try to understand how they will change over the next few years. While there will be many possible factors facing the organisation, it is important to focus on those that will have a major impact. It is sometimes argued that the macro environment is outside the control of an organisation. However, regardless of whether it is or is not outside their control, it is imperative that managers are aware of these developments and plan accordingly. It should also be noted that, while it may be outside the remit of any one firm, most industries have representative associations that lobby government and the EU on issues facing the industry. One just has to look at the various farmer groups in Ireland, such as the Irish Farmers

Association (IFA), to see the impact of such lobbying. Finally, the PESTEL framework is not just relevant when developing strategy here in Ireland, but any Irish company wishing to expand abroad would also need to use it to analyse the target country.

Political Political factors include the EU, government stability, and whether there is a favourable climate for business in the country. Obviously, the EU has, and will continue to have, a major influence on how business operates. Calls for tax harmonisation, if they were to be adopted, would significantly change the attractiveness of Ireland with regard to foreign direct investment. At present in Ireland, the rate of corporation tax is 12.5%, which is extremely low by international standards and has been very important in attracting foreign direct investment into the country. It is government policies such as these that have a major impact on the economy. Government policy directly affects the standard of living and quality of life of its citizens through investment in infrastructure and services such as health and education, which in turn influences people's decision to live and work in Ireland.

Government stability refers more to the *type* of government rather than any particular political party in power. A socialist government would have a different view of business than a centre-right party. A stable political system allows companies to plan for the future with a degree of certainty. It must also be remembered that governments are also major buyers of products and services in their own right, and this can have a strong impact on the economy. Through its laws and regulatory bodies, the government also plays a very important part in creating the environment in which business operates. In the section on Porter's Diamond above, we examined the essential nature of competition. There must be a level playing field for all companies to operate and prosper, underpinned by appropriate company law.

Illustration 5.2: Ireland's Corporate Tax Rate

A low rate of corporation tax has been part of the bedrock of industrial policy in Ireland since the mid-1950s. It began as an exemption on export sales profits in order to encourage foreign direct investment in Ireland. The incentive has continued in some form or another since then. The rate is currently 12.5% for all companies. Over the last number of years, the European Commission has been discussing the idea of a common consolidated corporation tax base (CCCTB) for Member States. This measure would include regulations on what may or may not be written off by companies for tax reasons. It would also include rules for multinationals as to how profits made in different countries would be apportioned between Member States for tax purposes. It is argued that the CCCTB would make it much cheaper and easier for businesses as they would effectively need to engage with just one tax system. However, others argue that it is the first step towards tax harmonisation, and it is believed that the amount raised by the Irish exchequer through corporation tax would fall significantly if harmonisation were introduced.

The low rate of corporation tax in Ireland has come under increasing pressure in recent times, particularly from the French and German governments. However, most European countries apply two rates of corporation tax: a nominal or headline rate and the actual rate paid by companies after all tax write-offs have been included. The rate in many European countries, such as France and Germany, is around 30%, but the actual rate is much lower, which reduces their tax take quite considerably. In Ireland, the effective tax paid by corporations is 11.9%, almost identical to the nominal rate.

The low rate of corporation tax has been an important factor in attracting foreign direct investment into Ireland, and in retaining such investment. For that reason, the Irish Government is reluctant to change the rate.

Economic Economic factors consist of interest rates, GNP/GDP, inflation, unemployment, disposable income, money supply, etc. The economic conditions in a country are of vital importance to the success of any company. In the EU, interest rates are set by the European Central Bank (ECB). There have been advantages and disadvantages to this but, in general, it has given Ireland great financial stability. However, there have been times when the rate set by the ECB for the EU as a whole had not suited Ireland's economic conditions at that time, particularly in the five-year period before the financial crash in 2008.

Unemployment and emigration were for many years seen as a fact of life in Ireland by successive governments. The various partnership programmes agreed between the Government, employers, trade unions and other bodies are largely credited with finally tackling this social and economic evil. While unemployment was coming down, the Irish labour force also grew from 1.49 million people in 1998 to 2.09 million in 2008. After the crash, it fell back to 1.8 million workers and has grown again since 2016. It now stands at 2.2 million – the highest ever number since the founding of the State. The expansion of the workforce has not only provided wonderful opportunities for individuals, but also enabled companies to expand. Indeed, such is the level of expansion that some industries are finding it difficult to recruit the amount of staff needed, which in turn may lead to wage inflation as companies seek to recruit staff with more attractive salaries.

The nature of the Irish economy has also changed a great deal in the last 30 years, with a shift in emphasis from manufacturing to the services sector. The International Financial Services Centre (IFSC) is an example of the importance of specialised services to the economy.

Sociological The factors that are relevant here are population, levels of education, income distribution and general socio-cultural changes that are taking place. The population of Ireland has changed enormously in percentage terms over the last 30 years for various reasons – not least being the reversal of what was an accepted policy of emigration. By 2019, the population in the Republic reached 4.8 million – the highest figure in well over a century. (By comparison, in 1961 the population was only 2.8 million.)

The structure and nature of the population has also changed significantly. Family size is much smaller, there are more one-parent families, and people are moving away from their home town searching for jobs, all resulting in a much higher demand for housing relative to the overall population size. In turn this impacts on the demand for a wide variety of services and products. The population of Ireland has a much higher proportion of young people than the majority of European countries, particularly Germany and Italy. This has important implications with regard to the type of products bought and the services required. For example, an ageing population will have a much higher demand for health-related products and services. The ethnic mix of the population has also changed dramatically in the last 15 years. These people entering Ireland have brought with them much needed skills and experience, but it has also brought challenges in terms of integration and the management skills required to manage a diversified workforce.

As stated above, the overall population growth has been a very necessary ingredient in the growth of the economy. However, one of the problems associated with this is the very large concentration in the greater Dublin area, and this has an impact on income distribution. Ireland now has a very high level of participation in third-level education in the school-leaving age cohort. This is also a very necessary ingredient of economic growth.

The increase in the workforce noted above can be partly accounted for by the fact that there has been a large increase in the number of women working outside the home. A corollary of this has been an increase in demand for relevant services and goods such as childcare and convenience foods.

The nature of employment is changing, with more and more people working part-time or on contract, rather than in permanent jobs. As a result of EU membership, there have been important changes in legislation dealing with employees, including protection of part-time staff, maternity leave, minimum wages and many more. All of these factors impact on costs and how companies are managed, as well as having important social implications. Finally, the culture of a country needs to be considered in as much as it overlaps with business. Business ethics and corporate social responsibility have already been discussed in **Chapter 4** and these are important considerations for society.

Technological This includes technological development and the rate of diffusion, the rate of obsolescence, spending on R&D, development of e-commerce, etc. Technology impacts on every type of organisation. Production methods are constantly changing and this has a knock-on effect on production costs, production times and the ability to customise products. Product life cycles are becoming much shorter, with products made obsolete much earlier than before.

Many products are also becoming smaller, as their capability increases. When mobile phones first appeared on the market, they were extremely bulky and unreliable. Now smartphones have huge functionality and are only a fraction of the size. Developments such as these can often lead to whole new industries. Such is the speed of diffusion that many new developments quickly become industry standard, putting pressure on other companies to follow suit. The importance of new product development will be dealt with in greater detail in **Chapter 9**.

There is a need for much greater emphasis on R&D in order to keep up with worldwide competition. Irish companies tend to lag behind in this regard. If we were to take out the spending by foreign-owned multinationals on R&D, such as in the pharmaceutical industry, it would show that the spending by Irish companies is very low. The section above on Porter's Diamond emphasises the importance of innovation and its link to R&D. One area of concern is the slow roll-out of the National Broadband Plan, as the lack of sufficient broadband speed in many parts of Ireland is having a detrimental impact on balanced regional growth.

In 1997, Harvard professor Clayton Christensen coined the phrase "disruptive technology" to describe the development of technology that radically changes how industries or business is operated (as opposed to incremental technological changes). Technology is becoming more centre stage for many companies. For some companies, technology is their core product, such as cloud-based solutions. For others, technology enables them to exploit their core product offering to a broader target market, as can be seen in **Illustration 5.3**.

Illustration 5.3: Technology Changing the Business Model – Salaso

Salaso Health Solutions®, based in Tralee, County Kerry, was established in 2011 by Aoife Ní Mhuirí, a Chartered Physiotherapist and lecturer in the Health and Leisure Department at IT Tralee. Salaso, supported by Enterprise Ireland, is growing at a substantial rate and currently employs 14 people (including physiotherapists and software engineers) and has customers in Ireland, Britain, Poland and the US.

Salaso believes that both targeted exercise and physiotherapy play a major role on the road to recovery – patient-specific exercises are more effective. The problem for many patients, particularly in rural areas, is the time required to undergo repeated bouts of treatment, which often involves long journeys to the physiotherapist. In addition, there are often constraints in the health system on the number of professionals available, and waiting lists are likely to grow as the population ages.

Salaso's solution to this problem involves transferring some elements of the treatment to the patient's own home and empowering them in self-care and self-management. 'Disruptive' technology facilitates this by providing support for physiotherapists to treat more patients and deliver high-quality care more effectively. It reduces costs considerably for the hospitals or clinics, and also for patients, who need fewer visits and less travel.

The initial consultation begins with a face-to-face meeting between the physiotherapist and the patient, and the physiotherapist then recommends specific exercises. A demonstration of the correct way to do the exercise is recorded and the video is uploaded to the Salaso system and is accessed by the patient via the website or app, along with clear, user-friendly instructions. This allows the patient to conduct the exercises at home, and their progress is monitored by the physiotherapist in real time. Exercise reminders can be sent by text message or email, and patients can keep a diary of their exercise programme.

The Salaso product can also be tailored for company wellness programmes, particularly for musculoskeletal conditions in the workplace, such as back and neck pain. Preventing such injuries can result in major savings for employers, reducing employee absence due to illness or injury; clearly, it is also beneficial for workers.

Salaso believes that, as a company, being agile is important, especially when it comes to customer care. The company is in constant contact with clients and is able to adapt its software in a matter of days when specific needs arise. Furthermore, the company has partnered with a number of teaching hospitals in Ireland and the UK in the development of its physiotherapy treatments. This ensures that the company is at the leading edge of research in this area, and patients are receiving the benefits of such developments.

Recovering from injury is always going to be difficult, but with the use of technology, it can be made a little bit easier and a lot less expensive.

Environmental This includes issues such as energy costs and consumption, environmental protection, disposal of waste material, etc.

The environment has taken on a new importance over the last couple of years for a variety of reasons. It is partly pro-active and partly reactive. In **Chapter 4** we discussed corporate social responsibility (CSR) and examined how companies are beginning to take a much broader perspective on how they relate with stakeholders other than shareholders. This includes taking responsibility for the environment in which we live, over and above what is required by law (CSR can even become a competitive advantage for such organisations). For those who do not regard such obligations as part of their remit, much tougher laws protecting the environment have come into play in recent years, and this trend will continue. When one considers the amount of illegal dumps that have been discovered in Ireland, many containing toxic materials, our record in this regard has not been exemplary.

What is of major concern to businesses and consumers alike is the impact that climate change is having on the planet. There will be enormous pressure put on companies to change their business models to more sustainable practices in order to reverse the negative impact of climate change.

Legal Health & safety, employment, consumer, company and competition law all come under this heading. Laws are put forward by the Oireachtas (the Irish Parliament) and signed by the President of Ireland. It is then up to the courts and the regulatory bodies to ensure that they are complied with. As a result of the numerous laws that have been passed in recent years, the HR function in companies has become quite a specialised area. Other areas of law and regulation, such as company law and competition law, often require more specialised outside advice as do the privacy and data protection regimes under key legislation such as the EU General Data Protection Regulation (GDPR). As with many of the other factors mentioned above, these all have important implications for how companies are run, and the responsibility rests with management to be informed about developments in relevant laws and regulations, and ensure compliance.

Implications for Organisations

As we have seen, there are myriad factors impacting on organisations that have to be taken into account when formulating strategy. They will all vary in terms of importance: some have little or no relevance; while others will be central to an organisation's competitiveness. Obviously, it is the latter that will require management's attention. The question needs to be asked: what impact will a factor have on the organisation? It must also be stressed that they are not static, and in some cases will be quite dynamic, particularly the economic factors. For that reason, management must be constantly aware of these issues and factor them into their decision-making. It is particularly important to try to understand how they may change in the next few years, as strategic decisions are, by their nature, long term. The point has already been made that there is a huge overlap in each of the six elements of the PESTEL analysis. Thus, it is not so much individual factors that have to be taken into account, but their combined effect.

Scenario Planning

Change is a factor that affects every organisation, some to a lesser extent, while others to a much greater degree. For every organisation, trying to predict the future can be difficult and, where there is a great amount of uncertainty, it can prove almost impossible. In such situations, the development of different scenarios can be particularly useful in helping organisations understand the nature of change.

 Scenarios provide an outline of alternative future developments and their impact on an organisation.

Scenarios can be used to examine developments at the macro environmental level and, perhaps, to a lesser extent at industry level, e.g. examining the effect on a business if a major competitor were to pursue a certain strategy. However, events at industry level are in most cases more predictable, and so the use of scenarios is more suited to examining major changes at global and national level.

Using scenarios is not about trying to predict the future. Scenarios take into account different perspectives on what might happen in the future, and examine the implications to the organisation if such an outcome were to happen. It is advisable to use an even number of scenarios, either two or four, as there can be a tendency to opt for the middle one, which may defeat the purpose of properly examining all possible future situations.

Scenarios should be constructed around events that would potentially have serious implications for the future of the company. An example of this would be the cost of oil for the airline industry.

Oil costs are entirely outside the control of the industry (even governments), but yet have major implications. High oil costs was one of the key reasons that, in 2019, Airbus announced it would discontinue production of the four-engined (and fuel-hungry) A380 from 2021, just 20 years after it entered production (Pfeifer, 2019).

In **Chapter 1**, when examining how strategy is formulated, the use of strategy workshops to debate the issues facing organisations was discussed. Such workshops can be particularly useful in developing and debating scenarios and play an important part in organisational learning. The ultimate aim is to develop contingency plans for each of the scenarios. One should avoid assigning probabilities to these scenarios, as it can confer a false sense of certainty to what is essentially an unpredictable future. As the circumstances become clearer with time and with more information, managers can then make a decision as to the most appropriate response to the unfolding circumstances. With the contingency planning completed, they are then in a position to react quickly, and develop a strategy that is suited to the particular scenario that is unfolding.

One obvious failure to properly utilise scenario planning was the collapse of the financial sector in Ireland. According to Jim O'Leary (2010), speaking about the time he was a non-executive director at AIB prior to the recession, directors of the bank did examine more malign scenarios but "they trusted the systems for monitoring and controlling risk ensured that banks would be adequately protected if such circumstances arose". While each of the banks probably did use scenarios, there clearly was a failure on the part of senior managers and directors to properly analyse the information and the implications for each individual company. Given that scenarios are designed to examine possible events that would have a very serious impact on an organisation, this represented a significant failure in not properly utilising this valuable strategic tool.

And the concept of using scenarios is not new. According to Macaro and Baggini (2010:51), the Roman philosopher Seneca believed:

> "It is important to envisage every possibility and to strengthen the spirit to deal with the things which may conceivably come about. Rehearse them in your mind: exile, torture, war, shipwreck."

THE MICRO ENVIRONMENT

As has been discussed above, the macro environment involves all of the factors affecting a company in a general way from a global and national perspective. However, analysis of the business environment needs to go deeper, as each industry will be facing different circumstances particular to that industry, and these must also be considered:

- Understanding the industry's economic structure
- Competitive forces – the Five Forces Analysis
- Industry life cycle

- Industry driving forces
- Market segmentation
- Strategic groups
- Critical success factors
- Opportunities and threats.

Understanding the Industry's Economic Structure

When discussing the characteristics of a particular industry, it is first necessary to have a clear understanding regarding the nature and boundaries of that industry. **Chapter 1** compared the nature of the cement industry with that of tourism. The cement industry is clearly defined – manufacturing bags of cement – whereas the definition of tourism is extremely broad, encompassing the provision of accommodation, meals, transport, entertainment, natural amenities, sport and leisure facilities, etc. Many of these constitute industries in their own right, e.g. the car rental industry. Where then does the tourism 'industry' begin and end? In other cases, different industries converge, such as when digital telephony and computing converged to give us smartphones.

Because each industry is different, we must first examine the overall structure of the industry within which we are operating, in order to get an understanding of that industry. Some industries are, by their nature, more profitable than others. Conglomerates are companies that are highly diversified. When examining the portfolio of conglomerates and the industries that they are involved in, the conglomerate may decide to concentrate more on one industry rather than another because that particular industry may present better opportunities. There are many factors that influence such profitability, such as the size of the industry and its growth rate. A big market is generally better than a small one (though niche markets can also be profitable) and growing markets are generally preferable to shrinking or slowing ones.

Companies will be reluctant to invest in an industry that is in decline. Competition too will play a very important part in deciding profitability, and this will be examined in detail below. Other factors include the level of technology and the rate at which it is developing. Some industries require economies of scale to be profitable, while others require strong learning curve effects. These, and many more questions, provide an overall understanding of the industry that will enable more informed judgement in making decisions about whether or not to invest in a particular industry. Indeed, it is the variation between one industry and another, and the complexity of understanding each of those industries, that makes managing conglomerates a difficult task.

Economic theory demonstrates that there are different types of competition. A **monopoly** is where there is only one firm in the industry and clearly there is no competition. An **oligopoly** is where there is only a small number of companies operating in the industry and, in effect, there is little or no competition. In these circumstances it is also difficult for new companies to enter the market. **Perfect competition** is where there is a large number of firms competing with each other and consumers have complete knowledge about prices. Entry and exit for companies is relatively easy in a highly competitive market. Competition is seen at EU and national level as being good for the consumer, and it is for that reason that markets that were traditionally restricted, e.g. electricity supply, are being broken up to allow for competition. This can be a slow process, however and the Government has put in place regulators in various industries, including telecommunications, energy, air travel, utilities, etc., to ensure a level playing pitch for smaller operators and for the consumer (see **Illustration 5.4**).

Illustration 5.4: The Commission for Regulation of Utilities

The Commission for Regulation of Utilities (CRU) is Ireland's independent energy and water regulator. It was originally established in 1997 as the Commission for Energy Regulation but its name was changed in 2017 to better reflect its expanded powers and functions.

The mission of the CRU is to regulate water, energy and energy safety in the public interest and it has a wide range of economic and safety responsibilities in the regulation of energy and water in Ireland. In that respect, the work of the CRU impacts on every Irish home and business by ensuring safe, secure and sustainable supplies of water and energy at a reasonable cost to the consumer. It also has to meet international obligations in relation to climate change.

The CRU is guided by six key strategic goals, which are that the interests of the public are protected by ensuring:

- energy and gas are supplied safely;
- the lights stay on;
- the gas continues to flow;
- a reliable supply of clean water and efficient treatment of wastewater;
- consumer prices for energy and water are fair and reasonable; and
- regulation is best international practice.

Organisational Structure

The CRU is led by up to three Commissioners at any one time. There are currently two Commissioners: Paul McGowan (Chairperson) and Aoife MacEvilly. The Commissioners are assisted in their duties by a staff of about 100, including four directors. The work of the CRU is divided into four separate divisions, with each division led by a director. These divisions are: water, energy markets, energy safety, and energy networks and legal. This structure reflects the CRU's varied economic, customer protection and safety responsibilities in energy as well as its role as economic water regulator.

Water Division

The CRU is the economic regulator for the public water and wastewater sector, covering the services provided by Irish Water. Its primary aim is to protect the interests of customers of Irish Water. The CRU seeks to ensure that Irish Water is run as efficiently as possible while providing appropriate water and wastewater services to its customers. It approves Irish Water's Water Charges Plan, which reflects the allowed revenue, connection charging policy and the domestic and non-domestic tariff regime.

Energy Markets Division

The Energy Markets Division is responsible for overseeing the wholesale, all-island Single Electricity Market (SEM) in co-operation with the Utility Regulator in Belfast. The division also monitors security of supply and generation adequacy in Ireland, the National Smart Metering Programme, and is also responsible for the monitoring and regulation of the energy retail market and the licensing of energy suppliers.

Energy Networks and Legal Division

This division is responsible for the economic regulation of the electricity and natural gas infrastructures in Ireland, including setting network development and connection policy, approving charges for access to and use of the networks and resolving connection disputes. It also has a general role in advising the organisation on all legal matters.

Energy Safety Division

The Energy Safety Division is responsible for the implementation of the gas safety framework and electricity safety functions. These include the safety regulation of gas supply, gas networks (including LPG), gas storage and the use of gas, the regulation of gas installers (including LPG) and electrical contractors. Furthermore, the division is responsible for the regulation of upstream petroleum exploration and extraction activities.

Source: Commission for Regulation of Utilities, 2019

Competitive Forces

Porter (1980:3) has developed a generic framework for examining competition in an industry. Competition puts a ceiling on profits, and the greater the level of competition, the lower the profits will be. It is relatively easy to look upon competition as just other companies operating in the industry. While this is totally valid, there are also other forms that must be taken into account. Porter describes five such competitive forces operating in any given industry. One important point about the Five Forces Analysis is that it should be used at the strategic business unit level rather than for the company as a whole, as competition will differ for each strategic group. One should not look at the forces in isolation, as there is a connection between them all. Similarly, there is often a connection between elements in the macro environment and the five forces that need to be considered.

Porter's **five forces** are:

1. The threat of new entrants
2. Rivalry among existing firms
3. The threat of substitute products
4. The bargaining power of buyers
5. The bargaining power of suppliers

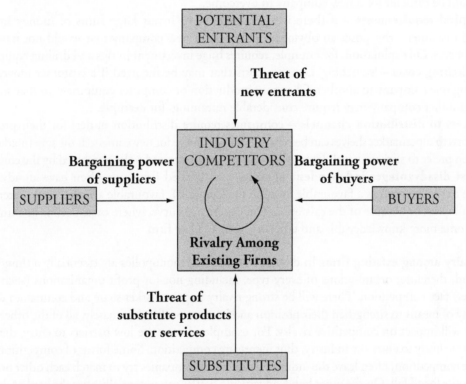

Source: Michael E Porter, *Competitive Strategy: Techniques for Analysing Industries and Competitors*, New York, The Free Press, 1980

Figure 5.3 *Five Forces Analysis*

1. The threat of new entrants The competitive market in any industry can often change as new companies enter, bringing with them extra capacity. When we examine many industries in Ireland, we see that a large amount of new capacity was added in the last 10 years. As a result, competition in these industries has intensified enormously. The likelihood of new entrants depends on the existence of barriers to entry – whether there are obstacles that they must overcome. Such barriers

179

should not be seen as permanent, but factors that will, at best, delay entry. According to Porter, there are six main barriers to entry:

- **Economies of scale** – some industries require economies of scale in order to be profitable. Economies of scale exist when unit costs come down as production goes up. It normally happens where there are high fixed costs. For example, pharmaceutical production requires large economies of scale in order to cover the very substantial investment required in R&D.
- **Product differentiation** – where a product is differentiated in the minds of the consumer, thus creating brand loyalty and allowing the company to charge a premium. Such brand loyalty would be difficult for a new company to overcome.
- **Capital requirements** – if there is a requirement to invest large sums of money in plant and machinery, this poses an obvious problem for a new company that would not have such resources. Oil exploration, for example, requires huge investment in rigs and drilling equipment.
- **Switching costs** – 'switching' costs are costs that may be incurred if a customer moves from using one company to another. Changing production or computer equipment to that supplied by another company may require considerable retraining, for example.
- **Access to distribution channels** – companies require distribution outlets for their products. Access to supermarket shelves can be very difficult to achieve for newcomers, as the supermarkets will often prefer to stick with well-known brands that are guaranteed to be purchased by the consumer.
- **Cost disadvantages independent of scale** – established firms can often have an advantage due to factors such as a favourable location (a restaurant), favourable access to raw materials or employees, or because of the existence of an experience curve, where costs decline as companies become more knowledgeable and efficient, such as a law firm.

2. Rivalry among existing firms In developed countries, monopolies are essentially a thing of the past and, therefore, organisations of every type, including not-for-profit organisations (such as aid agencies) face competition. There will be strong rivalry to gain market share and companies will use a variety of means to strengthen their position and increase profits. Ultimately, all of the other forces at play will impact on competitive rivalry. For example, if there are low barriers to entry, then new players are likely to enter the industry, thus increasing competition. Some forms of competition, such as price competition, often leave the industry worse off as companies try to match each other on price, and profits for all fall. On the other hand, advertising battles can potentially raise the level of demand generally. There are a number of factors that influence the level of competitive rivalry, including a large number of similar sized competitors, slow industry growth and high fixed costs or exit barriers.

While many companies will naturally focus their competitive attention on existing rivalry, it must be remembered that the nature of competition is changing rapidly with the emergence of new developing markets. This combined with changes in technology, particularly with regard to the internet, makes understanding the true nature of existing rivalry much more difficult. On the other hand, the use of technology can also present opportunities.

3. The threat of substitute products The existence of substitutes for products will ultimately put a ceiling on the price that can be charged for that product, particularly if consumers see the substitute as a close second. A substitute refers to a product that provides a similar function to other products.

There are different types of substitution. First there is product-for-product substitution. Regional flights in Ireland save a good deal of time for busy executives. In most cases there is probably only one operator flying between the regions and Dublin. For example, Aer Lingus currently has the contract to operate flights between Kerry and Dublin and, on the face of it, it would appear that there is no competition. However, in recent years, intercity rail has improved greatly, and while the actual journey does take longer, it is often less expensive and without lengthy security and check-in procedures, and so represents a viable alternative.

There is also substitution of need, where new developments may render other products obsolete, even though they are quite different, e.g. using a mobile phone instead of a watch to tell the time. Finally, it must be remembered that in a competitive world where people have only a certain amount of disposable income, choices have to be made with regard to spending. Thus, a garage selling cars is not only competing with other car dealers, but is perhaps competing with, say, the travel industry, as limited funds may require that a choice has to be made between taking a holiday or changing the car.

4. The bargaining power of buyers Organisations require customers to purchase their products and services. If those customers/buyers are in a position to exert pressure on the company to sell at a lower price, that represents a form of competition and places a ceiling on the price that can be obtained. The ability of buyers to obtain more favourable prices from their perspective depends on their bargaining power. A distinction needs to be drawn between the buyer and the ultimate consumer. A person dining in a restaurant and purchasing a bottle of wine is the ultimate consumer. The price paid is that marked on the wine list, and there is no negotiation. The restaurant, on the other hand, is the buyer and, particularly if it is part of a chain of restaurants, will buy the wine in considerable quantities perhaps directly from the vineyard, and will have strong bargaining power. The buyer will have high bargaining power if:

- there is only a small concentration of big buyers, which puts them in a powerful position;
- products are undifferentiated or easily switched from one seller to another; and
- there is easily available information on the internet regarding price.

5. The bargaining power of suppliers In many ways, the bargaining power of suppliers is a mirror image of the bargaining power of buyers. The next chapter will deal with the value network in detail, showing the relationship between an organisation and its suppliers. In this context, there are occasions where the supplier can exert considerable bargaining power in supplying the necessary raw materials or components to a company. Bargaining power is said to be high when there are only a few suppliers of components that are in strong demand, or those components are an important input into the buyer's business. In addition, high switching costs from one supplier to another means businesses tend to stay with existing suppliers.

Holistic Analysis

Analysis of each of Porter's five competitive forces will present different answers. The threat of new entrants might be high, existing rivalry might be moderate to low, etc. For that reason, it is necessary to form an overall judgement with regard to the level of competition, and thus the overall level of attractiveness of that industry. If competitive forces are weak, it will present a good opportunity to invest in that industry. It must also be remembered that competitive forces are dynamic – they can and do evolve. Companies must be constantly monitoring competitive developments and take appropriate offensive or defensive action to counter the threat. An example of an offensive move to counter competition is acquiring a rival company, thus reducing the level of competition being faced. On the other hand, increasing the level of advertising or investment in R&D would be regarded as defensive moves.

Five Forces Analysis does have limitations. The bargaining power of suppliers, for example, suggests an adversarial approach between a company and its supplier. Driving too hard a bargain with suppliers undermines the relationship and works against the level of co-operation that is needed to make just-in-time management succeed. With regard to the threat of new entrants and rivalry among existing firms, the nature of rivalry suggested by Porter is probably more reflective of rivalry as it existed pre-globalisation and, in particular, pre-internet, as many of the barriers to entry can be easily overcome as a result of the development of e-commerce.

Industry Life Cycle

Competition will also depend on the stage the industry is at in its life cycle. This variation is due to the number of competitor firms and the difference in consumer's buying habits. There are four main stages (as depicted in **Figure 5.4**):

- Introduction
- Growth
- Maturity
- Decline.

In the **introduction** stage, there may well be only one manufacturer in the market (particularly if the new product is patent-protected). Even if there are a few, the competitors will be more concerned with building up the overall market as there tends to be a small number of consumers due to a lack of familiarity with the product and high purchase costs.

In the **growth** stage, sales begin to rise rapidly and more companies begin to enter the industry. The emphasis will still be on trying to grow the market overall, but competitors will also start trying to vie for market share. The initial players in the industry will now begin to recoup their development costs. In response to more competition, prices begin to drop significantly, making it possible for a larger group of people to purchase the product.

In the **maturity** stage, the sales curve peaks and begins to decline. There are no new customers and the industry is dependent on repeat custom. Competition now becomes severe, and many of the weaker players will be forced out of the industry.

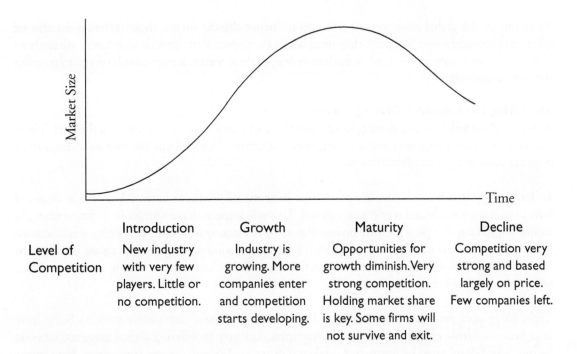

	Introduction	Growth	Maturity	Decline
Level of Competition	New industry with very few players. Little or no competition.	Industry is growing. More companies enter and competition starts developing.	Opportunities for growth diminish. Very strong competition. Holding market share is key. Some firms will not survive and exit.	Competition very strong and based largely on price. Few companies left.

Figure 5.4 *Industry Life Cycle*

The final stage of an industry's life cycle is the **decline**. There is a large drop-off in usage, and companies are concerned with minimising costs by cutting all advertising and minimising product offerings. There are likely to be only a few competitors left in the market at this point. (The product life cycle is discussed in greater detail in **Chapter 9**.)

Driving Forces

Both at international level and at industry level, there will be many changes taking place that will sometimes alter the business environment in a fundamental way. This can happen in a relatively short period of time, but generally it will be part of longer-term trends. If there are changes happening that are going to radically change the nature of the industry, it is vital that senior managers understand such changes and the impact that they are likely to have on the industry. These changes are often termed the industry's driving forces.

 Industry driving forces are those changes taking place that are altering the fundamental nature and competition of that industry.

As such, they will have a significant impact on the future success of the company. For that reason, senior management must first be able to recognise the forces driving change in their industry.

As factors in the global environment will also influence driving forces, these factors must also be taken into consideration. Secondly, they must assess the impact that those driving forces are likely to have. Lastly, once they have gained an understanding of these forces, action must be taken to position the firm accordingly.

Identifying the Industry's Driving Forces

As stated, there will be many driving forces, and these will vary from one industry to the next. There are, however, many common issues facing most industries, and perhaps the two most important ones are technology and globalisation.

1. Technology is constantly changing, not just in terms of product offering, but also in terms of how products are made and services are offered. This will impact on companies in different ways. As technology changes, it puts pressure on companies to constantly innovate. This point was discussed above in the context of Porter's Diamond. There is consequently a greater pressure on firms to innovate and upgrade their products to meet the demand of consumers. Failure to do so will see companies left behind.

Technology also provides opportunities. Electronics consumer companies such as Sony have now become firmly established in the photographic industry by offering digital cameras, whereas before, it was dominated by Eastman Kodak and other 'traditional' camera companies. Firms must also be mindful of their costs, and process innovation is also an important factor that should be considered. The steel industry has seen enormous changes in the recent past in the way the product is manufactured. It was once an industry that required huge capital investment, but the development of mini-mill technology has now made it possible for small steel producers to compete successfully with larger operators.

The internet has radically changed the way business is carried out in so many industries, along with the nature of competition. While high-speed broadband rollout has been slow in this country, the number of people that have access to broadband is growing constantly. It has changed the way in which companies interact with their customers. In many cases it has resulted in cutting out middlemen from the channel of distribution. It is, therefore, of vital importance that companies develop attractive websites that are easy for customers to navigate.

An aspect of technology that will have a profound effect on business is the development of **artificial intelligence** (AI). While still in its early stages, AI will radically alter how products are made, as well as the nature of employment as we currently know it. AI will impact on different sectors and industries in different ways, and the timeframe for development will also vary. It is vital that executives keep up to date with the opportunities and threats that AI presents for their business, and take appropriate action, for example by investing in this technology.

2. In the context of driving forces, globalisation has radically altered the nature of competition and demand. For many products, there is a homogenisation of demand around the world, brought about to no small effect by, for instance, the internet and satellite television, as well as the removal of trade barriers and tariffs as a result of the EU and World Trade Organization agreements. In turn, this puts pressure on companies to compete on a global basis in order to respond to the changing nature of competition, particularly with regard to economies of scale. From cars to computers, economies of scale are constantly rising in terms of the amount required by production runs and marketing. One way this manifests itself is through the outsourcing of production to countries with cheaper labour costs, such as China or the Philippines. Tax laws can also result in a form of globalisation, and Ireland has seen many foreign multinationals establish here to avail of the low rate of corporation tax.

The Impact of Driving Forces

Driving forces will impact on organisations in very significant ways, and this impact will increase over time. Ideally, organisations should be able to spot these trends in the early stages and take action that places them ahead of their rivals. It is a difficult call to make, as a distinction needs to be made between passing fads and underlying drivers of change. In the case of the latter, managers need to be able not just to identify the basic trends, but to understand the impact they will have on the industry and their company in particular.

It must also be remembered that while some forces will be pushing the industry in one direction, other forces may be pushing it in another. Thus, the overall impact of the various driving forces is what matters. Again, this highlights the importance of undertaking environmental analysis, as it is essential that managers fully understand the nature and impact of these driving forces in order to take effective action in response. The strategies that need to be considered by the organisation in light of these driving forces will be explored below.

Segmentation, Targeting and Positioning

Throughout this textbook, the importance of the customer is highlighted. In any market, whether it is a consumer market or a business market, different customers will inevitably have different needs. This concept is clearly illustrated by the vast range of items on sale in supermarkets, where there could be a large variety of any one item on sale, e.g. biscuits. Customers' needs must be understood by all companies operating in the market. While each individual will have their own specific requirements, these requirements can usually be grouped by companies into different segments. Therefore, when looking at the level of competition in an industry, it is necessary to examine the various segments that exist. The process by which companies identify different segments and decide which segments to pursue is known as segmentation, targeting and positioning.

Definition	**Segmentation** is the process by which diverse customers in a large market are divided into smaller groups that have similar needs.

Essentially, it is a group that has similar products or buying needs. There are many segmentation variables that can be used: age, gender, occupation, ethnic grouping, family size, life-cycle stage and many more. Segmentation may be by a single variable, for example a specific age group; or by multi-variable segmentation where more than one characteristic is used. The more variables that are used, the more homogenous will be the chosen group in terms of identifying their needs.

Once the market has been divided into segments, the next stage is identifying which of those segments the company wants to target with its product offering.

| Definition | The decision about which market segment(s) a company will focus on is known as **targeting**. |

The company can make a decision based on a concentration strategy, directing its marketing efforts towards a single market segment; or a differentiated strategy aimed at two or more market segments. Positioning is the final stage of the process.

| Definition | **Positioning** involves creating an image of the product or service in the minds of the customer that will form a central part of its promotional strategy. |

When the company has decided which segments to target, it must then meet the needs of those targeted customers with an appropriate marketing mix – a tangible mix of its products/services, place (where it is distributed), an attractive price – and promote it in a manner that will appeal to potential buyers. People will inevitably play a vital role in this process.

The InterContinental Hotel in Dublin, for example, has a target market that is primarily aimed at wealthy visitors to the capital. It is marketed as a luxurious, relaxing venue that provides individual customer service that is unparalleled in the industry.

Strategic Group Mapping

There is a close connection between segmentation, targeting and positioning on one hand, and strategic group mapping on the other. Segmentation, targeting and positioning is a response to customers' needs. Companies will make decisions on which market segments to focus on based on a number of factors, including their own strategic capability (see **Chapter 6**).

In examining the micro environment, it will become obvious that not all companies are alike in terms of size, market share, the range and quality of products, distribution channels, etc. This has implications in terms of assessing competition. Some companies will be direct competitors of a particular firm, while others will have little impact on it. Thus, when examining competition, the 'industry' is very often too large a concept to have any meaningful value. Therefore, the industry needs to be divided up by grouping together those players that possess similar characteristics and competitive approaches. They can then be analysed by way of strategic group mapping.

| Definition | A **Strategic group map** is a graphical depiction of the positioning of various companies competing within an industry. |

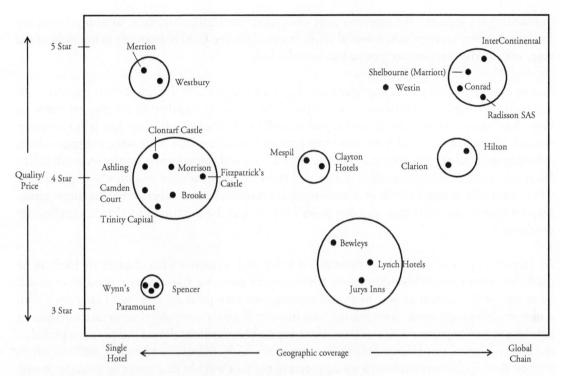

Figure 5.5 *A Strategic Group Map of Some of the Main Hotels in Dublin*

In positioning the rival firms, they can either be grouped together in a cluster or viewed separately, depending on the numbers involved.

There are many criteria for comparing companies, and by choosing different variables, an alternative competitive picture emerges. For that reason, the exercise is often repeated using various characteristics, resulting in a more comprehensive analysis. The analysis should be based on how the firms compete with one another, for example on price, product range, etc. Having chosen the most appropriate variables for comparison, the various strategic groups can be analysed on a two-dimensional chart (see **Figure 5.5**). Price/quality will often be chosen as one axis, while the other axis might represent, for example, product range or geographic coverage. The next stage is to examine all the companies operating in the industry and plot them on the chart according to the characteristics chosen. A circle is drawn around each one (or a group of rival companies when they display similar characteristics). The size of the circle should represent the size of market share that they possess in the industry. This will allow a quick, visual representation of the breakdown of the industry.

When selecting the variables for analysis, it is important to pick ones that are contrasting, otherwise the variables will be highly correlated along a diagonal axis on the map, and it will be of little value in analysing the industry. For example, price and quality are highly correlated, so with price on the x axis and quality on the y axis, it would result in a straight line from bottom left to top right of the map, with all the competitors grouped around the line.

Strategic group mapping is an important exercise in analysing where the real competition exists for any particular company. Those companies that are located close together on the map represent an immediate threat, while those located elsewhere will be of lesser significance. Just as importantly, strategic group mapping will show that some parts of the industry are more attractive than others, reflecting the level of competition in any one cluster. This will consequently impact on profitability. For a new entrant into the market, it may well show up opportunities to gain a strong foothold where competition may be weak or non-existent. It must also be remembered that a strategic group map represents the industry at any one point in time, but the situation can change significantly over time.

An important part of the analysis, therefore, is to try and anticipate what changes are likely to be made by competitors. This information is not easy to come by, but a certain amount of it will be in the public domain by way of annual reports, company press releases, radio interviews with senior executives and so on. Anticipating such moves will give a company time to take offensive or defensive action to protect their position. Another part of the analysis should include an appraisal of the different strategies of the various rival companies: which strategies are working well and which are not? A company that has been a strong player in the past will not necessarily be so in the future.

This will all be necessary in trying to understand the opportunities that potentially exist for a company. Such opportunities must also be looked at against a background of consumer needs, and ultimately the product or service being offered must meet the needs of the target group. These needs will also change over time. In any business, staying close to the customer and being aware of their needs is vital. Meeting these needs will also form the basis of the strategy being pursued by the company. For example, for the price-conscious customer, keeping costs down is a vital part of the company's strategy.

Key Success Factors

The importance of understanding customer needs was made above. These needs will differ between different segments. The relative importance that customers place on certain product/service features will also vary. Some will be considered essential, while other features will be of lesser significance. Thus, from a company's perspective, there must be a clear understanding of these features and their relative value among the target group.

Definition   **Key success factors** (also known as critical success factors) are the resources and competences required by an organisation to be successful in a competitive industry.

Key success factors (KSFs) are what separate the industry leaders from the minnows. KSFs will vary from one industry to another. For example, in the clothing industry, design and cost are of major significance, while in the food industry, branding and a strong distributive network are vital. When management have an understanding of the KSFs of the industry in which they are operating, they can gauge how well they are performing against the criteria which customers (and not the company) consider important. This analysis requires an understanding of the company's strategic capability and will be developed in the next chapter. Some of the most common types of KSFs include:

- Well-known brand name
- Range of products
- Customer service
- Supply chain management capabilities
- Quality control
- Skilled labour
- High utilisation of fixed assets
- Location (retail stores)
- Marketing skills
- Innovation in product design.

Generally, there are probably about three KSFs, and certainly no more than five, operating within a particular industry. It is, therefore, an essential part of strategic analysis that senior management identify the KSFs operating in their industry. It is obviously easier for companies to understand KSFs when dealing directly with their customers, rather than operating through intermediaries. It is the view of the ultimate consumer that is important. Companies must be conscious that their decisions are based on hard evidence, rather than assuming that they know best. Those decisions must also be based on what the customer is looking for rather than what is convenient for the company to provide. It should also be noted that KSFs will vary over time and managers need to be aware of these trends, and not stick rigidly to out-of-date assumptions.

The strategy being developed by the company should incorporate these KSFs in such a way that they form an integral part of their competitive approach. In comparing how one company is doing against its main rivals, Kim and Mauborgne (2002) advocate the use of what they term a "strategy canvas". This is a visual representation of how different companies compare against the KSFs of that industry. They argue that, rather than preparing large documents filled with detailed numbers and jargon, companies should instead build the process around a graphical representation of the key issues. Such a picture will yield better results. See **Figure 5.6** below.

According to Kim and Mauborgne, a strategy canvas assists in visualising a strategic plan and helps to understand the company's strategic positioning. It displays the following:

- Factors affecting competition among key industry players.
- Strategic profile of current competitors showing which factors they invest in.

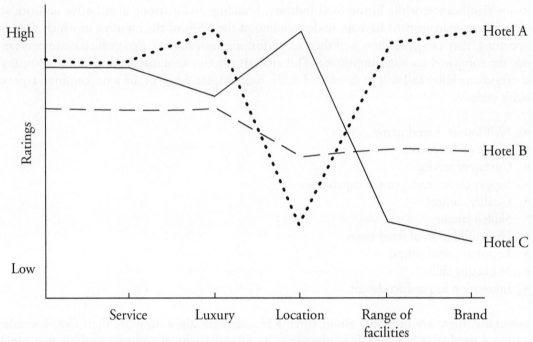

Figure 5.6 *A Strategy Canvas for Five-star Hotels*

Source: Adapted from Kim and Mauborgne (2002): "Charting your Company's Future": *Harvard Business Review*, Vol. 80, Issue 6, p.76–83

- It draws the company's strategic profile or value curve showing how it invests in the factors of competition and how it might do so in the future.

A strategy canvas assists the company to develop a clear focus on the areas in which it should concentrate when developing strategy. In particular, it shows where a company should distinguish itself from competition, rather than following others. In this way, it can develop uniqueness and stand apart, and may even create new ways of competing (e.g. Southwest Airlines began operating point-to-point travel between mid-size cities in the US rather than the traditional hub-and-spoke system).

A good strategy should also allow itself to be communicated clearly to customers. With Southwest Airlines, it is: "The speed of the plane at the price of a car." Southwest Airlines are a low-cost airline offering a basic, but inexpensive service.

The strategy canvas is a useful tool in visualising the type of strategy that an organisation might follow. Whether or not the organisation has the capability to pursue that strategy will be examined in **Chapter 6**. Care must therefore be taken when plotting a company's profile on a strategy canvas; it should be completed only after a thorough analysis of the company's strategic capability. In **Chapter 6**, we will also examine a competitive strength assessment, which in many ways is a similar exercise to the strategy canvas.

Opportunities and Threats

Throughout this chapter we have stated that the environment is constantly changing. Environment analysis must also be ongoing, both on a formal and informal basis. The purpose of such analysis is to identify the opportunities and the threats that exist. A key element in this analysis is not a listing of different factors, but an understanding of the implications that they have for a company.

Opportunities exist in many forms. The industry may be in its infancy with large growth potential, and regulatory factors may have opened up what was previously a closed shop. A company may have a well-known brand which places it in a strong position, or it could have a good deal of retained earnings that would enable it to make acquisitions, etc. Executives must also be on the lookout for opportunities wherever they exist. Very often, simple ideas can result in successful products or businesses, leaving other people wondering: "Why didn't I think of that?".

A company must also be mindful of threats. The competitive situation may have changed and become unfavourable – perhaps a large international player has come into the market, changing the dynamics. A downturn in the economy may make the entire industry vulnerable, particularly if the demand is elastic, such as in the tourism industry where a small increase in the cost of living can result in a big drop-off in demand for holidays as people struggle to buy the essential.

Threats can come from a whole range of sources. It is vital that management recognises the threats that exist – ignoring them will not make them go away. For single-business companies, it will be a case of trying to ride out the storm. For conglomerates, it may well mean deciding to exit a particular industry and concentrate on the other sectors in which it operates.

However, the existence of threats does not necessarily mean doom and gloom. What is important is how the company deals with them. The objective is to minimise the threats while capitalising on the opportunities. The next chapter will examine the competitive position of the organisation: the strengths and weaknesses and, together with the opportunities and threats, this completes the SWOT analysis. This analysis will subsequently dictate the choices that a company makes.

Illustration 5.5: Bord na Móna and its Changing Environment

Bord na Móna Plc is an Irish company that has recognised how the business environment has altered radically as a result of climate change. It was established in 1946 as a semi-state company to harvest peat, which at the time was an important source of fuel for heating homes and generating electricity. Two major factors have faced the company in recent years. First, the boglands that could be commercially harvested by the company have rapidly depleted. Secondly, and more importantly, the EU, and Ireland as a Member State, is moving towards low-carbon and zero-carbon sources of energy, such as wind farms. Peat bogs are now regarded as a vital resource in sequestering carbon dioxide from the atmosphere and thus will play a vital role in preventing climate change. Consequently, these bogs need to be protected.

As a result of these developments, Bord na Móna has been cutting back on peat harvesting and moving towards sustainable and renewable energy production. At the same time, it is mindful of its social obligations in that it employs a large number of people in peat harvesting in regions where there are few alternative sources of work available.

Since 1992, the company has opened a number of wind farms across the country – ultimately up to 9% of the company's land could be used for this purpose. In addition, it has established a 'waste to energy' plant at Drehid, County Kildare, which now produces energy to power up to 8,500 homes. The company is currently examining the potential of solar-power generation. Some of Bord na Móna's extensive landholding will be used for forestry, tourism and recreational use, though much of the land will have to be rehabilitated for its biodiversity potential. This is a complicated process, as the composition of each bog, its soil composition and water table vary considerably.

Though such developments are a marked change from the company's original purpose and objectives, the implications of climate change require a total change in how we use energy in all aspects of our lives. For Bord na Móna, such a paradigm shift could have been seen solely as a threat to its business model. Instead, it was grasped as an opportunity.

Source: Bord na Móna, 2019

The five illustrations in this chapter are typical of many companies in Ireland in terms of the challenges posed by a changing environment. It is, therefore, imperative that all organisations constantly monitor their environment, both from a macro and micro perspective, as the opportunities and threats that are identified are constantly evolving.

In Chinese, the symbol for crisis consists of two parts: danger and opportunity.

Figure 5.7 *Crisis: Danger and Opportunity*

Whether we determine something to be a crisis or an opportunity depends to a large extent on how we view things:

"For there is nothing either good or bad but thinking makes it so."

Hamlet, Act 2, Sc. 2

CONCLUSION

Even in times of recession, there are opportunities for companies to exploit. However, each company must be in a position to identify those opportunities, ideally before rival companies can spot them. Environmental scanning is, therefore, a vital part of the strategic management process. Circumstances are constantly changing, sometimes slowly, and sometimes major events can happen very quickly. Either way, managers must be constantly observing both the external environment within which they operate and interpreting how events will impact on their company. With many of these factors, managers will have very little direct control over them. On the other hand, they have control over how they act and, by taking appropriate action, they can minimise threats and position their company to take advantage of any opportunities. Monitoring the environment is a subjective process and managerial experience plays an important part in how events are interpreted. This judgement is built up over time. Thus, an important part of the process is creating a culture within the organisation where all these factors can be openly discussed and lessons learned from past experience.

SUMMARY

The **macro environment** examines what is happening generally in the global and national environment. There are many different **trading blocs** operating around the world, with the **European Union** of greatest interest to this country in terms of regulations, as well as providing a market of over 508 million people (this number includes the UK). The EU has been of huge benefit to Ireland in many ways. **Porter's Diamond** looks at how different countries develop a competitive advantage. It examines competitiveness under four headings: factor conditions; demand conditions; related and supporting industries; and firm strategy, structure and rivalry.

The **PESTEL framework** examines the political, economic, social, technological, environmental and legal factors that will impact on an industry. They are all inter-related and will vary in terms of importance. Some may have little or no relevance; others will be central to the organisation's competitiveness. It must also be stressed that they are not static and in some cases will be quite dynamic, particularly economic factors. Trying to predict the future can be difficult where there is a great amount of uncertainty. The use of scenario planning offers a way of determining how the business environment might develop in the future.

The **micro environment** considers all of the factors that affect a specific industry and is of immediate concern to any particular company. There are a number of issues that need to be examined, including:

- The **industry's economic structure** – an overall view of the attractiveness of the industry.
- **Five Forces Analysis** – Porter's model examines five competitive forces at play in an industry. They include the threat of new entrants, rivalry among existing firms, the threat of substitute products, the bargaining power of buyers and suppliers. These all put a limit on the amount of profit a company can make. Competition also depends on the stage at which the industry is at in its life cycle.
- **Industry driving forces** are described as those changes taking place that are altering the fundamental nature and competition of that industry. As such, they will have a significant impact on the future success of a company. These factors, such as globalisation, will have to be identified.
- Not all companies are alike in terms of size, market share, the range and quality of products, distribution channels, etc. This has implications in terms of assessing competition. **Strategic group mapping** is a technique for displaying market or competitive positions that rival firms occupy in the industry.
- **Market segmentation** is the process by which diverse customers in a large market are divided into smaller groups that have similar needs. There are many segmentation variables that can be used such as age, sex, occupation, ethnic grouping, family size, life-cycle stage, etc.
- **Key success factors** are the resources and competences required by an organisation to be successful in a competitive industry. Generally there are about three or four and include factors such as brand names, supply chain capabilities, skilled labour and many more.

Environmental analysis must be ongoing, both on a formal and informal basis, in order to identify the **opportunities** and **threats** that exist. A key element in this analysis is not only a listing of different factors, but understanding the implications that they have for a company.

DISCUSSION QUESTIONS

1. Explore the relevance of understanding the macro environment in formulating strategy.
2. Discuss the use of scenarios in strategic planning.
3. Critically analyse the role of Porter's Five Forces in understanding the competitive environment of an organisation.
4. Taking an industry of your choice, explore the nature of the driving forces that are impacting upon it.
5. Evaluate the use of strategic group mapping as a tool for analysing competition.
6. The identification of key success factors is a vital part of environmental analysis. Discuss how an organisation can use this knowledge to gain competitive advantage.

Evaluating an Organisation's Strategic Capability

LEARNING OBJECTIVES

On completion of this chapter, you will be able to:

- Evaluate a company's tangible and intangible resources
- Analyse an organisation's basic and core competences
- Assess the level of knowledge management within a company
- Critically examine the value chain and wider value system
- Undertake a review of a company's strengths and weaknesses

"Make your life an affirmation, defined by your ideals, not the negation of others. Dare to the level of your capability then go beyond to a higher level."

General Alexander Haig, US Secretary of State 1981–1982

INTRODUCTION

The previous chapter looked at the external factors affecting an organisation. The primary purpose of such analysis was to identify the opportunities and threats in the business environment. In order to avail of any such opportunities, the organisation must have the necessary strategic capability. Except in the case of start-up companies, there will be an existing strategy in place, and it is important to review that strategy to see if it is achieving the strategic goals set in its existing strategic plan. While some aspects of the existing plan will change, inevitably much of it can remain. This chapter is concerned with analysing the capability of a firm to achieve its strategic goals, and provide management with an understanding of how best to get there.

First, it is necessary to examine the resources available to a firm. These include human resources, physical resources, financial resources and intangible resources. While such resources are essential, on their own they are of little benefit – it is how they are co-ordinated and utilised by an organisation that is important. The next stage in the process, therefore, is to examine the competences with which a company uses those resources. It is the mixture of an organisation's resources and competences that define its capability and what separates a superior company from a mediocre one.

In a competitive environment, all organisations must be concerned with their costs. Analysing costs is an integral part of understanding strategic capability. The value chain, and the wider value network, will assist in this process. In the final analysis, the strategic capability of any company is relative, and so we must compare performance with rival companies. This can be done with the use of a competitor strength analysis. Having carried out this analysis, management are in a position to fully understand the organisation's strengths and weaknesses. Together with the identification of the opportunities and threats from the last chapter, this completes the SWOT analysis and allows management to position the company strategically.

Carrying out a critical evaluation of an organisation's internal capability is an essential element of formulating strategy. It is also very difficult, as it requires the organisation to view itself in an objective manner. There will inevitably be vested interests involved that will lead to a more subjective rather than objective appraisal. The use of the strategic tools described in this chapter should ensure that such bias is kept to a minimum. Such analysis should focus the attention of management on the areas of most need. The strategic goals and objectives for an organisation have been set, and management must now ensure that they utilise all its resources in an efficient and effective manner so that those goals and objectives can be achieved. The strategic capability of an organisation is ultimately dependent on its resources and competences.

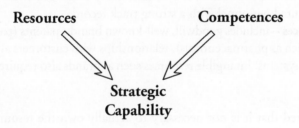

Figure 6.1 *Strategic Capability*

RESOURCES

The first stage of an internal analysis is a **resource audit**, examining all of the resources, both tangible and intangible, within an organisation. While it is necessary to examine all of the resources, the process is much more than just a listing of them. Ultimately, what is important is the value that they add to an organisation. The resources can be broken down into five main headings:

- **Human resources** – it is so often said by companies that their employees are their most important asset. For many firms it is little more than rhetoric, and yet the reality is that staff are vital to the success of any organisation. As Ireland moves further into what Drucker (1954) referred to as the "knowledge economy" and companies move higher up the value chain, people will become even more important. One significant difference with human resources compared to other resources is that the company does not own the people who work for it. Irrespective of employment contracts, it is relatively easy for employees to leave and join rival companies. As a result, careful consideration must be given to HR policies to make the organisation an attractive place to work for employees at every level of the organisation, and this needs to be supported by the culture of the organisation.

- **Physical resources** – includes buildings, plant, machinery, transport fleet, etc. There are a number of factors that need to be considered when examining such assets – their age, overall condition, location (buildings, for example, are specific to one particular location, which may or may not be an advantage). Their lifespan also needs to be taken into account. Perhaps the most important thing when considering physical resources is to examine their production capability, not just for present requirements, but also their future potential.

- **Business intelligence systems** – in recent years, there have been enormous advances in business intelligence systems and cloud computing. Such systems are now an integral part of the resources of companies and can provide them with a considerable strategic advantage. Such systems must allow them to fully integrate and utilise all other resources. With regard to personal data, the General Data Protection Regulation (GDPR) has introduced stricter requirements as to how and why such data is used and stored (see **Chapter 7**).

- **Financial resources** – such resources include the company's capital structure, retained earnings and other cash, debtors and creditors, as well as its relationship with its shareholders and bankers. Most options will involve substantial financial investment, and so financial resources are particularly important. Once finance is available, many of the other resources can be obtained, such as hiring talented personnel with a strong track record.

- **Intangible resources** – includes goodwill, well-known brands, patents (particularly important in some industries such as pharmaceuticals), relationships with customers and customer databases, as well as business systems. Intangible resources such as brands also require considerable financial investment.

It must be remembered that it is not necessary to actually own the resources. Many companies will only ever lease the physical resources that they need. In other instances, companies may sell the property and equipment and then lease them back, thus freeing up cash for investing in and developing the business. Lynch (2008:126) believes:

> "It is useful to explore the reasons for an organisation to possess and use any resources beyond the minimum amount to stay in existence. Arguably, in an efficient market, there will be outside, more specialised suppliers that will be able to sell some activities more cheaply to the organisation than it can make them for themselves."

Outsourcing some value chain activities is becoming more common. Benetton, the Italian clothing company, outsources much of its production to a network of small local producers. Similarly, Nike outsources production of its footware and apparel, but does so to developing countries. In the 1990s there was widespread concern among customers in relation to the working conditions in certain 'sweatshop' factories used by the company, which led to a very damaging consumer boycott of Nike goods (Crane and Matten, 2016).

As a company grows in size, the amount of resources it has will also grow. Having resources somewhere in the firm is not enough. They have to be deployed where they are most needed and, consequently, flexibility is a very important aspect that needs to be considered, particularly with regard to the workforce. Given the huge level of investment in resources, it is imperative that an organisation gains maximum efficiency in their use. It must also be remembered that many resources can be easily imitated by competitors and so, on their own, resources will not give a company a sustainable competitive advantage. The next stage, therefore, is to examine the competences of the organisation.

COMPETENCES

Prahalad and Hamel (1990) first coined the term 'core competence' in their *Harvard Business Review* article: "The Core Competence of the Corporation". They believed that "competitiveness derives from an ability to build, at lower cost and more speedily than competitors, the core competences that spawn unanticipated products". They regard core competences as the 'collective learning' in the organisation – the co-ordination of diverse production skills and integration of multiple streams of technology. It is about the organisation of work (particularly working across boundaries involving people at all levels and functions) and the delivery of value. In that sense they transcend business boundaries, such as SBUs, and allow a company to operate in what appear to be diverse areas. Canon, for example, has core competences in optics, imaging and microprocessor controls that has enabled it to succeed in diverse areas such as copiers, laser printers, cameras and image scanners.

The physical assets of any organisation deteriorate over time. However, core competences develop as they are applied and shared throughout an organisation, provided that those competences are nurtured by an organisation. They are built up over a long period of time, perhaps a decade or so, and this involves a process of continuous improvement; what the Japanese refer to as *Kaizen*.

According to Prahalad and Hamel, there are three tests to identify core competences. First, that they provide potential access to a variety of markets. Second, in terms of the end user, it should make a significant impact in terms of perceived benefit. Third, it should be difficult for competitors to copy the core competence. The above example of Canon fits all three criteria: they operate in a variety of different markets; their products are of very high quality and represent good value for the consumer; and it will be difficult for competitors to replicate its processes.

Similarly, Honda has built a whole range of products, from cars and motorcycles to lawn mowers and chainsaws, from its competence in engine technology.

The building of core competences requires a strategic decision about where to build competence leadership within the organisation. This can often be built up through strategic alliances, as many Japanese companies have clearly done. Tesco has developed a core competence in managing customer information and using that information to guide the company in making decisions about what products to sell in its stores (see **Illustration 13.1** in **Chapter 13**).

Every organisation will naturally have to have a basic competence in all of the activities that it performs across its value chain.

Definition A **basic competence** should be seen as the minimum level of competence required to satisfy customers' requirements.

In a competitive environment, these basic competences are clearly not sufficient to support a leadership position in its chosen markets. Therefore, the company will have to develop core competences in one or more areas of their activities. As the company develops experience in different aspects of its business, it will build on the competences it has and develop them into a core competence.

Definition A **core competence** is an activity that the company has developed into a specialised activity that gives it a competitive advantage in that field.

Core competences will play a central part in the company's strategy and future development. Over time, core competences can, of course, be copied by rival companies, thus eroding any competitive advantage. For many years, Volvo had a core competence for safety that gave them a strong competitive advantage. Now, many other car manufacturers such as Toyota, Renault, BMW, Mercedes, etc., have cars that are just as safe as Volvo's.

Wernerfelt (1984) was the first to discuss the importance of examining the strategic capability of a company from the perspective of its resources and the concept was further developed and popularised by Barney (1991). As with many management theories, the original ideas go through a number of further iterations. Johnson *et al.* (2017:101) suggest that there are four grounds for sustaining competitive advantage: value, rarity, inimitability and organisational support, known by the acronym 'VRIO'.

- **Value** – as in the value of a company's resources and capabilities. Such value must be of importance to a company's customers and at a price they are willing to pay. This will enable the company to take advantage of market opportunities.
- **Rarity** – if a company has rare resources or capabilities that are valued by its customers it will inevitably give it a competitive advantage that can be sustained over the long term. Restricted access to raw materials can confer such advantage, e.g. the use of nickel in the electronics industry. Patents are also important, particularly for pharmaceutical companies, to protect large investments in R&D. In reality, however, businesses will not normally be able to sustain such rarity for long, as rivals will likely develop other sources of supply and/or capabilities.
- **Inimitability** – how difficult is it to imitate the competences of another company? The low-cost model employed by Ryanair cannot be protected by a patent, and other low-cost airlines follow similar strategies, though none to the extent of Ryanair. With Ryanair, such practices are embedded in the linkages of its value chain and in its corporate culture. It is, in fact, very difficult to compete with Ryanair on a cost basis. While such practices can be identified, their full extent is often hard to discern and comprehend. This is what King (2007) refers to as 'causal ambiguity'.

- **Organisational support** – having a product or service of value to customers that requires rare resources and is inimitable is important for sustainable advantage, but it also requires the company to put support systems in place, such as IT systems, highly trained personnel, etc., that will allow it to exploit the other three factors to their full extent.

CAPABILITIES

It is a combination of resources and competences that give an organisation its strategic capability. It is with this capability that a company can take advantage of the opportunities that have been identified. Just as key success factors will change over time, it is important to realise that the capabilities required for market leadership will also evolve as the business environment changes. When examining the capabilities of an organisation, it is important that they are viewed from the perspective of the customer. If there is no customer willing to buy a company's products or services, then such capabilities are of little use. These capabilities can be found throughout an organisation, and so a functional analysis can be of benefit to identify areas where the organisation is performing particularly well.

Human Resource Management

Organisations do not create strategies – it is the people within those organisations that do. Having talented managers and employees is of vital importance to every organisation. However, their presence alone is not enough – what is important is how they work together to achieve organisational objectives. In terms of capability, it begins with leadership, both in terms of setting the vision and achieving objectives. Being able to pick the right people for the job is in itself a key competence, which involves not just having the right skills and experience but also being able to blend new employees into the existing team. Leadership also involves creating and supporting the culture within which people will work together in a productive manner. Leadership at every level is important, from the CEO down to front-line supervisors.

In examining the capability of people in an organisation to support its strategy, it is important to conduct such an analysis against the background of the culture that exists within that organisation. It can be difficult to fully understand the culture of an organisation, particularly for a manager joining the company from outside. Yet, it is essential to gain such an understanding in order to appraise the ability of the staff to support strategy. Johnson *et al.* (2017:175) refer to the '**cultural web**' as a means of understanding the culture that exists within an organisation. The cultural web involves examining the paradigm of the organisation – how it sees itself and the world around it. It also involves examining the organisational structures, power structures, control systems, rituals and routines, stories and its symbols. By analysing all of these elements, not just individually but collectively, a picture can be built up of the company's culture and whether it is likely to help or hinder a particular strategy.

In terms of capability, it is also important to understand the power structures at play as this will ultimately dictate what can be achieved. The adaptability of the people in the organisation is a crucial element in its ability to meet the changing needs of markets. It forms a central part of the ability to lead and manage change (this will be discussed later in **Chapter 14**). The growth in the diversity of the Irish workforce has brought with it challenges as well as opportunities. Most organisations are constantly looking at means of reducing staff costs by introducing automation. HR remains perhaps the most important function in relation to organisational capability as, with the right staff on board, everything becomes possible in terms of achieving strategic intent. According to the Organisation for Economic Co-operation and Development (OECD), Irish workers are among the most productive in the world. However, further investigation by the Central Statistics Office (CSO) draws a sharp distinction between the high levels of productivity achieved in foreign-owned multinational companies and the domestic sector where productivity tends to be lower (Burke-Kennedy, 2019).

Finance

There are a number of issues that have to be looked at in terms of financial capability (Ward, 2014). In most cases, strategic decisions are likely to require significant funding, and decisions have to be made with regard to the source of capital. Most organisations use a mixture of debt, equity and retained earnings to fund major strategic projects. There are advantages and disadvantages to each. For example, the interest on debt is tax deductible, but it also increases financial risk. The debt has to be repaid irrespective of the fortunes of the company. Sometimes such finance may be difficult to raise, particularly for small businesses, and there will be a certain level beyond which the risk increases substantially.

On the other hand, the issue of shares (whether to new investors or through a rights issue) does not carry financial risk to the company but is more expensive. This is due to the cost involved in the of issuing shares; dividend payment by the company is not tax deductible (unlike debt interest); and the fact that such shares (and dividend payment) are long term in nature, while most debt is paid off relatively quickly thus finishing interest payments. Retained earnings (profits accumulated over past years), if such exist, are an alternative way of financing projects. The overall cost of capital must be considered when evaluating the options using the weighted average cost of capital.

There is an opportunity cost involved in financing projects, in that once the funds have been committed to a project, those funds are not then available for other opportunities that might arise. Consequently, an important capability is being able to appraise the various options available and pick the optimum one for the company. Return on capital employed, payback period and discounted cash flow analysis are all techniques which are used to evaluate strategic options, and these will be discussed in **Chapter 12**. Managing cash flow is a vital financial skill, and problems with cash flow are all too often the reason why companies go into liquidation. Product lines and customers must also be screened to see where the company is making money and where the costs exceed the value.

Debtors must be constantly examined to ensure that they are paying on time. In recessionary times, many debtors will try to extend credit for as long as possible. Worse, there is a danger that some debtors' companies may go out of business, leaving large amounts of money outstanding and unsecured. The collapse of the British construction company Carillion in January 2018 left debts of £900 million and a pension deficit of £587 million. The closure had an immediate impact on 30,000, sub-contractors and suppliers, most of whom were small companies who could ill-afford such losses. This had a direct knock-on effect on the viability of suppliers, including some in Ireland

(Chapman, 2018). Even where a company is eventually getting paid by its debtors, it is important to remember that while the company may be profitable overall, any delay in debtors' payment could result in short-term insolvency and an inability to meet day-to-day liabilities, such as staff wages and electricity bills.

Costs cannot be controlled unless they can be identified. It is, therefore, essential that every company fully understands where all its costs are incurred. Management information systems play a vital part in providing such information. The use of the value chain (see below) can be used as a framework to examine where a company incurs its costs.

Marketing Concept

According to Dibb *et al.* (2006:17), the **marketing concept** is "a philosophy that an organisation should try to provide products that satisfy customers' needs through a co-ordinated set of activities that also allows the organisation to achieve its goals".

It has been said that marketing is too important to be left to *just* the marketers. Marketing is a way of thinking that covers all aspects of the organisation, and everything the organisation does must be market-focused. Without customers, there is no future for the business. There are many skills involved. First, a company needs to understand the market and customers' requirements. Sometimes this involves developing products for which customers have not yet identified a need. It also requires an ability to successfully segment the market, target and position the company. Developing the 'Five Ps' – product, price, place (distribution), promotion and people – is central to satisfying customers. In a competitive environment, building up and supporting brands is an essential element in separating companies and is directly tied in with the reputation of the company. Brands are capable of creating huge value for the company.

At the heart of any marketing function should be the customer. Over half a century ago, Peter Drucker (1954) identified the importance of the customer in *The Practice of Management* in which he stated that "a company's primary responsibility is to serve its customers... Profit is not the primary goal, but rather an essential condition for the company's continued existence". This approach is echoed by Martin (2010) who believes that the concept of maximising value for shareholders is inherently flawed and that shareholders actually do better when firms put the customers first. He believes that a better approach is to make customer value the top priority, and this in turn generates greater shareholder returns. He cites Johnson & Johnson and Procter & Gamble as examples of companies that have succeeded by putting customer value as their main focus. Staying close to the customer is an important part of customer value as it ensures that the company's products and services meet the needs of its customers.

Some companies deal directly with customers without the use of intermediaries, such as retail shops. One big advantage (apart from cost reduction) is that these companies can get direct feedback about what their customers *actually* want. For example, when people buy a Dell computer online, they can customise the specifications for that computer, adding in or leaving out components as required. This gives Dell a very accurate picture of what customers truly value in terms of its products and

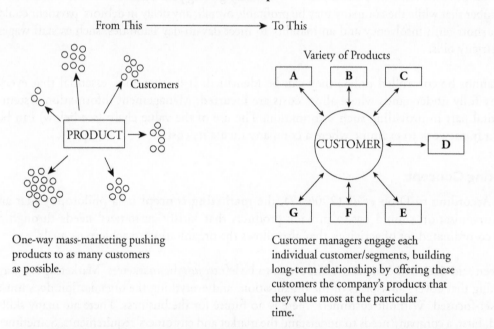

Product – Customer Relationship

From This ⟶ To This

One-way mass-marketing pushing
products to as many customers
as possible.

Customer managers engage each
individual customer/segments, building
long-term relationships by offering these
customers the company's products that
they value most at the particular
time.

Source: Adapted from: Rust *et al.* (2010) "Rethinking Marketing", *Harvard Business Review*, Vol 88, Issue 1, p. 96

Figure 6.2 *Product–Customer Relationship*

the items that those customers are willing to pay for. This information also plays an important part in Dell's research and development.

Rust *et al.* (2010) suggest that the focus on the customer requires a strategic shift within the organisation, with the customer rather than the product placed in the centre.

What is needed, they argue, is for the creation of a new position of chief customer officer, reporting directly to the CEO, but senior to all product/brand managers. The primary purpose of the chief customer officer is to engage individual customers or to narrow customer segments in two-way communications, building long-term relationships by promoting whichever of the company's products the customer would value most at any given time.

They propose new metrics for measuring the effectiveness of a customer-driven strategy. First there is a need to move the focus from product profitability to customer profitability. Secondly, pay greater attention not to current sales but to the customer lifetime value (the potential future profits that will come from a satisfied customer). Thirdly, the focus should move from brand equity (the value of a brand) to customer equity (the sum of the lifetime value of customers). Customer equity is also a good proxy for the value of the firm. Fourthly, the company should pay less attention to market share and more attention to customer equity share (the value of the company's customer base divided by the total value of the customers in the market).

The information required by the organisation needs to be tracked at a number of levels, from the individual to the aggregate market level which, in turn, will require very close integration of the IT function within the organisation. Such transformation clearly needs to be driven from the top down.

Operations

The operations of a company are the means by which inputs are converted into outputs, and are at the heart of every organisation, whether in manufacturing or services. Such operations have to be carried out efficiently (achieving objectives using the least amount of resources necessary) and effectively (ensuring that the organisation is pursuing the correct objectives). The use of technology plays a very important part, and decisions have to be made about the level of technology and its cost vis-à-vis the cost of labour. This is complicated by the rate of change in technology development. Companies such as Toyota have made enormous savings by the development of what is termed 'lean production' techniques.

There are a number of major decisions that have to be made. The first is whether to make or buy. Some activities should be done in-house, while other activities can be safely outsourced. Nike has outsourced its production and is effectively a very successful marketing company that has created a lifestyle image that people buy into.

Other decisions include how to manufacture and where. Relationships with suppliers are very important, particularly for companies such as Dell, who rely heavily on just-in-time management to minimise inventory costs. Product design and the design of the production process itself are also central to the issue of costs. While there are differences between services and manufacturing, many of the principles overlap.

These days, outsourcing is an integral part of many companies' operations and it has several advantages. However, it is important that the relationship between the company and its contractors is managed very carefully to ensure quality. It also has important ethical considerations in terms of the possible exploitation of labour by contracted companies (with regard to corporate social responsibility and outsourcing, see below under **Supply Chain Transparency**).

Research and Development

With product life cycles getting ever shorter, it is imperative that companies invest in R&D. It has been stated already that not enough money is being spent on R&D in this country in order to be competitive in a global market. The first decision, therefore, is the commitment to spending on R&D. Thereafter it requires making decisions on what areas to invest in. There will be many areas that can show potential, but not enough finance to support them all. Decisions will be required as to which areas to champion. Innovation is the life blood of any organisation and it requires a different way of thinking and a culture that supports it. As Albert Einstein put it:

"The significant problems we face cannot be solved at the same level of thinking we were at when we created the problem."

Business Intelligence

Throughout this textbook, the importance of business intelligence is a constant theme. Information systems must be thought of not as an optional extra, but as an integral component of the strategic framework that supports competitive advantage in any organisation. It follows then that any discussion on strategic capability has to examine the information systems of the company to see how it creates value for both the company and the customer. This can be achieved in a variety of different ways, from the use of data mining as a means of increasing sales, to control systems to minimise costs in the system. Yield management, which will be discussed later in this chapter, relies heavily on the use of business intelligence. Business intelligence is also a vital element in the quality of decisions made by managers. Various types of decision support systems are examined in **Chapter 12**.

Ireland has produced world-class companies that develop business intelligence systems and, given the peripheral nature of this island, e-business applications play an essential role in connecting Irish companies with their customers both at home and all around the world. This can be a major contributor to operational efficiency, productivity and customer service.

The above section has examined the various functional areas where capability might be located. There are two main capabilities that bring together, and underpin, all of those parts, and these need to be considered in developing an understanding of capability in the organisation: knowledge management and cost competitiveness.

KNOWLEDGE MANAGEMENT

The concept of the 'knowledge economy' was mentioned above. As Ireland moves further into the knowledge economy, how companies manage knowledge will be of great importance in developing a competitive advantage. Indeed, some organisations, such as accounting firms, rely almost exclusively on the development of organisational knowledge.

 Organisational knowledge is the knowledge, values, understanding and experience that has been built up throughout an organisation over a period of time.

There are certain challenges in how organisational knowledge is managed, particularly as the organisation grows and develops into more and more divisions. Information technology has made the sharing and use of knowledge much easier, but is still dependent on the goals that management has set with regard to knowledge sharing. At GE, it is a central goal for each manager to share knowledge gained through the operation of their strategic business unit with other parts of the organisation (Welch, 2001).

Knowledge can be shared in different ways. According to Nonaka and Takeuchi (1995), there is a difference between 'explicit' and 'tacit' knowledge. **Explicit knowledge** is expressed knowledge that is contained, for example, in standard operating procedure (SOP) manuals and texts. Franchise operations such as McDonald's depend on a replication of such standardised procedures in all outlets, and this is achieved through strict reference to such manuals. The development of SOPs can be time-consuming and costly, but they ensure that all parts of the organisation are in tune. The danger is that rival firms can obtain these manuals and gain an understanding of how the company is operated, or just replicate the same procedures. While there are ethical issues involved, it would be naive to believe that such practice does not happen.

Implicit knowledge, on the other hand, is knowledge that people possess, but is not expressed in any formal way. In the course of their work, professional people, for example, will build up an enormous volume of knowledge that will inform their judgement and decision-making. A barrister doing a cross-examination in court will base questions on a mixture of the knowledge of the law built up over the years, along with their experience of previous cases, and what the witness has already said. It would be extremely difficult to codify such knowledge.

The organisation needs to put in place mechanisms for the sharing of as much information as possible so that as many people as possible benefit from it. With explicit knowledge, it is relatively easy in that this can be written down in books, manuals and policy procedures. For implicit knowledge, it is more difficult and relies on a social process within the organisation. This takes many forms. In the above example of a lawyer, a newly qualified barrister is obliged to spend a year devilling (acting as an understudy) with an experienced colleague.

In a similar way, trainee doctors will shadow consultants doing their rounds in hospital wards. In both cases, it presents an opportunity to observe and ask questions and develop knowledge that would be very difficult to gain solely from books. Training seminars and in-house development programmes also provide an opportunity for people to mix together and share information. Ultimately, the value of the firm in terms of knowledge is the cumulative value of the knowledge of its entire workforce.

Information technology plays a pivotal role in how knowledge is managed within the organisation, and many companies are developing knowledge management systems (KMS) to assist them in managing organisational learning. According to O'Brien and Marakas (2008:63), knowledge management systems facilitate organisational learning and knowledge creation. In many cases, organisations have more than sufficient information to enable them to make decisions. The problem for most, however, is providing that information in a form that is both useful and timely. Systems include internet and intranet websites, data mining, knowledge bases and online discussion groups.

COST COMPETITIVENESS

Central to the concept of capability is cost competitiveness, which covers every single aspect of an organisation. The human resource – the employees – must be able to generate revenue that justifies their salaries. Production costs must be kept in line. In selling products or services, it must be done at a price that customers are willing to pay and still allows the firm to make a profit. Managers have to be able to control costs and to do it on a continuous basis to achieve a competitive advantage. Information technology is playing an increasing role in enabling managers to identify where the costs are being incurred and thus take targeted measures to reduce those costs. Johnson *et al.* (2018) state that attention must be paid to **cost drivers** in order to manage costs effectively:

- **Economies of scale** In situations where there are high capital costs, these need to be recovered over a high volume of output. Some industries traditionally require economies of scale to be profitable, including chemical and car manufacturing.
- **Capacity utilisation** Similar to benefits of economies of scale, if a company is able to operate at or near full capacity, it can lower unit costs by spreading the fixed costs over a larger number of units. This is essential for airlines and hotels, where the product is 'perishable', i.e. if a particular flight is only 70% booked the revenue potential of the remaining 30% is lost forever. (Yield management is discussed in more detail later in this chapter.)
- **Supply costs** Just-in-time manufacturing reduces overall costs by minimising the costs involved in supplying the necessary components. Scale is an important factor as well, in that companies buying in large quantities can negotiate more favourable prices. Location is also an important factor. Some manufacturing requires being located close to the raw materials because of the cost of transportation. Sheffield in England became synonymous with stainless steel as it was located next to plentiful supplies of coal and iron ore, both of which were required in the manufacturing process.
- **Product and process design** Streamlining product and process design can generate substantial savings. In the coming decade, there are likely to be enormous changes in product and process design with the greater use of AI. This will result in much greater automation, potentially making many existing jobs redundant. Such technology can also operate on a 24-hour basis. Many industries have already seen significant changes to process and product design. In banking, for example, ATM machines have provided a 24-hour cash-dispensing service for many decades and, more recently, the move to internet banking also provides a full 24-hour banking service without the need for expensive high-street real estate, and with greatly reduced levels of staffing.
- **Experience** The 'Experience Curve' describes how an organisation can reduce costs as it gains experience in whatever field it operates. As it gains this experience, it can operate in a more efficient manner and a shorter timeframe.
- **Culture** Organisational culture can play a big part in reducing costs in companies following a low-cost leadership position (see **Chapter 8**), where cost reduction becomes embedded in its culture.

VALUE CHAIN ANALYSIS

This chapter has already examined the capability of the organisation under each of the functional headings, such as HRM, finance, etc., but understanding this capability requires an holistic view of all of these functional areas *working together* to see where value can be created. Managers also need to understand *how* such value is created. Porter (1985) developed the concept of the 'value chain' to describe the activities of an organisation that are linked together to create value. It was originally designed to understand costs from an accounting perspective, but Porter suggested that it had wider application as a strategic tool. It enables managers to look at each part of the organisation to see where value is being created and, more importantly, to understand the linkages between the different parts. It is a generic tool in that it can be applied to any business, whether manufacturing or service, and adjusted to meet the needs of a specific company, with some parts being more relevant than others.

As shown in **Figure 6.3**, the value chain can be divided into two main parts: primary activities and support activities.

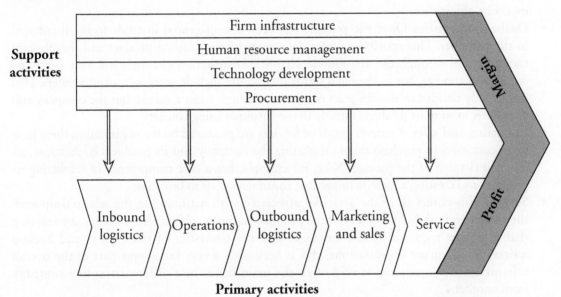

Source: Adapted from Michael E. Porter, *Competitive Advantage: Creating and Sustaining Superior Performance*, New York, The Free Press, 1985

Figure 6.3 *The Value Chain*

The **primary activities** consist of:

- **Inbound logistics** This is concerned with how the organisation interacts with, and receives goods from, its suppliers, as well as the inspection of those goods to ensure appropriate quality. It also covers all internal handling and inventory management as the goods are stored and distributed to the operations division when they are needed. Companies such as Toyota have a very close relationship with their suppliers, ensuring just-in-time delivery of all necessary stock. The company knows exactly what parts are needed and, through electronic data interchange (EDI), so does the relevant supplier. The components are then dispatched immediately, replacing those that have been drawn from the company's internal stores. Only the bare minimum amount of stock is in the system at any one time, thus ensuring that costs are kept as low as possible for both the supplier and for Toyota.

- **Operations** This is the heart of the organisation – where inputs are turned into outputs. It includes assembly, production, testing, packaging and getting the product or service ready for the customer. By carefully organising the operations, the firm can manage cost without impacting on the value obtained by the end user. For Dell, this means the assembly of the computer according to the specification requested by the customer. Nike outsources its production to manufacturing companies in Asia. For Nike, 'operations' is more concerned with controlling the relationship with its subcontractors, rather than being directly involved in the manufacturing process itself. Perhaps the biggest change in operations in most industries is the greater use of technology in automating many processes, and in providing real-time information on how to maximise efficiencies.
- **Outbound logistics** Once the product has been manufactured it needs to be distributed to the customer. This activity includes the storage of the finished product and the physical transportation through the distribution channel. Distribution channels will vary from one industry to another, but in the retail sector they would include wholesalers and retailers. Dell has recently decided to distribute its computers through select retailers, but the company still distributes most of its products directly to the customer using couriers.
- **Marketing and sales** Whatever goods or services are produced by the organisation there have to be customers to purchase them. Marketing the company and its products is, therefore, an essential element of the process. Nike, for example, has a core competence in marketing its products and creating a lifestyle image that consumers want to buy into.
- **Service** This covers all of the activities associated with maintaining the relationship with the customer, both before and after the product has been sold. It also includes any training that might be required by the customer and the provision of spare parts and backup assistance. For many organisations, this is becoming a very important part of the overall offering to customers, and is very often the main factor that differentiates one company from another.

By examining each of the primary activities, the organisation can see where value is created. Each of the primary activities is, in turn, assisted by the four **support activities**, which are:

- **Procurement** Many organisations will have a dedicated department for procuring all of the resources needed by all of the primary activities. It will source these resources at the best price from suitable suppliers and it covers everything from spare parts for production machines to paper for office printers.
- **Technology development** New products are the lifeline of every organisation as it adapts to changing circumstances. R&D and product design are integral to all parts of the value chain. (New product development will be discussed in detail in **Chapter 9**.) When Porter originally developed the value chain concept, technology played a comparatively minor support role. In the intervening decades, technology – particularly IT systems – have radically transformed the importance of this secondary activity into being an essential support mechanism for capitalising on all elements of the entire value chain.
- **Human resource management** This chapter has already covered the importance of human resources to the organisation. Every part of the company will need suitable employees from those involved in procurement to after-sales service. These must be recruited, selected, trained and

integrated into the organisation. Given the high costs associated with staff turnover, suitable staff must also be retained and rewards systems must be put in place to support their retention.

- **Firm's infrastructure** This section includes everything from the structure and control mechanisms in the organisation to finance, administration, and the IT systems required to support all aspects of a company.

On the right-hand side of **Figure 6.3** is the margin or profit that the company makes. The outer line is the end-price to the customer and the inner line represents the totality of the costs to the organisation. The difference is obviously the profit margin. To increase this margin, the outer line could be moved further to the right, to increase the selling price. In a competitive environment, this is very often not a feasible option. The alternative is to move the inner line further to the left, i.e. reduce costs.

By using the value chain, organisations can look at the various activities, both primary and secondary, to see where value is being created. It focuses management's attention on not just the different parts of the organisation but, just as importantly, on the **linkages** between those parts. The importance of linkages within the organisation cannot be overstated. It is imperative that the organisation is acting in a unified manner, with the customer at the centre of its focus. Kanter (2008) highlights the importance of being able to respond quickly and creatively to opportunities. This requires the co-ordination of all elements and business processes of the organisation, using various systems from common core values to IT platforms. Obviously, the focus on costs is very important, and by examining each component managers can isolate the costs for each activity, which supports the process of activity-based costing. These costs can then be compared to industry averages. The value chain for each company will differ due to the way each one is configured and how they perform each activity. These differences will further evolve over time. Later in this chapter, we will examine how parts of the value chain might be reconfigured to improve value and cut costs.

It is also important that managers examine value from the perspective of the customer. In a hotel, for example, 'service' is a *sine qua non* in terms of the customer, but a strict focus on costs may well trim back elements of the service that are considered to be essential by the customer. In particular, in some aspects of the value chain, such as the quality of the workforce or management, it may be very difficult to place a precise cost on such activities.

Michael Porter's value chain brought the focus on value creation to a strategic level in the minds of executives and created an important focus on the customer in the value chain. While Porter's contribution has been very significant, there are also some important limitations that need to be considered. The model represents a traditional focus on the organisation, placing marketing and service at the end, with the primary focus on the profit that is made when the product or service is sold to the customer.

Hines (1993) examined supply chains in Japanese companies and, adapting Porter's work, proposed an Integrated Materials Management System. He believes that a number of factors should be taken into consideration when examining the concept of value in terms of providing products or services. First, he believes that customer satisfaction and not company profit should be the main focus of the organisation. Secondly, while he acknowledges that Porter stresses integration between the different elements of the organisation, Hines believes the original model still shows a divided network, not just between the divisions within the company but also between the various companies in the value network. Thirdly, he considers the wrong functions are highlighted in the value chain.

Instead, Hines proposes that the value chain should be pointing in the opposite direction, placing the customer at the beginning of the process. His reasoning suggests that it is the final customer that defines what value is, not any of the groups within the value chain. Thus the Integrated Materials Management System moves away from the traditional 'push' system as emphasised by Porter, to a consumer 'pull' system. The entire system needs to be a fully integrated system with one common purpose: customer satisfaction. Thus, the relationship between the different companies in the wider value chain is one of collaboration, rather than an adversarial one.

In addition, Hines believes that the primary activities should reflect a collaborative approach to defining value, starting with the customer and working back through the entire system to the supplier organisations. Hines lists marketing, materials, engineering, quality, R&D and design as the primary activities. These jointly define value at each stage. The secondary activities are activity-based costing, human resource management (HRM), total quality managemant (TQM), electronic data interchange (EDI) and profit. Perhaps one of the major differences between Porter's value chain and Hines's model is that Hines believes profit is a facilitator and places it under the category of a secondary activity. He considers that a reasonable level of profit throughout the network is necessary to serve the consumer most effectively, stating that this is the approach most commonly taken by Japanese companies, reflecting a much more collaborative effort between all the different players in the system. Such collaboration is supported by a constant focus on innovation and the search to find better ways of delivering value to the customer. In so doing, it also combats many of the effects of the competitive forces at play within the industry.

One final observation that needs to be made about the value chain concerns IT. The capability of IT systems has transformed beyond recognition from the time Porter first proposed the value chain. IT must now be considered an integral part of any organisation from a strategic perspective. For example, the use of data mining (see **Chapter 13**) can greatly enhance the effectiveness of the Marketing and Sales part of the value chain. Those who have bought books through Amazon will have experienced how the company trawls though past purchases to pick new books that will suit the individual customer's choice. While there is a certain 'push' element to Amazon's strategy, it still ties in with the discussion above on the importance of working with customers to select products that match their requirements (Rust *et al.*, 2010).

The Value System

The above section dealt with the value chain of a single company. It would be quite unusual for one company to perform all of the value chain activities by itself.

The primary activities of inbound logistics and outbound logistics imply a relationship between the organisation and its suppliers and distributors. The price paid for a product by the customer also includes the cost of all parts of the entire chain from the supplier of raw materials/components to the retail outlet. This wider network is known as the 'value system' and must be included in the analysis by management in order to understand the totality of costs and value.

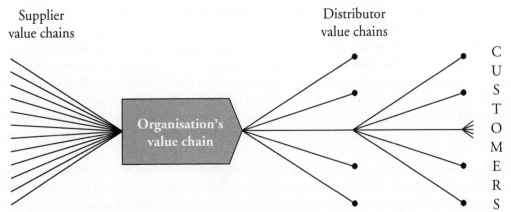

Source: Adapted from Michael E. Porter, *Competitive Advantage: Creating and Sustaining Superior Performance*, New York, The Free Press, 1985

Figure 6.4 *The Value System*

It is essential that all firms in the value system work closely together with a common aim of ensuring the final customer is satisfied and all regulatory requirements are met. Companies must be careful in selecting other companies in the value system as potential partners. According to Kanter (2008:49), in selecting external partners to work with, organisations require an open definition of purpose to "encourage exploration of partnership possibilities", which in turn requires managers to "think about the end-to-end possibilities to the whole ecosystem, from suppliers' suppliers to customers' customers and beyond – to society itself". It also provides opportunities to develop new products. Supply chains have become quite complicated and materials and components are often sourced from different regulatory regimes, which can complicate finished product certification. The pharmaceutical industry in Ireland, for example, sources many ingredients from the UK. However, divergent regulatory standards after Brexit may yet cause major problems for final certification. The US market is the final destination for many of Ireland's finished pharmaceutical exports. However, to receive approval from the US Food and Drugs Administration, every part of the manufacturing process has to be certified to the equivalent of EU standards (Connolly, 2017).

One of the major decisions that an organisation needs to consider is which parts of the value chain it will undertake itself, and which parts (if any) it will outsource. Only bigger companies can afford to have dedicated departments covering all aspects of the company's marketing activities. Smaller companies may employ a marketing manager, but all other aspects of the marketing function, such as advertising, are usually outsourced to an advertising agency. For most organisations, it makes sense to outsource advertising and PR to specialist companies who have the expertise and the necessary industry contacts. The main function of a marketing manager in this instance would be to liaise with the advertising/PR agency with regard to the specific needs of the company. The main advantages

213

for the company in outsourcing is that they are getting expert assistance when required, without the overheads of maintaining staff that would not be fully utilised at other times. Thus, any discussion about managing linkages refers not only to internal linkages, but also to external linkages.

A detailed knowledge of costs is an obvious requirement of making decisions on outsourcing. Generally, an organisation should not outsource an activity if it is a core competence, as this will be a vital part of the organisation's capability. Another major decision to be made is which companies might be suitable to form alliances with. Any breakdown in the relationship between the partners will have serious consequences, and so it is vitally important that such alliances are carefully chosen. Like all relationships, they need to be nurtured on an ongoing basis. Porter pointed out that many aspects of a value chain can be copied by competitors. However, the quality of relationships could make it very difficult for competitors to copy, and so give the company a competitive advantage.

While production is often outsourced to developing countries where labour is cheaper, companies are coming under increasing pressure to shorten supply chains. This is primarily due to environmental concerns and the carbon footprint involved in moving goods half-way around the world. Increasingly, however, energy costs are also a major factor. According to Ghemawat (2010:58), nearly one-quarter of all North American and European countries have taken steps to shorten their supply chain in recent years.

Supply Chain Transparency

It must be remembered that, from the perspective of corporate social responsibility (CSR), the company manufacturing products retains responsibility for its entire value system. Many companies have suffered significant reputational damage due to the actions of their immediate suppliers, or indeed companies supplying their suppliers. Thomas (2008) highlighted many unsavoury practices including *inter alia* the use of child labour in El Salvador in harvesting sugar cane that was used to supply Coca-Cola. Harvesting is hazardous and is classified as one of the worst forms of child labour by the UN. In its 2004 report on El Salvador, Human Rights Watch (2004:60), identified that while Coca-Cola did not directly use suppliers that employed child labour, the company did indirectly benefit from such labour in their value network.

Companies are beginning to take much greater care to minimise adverse environmental effects all along the supply chain (Fisher *et al.*, 2014; Crane and Matten, 2016). Previously, customers had a limited view of supply chains, but now they pay considerable attention to the provenance of the goods they are buying. This applies not just to suppliers but to all parts of the distribution network. As a result, companies must take an active part in thoroughly investigating not just the companies that they are dealing directly with, but also other companies that their suppliers are dealing with.

Changes in technology in recent times have made this all the more important. While many of the technologies are not new, they are evolving in such a way that creates both opportunities and threats for companies. These technologies include microscopic labelling devices, a new generation of barcodes that can be read with mobile phones, as well as radio-frequency identification (RFID) tags which are becoming smaller and smaller. Technology such as cloud technology can be used to store data directly and can be updated as it moves through the value chain. It can also be used to connect to a vast amount of web-based supporting data. This tracking of goods is already standard practice in many safety-critical industries where companies must be able to certify the quality of product components, such as in the aerospace industry and with pharmaceuticals and medical devices. As customers take greater interest in the origin and the authenticity of the goods they purchase, providing them with the means to track the supply chain can help increase brand value. Companies that fail to reveal this information may well have it exposed by activists who oppose certain supply chain practices and, in so doing, may cause enormous damage to corporate reputations (Human Rights Watch, 2004).

Activity Maps

The importance of linkages in the value chain was discussed above. Porter (2006) considers the creation of customer value in organisations as a series of inter-connected activities. The challenge then for managers is to develop a strategic positioning by choosing which activities to engage in that will differentiate the company from its rivals. Some of these activities may be inconsistent with each other and a trade-off between those activities will be required, e.g. in order for Ryanair to reduce airfares, it is necessary to minimise passenger service. Thus, senior managers must decide on the priorities, and also make decisions about what not to do. These priorities must then be communicated to all staff members.

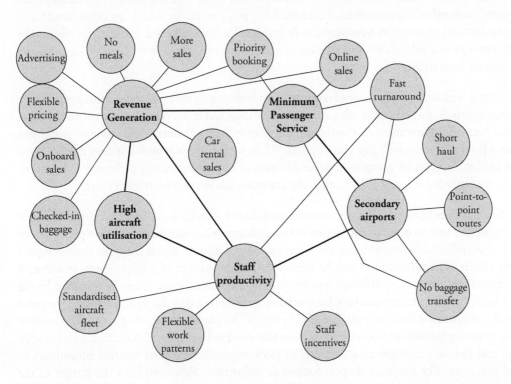

Adapted from Porter, M. E., 2006 "What is Strategy?", *Harvard Business Review*, November/December 2006, Vol. 74, Issue 6, p.73

Figure 6.5 *Activity Map – Ryanair*

These activities can be plotted on an 'activity map' which shows both the main activities and related activities. Note that an activity map is a different concept to the strategy map that was discussed in the context of the Balanced Scorecard in **Chapter 3**. **Figure 6.5** is an activity map that could be applied to Ryanair. One major advantage of such a visual representation is that it shows the connection between all of the activities and how changing one activity can impact on others. It reinforces the importance of the fact that a company's capability lies not in any one particular function. It is a whole system of activities, rather than a collection of individual parts. This inter-connection plays a vital role in preventing competitors from imitating a particular company. There is no element of Ryanair's strategy that is difficult to interpret and copy. Its strength lies in how the company combines all these activities in a unified offering to customers, thus creating sustainability. The content of activity maps can easily be created – digitally using proprietary software, physically on a white board or by using Post-it® notes. The content can then be debated internally with regard to the importance of each element and the connections between them.

BENCHMARKING AN ORGANISATION

The value chain and value network examine the notions of cost and value in an organisation and their relationship in the wider value network. The capability of an organisation is relative, and must be compared with other organisations. Benchmarking is a process by which an organisation can compare its internal activities to best practice. It involves looking at how a company performs the different activities in terms of cost and efficiency. There are a number of ways in which a company can benchmark its activities.

The first process is historical analysis, which compares performance in the current year with performance in the previous year. Activities such as sales, administrative costs and many others can be examined to see if there has been an improvement or deterioration in performance. Airlines could compare passengers carried on a particular route with last year's figures. While such analysis is useful, it does not present a complete picture. A particular company may have improved its performance by perhaps 5%. However, if the industry expanded at a rate of 10%, then the company has lost relative market share.

A better form of benchmarking is a comparison to industry standards, to see if an organisation is performing well relative to other organisations in that industry. Most industries will have performance indicators that individual companies would be aware of and against which they can then compare their own results. The information can be obtained from a number of sources, such as industry analysts, annual reports, other published reports, suppliers and customers. It can be obtained by the company itself, or there are companies who specialise in gathering data for benchmarking purposes and provide comparative data without identifying any of the participating companies. The analysis should focus management's attention on those areas that need to be improved. Discrepancies between company and industry averages could be due to poor implementation of internal procedures or outdated processes. The previous chapter looked at industry analysis and how the nature of the industry changes. It looked at how the photographic industry and the electronics industry converged and brought in new players such as Sony and Canon. Such changes in the boundaries of an industry have to be borne in mind when making an industry comparison.

One other drawback with industry comparisons is that the entire industry may not be performing to its potential. Prior to the deregulation of European airways, many national airlines such as Aer Lingus were very inefficient, but still profitable because of their protected position. Post-deregulation, huge structural changes were required to put these airlines on a sound commercial footing. In many industries there can be a resistance to change because the industry standards are regarded by participants as tried and trusted. Yet improvements in productivity can always be made. Therefore, benchmarking needs to go one step further and look at best practice, wherever that is found. The concept of just-in-time management was first implemented by Toyota after some of its executives had observed how supermarket shelves were quickly restocked after customers bought the products. Having observed the process, they saw that it could be applied to car manufacturers in their dealings with suppliers. As a result, just-in-time manufacturing is now an integral part of the car manufacturing industry.

Performance Metrics

There are different ways in which performance can be measured. One important measurement technique is to apply financial ratios to evaluate a company's financial performance and strength. Different ratios will measure different aspects of the business, and ratios will also differ according to the type of industry. These ratios can be used for internal historical analysis and for industry comparison. Some of the more common ratios are outlined in **Table 6.1**.

Table 6.1: *Financial Ratios*

Ratio	Calculation	What it measures
Gross profit percentage	$\dfrac{\text{Gross profit} \times 100}{\text{Sales}}$	Indicates the efficiency of the producing department as well as the pricing policy of the business. It is a fundamental measure of the effectiveness of an organisation. The higher the rate the better.
Net profit percentage	$\dfrac{\text{Net profit} \times 100}{\text{Sales}}$	After-tax profit as a percentage of sales. It indicates the relative efficiency of an organisation after deducting all expenses, but probably before interest and tax. The higher the better.
Expenses as a percentage of sales	$\dfrac{\text{Expenses} \times 100}{\text{Sales}}$	Measures the expenses involved in making sales. This should be kept as low as possible.
Return on capital employed	$\dfrac{\text{Net profit (before tax)} \times 100}{\text{Capital employed}}$	Shows the return the company is making on the total investment.
Return on shareholders' funds	$\dfrac{\text{Net profit (before tax)} \times 100}{\text{Shareholders' funds}}$	Shows the return the shareholders are getting as a percentage of their investment in the company.

Ratio	Calculation	What it measures
Earnings per share	$\dfrac{\text{Profits after taxes}}{\text{Number of ordinary shares}}$	Shows the profit attributable to each ordinary shareholder.
Price/earnings ratio	$\dfrac{\text{Current mkt price per share}}{\text{Earnings per share}}$	Shows the number of times' earnings a shareholder is willing to pay in order to purchase the share. The higher the rate, the greater the investor confidence.
Current ratio	$\dfrac{\text{Current assets}}{\text{Current liabilities}}$	Indicates the extent to which the amounts owed to short-term creditors can be met by assets which are expected to be converted into cash within the same time period.
Liquid or quick ratio	$\dfrac{\text{Current assets less stock}}{\text{Current liabilities}}$	The ability of the firm to pay current liabilities without having to sell stock.
Gearing	$\dfrac{\text{Total debt}}{\text{Total shareholders funds}}$	This is a term used to describe the extent to which the company's total capital is provided by fixed-interest finance. High ratios show excessive debt.
Stock turnover	$\dfrac{\text{Cost of goods sold}}{\text{Average stock}}$	Measures the number of times that stock is sold in the year.
Average collection period of debtors	$\dfrac{\text{Total debtors x 365}}{\text{Credit sales}}$	Indicates the average length of time it takes to convert debtors into cash.

Removing Cost Disadvantages

If an organisation is able to produce goods or services at a cost lower than its rivals, this will afford it a competitive advantage. On the other hand, if it is seen that the organisation is operating at a higher cost base than companies offering a similar product, remedial action needs to be taken quickly and decisively. Such cost disadvantages can occur anywhere in the company's value chain, or in the wider value system.

If the problem is internal, then managers have direct control over solving the problem. Using benchmarking, managers can identify best practice for the particular cost driver and make the appropriate changes. There can be numerous reasons for high costs: the company is carrying too much stock; administrative costs are too high; operations are badly designed; or manufacturing costs are too high. In the early part of this century, many Irish companies outsourced part of their service operations to countries in Asia. However, in recent years, some companies have brought these services home again, as the cost benefits did not always match service expectations from customers due to poor quality service and language problems.

Costs disadvantages may also be found in the area of component supplies and these also have to be rectified. The problem may be solved by finding a different supplier who can guarantee the same quality and service but at a cheaper price. The answer may also be found by working more closely with the supplier and operating a just-in-time delivery system that reduces costs for both parties. If the supplier is in a strong bargaining position, this puts the onus back on the organisation itself to see if its operations can be redesigned in order to reduce costs.

Costs may also be found in the forward distribution channel, as distributors or retailers may be adding on too much of a mark-up. The company should work with the channel members to see if there are ways in which costs can be reduced and so preserve existing margins. In some cases it may be necessary to bypass distributors and deal directly with the customer. Dell has traditionally operated in this manner. Likewise, Ryanair began using telesales in the late 1980s where passengers could phone and book their tickets, thus cutting out the 12.5% margin being made by travel agents (Ryanair has since reverted to working with travel agents). As the internet gained widespread usage in the 1990s, passengers switched to booking online and now the vast majority of Ryanair tickets are purchased in this way. By reconfiguring its value chain in this way, Ryanair made substantial savings in its cost base, which allowed it to pass those savings on to customers. In this manner, it turned a cost into a first-mover competitive advantage.

YIELD MANAGEMENT

The containment of costs is an essential capability of any organisation. By lowering costs, profits can be increased. The maximisation of revenue is also an important part of the equation of increasing profits. Most organisations are usually limited by competitive forces from increasing prices significantly. Therefore, in order to maximise revenue, the company must create a greater demand and sell more products at the standard, fixed price. If the demand is greater at certain times of the year, e.g. the Christmas toy market, then the products can be stockpiled in warehouses until they are needed. There are some industries that cannot stockpile goods for sale at a later date and, consequently, this could restrict their ability to maximise revenue. However, by using yield management techniques, greater profits can still be made by these organisations.

Definition | **Yield management** is the application of information systems and pricing strategies to maximise revenue from resources of a relatively fixed, but perishable, capacity, by anticipating and directing consumer behaviour.

Yield management was developed by the US company American Airlines in 1985 to enable it to compete with low-cost carriers following the deregulation of the airline industry. Throughout the late 1980s and early 1990s, yield management quickly spread to other airlines and transportation companies. Yield management is particularly relevant for sectors such as hotels, airlines, theatres, etc., that have relatively fixed capacity (over the short term). It is regarded as 'relatively' fixed as, for example, a 100-seater aircraft flying on a particular route is restricted to carrying 100 passengers on any one flight. Theoretically, the aircraft could be replaced by a larger aircraft if there was greater demand, but in the short term it is relatively fixed. Any seats that have not been sold on the flight are regarded as 'perishable' and cannot be resold on a later flight that might have a greater demand.

The same principle holds for many service industries where production and consumption is simultaneous, e.g. if U2 are playing in Croke Park, ticket holders must be present (consuming) as the concert is playing (production). If any fan was unable to make the concert on that night, the opportunity for that particular concert is missed forever.

With airline flights, demand is restricted by both capacity (the number of seats available) and time when the product is available, e.g. there are currently eight flights per day available on the Dublin–Stansted route. Inevitably demand will be higher or lower depending on the time the product is available. For example, airline flights on Friday evenings will usually have a greater demand as business people return home, and holidaymakers wish to depart. Some customers will be willing to pay more to travel at a specific time, while others are more price-sensitive and are happy to travel at other times at a cheaper rate. Demand can also be altered by imposing minimum stay requirements. In addition to situations of fixed capacity, yield management is also relevant when there are high fixed costs and fairly low variable costs. With airlines, for example, there are high fixed costs (capital costs) associated with providing the aircraft, while the variable costs involved are very low. Therefore, any additional passenger, even at a low ticket price, represents a contribution to fixed costs. Once break-even point is reached, the contribution that each additional passenger makes can represent a significant rise in profit for that particular flight.

According to Hayes (2010), yield management using demand-based pricing helps ensure an even distribution of demand for the product by shifting it away from peak-demand periods to times when demand is lower. In order to ensure that each flight is full, differential pricing is used, which means that customers using the same service at the same time can pay different amounts, depending on when they booked the service. The objective in both cases is to maximise revenue by using an appropriate pricing structure, information on the demand patterns of different market segments, information about historical demand and booking patterns, all of which are supported by an information system capable of handling such data. The computer system must be fully integrated into the overall IT structure of the company, underlining the strategic importance of information technology to the organisation.

Yield management requires a detailed knowledge of the market, which includes knowledge of segmentation – dividing the total market into different sub-groups that have similar needs or characteristics. It also requires the ability to forecast the requirements for the service using historical information to estimate future demand. Computer systems then analyse the demand on a real-time basis and adjust prices up or down accordingly.

While computers can assist in the process, yield management also requires subjective decisions by management and staff as some business will be last minute, e.g. direct enquiries by customers.

In that regard, it requires well-trained staff to make appropriate decisions, as pricing too low will not maximise revenue, and pricing too high may turn away the business. Good sales staff will know when to make the right call, and direct contact with the customer can also provide an opportunity for selling other products, e.g. car rental, and so further increase revenue. In essence, yield management allows for a more structured approach to pricing decisions, taking into account marketing, customer and operational decisions.

COMPETITIVE STRENGTH ANALYSIS

Benchmarking will show the company whether they are stronger or weaker than their main rivals and in which areas. Such comparison is important, but the emphasis tends to be quantitative. There are also other qualitative factors on which companies compete and these must also be measured to ascertain whether the company has a competitive advantage or not. Thompson *et al.* (2018) recommend carrying out a competitive strength assessment to compare a company with its rivals on a range of topics. These should include the key success factors for the industry (see previous chapter), and can also include other criteria that measure competitive strength.

The competitive strength analysis can be un-weighted or weighted. A weighted assessment is recommended as some of the factors will inevitably be more important than others and this should be reflected in the weighting allotted. The selection of the criteria, the weightings used and the scores allocated to each criterion, will inevitably be subjective. This might seem to undermine the purpose of the exercise. The process involved is, nevertheless, an important exercise in encouraging management to focus their attention on the important competitive issues facing their company. It should then direct action toward the areas that need strengthening.

There are a number of stages involved in constructing a competitive strength analysis:

1. List the industry's key success factors and most important measures of competitive strength/weakness. Up to 10 factors should be chosen.
2. Apply a weighting to each factor reflecting its overall importance. The sum of all the weightings should equal 1.0.
3. List each company that the company is in competition with. (Strategic group mapping will assist this process.)
4. Each company is then given an allocated score for each of the criteria chosen on the left-hand column. This is then multiplied by the appropriate rating to give a weighted score for that criterion.
5. The process is repeated for all the criteria to be compared.
6. The scores for each company are totalled for all the criteria. The company with the highest score is the most competitive, ranging down to the least competitive.

It will be seen in the example in **Table 6.2** that there is a difference in the scoring between the un-weighted and the weighted scores. The weighting takes into account the importance

Table 6.2: *Weighted Competitive Strength Assessment: Henry Morris Manufacturing Ltd*

(Scoring: 1 = very poor 10 = excellent)

Competitive Factor	Allocated weighting	Henry Morris Ltd Allocated score	Henry Morris Ltd Weighted score	Rico Ltd Allocated score	Rico Ltd Weighted score	Galmul Ltd Allocated score	Galmul Ltd Weighted score	Lowper Ltd Allocated score	Lowper Ltd Weighted score
Brand reputation	**0.20**	8	1.60 (8 × 0.20)	7	1.4 (7 × 0.20)	9	1.80 (9 × 0.20)	4	0.80 (4 × 0.20)
Product quality	**0.15**	7	1.05	7	1.05	8	1.20	4	0.60
Customer service	**0.15**	4	0.60	3	0.45	6	0.90	3	0.45
Distribution network	**0.05**	4	0.20	4	0.20	6	0.30	4	0.20
Overall cost position	**0.30**	5	1.50	6	1.80	5	1.50	4	1.20
Financial strength	**0.05**	6	0.30	6	0.30	4	0.20	2	0.10
Production capability	**0.05**	4	0.20	5	0.25	7	0.35	5	0.25
Range of products	**0.05**	8	0.40	5	0.25	7	0.35	6	0.30
Sum of weights	**1.0**								
Un-weighted strength		46		43		52		32	
Overall competitive score (weighted)			**5.85**		**5.70**		**6.60**		**3.90**

Adapted from Thompson *et al.* (2018:110)

of the various criteria in the mind of the customer and gives a more accurate reading. In **Table 6.2** above, Galmul Ltd is the strongest in the market with a score of 6.60; followed by Henry Morris Ltd at 5.85; then Rico Ltd at 5.70; and finally Lowper Ltd with a score of 3.90. The most important factor in the example is the overall cost position of the companies, which is given a weighting of 0.30.

An examination of the competitive strength assessment matrix will show the overall relative position of each company. It will also reveal the breakdown of where that strength lies and its importance from a customer perspective. Unlike the strategy canvas (see **Chapter 5**), it gives an overall assessment that includes a weighting in favour of the more important factors. This will give the company much more accurate feedback as to its true strengths and weaknesses, and consequently where it needs to take action. It will also guide management in making decisions about what type of action, either offensive or defensive, that needs to be taken. The information in **Table 6.2** can now be presented graphically in **Figure 6.6**.

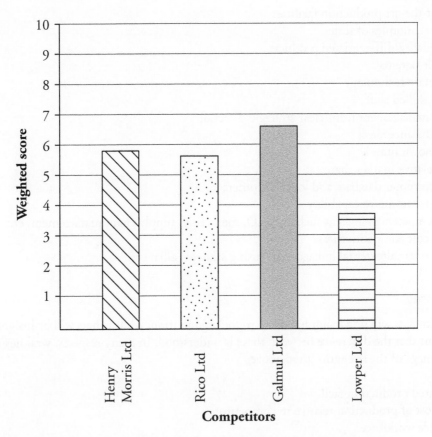

Figure 6.6 *Weighted Competitive Strength Assessment (Graphical Depiction of Table 6.2)*

SWOT ANALYSIS

A SWOT analysis lists the **s**trengths, **w**eaknesses, **o**pportunities and **t**hreats facing an organisation. In the previous chapter, we examined how opportunities and threats are identified from examining the environment. That chapter also looked at the organisation internally to examine its strategic capability. A number of strategic tools were used to analyse the resources and competences. The organisation is now in a position to draw all of these factors together in a SWOT analysis and this will form the basis of future strategic decisions. A SWOT analysis can be a useful strategic tool when it is properly utilised. It is **NOT** a mere listing of factors but a detailed analysis of the main issues facing the organisation as well as their impact and probability.

Strengths

The review of resources, competences, functional analysis, value chain and value network analysis, and benchmarking will show a number of possible strengths. Such strengths could possibly include:

- Prime location
- State-of-the-art production facilities
- Strong economies of scale
- High quality/differentiated products
- Valuable patents
- Proprietary technology
- Highly skilled staff
- Strong management team/clear strategic direction
- Strong balance sheet
- Well-known brand
- High relative market share
- Large customer database and loyal customers
- Strong e-commerce capability
- Core competences in areas such as R&D, marketing, supply chain management, etc.
- Strong cost competitiveness
- Strong internal/external linkages and strong strategic alliances.

Weaknesses

Some weaknesses will be a major handicap to the organisation, while others will be insignificant. It is important that the difference between these is understood. In many respects, weaknesses will be a mirror-image of the strengths listed above:

- Out-dated production facilities
- High cost of production relative to competitors
- Inflexible workforce
- Poor management team/lack of strategic direction

- High level of financial borrowing (highly geared)
- Falling profitability
- Poor/declining market share
- Poor brand image
- Lack of e-commerce capability
- Poor quality products/too narrow a product line
- Lack of core competences
- Poor competitive position.

Opportunities

The opportunities and threats will have been observed from the external analysis and will vary with industry conditions. It must also be remembered that opportunities can often be there around us – it is a matter of being able to spot them. In **Chapter 2**, it was shown how important it is to be able to seize the 'window of opportunity' when it arises. What may be an opportunity for one company may not be for another. Opportunities are also dependent on having the necessary resources to be able to exploit them. Opportunities may include:

- Expanding home market
- New market segments
- Growth in the economy
- Weak competitors/potential to expand relative market share
- Foreign markets
- Developing online sales
- Mergers and acquisitions
- Deregulation in the market
- Reduction in trade barriers
- New technologies
- Forward or backward integration.

Threats

The organisation will want to take advantage of any opportunities in the market, but it also needs to be aware of any potential threats. Some of the threats will be to the industry in general, others will be more specific. The threats will also vary in terms of their possible impact on an organisation. Threats that are potentially significant in nature will have to be faced as a matter of urgency. Possible threats include:

- Declining economic growth
- Deregulation
- New technologies
- Declining home market/falling demographics
- Competitors gaining market share/increased competition

- Shift in consumer tastes
- Globalisation.

SWOT analysis should not be just a listing of the various factors. Its use lies in the analysis and interpretation of those factors and the conclusions drawn. It is also about the action taken on foot of such analysis. The organisation will be trying to use its strengths to capitalise on the opportunities most appropriate to its situation, as that will give it the best chance of success. In particular, the company will need a strong match between its capabilities and the industry's key success factors.

When discussing PESTEL analysis in the previous chapter, it was stated that the organisation must examine the factors that are relevant now, but also those that will impact on the organisation in the years to come. The same situation arises with a SWOT analysis. Strategy is about the long-term direction of an organisation. While some options may be able to be seized straight away, it may take many months or indeed years to put in place an appropriate strategy. Management will have to focus on those issues that are most pressing.

"Things that matter most must never be at the mercy of things which matter least."

Goethe

CONCLUSION

In the introduction to Part Two of this textbook, there was discussion regarding which should come first: the process of setting strategic goals, or analysis of the external and internal environments. This textbook argues that to achieve long-term strategic success, it is important that the vision drives the strategy-making process. Geometry tells us that the shortest distance between two points is a straight line. For a company, however, it is not always possible to move in a straight line in terms of achieving its vision. Cognizance must be paid to the environment within which the company is operating. For that reason, having conducted a SWOT analysis, the organisation may well wish to revisit the (short-term) goals and objectives that have been set, particularly in light of the resources available. While the short-term goals may be modified following this analysis, the resources available should not restrict the vision. Thus, the first part of the company's strategic plan (see **Chapter 12**) should now be complete. The strategies for achieving those goals will be the subject of Part Three of this textbook. It is at that point that the strategic plan will be finalised.

SUMMARY

The previous chapter examined the external environment to identify opportunities and threats. This chapter looked internally to examine the strengths and weaknesses of the company. Together they comprise a SWOT analysis.

Every organisation needs resources such as buildings, machinery, transport, etc. It also includes valuable, but intangible, resources such as brand names. The competences of an organisation describe its ability to use these resources, and together they make up its strategic capability.

A resource audit examines all of the tangible and intangible resources of the organisation, which include:

1. **Human resources** – Employees are a company's most important asset and are vital to its success.
2. **Physical resources** – Buildings, plant, machinery and transport fleet. Their age and condition must be taken into consideration.
3. **Information technology resources** – IT systems that can confer a competitive advantage.
4. **Financial resources** – Financial resources include the company's capital structure, retained earnings and other cash, debtors, creditors, as well as its relationship with its shareholders and its bankers. Implementing strategy will involve substantial financial investment.
5. **Intangible resources** – Includes goodwill, well-known brands, patents, relationship with customers, and customer databases, as well as business systems. Intangible resources such as brands also require considerable financial investment.

Resources have to be deployed where they are most needed and, consequently, flexibility is very important, particularly with regard to the workforce.

A **basic competence** should be seen as the minimum level of competence required to satisfy customers' requirements.

A **core competence** is an activity that the company has developed into a specialised activity that gives it a competitive advantage in that field. Core competences will play a central part in the company's strategy and future development.

Strategic capability is the combination of resources and competences. It is with this capability that a company can take advantage of the opportunities that have been identified. Such capabilities can be found throughout an organisation, and so a functional analysis can be of benefit to identify areas where the organisation is performing particularly well. **Organisational knowledge** is "the collective experience accumulated through systems, routines and activities of sharing across an organisation".

Central to the concept of capability is **cost competitiveness**. Managers have to be able to control costs and do so on a continuous basis to achieve a competitive advantage. Attention must be paid to **cost drivers** in order to manage costs effectively.

The **value chain** describes the activities of an organisation that are linked together to create value. It enables managers to look at each part of the organisation to see where value is being created and, more importantly, to understand the linkages between the different parts. The value chain can be divided into two main parts: primary activities, including inbound logistics, operations, outbound logistics, sales and marketing and service; and support activities, including procurement, technology development, human resource management and the firm's infrastructure.

The **value system** covers the entire chain from supplier to the customer, and all the costs generated in between.

A **competitive strength assessment** compares a company with its rivals on a range of topics. These should include the key success factors for the industry and can also include other criteria that measure competitive strength.

A **SWOT analysis** lists the strengths, weaknesses, opportunities and threats facing an organisation. This will form the basis of future strategic decisions.

DISCUSSION QUESTIONS

1. Differentiate between an organisation's resources and competences.
2. Taking an organisation of your choice, explore the various elements of that organisation and discuss where its capabilities lie.
3. Critically analyse the use of the value chain as a method of understanding an organisation's capability.
4. Discuss the role of benchmarking in evaluating organisational performance.
5. Evaluate the use of competitive analysis as a qualitative tool in inter-company comparisons.
6. Discuss how a SWOT analysis assists organisations in drawing up strategic plans.

PART THREE

Developing Strategy

Introduction to Developing Strategy

In every organisation, there will be a whole variety of options available with regard to the development of strategy. All these options will have to be carefully analysed to ensure their implications are fully understood. More and more, companies are delegating power for decision-making to those parts of the organisation that deal directly with their customers. This provides a faster response time and helps ensure that the company is meeting the needs of its customers. Major decisions will still have to be taken in the company's headquarters to ensure uniform policy in important functions throughout the entire organisation. For that reason, Part Three of this book begins by looking at corporate-level strategy. The factors considered in **Chapter 7** will be relevant for all types of organisations. If the company is large, there will be a clear distinction between the headquarters and each of its strategic business units. **Chapter 8** will then discuss business-level strategy which is designed to deal with the competitive factors in a specific market. If the company is small, the distinction between corporate-level and business-level strategy will be blurred, and there will be a large overlap between the two.

Developing Strategy

In order to be able to build up market share, a company must develop a range of products and services that will satisfy potential customers. This concept is central to the company's existence and is examined in **Chapter 9**. The company must also build up the actual markets in which to sell those products and services. To compete in the marketplace, the company must approach these challenges in an innovative way that will enable the company to stand out from its competitors. The company must also be constantly trying to improve its capability to deliver products and services at a price that people are willing to pay and that will also deliver profit to the company. **Chapter 10** will then examine how some companies move away from their main product ranges and diversify into different products and markets. Such diversification has advantages, but also poses many challenges in terms of how it is managed.

Most companies will want to grow their market share, and there are a number of ways in which this can be achieved: internal growth, strategic alliances and mergers and acquisitions. These are examined in **Chapter 11**. With all these choices open to managers, it is important that these strategies are all properly evaluated and a decision is made that is in the best long-term interest of the company. There have been many examples in recent times of decisions being made that were not sustainable. **Chapter 12** will conclude Part Three by examining how decisions are made in a variety of settings.

It is important to remember that Part Three must not be examined in isolation. The options under consideration must be aligned to the company's vision, mission and its strategic goals and objectives. The internal and external analysis will also dictate what the priorities are and what the organisation

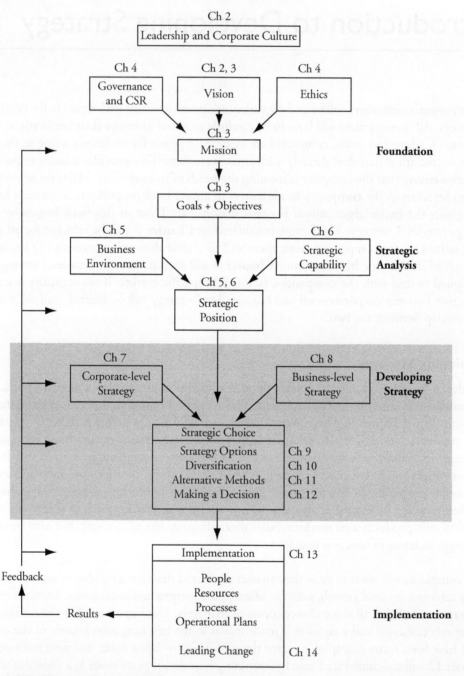

Figure 1.2 *The Strategic Planning Model*

is capable of doing in the immediate future. In one sense, examining and choosing these strategic options is a sequential process, but it is also an iterative one. Events in the last decade remind us just how quickly the business environment can change and the severe consequences of that change for every company. Flexibility and quick response times by managers are, therefore, essential.

Corporate-level Strategy

LEARNING OBJECTIVES

On completion of this chapter, you will be able to:

■ Distinguish between different types of organisational structure
■ Evaluate different parenting styles
■ Distinguish between the various financial decisions that are made at corporate level
■ Evaluate the level of risk that an organisation faces when considering a strategy

"It is not enough to have a good mind; the main thing is to use it well."

René Descartes

INTRODUCTION

There are many decisions that have to be made by a company in relation to its strategic direction. Managing a large corporation with many divisions brings with it very different challenges in comparison to running a small, single-business operation. It is inevitably a much more complex operation. This chapter is concerned with how the corporate headquarters makes decisions about the overall direction of the business. This begins with defining the scope of the business – where does the business begin and end? This process is directed by the vision that was outlined for the company and the objectives that were set. Strategy is all about the means towards fulfilling those objectives.

This chapter will also take an initial look at the structure of the organisation. The structure should support the strategy, and from that perspective it is normally discussed in the context of strategy implementation. However, it is being included here because it is important to understand the existing structure and the relationship between the various parts of the organisation and how these relate to the development of strategy. This chapter will also discuss the nature of financial decisions, the capital structure, dividend policy and management incentives, as these decisions affect the entire company. The culture of the organisation will also be set at this level.

When examining strategic options at corporate level, there are many strategies available to the company based on product development, market development and diversification. These matters will be discussed

233

in detail in **Chapters 9** and **10**. How the headquarters or corporate centre interacts with the different parts of the organisation and where the decisions are made, either centrally or by each of the strategic business units, will also be discussed in this chapter. One way or another, the corporate centre should provide guidance and expertise to each of its divisions, and ultimately should add value to each of them.

CORPORATE HEADQUARTERS – DEFINING THE BUSINESS

Corporate headquarters can vary quite considerably from one organisation to another. Some can be very small units that set financial goals for the different divisions; other companies can have very large headquarters that micro-manage the entire organisation. Irrespective of its size or approach, the corporate centre shapes the business in a number of inter-related ways that need to be examined under a number of different headings:

- Scope
- Corporate Governance
- Business Intelligence
- Data Protection – GDPR
- Leadership
- Employees
- Motivation
- Culture
- Creativity.

The last five of these headings, from leadership to creativity, share the common theme of people and how they can contribute to the success of the organisation.

Scope

The scope of an organisation refers to the range of activities that it performs internally, the breadth of its product and service offering, the extent of its geographic market presence and its mix of business (Thompson, *et al.*, 2018). The centre defines the personality of the organisation in terms of its culture and how it relates to the world around it through its policy on corporate social responsibility. Developing strategy for an organisation is a means of achieving the goals and the objectives that have been set. Those goals and objectives are, in turn, a means of realising the vision. These are the factors that will help define the business in terms of the markets it is serving and the products and services it is delivering.

Some companies will maintain a relatively narrow scope in terms of products and markets, while others will broaden out and diversify into entirely different lines. The level of diversification is a policy decision that is taken at corporate level as it ultimately brings many challenges in how such diversification is managed. Many companies, even large ones choose not to diversify (this topic will be discussed separately in **Chapter 10**). Either way, senior managers need to be clear about the type of growth they wish the organisation to achieve, and be single-minded in achieving it.

All of the work and resources of the organisation should be supporting that effort. One of the primary functions of a corporate headquarters is to provide a clear sense of direction for the entire organisation, and often this has to be achieved against a background of conflicting stakeholder expectations. This means establishing a vision for its future direction, and goals and objectives that will stretch the organisation in terms of what it can achieve.

As an organisation grows more diverse, providing clear direction becomes a greater challenge. Yet diversified companies like Richard Branson's Virgin Group and General Electric manage to achieve such direction. This textbook examines a wide variety of different strategies, each designed to achieve different objectives. The strategies will need to be tailored for each organisation, as not only will their visions differ, but so too will the resources available to help deliver the strategies.

Ultimately, the corporate headquarters should add value to the company as a whole, which is greater than the sum of the divisions of that company if they were operating separately. Value can be added by being able to provide finance for worthwhile projects in situations where finance might not otherwise be available. The centre can also supply expertise to guide the division, particularly in turbulent markets. On the other hand, the corporate headquarters does not produce revenue directly, and represents a cost. All of the salaries and other overheads of the centre must be paid for by the divisions that generate revenue. There is a danger that the headquarters may continue to grow in size and expense without adding extra value. The centre adds value through the decisions it makes in terms of providing overall direction, developing a strong corporate culture and management team, through mergers and acquisitions (M&As), and by directing or influencing the decisions of the various divisions.

Corporate Governance

Corporate governance is the control mechanism by which senior executives are held accountable to stakeholders for the strategic direction of an organisation and for legal and ethical compliance. Corporate governance plays a very important role in every company and there is an onus on the corporate headquarters to ensure the proper procedures are put in place to both direct and protect the organisation. While increased regulation is placing greater pressure on organisations to ensure compliance, it must be remembered that 'direction' is also an integral part of governance. Direction is of particular importance in the context of this chapter. This ultimately involves all stakeholders working together in achieving stated objectives. Another important aspect of governance is the need to build trust with all of the company's stakeholders and to protect its reputation. Given such high-profile failures in this regard in recent years, it is an area that now requires close scrutiny in future years as the need for compliance is greater than ever.

Business Intelligence

Business intelligence is a key and integral part of modern companies. According to Sharda *et al.* (2018:16), business intelligence is a broad term "that combines architectures, tools, databases, analytical tools, applications, and methodologies."

Information technology (IT), on the other hand, is a more specific term that refers to the hardware and software necessary for the system to operate. The nature of business intelligence is complex and constantly evolving. Consequently, while such business intelligence systems provide many opportunities, there can be enormous costs associated with them (see **Illustration 1.1** in **Chapter 1**) and so management needs to be clear on the purpose business intelligence systems are required to serve. Business intelligence systems must not be seen as an end in itself, but an integral part of the business process that will help deliver strategic goals. This was highlighted in **Chapter 6** when examining the value chain and the need for real-time information in making decisions. However, it must be remembered that no matter how sophisticated business intelligence systems might be, it still requires the executive to make the decision.

The benefits of business intelligence can have a positive impact on every part of a business. For that reason, rather than treating business intelligence as a separate topic, it is discussed in the context of each part of the strategy process throughout this textbook. There are some elements of business intelligence that need to be discussed at corporate level in terms of an overall policy framework.

One important issue that must be decided at corporate level is the nature and extent of the business intelligence systems that will be used in the organisation. If the company is divided into different strategic business units, it is imperative that there is an integrated system that is used throughout, and is capable of being expanded to meet future needs. When organisations merge, one of the big difficulties in post-merger integration is linking two business intelligence systems that were never designed to work together.

While dedicated systems can be very expensive, in general, overall costs are coming down as IT systems/applications have moved towards web-based IT applications delivered as part of cloud computing platforms and software as service (SaaS) models. Cloud computing is the term applied to IT applications and data storage that are delivered across the internet, often on a pay-per-use basis. This has the added advantage of no major implementation issues that can often prove quite challenging for IT managers.

The importance of good communication throughout organisations cannot be overstated. Though good communication is primarily dependent on the communication skills of the people involved, and no amount of technology can make up for a lack of these skills, IT networks can play a vital part in the communication process by linking all parts of the organisation, regardless of how remote those parts may be. IT can provide accurate information for decision-making instantaneously. Policy decisions need to be made by the corporate headquarters in terms of the type of resources needed, including the physical resources (hardware), the information processing systems (software), the communication channels (networks) and data storage (data resources). Financial resources will then have to be provided to fund the purchase or development of the systems that will deliver business opportunities. This process must be managed in a cost-efficient and ethical way.

In essence, there are three fundamental roles for business intelligence in any organisation:

- Support the business processes and operations of the company
- Support the decision-making processes
- Support strategies in achieving a competitive advantage.

These roles are integrated and mutually supporting. **Enterprise resource planning (ERP)** systems provide a common interface that integrates all aspects of the company, including planning, financial management, HR, inventory control, manufacturing, sales and customer service. Business intelligence should ultimately enable internet-based **e-business** (collaboration within a company and with customers and suppliers) and **e-commerce** (the buying, selling, marketing of goods and services over a variety of computer networks) systems.

There are important ethical considerations in the use of information technology in organisations, and clear guidelines must be provided for all employees on what is considered acceptable behaviour. The security of the system is also vital, and security measures must be taken to prevent fraud, etc. The financial and reputational consequences arising from a data breach under the EU General Data Protection Regulation (GDPR) are very significant for all organisations.

It must be remembered that IT is moving beyond internal corporate processes into the wider external social sphere, with businesses now integrating their IT applications with social networking platforms. As a result, the internal/external divide is starting to be broken down.

Data Protection – GDPR

One area that is of vital concern to senior executives are the provisions on data protection under the EU General Data Protection Regulations (GDPR), in force from May 2018. GDPR was transposed into Irish law under the Data Protection Act 2018. These provisions relate to the protection of personal data, which is regarded as a fundamental right by the EU. Article 8(1) of the Charter of Fundamental Rights of the European Union and Article 10 of the Treaty of the Functioning of the European Union (Lisbon Treaty) provide that everyone has the right to the protection of data that concerns him or her. The GDPR seeks to harmonise the protection of fundamental rights and freedoms of natural persons in respect of data processing rights. Many of the main concepts and principles of the GDPR are similar to previous Data Protection Acts (1998 and 2003). GDPR introduced new elements and significant enhancements.

All organisations are required to conduct a 'review and enhance' analysis of all current and proposed processing of personal data. The GDPR gives enforcement agencies and authorities (in Ireland, the Data Protection Commissioner (DPC)) more robust powers to tackle non-compliance: fines of up to €20 million or 4% of global turnover (whichever is the greater). The GDPR also makes it easier for individuals to bring claims against data controllers. **Personal data** means data relating to a living individual who is or can be identified either from the data or from the data in conjunction with other information that is in, or likely to come into, the possession of the data controller. Individuals have additional rights in relation to **sensitive personal data**. These relate to specific categories of data, which are defined as data relating to a person's racial origin; political opinions or religious or other beliefs; physical or mental health; sexual life; criminal convictions or the alleged commission of an offence; and trade union membership.

Under the GDPR, there are six principles of data protection. Personal data should be:

1. Obtained and processed lawfully, fairly and in a transparent manner
2. Collected only for specified, explicit and legitimate purposes, and used and disclosed only in ways compatible with these purposes
3. Adequate, relevant and limited to what is necessary
4. Kept accurate, complete and up-to-date
5. Retained for no longer than necessary for the purpose or purposes for which it was collected
6. Processed it in a secure manner that protects it against unauthorised processing, accidental destruction or damage.

Given the scale of the potential fines, it is imperative that organisations thoroughly embrace these principles in all aspects of how they handle personal data, not just electronically but also in paper/manual systems. In particular, data that is regarded as 'sensitive' (e.g. medical data) needs very careful consideration. Any data beaches must be reported to the DPC within 72 hours of discovering the breach. There are additional fines that may be imposed for non-reporting, separate to those outlined above. In January 2019, the equivalent of the DPC in France fined Google €50 million for failing to comply with the GDPR (*The Guardian,* 2019). Such fines are likely to be commonplace until companies embed the principles and practice of data privacy into their cultures.

Leadership

The importance of leadership is emphasised throughout this textbook. Leadership was defined in **Chapter 2** as "the ability to inspire and motivate others to work willingly towards achieving organisational goals". Those at the corporate headquarters must provide clear direction and leadership for the organisation. They need to foresee developments in the industry and understand the implications for the organisation. This will require being able to deal with ambiguity and uncertainty and an ability to make sense of it all. Those at the top must also build a business model that is sustainable.

Leadership must be nurtured and the development of leaders must be seen as an essential investment in the future of the organisation. This begins effectively at the recruitment and selection stages (Yarlagadda *et al.*, 2017). If the right talent is not selected initially, it will be difficult to develop those people in a manner that will meet the needs of a high-performance organisation. Kerry Group Plc (see **Illustration 7.1**) runs its own graduate recruitment programme. Kerry's mission is to be an absolute leader in its markets through technological creativity, product quality, superior customer service and the wholehearted commitment of its employees. Therefore, the company places great emphasis on recruiting the best people with the requisite skills to manage the business. Graduates are selected across a wide range of disciplines, including research and development (R&D), accounting and finance, operations, engineering, supply chain management, IT, procurement, sales and marketing, and human resources management.

Many other large multinational organisations also have their own leadership programmes, such as Johnson & Johnson's LeAD Programme, which is a nine-month training programme designed to coach, develop and test employees who have been identified as having the potential to lead business units within the next three years. Martin and Schmidt (2010) remind us of the importance of such training being driven and co-ordinated at corporate level. There are many reasons for this. Such development will involve giving individuals a broad experience that will involve the entire organisation, rather than just one single unit. There is also a danger that managers at the SBU level will, for purely selfish reasons, try to hold on to talented individuals and block their progress, even if only in the short term.

Employees

While leadership plays a central role in driving the strategy process, people throughout the organisation also play an essential part in helping it achieve success. Collins (2001) wrote about having the "right people on the bus", and in the right seats. Corporate headquarters must develop the human resources of the company in a strategic manner. Huselid (1995) argues that human resources management (HRM) practices direct performance in three key ways:

- Increase the knowledge, skills and abilities (KSAs) of employees
- Motivate employees to use their KSAs to benefit the organisation
- Empower the employees to take action.

HRM planning ties these three elements together. This implies designing the HR function so that it supports the objectives of the company. Liu *et al.* (2007) investigated numerous HRM practices based on data from 19,000 organisations, and concluded that HRM adds significant value to organisations, in particular where HR decisions are tied to strategy. Consequently, HR must be involved in the strategy-formation process to ensure the organisation will meet its future needs in terms of suitable personnel with the appropriate skills. It is vital therefore that the organisation plans well in advance to determine its HR needs. The future needs must be compared with present resources, taking into account the supply and demand for labour. The organisation can then draft a HR plan that will satisfy its needs from internal and external sources (Gunnigle *et al.*, 2017).

As well as vertical alignment in terms of strategy, there should also be horizontal alignment where all elements of the HR system support one another. It is critical that HR professionals understand how one element of their policy impacts on others, e.g. recruiting people with a certain level of skill will affect the level (and cost) of training needed. In particular, policies must not contradict one another. An example of this is encouraging teamwork while only rewarding employees on the basis of individual performance.

Each organisation will have its own unique people-requirements. For larger organisations, each division will also have its own separate needs. The corporate headquarters set overall policy with regard to its employees, no matter where in the organisation they work. This will include guidelines on all aspects of HR policy from recruitment criteria, continuous professional development (CPD), promotion, gender balance, grievance procedures and employee compensation (Hope-Hailey and Gustafsson, 2014). While each division may subsequently adapt the HR policies as needs arise, there must be an overall consistency that promotes fairness, equality and develops talent.

Motivation

Motivation is a key function of leadership. Long-term productivity gains will only be achieved by motivating those employed in the organisation. Motivation is a complex subject, and each individual will respond to different stimuli. Money clearly plays an important part in the overall mix, and in times of recession, the ability of managers to increase pay is clearly constrained. It is therefore important for managers to examine the components of motivation that are within their control. There is often a discrepancy between the factors that managers *think* motivates their employees, and what *actually* motivates them.

Multi-year research carried out by Amabile and Kramer (2010) listed the factors that managers considered to be significant in motivating knowledge workers: recognition, incentives, interpersonal support, support for making progress and clear goals. The number one factor listed by managers was recognition (both public and private recognition). The research also examined what the workers themselves considered to be the important factors in motivating them. Their view was different. The number one factor for employees was, ironically, the factor that was ranked last by managers: progress. The research showed that knowledge employees are driven most when they feel they are making progress in their job or when they receive help in overcoming obstacles.

Perhaps the most significant point about these findings is that progress is a factor that is largely within the control of managers. Managers have significant influence over the events within the organisation that will either facilitate or hamper progress. By having clear objectives, providing necessary resources and encouraging team members, managers can play an important role in facilitating progress (Yarlagadda *et al.*, (2017). The research shows that negative events have a greater impact on motivation than positive events. Managers must therefore be decisive in their actions; they should not change goals without consultation, or hold up resources that are needed. From an organisational perspective, the corporate headquarters should be mindful of the need for motivation as this will set the tone for the entire organisation. This is one clear way in which the centre can add value.

Culture

The nature of organisational culture was discussed in detail in **Chapter 2**. One important role for the corporate centre is establishing and maintaining a culture that is supportive of the strategy that is being pursued. Values are central to organisational culture and senior executives need to give careful consideration to the type of values they want to see practised within the company. While values will vary in their nature, there must be a strong ethical theme that runs through them. Executives need to be mindful of how they model that behaviour and also the importance of clear communication so that all employees fully understand what the company expects of them in their day-to-day operations (Hope-Hailey and Gustafsson, 2014; FRC, 2016).

It will be recalled that the main ways in which leaders embed culture is: through the issues they pay attention to; how they react to critical issues; how resources are allocated; rewards; recruitment and selection (and retention); and role modelling and coaching. Secondary factors include structure, systems, building layout and others (Schein, 2010). While subcultures may exist in larger organisations, those at the top must take effective action to develop a high-performance culture that drives success. That high-performance culture should include a focus on creativity and innovation.

Creativity

In a global and competitive environment there is a distinct need in every organisation for creativity, and it should exist right across all departments. Creativity is about the search for new ways of doing things and trying new approaches. A critical element in 'Blue Ocean' thinking, creativity is more than just thinking in a certain manner. According to Amabile (1998), there are three broad elements to creativity:

- Expertise – technical, procedural and intellectual knowledge
- Creative-thinking skills – these skills determine how people approach problems in a flexible and imaginative manner
- Motivation – in particular intrinsic motivation that will develop a passion to solve problems.

There are many roles for the corporate headquarters in developing creativity. Hiring creative people is an important first step. Unfortunately, many organisations kill creativity through rigid policies and procedures. The challenge for managers is how to manage and cultivate creativity in a way that will help their company compete. Amabile (1998) argues that there are a number of measures that can be taken to foster creativity, beginning with matching people to the right assignments that play into their expertise and skills in creative thinking. While the senior managers will decide on the direction to be taken, staff must be given autonomy as to how to solve operational problems.

Resources in the form of time and money will be needed. Time deadlines can often help the process – provided such deadlines are based on real competitive pressures; artificial deadlines can kill creativity. Careful attention must be paid to the design of work teams to provide sufficient diversity and mutual support. Motivation plays a central role in sustaining the interest of the group – their work must be recognised. Recognition should also include unsuccessful attempts where a lot of effort has been invested. In addition to motivation, wider organisational support should also be available – systems and procedures that emphasise the importance of creativity. Finally, organisational politics must not be allowed to hinder the process.

It must therefore be recognised that, while the importance of creativity may well be accepted by senior executives, creating such a culture within the organisation requires careful and deliberate nurturing. While creativity is important, Levitt (2002) reminds us that creativity on its own, is not sufficient. Businesses must also take into account the practical matter of implementation, translating creativity into tangible products and services that consumers want. (This will be discussed further in **Chapter 9** when discussing innovation.)

Structure and Strategy

The decisions taken at corporate headquarters will impact on the entire organisation. Depending on the type of organisation, they will have a direct or indirect effect on each division. It is therefore, necessary to have an initial examination of the organisational structure. It needs to be emphasised that the structure of the organisation must support the strategy that is being followed. According to Chandler (1962), "structure follows strategy". For that reason, the structure will have to be revisited when examining the implementation of strategy. In the meantime, it will benefit the reader to have an understanding of the organisational structure of a large corporation as this will help illustrate how decisions are made at headquarters that direct each part of the company. There is no prescriptive structural form for a company. Each company will have its own variation on some of the structures that will be examined here. What matters is not the shape of the structure *per se*, but whether it supports the organisation in achieving its goals.

ORGANISATIONAL STRUCTURE

The structure of a company, as depicted graphically by an organisational chart, is effectively the skeleton that provides shape and form to that organisation. It depicts the various departments, the layers of management and the lines of responsibility in the company. For somebody joining the company, they can get an overview of its shape. Other factors, such as culture and control types, are separate elements (these will be examined later in **Chapter 13**) and are not immediately obvious when examining the organisational chart. Some of the basic generic structures are:

- No formal structure
- Functional
- Multi-divisional
- Matrix.

No Formal Structure

Some types of company may have no formal organisational structure at all. In the initial stages of establishing a company, there may be only a few individuals involved, and there is no formal structure. For example, Michael Dell began his company assembling computer components in his college dormitory. Similarly, the founders of Google, Sergey Brin and Larry Page, started their search engine company operating out of Stanford University before moving to offices of their own at Palo Alto. Despite the prominence of the many large multinational corporations in this country, Ireland relies very heavily on small businesses. This reliance will grow in years to come and the Government, through various agencies such as Enterprise Ireland and local enterprise offices (LEOs), provides a lot of support for start-up enterprises. Many of these small companies may have only a few people working in them, certainly in the initial phase.

Such informality regarding structure works well in the early days, as maximum flexibility is required. Those involved in establishing a business will be punching in long days and will tackle each job as it arises. Sooner or later, the newly fledged company will need specialised personnel to deal with the different tasks that require specific skills such as finance, marketing, etc. In the case of Google, Larry Page and Sergey Brin realised that while they had the technical expertise to build the company, they also needed business expertise, and their first appointment was Eric Schmidt as CEO. In turn, Schmidt built up the structures of the company.

Some start-ups will remain forever small, but others will begin to grow. For those that do begin to grow, within a relatively short period of time a more formal structure will be put in place, and the most common form is the functional structure.

Functional Structure

The functional structure is based upon a division of responsibility according to various functional departments such as finance, marketing, human resources, operations, R&D and IT. The company is likely to develop such a structure early in its life as it will require the expertise of people with those specialised skills. While the company may grow into a larger organisation, this functional structure will stay, as that expertise will always be required. The head of each department would

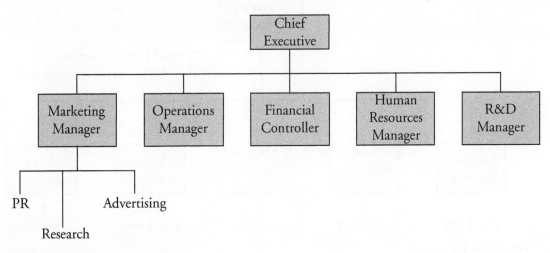

Figure 7.1 *A Functional Structure*

be responsible for running that department and would report to, and provide expert advice to, the CEO.

Each of these functional divisions may be further subdivided, depending on the size and requirements of the organisation. For example, the marketing department may have sections dealing with sales, advertising, public relations and market research. The CEO is ultimately responsible for the success of the company overall and must ensure co-ordination between each of the divisions. One danger with this type of structure is that the divisions become autonomous units existing in their own right, rather than supporting the firm with functional expertise. This is often referred to as creating 'functional silos'. There are also potential problems with this structure as the organisation grows into a divisional structure.

Multi-divisional Structure

As organisations grow in size, their structures must adapt. The most common form of structure is the multi-divisional one, which allows the company to deal with a diversity of products and/or geographical spread. This was first developed by General Motors (Chandler, 1962) and is now used in some form by most large organisations. It can be seen from the diagram in **Figure 7.2** that there is still a functional structure in place, not just at corporate headquarters, but also in each of the divisions. This might seem like an unnecessary and expensive duplication, but it is necessary, as each division will have its own specialised requirements. For a company like GE, which manufactures a vast selection of products, the marketing of jet engines to aircraft manufacturers will be very different to the marketing of financial products to individual consumers.

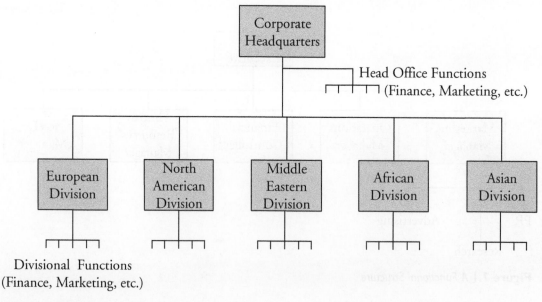

Figure 7.2 *Multi-divisional Structure*

One danger with the functional centre being in corporate headquarters is that HQ might try to impose policy decisions, where local decisions need to be made. An example would be in advertising, where not only does advertising have to be done in the local language, but it must also take into account local cultural sensitivities.

The multi-divisional structure gives the organisation flexibility in that divisions can be added or deleted as the need arises. In turn, each division may be subdivided into smaller divisions. Whether the divisions are based on product lines or geographical regions, it allows that division to develop particular expertise so that it can better meet the needs of its target market. Depending on the parenting style of the organisation, these divisions can operate as part of the greater organisation or as independent units. (This point will be developed later when examining portfolio management.) Either way, a structure such as this facilitates control and responsibility in each unit. In situations where companies own other companies, and allow them to operate autonomously, such parent companies are referred to as 'holding companies'.

In larger companies, this type of structure is important in giving potential senior managers the experience required by working in a variety of different divisions. Indeed, in most multinational companies such experience would be considered a prerequisite for promotion.

Illustration 7.1: Organisational Structure – Kerry Group Plc

From its beginnings in Listowel in North Kerry in 1972, Kerry Group Plc is now one of the world's leading agribusiness companies with annual sales of over €6.5 billion. It is headquartered in Tralee, employs over 25,000 people and has operations in over 30 countries around the world. The company is quoted on the Dublin and London stock exchanges and has a market capitalisation of over €16 billion. In recent years, Kerry Group has been restructured and is now organised into three divisions.

245

Kerry Taste & Nutrition is the largest division of Kerry Group with 130 manufacturing bases across the Americas, EMEA and Asia-Pacific regions, producing ingredients, flavours and integrated solutions. It is a leading supplier of ingredients to the major food and beverage companies around the world. The division employs over 800 food scientists who work in partnership with the Group's customers to develop new products. The division has grown substantially over the years using a mixture of organic growth and acquisitions.

Kerry Foods has manufacturing facilities located throughout Ireland and the UK. It is a leading supplier of value-added branded and customer-branded food products to the major supermarket chains, convenience stores and independent retailers. The division is subdivided into a number of business units that market its various food products and services. These include: Brands Ireland; Brands GB; customer brands; direct to store/Kerry Connect; meat and savoury provisions; meat solutions; food service and dairy products. Kerry Foods has some high-profile brands in its portfolio, which include Denny, Galtee, Low-Low, Dairygold and EasiSingles. The range of products is constantly evolving as it responds to meet changing consumer demand.

Kerry Agribusiness is based in Charleville, Co. Cork. Some 3,200 milk suppliers in the south-west of Ireland provide it with high-quality milk in line with EU dairy regulations. It works closely with its suppliers to reduce production costs while maximising the quality of the milk.

Source: Kerry Group Plc, 2019

Matrix Structure

One of the potential problems with the multi-divisional structure is that there can be conflicts between different geographical areas and product divisions as to the level of standardisation/ localisation required. Another problem can relate to the transfer of knowledge within the organisation. One way around these problems is the matrix structure, with its parallel reporting relationships, which combine different dimensions such as product lines and geographical regions.

The multinational company Royal Dutch Shell uses a matrix structure to co-ordinate its various geographical areas, including Europe, Asia and the US, with major product divisions such as chemicals, gas and oil. According to Bartlett and Ghoshal (1990), companies with a multi-divisional structure are organisationally incapable of carrying out the sophisticated strategies that they have developed, given the growing complexity of relationships between suppliers, customers, employees and governments. A matrix structure can overcome these problems.

With a matrix structure, the centre still has an involvement in decision-making and has different functional groups, such as finance, etc. The process facilitates the necessary co-ordination and decision-making between what are very different lines of demarcation. It should also speed up that decision-making process and ensure that the end result is more customer-focused than would otherwise be the case.

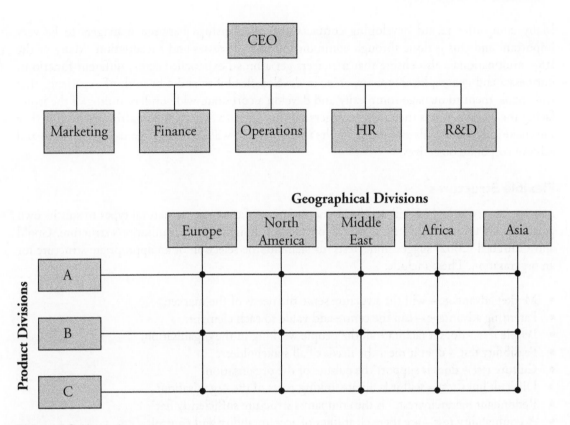

Figure 7.3 *Matrix Structure*

On the other hand, conflict can arise in matrix structures, such as personality clashes between key managers, and this can have the opposite effect. It can be further complicated by barriers of time, distance and culture. It will be necessary to have clear guidelines on who has responsibility for the final decision. As in all such situations, it is the responsibility of the CEO to ensure that the entire organisation is working towards common goals. As organisations grow in size, this can become increasingly difficult.

Bartlett and Ghoshal (1990) suggest that companies need to focus on the challenge of establishing an appropriate set of employee attitudes and skills, and linking them to carefully developed processes and relationships. They regard matrix management not as a structure, but as a frame of mind. The challenge for senior management is to provide clarity on the corporate vision, continuity in terms, sticking with strategic objectives and consistency in ensuring that everyone in the company shares the same values and objectives. The selection of the right people, along with their training and development (including managing complexity), is a vital part of the process. So too is charting a career path for them. IBM is one major multinational company that uses a matrix structure and the company regards itself as a "globally-integrated organisation".

Many companies regard developing contacts and relationships between managers to be very important and this is done through common training processes and socialisation. Many of the large multinationals also ensure that managers get a broad experience across different functions, businesses and geographical areas in order to develop flexibility and a breadth of experience that will enable them to manage complexity and develop a corporate-wide understanding of the issues facing the company. It is then that managers can operate successfully in a matrix structure as they can make judgement calls and negotiate the trade-offs that will drive the organisation forward and achieve corporate objectives.

Flexible Structures

As stated, every company will develop some variation of the many structural types to suit its own particular circumstances. There is no set formula for designing an organisation's structure. Goold and Campbell (2002) suggest nine 'tests' to facilitate the selection of an appropriate structure for an organisation. These include:

- Market advantage – will the structure serve the needs of the market?
- Parenting advantage – can the centre add value to each element?
- People test – does it facilitate all the people working in the organisation?
- Feasibility test – does it meet the needs of all stakeholders?
- Culture test – does it support the culture of the organisation?
- Difficult links test – will it facilitate linking parts of the organisation?
- Redundant hierarchy test – is the company's structure sufficiently flat?
- Accountability test – are there clear lines of accountability and control?

Over a period of years, it is natural that the structure of organisations will evolve. On the other hand, it is important to have some continuity so that organisational members will understand the structure of the company and, in particular, the lines of responsibility. The challenges facing the organisation will vary and every situation will be different. A greater degree of flexibility is therefore required than such structures provide. To facilitate such flexibility, most organisations will leave the basic structures in place, but create special multi-discipline teams to cater for specific eventualities. Team members operate together to deal with tasks such as new product development, where a wide variety of knowledge and experience is required.

In many organisations such teams are standing teams, where the team meets on a regular basis and the members are constant (allowing of course for normal transition due to people moving appointments or retiring). In other situations, special teams are put together for a specific project and are known as project teams or taskforces. Government departments use a variety of teams and taskforces to co-ordinate cross-departmental functions where a number of different departments may have a role. For example, the Department of Children and Youth Affairs would have to work with other departments, such as Education and Skills, Justice and Equality, and Employment Affairs and Social Protection, in order to develop an holistic approach to child welfare.

Information technology plays an integral part in linking the various parts of an organisation. According to O'Brien and Marakas (2008:60), forming a 'virtual company' can be "one of the most important strategic uses of information technology". A virtual company uses information technology to create links between people inside and outside the organisation using a variety of facilities, including the internet, intranet and cloud computing services.

Kaplan and Norton (2006) believe that the search for new organisational structures is driven by changes in competition and in the economy. Companies now derive their advantage not so much from managing physical and financial assets but more from how they align intangible assets such as knowledge management, R&D and IT to the demands of their customers. In addition, the opportunities and challenges that globalisation brings are making many companies revisit many long-held assumptions about the management and control of both physical and intangible assets. They suggest that restructuring a company can be both expensive and distracting, and believe that it is far more effective to choose a design that works reasonably well, and then develop a strategic system to tune the structure to the strategy. To that end, they argue that the Balanced Scorecard framework (see **Chapter 3**) is the best way to align strategy and structure.

One way or another, the structure of the organisation is an important element in the implementation of strategy and must be designed to support it (see **Chapter 13**). Hamm (2006) believes that organisational charts represent much more than just the shape of the organisation. They also represent individual power and influence. Therefore, when change in the structure is needed, the CEO needs to take quick and decisive action, otherwise the organisation will grind to a halt while employees await decisions on who will be reporting to whom, and managers jostle for position. It then becomes a source of anxiety for all, rather than a supporting mechanism for strategy. Ultimately, it is about optimising the use of resources within the organisation.

In **Chapter 6** the importance of linkages in the value chain was highlighted. Regardless of the type of structure chosen, such linkages must be created and strengthened. In response to pressure to adapt products and services to meet the specific requirements of different markets, many multinational companies are driving decision-making down the line to country managers. This allows for more responsive decision-making to meet the needs of each particular market, though it will place extra strain in terms of managing those important linkages. One essential task for senior management is to ensure that proper communication channels are developed, a process that can be difficult when different national cultures and languages are involved. It again highlights the importance of leaders having cultural intelligence (see **Chapter 2**). In addition to structure, the company's internal control systems and how the company relates to other organisations is also important.

CONTROL STYLES

It was stated above that the corporate parent does not add value directly in its own right, but does so through interacting with the various divisions. Now that we have examined the different types of structure that organisations might adopt, it is important to explore the type of relationship between the corporate headquarters and each division. Central to this relationship are the concepts of centralisation and decentralisation.

With centralised decision-making, the corporate headquarters makes strategic and operational decisions that provide direction for the entire organisation. It is highly prescriptive and works on the basis that executives in the headquarters have greater knowledge and experience and thus can make more informed decisions. It is authoritarian and relies on a traditional command-and-control structure. It exerts tight managerial control over the organisation; it is bureaucratic and slow in making decisions, and it is a somewhat obsolete structure for modern organisations.

At the other end of the spectrum is decentralised decision-making. Here the authority to make decisions is pushed down to the lowest level in the organisation that is capable of making such decisions. It means that unit managers are then responsible for what happens in that division, but takes into account that each market is different and these managers are best equipped to make decisions by considering all relevant factors. Because decisions do not have to be referred 'up the line', decision-making is much quicker.

Individual companies will differ in how they relate to their units. Goold and Campbell (1987) suggest different styles that describe the relationship between the centre and the different divisions:

- **Strategic Planning** This is a highly centralised approach where all the major decisions are taken by the corporate headquarters and then prescribed to each of the divisions. It relies on the formal, traditional approach to planning, and the centre provides the necessary services by way of structure, operating procedures, finance and other resources. It can be appropriate where the executives in the centre have an in-depth knowledge of the business units and where all elements of the company are homogenous, e.g. a multinational hotel chain such as Hilton Hotels and Resorts. However, it can destroy value where the business units are quite different in terms of industries and markets, as headquarters staff could not possibly know more than unit managers and the cost of a bureaucratic headquarters would not be justified. It would also be very demoralising for divisional managers. In reality, most commercial organisations are moving away from this parental style.
- **Strategic Control** This is a mid-point between strategic planning and financial control and probably reflects a majority of major organisations. Here the centre will set the overall direction for the company, but work in tandem with the various business units in developing an agreed strategic plan. Part of the plan will include specific goals and objectives for each part of the organisation. The goals of each unit should support the overall goals of the corporation. In terms of resources and support, there will be a certain balancing act between the SBUs in proving those resources and the markets in which each is involved. The centre will endeavour to create linkages between all of the different elements of the company and facilitate organisational learning.
- **Financial Control** This is the parenting style normally associated with holding companies or highly diversified conglomerates. In such cases, the constituent companies will differ greatly in the nature of the industries that they are involved in, and the corporate centre could not

possibly hope to add value by being directly involved. Instead, it sets financial objectives for each, and places responsibility on the management of those companies to deliver the results. The individual managers have complete autonomy on how they achieve the results. One of the big drawbacks with this type of parental style is that there tends to be a short-term focus on results, often to the exclusion of longer-term development.

Culture can play a very important role in organisational control by ensuring work is done in a certain way and to a certain standard. This can be even more powerful than traditional methods of control that would be exercised through organisational structure, and does not require constant supervision. The 'Kerry Way' is a 200 km walk through Ireland's most scenic county. It also refers to the culture in Kerry Group Plc and how things are done in one of Ireland's most successful companies.

ALLOCATING RESOURCES

It will be seen from the above section that an important role for the corporate headquarters is in allocating the necessary resources to, and developing the potential of, each SBU. There are a number of factors to be considered in this regard. First, there is finance. Strategic objectives will generally require substantial funds, and individual SBUs or companies within the overall organisation may not have sufficient finance to achieve their objectives. The headquarters will have to take an overview, looking at where the greatest profit potential lies and then investing in those SBUs. This point will be further developed later in **Chapter 10** when looking at portfolio analysis.

The second point to consider, related to profit potential, will be a decision on the markets within which the company will compete. If the company intends to operate outside its home market, choices will have to be made on which market to enter. Some markets grow faster than others.

Thirdly, decisions will be required on the product range on offer. Should the current product range be broader or narrower than it currently is, and what new products should be developed (again requiring considerable finance)? Sometimes, organisations reach **strategic inflection points** that point them in a totally different direction. Bord na Móna was established to harvest peat from Irish bogs for burning in power-generating plants and domestic fires. It is now recognised that bogland plays a vital role in carbon sequestration and Bord na Móna is shifting from peat harvesting to renewable energy products. See also **Illustration 5.5** about Bord na Móna in **Chapter 5** and the case study on Fairfield/Decom Energy at the end of this textbook.

Finally, human resources play a very important role in the development of the organisation. This involves two dimensions: first, ensuring that each part of the organisation has the right people-mix and skill range required at any one time; and, secondly, it is about developing future leaders by ensuring they have the right experience in terms of different product areas and geographical regions.

All of these factors have to be balanced by the corporate headquarters. Sometimes hard choices may have to be made that will not be popular with particular SBUs, but which are in the best interests of the corporation. Many factors will influence the decision, but much of it will be based on financial appraisal methods such as internal rate of return (IRR) and net present value (NPV). There will be more detailed discussion about methods for selecting particular strategies (**Chapter 12**) as well as product and market decisions later (see **Chapter 9**).

However, as a general principle, it can be taken that with a severe downturn in so many markets and the smaller margins that result, companies will have to be far more selective about investment decisions. This will have implications for portfolio management (see **Chapter 10**).

FINANCIAL DECISIONS

According to Ward (2014), there are other decisions required at corporate headquarters level relating to the financing of the organisation, including:

- Capital structure
- Policy on dividends
- Incentive schemes for managers
- Managing risk.

These will impact on all other corporate decisions.

Capital Structure

The gearing ratio of the firm refers to the relationship between debt and equity. The appropriate gearing ratio will differ according to the industry that it is operating in and the ability of the company to generate cash. Lenders will also take the company's credit history into account. The greater the level of debt, the greater the business risk. Ultimately, companies can decide not to issue dividends, but any loans must be repaid. If the company is experiencing difficult trading conditions, it often results in cut-backs in areas such as R&D, training or advertising. This will help the short-term position with regard to cash, but impact on its long-term growth. Even a temporary inability to pay debt would have very serious consequences for a company, and its ability to raise further debt in the future.

Every company will have a certain level of debt on its balance sheet and there are benefits to having some debt. The interest on debt can be put into the profit and loss account and so reduce the tax payable. The tax benefit will obviously depend on the tax rate applicable – the greater the rate of corporation tax, the greater the saving for the firm. With such a low rate of corporation tax in Ireland, it does not confer the same benefit as other jurisdictions. Debt is considered to be a cheaper form of finance than equity. There is also an argument that suggests that taking on debt will concentrate the minds of executives to ensure that they are getting a higher rate of return than the cost of debt. One of the biggest challenges at present, particularly for smaller businesses, is getting access to borrowing. Banks have not been lending in a way that meets the needs of these companies.

Gearing ratios are also influenced by the nature of the investment required. Heavy investment in capital equipment will normally require a greater use of equity than debt. The amount of debt that lenders are willing to give will also depend on the nature of the assets. If they are tangible assets, banks can place a mortgage on them, and the more liquid those assets are the better. However, intangible assets, such as brands or goodwill, do not have the same attraction to lenders. Finally, there will be international differences in the amounts that banks will lend. In Ireland, Britain and the US, the relationship with banks tends to be purely contractual. While companies may have a long-term relationship with a particular bank, each loan is essentially a separate contract between the company and the bank. In Germany and Japan there tends to be a greater involvement by banks in the shareholding of companies that they do business with and, consequently, they have a much greater interest in the long-term development of those companies.

Dividend Policy

Another major decision to be made by companies relates to their dividend policy. Each individual company must decide if it will pay a dividend and, if so, how much? Some companies on the Irish stock exchange, such as Ryanair, Delata Hotels and FBD, do not pay a dividend. Investors must rely on the capital growth in the value of the share to get a return on their investment. Not paying a dividend, or paying just a small dividend, allows the firm to reinvest profits back into the company. In practically all cases, strategic decisions will require the investment of retained earnings in addition to loan capital to fund the project. Large dividends will be attractive to investors, but will lessen the amount that can be reinvested for the future growth of the company.

There are occasions where there may not be any suitable investment opportunities to hand, in which case there is a strong argument for returning the money to shareholders by either dividend payment or a share buyback. Traditionally, Ryanair is one of those companies that does not pay a dividend. In 2010, it broke with its own tradition and paid a dividend to its shareholders, a decision taken after negotiations with Boeing to purchase new aircraft failed to secure a deal and the company decided to return some of its cash to its shareholders. Share buyback has the advantage (in most cases) of increasing the capital value of the share and being more advantageous where the marginal rate of personal tax is greater than capital gains tax. Senior executives also need to be aware that a dividend policy sends out important signals with regard to the future growth prospects of the firm. If the dividends are too high, it could be perceived that the company has no better use for the money, and needs to return it to the shareholders. If the dividends are too low, the markets may interpret that the future may not be as bright and the company needs to hold on to the cash. Finding the right balance can be difficult. In all cases, clear communication with shareholders and investors is vital.

Management Incentive Schemes

Another corporate financial decision concerns incentive schemes for managers. Many large organisations will include share options as part of the remuneration package of senior executives. A share option is where the executive has the option of buying a specified number of shares in the company at a future date at a fixed amount (called the exercise price). The exercise price is set above the current share price. When the share price rises in value above the exercise price, the executive can take up the option to buy the shares at the exercise price and so make an immediate profit. The purpose is to provide an incentive to managers to make decisions that will increase the value of the company and such options effectively align shareholders' objectives with their own objectives. There are certain restrictions that must be adhered to and options also raise the issue as to how they should be treated in the company accounts.

One problem with regard to the efficiency of share options as a management incentive scheme is that they can reward mediocre performance. For example, the share price might go above the exercise price, thus rewarding the executive. However, the performance of that particular company could be lagging behind that of the industry in general. It is important to set the exercise price at a level that will stretch the executives' skills in attaining the share price and to include malus and clawback provisions.

The TASC report *Mapping the Golden Circle* (Clancy *et al.*, 2010) and also O'Higgins (2012), poses the question as to whether there is a ceiling beyond which no further level of motivation will occur and also draws attention to the traditionally high level of remuneration that occurs among board members of Irish companies, particularly in the financial sector. The payment of high salaries and bonuses to bank employees in Ireland generated significant controversy at the time of the financial crash, with the Minister for Finance at the time directing that no further bonuses be paid by banks receiving State aid. The *UK Corporate Governance Code*, which also applies to Irish quoted companies, states: "Executive remuneration should be aligned to company purpose and values, and be clearly linked to the successful delivery of the company's long-term strategy" (FRC, 2018).

It must also be remembered in relation to the banking crisis that there is a strong link between the level of bonuses paid and the level of risk facing the company. Bonus payments were linked to the amount of lending by managers – the more money that was lent to customers, the greater the bonus. Such short-term incentives overrode sound judgement and proper risk assessment, and in many cases were what is known as 'perverse incentives' whereby the incentives promote the wrong type of behaviour.

While many organisations will retain incentive schemes for managers, a more prudent approach would be to create a much longer timeframe between the action that triggers the incentive, and its actual payment. A gap of a number of years would determine whether that action increased long-term shareholder value or not.

MANAGING RISK

Strategic decisions are long-term decisions. The company may be analysing the environment now and trying to extrapolate what the future is likely to hold in terms of return on investment. By using the appropriate strategic tools, the company may hope to gain a reasonably accurate insight into the future. But inevitably there is a level of uncertainty in such prediction and sometimes events happen that could not have been foreseen. Accordingly, risk is an inherent part of every strategic decision, which can result in consequences different from those intended. Such risk can come about from changes in the environment, through selecting inappropriate options or through the poor implementation of the chosen strategy.

In general terms, there is a strong correlation between risk and return – the higher the potential return, the greater the level of risk. Drawing on a horse racing analogy, the horse that the bookies have put at 100/1 will potentially give a very healthy return to the punter, but the chances of that horse winning are fairly slim. Managers then need to balance the risk and return relationship.

Some decisions will encounter very little risk. Pension fund managers, for example, will transfer a person's pension into bonds and cash as he or she nears retirement in order to minimise the risk involved. In order to grow the pension in the earlier years, a portion of it will be put into speculative stock as the potential return will be far greater than normal run-of-the-mill investments. It is the same with all strategic decisions – the level of risk will vary depending on the nature of the decision. The level of risk will have to be balanced against the circumstances, and the implications involved.

The risk profile of every company will differ. Some will be risk-averse, some risk-neutral and others will be risk-takers. There is no right answer in terms of what is an appropriate level of risk, as there are so many factors that need to be taken into account. In some cases, the future of the organisation may ride on a particular decision. For example, in aircraft manufacture, because of the enormous costs involved in the development of a new commercial aircraft, a wrong decision with regard to the type of aircraft to be manufactured (e.g. decisions on whether to develop wide-bodied, large-capacity aircraft, or aircraft that can achieve greater speeds) could spell the end of the company. In other cases, the level of risk involved may not threaten the existence of the company, but may still have a very significant impact on it, such as the rising cost of fuel on airlines.

There are different forms of risk other than examining whether a company will get an expected return on investment. In examining corporate social responsibility, we saw that companies are liable to suffer risk to their reputation, and companies can lessen this risk by acting in a manner that embraces all stakeholders. The nature of modern communications means that a company's reputation could be severely battered in a very short space of time as a result of environmental damage.

The strategic capability of an organisation could well rest on having very talented and experienced personnel working in the company. In such a case, it will need to ensure that its HR policies provide sufficient incentives to hold on to those personnel. Related risk would include health and safety issues. The cost of inputs can pose a big risk to companies. As mentioned above, it is common in the aviation sector to hedge on the price of fuel because it is such a large percentage of their total costs. With electricity costs soaring, many companies will be under pressure on costs over which they have little or no control. Fraud is an increasing risk for many companies. According to the *Financial Times*, the collapse in 2019 of Patisserie Valerie in the UK was due to finance staff and suppliers colluding to produce false invoices. It resulted in a £40 million fraud and 3,000 job losses (Marriage and Beioley, 2019).

There is also a risk involved in doing nothing. There will be occasions when executives have reviewed a situation and come to the conclusion that 'steady as she goes' is the best course of action. Perhaps one of the biggest dangers is that, when direction is required in a company, managers do not take the appropriate course out of fear of making the 'wrong' decision. They keep putting off the decision, looking for more and more information before taking action – what is known as 'paralysis by analysis'. We should learn from Hamlet's soliloquy:

> "... Thus conscience does make cowards of us all; and thus the native hue of resolution is sicklied o'er with the pale cast of thought, and enterprises of great pith and moment with this regard, their currents turn awry and lose the name of action."
>
> *Hamlet*, Act 3, Sc. 1

In all cases, senior executives must examine all of the relevant information and assess the level of risk involved, including the likelihood of that event occurring and the consequences if it does happen. On a personal basis, we insure our homes against a variety of risks. Most people would hope never to have to claim on their policy, but the insurance is still taken out. A fire, for example, would have a devastating impact on the home owner if there were no insurance in place. Likewise, a company must assess the different types of risk that it faces, such as business or financial risk. Once a proper risk assessment has been carried out, appropriate steps can then be taken to control or mitigate such risk.

The assessment of risk by many Irish companies in the last few years leaves a lot to be desired, particularly in the financial sector. The recession has left many of these companies dangerously over-exposed. In the case of the banks, the exposure to risk left them totally dependent on state aid to continue in existence. In turn, this has had a devastating impact on the entire economy.

Ultimately, when evaluating any strategy for a company, it is the responsibility of the board of directors and senior managers to satisfy themselves as to an appropriate level of risk. Commenting on the Irish business environment prior to the financial crisis in 2008, Clancy *et al.* (2010:2) state:

> "The Irish business environment, exemplified by a culture of excessive risk-taking in key sectors, together with a system of so-called 'light-touch' regulation, helped foster a weak and

inadequate system of corporate governance. Some of the resulting failures have contributed to the economic crisis in Ireland."

They further state that "a high-pay culture also appears to have affected companies at the centre of the recent banking crisis by promoting a culture of short-termism." Clearly, all companies will have to review their procedures for evaluating risk. While the economy has improved considerably since the financial crisis, the sentiments expressed in the Clancy *et al.* report still remain valid today. This is particularly so with the uncertainty surrounding Brexit.

Procedures for Managing Risk

The board of directors and executive management team of each company must determine the risk appetite and risk capability, taking into account the advice of the risk committee. **Risk appetite** is the amount of risk a company is willing to take in the pursuit of its strategic goals. **Risk capability** is the amount of risk the organisation is capable of tolerating before it endangers its own sustainability. The plenary board retains overall responsibility of the management of risk, and risk should be a regular item high up on the board's agenda (Duffy, 2017).

The risk committee, or the board itself if there is no risk committee, should engage with management and employees in the identification of risk as it will have first-hand knowledge of many of the risks facing the organisation on a daily basis. Ultimately, there is an important link between identifying and managing risk and a culture of 'speaking up' in the organisation. Every member of the organisation should 'own' risk, and play their part in minimising it (Tricker, 2015). The organisation may also need to enlist any outside expertise deemed necessary to assist it in its tasks, such as risk identification and mitigation.

The executive management of the company must review and assess all of the risks facing it and make recommendations on risk management to the board, taking into consideration the board's overall risk appetite, the current situation of the company and its capacity to manage and control risks at the present time. These risks include, *inter alia*, financial, health & safety, information technology, data protection, cybersecurity, human resource, brand and reputational risks, and management risks.

There are a number of areas of risk management that should be of key concern to the board, namely:

- Developing the organisation's approach to and appetite for risk
- Knowing the extent to which the executive management team has established effective enterprise risk management systems
- Reviewing the company's risk portfolio
- Considering the level of risk arising from the executive incentive schemes that are in place, and in particular, what are known as 'perverse incentives' (i.e. is the organisation rewarding behaviour that delivers value to all stakeholders?)
- Being apprised of the significant risks and the response of management to those risks
- Reporting of the risks to relevant stakeholders.

In developing a risk analysis process, there are a number of iterative stages that need to be undertaken as illustrated in **Figure 7.4** below.

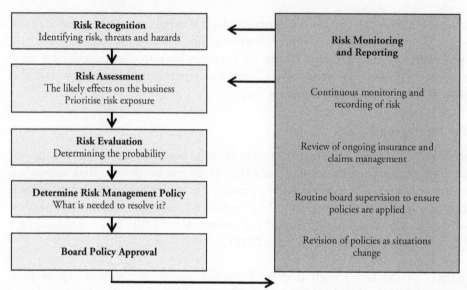

Source: Adapted from Tricker (2015:204), *Corporate Governance. Principles, Policies and Practices,* 3rd Edition. Oxford, Oxford University Press.

Figure 7.4 *Risk Analysis Process*

Both qualitative and quantitative analysis should be used as part of the company's **risk assessment** approach and any recommendations should be comprehensive and complete (Duffy, 2017). This should include an assessment on the likelihood of the risk event happening and the potential impact on the organisation. Each risk should be identified separately and plotted on a matrix. Each risk can be allotted an identifying number, e.g. R1 Brexit; R2 a 3% rise in interest rates; R3 data breach, etc. This can be presented in a matrix form such as the example in **Figure 7.5** below.

Impact on the Organisation

		Low	Medium	High
	Certain	R4	R8	R1
Likelihood	**Possible**		R3 R7	
	Unlikely	R5	R6	R2

Figure 7.5 *Risk Matrix*

Such assessment should include examining different scenarios covering all potential risks and what the organisation will do in response. These risks would be recorded in a **risk register**, which should be updated on a regular basis.

The management should communicate regularly with relevant stakeholders on likely risks that the organisation faces, along with the strategies in place to deal with those risks. Management must ensure that the organisation is compliant with all relevant laws, regulations or codes that apply to its functions. This review should include assessing the likely impact of potential regulatory changes in the sector.

The management should review the effectiveness of the **risk-management framework** within the company and particularly the mechanisms by which staff can raise concerns regarding the management of any risks. A culture of health and safety is an essential element of risk management, and if things go wrong, all staff involved must be treated fairly, with an emphasis on learning and continuous improvement. It is also necessary to develop contingency plans in the event of a major **risk event** impacting on the organisation. This **disaster recovery plan** should include a communications plan for dealing with all stakeholders, including the media.

The greatest risks to an organisation are ones that may cause it to fail at a strategic level. The use of social media can result in incidents going 'viral', resulting in immediate and very significant reputational damage. A vital element, therefore, in recognising risk is a corporate culture that places risk management at the centre of the organisation. In addition, IT-based risk management solutions are now commonly used, which link all parts of the organisation to provide an holistic overview of risk throughout the organisation (Tricker, 2015). However, a word of warning: while risk-management systems can be very effective, reports into the banking crisis have highlighted that such risk-management systems were in place in all the major banks. Such systems are dependent on directors and senior managers being able to interpret the data and making the appropriate decisions in relation to risk and governance (Nyberg, 2011).

Once risk has been identified, action can be taken. This may take the form of:
- **Avoid the risk:** taking action to avoid the risk in the first place. However, this is often not a viable alternative, particularly for public services as they are obliged to provide services to the community, whereas private sector companies may choose not to provide particular services because of the risk involved.
- **Transfer the risk:** taking out insurance or outsourcing the activity to another third party who will then assume responsibility for managing the risk.
- **Mitigate the risk:** taking action to minimise the impact and or probability of the risk, e.g. by having appropriate safety systems or equipment in place.

Uncertainty

A distinction needs to be drawn between risk and uncertainty. Lunn (2008) suggests that risk is similar to playing roulette in a casino. With a roulette wheel, one knows how many red and black numbers there are. As a result, the level of risk can be calculated. However, when operating in global markets, there is a great deal of uncertainty. People do not know the odds. It is like playing poker without knowing how many aces are in the pack. Risk can be quantified, uncertainty cannot. So much of what is happening in global markets involves uncertainty. It is an important distinction that should be borne in mind by executives when making strategic decisions. At the time of writing,

Ireland is facing the prospect of the UK leaving the European Union without a deal in place – a so-called 'hard Brexit'. The implications of such a scenario for businesses on the island of Ireland are enormous, but the full extent is unknown. For executives trying to plan their strategy for the next few years, the uncertainty surrounding Brexit makes it an almost impossible task. It will, most likely, take many years for the true impact on Irish businesses to unfold.

CONCLUSION

The corporate headquarters is the force that co-ordinates and drives the entire organisation. It creates the internal environment where all divisions can work together to achieve a level of synergy that ultimately enables the organisation to successfully implement its strategy. The issues dealt with in this chapter are general policy issues faced by organisations at the corporate level. The centre defines the personality of the organisation in terms of its culture and how it relates to the world around it through its policy on corporate social responsibility. One of the primary functions of a corporate headquarters is to provide a clear sense of direction for the entire organisation and this often has to be achieved against a background of conflicting stakeholder expectation. This means establishing a vision for the future direction of the organisation and also establishing goals and objectives that will stretch it in terms of what it can achieve. Ultimately, the corporate headquarters should add value to the company as a whole, which is greater than the sum of the divisions of that company if they were operating separately.

The next chapter will examine business-level strategy, either as a stand-alone competitive strategy or as part of the competitive strategy of a larger group. **Chapters 9** and **10** will then examine a number of strategic directions that are open to the company to help it achieve its strategic objectives. **Chapter 11** will examine the different methods by which companies can choose to pursue those directions. **Chapter 12** will then consider the different tools that can assist in the decision-making process as the firm tries to choose the optimum solution given its particular circumstances.

Thereafter, the remaining chapters will consider the actions required to implement the strategies that a company uses, from gathering the right team together to the resources required to support them, the structure of the organisation and the control processes. This part will also include a chapter on change management. However, while change will be examined separately in order to understand the process better, it must be remembered that change is an ongoing process that affects every organisation to some degree or other. For that reason, when executives are looking at making corporate decisions, flexibility is essential in that process.

SUMMARY

This chapter examined how the corporate headquarters defines the business in a number of ways:

- Scope – in terms of products and markets and whether it diversifies
- Leadership – how the centre provides leadership for the entire organisation

- Employees – recruiting the right employees is of vital importance
- Motivation – motivating the people in the organisation to achieve success
- Culture – instilling a high-performance culture
- Creativity – creating the environment where people will solve problems in creative ways
- Corporate governance – ensuring legal and ethical compliance
- Information systems – to achieve maximum efficiency and effectiveness
- Data protection – ensuring compliance with GDPR.

The structure of a company, as depicted graphically by an organisational chart, is effectively the skeleton that provides shape and form to that organisation. It depicts the various departments, the layers of management and the lines of responsibility in the company. Some of the basic structures are:

- **No formal structure** – start-up companies with just a couple of people working in them. Sooner or later it will have to adopt some form of structure.
- **Functional** – where the organisation is divided up into different functional areas such as marketing, finance, production, etc. The organisation requires this form of functional expertise and this structure is likely to remain in place regardless of how the company grows.
- **Multi-divisional** – where the organisation is divided along geographical or product divisions. It allows the company to grow and there is flexibility in how more divisions are added. It facilitates the company concentrating its efforts in separate divisions.
- **Matrix** – a combination of, say, geographical divisions and product divisions that allows the company to adapt products for specific markets.

Every company will develop some variation of the various structural types to suit their own particular circumstances. There is no set formula for designing an organisation's structure. Goold and Campbell suggest nine 'tests' to facilitate the selection of an appropriate structure for an organisation. Over time, it is natural that the structure of organisations will evolve. On the other hand, it is important to have some continuity so that organisational members will understand the structure of the company and, in particular, the lines of responsibility.

With **centralised decision-making**, the corporate headquarters makes strategic and operational decisions that provide direction for the entire organisation. It is highly prescriptive and works on the basis that executives in the headquarters have greater knowledge and experience and thus can make more informed decisions.

At the other end of the spectrum is **decentralised decision-making**. Here the authority to make decisions is pushed down to the lowest level in the organisation that is capable of making such decisions. It means that unit managers are then responsible for what happens in that division, but takes into account that each market is different and these managers are best equipped to make decisions by considering all relevant factors. Individual companies will differ in how they relate to their units. Goold and Campbell suggest different styles that describe the relationship between the centre and the different divisions.

An important role of the corporate headquarters is in allocating the necessary resources to, and developing the potential of, each SBU. There are a number of factors to be considered in this regard, including finance, deciding which markets to compete in, and the product range on offer.

Financial decisions required at corporate headquarters level relate to the financing of the organisation including:

- Capital structure – how the corporation is financed between debt and equity
- Policy on dividends – a decision to be made by each individual company with regard to whether they will pay a dividend and, if so, how much
- Incentive schemes to attract and retain top managers and employees
- Managing risk, recognising that the risk profile of every company will differ. Some will be risk-averse, some risk-neutral, and others will be risk-takers.

All of these factors will impact on the other corporate decisions that are made.

DISCUSSION QUESTIONS

1. Differentiate between the various types of organisational structures and state the circumstances in which each type might be appropriate.
2. Distinguish between the different types of parental control that a corporate headquarters might use in controlling a subsidiary company.
3. Explore the various types of financial decisions that need to be made at corporate level.
4. Financial incentives have come in for a lot of criticism in recent times. Explore the role of such incentives in motivating managers.
5. Distinguish between risk and uncertainty.

Useful Websites

The following organisations have been referred to in this chapter:

- GE: www.ge.com/company
- IBM: www.ibm.com/us/en/
- Kerry Group Plc: www.kerrygroup.com
- Shell: www.shell.com
- Ryanair: www.ryanair.com/ie
- Virgin Group: www.virgin.com

Business-level Strategy

LEARNING OBJECTIVES

On completion of this chapter, you will be able to:

- Distinguish between business-level strategies and corporate-level strategies
- Differentiate between the various strategies that can be adopted at business unit level
- Analyse the extent to which each strategy will contribute to the competitive advantage of an organisation
- Critically examine the overall suitability of a particular business-level strategy for an organisation

"So much of what we call management consists of making it difficult for people to work."

Peter Drucker

INTRODUCTION

Throughout this textbook there are examples of organisations that are both large and small. The subject of this chapter is smaller, single-business organisations where the business-level strategy is the same as the organisation's strategy. This also applies to much larger organisations that are divided into different strategic business units (SBUs). Each of these SBUs is operating in a different market, with its own set of customers and different customer needs. The competitive environment will differ from one market to another and the strategy and business model being pursued must also be tailored for that market. The purpose of the strategy is to create value for the customer and generate profit for the company. If it can outperform rivals in so doing, it will achieve above-average profitability.

The concept of generic strategies was first developed by Michael Porter in his 1980 book *Competitive Strategy: Techniques for Analysing Industries and Competitors*. He described **three internally consistent, generic strategies** that could be followed by any business:

- Cost leadership
- Differentiation
- Focus.

The first two ('cost leadership' and 'differentiation') were aimed at a broad market segment, while 'focus' was aimed at a narrow market segment. By 'internally-consistent', Porter meant that the strategy should form the basis of everything the SBU does and requires total commitment. They were termed 'generic' as they could be applied to any business situation, and companies should choose one of those options.

In the 1980s, Porter's work was considered to be seminal but, like many theories, it has since been developed by others, reflecting the many changes that have taken place in industry in the intervening time. Johnson *et al.* (2017) refer to the "strategy clock", which is adapted from the work of Bowman (1995). This is a four-point clock representing different positions (generic strategies) in a market that reflects different customer requirements in terms of the price paid by the customer and the perceived product/service benefits. However, many writers, including Lynch (2018), Hill and Jones (2004), Thompson *et al.* (2018) and others, have taken Porter's original framework and developed it further. Despite their criticisms (some of which will be discussed here), it remains an important piece of work as part of a broader analysis in generating strategic options. According to Lynch (2018:307) it "forces exploration of two important aspects of corporate strategy: the role of cost reduction and the use of differentiated products in relation to customers and competitors."

GENERIC STRATEGIES

According to Thompson *et al.* (2018:134), there are five generic strategies. They are:

1. **Low-cost provider strategy.** This strategy involves attaining overall lower costs than rivals and appealing to a broad segment of consumers by charging a lower price.
2. **Focused low-cost strategy.** This is based on low price and is aimed at a narrow market niche, the needs of which are not being met by the companies pursuing a broad-based cost leadership strategy.
3. **Broad differentiation strategy.** With this strategy, the product is differentiated from rivals by way of quality or service that appeals to customers, thus allowing the provider to charge a premium price.
4. **Focused differentiation strategy.** This strategy is also aimed at a niche market, but which has differentiated needs that are not being met by companies pursuing a broad differentiation strategy.
5. **Best-cost provider strategy.** This strategy involves a combination of good quality at a competitive price (a strategy likely to be considered undeliverable by Porter).

Each of these strategies will require different distinctive competences to implement them successfully, and will now be discussed in detail.

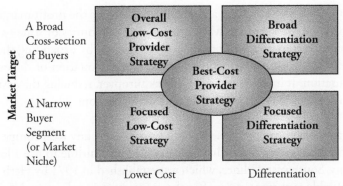

Source: Thompson *et al.* (2018:122) *Crafting and Executing Strategy: The Quest for Competitive Advantage Theses and Cases*, 16th Edition, Boston, McGraw-Hill

Figure 8.1 *Five Generic Strategies*

Low-cost Provider Strategy

Chapter 6 examined in detail how an organisation can reduce its costs to become competitive. In every industry there will be a segment that is price sensitive, either out of necessity, or because it is regarded as being the product or service to be worth only a certain price and no more. There are two different ways in which pursuing a low-cost strategy can work. First, charge a lower price than rival companies and so attract customers. Any organisation can sell products or services at a low price. The acid test is whether it can do so and still make a profit. Secondly, once the company has attained low costs, it can also charge the standard industry price and make a much larger profit.

To achieve a low-cost provider strategy, the company must examine its cost base to see where costs can be reduced, or even eliminated in some cases. A low-cost provider strategy is attained when the organisation becomes *the* low-cost provider in the industry. It involves a relentless pursuit of reducing costs to the bare minimum throughout the entire organisation. Once this has been attained, the company then has a competitive advantage. It should be noted that costs will vary with each industry, so any discussion about cost will be relative to rival companies in that industry.

Cost leadership requires a business model based on lowering the company's cost structure, and developing a distinctive competence that will separate the company from rivals, based on the price paid by the customer. The value chain (see **Chapter 6**) is a useful strategic tool to examine the organisation to see where costs are generated and value is created. As such, it can be used to apply a generic strategy to the organisation. **Illustration 8.1** highlights many aspects of Dell's strategy to reduce costs. Each of the primary and secondary activities of the value chain can be examined to see where costs might be minimised. This can be achieved either by performing elements of the value chain better than rivals, or through bypassing some of the activities, e.g. originally, Dell used to only ship computers directly to its customers, thereby cutting out the retail distribution channel (and the associated costs); it now uses retail channels in addition to direct shipment. There are numerous ways in which an organisation can reduce costs. The product or service is generally a standard, 'no-frills' product that will appeal to a large segment of the target market.

Generally, cost reduction requires attaining a large market share, as the profit margin per unit sold tends to be small. The large market share will, in turn, reap economies of scale (where unit costs decrease as production increases) and economies of scope (gained by expanding the scope of their activities and managerial skills). Cost reduction also requires exploitation of the experience curve and high capacity utilisation. It involves increasing stock turnover, reducing the cost of goods sold, skilled materials' management and flexible manufacturing/operations.

All of these methods are not proprietary, i.e. they can be copied by any rival company. Ryanair did not invent the low-cost strategy for the airline industry. The first airline to use a low-cost strategy was the Texan company, Southwest Airlines, which was established in 1971 by Herb Kelleher. It has been consistently profitable ever since, even after the events of 9/11 when the US airline industry was in turmoil. In the early 1990s, Ryanair's CEO visited Southwest Airlines to observe how they operated and then replicated its business model. There are other low-cost airlines operating in Europe, but none has been as profitable as Ryanair. What separates it is the determination of Ryanair to minimise costs throughout the entire organisation at every juncture.

Illustration 8.1: Low-cost Provider Strategy at Dell

The computer manufacturer Dell pursues a low-cost provider strategy by minimising costs across its entire business model. The strategy has evolved over the years, and the company is constantly seeking to cut costs from its system. Some of the principal ways in which this is achieved include:

- **Links with Suppliers** Dell works very closely with its suppliers and establishes long-term relationships with them. It limits the number of its suppliers and maintains relationships as long as suppliers keep at the cutting edge in terms of technology development.
- **Just-in-time** Dell has built up a perfect just-in-time relationship with its suppliers, many of whom are located close to Dell's manufacturing plants. The just-in-time arrangement ensures that a minimum amount of money is tied up in its supply chain, benefiting both the suppliers and Dell.
- **Operations** Dell operates with a minimum supply of parts on site, and as soon as these parts are used, just-in-time arrangements replace them. Working closely with its suppliers, Dell has consistently reduced the amount of stock it holds, consistent with its 'just-in-time' arrangements with its various suppliers. Dell's operations are primarily based on building computers to order, which allows them to customise the computer to meet the needs of the customer while being able to capitalise on mass production efficiencies. Working to order also allows the company to track latest trends in terms of what customers want.
- **Research and Development** In addition to the feedback from customers' orders, the company also has a dedicated R&D unit employing a few thousand engineers to develop new products that leverage off existing production facilities and expertise.
- **Payment** With direct customer orders, Dell assembles its computers only when it has received payment from the customer. This up-front payment minimises the amount of working capital required in the business and also ensures that there are no bad debts.

- **Direct sales** While the company has recently modified its sales strategy, it is still primarily based on direct sales to customers. This allows Dell to remove the cost of distribution from its value chain. Its sales staff deal with all segments of the market, including home use, small businesses, large corporations, government departments, etc.
- **Customer service** The company provides an online after-sales service and uses contracts with local service providers to facilitate on-site business repairs. Its direct link to customers also allows the company to target existing customers for replacement models and computer peripherals such as printers.

Low-cost provider strategy requires a company to scrutinise each cost to see how it can be reduced or eliminated. It also requires creating a corporate culture that supports such attention to costs. It must be remembered that costs change constantly, and so the model must also change. For example, technology is constantly evolving, but it also creates opportunities to further reduce costs. However, in cutting costs, the organisation needs to have a good understanding of what the customers consider to be an integral part of the product/service and what is an optional extra.

Customer sensitivity to price will also vary over time as living standards increase. In recent years, Dunnes Stores, particularly its household department, has moved upmarket, with designer labels reflecting the increased prosperity in the country. On the other hand, Penneys still concentrates on a price-sensitive market. Other examples of cost leadership companies include Wal-mart, Lidl and Aldi in supermarkets, Bic in ballpoint pens and razors, Nucor in steel production and Briggs & Stratton in small petrol engines.

Focused Low-cost Strategy

The discussion above on overall low-cost provider strategy centred on a broad market segment. The target segment with low-cost focus and focused differentiation is directed at a niche market whose needs are not being met by the bigger players. The niche market can be segmented on the basis of geographical area and special product or user requirements. It requires a clearly defined target market.

With focused low-cost strategy, the company needs to achieve lower costs than rivals for that particular market segment and, in so doing, can achieve a competitive advantage. From a cost perspective, the methods of achieving low cost are similar to those used in overall low-cost provider strategy for the broader market.

While there has been an enormous increase in the number of '4×4' sports utility vehicles in the last number years, the vast majority will be used only in an urban environment. Land Rover has been around for the last 70 years and caters for those who need a rugged 4×4 off-road vehicle. The Land Rover Defender is used by organisations and individuals that require such capability, but are not prepared to pay for the luxury found in many prestige SUVs.

Broad Differentiation Strategy

With a broad differentiation strategy, companies are trying to achieve a competitive advantage by selling a product or service that customers perceive as being different and are willing to pay a premium for that difference. By building up brand loyalty, they can create an advantage over rivals. Costs are the main concern with cost leadership; and remain important with differentiation, but they are not the primary concern. Differentiation can be achieved through a number of different approaches:

- Superior design and performance – Mercedes and BMW cars
- Superior service – Four Seasons hotels, FedEx logistics
- Innovation and technological leadership – 3M
- High-quality durable products – Caterpillar earth-moving equipment
- Prestige design or brand image – Rolex watches, Fieldcrest towels and linen.

The more attributes that a company can use to differentiate itself from rivals, the more difficult it will be for those rivals to imitate that product or service. All of these differentiating factors increase the cost. In including extra product features, the company must still be mindful of costs as the selling price has to cover the total costs involved. There is, generally speaking, a ceiling to the price that customers are willing to pay for the product if the differentiation is based on product features, as customers will compare the various products. When the product conveys a prestige image that conveys status, people are less price-sensitive and in many cases the product would lose some of its appeal if the price were to be dropped. Modern digital watches are probably as accurate as Rolex watches, but do not have the image that allows Rolex to charge a premium price.

The value chain can also be used to identify opportunities for differentiation. In terms of quality, it begins with the design of the product (R&D) and the sourcing of the components (high specifications). In operations, there has to be strict adherence to quality and attention to detail. The marketing of the product has to be in keeping with the image being portrayed, and there needs to be a high level of customer service. The linkages between all of the elements of the value chain are also very important, because differentiated products are more expensive and companies following such a strategy have smaller market share. The premium price, however, allows the company to make significant profits on each item sold.

Illustration 8.2: Differentiation Strategy – Four Seasons Hotels and Resorts

Four Seasons Hotels and Resorts is a Canadian company that operates an international chain of luxury hotels. It was founded in 1960 and has grown continually since then. Four Seasons is an example of a company operating a differentiation strategy. The group is dedicated to providing the highest standards of hospitality and instils a culture of dedication and service among its employees. Four Seasons currently operates over 100 hotels in 38 countries, with many more under development. It is considered a leader in the hospitality industry in terms of quality and service, and is the recipient of numerous prestigious awards.

Its founder, chair and CEO, Isadore Sharp, has based his approach on four strategic decisions, which he has termed the 'Four Pillars'. First, it only operates medium-sized hotels of *exceptional quality*, and aspires to be the best. Secondly, Four Seasons distinguishes itself by the quality of its service – and builds a competitive advantage based on that service. Thirdly, its values (its golden rule) are based on helping others, and there is also a code of ethics that forms the basis of its corporate culture. This is something that is universal and transcends national cultures. Finally, from a customer perspective, the brand is synonymous with quality that reflects the people working in the organisation. It recognises staff contribution and is quick to share the credit.

In terms of its strategies, how then does Four Seasons differentiate itself from its competitors?

Central to the concept of quality are the people working in the organisation. This begins at the recruitment and selection stage. Employees are hired for their attitude – people who have a natural affinity for customer service. Whether at recruitment stage or being selected for promotion, each employee is interviewed by four managers, including the hotel's general manager. Training is also an essential element in the provision of a quality service. There are two distinct aspects to training. First is customer service: developing the emotional connection to people. Second is developing the technical skills required. Taken together, it ensures that the level of consistency and service exceeds customer expectations and builds on the reputation for quality. Refinement of the process is also important – examining procedures to ensure there is constant improvement on what they do. Staff who are professional and deliver a consistently high quality of work will inevitably derive great satisfaction from that work. The acid test is in staff turnover. Four Seasons has an exceptionally low turnover of staff – the lowest in the industry among the big brands. In the words of Isadore Sharp: "That which we do not own is our most valuable asset. They stay by choice because they are all highly qualified."

Delivering on customer service is essential. However, it must be remembered that Four Seasons is a business like any other. Four Seasons was a public company but it was taken private in 2007 by investors, including CEO Isadore Sharp and Bill Gates. It was bought at 40 times' earnings, which demonstrated tremendous confidence in the potential of the brand. Indeed, the hotel group is a market leader with regard to financial returns – approximately 25–30% RevPar (revenue per available room) above other branded competition. Four Seasons charges a premium that customers are happy to pay in return for a blend of luxury combined with exceptional service levels. Four Seasons aims to be the best hotel in each market in which it operates. For the investors who own the hotel buildings (the company has a management contract to run the hotels on behalf of the owners), they too get an exceptional return as the brand generates a valuation premium on their investment.

Source: www.fourseasons.com and interview with Mr John Brennan,
former Regional Vice-President with Four Seasons Hotels and Resorts

(See also the Four Seasons Hotels and Resorts case study at the back of this textbook.)

Focused Differentiation Strategy

Focus differentiation strategy caters for a niche market that is willing to pay premium prices. By meeting the specific needs of this niche group, a company can attain a competitive advantage and above-average returns. Keeping with the example earlier, a Range Rover vehicle has excellent off-road capability for pulling horse boxes, while encompassing top-of-the-range luxury. Porsche manufactures sports cars that have enormous engine power suited to German autobahns in a way that other sports cars could not match. Gore-Tex clothing is upmarket outdoor clothing that combines durability and quality for those out in extreme weather. Fisher-Price manufactures electronic equipment for young children. Tag Heuer aims its products at those desirous rugged waterproof watches.

Best-cost Provider Strategy

Porter (1980:41) suggests that companies need a clear understanding of their strategy, be it low-cost or differentiation, and should pursue that strategy rigorously. To do otherwise is to be "stuck in the middle" and involves "almost guaranteed low profitability". Many writers now see this as being inaccurate. It is possible to attain lower cost *and* differentiation simultaneously.

Since the 1980s, when Porter developed his theory on generic strategies, much has changed with regard to the notion of costs. The previous chapter examined many ways in which costs can be reduced in an organisation through processes such as outsourcing, total quality management (TQM) and business process re-engineering (BPR) – see **Chapter 13**. Such processes deliver improved quality and reliability, particularly for Japanese companies, while at the same time reducing costs. Thus the combination gives customers more value for their money. It requires manufacturers to include features at a lower cost than rivals as well as quality and performance. It meets the needs of buyer segments that are looking for quality but are more price-sensitive than those in the differentiated bracket.

When Toyota launched Lexus, they created it as a separate brand in order to be able to compete with prestige brands such as Mercedes, BMW and Jaguar. While Lexus is marketed as a separate brand, it is still able to benefit from the entire R&D, sourcing and production economies of scale available to Toyota. Lexus has won many awards for quality and reliability, and because of its lower manufacturing costs, its cars are sold at a more competitive price than its prestige rivals.

Toyota has successfully pursued a best-cost provider strategy, but this is a difficult strategy for many organisations to achieve. The danger with pursuing a best-cost strategy is that a company may not achieve low enough costs while not having enough product features. Consequently, it appeals neither to price-sensitive buyers or those willing to pay a premium for top quality. Nevertheless, it can be achieved. For example, many international brands operating in the four-star hotel market are able to blend economies of scale that provide competitive prices, with a level of comfort bordering on five-star hotels.

Managerial Skills

Different core competences will be required for managing individual strategies. For an overall low-cost strategy, the main emphasis is on cost reduction and a company will require very tight control mechanisms to ensure that all costs are kept to a minimum. Staff training and control will be very prescriptive, and standardised manuals will direct staff in particular situations. For a broad differentiation strategy, costs still need to be managed, but the emphasis here is on the quality and service for which people are paying a premium price. It requires a core competence in customer service. It needs a totally different type of staff training – one that develops individual initiative and responsibility. As managers cannot be everywhere at the same time, there needs to be much greater latitude on the part of management with regard to the decisions made by staff in an effort to please the customer.

It is often a moot point as to whether a company is following an overall low-cost strategy or a focused low-cost strategy and similarly for broad differentiation and focused differentiation strategies. The theory of the broad versus narrow segments is often clearer than the reality. Are they distinguished by the size of the market or limited to geographical location or customer type? Apart from developing an appropriate marketing strategy, such distinction has probably little value. As with many aspects of strategy, the environment is constantly changing and organisations must be mindful of these changes. For differentiation strategies, the image created by marketing is central to generating a demand for the product or service. It has to create a sophisticated message that will appeal to wealthy customers. In some instances it will be a global appeals such as in high-end fashion. In others, it will have to be tailored for a specific group and so cultural awareness will be important (Early and Mosakawski, 2004).

Information technology plays an important part in the management of generic strategies. For a cost leadership strategy, managers need to have accurate, real-time information about costs, so that measures can be taken to reduce them. O'Brien and Marakas (2008:364) describe the attributes of information quality along three dimensions:

- Time – information should be up-to-date and available when needed and it should cover past, present and future performance
- Content – it should be accurate, relevant, complete and concise and it should reveal performance by measuring activities, progress made or resources accumulated
- Form – it should be clear and presented in a form that contains sufficient detail for the level of manager concerned.

Yield management will also play a very important role in industries such as the airline industry. See **Chapter 6** for a discussion on yield management.

Linking with Corporate Level

For smaller companies with a single-business market, there will be an overlap between the generic strategy it is pursuing and corporate-level strategies. In essence, they will be woven into one overall strategic approach. For business units that are part of a much larger organisation covering many different markets and possibly different industries, there will be some degree of autonomy in the decisions that the SBU makes. There are many factors that will dictate the level of autonomy that applies, and this will vary greatly from one organisation to another. Regardless of the amount of decision-making latitude involved, the objectives set by the SBU must support the overall objectives of the corporation.

Having decided on a particular generic strategy, the organisation must then consider the possible strategies that will enable it to achieve its overall corporate objectives, and these will be considered in **Chapter 9**. There are a variety of factors that need to be considered and, while there are many strategic tools that will assist in the process, experience and judgement will also play an important role.

SUMMARY

Business-level strategies apply to smaller, single-business organisations. In such cases, the business-level strategy is the same as the organisation's strategy. It also applies to much larger organisations that are divided into different strategic business units (SBUs). Each of these SBUs is operating in a different market, with its own set of customers and different customer needs. The competitive environment will differ from one market to another and the strategy and business model being pursued must also be tailored for that market. The purpose of the strategy is to create value for the customer and generate profit for the company. If it can outperform rivals in so doing, it will achieve above-average profitability.

The concept of generic strategies was first developed by Michael Porter, who used the term 'generic' in that they are strategies that could be applied to all types of organisations. Thompson *et al.* (2018) and others have taken Porter's original work and developed it further and now refer to the five generic strategies, which are:

Overall low-cost provider strategy This strategy involves attaining overall lower costs than rivals and appealing to a broad segment of consumers by charging a lower price. It appeals to price-sensitive buyers. To achieve cost leadership, managers must target costs throughout the organisation. The value chain will help identify where costs are being generated. The strategy requires tight managerial control.

Focused low-cost strategy This is based on low price and is aimed at a narrow niche market whose needs are not being met by the companies pursuing a broad-based cost leadership strategy. It requires having a clearly defined market niche.

Broad differentiation strategy In this case, the product is differentiated from rivals by way of quality or service that appeals to wealthy customers, thus allowing the provider to charge a premium price. Costs remain important, but they are not the primary concern. Differentiation can be achieved in many different ways.

Focused differentiation strategy This strategy is aimed at a high-end niche market, but with differentiated needs.

Best-cost provider strategy This strategy would have been considered unattainable by Porter, but involves a combination of good quality at a competitive price. Developments over the last 15 years or so have led to improved quality while keeping costs low. A best-cost provider strategy is difficult to achieve and sustain as there is the possibility of failing to achieve low costs and high quality simultaneously.

Each of these strategies will require different distinctive competences to implement them successfully.

DISCUSSION QUESTIONS

1. Evaluate the importance of developing business-level strategies for an organisation.
2. Differentiate between the different generic strategies.
3. Critically analyse an overall low-cost leadership strategy and the managerial competences required to underpin the strategy.
4. Evaluate the best-cost provider strategy and state whether you think such a strategy is sustainable or is 'stuck in the middle'.

Activity

Taking the example of Dell in **Illustration 8.1**, use the value chain (see **Chapter 6**) to examine where Dell reduces its cost base.

Developing Strategy Options

"Success is on the far side of failure."

Tom Watson, Founder, IBM

INTRODUCTION

This chapter examines the different strategy options from which a company can choose. These include: consolidating what the company has already achieved and increasing market share; developing a range of products to keep abreast with new technology; and developing new markets and going international. In making the decision to enter foreign markets, there are many factors that need to be taken into consideration. This chapter examines the choices available to enter new markets: exporting, licensing and franchising, strategic alliances and joint ventures, and also foreign direct investment. There are also different strategic options for operating internationally: global strategy, transnational strategy and multi-domestic strategy.

Chapter 10 will continue this theme of strategy development and examine the nature and types of diversification.

The strategies discussed in **Chapters 9** and **10** are by no means mutually exclusive, and companies will develop along a number of these lines simultaneously. **Chapter 11** deals with the different options open to an organisation to help achieve these strategies, such as organic growth, mergers and acquisitions, and strategic alliances. **Chapter 12** then looks at a number of different evaluation tools that executives can use to help select the strategy best suited to the circumstances under which a particular firm is operating. These circumstances and the resources available will differ significantly from one organisation to another and, while the various strategic tools will assist in the selection process, the ultimate decision still requires managerial judgement.

CORPORATE STRATEGY DIRECTIONS

In 1965, the Russian-born writer H. Igor Ansoff published his famous work *Corporate Strategy* (it was subsequently republished in 1988 as *The New Corporate Strategy*). Having worked for the Rand Foundation and Lockheed Electronics Company, he subsequently taught at the Carnegie Institute of Technology. Along with his other books, his teaching on strategy and corporate planning was regarded as seminal. He argued that there are four broad strategic directions open to a company (known as 'Ansoff's Matrix' – see **Figure 9.1**):

1. **Market penetration** – consolidating the company's position in the market and developing a larger market share.
2. **Product development** – developing new products to meet market needs.
3. **Market development** – developing new markets (including international markets) as well as new market segments and new uses for products.
4. **Diversification** – related and unrelated diversification (see **Chapter 12**).

While these are listed as alternative directions, in reality, companies will pursue most, if not all, options possibly at the same time. These options will now be looked at in detail.

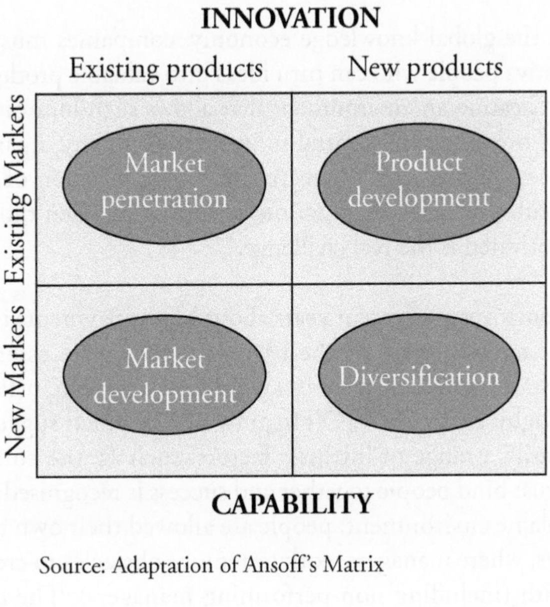

Source: Adaptation of Ansoff's Matrix

Figure 9.1 *Ansoff's Matrix*

CAPABILITY AND INNOVATION

Capability

The capability of the organisation was examined in **Chapter 6**. In pursuing the various strategic options outlined in this chapter, it is assumed that a company has the strategic capability to follow through on their chosen strategy. If such capability does not currently exist, the company will need to develop or acquire that capability. If, in the short-term, such a capability cannot be obtained, the company will have to settle for a more realistic option. However, care must be taken that the company is not always pursuing the safe option. Attaining 'stretch' goals requires that a company move out of its comfort zone to reach difficult targets.

The various options presented here: market penetration; product development; market development; and diversification, all require an innovative approach by the organisation to differentiate itself from competitors. It requires fresh thinking by managers to spot and develop new approaches and the determination to pursue them.

Innovation

There is a distinction between invention and innovation. According to Smith (2006:5), invention is the discovery of a new product. Innovation goes one step further in bringing that new product, process or service into use. The economist Joseph Schumpeter defined innovation as "getting things done". It is an important distinction. An invention may be a piece of great ingenuity, but the primary focus here is on the commercial viability of new products in the marketplace.

As Ireland competes in the global knowledge economy, companies must realise that their most important assets are creative people who can turn ideas into valuable products and services that will satisfy their customers. Creating an environment that allows such innovation is a major challenge for the leadership of any organisation. Central to innovation in any organisation is the quality of its workforce. That process begins with the recruitment and selection of people who are creative and will fit in with the culture of the organisation. It continues when those people decide to stay. Keeping such people motivated is the real challenge.

There has been much controversy in recent years about bonus payments in banks. Such payments were justified by senior management on the basis that they were essential to motivating and holding on to talented staff. However, there is a good deal of research (Floriday and Goodnight, 2005; Catmul, 2008; Rigby *et al.*, 2009; O'Higgins, 2012) which suggests that what motivates creative people is primarily a range of intrinsic factors, such as: the culture of the organisation where collegiality and trust bind people together and success is recognised; where experimentation can take place in a no-blame environment; people are allowed their own time for creativity rather than fixed to 9-to-5 days; where managers work to remove obstacles to creativity; and where non-performers are dealt with (including non-performing managers). The challenge for managers, therefore, is to keep creative people intellectually engaged. The culture of the organisation is clearly an essential element in facilitating innovation, along with open communication where ideas can be shared and discussed.

Staff motivation is important, but so too is keeping the customer satisfied. Customer loyalty can have immense benefits for any organisation. Engaging with customers allows the organisation to understand precisely what their needs are. Working with customers and listening to their problems can also be a key source of innovation.

Innovation comes about in many ways. Smith (2006:86) suggests that innovation is not usually a particularly structured process, but comes about as a result of developing an "insight" that might follow years of painstaking research. Such insight can manifest itself in various ways:

- Association – when people make an association between two apparently unconnected things
- Adaption – by adapting an existing product for a different use
- Analogy – where a principle in one situation is used for a completely different process
- Serendipity – when people discover something purely by chance.

The danger for many companies in the middle of a recession is that they will cut back on investment in innovation. Chesborough and Garman (2008) suggest that "the companies that continue to invest in their innovative capabilities during tough economic times are those that fare best when growth returns". They suggest that not all of the investment need come from internal resources and instead companies can look at entering into partnerships with other organisations, while other projects can be spun off as separate ventures that will allow retention of some equity. Innovation can be hard to manage and also hard to measure, and the temptation is to cut back on investing, but it must be seen as of long-term benefit. The real challenge according to Rigby *et al.* (2009) is how to evaluate the merit of projects, and that too often decisions are made by overly analytical leaders. They suggest that executives require complementary – creative and analytical – styles. Innovation should be seen as core to business, not a marginal activity.

In **Chapter 4** we examined the importance of corporate social responsibility, and how it can bring benefits to the organisation as well as the wider community. It is also important that executives view sustainability not as a burden on the bottom line, but that being environmentally friendly can lower costs and increase revenues. Nidumolu *et al.* (2009) believe that sustainability should be the "touchstone for all innovation". They see it as a five-stage process:

- Viewing compliance as opportunity – ensure that compliance with norms becomes an opportunity for innovation
- Making value chains that are sustainable – increase efficiencies in the value chain
- Designing sustainable products and services – make them eco-friendly
- Developing new business models – try to find novel ways of delivering value to the customer and that will change the basis for competition
- Challenging existing paradigms and creating next-practice platforms – critically examine today's accepted way of thinking and develop innovative solutions.

A culture of innovation is a critical aspect of any business operating in a competitive environment. Such a culture is pervasive throughout the organisation and not confined to those involved directly in research and development (R&D). It requires a constant search for better ways of doing things, and staying ahead of rival companies in all aspects of their operations.

MARKET PENETRATION

Market penetration discusses how a company will grow its share of its current market. In order to do this it may also require consolidation or even withdrawal from other parts of the market.

Market Penetration

Market penetration is a growth strategy dealing with the development of the company using existing products and in existing markets. In essence, it is about gaining customers from a company's competitors. It can also be achieved by convincing existing customers to buy more of your products or services. This can be done through increased advertising or direct selling. Market penetration is perhaps the option with the least amount of risk.

Most companies will try to develop greater market share, the main reason being that there is a strong correlation between high market share and profitability. This is primarily due to fixed costs, which can be spread over a greater number of units. Once market share has been built up, companies will want to protect their investment and ensure that competitors do not erode any advantage. Companies can defend their position in many different ways, such as increasing advertising, price cuts or building in customer loyalty, e.g. with loyalty cards. In most instances, companies operating in an industry will each have only a relatively small slice of the market. Perhaps the best way to protect that market share is to gain an even greater share (and so increase profitability, which in turn can be reinvested). Each company has the advantage that it knows the market well and will spot opportunities when they arise. Though most Tesco stores are large outlets in out-of-town retail centres with ample parking, the company has also targeted underserved segments in urban centres with smaller outlets designed for convenience shopping for those who may not have cars, and thus access to the larger stores. In this way, Tesco is achieving even greater market penetration than they could by just building the larger stores.

In a static market, if one company gains market share it will be at the expense of another, and so they can expect retaliation. Increased advertising or price reduction by one company is usually met with a similar tactic by competitors, resulting in smaller profits made in the market and a more competitive environment for consumers.

An easier method of gaining market share is to acquire other players in the industry, as this does not directly impact on the market share held by competitors, at least not in the short term. In the longer term, the consolidated company will have a greater combined market share and profitability. If the market is growing, it is easier for one particular company to gain market share, as other companies are also expanding but not at the same rate. For rival companies, they might be perfectly happy with increased sales, and not too concerned about their overall share of the market, which has fallen in relative terms.

Consolidation

While the ultimate objective of market penetration is to increase market share, it may not always be possible and companies may be forced to consolidate part of their current market share. Consolidation is a defensive measure (and should not be regarded as a primary objective in itself). It is important that what the organisation has, it holds. In a mature market, where demand is static or falling, a company may want to close some spare capacity in order to reduce costs and concentrate on other production facilities. Likewise, in mature markets many smaller or weaker firms will either go out of business or be taken over by larger competitors, leading to a consolidation of the industry. This can lead to problems with the Competition and Consumer Protection Commission or the European Commission if it is seen that one particular company is becoming dominant in the marketplace. The result can be the blocking of a particular move or forcing the company to sell other related businesses to bring its overall holding back down to an acceptable level. Some industries are seen as being very sensitive in this regard, such as the media, where a dominant position can place a company or individual in a very powerful position. Consolidation takes place in service industries as well as manufacturing. Over the last 15 or 20 years, many accountancy firms have merged in an overall consolidation of the industry.

Withdrawal

On some occasions, in order to consolidate the main business, it may become necessary to withdraw from certain markets to concentrate on core markets or business units. Bank of Scotland Ireland (BoSi), a subsidiary of Halifax Bank of Scotland, expanded very rapidly in the Republic of Ireland from 2000–2007. This subsequently become one of the bigger casualties in the collapse of the banking sector in Ireland. The problem for Halifax was that this expansion was not based on proper risk analysis, and when the financial crisis erupted, BoSi began losing enormous sums of money, as did its parent company, which was subsequently taken over by Lloyds Banking Group in January 2009. In order to stem the losses, Lloyds Banking Group took the decision to close down the retail and commercial sections of BoSi, and transferred the debts to a new company, Certus, whose function is to collect as much of the outstanding loans as possible. In 2015, Certus lost the £5.5 billion contract with Lloyds, and the servicing of the mortgages was transferred to an Australian loan administrations company Pepper. Certus subsequently ceased operations. Having acquired Halifax Bank of Scotland, along with all its debt, Lloyds Banking Group now wishes to consolidate its core banking business, and withdrawing from the Irish market is central to that strategy.

In February 2019, the Japanese car manufacturer Honda announced that it would close its UK plant in Swindon. While there was much speculation that the prospect of Brexit was a reason, Honda stated that it manufactured only 161,000 cars in Swindon out of a total global production of 5.3 million. It is estimated in the industry that a production rate of 250,000 cars a year in a plant is necessary to achieve sufficient economies of scale. In January 2019, Nissan announced that it would cease production of its X-Trail SUV in Sunderland. In both instances, production will continue in their Japanese plants (Pfeifer *et al.*, 2019).

Not all withdrawal situations are similar, however. Sometimes companies diversify into sectors that at the time seem promising, but later prove difficult from a corporate parenting perspective. The business itself may be reasonably profitable, but prove challenging for the corporate parent to derive full value from it. In such cases, it can make sense for the corporate parent to divest the under-performing company, and concentrate on areas in which it is strong. This is what Peters and Waterman (1982) meant by their phrase: "stick to the knitting".

An example of a company refocusing its business operations is when DCC, an Irish-owned Plc, disposed of its food and beverage division in 2014 in order to concentrate on the management of its four main business divisions of LPG, retail and oil, health care and technology. (**Chapter 10** examines portfolio issues in greater detail.)

PRODUCT DEVELOPMENT

Product development should be seen as an integral part of what a company does, rather than being viewed as an optional extra. By product development we mean developing brand new or modified products for existing markets. This textbook has already looked at how product life cycles have become shorter and shorter. Consequently, in a competitive environment, any firm that does not keep up to date with new product development will quickly lose market share and risks going out of business as other companies innovate. Customer demand is not just for new products, but also for updated existing ones. Computers double their processing power every 18 months, and customers expect that all manufacturers are constantly improving their product. Otherwise a company would very quickly lose market share to competitors.

While new product development may be regarded as essential, it does present certain problems in terms of cost and the management of products coming on stream. The process is very much linked with the environmental analysis carried out in **Chapter 5** and the strategic analysis in **Chapter 6**, as companies have to be aware of opportunities in the market and their own capabilities in terms of being able to exploit such opportunities for profit.

There are a number of issues that need to be taken into consideration. These include:

- Definition of products
- Product line and product mix
- Research and development
- Product life cycle
- First-mover advantage
- Brand management.

Definition of Products

According to Kotler *et al.* (2016:520), **a product** is "anything that is offered to a market for attention, acquisition, use or consumption and that might satisfy a want or need and consists of a set of attributes, including physical goods, services, experiences, events, persons, places, properties, organisations, information or ideas".

Products include more than just tangible goods. Broadly defined, products include physical objects, services, persons, places, organisations, ideas or mixes of these entities. In marketing terms there are five different levels to a product:

1. **Core product** This is the essential part of the product – the core benefits that consumers are really buying. The core product of a car is an independent means of transport.
2. **Actual product** This includes the brand name, the quality of the product, its features and other attributes that combine to deliver core product benefits, for example, a Nissan X-Trail or Volvo V70.
3. **Expected product** The set of attributes and conditions that buyers normally expect when they buy a specific product, e.g. when buying a car, people will now expect certain features to be included such as ABS brakes, satellite navigation, etc.
4. **Augmented product** Additional consumer services and benefits that come as part of the overall package of the core product and which augment it. When we buy a car, it will come with a warranty, after-sales support, there may be credit provision, etc. These will differ from one manufacturer to another.
5. **Potential product** This encompasses all of the potential benefits that the product may have in the future, for example at the time of writing, Nissan have an offer whereby a person who buys a 2019 model can trade it in the following year and get an equivalent 2020 car at no extra cost.

In terms of new product development, it is often a moot point as to whether it is a 'new' product or a modification of an existing one. When a new car model comes out, it is generally a modification of an existing model (described in motoring terms as 'evolutionary'). In other cases, the product on offer simply did not exist before, as when the Apple iPad first appeared on the market. Sometimes the core product remains the same but the actual product is quite different. For example, as a core product, a smart-screen television is still a television, but the quality of picture is far superior and the technology involved is quite different from the technology in older flat-screen televisions.

A distinction needs to be drawn between a **product innovation**, which is a change made to an existing product, and a **process innovation**, which is a change made to the way that the product is manufactured or distributed.

Hayes and Wheelwright (1979) suggest that in the early stages of industry development, product innovation is very important as firms try to create technological advantage. Over time, this becomes less important and the emphasis switches to process innovation. Here the emphasis is on streamlining the operation and, in particular, reducing costs.

In the banking industry, when interest-only mortgages were first introduced, they represented a product innovation. Prior to that, mortgage holders were required to pay back interest *and* capital each month. It allowed people to borrow much more than they previously would have been able to do on the basis that, after a few years, their salary would have risen and they would then be able to switch to an annuity mortgage. Internet banking when it was brought in represented a change in the process by which banks interacted with their customers. It was a process change designed to reduce costs as internet banking costs are a mere fraction of the cost of operating a high-street branch.

Product Line and Product Mix

It is important to look at new product development in the context of the overall products sold by a company. In broad terms, products can be directed at industrial (business-to-business) markets or consumer markets. There are a number of marketing terms used to distinguish the different aspects of product offerings.

Definition According to Dibb *et al.* (2006:302), a **product item** is a specific version of a product that can be designated as a distinct offering among a business's products, for example, a particular type of biscuit such as a cream cracker.

Definition A **product line** is a group of closely related product items that are considered a unit because of marketing, technical or end-use considerations. This would include all the different types of biscuits manufactured by the company.

Definition A **product mix** is the total group of products that a company manufactures for its customers. The product mix can be divided into product mix width and product mix depth.

The **width** of a product mix is the number of different product lines that it offers, while the **depth** means the number of different products offered in each product line. Procter & Gamble are a large multinational consumer company whose product-mix width includes laundry detergents, toothpastes, soaps, deodorants, shampoos and tissues. If we take one of those product lines, say shampoos, the depth includes five different brands, among them Head & Shoulders, Pantene, Vidal Sassoon, Pert Plus and Ivory.

Making decisions about the type of products, product lines and product widths are very important choices for the company in terms of building up a market profile and the revenues that will follow from the sales. On the other hand, it also has to consider the costs involved, as well as the resources needed to manage those brands.

Research and Development

Product development requires considerable investment in R&D. This investment takes two forms. First is the investment required in the actual R&D facilities and, with the larger multinationals operating in Ireland, this can amount to tens of millions of euro in building and equipment costs. Secondly, there is the cost of the R&D activity itself.

In general, any new R&D jobs created are for graduates, often requiring people with PhDs. This is obviously good for the economy as they are high-end jobs. In turn, it requires a high level of investment by the government in third-level facilities to produce the required number of suitably qualified graduates.

The cost of R&D will vary from one industry to another. In the pharmaceutical industry, it can take around €2 billion and up to 15 years to bring a drug from concept stage to where it can be sold to the public in pharmacies. For other industries it may not be so expensive. Either way, it still requires specific funding that may not show an adequate return on investment and so there is an inevitable level of risk involved in the process. For decades, Eastman Kodak had a strong lead in traditional cameras, but did not invest heavily enough in digital photography. As a result, they lost out in the digital age to companies like Sony and Canon.

Illustration 9.1: Research and Development

With technology evolving at an ever-increasing rate, it is imperative for companies to invest in R&D. Artificial intelligence and virtual reality are two examples of areas that are rapidly changing the nature of many industries. For a small, open economy like Ireland, R&D is a vital component in our international competitiveness across all sectors. With Brexit looming, the food industry in Ireland is particularly dependent on the British market. However, the structure of the industry has evolved significantly in the past couple of decades from low-value-added primary products to being a world leader in processed foods and food ingredients, with Kerry Group Plc being a prime example. The problem for many smaller companies is that R&D is extremely expensive, and often takes many years to reap the benefits.

The result of Brexit will have an enormous impact on many industries in Ireland. In previous decades, almost all of Ireland's food exports went to the UK, although the last two decades has seen a reduction in both the volume and makeup of agricultural exports going there. However, the UK market is still important for Irish exporters. For example, in 2019, 70% of Irish-produced cheddar cheese goes to the UK; 54% of Irish butter; 50% of Irish beef; and 65% of prepared consumer foods. Other industries will also be hit by Brexit. Pharmaceuticals is Ireland's most valuable export, and while only 7% of Irish exports go to the UK, 23% of Irish supply chains are sourced in the UK. Barriers and tariffs are not the only problem here. If there is regulatory divergence after Brexit, this will have major implications with the US Food and Drugs Administration in regard to the certification of Irish exports to the US, which is Ireland's most important export market for pharmaceutical products. This will mean that Irish pharmaceutical companies will now have to manufacture these ingredients in-house or else source them from other European countries (where common certification exists under the EU Single Market).

The State recognises the importance of R&D and in 2018, Science Foundation Ireland announced the creation of five new world-class research centres, representing an investment of €74 million from the Department of Business, Enterprise and Innovation, and the Department of Agriculture, Food and the Marine over a six-year period, along with a further investment of €40 million from industry (Science Foundation Ireland, 2019). These will cover R&D in areas such as smart manufacturing, neurological diseases and the bio-economy, and will involve indigenous and foreign-owned companies of all sizes.

Because of the high cost of R&D, much of it is a collaborative effort between the State, industry and third-level institutions. In addition, Ireland has received significant funding from the EU's €70 billion 'Horizon 2020' programme, which was designed to promote greater levels of R&D throughout Europe. In addition, 'Project Ireland 2040', a government initiative to maximise Ireland's social and economic development, will also be providing funding through its 10 strategic priorities (Government of Ireland, 2019).

However, at 1.3% of GDP, Ireland's expenditure on R&D is still low when compared internationally. Top spenders such as Israel, Singapore and Finland typically spend 3% of GDP on research. According to the OECD (2018), R&D capacity in indigenous businesses in Ireland is particularly weak, which reduces their ability to innovate and adapt new technologies from the foreign-owned multinational companies located in Ireland. This partly reflects the fact that state support for R&D is largely funded through tax incentives rather than grants or loans (IDA Ireland, 2019), although Enterprise Ireland offers research innovation vouchers worth €5,000 and innovation partnerships worth up to €200,000 (Enterprise Ireland, 2019).

State support is clearly important to the further development of R&D in the indigenous business sector, but the primary impetus must come from each company. Senior managers must recognise the importance of ongoing investment in this area to ensure a constant flow of future products that are internationally competitive.

The risk involved in new product development can be quite substantial as it is estimated that the majority of new products fail. It is difficult to measure precisely the level of new product failure, but according to Dibb *et al.* (2006:307), it could be between 60% and 90% depending on the nature of the industry. However, companies must persist. Tom Watson, the founder of IBM once said: "Success is on the far side of failure." The reasons for this high level of failure are many. Perhaps the main one is the company's failure to match the product offering to customers' need. Other reasons include ineffective branding, technical or design problems, poor timing, over-estimation of market size, ineffective promotion, and distribution.

Failure to meet customers' needs raises a fundamental question for the company. What factors are driving the development of new products? There are different levels of new product failure. Some products can be outright failures where the company loses considerable money on a product that just never takes off with consumers. Other products may make a small profit, but fall well short of the financial and market share objectives that have been set for it. While the product may be making a profit, it must be remembered that there is an opportunity cost in terms of resources and management time for the company in continuing with production.

In some companies, researchers are given large amounts of money to pursue development in certain areas. Over a period of time, knowledge and expertise in the area is built up and eventually a new product is developed. This product is then launched onto the market. There are occasions where these products can be very successful, even though a prior need was not identified.

Post-it® notes are a simple example. These were developed by the US company 3M as a result of experimenting in the production of a batch of glue for binding books. An internal memo was sent around describing the characteristics of the glue (particularly that it did not stick very well and could be peeled off without leaving any residue) and inviting suggestions as to what could be done with it. One 3M employee who sang in a church choir used torn pieces of paper to mark pages in his hymn book, but these often fell out. Post-it notes solved that problem for him. The result was a new product that has been a huge commercial success. In general, however, with such a high rate of failure in new product development being due to those products not meeting consumer needs, a 'push' strategy is generally not the best approach.

Ohmae (1982) believes that customer-based strategies are at the heart of all strategy. He refers to the 'strategic triangle', consisting of the company, its customers and competition. Responding to customer needs is clearly an integral element of R&D. This means listening to customers, directly and indirectly. Sales personnel are coming into daily contact with customers and obtain feedback about the adequacy of current products and services and, in particular, what requirements are not currently being met. Companies can also receive information on customer requirements indirectly through market research. In relative terms, the costs involved in market research are little (when compared to the cost of product failure) and could mean the difference between success and failure. Having an understanding of customer needs is one thing; fulfilling those needs is another. Research should therefore be directed to those areas where there is a clearly identified need.

According to Tansey (2008), innovation is market-led, not science-based. The traditional view was that science caused innovation by increasing the flow of new knowledge. A 2005 report by Forfás entitled "Making Technological Knowledge Work" challenged this view. It believes that innovation can be stimulated in two ways. First, competition must be strengthened and the domestic market liberalised as this competitive pressure will force firms to innovate. Secondly, the absorptive capacity of enterprises must be improved so that they can utilise, in a creative manner, the existing stock of knowledge. This requires a more extensive investment in education as innovation requires better educated managers and workers.

The section dealing with organisational structures above included a discussion on project teams. Cross-functional project teams are an important part of new product development as it is imperative that the different functional areas of the company have an input right throughout the process, from the very beginning right through to when the product is launched. Such an approach will greatly increase the chances of the product being commercially successful. Kotler *et al.* (2016) suggest that there are a number of stages in the development of a new product, including:

- **Idea generation** – the process by which businesses seek product ideas that will help them achieve their objectives
- **Screening ideas** – assessing which product ideas match organisational objectives and resources
- **Concept testing** – seeking potential buyers' responses to a product idea
- **Business analysis** – evaluating the idea to determine the likely commercial benefit to the company in terms of sales and contribution to profits

- **Product development** – examining the feasibility of the company actually making the product
- **Test marketing** – a limited introduction of the product in specific regions picked to represent the overall market. The purpose of test marketing is to confirm that there is an actual demand for the product and to ascertain whether any modifications need to be made before full-scale production
- **Commercialisation** – making the final changes prior to production.

Very often companies are formed as a result of an entrepreneur coming up with an idea for a new product. The big challenge then for such people is to ensure that it is not just a once-off product and that other product ideas will follow, e.g. the Dyson range of different vacuum cleaners and other products such as hair dryers. Trying to obtain funding to establish a company to develop products can be particularly difficult as banks are often reluctant to lend money to people who do not have a proven record in business. The gap is often filled by venture capitalists who will lend money to the entrepreneur. This is usually done by taking a stake in the new company with an exit mechanism in place to realise their investment.

The primary focus here is on existing organisations that need a constant stream of products to satisfy consumer demand. Different companies will have different policies for new product development. Some will have dedicated R&D departments whose remit will be to come up with a succession of products. In other cases, organisations may allow employees follow up on ideas that they have in their spare time and provide them with the facilities and funding they require.

This policy of allowing independent development to take place within the organisation is known as **intrapreneurship**. In situations where the product proves successful, the person behind the idea would generally share in the revenues that accrue to the company. It generally requires a champion for it to succeed. A champion is a senior executive in the organisation who personally backs the project in terms of mentoring and providing the resources required by the intrapreneur, as well as facilitating the process through the bureaucracy of the organisation. In some situations, if the product development is different to the existing range, the organisation may establish a new spin-off company to exploit the concept. This might be for various reasons, such as a requirement for different plant and equipment, or because it requires the support of a different culture to that of the parent organisation. Whatever forum is used for new product development, it requires a policy by the organisation that is actively promoting new ideas and encouraging independent thinking.

Product Life Cycle

Every product goes through a life cycle, consisting of four phases (see **Figure 9.2**). The purpose of product life cycle analysis is to assist managers to plan the most appropriate development and advertising strategies for the product, depending on where in the life cycle it happens to be at that point. The four phases are introduction, growth, maturity and decline. First is the **introduction** stage when the product is introduced to the market. The company will be making a loss on the product at this point as all of the development costs will have been incurred, but sales are only beginning. The **growth** stage comes next, when sales begin to rise rapidly. It requires aggressive advertising to help promote sales. The pace of diffusion will vary greatly depending on the industry and product type as well as a wide range of consumer factors. Nichols and Roslow (1986) refer to the 'tipping point' when there is a rapid increase in sales. The next stage is **maturity,** when the sales curve peaks and starts to decline. Competition is extremely strong at this stage. The final stage is **decline** when sales fall rapidly. Promotion is generally kept to a minimum and the company has to make decisions on the withdrawal of the product from the market – either an immediate or a phased withdrawal.

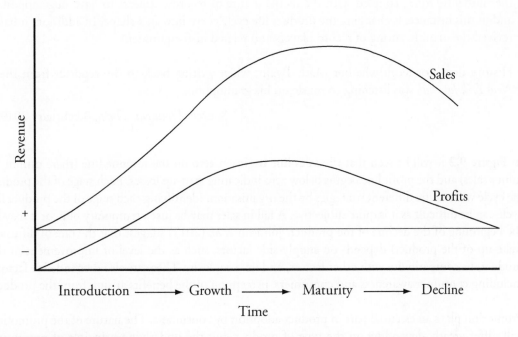

Figure 9.2 *Product Life Cycle*

Illustration 9.2: The Product Life Cycle and the Return of Vinyl Records

The American writer and humourist Samuel Langhorne Clemens, better known by his pen name, Mark Twain, was in London in 1897 when word spread back to the US that he was seriously ill and had subsequently died. The English correspondent for the *New York Journal,* Frank White, made some enquiries, only to discover Twain was still alive and contacted the famous writer. Twain wrote back to White and his letter was published in the *Journal.* While acknowledging that he had been ill, Twain finished his letter with the line: "The report of my death was an exaggeration" (often misquoted as "rumours of my demise have been greatly exaggerated"). So, too, have the rumours of the demise of vinyl records.

For some of the generation now accustomed to digital streaming of music, the vinyl records that they perhaps once noticed in their grandparents' house are now making a comeback. The record company HMV was bought out of bankruptcy in February 2019 by the Canadian company Sunrise Records, and it hopes that the demand for vinyl will help revive this well-known brand. The UK record company Rough Trade reported a 25% rise in the sale of vinyl records in 2018, and in the US, 17 million vinyl albums were sold in 2018, a rise of 15% from the previous year. While classic albums such as Pink Floyd's *Dark Side of the Moon* and Fleetwood Mac's *Rumours* top the sales of vinyl albums each year as baby boomers relive their youth, Millennials are also purchasing vinyl in large numbers. The rediscovery of what many devotees refer to as the 'authentic tone', coupled with the tactile nature of records, appears to have huge appeal, and in this instance, is changing the product life cycle curve into an s-shape. In addition, it has revived the manufacturing of record players and related hi-fi equipment.

History does not recall whether Mark Twain, when writing back to the reporter from the *New York Journal*, was listening to music on his gramophone.

Source: *Financial Times*, 8 February 2019

In **Figure 9.2** it will be seen that the sales line begins at zero on the revenue line (there cannot be minus sales) and the profit line begins below zero indicating start-up losses. Each stage of the product life cycle will require different strategies by the organisation. Identifying each stage of the product life cycle can be difficult as it is quite subjective. A fall in sales may be just a temporary blip, or it may be the beginning of the decline of the product. Johnson *et al.* (2017) suggest that the rate of diffusion (take-up of the product) depends on supply-side factors, such as the level of improvement in the product, its compatibility with other factors, and its complexity. There are also demand-side factors, including consumer awareness and consumers' perception of the benefits arising from the product.

Promotion plays an essential part in product adoption by consumers. The nature of the promotion will differ greatly depending on the type of product, but the underlying principle of promotion is essential, regardless of product category. There is a five-stage product adoption process that includes awareness of the existence of the product, interest in it, evaluation, trial and adoption. In promoting the product, the company will bring to the attention of the market that the product exists in order to generate a need in consumers' minds for the product category. Once there is that need, advertising will try to create a favourable attitude towards the company's brand and then encourage consumers to make the actual purchase decision. If they are happy with the product, they will hopefully buy it again and again, thus building up brand loyalty.

For a product to be a commercial success, there has to be a large take-up in the target market. This can be a gradual process as not everybody will buy new products at the same rate. Dibb *et al.* (2006:519) describe consumers according to five product-adoption categories. The figures in brackets represent a typical breakdown of a market:

• Innovators (2.5%) – the first to adopt a new product
• Early adopters (13.5%) – they choose new products carefully and are seen as 'the people to check with' by others

- Early majority (34%) – they buy just before the average person
- Late majority (34%) – somewhat sceptical about buying and do so out of social pressure
- Laggards (16%) – these are suspicious of new products, and when they get around to eventually buying them, newer products are coming out.

First-move Advantage

In Ireland, the US company Hoover and vacuum cleaners will forever be associated. 'Hoover' is the registered trade name of the company that invented the cleaning device, and the brand name became a generic term for vacuum cleaners. In the process, a new verb was created: to hoover. (Ironically, Americans would use the term 'vacuum' to 'hoover' a carpet.) Being the first to the market has many benefits, known as '**first-mover advantage**'. At this stage, there are probably no other suppliers, so the company is the only company meeting consumer demand, generating strong brand recognition and loyalty.

Brand loyalty can confer huge benefits in terms of repeat sales and in referral for new customers. The ultimate in brand recognition is when the brand name becomes a generic term in the industry, such as with Hoover, or Biro (made by the French company Bic) for ball-point pens. In addition, the first mover may also have patent protection, slowing down the entry of rivals into the market.

First-maker advantage means the company can also gain considerable experience (the concept of the experience curve has already been discussed) and, when rivals do enter the market, the company will have a strong lead over them in this respect. They can use the experience to modify and improve the quality of the product, as well as build up greater knowledge of the nature of consumer demand for the product. An early lead in sales volume can allow the company to reap economies of scale, and allow them to use the financial gain to either improve quality or reduce price or both. This will further differentiate the first mover from later rivals.

However, first-mover advantage is more than a myth, but also far less than a sure thing. For every success story there is an equal number of examples of first movers who lost out to later followers. For many years, Xerox, a company with a strong brand name and resources, enjoyed first-mover advantage in photocopying. In fact, its name had become a generic term and turned the brand name into a verb: to xerox a page meant to photocopy it. However, it failed to hold on to the first-mover benefits, with latecomers like Canon taking away its market share (Suarez and Lanzolla, 2005: Kotler *et al.*, 2016).

Building a first-mover advantage depends on whether a company can build a durable or a short-lived advantage. With slow-moving markets and technologies, a durable advantage is more likely. Industry dynamics are also crucial. Where the technologies involved are changing rapidly, first movers are unlikely to enjoy lasting benefits. Sometimes those coming afterwards have the advantage. They are able to evaluate what worked well for the pioneers and, just as importantly, what did not work. They can learn from other people's mistakes. They can also benefit from learning about the processes involved in manufacturing. Patents often give just limited protection and there are many countries around the world that do not respect patent rights.

While first-mover advantage often confers great benefits on the company in question, it does not always follow that such benefits will accrue. The question then is does the company try to be a first mover, or follow behind? And a much more important question is the level of new product development that the company engages in. The industry that the company is operating in will have some bearing on the issue, as some industries change faster than others. While the pace may vary, the development of new products has to be an integral part of every company's continuing existence.

Brand Management

According to Kotler *et al.* (2016:423), a **brand** is "a name, symbol, logo, design or image, or any combination of these, which is used to identify a product or service and distinguish it from those of competitors".

In developing new products, it is very important that the company protects those products by branding them. Branding helps buyers by enabling them to identify and evaluate products, and it facilitates repeat purchases. The ultimate aim of a company is to try and engender brand loyalty among its customers, so that they will buy only from that company. Promotion, be it in the form of advertising, public relations, publicity and other marketing devices, plays a very important part in building up brand recognition and loyalty. Brand names can be legally protected by registering those brands and trademarks.

Illustration 9.3: Brand Name Protection

The right to register a brand name as a trademark and have it legally protected is underpinned by legislation. This legislation is designed to protect the goodwill and investment a company has built up in its brand. If a rival company uses the same or a similar trademark, the company that registered the name can sue for trademark infringement as the similarity may cause confusion with customers and damage the value of brand. In the case where a business name is not registered as a trademark, and another company uses the same or a similar company name, redress can be sought in the civil courts under the common law of tort in what is known as 'passing off'. One exception is where a company owner can use his or her family name as a company name even through there may be other similar names in existence.

Companies go to great lengths to protect their brand names, and McDonald's with its golden arches and its 'Big Mac' brand is no exception. A Galway-based fast-food chain, Supermac's, had trademark protection for its brand name in Ireland, but was previously prevented by the US multinational McDonald's from using it in any other country as it was deemed to be too similar to McDonald's and the 'Big Mac'. In 1996, McDonalds had registered the 'Big Mac' as both a food and under a category for restaurant names. (The name 'Supermac's' is derived from the school nickname of its owner, Pat McDonagh.)

However, in January 2019, Supermac's won a landmark battle in its bid to extend the scope of its trademark brand name. A judgment from the European Union Intellectual Property Office (EUIPO) said that McDonald's had produced insufficient evidence to establish general use of the trademark 'Big Mac' as a burger or restaurant name. It initially appeared that Supermac's was now free to use its name throughout the EU. In March 2019, though McDonald's had lodged notice of appeal to the EUIPO, it had yet to lodge the actual grounds of appeal. Once lodged, it is expected to take at least one year for the EUIPO to decide on the appeal. In the meantime, the EUIPO has written to both parties and stated that Supermac's trademark application will not be finalised until the matter with McDonald's 'Big Mac' trademark has been resolved.

Source: Hamilton, 2019; Deegan, 2019

Companies can choose different options when branding their products. Some opt for what is termed **family branding**, where all of the company's products include the name of the company, for example, Campbell's Soups. With Campbell's, the labels are similar, differing only in describing the type of soup, such as mushroom or tomato, but they all have the name Campbell's prominently displayed. This approach facilitates adding new brands to the line-up as consumers will instantly associate the new product with the company. Branding applies to companies as well as to products. The Virgin Group applies the brand name 'Virgin' to all its companies.

Other companies, such as Procter & Gamble (see section on product mix above), use different brand names for each product, and there is no visible association with the company on the product label. It does not confer the advantage of existing brand recognition when launching a new brand. However, if the new product is a failure, it will not damage the existing brands.

Brands (and products) have to be actively managed. The company has to take an overview of all of its products and make decisions about the allocation of resources. There are a number of tools available to enable managers to manage the company's product and brands, such as the Boston Consulting Group Matrix (see **Chapter 10**) and others. These strategic tools will be looked at later on in the context of managing SBUs and companies.

MARKET DEVELOPMENT

From a business perspective, Ireland is a very small market, and for many Irish companies development inevitably means looking overseas in order to grow the market for their goods or services. In a globalised world, this is increasingly becoming the norm. The main theme of this section will deal with developing international markets. In addition to developing international markets, Johnson *et al.* (2018) identified two other forms of market development that are important and must also be examined: new segments and new uses.

New Segments

In any market, there will be only certain groups of people who are interested in a company's products. This is because the needs and wants of people will vary considerably and their purchasing habits will reflect that. Segmentation of the market is a central part of what companies do to identify the different groups and exploit market opportunities. It allows for better planning and a much more effective use of resources, and hence profitability. Those segments that the company is able to satisfy with its products and services are prioritised and targeted. The company will then develop a marketing mix that will suit the targeted segment(s). The marketing mix is the combination of: the product, how it is promoted, its price, how and where it is distributed and the people providing the service that goes with it. If a company can sell its products to a wider variety of segments than originally designed, it will obviously achieve a greater number of sales – the object of the whole exercise.

Targeting can involve a concentration strategy where the company directs its efforts towards either a single market segment by using a single marketing mix, or a differentiated targeting strategy where it develops different marketing mixes for different segments. In both cases, the company needs to have the strategic capability to satisfy those needs. Once the company has decided which segments of the market to target, it must then position the product or service to create a clearly defined image in the minds of its chosen potential customers. This is particularly evident in the fashion industry, where companies are not just selling clothing; they are selling a whole lifestyle image.

A product will be developed for a specific market segment or segments and may satisfy those segments very well. As time passes, the company may identify other segments of the market to which they could also sell. Satellite navigation systems have now become very popular with motorists. The technology for these devices was initially developed for the US forces in the first Gulf War in 1991. The problem with navigation in deserts is that very often there are no clearly defined reference points. One sand dune looks like the next, and these dunes are constantly shifting in strong winds. Global positioning system (GPS) technology was developed using satellites to determine one's position. Having been developed for military use, it was subsequently adapted for civilian use for hill walkers and boating enthusiasts, and then for motorists. It is essentially the same technology, but it is now being targeted at a much wider range of segments.

Another example is the drink Lucozade®. When Lucozade was first developed it was aimed at people convalescing in hospital. It is a glucose-based drink and glucose is the most basic form of energy used by the body. It does not require any breakdown by the body and because it is isotonic it can be absorbed straight through the stomach wall into the blood stream. The company repositioned the product and it is now seen as an energy-replacement drink for people leading active, sporting lives (the opposite segment for which it was originally designed!). While the company added some extra flavours such as orange, the product is still a basic glucose drink. The brand was extremely successful and now sells to a much larger market segment, in addition to the original segment.

New Uses

New products are normally developed with a specific use in mind. Again, with the passage of time, new uses for products can appear that were not there when the product was first developed. There are some similarities between 'new uses' and new segments. Throughout the 1980s, silicon chip manufacturers and consumer electronics companies put much effort into reducing the size of electrical appliances. This involved both improving existing technology but, more importantly, developing new technology. This technology was then taken, modified and used to create totally different products such as smartphones and MP3 players. Such devices would not have been possible without the process of miniaturisation, but that was not the original intended purpose.

Stainless steel is another example. Stainless steel was first used to manufacture mass-produced cutlery, and for years was synonymous with Sheffield in England. It was later used for beer kegs. While wood is necessary for the maturation of spirits such as brandy, there is no need to mature beer. The manufacture of wooden barrels is a skilled trade for coopers, and so wooden beer kegs were expensive to produce and very brittle. Steel kegs are extremely robust and last for years. Stainless steel is also used in the automotive and the aeronautical industries. Such industries (and uses) were not envisaged when the product was first developed, but have greatly increased the size of the market for the product. Finally, researchers at General Electric adapted technology for aircraft engine fan blades into the blades used by wind turbines (of which GE is one of the world's leading manufacturers).

International Markets

In the middle of a severe downturn, many companies will retrench and focus on home markets. While this may be necessary, the company should be certain that growth opportunities do not exist elsewhere. In terms of market growth for Irish companies, by far the most important way of growing markets is to look at international markets for opportunities. International expansion is a form of diversification, and this will be developed in detail in **Chapter 10**. The strategic tools used in carrying out environmental analysis and understanding strategic capability are an important foundation for identifying possibilities for future expansion (see **Chapter 5**). Ultimately, international expansion should exploit environmental opportunities.

Chapter 5, in discussing the European Union, highlighted the opportunities available to Irish companies in terms of the sheer size of the market that is available without any restrictions such as tariffs or barriers, or import quotas. In the early years of EU membership, Ireland saw many of its indigenous industries close, as they could not compete with more competitive European companies. Over the last couple of decades, Irish companies gradually, but consistently, improved to a point where the quality of its products and the productivity of its workers could match the best. Clearly, exposure to the international arena of the European Union has been very beneficial to Ireland, apart from benefits such as the structural funds that Ireland received in the 1980s and 1990s.

Now Irish companies are competing very successfully on international markets and, once the home market is saturated, this allows Irish firms to gain access to potentially much larger markets. Opportunities are not just restricted to the EU. In recent years, many Irish companies have established a strong presence in China, which has a population of 1.4 billion people (see **Chapter 5**). Emerging markets are likely to increase in importance quite substantially in the future. Apart from increasing the size of the market, operating in international markets can play a large part in reducing risk, as the company is no longer dependent on one particular market if there is a downturn. It can also increase the life cycle of a product that may be reaching decline in the home market, but could still be in the growth or maturity phase in a less developed country. As the development costs of the product will have been well recouped, it can offer great possibilities as a 'cash cow' (a product generating large profits — see **Chapter 10**). In developing foreign markets, cultural intelligence is vitally important in terms of forging relationships with potential buyers. Cultural intelligence (Earley and Mosakowaski, 2004) was discussed in **Chapter 2** in the context of leadership.

International Drivers

Yip (2003) refers to various factors that are driving internationalisation. While these will vary from one industry to another, they provide a useful insight into the nature of how international factors are impacting on Irish companies, and how they need to respond.

The Irish economy is a very open one (it exports and imports a very high percentage of its GDP), and even in terms of protecting market share of the home economy, Irish companies must be able to compete with the best international businesses. The section on Porter's Diamond in **Chapter 5** highlighted the importance of competition in developing the strategic capability of a firm. Irish companies have made enormous improvements in this respect in the last couple of decades. From that perspective, Irish companies can be confident that they can compete in the international arena. The World Trade talks are also aimed at reducing restrictions on international trade and increasing greater interdependence between countries. Technical specifications are becoming increasingly standardised and this also facilitates greater trade.

Satellite television and the internet have played an important role in opening up Western culture to other parts of the world, and the reverse is also true. This has contributed enormously to what can be termed a 'mass homogenisation' of global demand for products, ranging from consumer goods to clothing to music. Electronic goods come with instruction booklets printed in perhaps 20 different languages, reflecting the fact that the same item is sold in Tokyo and in Dublin.

Driving down costs is an essential element of running any organisation. The value chain and value system is increasingly becoming globalised as firms strive to find the lowest costs, wherever they may be in the world. International expansion can help an organisation to lower costs by selecting the optimum location for every part of its value chain. By selling to a global market (with its size implications), it provides enormous possibilities for achieving economies of scale in manufacturing. This is critical in the pharmaceutical industry where development costs are so high that it is essential for each company to achieve global sales. There are also economies of scale in marketing. Large international hotel chains such as the Marriott Group, which has a few thousand hotels around the globe, can reap huge economies in marketing, as well as other areas such as purchasing.

Competitive Advantage

One main objective in operating on an international basis is to develop a competitive advantage. Porter's Diamond looked at how some countries can be more competitive than others, and within those countries some industries are more competitive. These are important factors in deciding competitive advantage. Many Irish software companies have located in Silicon Valley to be at the cutting edge of developments in the industry. This allows companies access to technology and know-how that they otherwise may not have, and leverages the core competences that they have developed. As a result, once Irish companies can compete there, it means that they have developed a level of expertise and competences that can allow them to compete successfully anywhere in the world.

While most of the pharmaceutical companies in Ireland are foreign-owned multinationals, the development of clusters has resulted in a competitive advantage, and it is Ireland's most important industry in terms of the value of exports. As with the software industry, this in turn has led to the development of many related and supporting domestic industries. Similarly, horse-breeding is very much an indigenous industry in which Ireland is regarded as a global leader and is responsible for considerable employment while supporting many other businesses indirectly.

The discussion on the value system can also be widened to look for international benefits in locating elements of the value chain that will yield greatest advantage. Many Irish companies are outsourcing part of their value chain to lower cost economies, particularly to avail of cheaper labour. Improvements in information technology are greatly facilitating this process. Differences in labour costs, taxation, energy costs, productivity rates, inflation and the environment for doing business are all factors that will create large variations from one country to another. While labour costs are high in Ireland by international standards, other factors such as the low rate of corporation tax, and a highly educated and productive workforce place this country in an advantageous position compared to developing foreign markets. Many foreign companies are locating R&D facilities in this country because of the above-mentioned factors. The presence of foreign multinationals operating here has had a highly beneficial impact on Irish companies, which in turn has brought them to a level where they can operate successfully in the international arena.

Selecting Markets

Notwithstanding the discussion on the drivers of globalisation, there remain many differences between various markets. Cultures and lifestyles still reflect national variations and, while they may have been eroded somewhat, they still exist. One major difference between markets is their purchasing power, so even if the desire for certain goods exists, the purchasing power may not match that desire. Markets have to be prioritised in terms of their attractiveness. Johnson *et al.* (2017) differentiate between market characteristics and competitive characteristics.

Market characteristics The market characteristics (using the PESTEL framework (see **Chapter 5**)) take into account the relative attractiveness of each particular market. From a political perspective, various countries will have very different business environments that may or may not be attractive for a company doing business there. This environment can also change significantly with a change in government. While the overall size of a market is important, economic factors will vary a great deal. As stated, there must be sufficient purchasing power available in a particular market, otherwise it will be of no benefit. (For example, though the people of a certain country may have a passion for horseracing, it does not follow that they can afford to buy Irish racehorses, and so there will be no market.) Economic indicators such as GNP/GDP, inflation rates, interest rates, and currency rates will give a good indication of the attractiveness of a country. Social factors, including favourable demographic segments, suitably qualified workers and cultural factors are important. Finally, the legal situation is important from the perspective of protecting and enforcing commercial contracts and intellectual property.

Ghemawat (2001) has stated that these factors are important, not just in terms of comparing one country with another to prioritise them, but also the compatibility in terms of culture and language between the country and the company that is considering operating there. If we examine this from the perspective of American companies such as Intel operating in Ireland, there is a very strong compatibility in language, culture, work ethic, education, etc.

Cultural variations can be important factors to consider from a number of perspectives. In dealing with people, either customers or employees, one must be conscious of major differences in things such as body language, how people greet one another, the use and meaning of different colours and the significance of numbers, as well as shapes and symbols. These are particularly relevant in the use of advertising. In addition to being aware of cultural variations, companies must make a conscious effort to bridge any cultural divide, while respecting the differences.

Competitive factors The factors affecting competition are also just as important for foreign markets as they are for the domestic market. Porter's Five Forces Analysis can be used to determine the existence of competitive forces and their intensity. If the level of competition in a country is deemed to be very high in a particular industry, then that particular market would be an unattractive location to establish a presence. Johnson *et al.* (2017) suggest that one must examine the likelihood of retaliation from other competitors in that market, along with their power to fight back. This is usually related to their share of the market. The likelihood of retaliation and their power in the market can significantly modify the attractiveness of choosing a particular country to enter. This analysis can also be used to determine the benefits of expansion in an existing foreign market.

Emerging markets and the BRIC countries (Brazil, Russia, India and China) have a growing middle-class population with high disposable incomes and so offer enormous opportunities for

Irish companies. Part of the remit of Enterprise Ireland is to help Irish companies expand abroad. They can provide significant assistance by way of country-specific market information as well as supporting companies in the process.

Risks

There are, however, certain risks that are part of international operations which need to be taken into consideration. Dess *et al.* (2004) suggest that there are four risks:

Political risk – forces such as conflict and military action, terrorism, social unrest, etc., make some countries across the globe unattractive as locations in which to become involved. For example, there have been numerous kidnappings of western workers in Iraq, and companies would have to bear this in mind if considering locating there. Host countries may impose restrictions on the amount of trade that can take place or impose tariffs to protect home companies from competition. Other restrictions may require foreign companies to operate as part of a joint venture, or there may be stringent bureaucratic requirements.

Economic risk – when the political situation is unstable it also increases the economic risk to a company. Destruction of property, non-payment of debts or loss of revenue through piracy of intellectual property can result in significant financial loss.

Currency risks – currency fluctuations can pose serious risks to a company. Since the referendum in the UK in regard to Brexit, there has been a substantial devaluation in the value of pound Sterling vis-á-vis the euro. This means that Irish goods are a lot more expensive in Britain compared to British goods. If tariffs are put in place after Brexit, this will add to the currency differential making Irish goods uncompetitive in the UK.

Management risk – the cultural variation (discussed above) adds to the complexity of managing an international workforce, and other factors such as distribution systems, customer preferences, etc., can all make the process of managing a company more difficult.

These risks will vary with the level of involvement in a particular foreign country. If the company is just exporting, the risk will be relatively low and confined primarily to currency devaluation or non-payment for a consignment. The company can then make a decision to withdraw from operating in that country. At the other end of the scale, a wholly-owned facility will expose the company to considerable risk.

STRATEGIES FOR ENTERING FOREIGN MARKETS

In **Chapter 7** we were introduced to organisational structure. It must be remembered that the structure of an organisation should support the strategy it is pursuing. The structure will therefore have to change, depending on the nature of its geographical operations, probably to some form of multi-divisional, transnational, or matrix structure. The structure will reflect the level of involvement in international markets. There are many choices available and each one requires a different level of organisational resources:

- Exporting
- Licensing and franchising
- Strategic alliances and joint venture
- Foreign direct investment (wholly-owned subsidiary).

Licensing and franchising, along with strategic alliances and joint ventures are discussed in detail in **Chapter 11** and, consequently, are only briefly covered here.

Exporting

Exporting involves manufacturing goods in one country and selling them in another. Exporting is the most flexible form of international trade, involving the least amount of risk as the exporting company generally does not make any large capital investment in the country to which they are exporting. Companies will normally begin the process of going international by exporting to a neighbouring country. For many decades, Irish companies would have exported to the UK, particularly agricultural produce. This process would have been facilitated by a common language and geographical proximity.

Though during this century Ireland's dependence on the British market has fallen significantly, at the beginning of 2019, it still remains the Republic's largest export market, with 34% of exports going to Britain. Brexit is likely to, out of necessity, reduce this dependence considerably, although there are still huge trade interdependencies between Northern Ireland and the Republic of Ireland, particularly in relation to food products.

According to the Central Statistics Office (CSO) (2019), the total value of goods exported from Ireland in 2018 was £141 billion, up from €123 billion in 2017. The total value of imports in 2018 was €90 billion, leaving a trade surplus of €51 billion, which demonstrates the high value-added nature of Irish exports. The pharmaceutical industry is Ireland's top exporter and is responsible for over €55 billion of exports. Other important industries include the medical technology sector, software products, information and telecommunications technology, aircraft leasing, financial products and the agri–food sector. In total, IDA Ireland client companies account for over 66% of total exports. However, exports from indigenous Irish companies also make an important contribution to the health of the economy.

While Britain remains the largest export market, Enterprise Ireland has made a considerable effort to help Irish companies find alternative markets ahead of the Brexit deadline. The eurozone accounts for 20% of total exports and this saw strong growth of 9% in 2018. Almost 90 companies exported to the eurozone from Ireland for the first time in 2017, reflecting the move away from dependence on Britain. The US and Canada account for 17% of Ireland's export markets and this grew by 7% in 2018. Exports to central and eastern Europe and to Asia were up by 9% in 2018. In addition to

Enterprise Ireland, the Irish Exporters Association also assists its members to grow their exports to world markets by providing a wide variety of export services.

Exporting increases the market for a company's products, allowing them to reap economies of scale without any major financial exposure. The internet has greatly facilitated this process. As such, exporting is a relatively inexpensive way of entering the market, especially if a foreign wholesaler with experience in distributing imports is used, although the exporter may choose to set up their own distribution network. Export agents bring together buyers and sellers from different countries, earning a commission for their work. Compared to other methods of entering foreign markets, it is very cheap. An export house and export merchants buy products from different companies and then sell them in other countries. Certain modifications may be needed for packaging and labelling in order to sell into other markets. Market research should be carried out to ascertain the level of demand and to see if there are any problems with regard to brand names, etc. Brand names often do not have the same meaning in other languages and may have negative connotations. For that reason, companies sometimes make up brand names that have no inherent meaning as such, e.g. Kodak or Esso.

There are also some drawbacks to exporting. Manufacturing costs in the home country may be more expensive than the host country. This is often the case with Irish goods at present, as labour costs here have increased dramatically in recent years compared to other countries. In addition, any depreciation of the US Dollar and Sterling can make Irish exports more expensive in those countries. Fortunately, this does not apply in the eurozone. Being an island nation, there are also higher transportation costs than, for example, French goods being sold in Germany. In most cases, companies will begin to export after they have established a solid presence in the home market, but there are exceptions. Some companies might be very specialised in their nature and the home market might be too small. The internet has also changed the nature of exporting and, for many companies, their goods can be sold across the world just as easily as in the home market.

Licensing and Franchising

There are occasions when a company may not have the resources or organisational capability to operate directly in another country. In such cases, it may license a company in the target country to manufacture the product and use its trademark in return for a royalty. This also has the advantage of minimising financial exposure as it does not involve committing resources. In some cases, it may be a government condition to operate in that market. Licencing and franchising will be dealt with in greater detail in **Chapter 11**.

Strategic Alliances and Joint Ventures

Joint ventures and strategic alliances involve sharing risk with a partner and have become increasingly popular as a way for companies to enter foreign markets. They differ in that strategic alliances comprise two companies working in co-operation with each other, while joint ventures involve setting up a new company that is jointly owned by the parent companies. By combining resources and expertise, companies can do better together than they could by operating on their own. Together, they can develop new core competences that will allow them to compete. In some cases it is a requirement by the host government before granting permission to operate in that country.

Foreign Direct Investment

A company may decide to invest directly in a foreign market. This can be achieved by purchasing an existing company or establishing a greenfield site where it builds a manufacturing facility from scratch. It involves a good deal of risk, which, unlike a joint venture, is borne solely by the parent company. On the other hand, it allows full control of the facility and distribution network. Potentially, it also offers the highest level of return. Acquisition is quicker than developing a greenfield site, but it can create problems in regard to integrating separate corporate cultures. A greenfield site would allow the company to build a state-of-the-art facility, and this could give the company a competitive advantage.

In addition, and depending on the host country, there may be financial incentives available to attract such investment. (Companies like Intel received millions of euro in grants from the IDA to attract them to Ireland.) Either option still involves a considerable financial outlay, so it is extremely important that the parent company has carried out sufficient research on the market beforehand.

STRATEGIES FOR OPERATING INTERNATIONALLY

Operating internationally raises issues as to whether the company should localise its products and services for each individual market, or whether to offer the same product around the world without any modification. There are three possible strategies, ranging from standardised products sold globally, to products that are adapted for each individual market:

- Global strategy – standardised throughout the world
- Transnational strategy – a global strategy adapted for individual markets
- Multi-domestic strategy – a localised approach to each individual market.

These are part of a continuum rather than discrete strategies, and there is considerable overlap between them. The strategies highlight the different approaches required by companies, which depend on a whole variety of factors and conditions. This will be examined in greater detail below, having first looked at the three approaches.

Global Strategy

A global strategy involves treating the world as a single, large market. It is sometimes referred to as a 'think global, act global' strategy. It is based on the premise that demand for products throughout the world is similar and companies can achieve lower cost and reap large economies of scale by manufacturing standardised products (and quality) that can sell around the globe. While minor changes might sometimes be made, it would not be appropriate if there is a requirement to make major changes to suit the local market.

Global strategy is a highly centralised strategy that is defined in the corporate headquarters and involves strong co-ordination between all units. It requires the same competitive approach and utilises the same capabilities across all markets. Global strategy is particularly relevant to industries that have large R&D costs, such as the pharmaceutical and semiconductor industries. It is also relevant to the fashion industry. Gucci products are in demand around the globe and the same items are sold in Japan and the US. Likewise, it is the same demand for Rolex watches that entices buyers in Dublin and New Delhi. However, Ghemawat (2010) believes that many changes have taken place in terms of the nature of global demand and that it makes sense to adopt a vision in which national differences remain pronounced. The primary challenge for organisations is how to manage those differences. It will require a fundamental shift in strategy to cater for regional varieties of offering in terms of taste, price sensitivity and infrastructure for service and delivery.

Transnational Strategy

In reality, there are very few truly 'universal' products that can be sold unaltered around the world. Products such as commercial aircraft seem universal, but each airline will want different layout configurations and will have different specifications for on-board equipment. A transnational strategy takes the benefits of a global approach, but adapts it to the different markets in which it is operating. It is a 'think global, act local' approach. It is a trade-off between the scale efficiencies that can be gained from a global product and the benefits from increased sales due to local adaptation. In essence, it overcomes the limitations of global and multi-domestic strategies. Competition will differ in each country. It recognises the importance of being responsive to the needs of various markets, but only as a means of achieving greater global sales in the international arena. A certain amount of knowledge transfer can take place between various parts of the organisation around the world, but the peculiarities of the different markets can make this difficult to achieve in reality. The company will operate globally and establish its activities in the most beneficial locations for each. For example, manufacturing could be in a low-cost country, while R&D is located where there is a ready supply of suitable graduates.

A transnational strategy is much less centralised in terms of decision-making, which is pushed down as far as possible in the organisation. At the same time, it recognises that such decentralisation increases the complexity (and costs) of its operations. Not all aspects of decision-making are decentralised. Value-chain activities can be divided up between those that are kept central, such as supply-chain activities and operations (as these will reap economies of scale), and other activities that can be devolved, such as marketing and customer service (these will help make the product more appealing to customers in each market).

Sometimes product modifications will be needed. Cars being sold in the UK and in Ireland require the steering column on the right-hand side, compared to the left in European and American markets. There is even a further difference in the right-handed version. In Ireland, the speedometer is in kilometres per hour, while in the UK it is in miles per hour. In most European countries washing machines are front-loaded, while in France they are traditionally top-loaded. These are relatively basic, but necessary modifications that are needed to succeed in each market. The clothing company Benetton has its operations configured to allow for maximum flexibility, while minimising costs, in catering for differing demands in each country.

Marketing will obviously differ in each market, taking into account language, culture, religious beliefs and social norms. Sometimes the advertising content needs to be adapted, as different markets will respond to different unique selling propositions (USPs).

A **unique selling proposition** is the unique product benefit that the company promotes in a consistent manner in a target market.

Ideally, a USP will travel across different markets. For example, the Procter & Gamble brand, Head & Shoulders, is based on its clinical ability to clear dandruff. This would appeal to all markets and differentiates it from other shampoos.

Multi-domestic Strategy

In some instances, there are considerable variations in tastes between different regions and, consequently, companies will need to respond with a range of products to reflect those needs. The company will tailor its competitive approach and product offerings to fit the specific conditions in each country in which it operates. It is a 'think local, act local' approach that produces goods locally for independent markets. There are many reasons for such localisation.

Demand for items and competition will differ in each market and businesses need to respond to that. As markets are in different stages of development, product life cycles can also vary. In developing, or less affluent, markets consumers often prefer purchasing smaller quantities rather than larger economy packs, which might be better value but cost considerably more. Sometimes, it might be a requirement of the host government, which may have strict specification requirements; or there may be tariffs or quotas to be circumvented by sourcing materials locally.

For clothing items, climatic conditions will vary considerably and this will be reflected in wide variations in demand. Generally, food items require considerable localisation as tastes differ according to ethnic background and culture. Other products such as car lubricants also require adaptation for local climate conditions, vehicle types and equipment applications. Castrol, for example, has an enormous number of different product variations to suit different local climatic conditions, variations in vehicle types and equipment uses. Services are different to tangible products, and various economic, legal and social structures will mean that services will usually have to be tailored for each country in which they are being provided. This will diminish the ability to achieve global economies in service provision.

Under a multi-domestic strategy, a company's regional managers will have considerable latitude in making decisions concerning what changes are required allowing for local tastes and preferences, as they are considered to know the market best. Co-ordination between the different parts of the company may be quite loose, given the varying conditions, and there is little opportunity for knowledge transfer as the competences required for each market can be different. A 'localisation' strategy will add considerable expense to the product, but is necessary if the company is to sell its products in that market. From that perspective, it is generally not suited to a low-cost strategy unless the company has the ability to customise products and still reap economies of scale. Finally, as consumer demand does become more globalised, the degree of customisation will change over time. In recent years, the Chinese market has become much more 'Western' in its outlook, and demand is reflecting those changes.

Globalisation or Localisation

Various writers on strategy have their own views on the globalisation/localisation debate. An examination of the literature suggests that, in reality, while there are examples at either end of the continuum, the majority of international companies operate on the basis of having a global strategy that is adapted to a greater or lesser extent to the needs of the various locations in which they are operating.

Earlier in this chapter we examined the international drivers that promote globalisation: common customer demand, competition, the need to minimise costs and moves by governments and international bodies (Yip, 2003). The move towards global demand is not a new phenomenon. Back in 1983, Levitt believed that a company could develop a sustainable competitive advantage by operating globally because of a similar demand worldwide and the efficient use of resources. Likewise, Ohmae (1989a) suggested that "most managers are near-sighted" and they should be looking at home and overseas markets as "equidistant". He suggests that, through the flow of information, people have become global citizens that demand universal products. However, while the product may be universal, it often requires approaching each market differently and building a complete local infrastructure to create local demand. Profits too will vary from one market to another, and companies need to adjust their expectations. Ohmae (1989b) also suggests that the best way to achieve globalisation for most companies is to form strategic alliances. Fixed costs in many industries have grown so large that it is better to share the burden by collaborating with other companies and, through such collaboration, increase global sales.

Ghemawat (2003) believes that the world is not so homogenous. He believes that there are opportunities to be gained by exploiting differences and that there are "many forms of arbitrage that offer sustainable sources of competitive advantage". These include cultural, administrative, geographic and economic arbitrage.

Rigby and Vishwanath (2006) suggest that, in the past, consumer markets were dominated by companies that pursued strategies of standardisation. This is no longer the case and success for retailers and product manufacturers now rests on their ability to adapt for local preferences while maintaining economies of scale: "Combining sophisticated data analysis with innovative organisational structures, they're gaining the efficiencies of centralised management without losing the responsiveness of local authority." They believe that standardisation undermines innovation throughout the supply chain. Technological advances now provide both retailers and suppliers with considerable information about consumers' buying habits and preferences, and this facilitates the process of localising stores, products and services with precision.

It is important to get the balance right. Too much localisation can dilute the brand and lead to escalating costs. Too much standardisation can diminish market share and profitability. It is vital that managers understand the business in terms of the cost involved in localisation and what impact it will have on sales. Store-by-store customisation is very expensive. (Though it is worth noting that artificial intelligence (AI) will provide enormous opportunities to customise products for individuals at little cost once the initial investment in AI has been made.)

They suggest that one way around the problem is to use clustering techniques. Companies analyse data to identify communities or clusters that display similar buying habits, and products are then customised on the basis of clusters. This simplifies the process and the company still benefits from economies of scale, reducing costs considerably. The company collects as much data as possible on key elements of each store's business over a period of time. From this data, they then identify perhaps three to five different cluster types for customisation opportunities. VF, the apparel maker that owns brands such as Lee, Wrangler and The North Face, combines "demographic and lifestyle data with daily store-level sales data, extensive consumer research and competitor analysis to develop localisation strategies". As a result, they have reported an improvement in sales by up to 50% while reducing store inventories and markdowns. Tesco gains an enormous volume of data from its loyalty cards, and using that knowledge has built specialised food formats in the UK, clustered to meet local demand.

Rigby and Vishwanath (2006) believe that too much decentralisation can backfire as local managers lack the level of skill and data to make the right decisions on a constant basis. It also makes the process too complicated and costly. Most decisions need to be co-ordinated centrally by managers who have a good overview of the entire business and demand patterns. Central co-ordination is also essential in developing relationships between suppliers and retailers. Store managers play an important part in information gathering about local events and market conditions. By having most of the merchandising decisions made by headquarters, it frees up store managers to concentrate on running the daily operations and engaging with customers.

Finally, Rosabeth Moss Kanter (2003) looks at the effect that globalisation has on communities. She believes that companies can meet global standards and tap into local networks. It is a symbiotic relationship that develops the local communities in which global companies are based, and these communities provide the company with one or more of the intangible assets that make customers loyal: concepts (leading-edge ideas); competence (the ability to translate ideas into applications); and connections (alliances among businesses to leverage core capabilities). Her research looked at five American communities or regions that have become world-class centres for manufacturing, including Spartanburg-Grenville in South Carolina where BMW established its first-ever manufacturing facility outside Germany. These clusters develop over time, which in turn attracts more foreign direct investment. It also leads to greater assimilation of the global company into the local community. She believes that there are four factors critical for success:

- Visionary leaders in the community who have a very clear economic development strategy
- A hospitable business climate and work ethic
- Customised training and development of workers' skills
- Collaboration within the business community, and between business and government, to improve quality and business performance.

This outside investment develops local communities, which has a positive spin-off effect on the local economy. Communities need to be able to attract these companies in the first instance, and then provide a forum which brings them all together to develop the common good. There are many similarities between her findings and the effect that foreign direct investment has had on Ireland in the last 20 or so years.

CONCLUSION

Nothing stays the same in the business world for very long. Companies must be constantly reviewing their position and developing new strategies to achieve their organisational objectives. In times of a downturn in the economy, some companies will want to consolidate their business and are happy to tread water until the economy shows signs of improving. Others will constantly look for opportunities to increase their market share.

With improvements in technology, product life cycles are getting ever shorter. Organisations must be constantly monitoring the markets in which they operate to develop a good understanding of what their target market is looking for. If the company cannot develop new products and services to satisfy consumer demand, customers will move their business to rival companies. The dilemma for companies then is to understand and meet consumer demand with a range of products in a profitable manner. New product development in most cases is expensive and firms need to make decisions balancing the need for consumer-driven demand with keeping costs under control.

The Irish market is small and puts a limit on the amount of growth a company can achieve unless it looks to foreign markets. Indeed, in many industries, international drivers are putting competitive pressure on companies to operate on a global basis. Because of the nature of some companies' product and technology, they have no option but to start on an international footing. Indeed, Irish companies are succeeding very well in the international arena. There are a number of strategies that companies can use to compete in foreign markets, but one policy issue they have to decide is whether to adapt their products for each market or operate with a global product.

Many companies will operate in one particular industry and build up expertise that cements their reputation in that industry. Others will diversify into related or unrelated industries. Unrelated diversification requires very different corporate parenting skills by the centre, and the portfolio of companies has to be actively managed.

Chapter 11 will examine how these four broad development directions can be achieved by an organisation, either through organic growth, strategic alliances or mergers and acquisitions. Once again, companies will use a variety of these methods, depending on the particular circumstances, to achieve their objectives.

SUMMARY

H. Igor Ansoff argued that there are four broad strategic directions open to a company:

- **Market penetration** – consolidating the company's position in the market and developing a larger market share.
- **Product development** – developing new products to meet market needs.
- **Market development** – developing new markets (including international markets) as well as new market segments and new uses for products.
- **Diversification** – related and unrelated diversification (**Chapter 10**).

While these are listed as alternative directions, in reality companies will pursue most, if not all, options, possibly at the same time. They are driven by innovation and organisational capability.

Market penetration Most companies will try to build up a greater share of the current market with their current products. There is a strong correlation between high market share and profitability. In turn this profitability can be reinvested and so build up further market share. Once market share has been built up, companies will want to protect the investment that they have made. This is done by increasing advertising, price cuts or building customer loyalty. While consolidation is a defensive measure, it is important that what the organisation has it holds. Consolidation may also include withdrawing from certain markets to concentrate on core areas. There can be a speculative reason behind divesting. In some instances, it makes sense for companies to divest underperforming subsidiaries.

Product development The development of new products should be seen as an integral part of what a company does. This involves developing brand new or modified products for existing markets. In a competitive environment, any firm that does not keep up to date with new product development will quickly lose market share and may go out of business as other companies innovate. Invention is the discovery of a new product; innovation goes one step further in bringing that new product, process or service into use. New product development presents certain problems in terms of cost and the management of products coming on stream. There are a number of issues that need to be taken into consideration, including: definition of products; product line and product mix; R&D; product life cycle; first-mover advantage; and brand management.

Market development There are three forms of market development: new segments, new uses, and geographical spread. Segmentation of the market is a central part of what companies do to identify different groups and exploit market opportunities. New segments can be identified. Targeting can involve a concentration strategy where the company directs its efforts towards a single market segment. It must then position the product or service to create a clearly defined image in the minds of its chosen customers.

Going international There are various factors that are driving internationalisation and there are a number of different factors that must be taken into account in choosing which markets to enter. There are certain risks with international operations that need to be considered. Strategies available for entering foreign markets are: exporting; licensing and franchising; strategic alliances and joint ventures; and foreign direct investment. There are three possible strategies, ranging from standardised products sold throughout the world to products that are adapted for each individual market:

- Global strategy – standardised throughout the world
- Transnational strategy – a global strategy adapted for individual markets
- Multi-domestic strategy – a localised approach to each individual market.

These are part of a continuum rather than discrete strategies, and there is considerable overlap between them.

DISCUSSION QUESTIONS

1. Differentiate between the various elements of a market penetration strategy.
2. Critically analyse the importance of research and development in supporting product development as a strategic option.
3. Discuss the factors that need to be taken into consideration in managing new product development.
4. Evaluate the importance of market development as a strategy for Irish companies.
5. Discuss the various factors that need to be taken into consideration when selecting foreign markets.
6. Explore the various options open to Irish companies when entering foreign markets.

CHAPTER 10

Diversification

LEARNING OBJECTIVES

On completion of this chapter, you will be able to:

- Assess when diversification is an appropriate strategy for an organisation
- Distinguish between related and unrelated diversification
- Critically analyse the impact diversification has on performance
- Evaluate the different methods of portfolio management

"Sometimes it's better not to listen when people tell you that something can't be done. I didn't ask for permission or approval. I just went ahead and did it."

Michael Dell

INTRODUCTION

As organisations grow in size, they often develop in different ways compared to their original business. **Chapter 9** dealt with companies expanding into other markets, but companies can also branch into different types of businesses or technologies, becoming diversified. According to Fitzroy and Hulbert (2005:244), "the degree, nature, and direction of diversification are some of the most important corporate strategy decisions" that a company will have to make. Strategy-making becomes a much more complicated affair for diversified companies. It involves assessing a number of different business environments and developing strategies for each business and for the overall corporation.

Chapter 10 examines the impact diversification has on corporate parenting styles, including the reasons why a company might diversify. There are two main types of diversification: related and unrelated. However, the distinction between the two types can often be blurred. In turn, related diversification can be subdivided into horizontal integration or vertical integration. The impact of diversification on performance is also examined in this chapter. Each form of diversification requires different types of managerial skills and corporate parenting styles. The aim of any strategy is to add value to the organisation, and so the type of corporate parenting style must be aligned to the specific nature of diversification in the company.

This chapter also discusses various strategies by which diversification can take place: internal start-up, joint ventures, and acquisitions. As the diversified company grows in size, managing the portfolio is a vital component of the success of the business and different techniques of managing the portfolio are examined.

CHOOSING A DIVERSIFICATION STRATEGY

As companies grow, they will sometimes develop in different directions from their original business. Such development is known as diversification and it can take many forms. In some instances there may be a strong common theme running through the different businesses – related diversification. On other occasions, the expansion may be into business areas that have no relationship with the original business.

Definition **Diversification** is a strategy whereby a company expands from being a single business operation into different businesses of varying relatedness.

The parenting style for each organisation will differ considerably as to how centralised or devolved the decision-making process is. This is generally related to the level of diversification in the company. It may involve detailed planning by the corporate headquarters for each business unit, or at a minimum giving approval for plans drafted by the SBU. Either way, the corporate parent must have a vision and a coherent plan for the entire organisation towards which all elements of the company focus their attention.

According to Thompson *et al.* (2018), the task of crafting a diversified company's overall strategy involves four distinct aspects:

1. Picking new industries to enter and deciding on the means of entry. Should the focus be a broad or narrow diversification, and should it be achieved by organic growth or acquisition?
2. Initiating actions to boost the combined performance of the businesses the firm has entered. It must strengthen the long-term competitive position of each company and the overall group.
3. Pursuing opportunities to create cross-business leverage – looking for ways to reduce costs and create efficiencies.
4. Establishing investment priorities and steering corporate resources into the most attractive business units.

Reasons for Diversifying

There are a number of reasons why a company might diversify. The acid test is ultimately whether diversifying increases shareholder wealth (other stakeholders' interests must also be taken into account). It can achieve such an increase in wealth in a number of ways, primarily through efficiency gains obtained from better utilisation of the company's resources in achieving economies of scope (where the company has underutilised resources or competences that can be deployed elsewhere in the company, such as management skills or financial resources). There can be opportunities to expand into related businesses that complement the current product line and technology.

Later in this chapter we will examine portfolios which can provide opportunities to cross-subsidise businesses that show potential. The company may also have an established brand name that can be applied to other businesses in a profitable manner, such as the Virgin Group. On occasion, a company may have exhausted all opportunities to further expand in its present business and, in order to achieve further growth, it will have to diversify into other areas. Likewise its current market may be in decline. Finally, by diversifying, a company is spreading risk across a number of industries. Most industries are cyclical to some degree, but not to the same extent and timing. By increasing the range of businesses, a company is lessening the impact that a downturn would have on its profitability.

According to Markides (1997:94–9), there are six questions that a manager should ask when considering diversification:

1. What can the company do better than any of its competitors in its current markets? Managers must have a clear definition of their business and of what sets them apart from their competitors. This will increase the likelihood of success.
2. What strategic assets do we need in order to succeed in the new market? Success in one market does not ensure success in another unless the company has the strategic assets it requires.
3. Can we catch up to or leapfrog competitors at their own game? If we lack some strategic assets, can they be bought or developed?
4. Will diversification break up strategic assets that need to be kept together? By breaking up strategic assets, will this diminish their overall effectiveness?
5. Will we be simply a player in the new market or will we emerge a winner? Can our competitors imitate our strategic assets and outperform us?
6. What can our company learn by diversifying, and are we sufficiently organised to learn from it? Diversification is potentially a learning experience that can improve overall organisational efficiency.

TYPES OF DIVERSIFICATION

Diversification can be divided into two broad classifications:

*   **Related diversification** where there are common links between the value chains of each company. There are two subdivisions:
    o   Vertical integration, either forward or backward integration
    o   Horizontal integration.

*   **Unrelated diversification** where the company moves into a business where there is no common link in their value chains.

Related Diversification

Related diversification is seeking to develop a strategic fit between the value chains of similar companies. This strategic fit can be in areas such as marketing or using a common brand name, sharing R&D resources, transferring valuable skills or know-how between companies and building up common capabilities.

Vertical integration Vertical integration describes the company moving either backwards or forwards along the value system. The inbound logistics of a company describes the movement of goods from a supplier to a manufacturer. **Backward vertical integration** is where the manufacturer moves back along the value system and takes control of a company that supplies it with raw materials, components or machinery. This might be done in a situation where the supplier has strong bargaining power and is demanding high prices. By moving back along the supply chain, the manufacturer is now achieving control over its inputs, particularly quality. A brewing company might take over farms supplying it with grain in order to ensure that its grain is of an appropriate quality and standard.

Outbound logistics is where a company interfaces with its distribution network in the value system. **Forward vertical integration** is where a company moves forward along the value system and takes over distribution systems or retail outlets. In the UK, many breweries own public houses (known as tied houses) which promote the beer of their parent companies. McDonald's supplies all its restaurants (most of which are privately held by franchisees) with all of the food and beverage supplies that are required.

Horizontal integration Horizontal integration involves moving into activities that are either competitive products or complementary products. Examples of companies/products competing with one another include some of the international hotel companies that own different chains offering different facilities and levels of comfort. While different star ratings are aimed at different segments, there is a large overlap between those segments and they are effectively competing for customers in the same industry. We previously examined the product mix of the fast-moving consumer goods company Procter & Gamble. The company manufactures a number of different washing powders, including Bold, Dreft, Tide, which are individually branded products that also compete with one another.

An example of related diversification into **complementary products** is Phonewatch. Eir, the former semi-state organisation, is a telephone operator involved in voice telephony. While home security alarm systems is a different industry, its effectiveness as a deterrent is largely dependent on telephone contact between the security company and the Gardaí to notify them that there has been a break-in at the house. The alarm system is connected to the phone system and there is a technological similarity in monitoring the alarm through the phone network. It is a complementary product that builds in 'switching' costs and reinforces the relationship between the company and the customer.

Synergy Related diversification (and to a lesser extent, unrelated diversification) should produce synergy. Synergy is achieved when the total is greater than the sum of the parts. In terms of diversification, the capability of the combined organisation should be greater than the capabilities of all the individual companies. However, research carried out by Goold and Campbell (1998:131) suggests that "synergy

311

initiatives often fall short of management's expectations". Rather than assuming that synergies will exist, managers need to adopt a more sceptical view. When synergy is not realised it is usually due to the corporate executives. They suggest there are four common pitfalls that make synergy seem more attractive than it is:

- **Synergy bias** – overestimating the benefits and underestimating the cost involved
- **Parenting bias** – a belief that synergy will be obtained only by forcing the business units to co-operate
- **Skills bias** – the assumption that the competencies and know-how required are available in the organisation
- **Upside bias** – when executives concentrate on the potential benefits and overlook the negative aspects.

The company needs to be clear about the objectives and benefits of the potential synergy that they have identified. They also need to be clear about how and when they should intervene in terms of extracting the benefits, and should take into account the skills of the managers involved. When synergy can be achieved, it can create additional value with existing resources, but it is often difficult to realise in practice.

It should be stated, in examining related and unrelated diversification, that the two types are not dichotomous, but are part of a continuum. At first glance, it may appear that there is no relationship between particular businesses, but on closer examination, a connection can often be found. With Procter & Gamble, for example, the product mix includes laundry detergents, toothpastes, soaps, deodorants, shampoos and tissues. They also used to manufacture the well-known snack item, Pringles crisps, but it sold this product to Kellogg's in 2012. The raw materials and manufacturing processes for all these products are quite different, and it would appear that there is little synergy involved. However, they are all classified as fast-moving consumer items and all are sold in supermarkets. There is little or no difference from a marketing perspective in terms of brand management, advertising and logistics. Therefore, it can be argued that it is related rather than unrelated diversification.

With a large, diversified company there can be some parts of the group that conform to related diversifications. There can also be other parts that are clearly unrelated companies and there is no synergy with the remainder of the company. In reality, most conglomerates are probably a mixture of related and unrelated diversification, and they also vary considerably in size. The make-up of individual companies can range from one core business accounting for most of the revenues, with a small number of other diversified companies. Other companies might be narrowly diversified, with around three or four businesses that may or may not be related. Finally, there can be larger companies that are diversified into a number of unrelated areas, but within each area there can be clusters of related companies. A good example of the latter type is the US company GE.

Unrelated Diversification

Unrelated diversification occurs when a company expands its portfolio into businesses where there is little or no relationship between the various companies. It is often referred to as a **conglomerate**, and many holding companies fall into this category. Conglomerates became very popular in the US and Britain in the 1980s as many large companies expanded across industries and geographical markets. The following decade subsequently saw many de-mergers (for reasons which we will examine) where the conglomerates were split into separate companies that allowed for a more clearly defined core business and market focus – what Peters and Waterman (1982) referred to when they coined the phrase "stick to the knitting".

The main rationale behind unrelated diversification is that the company headquarters can make better capital allocation to the various units than financial markets could if the businesses were separate companies. With a spread of businesses, and industries, there should be a more even flow of cash compared to a single business where it can be quite cyclical.

Economic cycles are effectively beyond a chief executive's control, but what they do have control over is the scope of the business. Apart from cash flow, diversification also spreads business risk across a number of different businesses and, using its corporate parenting skills, the conglomerate can invest in industries that are showing attractive returns rather than restricting growth to related industries.

While industries appear different, there can be opportunities to exploit what Bettis and Prahalad (1995:5–14) referred to as "**the dominant logic**". The research in their original paper in 1986, and then revised in 1995, drew attention to managerial rather than economic forces in environmental-driven organisational change and the problems they face. Information technology has led to "information-rich but interpretation-poor systems" that lack appropriate actionable knowledge. They define the dominant logic "as the way in which managers in a firm conceptualise the business and make critical resource allocation decisions". It acts as an information filter that focuses organisational attention only on data deemed relevant by the dominant logic, which in turn is incorporated into the strategy of the organisation. This can direct organisations in certain directions but can also prevent them from taking certain action. They cite IBM in the early 1990s as an example of the latter, where for many years its dominant logic revolved around the centrality of the mainframe business (rather than personal computers) and which became embedded in their strategy. In such cases, the dominant logic prevents new learning and must be changed.

Performance

There has been much research into the correlation between diversification and performance. Focused companies are subject to the cyclical effects of industry and declining industries. To generate further growth, they have to diversify. In general (and there are many exceptions), limited related diversification produces better results than either single-business companies or highly diversified companies. This is often depicted graphically as an inverted 'U' with the vertical axis representing performance and the horizontal axis representing the level of diversification. This suggests that profitability increases with diversity, but only to the point known as the 'limit of complexity'.

Harper and Viguerie (2002:30) found that "moderately diversified companies share a common approach to managing scope – an approach applied at the right time in the life cycle of a business, generates superior returns through higher growth that is both realised and anticipated by capital markets". They refer to the balance between focus and diversification as a "strategic sweet spot", but finding that balance can be difficult as it varies widely from company to company and from point to point in the stages of a business's life cycle. It is not a steady state and needs to be managed. Their research, carried out on 412 S&P 500 companies, found that, on average, moderately diversified companies notched up 13% per year in annual excess returns compared to highly diversified companies.

Managing conglomerates is extremely challenging, given the wide variety of industries and business environments. Increasing the variation of companies adds to the complexity involved. The greater the spread, the more difficult it is for corporate managers to have an understanding of the individual businesses and to keep abreast of the changes taking place. As a result, they are not in a position to properly evaluate proposals from individual companies. For that reason the form of parenting style known as 'financial control' is most suited where the role is that of a portfolio manager. The corporate headquarters would set financial objectives for the companies and allow the company to develop its own strategies to achieve the required results.

There are many arguments that suggest that investors allocate capital across different businesses more effectively than a conglomerate can do. Markets often discount the valuation of conglomerates as they perceive that the full financial benefits do not materialise due to a number of shortcomings associated with broad diversification, such as the cross-subsidisation of unprofitable businesses.

According to Jolly (2018), GE, once the biggest company in the world, making a range of products from jet engines to refrigerators, has suffered from a series of set-backs over the last decade due to overly expensive acquisitions and under performing subsidiaries. By June 2018, the company had built up a debt pile of $115 billion and it dropped out of the Dow Jones Index for the first time in 110 years. Originally founded by Thomas Edison as General Electric, GE has gone through three successive CEOs in an 18-month period. The company requires major restructuring to reduce its debt and ensure its survival.

There are occasions when diversification across a broad spectrum can produce superior results, such as when it takes over a company that has undervalued assets or is in financial distress. In 2008, the value of many Irish companies, and in particular banks, dropped very significantly. In such situations companies are always vulnerable to a takeover bid. In 2011, US multi-billionaire investor Wilbur Ross bought a significant amount of Bank of Ireland shares in the aftermath of the financial crash and sold them a number of years later at triple the price, making a $500 million profit (Duffy, S., 2017).

Adding Value – Diversification

Examining the performance of diversified companies again raises the issue of corporate parents and whether they add or destroy value. As public companies can be taken over if they are under-performing, corporate parents must demonstrate that they are able to contribute to the value of the company. Goold *et al.* (1994) suggest that a corporate parent can add value by: providing a clear vision and strategic intent for the organisation; developing strategic capabilities and synergies; providing financial support and expertise; monitoring business performance; and making necessary interventions. Corporate parents can also destroy value: in that they add to the cost as they do not generate revenue in a direct way; they slow down decision-making and add to the "bureaucratic fog"; and internal cross-subsidisation can cover poor performance in parts of the organisation.

The more related the various companies are to each other, the easier it can be for the corporate parent to intervene in a meaningful way in businesses that they understand – what Goold *et al.* refer to as 'parental development'. In a hotel chain, executives at head office will have worked in the group in different positions and locations, giving them a wealth of experience that they can apply to an individual hotel that is not performing to its potential. In addition to providing expertise, a strong brand and the ability to provide finance can assist the individual units. For a highly diversified company, however, this form of parenting would do great damage and instead requires, what Porter (1987) termed, a 'portfolio manager'.

There are many examples of major conglomerates that are very successful. DCC plc and CRH plc are examples of highly diversified Irish companies that have experienced sustained growth since their establishment (1976 and 1970 respectively). See **Illustration 10.1** below for more information about DCC and the case study on CRH at the back of this textbook.

Berkshire Hathaway, another very successful conglomerate, is run by one of the richest men in the world, Warren Buffet. Each year, at the company AGM, analysts as well as shareholders wait with bated breath to listen to 'the sage of Omaha' and hear his views on a wide range of economic issues. Buffet, who is almost 90-years old, is a self-confessed technophobe. No one should use that as an excuse for ageism. During the 1990s when billions of dollars were being invested in dot-com companies, he stayed clear of them stating that he did not understand them and therefore would not invest (they were outside his 'dominant logic'). His judgement proved correct when the dot-com bubble burst and proved that many of these companies lacked a sound business model. While the personal wealth of many other big names has decreased, Buffet's has increased each year. He also wants to give his wealth away while he is living, rather than set up a trust that would disperse it after his death. He claims that attempting to control the spending of his money after his death would give a new meaning to the term 'thinking outside of the box'!

Illustration 10.1: DCC – A Diversified Irish Company

A highly diversified Irish company, DCC plc is a leading international sales, marketing and support services group with a focus on performance and growth. A constituent of the FTSE 100, DCC is listed on the London Stock Exchange. In the financial year ending 31 March 2018, DCC generated revenue of £14.3 billion and an adjusted operating profit of £383 million.

DCC was established in Dublin in 1976 by Jim Flavin, originally as a venture capital business. It currently employs 11,500 people. A year after its foundation, the company invested in the energy sector with the acquisition of Flogas, an Irish LPG business. In 1982, it invested in Hospital Enterprises, the forerunner of today's DCC Vital within its healthcare division. In 1988, the company invested in the technology sector in Ireland and the UK, and by 1990 it was involved in the food sector. In 1994, the company listed on the London and Dublin stock exchanges.

In 1999, DCC acquired two UK health and beauty businesses, and two years later it entered the UK oil distribution business with the purchase of BP's business in Scotland. The following year it bought BP's LPG business in the UK; in 2005, it bought Shell Direct, making it the largest independent oil distributor in Britain. The company has also become the largest consumer software distributor in Britain. Between 2007 and 2012, DCC expanded into continental Europe in a number of different sectors and, in 2019, Europe accounted for 20% of the group's profits. The company saw a significant expansion in the UK with the acquisition of Kent Pharmaceuticals. The company has continued its expansion in the UK and continental Europe, including the Nordic countries. In 2014, DCC decided to divest its food and beverage division in order to focus on other areas of operations (see **Chapter 9**). By 2015, its success led to the company becoming part of the FTSE 100.

The company has a focus on building strong routes to market for its products and investing in businesses that have strong cash flows that can be reinvested in new ventures. According to the company, its growth objective is based on five principles:

- the creation of shareholder value through growth in share price and dividends;
- enhanced levels of customer service;
- strengthening relationships with suppliers;
- increased career and development opportunities for all employees;
- a positive impact on the wider community in which it operates.

The growth of DCC is based on utilising its resources by combining its people, capital, facilities, business partners and its products as integral parts of its business model. It has five strategic priorities:

1. To be the number one or two operator in each of its chosen markets by increasing its market share through acquisitions that generate superior returns
2. Operational efficiency achieved by benchmarking its business against specific KPIs (key performance indicators)
3. Extending its geographical footprint on a selective basis
4. Financial discipline that maintains relatively low levels of financial risk throughout the group
5. Developing and investing in the leadership capability and skills of its employees.

According to DCC, its actions are based on four core values: the safety of its people, integrity in its business dealings, partnership with its stakeholders, and excellence in everything it does. The company now has four divisions:

1. **DCC LPG** – a leading LPG sales and marketing business with operations in Europe, Asia and the US, and a developing business in the retailing of natural gas and electricity. This division generates 44% of the group's profits
2. **DCC Retail & Oil** – a leader is the sales, marketing and retailing of transport and commercial fuels, heating oils and related products and services in Europe. This represents another 30% of group profits
3. **DCC Healthcare** – a leading healthcare business, providing products and services to healthcare providers and health and beauty brand owners. The healthcare division generates 14% of group profits
4. **DCC Technology** – a leading sales, marketing and services partner for global technology brands. This division accounts for the remaining 12% of profits.

As of 2019, all four divisions are showing a growth in profits, year-on-year. In regard to the company's geographical spread: Ireland accounts for just 5% of total profits; the UK for 45%; and continental Europe/other for the other 50%.

Source: DCC plc (2019)

Competences

Clearly, there is no obvious synergy of activities across DCC. However, when analysing conglomerates, there are certain competences that are required by all constituent businesses, and by corporate headquarters in managing them together as a portfolio. These apply also to single businesses, but given the complexity involved in managing conglomerates, they are particularly important here.

The first competence needed is **financial**. Financing structures, cash flows, profits, control measures, etc., will differ from one industry to another, but the basic underlying skills are common to all. In dealing with individual business managers, it is vital that head office executives have the ability to understand the financial implications of decisions that are being made and the financial information that is coming to them. DCC has stated that one of its strategic priorities is financial discipline and maintaining a low level of risk. This allows it to fund targeted acquisitions while maintaining a healthy balance sheet.

The second competence required is **leadership**. In a diversified company, it is very difficult to forge a common vision that unites all the elements under one banner. The Virgin Group achieves it under a common brand that signifies an innovative approach to established businesses. GE achieves it to some extent by requiring each business to be number one or number two in the industry in which they operate.

DCC has also built up a strong brand image that unites the various divisions. There has to be strong leadership from the centre that motivates and inspires each company to achieve good results.

Part of such leadership is the ability to spot talented people. Each company is only as good as its management team and staff, and so picking the right people and keeping them motivated is a vital ingredient. In **Illustration 10.1** above, we see that DCC places a strong emphasis on the development of leadership and other skills of its management and staff.

STRATEGIES FOR ACHIEVING DIVERSIFICATION

There are different methods for achieving diversification in a company, including:

- internal start-up (organic growth),
- joint ventures, and
- acquisitions.

These will be discussed briefly here in the context of diversification. As they are also general strategies for all types of companies, they will be dealt with in greater detail in **Chapter 11**.

Internal Start-up

An internal start-up is where a company builds up a new subsidiary company (different from the parent company) from the beginning. It involves the parent company investing considerable time and resources to build up all aspects of the new company internally, and externally in forming relationships with suppliers and distributors. An internal start-up takes a considerable period of time compared to making an acquisition, so time cannot be a critical factor as it would be in a highly competitive and fast-moving industry. The response from competitors will also be related to time. The parent company must already have all the necessary skills and competences to compete in an area different from its own or else be able to hire people with those skills.

Joint Venture

A joint venture involves forming a new company that is jointly owned by two or more companies. In some countries, the host government makes a joint venture with a local company a requirement for foreign companies wishing to operate there. This method of achieving diversification is particularly useful where a company does not have all the necessary skills to operate in a new venture. This is often the situation in technology-related areas where the boundaries of current industries are constantly changing and merging with other industries. Sometimes these ventures can be extremely expensive and so it also spreads the risk involved. There are a number of pitfalls in joint ventures, which will be dealt with in the main discussion on the topic in **Chapter 11**.

Acquisition

Acquisitions of existing companies is probably the most common form for achieving diversification. It is quick, and in taking over an existing company the new parent is acquiring all of the assets, resources, personnel and know-how as part of the deal. It also means that the company has an immediate relationship with suppliers and distributors, who no doubt will want to continue doing business with the company. (It can be seen in **Illustration 10.1** above that the predominant means of growth for DCC is by acquisition.)

The above strategies can be used singly or in combination. Decisions have to be made with regard to the scope of the diversified company. It may decide to broaden the base of the company through further acquisitions in new areas or complement the existing line-up. If some companies are not performing, it may decide to divest those areas and concentrate its efforts on those parts that are performing. It might also look at keeping the existing range of businesses, but perhaps pursue international diversification. The environment is constantly changing and diversification requires constant management of the portfolio.

MANAGING THE PORTFOLIO

In a conglomerate, not all constituent companies are going to have the same characteristics and perform at the same level. Therefore, the corporate headquarters needs to maintain a watching brief on the entire organisation and take corrective measures in individual companies whenever necessary. This will also involve adding or subtracting companies from the portfolio to keep an overall balance. As a result of the recession, many companies may find that some parts of their portfolio subtract rather than add economic value. Ghemawat (2010) believes that companies will have to be more ruthless about terminating long-standing loss-makers – and pursuing new opportunities. Some of this can be achieved by creating more stringent investment criteria and adopting more realistic assumptions about future growth. There will still be opportunities for growth but, in order to pursue these opportunities, other avenues may have to be closed off.

There are a number of different techniques to assist managers in the process. The original model was developed by the Boston Consulting Group (BCG), which developed a growth/share matrix. It was initially designed to manage a portfolio of products, but it can equally be applied to manage a range of businesses in a company's overall portfolio.

Boston Consulting Group Matrix

The BCG Matrix plots each business on a two-dimensional basis, showing market growth rate and the market share held by each company, resulting in a four-quadrant matrix – see **Figure 10.1** below.

Market share is important as there is a strong correlation between high relative market share and profitability. Growth rate is important for the future success of a company. In putting resources into a company, it is obviously better to invest them in one that is located in a growing, rather than a contracting, industry. It will, however, require a good deal of investment to ensure growth. The purpose of the matrix is to get an overview of the entire portfolio so that managers can see where resources are needed and where they emanate from. Individual businesses within the company are allocated to the different quadrants according to their characteristics.

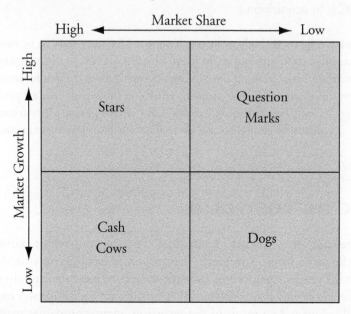

Figure 10.1 *The Boston Consulting Group (BCG) Matrix*

The resulting quadrants are labelled 'stars', 'cash cows', 'question marks' (also called a 'problem child') and 'dogs'.

Stars A 'star' is a business that has high market share and high market growth. This is a good position to be in as it has high market share at present (which makes the company more likely to be profitable) and it is also in an industry that is growing, thus showing future potential growth for the company either in just maintaining its existing market share percentage or in growing it. However, that is by no means guaranteed. Rival companies will also try to increase their market share, so the future position is by no means secure and it will require substantial investment to maintain a favourable position. High market share should mean good profitability, and these profits can be reinvested, but it will probably require additional investment from the cash cows quadrant.

Cash Cows A 'cash cow' is a business that has high market share, but one that is located in a mature market that is no longer growing. High market share means that it is in a dominant position and is yielding worthwhile profits. As the market is mature, it can be taken that all development costs such as R&D have been well recouped and it is now generating good profits. These profits are not required for reinvestment in the business and so they can be diverted to help support 'stars' and 'question marks'. One drawback to this transfer of funds from cash cows is that it can have a de-motivating effect on the management of cash cow companies as they see their hard work going to other companies that may not put in the same effort.

Question Marks (or Problem Child) A 'question mark' has low market share in a growing industry. The low market share needs to be built up to a star position, where it will be much more profitable. To achieve this, it will require substantial investment in marketing, particularly in advertising, and in developing technology. However, such investment is certainly not guaranteed. While some question marks will go on and become successful, others will fall by the wayside. For example, when new technology is being developed in an industry, it often happens that different companies are developing variations of the technology simultaneously. The industry will opt for one particular type, which will become the 'industry standard', and the company that has developed that technology will quickly move into a star position. For the others, it often means being left behind. This happened in the development of video recorders in the early 1980s, followed by the development of DVD technology and latterly by streaming services such as Netflix.

Dogs 'Dogs' have low market share and are in a static or declining market. This is the worst possible position to be in from every perspective, and the business will at best be breaking even, but most likely is making a loss. Thus, it drains cash from the other companies in the portfolio. With the market declining, there is little or no prospect of a turnaround. The accepted wisdom in dealing with business in the 'dogs' category is to sell them or close them down, provided other businesses in the portfolio are not dependent on them. However, the most rational decision is not always taken, as there are often political considerations to be taken into account. For example, the chief executive could have been associated with that company in the past, might have a strong emotional attachment to it, and it could be that no one in the company wants to state the obvious! There are occasions when such a company may be held on to for strategic regions; for example, it might have a valuable distribution network in a particular market that could be used for new products about to come on stream in another company within the group.

The BCG Matrix can be a useful tool for managers to gain a good overview of the entire portfolio of companies, not just singly but in how they relate to one another in the group in terms of the transfer of resources. It is not just financial resources that can be transferred. Earlier in this chapter, attention was focused on how corporate parents may intervene in a particular company to help turn it around. Such intervention may require moving managers with particular skills from one company to another. It is standard procedure in large multinational companies for executives to be moved from one company and location to another. While this is done to give executives personal experience for future promotion within the company, it is also done for very practical reasons, such as bringing their expertise to parts of the company that need it.

There are some limitations with the BCG Matrix as a tool. First, it examines only two variables: market share and market growth rate. While these are very important, there are also other important criteria that should be considered. These will be discussed below when considering the GE matrix. Secondly, high market share and high market growth are often very subjective terms. In some industries, it is possible to calculate these criteria reasonably accurately. In the motor industry, for example, because all new cars have to be registered and taxed, it is possible to get accurate figures on the total amount of new cars sold which can be compared with previous years to determine growth in the market. It will also show the relative market share of each car manufacturer. However, the car industry is something of an exception in that regard, and such accurate figures will often be unavailable for most industries. As a result, it requires a lot of speculation, which may not present an accurate figure. As Mark Twain once quipped: "Get your facts first, then you can distort them as you please."

Thirdly, the BCG Matrix perhaps implies that the resources needed by one company must come from others in the group. In many situations, financial resources may well be raised by the company itself through bank loans or share issues. This can have the benefit of focusing the attention of management in that company to the issues facing it, rather than automatically assuming that if resources are needed they will be provided by the corporate head office. If a company believes that a certain decision could secure its future or, on the other hand, mean its demise, it will think very carefully before making that decision. The other side to transferring resources from one company to another is, as mentioned above, that it can have a de-motivating effect on the management in the company that is providing the resources. They may resent having to give over those resources having worked hard to build them up in the first instance.

Directional Policy Matrix

McKinsey, another consultancy company, in conjunction with GE, developed the Directional Policy Matrix, also known as the Industry Attractiveness–Competitive Strength Matrix. The GE/McKinsey Matrix looks at different companies in the portfolio and places them according to:

1. The attractiveness of the market in which the company is operating.
2. The competitive position of the company compared to others in the market.

The attractiveness of the industry can be termed as high, medium or low and it is an overview of that industry taking many different criteria into account. **Tables 10.1** and **10.2** show some of the criteria that should be included in the analysis. The level of detail here is considerably greater than the BCG Matrix and consequently should provide a much more comprehensive picture to executives. The information is plotted on a nine-box Industry Attractiveness–Competitive Strength Matrix (see **Figure 10.2**).

Each company or SBU is shown graphically on the matrix as a circle. The size of the circle represents the size of the market that the SBU is operating in; the size of the 'wedge' within the circle represents the size of the market share of the SBU within that market. The matrix also gives guidance to managers with regard to each business. The company should invest in strong, attractive industries (top left). At the opposite end of the scale, those that are not in attractive industries and are weak should be divested (bottom right). For those companies in the middle, the decision is not so clear-cut. This is illustrated in **Figure 10.3**.

The following are some of the criteria that should be included in the analysis.

Table 10.1: *Market Attractiveness*

Factor	Impact
Market growth rate	As discussed above in the BCG Matrix.
Market size	A big market will have greater potential than a small market.
Competitive structure and profitability	Looking at Porter's Five Forces to determine the competitive structure of the industry and to see how profitable it is.
PESTEL	Using the PESTEL framework to gain an overall understanding of the factors affecting the industry. For example, economic factors will determine profitability, but this can be moderated by other factors such as political or sociological forces, etc. The most relevant factors should be included.
Cyclicality	Many industries are cyclical in nature. In terms of entering a particular industry, the optimum time is just as it is about to emerge from a downturn. For divestment, the time to get out is when it is still on top of the cycle and is attractive to buyers.

Table 10.2: *Relative Strength of the Company*

Factor	Impact
Market share	As per BCG Matrix above.
Financial resources	A major benefit of a portfolio is having financial resources that can be transferred from one company to another in the group.
Research and development	In discussing new product development, it was stated that new product development is the lifeline of any company, and with product life cycles getting ever shorter, it is imperative that companies have a constant stream of new products in production.
Managerial strength	Corporate parenting skills are very much dependent on the calibre of the management team in the corporate HQ.
Marketing	Marketing ties in with R&D to ensure that the products being developed will have market appeal. It is also vital that when they are developed they will be marketed effectively, and the public has a positive image of the company.

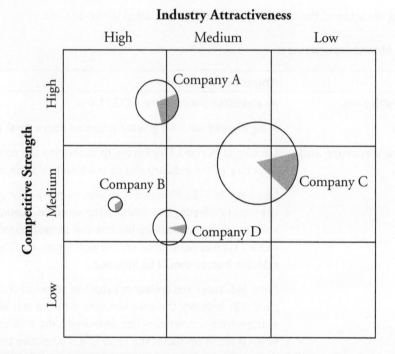

Figure 10.2 *Industry Attractiveness—Competitive Strength Matrix*

Industry Attractiveness

	High	Medium	Low
High	STRONG INVESTMENT	INVEST	SELECTIVE INVESTMENT
Medium	INVEST	SELECTIVE INVESTMENT	HARVEST/ DIVEST
Low	SELECTIVE INVESTMENT	HARVEST/ DIVEST	DIVEST

Figure 10.3 *The GE/McKinsey Matrix*

Once again, much of the information that is fed into the criteria can be quite subjective. However, the object of the exercise is to gain a good, overall understanding of the position of each company in the matrix. This textbook has already discussed the importance of ongoing environmental analysis. Executives should have a reasonably accurate picture of the information required, and it will assist them in making the decisions that are needed to develop the portfolio. This information can be discussed and debated by executives until there is some form of consensus with regard to the issues facing the company (from **Chapter 1**, it will be recalled that, in general, organisations are moving towards a more pluralist approach to strategy-making rather than a top-down approach by the CEO).

Corporate Parenting

We saw in **Chapter 7** that the main function of the corporate headquarters is to add value to the organisation as a whole. According to Grant (2010) one major drawback with both the BCG Matrix and the GE/McKinsey Matrix is that they regard each of the business units in the matrix as being a separate entity, while one of the most basic arguments in favour of a multi-business organisation is the existence of synergy between all the various companies. There is an implicit assumption in the above models that there is a balance between each of the companies in the portfolio. However, there may not be any synergy present, and the inclusion of any one company in a portfolio does not automatically represent added value. To overcome these weaknesses, Campbell *et al.* (1995) proposed a parenting framework to examine where companies create value in the portfolio of businesses they own. The focus is thus on the competences of the corporate parent and the value created from the relationship between it and its businesses. Where there is a good fit between the parent and the business, value will be created. If none exists, then value will be destroyed.

The corporate parenting framework assessment process has two parts. It begins with identifying the key success factors (KSFs – see **Chapter 5**) of each business in the portfolio. Every business has activities that are critical to its performance and the creation of competitive advantage, and these will vary in different industries. (A corporate parent that does not understand the KSFs in a business is likely to destroy value.) Identifying KSFs will also enable the headquarters to compare how similar the KSFs are among the various businesses and where there is a parenting opportunity.

In the second part of the parenting framework process, the parent examines where performance can be improved – where it can add value to the business. This might be in a wide variety of areas, such as reducing costs or creating economies of scale in marketing, better management, providing a clearer business definition, common capabilities, access to finance or perhaps the business may need to undergo a major restructuring.

A business may be performing well or poorly without the parent having any real influence on that performance. It can therefore be difficult for companies to judge exactly the level of value added by the parent. Campbell *et al.* recommend that the performance of the business in the portfolio is compared with the industry average return on investment using the Profit Impact of Marketing Strategies (PIMS) methodology. PIMS is a database containing detailed information about various aspects of performance submitted confidentially by participating companies. These results are combined and companies can then compare their results, thus indicating whether their performance is on par, above or below the average for that industry.

The examination of the compatibility of KSFs and where the parent can add value can be brought together in a Parenting Matrix (see **Figure 10.4**).

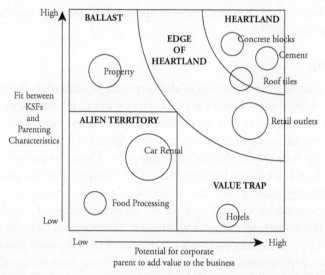

Source: Adapted from Goold A., Campbell A. and Alexander M. (1995), "Corporate Strategy: The Quest for Parenting Advantage", *Harvard Business Review*, March/April 1995, Vol. 73 Issue 2, pp. 120–132.

Figure 10.4 *Parenting Matrix: (the Ashridge Portfolio Display) A Diversified Buildings Material Group*

Each business in the portfolio can be plotted on the matrix and its position can then direct corporate strategy for those businesses. Campbell *et al.* categorise them as follows:

Heartland businesses – these are the core of the company's strategy, as the parent understands the KSFs very well and there are ample opportunities to add value. In **Figure 10.4**, the concrete block and cement businesses are central to the company.

Edge of heartland – judgement is difficult here as some businesses will fit and others may not match very well. In the example in **Figure 10.4**, the retail outlets can benefit in many ways from the corporate parent but there is some gap between the KSFs of the parent and the retail business. This can take up a lot of management time in the beginning as the corporate parent tries to understand it better. If they succeed, the retail outlets business may move into the heartland.

Ballast – here the potential for further value is low, but the business sits well in terms of the KSF fit with the parent. The important thing is there is also little opportunity to destroy value as the parent is familiar with, in this case, the property business. Ballast businesses are usually a good source of cash flow and steady earnings, but slow growth can be a drag on the company and they may drift into alien territory or be taken over.

Alien territory – there is little potential for adding value and there is a poor match between the KSFs of the business and parenting characteristics, as depicted by the food processing and car rental business in the example in **Figure 10.4**. These companies may well be quite profitable, but in all probability, the parent will be destroying value by having them in the portfolio, and in most cases would be better off divesting them.

Value trap – here there are opportunities to add value, but there is little fit between the KSFs of running a hotel (such as service and yield management) and the building materials businesses. The opportunity to create value often blinds senior managers to the risks involved. Value is usually destroyed and the business usually ends up worth a good deal less.

Portfolio frameworks such as the BCG Matrix and the GE/McKinsey Matrix look at companies primarily as stand-alone entities rather than addressing the more fundamental question of whether the businesses are better off as a result of the influence of the corporate parent. The Parenting Matrix addresses this important issue. Parenting skills are usually developed from deeply held values making change difficult. In most cases, therefore, it is easier to change the company mix in the portfolio to suit the corporate parent rather than trying to get the corporate headquarters to develop new parenting skills. As a result, the corporate parent can then develop strategy that is more likely to create value across its portfolio because it is using parenting fit as the criteria rather than an excess of cash on its balance sheet prompting the company to make acquisitions.

CONCLUSION

For many conglomerates, the path to diversification was probably due more to emergent strategy than any particular design. Such diversification poses many challenges for managers as they try to maximise the value from the overall group. In many cases, value may well be increased by divesting some of the companies. Perhaps one of the biggest challenges for senior executives is developing enough expertise in all of the different industries represented by the group's constituent companies. Providing such depth of knowledge is a very difficult process and, in reality, those at the top are highly reliant on the CEOs of the various companies in the group. Consequently, it requires a more hands-off approach to corporate parenting and, again, this highlights the importance of selecting the right people that will fit in with the organisation. Larger companies such as GE also go to great lengths to develop its managers so that they can assume such responsibility.

SUMMARY

As companies grow in size, they often develop in different ways from their original business, branching into different types of businesses or technologies and becoming diversified. The task of crafting a diversified company's overall strategy involves four distinct aspects:

- Picking new industries to enter and deciding on the means of entry. Should the focus be a broad or narrow diversification and should it be achieved by organic growth or acquisition?
- Initiating actions to boost the combined performance of the businesses the firm has entered. It must strengthen the long-term competitive position of each company and the overall group.
- Pursuing opportunities to create cross-business leverage – looking for ways to reduce costs and create efficiencies.
- Establishing investment priorities and steering corporate resources into the most attractive business units.

There are a number of reasons why a company might diversify. The acid test is ultimately whether diversifying increases shareholder wealth. Diversification can be divided into two broad classifications:

- **Related diversification**, where there are common links between the value chains of each company. There are two subdivisions:
  - o Vertical integration, either forward or backward
  - o Horizontal integration.

- **Unrelated diversification**, where the company moves into a business where there is no common link in their value chains.

There are different methods for achieving diversification in a company, including internal start-up (organic growth), joint ventures and acquisitions. In a conglomerate, not all constituent companies will have the same characteristics and perform at the same level. Therefore, the corporate headquarters needs to maintain a watching brief on the entire organisation and take corrective measures in individual companies whenever necessary.

The Boston Consulting Group (BCG) Matrix and the GE/McKinsey Directional Policy Matrix can be useful tools for managers to gain a good overview of the entire portfolio of companies, not just singly but in how they relate to one another in the group in terms of the transfer of resources. The Parenting Matrix examines whether the corporate parent can add value to businesses in its portfolio and whether there is an understanding of the KSFs of that business. Those businesses that fall into the 'heartland' category will benefit from the parenting skills, and consequently add value to the corporate parent.

DISCUSSION QUESTIONS

1. Critically analyse the reasons why a company might choose a strategy of diversification.
2. Differentiate between the various forms of diversification.
3. Select a diversified company and identify its various constituent businesses. Identify any common theme that links the various elements together.
4. With reference to question 1 above, in your opinion does the corporate parent add or destroy value?
5. Discuss how an organisation might analyse the contribution of various businesses in its portfolio.

Alternative Methods of Developing Strategy Options

LEARNING OUTCOMES

On completion of this chapter, you will be able to:

- Critically examine the various methods of strategic development
- Distinguish between the different types of strategic alliances and the circumstances in which each is appropriate
- Undertake an appraisal of an acquisition and ascertain its effectiveness
- Analyse industry conditions with a view to selecting a suitable strategy for a company

"Interdependence is and ought to be as much the ideal of men as self-sufficiency."

Mahatma Gandhi

INTRODUCTION

Chapter 9 looked at Ansoff's Matrix to explore the four possible strategic directions a company can take: market penetration, product development and diversification. There are a number of methods by which these strategies can be achieved:

- Internal development (also known as organic growth) is concerned with how a company grows incrementally year after year using its own resources, such as retained earnings, along with borrowings. It is a very important method of achieving growth for the vast majority of companies.
- Strategic alliances involve teaming up with other companies and pooling resources in a mutually-beneficial way. They can take many different forms and vary in duration from short-term arrangements to ones lasting many years.
- Mergers and acquisitions are where one company takes control over another. As the Irish economy grows, so too do the number of M&As each year.
- Particular industry conditions will mean the tailoring of specific strategies to accommodate those conditions.

Each of these methods will be examined in detail and it will be seen that they are quite different from one another in a number of respects. Once again, the methods shown here are by no means mutually exclusive and it would be quite common for a company to pursue a number of these methods simultaneously.

Strategy is largely dependent on the context surrounding the organisation. The final part of this chapter deals with various industry conditions and examines which method is more appropriate for any given situation.

INTERNAL DEVELOPMENT

Internal development, or organic growth as it is sometimes called, is common to every type of organisation and is generally the main method of development. It involves the company growing using its own resources and capabilities. Internal development can be used as a means to achieve all of the directions discussed in the last two chapters: growing market share, developing new products, market development, or diversification. Normally, the investment in organic growth can be either for offensive (taking the initiative) or defensive (reacting to moves by competitors) reasons.

The funding required for internal development may come from a number of sources. For most established companies, funding would come from retained earnings (profits built up over a few years) along with bank borrowings. The level of bank borrowings by a company depends on a number of factors, including the availability of funds for lending by the banks, the rate of interest being charged and the amount of existing borrowing by that company. In addition, banks will want the company to invest a portion of their own funds into a project before lending – what is often referred to colloquially as 'skin in the game'. In essence, both the company wishing to invest and the bank that is providing the funds need to assess the level of risk involved.

If large amounts of funding are needed the company may raise fresh equity, probably in the form of a rights issue. (Issues about the nature of funding have been discussed in **Chapter 7**.) Suffice to say, retained earnings will form an important element of the funding as companies will want to reinvest this money to create greater profitability in the future. The amount of funding raised in the various forms would depend on the nature and scope of the growth involved, depending on whether it is incremental or adding a major amount of new capacity. Especially in the case of incremental development, it has the advantage of spreading the cost over a greater period of time, thus easing pressure on cash flow in any one particular year. While borrowing has positive tax implications (interest payments can be offset against tax), it does place a level of financial risk on the company, and this is minimised when the development takes place over a number of years.

Organic growth avoids one major issue that occurs with the various forms of alliances and with mergers and acquisitions, and that is cultural compatibility. (The implications of this are presented in greater detail below.) Any new staff being recruited as a result of the development will, as part of their induction and training, be slotted into existing structures and work patterns and will be absorbed into the culture of the organisation. As a consequence, growth does not have a disruptive effect in terms of the internal politics of the company (the impact of company politics on organisational strategy was examined in **Chapter 1**).

When expanding into international markets, a business may initially use an indigenous company to distribute its exports or maybe form a joint venture. This is often the practice as the business may have very limited knowledge and experience in operating in such a market. In further developing that market, it may decide to do so by internal development and establish its own greenfield site. This would then give an organisation far greater control in that it is not dependent on any other company and can therefore develop at its own pace. In turn, this will build up the company's own internal capability and knowledge, which will assist it in further development either in that market or in others.

There are situations where there is no other choice open to a company if it is to grow. In the case of brand new technology, it may well be that one company is far more advanced than any of its rivals, and there are no suitable firms to acquire or with which to form a joint venture in terms of advancing the development. As a result, there is no option but to continue the development internally. On other occasions, a suitable acquisition opportunity may just not present itself.

Illustration 11.1 below concerns Dairymaster, an Irish company that has grown organically since its foundation.

Illustration 11.1: Dairymaster and Organic Growth

Dairymaster is a family-owned company located in Causeway, a small village north of Tralee in County Kerry. The business was established in 1968 by Ned Harty to meet the needs of dairy farmers in providing equipment to streamline the labour-intensive process of milking cattle. Dairymaster has reinvested profits into building up the business and the Dairymaster plant has grown gradually and it now occupies an 11-acre facility, employing over 400 people. It is internationally recognised as a world-leader in dairy equipment manufacturing, with customers in over 40 countries around the globe. Dr Edmund Harty (its current CEO and son of the founder) was the Ernst & Young *Entrepreneur of the Year* in 2012.

Dairymaster's product range includes milking equipment, feeding equipment, automatic manure scrapers, milk cooling tanks and health and fertility monitoring systems. Through the use of technology, farmers are able to increase milk yield, reduce milking times, cut energy costs, decrease labour and improve the overall health of the dairy herd, and also improve conception rates. Given the nature of the farming business, its product range is supported by a 24/7 technical back-up team (mechanical and software) to give farmers immediate assistance, while the sales team can advise farmers on the specific needs of their operations. The company's products have received multiple awards in the markets in which it operates.

With the world's population growing at a substantial rate, the requirements for more food must be balanced with sustainable food production. Innovation is central to providing such solutions for the farming sector. Dairymaster, with its strong emphasis on innovation, invests significant amounts of money in research and development in the dairy sector. The company has over 90 patents for its products, resulting in technologically advanced, high-performance equipment. All of this expertise, from robotic production equipment to laser technology, has been created in-house over the years in Dairymaster.

Dairymaster has been built up by the Harty family and their team over the past half century. Being leaders in its field, and given the pioneering nature of the products it manufactures, there were no suitable opportunities available to Dairymaster to acquire similar companies either in Ireland or abroad. Nor as a private, family-owned company was it able to leverage the financial or marketing strength of a corporate parent. As a result, the only real option open to Dairymaster was to expand through internal/organic growth.

When expanding abroad, the company establishes (and trains) a dealer's network to be able to provide local support for farmers who buy its products. This is important: the nature of dairy farming requires prompt service as cows require milking twice a day. These dealers are able to advise farmers on the type of equipment that would best suit their needs, and then provide full back-up service to them, ensuring a high level of customer service and satisfaction.

With sales all around the globe, and numerous industry awards, the organic growth achieved by the Harty family is something they have managed very successfully.

Source: www.dairymaster.com (2019)

STRATEGIC ALLIANCES

Strategic alliances have grown enormously in popularity over the last 20 years or so. Not only are more and more companies recognising the benefits of entering alliances; some larger companies can be involved in dozens of different alliances simultaneously. Strategic alliances can be contractual, involving ownership, or looser collaborative arrangements between companies.

Definition A **strategic alliance** is when two or more separate companies agree to collaborate on a strategic basis and share resources, risk and control for their mutual benefit.

Globalisation has changed the nature of competition and, according to Ohmae (1989), "in a complex, uncertain world filled with dangerous opponents, it is best not to go it alone". In a globally competitive industry, it can be particularly useful for launching a product around the world simultaneously rather than using a 'cascade' effect moving from one market to another.

As with internal development, strategic alliances can be used by companies in achieving the four different development directions discussed in the last chapter:

- Consolidation – loose, non-contractual agreements to protect market share
- Product development – defraying the huge cost and risk involved in research and development and speeding up the development process
- Market development – entering new markets internationally using joint sales and distributions systems
- Diversification – developing the skills and resources needed to diversify from the main line of business.

There are many benefits from alliances. Generally speaking, they are a much quicker form of development than internal development. In technology markets in particular, speed is of the essence in developing new products and this can be achieved by collaboration. Alliances are also used to improve various value chain activities and can reduce costs in production and marketing as well as research and development. These costs savings make the members of the alliance more competitive. As mentioned, when discussing entering international markets, alliances can sometimes be a requirement by host governments in foreign markets, either by way of joint ventures or other forms. In other cases, it may not be an actual requirement, but it can help the company in navigating its way through the cultural peculiarities of a foreign market or through the layers of bureaucratic red tape, or both. The need to adapt products for particular markets was also examined and, where a company lacks experience of a certain market, alliance with foreign companies can assist in the process of adaptation.

As with all the other options being examined, strategic alliances should be seen as a means to an end – to achieve a specific and important goal for the organisation. An alliance can either be an offensive move to take advantage of an opportunity, or defensive to ward off a threat.

Types of Alliance

There are a wide variety of types of alliance from which to choose. Alliances can vary from long-term agreements to temporary arrangements. Generally speaking, they tend to be long-term when the companies involved are collaborating on either supply or distribution contracts. Alliances based on the development of technology tend to be shorter as the companies realise the benefits in terms of new products coming on stream and then they move on. The different types of alliance include:

- Consortia
- Joint ventures
- Licensing
- Franchising
- Outsourcing
- Networking.

Consortia

Contractual alliances involve consortia and joint ventures. A consortium is a group that consists of two or more companies that have come together for a particular purpose, such as developing a large venture. A Public Private Partnership (PPP) is a type of consortium between the state and a private company to develop, for example, hospitals and schools as well as major infrastructural projects. In many cases, because the cost of the project is so immense, a number of banks would be part of the consortium, as the financial risk would be too great for any one bank to bear on its own. The total cost of completing the Dublin Port Tunnel was approximately €700 million (which was almost twice the original estimate) and development costs such as this are best spread over a number of different groups.

The Gulf of Mexico, Deepwater Horizon, oil rig explosion in 2010 remains one of the biggest ecological disasters in the history of oil exploration and involved a number of companies operating as a consortium. While BP took the brunt of the criticism for the disaster, the Deepwater Horizon rig was in fact owned by a consortium comprising BP (65%), Anadarko (25%) and the Japanese group Mitsui (10%). There are many other companies actually involved in the extraction of the oil. The Deepwater Horizon rig was built by Hyundai and was supplied by the world's largest offshore drilling contractor, Transocean. In turn, the US company Halliburton had responsibility for cementing the rig in place. The blowout preventer was manufactured by Cameron International, a specialist engineering company. BP is hoping to share the cost of the damage with its consortium partners, but this is being disputed by the other members.

For expensive projects such as this, consortia are a common method of development, as it spreads the risk between a number of individuals and institutions.

Joint Ventures

 A **joint venture** is when two companies come together and create an alliance in the form of a third company that is jointly owned and managed by the two parents, who remain separate entities.

In a joint venture, both companies will contribute dedicated assets and resources in order to spread the risk involved. In recent decades, foreign firms wishing to enter some markets, such as China, were often required by the government there to form a joint venture with a domestic manufacturer. Many of these countries are transitioning to market economies and joint ventures are seen as a means for domestic companies to develop the resources and skills required to compete in global markets. With its population of 1.4 billion, it is perhaps not surprising that China is the biggest car market in the world and continues to grow. According to the French car manufacturer Renault, which has a joint venture with a Chinese car manufacturer Dongfeng, along with two other companies, over 28 million cars were sold in China in 2018 (Renault, 2019).

The four main domestic car manufacturers operating in China are: Dongfeng Motors, Changan Automobile, FAW Group and SAIC. Each of these companies manufacture a vast array of different cars models, many of them in partnership with the main international brands such as Renault, BMW, Nissan, Volkswagen, Honda, General Motors, Jaguar Landrover, Mercedes and many more. Volkswagen, in strategic partnership with both FAW Group and SAIC, is the largest foreign car manufacturer in China. In 2018, China relaxed its decades-old requirement for foreign companies to operate as part of a joint venture with a Chinese company, and foreign companies could not hold more than 50% of the joint venture. However, the partnership with foreign car manufacturers is expected to continue investment by international brands is expected to grow. Following the relaxation of the rule, BMW announced it was increasing its investment in its joint venture to 75% and extending the agreement until 2040 (Handcock and Woodhouse, 2018). Luxury car brands are particularly popular among wealthy Chinese, but these are now very heavily taxed as the government in China is putting enormous resources into the development of electric vehicles as a means of combating serious air pollution, particularly in the big cities.

Some Irish semi-state companies have entered into joint ventures abroad. One such company that has engaged in many joint ventures in foreign countries is ESB International (a subsidiary of the Electricity Supply Board), which provides consultancy services overseas in building and managing power plants. Since its establishment in 1973, ESB International has been involved in over 150 countries. Another company involved in joint ventures abroad is Aer Rianta International, a subsidiary of the Dublin Airport Authority. It has developed airports and duty-free facilities in cities around the globe. Joint ventures can create great opportunities for many companies who are trying to access foreign markets.

Illustration 11.2 below is an example of an Irish company that has expanded using a variety of different methods, primarily through strategic alliances.

Illustration 11.2: Insomnia Coffee Company

Insomnia Coffee Company was established in Galway in 1997 by four Irish entrepreneurs who identified an opportunity in the rapidly growing market for premium coffee. They opened their first outlet in Galway and this was quickly followed by six outlets in the Dublin area. In the intervening years, Insomnia has grown significantly through internal development and through partnerships with Spar and Eurospar, in addition to a number of other Irish retailers. In addition, the company has over 400 self-service units in Ireland and the UK. Insomnia is now the largest premium coffee and sandwich retail chain in Ireland and has a significant presence in Britain.

In 2003, the company merged with the gourmet sandwich company, Bendini & Shaw, to combine quality snacks with its hot beverage range. They offer 29 different varieties of homemade sandwiches and a selection of 11 different breads; to ensure quality, the sandwiches are made freshly throughout the day. There is also a large variety of freshly baked bagels, pastries and deserts.

In 2005, Insomnia acquired Perks Cafés; also in that year, Insomnia signed a deal with Fairtrade Ireland, a deal representing 20% of all Fairtrade coffee business in Ireland and, indeed, the country's biggest Fairtrade deal.

In 2012, the company launched the Insomnia High Street franchise with a target of opening 15 franchisee stores in five years. In 2015, Insomnia announced a partnership with Debenhams, with the first store opening at Debenhams in the Mahon Point Shopping Centre in Cork. This was then followed by a number of openings in Debenhams in the UK, in Bradford, Cardiff, Bristol, Brocklebank, Watford, Stockport and Leeds. As well as Debenhams, Insomnia also has a partnership with leading Irish clothing retailer, Penneys, and they have opened in several Penneys stores, including Waterford, Swords, Liffey Valley and Athlone.

The company has won, or been short-listed for, a number of awards including:

- Franchisor with Outstanding Social Responsibility at the 23rd Annual Irish Franchise awards in 2018.
- Winner of the 2017 National Café Chain of the Year for the second consecutive year in the Irish Food Service Awards.
- Best Indigenous Irish Franchise 2017 at the 22nd Annual Irish Franchise Awards.
- Finalist in the 2018 Waste Management & Recycling awards, with the launch of their 'Mission Compostable' initiative.
- Finalist in the Retail Excellence Awards 2019.

Source: www.insomnia.ie (2019)

One of the main issues to be decided in forming a joint venture is the management of the assets being dedicated to the joint venture, and how the assets of the joint venture relate to, and can be separated from, the parent companies. While the joint venture might spread risk on one hand, this form of alliance also brings risks in terms of the management of the assets and whether one side might take them for their own exclusive use.

Licensing

In **Chapter 9** it was stated that there are occasions when a company may not have the resources or organisational capability to operate directly in another country, and it may license a company in another state to manufacture the product and use its trademark in return for an initial fee and an annual royalty based on production. It also has the advantage of minimising financial exposure as it does not involve committing resources and, as such, is an alternative to foreign direct investment. As discussed above in the section on joint ventures, it may be a government condition to operate in that market. In other cases, it may just suit a company to issue a licence to another company in order to reduce the production or distribution cost, as in the case of Carlsberg, a global brewer. The capital cost of building a brewery is quite substantial, and by licensing its product, Carlsberg avoids this huge capital cost and large transportation costs in what would be a relatively small market for its product. Another licensed product that consumers in Ireland would be familiar with is the French yoghurt, Yoplait.

Licensing can also be particularly useful in a situation where the political climate in a country is somewhat unstable. It is then seen as an attractive alternative to foreign direct investment as it minimises the financial exposure involved. Licensing is normally more common with technological products. Airlines now have the ability to allow passengers to use mobile phones on board aircraft. The technology underpinning this was developed by Altrobridge, a Tralee-based company founded by entrepreneur Mike Fitzgerald. The technology, which creates a base station and then uses satellites to create links, has been licensed to airlines, shipping companies and emergency services. The company is now targeting remote villages in developing countries in conjunction with large mobile phone operators. Licensing allows Altrobridge (a company of 130 employees) to expand at a much greater pace than would otherwise be possible.

Franchising

 Franchising is a form of licensing whereby the franchisor grants the franchisee the right to use certain intellectual property rights, such as brand names, copyrights, patents, etc., in return for various fees.

Franchising is another alternative to direct investment and one that is growing worldwide at a phenomenal pace, particularly in various service industries. Brand recognition is an inherent part of franchising. The examples listed in **Table 11.1** below are all well-known brand names. According

Table 11.1: *A Selection of Franchise Businesses Operating in Ireland*

Abrakebabra	Avis	Sherry Fitzgerald
Burger King	Budget Rent-a-Car	Chemdry
Domino's Pizza	Snap Printing	The Wine Buff
Four Star Pizza	Mace	Pitman Training
McDonald's Restaurants	Fairplay	Home Instead, Senior Care
Supermac's	Centra/Supervalue	Radisson
Pizza Hut	Spar	Senator Windows
O'Brien's Irish Sandwich Bars	Card Connection Ireland	Tilesavers
Sign Express	Cleaning Doctor	Value Tile
Fastway Couriers	Weight Watchers	
		Source: Irish Franchise Association

to the Irish Franchise Association (2019), there are now over 300 different franchise operations in Ireland, employing over 40,000 people.

By comparison, in the US there are over 3,000 different franchise operations, and many of the franchises operating here in Ireland originate in the US, including McDonald's. Indeed, only 14% of franchise systems in Ireland originated here. Indigenous franchise businesses include Supermac's, O'Brien's Irish Sandwich Bars and Butlers Chocolates. McDonald's is the largest franchise system in Ireland with 80 outlets, employing over 1,000 people. Approximately two thirds of these are franchised operations and the remaining ones are operated directly by McDonald's Ireland. This part-owning, part-franchising arrangement is quite common among companies that have franchised their business.

Franchising is an ideal way for someone with limited commercial experience to start a business, as they are buying into a tried and tested business model, with training and support, and a marketing network. This expertise and support reduces the time required to set up a successful business. There would also be a performance clause to ensure that the conditions and standards must be met, particularly, for example, in food safety, hygiene and storage arrangements.

While franchising is a very good idea for someone setting up in business, there are also some downsides. The franchise agreement is quite prescriptive in how the business is operated, and any deviation from the required model would terminate the franchise. Thus, it offers little scope for initiative by the franchisee (the person taking out the franchise). If there is any damage done to the franchise brand in general, it will obviously impact directly on the franchisor (the company that is franchising its business) as well as on each franchisee of that brand. Unlike a normal business, the franchisee does not have the freedom to sell the franchise without the prior agreement of the franchisor, and goodwill would not be part of the sale price as it remains with the franchise owner. It is important that care is taken in selecting franchise operators as there must be compatibility between the two parties to ensure a smooth operation, as it is, after all, a binding legal agreement.

The fees involved vary considerably depending on the franchise but would normally include an initial franchise fee. According to the Irish Franchise Association, these fees vary from €2,500 to €500,000, with an average fee around €25,000. The franchisee would also be expected to have sufficient working capital to operate the business on a day-to-day basis. There will also be other investment requirements to fit out the premises to the standard required by the franchisor as part of the business concept, and to fund equipment and vehicles. This could amount to perhaps €500,000 for bigger operations, but for most businesses the average would be about €150,000. In addition, a percentage of the turnover would be paid as a royalty fee (typically 6.5%) and a marketing fee (typically 2.5%). Normally the franchisee would also be obliged to buy all its supplies and materials from the franchisor (an additional form of income for the franchisor). Because of the split of income between the franchisor and franchisee, the franchise arrangement can only operate in an industry with reasonable margins. Generally speaking, the franchisee would have exclusive rights to a certain geographic area, so that two franchise operations are not competing for the same customer base.

According to McGarry (2007), there are certain preconditions necessary before considering franchising a business. It must have:

- A profitable track record to allow for profits for both the company and investors.
- Name protection, so that the company has exclusive rights to that trademark.
- A clear identity that separates the business from competitors.
- Transferable operations – those that can be transferred from one location to another while delivering consistency of product or service to the customer.
- Management depth to provide potential franchisees with training, and all of the operating manuals and other material that they need.

From a strategic perspective, franchising is an ideal way to rapidly expand a business while incurring little risk in the process. It is each individual franchisee that is putting up their own capital to invest in the business, while the franchisor gets the fees. The total amount raised by the fees may not be the equivalent of the profits from owning businesses outright, but they still amount to considerable profit providing the business concept is sound and it has good consumer appeal. In 1987 Starbucks was a modest nine-store operation in the Northwest of the United States. In the intervening time, Howard Schultz, its founder and chair, has transformed the company into a multinational enterprise which by 2019 had grown to 29,000 stores around the world. This enormous expansion could not have been achieved by organic growth alone, leaving aside the inherent risk involved in such rapid growth. It is easy to see why franchising is becoming such a popular strategy for expanding businesses.

Outsourcing

Outsourcing is a form of alliance that is becoming more and more popular with a wide variety of firms. This is when a company makes a decision not to perform some value chain activities itself and subcontracts them to another business specialising in that activity. Many companies are gaining a better understanding of their strategic capabilities and, just as importantly, any value chain activities in which they do not excel. Traditional economic theory would suggest that it is better to spend time and effort concentrating on those parts of the operation where one has a comparative advantage. The remaining activities can be farmed out to a company that can perform them better or cheaper than they can be in-house.

The company providing the service can also be expected to keep up to date with all aspects of that service and any new developments. This reduces the risk to the main company regarding any changes in technology that may take place within the outsourced activity area. The other side to the decision to outsource is that it then allows the company doing the outsourcing to concentrate on the core areas that are critical to its success. In cases of expansion into new markets or product areas, it also gives the company the flexibility to acquire access to the skills that they need but may not have already. The one critical factor is picking the right activities to be outsourced.

In choosing to outsource activities, it is best to pick ones that are non-crucial to the firm in achieving competitive advantage. A common example of an activity suitable for outsourcing is office cleaning. Offices need to be cleaned in the evening when most staff have left. By outsourcing this activity a company is not employing cleaning staff that are underutilised for long periods of time. Instead, cleaning companies will have a team that can get through the offices in a very short time and then move on to the next office block.

Companies can outsource many other activities. Various administrative functions such as payroll activities are outsourced. A company that passes on all legal matters to a particular firm of solicitors is effectively outsourcing. We have already seen in **Chapter 6** how Nike outsources its manufacturing process to companies mainly situated in Asia. At first glance, the manufacture of its product line might seem like a critical activity and one that should not be outsourced. However, the actual manufacture of clothing apparel is an activity that could be carried out by many manufacturers. What is critical to Nike is the design of its clothing and the lifestyle image that it is creating, and it is that image that people are buying into.

In developing relationships with suppliers, a firm is building up a strong, dedicated arrangement with those suppliers to ensure delivery of goods at the right quality and the right time. This is a central part of the process in controlling cost and quality of the brand. It is also a departure from a more adversarial arrangement based purely on the cheapest price. Just-in-time supply chains requires a very close relationship where much information is exchanged between the two companies – it is in effect an alliance between the manufacturing company and the supplier for the delivery of its inputs. As with most other types of alliance, it is critical to pick a suitable partner.

Networking

The final type of alliance is networking. This is very much a non-contractual arrangement that is extremely loose, but nevertheless is beneficial to all concerned. Each company maintains full control over its activities. There are many different types of networking arrangement. Most industries have representative bodies acting on behalf of all members in areas of common interest. Take licensed premises, for example: each pub is in competition with all other rival pubs for business. Like other industries, there are also areas of common concern on which publicans would like to see action taken, such as the level of excise and VAT. In these cases, their representative bodies provide a forum for each industry to voice its concerns.

Code-sharing agreements between airlines is another type of networking. Code-sharing agreements are where airlines feed business into rival airlines that are members of the network but are not competing on the same route. They will sell tickets that can be used by passengers using the other airlines and would recognise each other's frequent flyer miles, etc. The Star Alliance currently has 27 member airlines, including major airlines such as Lufthansa, Singapore Airlines and Swiss. Within the European Union, code-sharing arrangements are covered by EU Regulation 261/2004. The code-sharing agreement works on the basis that a business person going on a work trip to a number of destinations might book a ticket through, say, British Airways to fly from London to

Singapore, then go to a meeting in Tokyo with JAL and then on to Melbourne with Qantas – all on the one ticket.

Managing Alliances

There is a wide variety of possible alliances and each one has its own requirements in terms of how it might be managed. Some large organisations may have a number of alliances operating simultaneously and so the process needs to be managed similar to a portfolio. At the outset, senior management needs to be very clear about what it hopes to achieve in terms of strategic and financial objectives from an alliance and, indeed, as to whether an alliance is the best way to achieve those objectives. According to Dyer *et al.* (2004:109), "alliances typically create very little wealth for shareholders". Thompson *et al.* (2008:167) quotes research carried out in 1999 by the global consulting company Accenture in saying that "61% of alliances were either outright failures or 'limping along'." Oscar Wilde's observation on marriage would appear to have some similarities:

> "Men marry because they are bored. Women marry because they are curious. Both are disappointed."

All parties to the arrangement must have a shared understanding of what it will bring to them. It will take a considerable amount of management time to make it work and to achieve the synergies involved. The previous chapter looked at how synergies can be greatly over-estimated in diversified companies. This can also apply to managing alliances. It will be easier to achieve synergies when management has definite objectives in mind, before crafting the alliance to achieve them. Both sides will need to be clear about the rules for decision-making in terms of the scope of decisions, as well as what level in the organisation they are made and the process by which those decisions are made. It is also important that the mechanism allows for decisions to be made in a timely fashion.

Cross-business teams will have to work closely together on all aspects of the relationship. As people get to know one another, it is easier to iron out potential problems. Different corporate and national cultures complicate the process and this will have to be worked on to ensure that both parties are culturally sensitive to the other. Choosing partners is not just about the sharing of technology but also the compatibility of people. Kanter (1994) believes that top executives spend more time screening potential partners in financial terms than in managing the partnership in human terms. "They worry more about controlling the relationship than about nurturing it." It is therefore important to choose potential partners with great care. Alliances are about organisations working together and that implies trust.

It takes time to build trust and, according to Ohmae (1989), one problem many organisations have is a fixation on control of equity, which "equates 51% with 100% and 49% with 0%". The trust has to be maintained for the duration of the alliance. For a successful alliance to happen, both parties must be able to see things from the perspective of the other side and to continue to live up to their commitments.

In **Chapter 3** we discussed the Balanced Scorecard. Kaplan and Norton (2010) also recommend the use of the Balanced Scorecard for managing strategic alliances as a means of increasing the chances of success. They argue that an alliance usually gets defined by service level agreements that focus on what each side will contribute to the arrangement rather than what they hope to gain. By developing a Balanced Scorecard specifically for the alliance, it shifts the emphasis from operational performance metrics to a strategic focus that cuts across organisational boundaries.

Circumstances can very often change an alliance. There has to be flexibility built into the arrangement so that it can evolve as the environment takes on a different shape. Technology is constantly developing and nothing stays proprietary for very long. Similarly, market conditions change and companies must be in a position to respond. Some alliances may be intended as short-term arrangements. This is often the case where the arrangement is based on technology, with quickly changing conditions. Other alliances, for example between suppliers and manufacturers, have long-term potential, provided that the relationship can evolve in a way that remains satisfactory to all sides.

MERGERS AND ACQUISITIONS

Mergers and acquisitions happen when two organisations come together, but differ in terms of ownership and management.

Definition A **merger** is where the companies involved, normally similar in size, agree to come together to form a new company, generally changing the name in the process.

While a name change is usual, there are examples of mergers where the companies still retain their original names. For example, the $62 billion merger between Kraft and Heinz in 2015, which created the third largest food and beverage company in the world. Unlike an alliance, mergers are a reasonably permanent arrangement, although there are circumstances when the companies subsequently de-merge.

Definition An **acquisition** is where one company takes over or acquires another one.

Generally, acquisition involves a large company acquiring a smaller company and absorbing it into its own operations. The acquired company may continue to trade under its own name or it may be changed to that of its new owner. When Aer Lingus was taken over by International Airlines Group (AIG), owners of British Airways and Iberian Air, it still kept the brand Aer Lingus. The name would have particular resonance with not just Irish passengers, but would be a well-established name in the US, particularly among the 40 million or so Irish–Americans.

Occasionally, there can be a 'reverse takeover' such as Alpyra's reverse takeover of Cardpoint Plc in 2007 to create Payzone, a consumer payment and cash distribution group. A reverse takeover is the purchase of a publically traded company by an unlisted one.

Worldwide, there are tens of thousands of mergers and acquisitions each year. It is not just manufacturing companies that engage in mergers and acquisitions. Professional firms, for example of accountants or lawyers, often merge to achieve greater scale and synergy. Merger and acquisition activity in Ireland was very subdued for a number of years after the financial crisis in 2008. However, in the last couple of years there has been a marked increase in activity. In the first half of 2018 there was €70 billion in deals, most of which were in the mid-market range up to €250 million (*Business and Finance*, 2018).

Benefits of Mergers and Acquisitions

There are many benefits to mergers and acquisitions (M&As). The premier one is the timeframe involved. Like alliances, M&As allow a company to expand much more quickly than would be possible solely with internal development. With an ongoing target acquisition process to identify suitable candidates for possible acquisition, negotiations may be conducted, due diligence carried out and the whole deal completed in a matter of months. Depending on the size of the merger or acquisition, this could substantially increase the size of the organisation. Irish multinational companies such as Kerry Group Plc and CRH Plc have both expanded significantly over the past number of years through acquisition, mostly in foreign markets.

M&A can also be used as a means of acquiring skills or expertise that a company does not currently own but needs for future development. This is particularly important when industry conditions are changing rapidly. Then speed is of the essence, and internal development may not be a viable option; while an alliance may not provide the desired level of control.

In the previous chapter it was seen that the share price of a company can sometimes fall significantly for a number of reasons. If there is no immediate prospect of it rising again, its shareholders may wish to sell the company in order to realise their investment. This could present an immediate opportunity for a company to acquire another at a considerable discount, integrate it into its own operations or, in some cases, strip its assets. Likewise, the privatisation of former semi-state companies provides opportunities for acquisition. Having changed hands on a number of occasions, the Australian finance group Babcock & Brown paid €2.4 billion in 2006 for the former state telecommunications company Eircom. Eircom, or Eir as it is now known, has been taken over on a number of occasions since privatisation, the latest being in 2018, when French billionaire Xavier Neil purchased 64.5% of the company for €3.5 billion.

An acquisition can be a good way for a company to enter a static market. Generally, competitors will not see it as a direct threat as it does not increase the capacity of that market and thus provoke retaliation by incumbent players. It is also a way in which a fragmented market can be consolidated.

The concept of synergy was discussed in detail in **Chapter 10**. Acquiring or merging companies can be a way of realising cost efficiencies in a number of areas such as advertising, sales, distribution and transport, research and development and managerial/administrative processes. In 1997, two of

Ireland's leading publicly quoted dairy companies merged to form Glanbia: Waterford Foods Plc and Avonmore Foods Plc. These two companies, in the same industry, were located in close geographical proximity to each other, so the merger allowed considerable efficiencies to be gained. In the 20 plus years since the merger, Glanbia has grown enormously and is now a global nutrition group operating in 34 countries, employing almost 7,000 people and with revenues of €2.5 billion.

One big danger with M&As is that executives will pursue them to increase their own power base rather than for the benefit of the organisation. For that reason, board approval should only be given when there are demonstrable benefits to be obtained from the process.

Variety of Mergers and Acquisitions

A common mistake managers make is to consider all mergers and acquisitions to be the same. Bower (2001) conducted a considerable amount of research on M&A deals and identified the following five categories:

The overcapacity M&A These account for 37% of all deals. The strategic objectives of the acquiring company are to eliminate excess capacity, gain market share and create a more efficient company. It requires the merged company to decide quickly what needs to be rationalised. This will present a number of problems, particularly in the battle for control by managers, as will the merging of different cultures.

The geographic roll-up M&A This may appear similar to the above category but it differs substantially as it generally occurs earlier in the industry's life cycle. It involves the company expanding geographically into desired locations. The acquired companies remain local and maintain their relationship with their customers. In areas of overlap, duplicate facilities can be closed. In both cases, it is creating scale and scope efficiencies. Irish banks expanded in this manner.

Product or market extension M&A This is the next biggest category at 36%, and it is done to extend a company's product line or international reach. It is different from geographic roll-up as it involves bigger companies and moving into different countries, not just adjacent towns and cities. It is more difficult to execute as there will be greater cultural differences and, because it is further from home, difficulty in assessing the deal. Likewise, expanding into new product lines that are different from existing ones can cause difficulties. The company must know what it is buying. It will also require a lot of consideration to develop the acquisition to its full potential. The bigger the acquiring company is compared to its target, the easier the integration process will be.

The M&A as R&D In this case, the acquisition is a substitution for in-house R&D, and allows the company to build market position quickly. Many biotech and IT companies expand in this manner (research shows that it is particularly suitable for IT). The company needs a robust evaluation process in order to ensure that it is acquiring the specific technology that it requires. It does not allow for a slow assimilation of the new company. It is imperative that the company holds on to its human talent in order to reap the entrepreneurial and technological benefits.

The industry convergence M&A In this case, a company anticipates that a new industry is emerging and tries to establish a position by culling resources from existing industries whose boundaries are eroding. The acquirer should rationalise the non-essential elements and install its own accounting and control processes. Thereafter, it requires giving the subsidiary a considerable amount of freedom, and choosing links carefully and diplomatically. Integration should be driven by specific opportunities to create value, not by a perceived need to create a symmetrical organisation.

Process

In **Chapter 1** we saw that there is often less emphasis now on the role of detailed format planning in developing corporate strategy. However, any form of alliance or acquisition requires a considerable degree of planning. There are various frameworks to guide the acquisition process. In most instances there are six main elements that are generic to acquisition programmes:

- Strategic review
- Identifying a suitable company to acquire
- Carrying out due diligence
- Making the acquisition
- Integrating the acquired company
- Review of acquisition.

Strategic Review In Part One, we looked at the process of how a company sets strategic and financial goals that it hopes to achieve. Strategy represents the process by which these goals are attained. In that regard, acquisitions like alliances should be seen as a means to an end. They must add value to the company. Thus, there must be a good reason for any proposed acquisition that fits in with the organisation's well-defined strategy. Developing an acquisition strategy requires a full understanding of the business environment and strategic review of the organisation. Uhlaner and West (2008) believe: "One of the most often overlooked, though seemingly obvious, elements of an effective M&A programme is ensuring that every deal supports the corporate strategy". As with strategic alliances, senior managers need to be very clear as to what their strategic and financial objectives are in relation to acquisitions and what they hope to achieve, e.g. a 7% increase in market share. In the last decade, companies such as Kerry Group have achieved significant growth through acquisitions. This is part of a clear strategy of expansion using acquisitions as a vehicle – it would not be possible to achieve the same level of growth within a short timeframe though internal development alone.

Part of the strategic review should be the development of a synergy plan. If the acquisition is to add value, then clear synergy objectives need to be identified. In the previous chapter it was noted that Goold and Campbell (1998) had stated that synergy is often overestimated. The possible synergies that are identified as part of the strategic review should be confirmed during the due diligence process.

Once a decision is made with regard to acquisitions, management then needs to establish criteria to identify the types of opportunities that they could realise. Different deals will involve different approaches and execution, and will have to be tailored for the specific circumstances that currently exist. The company will also need to develop an acquisitions team representing various business functions and SBUs that will search for suitable targets. It is important to get the number and combination of this team correct. Given the huge cost of the acquisition, the process has to be right. This team will need clear guidance as to their function, and will often be assisted by consultancy firms specialising in mergers and acquisitions. Deals will need to have approval in principle from the board of directors.

Identifying a suitable company to acquire In addition to identifying particular companies that may be suitable in terms of strategic and financial objectives, the company must be realistic about what it can achieve in terms of price and the skills required in making a deal. Therefore, they will need specific parameters to guide their search, and a priority listing of the various factors. The target company may well be one with which they have a strategic alliance already in place already. The team may examine a few dozen companies. It will draw up a list of possible candidates and this will have to be examined and reduced to a shortlist of those companies that are most likely to fulfil the company's objectives and achieve both a strategic and cultural fit. This will obviously require considerable resources, which must be put in place if the process is to succeed. Eventually, the team will come up with a preference. Procedures for opening discussions and conducting negotiations will also have to be formulated. This will have to include price limits. Initial plans should be made for how the new company will be integrated if the deal is completed.

Carrying out due diligence When the company has identified a specific target that fits the appropriate criteria, it will carry out a process of due diligence on that firm. Due diligence is an essential part of purchasing any company in order to ensure that it will form a proper strategic fit in line with the objectives and to ascertain a reasonable price for the acquisition. It needs to identify the synergies to be realised and how the deal will generate value. It involves doing a review of all aspects of the company's operations in all its functional areas, including product range, sales and marketing, research and development, human resources and finances (in particular its liabilities). The importance of doing proper due diligence is borne out by the following example.

In 1983, AIB, which had a stake in the Insurance Corporation of Ireland (ICI), bought the remaining shares for £40 million and, according to Carswell (2006), carried out only 'superficial' due diligence. It used auditors Ernst Whinney to value the company. ICI had become a large organisation, covering a wide variety of risk in Ireland and the UK. However, it was poor at evaluating the risk it was underwriting. By 1984, ICI was building up huge losses, particularly in London, and did not have the cash reserves to cover those losses. By the end of the year, the losses were out of control and AIB had to plough another £40 million into the company. The problem was compounded by the fact that insurance is a 'long tail' business, meaning that it is often years after an event that the insurance cover is paid out.

By March 1985, given the enormous scale of the losses in ICI to date, along with unknown future liabilities, AIB informed the Government that it would not underwrite its subsidiary any longer. The scale of the problem was such that it would have brought down AIB, Ireland's largest bank, along with the entire Irish banking industry. The potential impact was so great that the Fine Gael-led Coalition Government was effectively forced to buy ICI from the bank (which wrote off its £86 million investment) for a nominal £1. In so doing, the State also took responsibility for its massive debt. By October 1985, it was estimated that debts would amount to £164 million. The Central Bank set up a rescue package and a new administration company, Icarom, was established to look after the winding up of ICI to meet its ongoing liabilities. In the early 1990s, AIB had agreed to contribute to the cost of the administration and, by 2004, had contributed €134 million with another €80 million due. Ernst Whinney was sued by AIB over the due diligence it had carried out on ICI. In 1993, Ernst Whinney settled out of court, without admission of liability for £39 million (Carswell, 2006). Clearly, it was an expensive exercise for all concerned. It is a sad irony that a quarter of a century later AIB had to be bailed out once again by the citizens of the State when in 2009 it had to be recapitalised to the tune of €20.8 billion as a result of the collapse of the banking sector in Ireland. Both of these incidents highlight the critical importance of proper governance structures.

Making the acquisition Once the company is satisfied that the target company represents good value and will help the company achieve its objectives, it can proceed with the deal and finalise arrangements with the company being acquired. All items included in the sale will have to be clearly stated. The company also needs to determine how the deal will be structured and financed. The acquisition will need the approval of the board of directors and other relevant stakeholders. Legal agreements will have to be drawn up by solicitors for both parties, and arrangements made for the closing of the deal.

Integrating the acquired company The acquiring company must act quickly to integrate the new acquisition as seamlessly as possible. It needs to draw up long-term, medium-term and short-term objectives. A priority of work also needs to be established, with an emphasis on the tasks that need to be tackled immediately. Integration involves a considerable amount of change, especially for the acquired company, and this process needs to be managed carefully.

According to Ashkenas and Francis (2000), the integration of an acquired company is a delicate and complicated process. The problem for most organisations is that the team that makes the acquisition then hands over to a management team, which will eventually run the merged organisations, but often, no-one is responsible for the integration process itself. They recommend appointing an integration manager, or what Uhlaner and West (2008) call a 'deal owner' – a senior, experienced, manager who will oversee the process from the very beginning to when integration has been completed. Functional heads would deal with the issues pertaining to their area of responsibility but report to the deal owner who would coach all those involved along the way.

Merging the two cultures is not an easy process. The two companies will have different objectives and priorities. Their corporate values will also be different, as will the way they approach work. Both management and staff in the new company will naturally be fearful. Their tenure needs to be clarified as soon as possible and expectations made clear. Bower (2001) has stressed the importance of holding on to talented personnel. The company will have to make a determined effort to hold on to key people by putting appropriate measures in place.

As with all aspects of management, good communication is vital, so there is a need to develop a communications plan for both organisations to ensure that all people have the information that they need and when they need it. In particular, each employee must understand what the priorities are and how it impacts on their work. Choosing the most appropriate medium for communicating is also important. In some situations, an all-staff email might suffice; on other occasions, it will require face-to-face meetings.

The integration process will involve a merging of the two corporate frameworks as well as each of the functional areas. The type of decisions required will include the desired locations for areas such as production facilities, R&D and the various staff functions. There will have to be a review of all contracts for supplies, distribution, advertising, training, etc. One of the most important areas for consideration is a review of operations to identify opportunities for synergies and then ensure that those synergies are created. While each of the functional areas will develop their own objectives, these must be developed in a co-ordinated fashion using frameworks such as the Balanced Scorecard. This can be used both as a planning and a control device to check progress.

Another consideration that must be taken into account is what technology will be used by the company after the acquisition. It may well be that the acquired company has better technology or systems in place than the parent company. A decision should be made to adopt the best technology/systems regardless of their origin. This needs to be done as quickly and seamlessly as possible.

Finally, it must be remembered that with larger organisations there may be a number of acquisitions being integrated at the same time. This obviously complicates matters quite considerably. According to Uhlaner and West (2008), in 2007, IBM's software group was integrating 18 acquisitions simultaneously, involving over 100 full-time experts in a variety of functions and locations in addition to the specialised teams mobilised for each deal.

Review of Acquisition

The importance of constantly monitoring the environment is stressed throughout this textbook. Circumstances change and, as a result, so too must the organisation. This ongoing review should also take into account the strategic capability of the organisation, as that too will evolve. The nature of an acquisition means that the organisation will change and, depending on the size of the acquisition, that change can be substantial. In some cases, an acquisition will be a rare occurrence that may happen only once in the lifetime of the organisation. For other companies, such as Kerry Group, acquisitions are a very regular occurrence and there may be a number of them carried out in any one year. In all instances, a review of the process should be carried out to ensure that it is realising the value and benefits that were expected. This review should be done at a strategic level to see whether an acquisition was the most appropriate way to achieve the strategic and financial objectives of the company and also to review whether the target acquisition process identified the most suitable target. At an operational level, the integration process itself also needs to be reviewed to see if any improvements can be made to the company's performance. It can be compared against any previous acquisitions completed by the company and it can also be benchmarked against similar acquisitions carried out in the industry by other companies. Any issues arising from the review need to be tackled without delay by senior management.

The concept of the learning organisation has already been discussed in this textbook. With regard to the learning organisation, the review process is not just about examining the performance of a particular acquisition: it should also be a learning experience to see what lessons can be put to use for the future direction of the organisation and whether acquisitions will form part of that. There will be lessons drawn from every deal, and it is important that these are shared throughout the company so that organisational learning takes place.

M&A Approval

When companies merge or are acquired, it can create a dominant position for that company in the marketplace. Such dominance is open to potential abuse, and for that reason both the European Union and national governments encourage as much competition as possible. If a merger or acquisition is likely to create such dominance, it must receive approval from the Competition and Consumer Protection Commission (in 2014, the Competition Authority merged with the National Consumer Agency to form the new body) before it can proceed (the UK equivalent is the Competition Commission). The Competition and Consumer Protection Commission (CCPC) received 98 merger notifications in 2018, an increase of 36% over the previous year. The main areas were real estate, information and communications, healthcare, and financial services (CCPC, 2018).

The CCPC has a two-phase process for vetting M&As. The majority of referrals are cleared after an initial Phase One investigation, but it has the power to carry out a full investigation if one is deemed necessary. In many cases, it may impose conditions on any approval given. For larger or international deals, approval may be sought from the European Commission before the deal can proceed. During 2018, the CCPC monitored a number of European merger activities that there deemed to be of significance to Ireland. Among those mergers monitored were: Bayer/Monsanto; Kennedy Wilson/AXA JV; and Siemens/Alstrom.

While the majority of M&As that are referred to the CCPC receive approval, occasionally some deals do not get the go-ahead. In August 2008, Kerry Group's proposed €165 million acquisition of Reox's Breeo Foods was blocked by the then Competition Authority, who held that it would "substantially lessen" competition in consumer markets for cooked meats and processed cheese. The deal would have seen Kerry Group add Dairygold, Galtee, Shaws, Mitchelstown cheese and Sno yogurt to their line-up. Kerry Group already owns well-known brands such as Denny, Dawn, Ballyfree, Charleville, Cheesestrings and Low Low. The failed acquisition netted Reox €20 million in a non-refundable deposit, which was agreed when the company entered into discussions about the takeover. When a deal such as this is turned down by the CCPC, there is potential redress for the companies concerned in the High Court (Curren and Daly, 2008). Lawyers for Kerry Group appealed the decision of the then Competition Authority to the High Court. In March 2009, the High Court overruled the ruling by the Competition Authority and it allowed the acquisition to proceed.

Illustration 11.3 Google Fined

In July 2018, Margrethe Vestager, the EU Commissioner for Competition, announced after a three-year investigation, that Google had been fined €4.3 billion by the European Commission for abuse of its dominant market position with its Android mobile phone operating system. According to the EU Commission (2018), more than 80% of smartphones devices in Europe and world-wide run on Android, and Google has more than a 90% market share for "general Internet search throughout the European Economic Area (EEA)".

This was the largest anti-trust fine ever imposed by the EU, equating to approximately 40% of Google's €12.6 billion profits in 2017. It was designed to send out a strong message about the need to comply with the EU's competition rules. Google was given 90 days to rectify its exclusive licensing arrangements with manufacturers or face fines of up to 5% per day of the global turnover of its parent company, Alphabet. Alphabet has annual revenues of $111 billion. Google was fined in 2017 by the European Commission for abuse of its market position in favouring its own shopping services in Internet searches.

The European Commission found against Google on three counts:
1. Google's requirement of manufacturers that they must pre-install the Google search engine and browser (Chrome) as a condition for licensing Google's application store (Play Store).
2. Google paid manufacturers not to pre-install any other system and to favour Google services, including the Chrome browser application.
3. Google prevented manufacturers wishing to pre-install Google applications from selling any smart mobile device running on alternative versions of Android that were not approved by Google.

As a result, the Commission determined that Google was abusing its dominant position. Google, while denying any wrongdoing, had to lodge the €4.3 billion into an escrow account pending an appeal to the Court of Justice of the European Union.

Source: Smyth, 2018

Alliance or Acquisition

Alliances and acquisitions are alternative strategies. There are certain similarities between them, but both often fail to deliver the promised results. According to Dyer *et al.* (2004), acquiring companies experience a wealth loss of 10% over five years after a merger. In contrast, after an acquisition is announced, the target company's share price rises by 30%, implying they are taking home most of the value. It is estimated that up to 55% of alliances break down prematurely. One of the main problems, suggested by Dyer *et al.,* is that executives do not treat alliances and acquisitions as alternative mechanisms, and do not compare them before picking one. "Consequently, they take over firms that they should have collaborated with and ally with those that they should have bought." They both differ in many ways.

Acquisitions are competitive and, being based on market price, they are risky. On the other hand, alliances involve two companies that are co-operating, which is less risky.

As outlined above, few companies appoint an integration manager or 'deal owner' who can steer the process from the very beginning through to the end. With no one taking overall charge, the deal will most likely fail. To help in deciding whether an alliance or an acquisition is more appropriate, Dyer *et al.* (2004:110) developed a framework which considers three sets of factors: resources and synergies; the marketplace; and competences at collaborating.

Resources and synergies The company must first decide on the type of synergies that potentially can be achieved:

- Modular synergies where resources are managed independently and later pooled for profits, such as an airline and a hotel chain working together to generate business for each other. In this case a non-equity alliance is best.
- Sequential synergies where one company completes its task and submits it to the other partner, as in biotech companies producing drugs for larger pharmaceutical companies who will then market them. These require equity-based alliances.
- Reciprocal synergies where companies work closely together and share knowledge. Here companies are better off combining all assets in a merger or acquisition.

Synergies are achieved by combining resources, so the company must distinguish between hard resources, such as manufacturing facilities, and soft (human) resources. With hard resources, acquisitions are a better option as they are easy to value and the synergistic effect is achieved by combining the resources and eliminating any excess capacity. Mergers and acquisitions are the best and quickest method of doing this. For example, in 2001 Hewlett-Packard, under CEO Carly Fiorina, initiated a $25 billion merger with Compaq, which at the time was intended to make it the top IT company in the world. Making mergers work in reality is extremely difficult and this merger failed to realise the benefits that were originally envisaged by the two companies. In 2013, HP discontinued using the Compaq brand name in the United States and in 2015, the Argentinean company, Grupo Newsan, aquired the brand's licence. Grupa Newsan has since ceased trading.

If the synergies are dependent on talented people working together, acquisitions should be avoided and equity alliances used instead. Research shows that when a company is acquired, many of its most talented people leave within a three-year period. An equity stake allows for better control and alignment of interests, without causing dissatisfaction among staff.

Marketplace Companies need to consider market uncertainty and competition. If there is market risk involved in the process, the companies are better off collaborating using an equity or non-equity alliance as this limits their exposure. If, later on, the level of certainty increases, they can then consider a merger or acquisition. An acquisition is based, among other things, on the market price of the target company. In a competitive environment there may be rival companies also interested in the same target and this can push the price up to a level that may not be justified.

Competences at collaborating According to Dyer *et al.*, the third consideration is the experience the company has in managing acquisitions or alliances. Previous experience tends to drive companies in a certain direction. If, in the past, the company negotiated a successful alliance, there is a strong likelihood that all future arrangements will be alliances rather than considering whether an acquisition would be more appropriate. The opposite also holds true. It is important that the company develops skills in both areas so that it has the competence to deliver on an acquisition or an alliance, whichever is the more appropriate in the circumstances.

This again highlights the necessity to have one senior executive in charge of the entire process, with different expert teams reporting to them. Cisco is a company with significant experience in growing through alliances and M&As. The company has a centralised process-driven approach to managing M&As based on three activities:

1. Discovery and planning – from the initial scoping and business modelling to conducting due diligence and integration planning
2. Execution of the plan – ensure the organisation is ready and all of the resources are in place
3. Monitoring – ongoing measurement and adjustment of the integration of the new company.

INDUSTRY CONDITIONS: TAILORING APPROPRIATE STRATEGIES

The last couple of chapters looked at the different directions in which a company could develop and the various methods by which it could achieve its strategic objectives. These are all possibilities for a company but depend on so many other factors. Ultimately, it depends on the strategic and financial objectives that have been set. The company must also consider the particular industry conditions that prevail, as well as their own capabilities. The firm must then adjust its strategies accordingly.

Porter (1980) drew attention to the concept that the structures of industries change, often in fundamental ways, as they evolve through the phases of introduction, growth, maturity and decline. This has "critical importance for the formulation of strategy", and it impacts on buyer behaviour, products and product changes, marketing, manufacturing, R&D and overall strategy. These strategies were further developed by Thompson *et al.* (2018).

Emerging Industries

In emerging industries, companies are trying to discover the nature of that industry as there are no set rules in place and each company is trying its own approaches. Examples of emerging industries include nanoelectronics and electric car engines. Different companies will often be coming up with their own version of the technology, hoping that their particular technology will eventually become industry standard. In general, companies will try to get the technology right and may well form alliances or acquire other companies to get the expertise that they lack. In order to recoup high R&D costs, the company will try to expand the market as quickly as possible, both at home and abroad (again possibly through alliances). One of the biggest hurdles for young companies in emerging industries will be raising sufficient finance to fund the establishment of their operations until such time as they reach break-even point.

Growth

When the market starts growing, the company will try to achieve a greater level of growth than the industry average. To entice more customers it is important to reduce price (through cost reduction). The company will also have to build up additional markets and distribution channels. As it receives feedback from sales, it will continue to improve upon the product and increase the range of models available so as to appeal to wider segments. In order to take advantage of a growing industry, companies may have to look at expanding out of the markets that they currently operate in. This is particularly relevant for Irish companies as the home market will invariably be too small. The methods by which this can be achieved have already been discussed in this chapter.

Maturity

When the market reaches maturity, sales will slow considerably as the last of the 'late majority' and 'laggards' buy the product. Other than that, it is dependent on repeat purchases from those who bought earlier on. Competition will be very strong as rival companies (including foreign ones) are well established and customers are much more discerning. The emphasis will then switch to service and cost, and profits will begin to fall considerably. The company needs to respond by cutting out marginal products from their range and concentrating on those that produce the greatest profit margin. Costs will have to be reduced considerably by examining every aspect of the value chain to see where efficiencies can be made without compromising quality. Economies may be achieved by acquiring rival companies that are struggling. There may be opportunities for increasing sales in less developed markets that are in a different stage of the industry life cycle. Foreign expansion could be achieved by foreign direct investment or through alliances or joint ventures. There will usually be a considerable amount of consolidation in the industry, as smaller or less efficient companies are taken over by their larger rivals.

Whatever action is being taken, it is important to respond quickly and to have a clear strategy. The maturity phase may well be extended as new technologies emerge that effectively prolong the life of the industry. For example, the TV industry continues to provide entertainment, while embracing new technology, such as smart TVs, thus prolonging the maturity phase of the industry. It is similar for the motor car: though manufacturers are switching to engines based on green technology, the car industry adapts and continues.

Decline

Declining industries see sales drop off considerably. This can be for a variety of reasons: changing customer tastes and lifestyles, demographics, or improved substitute technology (e.g. personal computers replacing typewriters). Costs will have to be driven down further, but there may be segments of the market that still remain profitable. The pace of the decline can be slow (where good profits can still be made) or fast, and consequently the company has to make a decision as to how it will exit the industry. In a slow-exit strategy, a company may curtail any new investment and harvest as much cash as they can. In a fast-exit strategy, it sells out as quickly as possible and concentrates resources in other industries.

In picking appropriate strategies, the situation is further complicated by additional factors such as whether the industry is turbulent and changing rapidly or if it is concentrated or fragmented. The position of the company in the industry will also have a bearing on the matter, depending on whether it is the industry leader, a close second or a small player. Companies that are in a weak position need to make a fundamental decision about remaining in the market and trying to improve their situation or making a decision to quit.

Thompson *et al.* (2018) point out that some strategic options are more suited to certain industry conditions and environments than others, while the company must also take into account its own particular circumstances to create a tight strategy–situation fit. They suggest that the company pose four questions to point it in the right direction:

1. What competitive edge can it realistically achieve?
2. Which strategy best suits the company, given all of the different issues that it faces?
3. What offensive actions can be taken to capitalise on rivals' weaknesses?
4. Does it need to take any defensive action to protect its position?

Having assessed the general situation, the company must be clear in what it is trying to achieve in terms of strategy. It is important that it achieves its potential, but at the same time it should formulate a strategy that does not push its capabilities too far. Ideally, it should stick to what it knows best and has experience in, as this will lessen the risk involved. However, it may be that a familiar strategy is causing problems, so executives must also be prepared to develop in a radically different direction if necessary.

CONCLUSION

There are many strategic options open to companies to achieve growth. Internal growth will play an important role for every company, and for many it may well be the only way that it achieves growth – particularly smaller and family-run businesses. Strategic alliances are growing in importance as many companies realise that it is neither desirable nor possible to develop all the competences required to operate in particular markets. For bigger companies, many may choose mergers and acquisition as a means of expanding quickly or acquiring skills and resources that they do not currently have. While M&As can achieve rapid growth, they also need to be managed very carefully, as they do not always achieve the benefits that are expected.

Perhaps the key requirement is for managers to have a clear vision of what exactly it is they want to achieve for the company and then to analyse each of the options available to see which method can best deliver on their strategic objectives. As with all strategies, they must be tailored for the specific conditions within which the company is operating.

SUMMARY

There is an extensive range of choices available for a company in deciding how it is going to achieve further growth. This chapter looked at the three main methods of strategic development: internal growth, strategic alliances and mergers and acquisitions. Each has different characteristics and will achieve different objectives for the organisation.

Internal development is the main method of development for most organisations. It involves the company growing using its own resources and capabilities. Internal development can be used as a means to achieve all of the directions discussed in **Chapter 10**. The funding required for internal development usually comes from a number of sources, including retained earnings, borrowings and, perhaps, fresh equity.

Strategic alliances can be contractual, involving ownership, or looser collaborative arrangements between companies. A strategic alliance can be defined as 'a formal agreement between two or more separate companies in which there is a strategically relevant collaboration of some sort, joint contribution of resources, shared risk, shared control and mutual dependencies'. It is a much quicker form of development than internal development, which can be especially important in the technology industry. Alliances can vary from long-term agreements to temporary arrangements, including:

- **Consortia** – groups that consist of two or more companies that have come together for a particular purpose, such as developing a large venture.
- **Joint ventures** – two companies come together and form an alliance in the form of a third company that is jointly owed and managed by the two parents who remain separate entities.
- **Licensing** – involves allowing another company to manufacture the product and use its trademark in return for an initial fee and an annual royalty based on production.
- **Franchising** – a form of licensing whereby the franchisor grants the franchisee the right to use certain intellectual property rights, such as brand names, copyrights, patents, etc., in return for various fees.
- **Outsourcing** – when a company makes a decision not to perform some value chain activities in-house and subcontracts them to another company that specialises in that activity.
- **Networking** – there are many different types of networking arrangements where firms maintain full control over their activities and benefit one another.

Mergers and acquisitions occur where two organisations come together in terms of ownership. A **merger** is where the companies involved, normally similar in size, agree to come together to form a new company, generally changing the name in the process. An **acquisition** is where one company takes over or acquires another one. M&As allow for quick expansion and for acquiring skills that the business does not currently have at its disposal.

Achieving **synergy** is perhaps the most important reason for M&As, though experience shows that it is much more difficult to achieve in reality than on paper. M&As require a significant amount of planning in order to be successful. The process involves a number of stages:

- Strategic review
- Identifying a suitable company to acquire
- Carrying out due diligence
- Making the acquisition
- Integrating the acquired company
- Review of acquisition.

Before a company can proceed with a merger or acquisition, it may, depending on its size, require regulatory approval.

DISCUSSION QUESTIONS

1. Critically analyse the advantages and disadvantages of organic growth as a method of development.
2. Ohmae (1989) stated: "In a complex, uncertain world filled with dangerous opponents, it is best not to go it alone." Discuss the importance of strategic alliances.
3. Differentiate between the various forms of strategic alliances.
4. Explore the role that franchising has played in the development of businesses in Ireland.
5. Critically analyse the importance of acquisitions in the strategy of multinational companies.

CHAPTER 12

Decision-making

LEARNING OBJECTIVES

On completion of this chapter, you will be able to:

- Examine the factors involved in the decision-making process
- Evaluate the rational model for decision-making
- Differentiate between individual and group decisions
- Critically assess the various factors that should be considered when making strategic decisions

"Time for you and time for me, and time yet for a hundred indecisions."

T. S. Eliot

INTRODUCTION

The previous chapters have examined the many possibilities for an organisation in terms of directions, methods and industry conditions. Such options offer an enormous choice, but it is essential that a company tailors its strategy to suit its own particular circumstances. This inevitably entails making a decision about its future. This chapter examines the process involved in making those decisions. It begins with examining the decision-making process itself: how do people and organisations make decisions?

The second section of the chapter goes on to explore the factors that managers need to consider in making specific choices. This section looks at ensuring that the strategies fit with the company's strategic position, which was explored earlier in **Chapters 6** and **7**, and ensuring that all possibilities are in line with the established strategic and financial objectives. Financial objectives are reasonably straightforward, in that financial analysis will indicate whether each option is giving an acceptable return on investment. A number of tools that evaluate financial returns will be examined. Strategic returns are more subjective and therefore somewhat more difficult to analyse, but must also be considered as they are equally important.

Stakeholders will have differing expectations of an organisation and these also need to be considered. The purpose of this chapter is to show what executives will need to do in order to make decisions that can capitalise on any opportunities that may arise, or to protect a company from possible threats. Either way, informed, decisive action is a vital part of success.

DECISION-MAKING PROCESS

In **Chapter 1**, the strategic process was described as the long-term action of an organisation and also as usually involving significant spending. Strategic decisions are rather complex and executives must consider many different factors. They involve both analysis and judgement. The implications of strategic decisions on the organisation can be quite profound. For that reason, they must be right.

Definition | **Decision-making** can be defined as "the selection of a course of action from among alternatives" (Weilrich and Koontz, 1993:199).

Before examining various techniques for analysing strategies, it is first necessary to look at the conditions under which decisions are made, including: uncertainty, risk, the amount of information available and the reaction of various stakeholders.

There is inevitably going to be a level of uncertainty involved in strategic decisions, and the greater the timespan involved, the greater the level of uncertainty. In studying the macro environment of an organisation, it may be seen that there are many factors outside its control, such as the cost of oil. A hurricane in the Gulf of Mexico or the threat of conflict in the Middle East can send the price soaring. As we have seen, this impacts on all businesses, sometimes in a major way. For a haulage company planning expansion, the cost of oil is extremely uncertain and will have serious implications for the company if the price rises significantly. While there are some decisions made where the outcome is reasonably certain, in reality there is some level of uncertainty in most strategic decisions.

Executives also have to look at the amount of risk involved in the process. **Chapter 7** examined how companies treat risk at the corporate level. The tolerance for risk must be factored into decision-making. There could be a course of action that potentially promises great returns, but as we have already seen, there is a strong correlation between risk and return. For that reason it may be decided that the level of risk involved is too great as it could endanger the entire future of the organisation should things go wrong. Even within the same organisation, different executives will have alternative approaches to risk.

When we examine the rational model for decision-making, we will see that a presumption is made that the relevant information is available to the executives. Strategic decisions are, for the most part, non-programmed decisions. At the operational level, most decisions are programmed decisions, where the manager has made similar decisions before and, if necessary, refers to operations manuals for guidance. Strategic decisions, on the other hand, are generally once-off, with no precedents for guidance. As a result, it is very difficult to ensure that all the relevant information for a decision has been gathered.

Various stakeholders can be expected to have different expectations from an organisation and there may be considerable opposition to a certain strategy from interested groups. Strategic decisions will often be modified to include the views of powerful stakeholders, such as unions or the government. All of these factors will modify the final decision, regardless of how objective the decision-makers perceive themselves to be.

THE RATIONAL MODEL

The rational model for decision-making originated with the Greek philosopher Plato. It assumes that people use a rational, sequential process in making decisions, and is often referred to in modern economics as 'homo economicus'. This model involves a number of stages, including diagnosing the problem, identifying all solutions, evaluating each one, making the optimum choice, implementing it and, finally, evaluating the decision.

Diagnosing the Problem

Executives have first to be aware that a problem exists (and this also implies that they are willing to take action to resolve that problem). A problem can be said to exist when the actual situation differs from the desired situation. It is important to diagnose the exact cause and nature of the problem rather than just the symptoms. High staff turnover can be a major problem for companies, but this may just be a symptom of a greater underlying problem with the quality of management. There will be considerable data from which executives can identify the problem, such as historical analysis and benchmarking. However, listening to staff and to customers can often highlight the existence of a problem, once the company has mechanisms in place for this information to filter through. It should be stated that a company that is intent on being a market leader should not have to wait for problems to arise, but should take initiatives to prevent them.

Identifying Different Solutions

The next stage of the process is to identify as many solutions as possible. It can often happen that the best solutions are not the most obvious, so for that reason, by generating as many potential solutions as possible the correct one can be more readily identified. They will be evaluated in the next step. It will be seen later that groups can often generate a greater number of possible solutions. Techniques like De Bono's 'Six Thinking Hats' can be useful for generating alternatives that may not otherwise come to mind. While most interpretations of the rational model suggest that many possible solutions are generated, it must be remembered that this can complicate the process and can also delay it considerably. The danger is that the search for an exhaustive list of solutions can lead to 'paralysis by analysis' – a situation where executives become so immersed in the minute detail of analysis that no decision is made. Time is often not on the side of a company, and so the executive does not want to be always one consultant's report short of a decision.

Evaluating the Alternatives

Once the various alternatives have been identified (bearing in mind that there may be some possible solutions that have not been included), the next stage is to evaluate them in order to come up with the solution that offers the greatest value to the company. This is sometimes referred to as 'maximising the expected utility of an outcome'. The problem with this is that it can be quite a subjective process, as many of the values are not numerical. Consequently, the alternatives have to be weighed up in an holistic manner in terms of the ultimate benefits. The use of cost–benefit analysis should be part of the process. (This will be developed later in the chapter.) As a result, the final decision will probably be a mixture of objective analysis and the executive's own gut feeling. Thus, experience can play an important role in making the correct decision.

Making a Decision

Rarely will an organisation have the luxury of a long period of time with which to reflect on all aspects of a problem. More often than not, there will be only a narrow window of opportunity to make a decision and implement it. Thus, an important function of management is the decision-making capacity. The executive needs to be decisive. There are circumstances where executives may rightly feel that there is genuinely not enough information to make a decision. In that case, they will have to revert to stage one to ensure that they have correctly identified the problem, or stage two in order to generate further options. While all this is time-consuming, it may be the best course of action. On the other hand, if they have the information, the decision should quickly follow.

Implementing the Decision

Once the executives have made their decision, and they are happy that it is the correct one, it must now be implemented. It is not a simple process of issuing an edict. Buelens *et al.* (2011) suggest that there are three managerial tendencies that reduce the effectiveness of implementing solutions. These are:

- The tendency not to ensure that everyone understands what needs to be done. Ideally, the decision-making process should be inclusive, but, one way or the other, the decision must be communicated clearly to all concerned so that there is no ambiguity about what is required.
- The tendency not to ensure the acceptance or motivation for what needs to be done. Once again, an inclusive approach to decision-making will allow for greater acceptance of that decision. This will increase ownership and overall acceptance.
- The tendency not to provide appropriate resources for what needs to be done. There are two aspects to this. First, the manager must provide adequate staffing and financial and physical resources to complete the job, as well as a realistic timeframe. Secondly, there need to be proper structures in place to ensure cross-functional/departmental co-ordination.

These points will be addressed in Part Four of this textbook which deals with the implementation of strategy. Successfully implementing the chosen strategy is an integral part of the overall process of guiding an organisation towards its chosen objectives.

Evaluating the Outcome

Feedback is an essential element of any process. In decision-making, the aim of feedback is to assess the effectiveness of the choices that were made, ensuring that an organisation is on target to achieve its objectives. Circumstances are constantly changing and, for that reason, adjustments will often have to be made to get back on course. This evaluation process should include re-evaluating the diagnosis of the problem in the first instance. If the original summation of the problem was incorrect, then a different solution will, in all probability, have to be found. The process of monitoring the decision should continue until the objectives are finally achieved.

Limitations of the Rational Model

The rational model for decision-making, as described above, is a logical process that should be used in examining potential strategies. It makes the assumption that, when executives are making decisions, they are trying to find the optimum solution. It also makes the assumption that those executives have full knowledge of the issues facing them and all of the relevant information to make the decision, as well as understanding the consequences of each alternative. The model also implies that the executives concerned have the intelligence to weigh up all of the factors and choose the optimum solution. However, as in many instances, the theory and the practical reality are often different for a number of reasons. In **Chapter 2** we saw that there is a strong link between politics and business, as political decisions ultimately create the environment within which business operates. Such decisions often take into account various political factors, many of which can over-ride better judgement. Barry (2010) catalogues a series of disastrous policy decisions that were taken by the Irish Government during the boom period in the 2000s that ultimately had a devastating impact on the economy. Simon (1979) suggests that, as such, the rational model is effectively aspirational as it largely ignores the human element in decision-making.

Decision-makers are limited by what March and Simon (1958) termed '**bounded rationality**'. Bounded rationality implies that the executive, when making decisions, is 'bounded' or limited by a number of different constraints. These include the environment within which executives are working, which is often outside their control. Individuals also have limited mental and emotional capacity. It will be very difficult to solve the problem, for example, if the problem is not clearly identified by the executives in the first instance. It may be that the problem is too complex for them to understand fully. Fatigue can also impair sound judgement. According to the Road Safety Authority, one in five driver-deaths in Ireland is due to driver fatigue (RSA, 2018). As a result of improvements in MRI technology, there has been a considerable amount of research conducted in recent years by the World Health Organisation, Berkeley University and Harvard Medical School on the negative impact that the lack of sleep has on decision-making. Many business people suffer from sleep deprivation as a result of the pressures of work, long-distance travel and what is termed poor 'sleep hygiene', primarily as a result of the use of electronic devices such as smartphones and iPads late at night (Czeisler, 2006; Walker, 2018). Four centuries before we had access to such technology, Shakespeare seems to have come to a similar conclusion:

> "Sleep that knits up the ravelled sleave of care, The death of each day's life, sore labour's bath, Balm of hurt minds, great nature's second course, Chief nourisher in life's feast."
>
> *Macbeth*, Act 2, Sc. ll

McShane and Von Glinow (2009) suggest that difficulties with problem identification include the fact that people sometimes block out bad news as a defence mechanism; people also develop mental models to help them cope with the outside world, but these also produce assumptions that can limit people's ability to think clearly. These assumptions can produce biases which will affect their judgement. The reaction of different stakeholders will often impact on corporate decisions, as we saw in **Chapter 1**. A certain course of action could well prove to be unacceptable to particular stakeholders, be they investors, unions or government. As a result, anticipation of their reaction is likely to have a modifying effect on the various outcomes that are being considered.

As a result of problems such as these, executives find it difficult to process all of the information, making it difficult to come up with an optimum solution. Instead of continuing the search for the best solution, people tend to 'satisfice' (Simon, 1956:9), coined the word from "satisfy" and "suffice". '**Satisficing**' is choosing a solution that meets the minimum, rather than the optimal solution: one that can be described as sufficient.

Time Requirement in Decision-making

Time to make decisions is another major constraint on people. One of the biggest economic decisions ever taken by an Irish Government was taken in an incredibly short timeframe. The €440 billion blanket guarantee for Irish banks given by the Government in the early hours of 30 September 2008 has been the subject of a lot of debate over the last decade. The chairs and chief executives of Ireland's two biggest banks, AIB and Bank of Ireland, had approached the Government on the previous evening. They believed that the collapse of Anglo Irish Bank and Irish Nationwide was imminent and that this would have a domino effect on the entire Irish banking system; they needed State support to ensure the future of AIB and Bank of Ireland. The decision to provide liquidity for the banks had to be taken before the markets opened at 7am on 30 September (at that stage the banks insisted it was just a liquidity issue rather than the major recapitalisation that would subsequently be required). Though that decision solved the immediate problem, the crisis continued to deepen, involving a €64 billion bank bailout the following year.

Time given to decision-making also has broader implications for corporate governance. Clancy *et al.* (2010), in discussing the number of cross-directorships in top Irish companies, point to the danger that, because of the workload involved in each directorship, not enough time is given by these directors to the problems actually facing the companies in question. They showed that some directors were sitting on the boards of five Plcs or semi-state companies at the same time, in addition to which they were directors of up to 10 other companies. Some of these were in full-time positions as CEOs while also serving in multiple directorships. The capacity of individuals to undertake multiple directorships depends on the competence and experience of the individuals concerned, as well as the complexity and diversity of each company. The degree of change being undertaken by companies will also impact on the amount of time required by directors and managers to make decisions. According to Clancy *et al.* (2010:20): "Some of them may have been over-extended, and thus unable to fulfil all of their roles as directors effectively, which is in itself a serious issue for good corporate governance."

The Walker Report (2009:14-15) in the UK also recommended that non-executive directors of boards need to give much greater time commitment than has been the case before. They suggest that directors of banks should commit between 30 to 36 days per year. A chair is recommended to commit a minimum of two-thirds of his or her time. Under the Companies Act 2014 in Ireland, a person may not be a director of more than 25 private limited companies at any one time.

Escalation of Commitment

When a decision has been made, there is often a tendency to stay with that decision, no matter what. The final stage in the rational model outlined above is the necessity to review decisions to see how successful they are. In some instances, it will appear that it was a wrong decision.

Definition The term '**escalation of commitment**' refers to the tendency to stay with a particular course of action even though it now appears to be a poor decision.

Ross and Straw (1993) suggest that there are four reasons underlying escalation of commitment: the ego of people involved in the decision-making process; internal politics and poor communication; the nature of the project itself and a natural tendency to stick with it and see it brought to a conclusion; and, finally, factors outside the organisation that may put pressure on them to continue.

An example of the concept of escalation of commitment on a grand scale was the American involvement in the Vietnam War. It began with the involvement of the US Army as advisers to the ARVN – the Army of the Republic of Vietnam (South Vietnam), and this led to the gradual introduction of US combat troops. In response to calls for additional troops by General Westmoreland, the US Commander in Vietnam, the Johnson Administration committed ever-increasing numbers to the war during the 1960s. There were a number of indications throughout the decade that should have alerted the Administration to withdraw the US troops. There was extremely strong Viet Cong resistance, particularly in the Tet Offensive in 1968, resulting in heavy American casualties, and diminishing international and domestic support for the war (Maclear, 1981; Hastings, 2018). Ricks (2006) draws similar conclusions about America's involvement in Iraq following the US-led invasion in March 2003:

> "It now seems more likely that history's judgement will be that the US invasion of Iraq in the spring of 2003 was based on perhaps the worst war plan in American history. It was a campaign plan for a few battles, not a plan to prevail and secure victory. Its incompleteness helped create conditions for the difficult occupation that followed. The invasion is of interest now mainly for its role in creating those problems."
>
> Ricks (2006:115)

The 2003 battle to take Iraq lasted just a couple of weeks. However, there was no coherent plan to govern the country after Saddam Hussein's regime fell. In the aftermath of the invasion, more and more American troops were required to maintain order in Iraq. Once again, military commanders requested a 'troop surge' to guarantee stability in the country. Six years later, the US still had a significant presence with over 100,000 troops in the country. It took a change in the administration in the US to announce a withdrawal from Iraq, with President Obama pledging to withdraw all combat troops by August 2010 and all remaining troops to have left the country by the end of 2011 (Staunton, 2009). However, in 2019, US troops are still serving in Iraq (and are still suffering casualties).

The development of the National Children's Hospital represents a commercial example of escalation of commitment. While the project was initially held up by planning objections, it expanded in scope and costs spiraled out of control even before the building work began. Yet at no stage were any restrictions put in place by the State that would have prevented such an escalation of resources and costs. (See the case study on the National Children's Hospital Project at the end of this textbook.)

Escalation of commitment can clearly have disastrous consequences for an organisation. The development of the National Children's Hospital by a private organisation would clearly have destroyed the company financially. In making decisions in an organisation, it is important that people are aware of the characteristics of escalation of commitment. It is important also that there is a supportive 'no blame' culture in the organisation that facilitates withdrawing from a project despite previous financial and emotional commitment to it. Such a culture can help reduce the potential negative impact. In addition, it can be useful to have other senior executives, not involved in the original decision, to review progress to determine if it is matching the original expectations. In the case of the development of the National Children's Hospital, the project could not have been pulled because of the urgent need of modern pediatric facilities in 21st Century Ireland, but the project certainly should have been managed better.

GROUP DECISIONS

Many decisions will be taken by groups such as committees or work teams. According to Kreitner (1998:234), there are a number of advantages and disadvantages to groups making decisions. The advantages include:

- 'Two heads are better than one.' Groups will, generally speaking, have a greater amount of knowledge and experience than an individual, and the group will be able to process more information than an individual.
- Groups will often have greater understanding of the issues under discussion and of the possible courses of action.
- Each member will have a different perspective on the issue.
- This greater comprehension should, in turn, lead to greater ownership and make the implementation process easier.
- Decisions can provide training for younger and less experienced team members.

It is said that a camel is a horse designed by a committee. It does not always follow that group decisions are better. Some of the disadvantages include:

- Groups can often be dominated by a few strong personalities.
- The contribution of individual members may be limited by social pressures to conform to group norms.

- Internal politics (see **Chapter 1**) can take precedence over the objectives of the group.
- Decision-making by groups can lead to what is described as 'groupthink' (see below) where the desire for unanimity overrides sound judgement.

Groupthink

The latter point is significant and requires further examination. The term '**groupthink**' was coined by Janis (1982) and he describes it thus:

Groupthink is "a mode of thinking that people engage in when they are deeply involved in a cohesive in-group, when members' strivings for unanimity override their motivation to realistically appraise alternative courses of action."

Groupthink impacts on the effectiveness of decision-making in a considerable way and can lead to ignoring reality, resulting in serious errors of judgement.

Illustration 12.1: Groupthink – The Irish Banking Crises

The collapse of the Irish banking industry over a decade ago has had severe repercussions for both Irish society and the economy. The bailout of the banks cost the Irish State €64 billion at the time, a great deal of which will never been recovered. Many companies went into liquidation in the years following 2008, and almost all other companies suffered severe direct negative consequences, along with untold lost opportunities.

Like all such systemic crises, the reasons behind the Irish banking crises are complex and varied, caused as it was by many public and private institutions, companies and individuals (both internationally and domestically) simultaneously following unsound commercial practices and poor risk management. The 2011 *Report of the Commission of Investigation into the Banking Sector in Ireland* (the 'Nyberg Report') into the banking crisis is quite clear: while international developments helped precipitate the crisis, they did not of themselves cause it.

While each organisation is responsible for its own decision-making process, the cumulative effect is often the result of 'herding' and a 'bandwagon effect'. This was the case with the Irish banks. In the years prior to the crash, domestic and foreign competition increased significantly in the Irish financial services industry. The banks systematically began to accept higher levels of risk through ever-larger loans, primarily for commercial property deals, and this led to an increasing fragility in their capital structure. The response by each of the banks was to adopt lower credit standards in order to maintain or grow market share, and this allowed the quality of risk management to be gradually eroded. Property speculation was rife, and the assumption widely held in Ireland was that property prices, which were already incredibly high by international standards, would continue to rise.

In 2007, when cracks began to appear, they were initially seen as liquidity issues rather than structural, and it was deemed there would be nothing more than a 'soft landing'. There were few contrarian views expressed, such as those voiced by economists Dr Alan Ahearne in National University of Ireland Galway and Dr Morgan Kelly from University College Dublin, but who were roundly dismissed as prophets of doom. Quite surprisingly, there seemed to be no contrarian views expressed by the directors of the various banks, who had direct responsibility for the long-term sustainability of their organisations (see interview with Niall Fitzgerald, former CEO of Unilever in **Chapter 4**).

One of the main contributory factors leading to groupthink is the lack of diversity in the makeup of a group in terms of background, experience, gender, etc. This is something that was highlighted by the TASC report (2010), *Mapping the Golden Circle* (see **Chapter 4**). A more recent investigation by Jones *et al.* (2016) found that gender balance was essential to good communication and reduced conflict in the effectiveness of team output by medical personnel. The research supported the careful selection of team members to ensure a good mix of male and female members and by encouraging more females to enter male-dominated professions (and presumably by removing any glass ceilings that prevent women from securing such leadership positions).

The Nyberg Report was quite damning in relation to the banks. It found there was a "pervasive pressure for consensus" throughout, and there was "little evidence of original critical analysis". One major function of directors is to debate various strategic options and the assumptions underpinning them. However, the Nyberg Report found there was a widespread lack of critical discussion within many banks and authorities, which indicates a tendency to 'groupthink'.

Sources: Nyberg Report, 2011; Jones *et al.* (2016)

Clancy *et al.* (2010:2) refer to the danger of groupthink when boards of directors are drawn from a small group of people and there are many cross-directorships and where there is a lack of diversity due to gender imbalance: "Similarities in world view and experience, risk persistent 'groupthink' which may diminish willingness to challenge decisions and may lead to a failure to understand and protect either the shareholders or the wider public interest." The Financial Reporting Council in its *Guidance on Board Effectiveness* (FRC, 2018) also suggests other factors that can distort group decisions, including where members have conflicts of interest, emotional attachments to certain courses of action, an unconscious bias or relying inappropriately on previous experience and decisions.

Notwithstanding the example of groupthink in **Illustration 12.1**, it is important to look at group decisions in a balanced manner. There are both advantages and disadvantages in group decision-making, and whether it improves the quality of decision-making in an organisation depends to a great extent on the particular context. In general, additional people should be included in the process if the information they possess would increase the quality of the decision being made.

Chapter 1 examined the political nature of organisations and the development of strategy. There are times when acceptance of a decision by a particular group is vitally important, and so inclusion of those people in the process facilitates acceptance of the final decision.

One interesting point to note is that hierarchical organisations that do not involve employees in the decision-making process still have group decisions made by their boards of directors.

Buelens *et al.* (2011) suggest that, in general, decisions made by groups are superior to decisions made by individuals. They further state that participative management and employee empowerment are highly touted as a means of improving organisational productivity. There are some important considerations here. First, groups tend to be less efficient than individual decision-makers. Time constraints would be a key factor in this regard. Secondly, groups are more confident about their decisions, but this does not guarantee quality. Thirdly, group size has an impact and there is a negative correlation between size and quality. Fourthly, group decision-making is better when the members know a great deal about the subject matter and group leaders can effectively evaluate individual contributions. Lastly, composition of the group is important – decisions are better when members possess lots of unique, rather than common, information. According to Parker (1990), in making decisions groups generally try to reach a consensus. There are different techniques that can be used to facilitate group decision-making, including brainstorming, the nominal group technique, and the Delphi technique.

Brainstorming The concept of 'brainstorming' was developed by Osborn (1979) to increase creativity in the advertising industry, and is a technique used to facilitate the generation of many different ideas and solutions. The emphasis is on the generation of the ideas rather than evaluating them, and the process involves a lot of interaction by the group.

Nominal group technique In contrast, the nominal group technique separates the brainstorming from the evaluation. It gets people to work individually on the problem. Afterwards, their ideas are recorded on a flip chart and the group discusses each one. People are free to criticise or defend these ideas. Finally, the group members vote anonymously on their choice, using a weighted voting system, and a decision is made.

The Delphi Technique The Delphi Technique was developed by Dalkey *et al.* (1972) and is an iterative, group process involving experts who generate ideas anonymously from individuals who are physically separate from one another. Members are asked to fill in questionnaires and return them to the co-ordinator. This allows ideas to be generated without interference from groupthink. The findings are summarised and returned to the members for further evaluation. The process continues until there is a clear consensus on the way forward.

DECISION-MAKING STYLES

As discussed in **Chapter 2**, leadership at every level involves decision-making and is an essential element in the running of organisations. This chapter has examined the rational model of decision-making and some of its limitations, as well as comparing individual and group decisions. Inevitably, various individuals will have different decision-making styles. According to Brousseau *et al.* (2006), it is essential that the style of decision-making evolves as people move to higher levels in the organisation.

Brousseau *et al.* carried out extensive research on the decision-making styles of over 180,000 executives across the globe. They found that decision-making styles differ in two fundamental ways: how people use available information (whether they tend to maximise the amount of information available to them before making a decision, or do they 'satisfice'); and how they create options (single focus on one option or multi-focused – generating lists of options and pursuing multiple courses). Using these two dimensions of information, use and focus, they categorised four styles of decision-making:

- **Decisive** – value action, speed and efficiency. The decision is made and they move on to the next decision
- **Flexible** – focuses on speed and also on adaptability. This kind of decision-maker will use enough information to make a decision and will change course if necessary
- **Hierarchic** – they do not rush to judgement, but analyse a great deal of information and expect others to contribute. Their decisions should stand the test of time
- **Integrative** – not necessarily looking for a single best solution. They frame every situation broadly, taking multiple elements that overlap into account. Decisions are broadly defined and consist of multiple courses of action. When working with others they require extensive input, even when it conflicts with their own view. Decision-making for them is not an event, but a process.

Managers need to be able to adapt to all four styles of decision-making depending on circumstances, e.g. an entrepreneur may not have the time for lengthy analysis, while periods of uncertainty may require a multi-focus approach. The main part of the Brousseau research focuses on how decision-making styles evolve as managers progress. In general, as managers rise in the organisation, there is a steady progression towards openness, diversity of opinion and participative decision-making. This reflects a move away from the type of direct, immediate action required from lower-level managers, to more analytical, creative and exploratory decision-making. As the career of the manager progresses, there comes a point where all four styles of decision-making converge. Some managers can continue to adapt while others remain at this point. For those managers who cannot make the transition in style, it usually means the levelling off of their progression within the company. Successful managers can adapt and develop new styles. **Figure 12.1** illustrates the changes in leadership styles for successful managers (in their research, Brousseau *et al.* picked high financial compensation as an inexact measure for success).

While the information in **Figure 12.1** was based on US executives, the results for European and Asian managers were reasonably similar. Latin American executives, on the other hand, showed a similar convergence at manager level, which did not subsequently fan out at more senior levels. The chart reflects different people at different levels, not the same people over the course of their careers.

This research has implications for organisations and how potential leaders are groomed for higher positions – how their competences are developed.

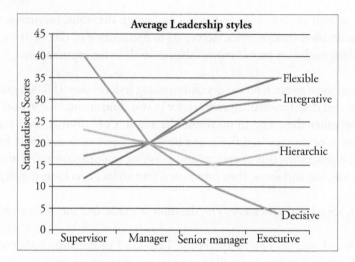

Source: Adapted from Brousseau *et al.* (2006) "The Seasoned Executive's Decision-making Style", *Harvard Business Review*, Vol. 84 Issue 2, p.116

Figure 12.1 *Average Decision-making Styles for Highest Compensated 20% of Managers*

BUSINESS INTELLIGENCE SYSTEMS

Sufficient, accurate information is an essential element in decision-making. In some cases executives may be lacking the information they require, but in most situations there are vast amounts of information potentially available to them, though perhaps not in a format that facilitates the decision-making process. Business intelligence systems can greatly assist executives in making sense of this information.

People at different levels of the organisation will vary in their requirements of report formats and information when making decisions. There are a number of reporting alternatives available, including periodic schedule reports, exception reports, demand reports, and 'push' reports (where reports are 'pushed' to appropriate individuals, e.g. by email). Such systems enable managers to use a number of analytical modelling techniques ranging from 'what if' analysis to optimisation analysis (O'Brien and Marakas, 2008). In addition, data mining can analyse vast amounts of data and search for patterns, trends and correlations. This can provide very valuable information to managers on which to base decisions (see **Chapter 13, Illustration 13.1: Data Mining at Tesco**).

Such technology has been constantly evolving since the 1970s when the primary aim was to provide periodic, structured reports for managers that focused on past performance. These were generally referred to as management information systems (MIS) (later decision support systems (DSS)), and were designed to help managers utilise data and models to solve unstructured problems. The technology continues to evolve and such systems are now generally referred to as business intelligence systems.

The main problem with these systems was that they were usually disjointed in terms of capturing information from different departments or functions in the organisation. In the 1980s, these systems developed to integrate information from different sources in relational databases in what became known as **enterprise resource planning** (ERP) systems. These allowed more specialised reports to be generated. Further developments in the 1990s created **data warehousing** and also allowed visual displays or dashboards to facilitate decision-makers to track performance. By the 2000s, as hardware and software systems continued to evolve, these technologies began to be called **business intelligence systems**. In turn, this increasing capacity allowed for 'data mining'. Since 2010, there have been further developments in the way in which data is captured and used. New data sources such as radio-frequency identification (RFID) tags, digital energy meters, clickstream web logs, 'smart' home devices, as well as social networking and social media are providing endless possibilities in the use of data – often referred to as '**big data**'. Big data is essentially data that cannot be stored in a single storage unit and covers data that comes in many different types of format. Big data refers to very large data sets that can be used to reveal patterns, trends and associations, especially relating to human behaviour and interactions.

Business intelligence systems is a broad term that combines "architectures, tools, data-bases, analytical tools, applications and methodologies" (Sharda *et al.*, 2018:16). Such systems provide interactive access (and sometimes real-time access) to data and so enable managers to get valuable insights that will allow them to make better and more informed decisions. A business intelligence system has four major components:

- a data warehouse with its source data;
- data analytics – tools for manipulating, mining and analysing the data in the data warehouse;
- business performance management (BPM) for monitoring and analysing performance; and
- a user interface or dashboard for presenting the data.

There are many pressures on businesses in capturing, analysing and understanding their data to provide them with a competitive advantage. These include legal imperatives, such as the requirements of the EU General Data Protection Regulation (GDPR), as well as shorter business cycles to analyse market trends and competitive pressures. This information has to be the right information, at the right time and in the right place and allow sophisticated analysis to support decisions. There are essentially three forms of data analytics:

- **Descriptive** – clearly defined business problems and opportunities. What is happening in the various departments of the organisation?
- **Predictive** – accurate projections of what is likely to happen in the future, based on statistical techniques that are generally referred to as 'data mining' (an area of activity in which there has been significant growth in recent years).
- **Prescriptive** – advising on the best possible decisions and actions to be taken to optimise performance.

Some business intelligence systems can combine multiple analytics models, such as social media analysis and 'stream mining'.

While business intelligence is providing wonderful opportunities for organisations, it can also present challenges, not least being the provisions of GDPR and the complaint storage and use of such data. This, in turn, raises many ethical issues that must be addressed by the company. Breaches in these areas can result in very significant financial penalties, and also serious reputational damage. However, by having robust policies and procedures in place that are properly implemented, firms can capitalise on the enormous potential that rich data can bring to decision-making.

STRATEGY EVALUATION

The process of evaluating different options is an important part of the process of developing and implementing strategy. It is likely that the development process may have thrown up many possibilities, and there is a need for a framework to consider each one and pick the one most appropriate to the organisation's position. Collins (2001:69) believes executives should display two disciplines of thought in evaluating strategy. First, they must infuse the entire process with the brutal facts of reality; and secondly, there must be a "simple, yet deeply insightful, frame of reference for all decisions". Executives must have a clear vision of what the organisation is trying to achieve.

Lynch (2018) distinguishes between content and process in strategy selection. So far, this chapter has looked at the decision-making process in general, both at individual and group level. The content refers to what strategy is selected and what proposals it contains. The purpose of looking at decision-making is to ensure the organisation will be able to choose the best course of action from the various options available and, in so doing, meet its strategic objectives.

Each organisation will have its own methods of assessing strategy. The framework outlined here is adapted from Lynch (2018) and will give some structure to the process. It should not necessarily be considered as a sequential process; rather, these are the factors that need to be taken into consideration when examining the different options. Thus, if it appears at the beginning of the evaluation process that the strategy under consideration is too risky or would be unacceptable to key stakeholders, then it is likely that it will not be considered any further. On the other hand, an option may appear to be suitable under the present circumstances, but may not be consistant with the mission. While the mission gives consistency to the organisation, it could be that the time has come for the mission to be reappraised.

Consistency

The process of evaluating a strategy begins with examining its 'consistency' with the organisation's vision, mission, goals and objectives. **Chapter 3** looked at setting a vision for the organisation. Part of that process involved the purpose for which an organisation exists. There needs to be a clear understanding by executives of what that purpose is and the objectives that have been set. The strategy that they choose should be consistent with those objectives, regardless of whether it is in the commercial sector or the not-for-profit sector. There should be an overall consistency from the vision through to the strategies that an organisation is following. If this consistency is lacking, the question must be asked as to why the proposal is being considered. Values are an integral part of the vision and they guide decision-making. Such values can range enormously from highly ethical ones to those without any element of integrity. Decisions being taken by people in an organisation should, therefore, be consistent with the values of that organisation, which should also reflect a sound ethical foundation.

Suitability

Suitability refers to how the various options relate to the business environment within which the organisation is operating and its strategic capability. **Chapter 5** examined the business environment in great detail from the macro and the industry perspectives. **Chapter 6** then examined the organisation's strategic capability to understand what the organisation is capable of achieving at the present time. The strategies under consideration need to be in line with the information resulting from this environmental analysis and examination of the organisation's strategic capability. For example, when the economy is stagnant or in recession, the strategies that an organisation should be concentrating on would probably be based more on consolidation than expansion. The following table is a broad outline of the major factors that would need to be taken into consideration.

Table 12.1: *Determining the Suitability of Strategic Options*

STRATEGIC TOOLS	USE IN DETERMINING STRATEGIC OPTIONS
External	
Global environment, Porter's Diamond, PESTEL analysis and scenario planning	While most of the information here will normally be outside the control of an organisation, it can have a major impact on the future profitability. While they cannot be controlled, they have to be taken into account when assessing opportunities and threats.
Industry economic features, Five Forces Analysis, industry driving forces, strategic groups, market segmentation, and key success factors	These are more applicable for a single company operating in a particular industry, or a diversified company considering moving into that industry. As above, consideration of these analytical tools should give a good indication of the suitability of the various options under consideration.
Internal	
Resources, competences, capabilities, cost competitiveness, value chain and value system analysis	These factors look at the internal strengths and weaknesses of a company. It must be remembered that, while there may be some great opportunities in principle, it depends on the resources and competences of an organisation to capitalise on those opportunities.

Source: Adapted from Johnson *et al.* (2017:381)

The internal and external analysis will have thrown up the main issues facing an organisation and its ability to respond. The purpose of using the strategic tools listed above is to help develop a proper understanding of all of the factors that need to be taken into account when developing strategy. Any of the strategic options under review should be in line with the environment and the capability of a company to exploit any opportunities. Judgement will play an important part in the process as there are many factors that need to be considered. It is also likely that there may be many different possibilities facing a company. In the vast majority of cases, resources will be limited, so decisions will have to be made with regard to the relative suitability of each one. One useful way to consider which ones should be exploited is to rank them against appropriate criteria. Those with the highest marking are ranked number one and so on down the line. The purpose of looking at the suitability of the options is to get an overall understanding of them. There are also other factors that need to be considered before a final decision is made.

While Lynch (2018) refers to 'validity', there is an overlap between suitability and validity. In considering the suitability of different strategies, much will depend on the assumptions underlying the future facing the organisation, the industry and indeed the macro environmental factors. It is important that the executives consider the validity of the assumptions that they have made. In other words, are the assumptions grounded in accurate information rather than what the executives would like to happen? Once again, this is something that will require sound judgement and experience.

Feasibility

There are a number of different factors that need to be considered under the heading of feasibility. First we must look at resources. A firm has to have sufficient resources, particularly the necessary human resources, to pursue the strategy in question. A resource deployment analysis can assist in the process of identifying the resources required and where they may be obtained. In larger companies, it will often be the case that the resources are present somewhere in the organisation but will need to be located and redeployed. Such moves have to be planned, particularly if it means moving managers with specific skills and experience. This process must also be supported by the culture of the organisation, where such redeployment is considered a normal part of working in that corporation. Not every company would have the necessary flexibility to be able to respond quickly.

Specific strategies will require specific resources, which may not be present within an organisation. Implementing an IT programme, for example, would require people with specialised skills. If it is the case that staff with specific skills are required, but are not available within the organisation, then a recruitment process will have to be put in place in sufficient time to allow new members to be employed in the company when they are required. It is not just a case of specialised skills that may be needed, but also the managerial competences necessary to support particular strategies, and at the appropriate level. In **Chapter 8** we saw that the different generic strategies require very diverse managerial competences. This will all have to form part of the overall consideration.

If the strategy under consideration is a merger or an acquisition, then it will most probably be the case that there will be excess personnel, in which case it will require an integration plan that will most likely entail redundancies. Once again, this is a process that needs to be planned very carefully to ensure that the company ends up with the right people remaining. Redundancy payments will form part of the financial consideration, as well as HR planning. This process can be complicated when it is a cross-border situation where different laws apply. Communication is an integral part of all moves concerning the people working in an organisation. Lack of communication, or poor communication, may cause many problems down the line that can easily be avoided.

Supporting a strategic move will also require adequate financial resources. This will probably be a mixture of an initial capital allocation and ongoing working capital requirements. The timing of cash flows in and out of an organisation can be critical to the feasibility of a strategy. The ability of an organisation to raise the necessary finance is critical.

In **Chapter 7**, we saw that finance for strategies can come from a number of different sources, and probably a mixture of sources. For strategic business units within a larger organisation, it may be the corporate headquarters that supplies the necessary funding. Strategic options will not be considered in isolation but in the context of other, previous strategies, and moves that are likely to come in the near future. Committing finance to a strategic project will tie it up for a period of time. Strategies implemented a couple of years ago may well be yielding positive cash flow that could support the strategy now under consideration.

External to a company, there are also factors that may curtail the feasibility of a strategic option. Some takeovers may require regulatory approval because of their size, and such approval may not be forthcoming. Such moves must also be made with regard to relationships within the value system, particularly suppliers and distributors.

Business Risk

Every strategic move is going to entail some level of risk. This is considered to be a normal part of business.

 Business risk can be defined as the risk of loss or failure due to pursuing a particular strategy.

We have already seen that different organisations will have different tolerances to risk, and this will have to be taken into consideration when making a decision. A company will have to carry out a risk assessment to ascertain the exact level of risk involved. This assessment should also include examining ways in which the risk can be reduced or removed. When examining corporate social responsibility, it was seen that certain moves could damage the image of a company, and that such damage could have serious financial consequences. Inevitably, financial risk will be a central part of this process.

In the previous section, it was seen that strategies require considerable financial investment. The ability of a firm to raise the necessary cash is central to the whole process. Putting money into a project inevitably produces risk, particularly when the nature of the financial package is taken into account. Debt finance can be offset against taxation, but it must be repaid regardless of the success of the project. This could place a considerable financial burden on a company.

Cash flow analysis is an essential part of this process. An operation can be profitable overall, but at times illiquid, and such illiquidity could bring about the demise of the company. Break-even analysis is another important criterion to consider. Break-even analysis examines the volume of sales required at a particular price to break even on the original investment, and before it starts making profit. Various financial ratio analyses should also be undertaken to examine all aspects of a project.

Sensitivity analysis should be applied to a project to examine the consequences if things do not go according to plan. It is often referred to as 'what if' analysis and it explores the impact that different factors would have on the strategy if they deviate from planned assumptions. For example, the project may necessitate borrowing a considerable amount of money. For a number of years, the European Central Bank's rates have been at an historical low rate. In recent times they have begun to rise. This obviously has a considerable knock-on effect on the financial viability of the strategy, and needs to be factored in when making the decision. Other factors that may not go according to plan are projected sales, economic growth, and currency movements. It is important to take a realistic view of all of these factors when considering a particular course of action as they could have a material effect on the financial viability of the plan.

Financial Return

For any commercially focused organisation, return on investment will be an essential part of its *raison d'être*. It is not just the shareholders that will be looking for a satisfactory return, but the future viability of the company and its ability to employ staff rests on its capacity to pursue profitable strategies (Ward, 2014). For that reason, the process of evaluation must consider the expected returns for each of the options under consideration. There is a very strong correlation between the level of risk and return. There is an old adage: 'If it looks too good to be true, it usually is'.

There are a number of different financial analyses that can assist managers in their appraisal. In general, they can compare the capital investment involved with the expected return. It is worth bearing in mind that, while the different appraisal techniques might appear objective, they rely on projections that might be subjective and are based on predictions about the future. Such predictions will be coated in uncertainty as there will be many circumstances outside the control of a firm. These calculations are based on factors that can be measured in financial terms. Not all factors can be reduced to monetary value. This will be developed further in discussing cost–benefit analysis.

Before examining specific techniques, there are a few general considerations to be taken into account:

- For the most part, the financial outlay will be quite substantial, so care must be taken to make the correct decision.

- Along with the size of the investment, it must also be remembered that these decisions are generally long-term, which will have implications with regard to tying up finance for the duration of the project.
- The decision to invest will have to be taken against the background of all other financial decisions as there is an inter-relationship in terms of cash flow and total borrowings.
- There is an opportunity cost in making an investment. The money allocated cannot be used for other purposes for the lifespan of the investment. There may be other opportunities available that have not been considered.

These different techniques act as a guide to decision-making. They assist in the process, but it still requires managerial judgement. Each technique needs different types of information and they lead to different conclusions. Thus, it is useful to employ a number of different techniques, including:

- Payback period
- Accounting rate of return
- Discounted cash flow methods.

Payback Period It was stated above that when money is invested in a project there is an opportunity cost involved, and this also involves risk that the investment may not be recouped. From a risk perspective, it is preferable that the amount of time involved is kept to a minimum as the longer the finance is tied up in the project, the greater the risk involved. The payback method is based on the amount of time it will take for the cumulative cash flows to equal the initial investment. From that point on the project will be making a positive contribution. The payback period is arbitrary: the nature of the industry and the particular circumstances of the company will dictate what an acceptable payback period would be. The following is an example.

A factory is considering investing €10 million in a large extension. Using the projected net cash inflows each year, it wants to know how long the payback period will be.

Table 12.2: *Payback Period*

Year	Net annual cash inflow (€)	Net *cumulative* cash inflow (€)
1	500,000	500,000
2	900,000	1,400,000
3	2,600,000	4,000,000
4	3,500,000	7,500,000
5	1,500,000	9,000,000
6	3,500,000	12,500,000
7	3,500,000	16,000,000

It can be seen that the time is somewhere between five years (which is €1 million short of the original investment) and six years (which is showing a cash inflow of €3.5 million). It can be estimated as:

$$\frac{1,000,000}{3,500,000} = 0.29 \text{ years}$$

Hence, the total payback period is 5.29 years.

The payback method is easy to use and it shows the amount of time the money will be tied up for, thus introducing some caution into the decision. Two major drawbacks of the method is that, first, it does not take into consideration the total net cumulative cash inflow; and secondly, it ignores the timing of cash flows. In the above example, there could be very high cash flows in years 8, 9 and 10 by which time there could be a theoretical return of €50 million (which would be an extremely satisfactory return on investment).

Accounting Rate of Return The accounting rate of return looks at the overall profitability of an investment. There are different definitions of the return and different definitions of the investment. The profitability is related to the amount of money invested in the project and the amount of time for which it is required. Depending on the cost of capital, the company will set a required rate of return. For example, the cost of capital in XYZ Ltd is 5% per annum, the company will accept the project under consideration if it yields a return of 5% or greater. Using the example from the payback method above:

Total cash inflow from the project	€16,000,000
Deduct the initial caapital investment	€10,000,000
Profit	€ 6,000,000

The investment earns €6 million over the seven-year life span, yielding €857,143 per annum. The initial investment was €10 million. The amount invested at the end is zero as the initial cost has been recouped, plus yielding a profit. Therefore, the rate of return is:

$$\frac{\text{Average annual profit (cash inflows less depreciation)}}{\text{Initial investment}}$$

$$\frac{€857,143}{€10,000,000} \times 100 = 8.57\%$$

As a return of 8.57% is greater than the cost of capital at 5%, this project can be accepted.

One advantage of the accounting rate of return method is that it takes the overall profitability of the project into account. However, one major weakness is that it does not take the pattern of cash flows into account.

Discounted Cash Flow Methods There are two methods of using discounted cash flow to evaluate capital investments:

- Net present value
- Internal rate of return (IRR).

Usually the methods yield the same result, though there are advantages and disadvantages to each appraisal method. The main advantage of the IRR method is that the information it provides is more easily understood by managers (especially non-financial managers). The main disadvantage is that it ignores the size of the investment. The net present value method takes into account the total size of the investment and is superior for ranking mutually exclusive projects. For these reasons it will be the method demonstrated here.

The one big advantage of the net present value method compared to the other methods used is that it takes the time value of money into account. Thus, projects that yield a good cash flow early on are preferable to others where cash inflows come later in the project. This brings us to the concept that money has a time value. There is a cost involved in having money tied up for a particular time period – the cost of capital. The longer this period will be, the greater the cost, and therefore the return from the project will be less valuable as time progresses.

The timing of cash inflow is important, assuming the money is going to be reinvested in further projects. While a particular project may produce a satisfactory profit over its lifetime, the company may have to wait a long time for cash inflows. If significant cash inflows are received earlier in the project, this will allow the company to reinvest that money in further projects and, consequently, is of far greater value to the company.

If we use a cost of capital of 10%, then a euro in one year's time is the equivalent of just 90.9 cent today, while a euro in two years' time would only be worth 82.6 cent today, and so on. This can be calculated using tables or using the formula:

Year one:

$$\frac{€1 \times 100}{110} = \frac{1}{1.10} = 90.9c$$

Year two:

$$\frac{€1}{1.10^2} = \frac{1}{1.21} = 82.6c$$

This can be extended to cover the number of years that the project will last. Taking the example used earlier of an initial investment of €10 million (**Table 12.2**), but this time using *annual* (rather than cumulative figures, which were used above in the payback method):

Table 12.3: *Net Present Value Method*

Year	Cash Inflow €	Discount Rate 10% (from tables or the formula)	Present Value of Cash Inflows
1	500,000	.909	454,500
2	900,000	.826	743,400
3	2,600,000	.751	1,952,600
4	3,500,000	.683	2,390,500
5	1,500,000	.621	931,500
6	3,500,000	.564	1,974,000
7	3,500,000	.513	1,795,000
Total	16,000,000		10,241,500

Present value of inflows = **€10,241,500**

The present value of the €16 million cash inflow is reduced to just €10.24 million using the discounted cash flow method. The net present value is equal to the present value of the cash inflows (€10.24 million) less the present value of the cash outflow (€10 million). In this case, the original investment was €10 million, so the project is just about breaking even over the seven-year period, using a cost of capital of 10% and the projected income outlined above. In the above example, the initial investment of €10 million was made at the beginning of the project. It will often be the case that the investment will be spread over a few years in the life of a project, in which case it is the net figure (the expenditure in that year less net cash inflow) that is discounted by the appropriate rate). It must also be remembered that, in addition to the capital investment, there may also be a requirement for working capital that should be taken into consideration.

These examples demonstrated different ways of evaluating various strategic projects from a financial perspective. The project was examined looking at its merits in isolation.

Mutually Exclusive Projects

It will often be the case that one project will have to be compared with another because of capital rationing or where they are mutually exclusive. According to Ward (2014:93), **capital rationing** "occurs when a company has a restricted supply of cash available for investment purposes". An example of this is the enormous overrun in the cost of building the National Children's Hospital in Dublin which will result in a number of other capital investment programmes in hospitals and community care projects being postponed. **Mutually exclusive projects** are where the acceptance of one project means that a company cannot accept another project. In this instance, a decision will have to be made as to which one is the most suitable. One other factor that needs to be considered when investing in a strategic project is that circumstances may change substantially and the project may have to be abandoned. Having invested what is perhaps a considerable sum, it may be difficult to do this. However, if it is no longer viable, it is better to treat it as a sunk cost and not waste further investment that could be used more productively elsewhere.

Cost–Benefit Analysis

The financial return from a project is obviously a very important consideration. It is not, however, the only issue that should be taken into account. A company should also take a strategic overview of its entire portfolio and look at the project against that background. For example, entering a new market using direct investment might be extremely costly for a SBU. However, once established, its distribution network may be of considerable benefit to other SBUs in the organisation. As a result, all of the costs and benefits, both tangible and intangible, should be taken into consideration when examining a strategic option. Cost–benefit analysis attempts to put a monetary value on all the costs and benefits of a project, whether they are tangible or not.

This applies to commercial bodies as well as to the public sector. Indeed, in the public sector, many facilities would never be built if a purely financial perspective were taken. Many of these facilities and services play an important part in society. Many small post offices, for example, do not make a profit, but it is felt that they play a very important social role in rural communities. Flights from many regional airports to and from Dublin are subsidised under a public service contract administered by the European Union, as they also are deemed to provide an important service in linking the regions. Without the subsidy, the cost of the flights would be regarded as prohibitive. The process of assigning a monetary value to intangible benefits is obviously difficult, but it does ensure that managers take a more holistic approach to decision-making rather than focusing purely on costs and revenues.

Stakeholder Reaction

In **Chapter 5** we examined the role of the different stakeholders in an organisation. It was seen that they will have very different views on the strategies chosen. It follows then that these views must be taken into consideration when developing strategies. The use of stakeholder mapping is a useful tool that can be used to anticipate support or opposition to a strategy. Once again, the importance of communication must be stressed, as often opposition can result from a lack of understanding. Communicating openly and clearly with all concerned may well alleviate any fears particular stakeholders may have. It should also be stressed that just because there will be opposition does not mean that a certain course of action should not be pursued, particularly if it is the correct course of action. However, being aware of the issues in advance can allow appropriate action to be taken.

Some of the obvious measures that will likely cause strong reaction are those involving major changes to the organisation – particularly those that will require redundancies, such as mergers and acquisitions, outsourcing or closing down production facilities. If an organisation takes a more inclusive approach then it should be able to reduce or even eliminate any negative repercussions.

STRATEGIC PLAN

An organisation should now be in a position to finalise its strategic plan. A strategic plan charts the direction in which a company is developing, establishes strategic objectives, and outlines its strategies (and necessary resources) that will be pursued to achieve those targets. A written plan in place will assist senior managers in terms of clarity of thought, and it will also play an important part in the communication of that plan to all staff members in the relevant parts of the organisation. There is no specific template *per se*, but the following framework is adapted from Thompson *et al.* (2018:267) and should provide guidance to those developing the strategic plan.

Table 12.4: *Strategic Plan*

	Content	Comments
1	**Strategic vision, mission and ethical stance**	This sets clear guidelines for the organisation and where it should be deploying its resources, and how the organisation should be conducting its affairs.
2	**Strategic goals**	These should be divided into different categories based on the Balanced Scorecard, and should include long-, medium- and short-term goals.
3	**Strategic objectives**	Stemming from the goals in stage 2 above will be the specific objectives that need to be set. Being specific, they are easier to measure. These should also be divided into long-, medium- and short-term objectives.
4	**Overall business model**	This should articulate the overall business model for the entire organisation and the specific strategic business units. It should cover what type of generic strategies will be used, as well as laying out the different directions and methods by which the organisation will achieve its goals.
5	**Functional strategies**	These are the various functional strategies to support the corporate and business strategies. Separate plans are made out for each functional division in the organisation: Operations, Marketing, Human Resources, Finance, Research and Development etc. As well as being specific departmental plans, they obviously need to be co-ordinated if they are to support the overall corporate plan.

	Content	Comments
6	**Monitoring**	It was seen from **Figure 1.2 (Chapter 1)** that feedback is an integral part of this process. As the plan is being implemented, it must be carefully monitored to ensure that it is working as it was originally intended. In most cases, changes will have to be made in light of the feedback being received. Developing a strategic plan on paper is relatively straightforward, but implementing it is quite a different process. Plans rarely fail because of the quality of the plan itself; most fail because they are poorly implemented, often complicated by a business environment that is changing as the plan is being rolled out. Therefore, monitoring the plan is an essential part of the process to ensure the strategic objectives are met.

Developing the text of a strategic plan is one thing, but implementing it is quite a different process. Plans rarely fail because of the quality of the plan itself; most fail because they are poorly implemented, often complicated by a business environment that is changing as the plan is being rolled out.

CONCLUSION

Strategic decisions have long-term implications for the organisation and generally involve considerable sums of money. Managers must therefore get them right. In the real world, this does not always happen, for a variety of reasons. Decisions must be taken by those running the organisation and, once people are involved, it is inevitable that the quality of decision-making will vary greatly from one situation to another and from one company to another. If people follow a logical framework, such as that proposed in this chapter, the probability of making a correct decision will be greatly enhanced. Ultimately, however, strategic decisions are usually quite subjective in nature, and it is hard to argue definitively whether a particular decision was the 'optimum' course of action. Perhaps the biggest factor in deciding whether the decision is a correct one or not, is the professionalism with which that decision is implemented. The implementation of strategy is the subject of Part Four.

SUMMARY

Strategic decisions generally involve a considerable amount of money and have significant long-term implications for an organisation. For that reason, it is important that executives choose the correct course of action. **Decision-making** is "the selection of a course of action among alternatives". Uncertainty and risk make decision-making a difficult process, and tolerance to risk will vary from one organisation to another.

The **rational decision-making model** assumes that people use a rational, sequential process in making decisions. It involves diagnosing the problem; identifying all solutions; evaluating each one; making the optimum choice; implementing the decision; and monitoring its outcome.

Decision-makers are often limited by what is termed '**bounded rationality**', which implies that executives are limited by a number of constraints including the capacity of the executive and the environment. As a result, people tend to '**satisfice**', i.e. choose an acceptable solution rather than the optimum solution. Stakeholder reaction and the time available to make decisions must also be taken into account.

Escalation of commitment is where more and more resources are allotted to a project, despite evidence that it is no longer viable. **Groupthink** occurs when a group of those involved see a problem from one perspective only, and their view turns out to be flawed. In general, however, group decisions achieve better results. **Business intelligence systems** play an important role in helping executives make decisions based on accurate and up-to-date information.

Strategic decisions must be consistent with the organisation's mission and objectives, and require a number of factors to be considered. They must be suitable and feasible. The level of business **risk** must be considered along with the potential financial return, appraisal approaches for which are the **payback method**, the **accounting rate of return** and **net present value (discounted cash flow)**.

Cost–benefit analysis examines decisions in an holistic manner and takes into account total costs and total revenues. The views of all relevant **stakeholders** should be considered. The organisation should then develop a **strategic plan** that can best position itself to seize all opportunities.

DISCUSSION QUESTIONS

1. Critically analyse the rational model as a tool for decision-making.
2. Differentiate between group decisions and decisions made by individual executives, and state under which circumstances one approach might be more suitable than the other.
3. Evaluate the various stages involved in choosing a particular strategy.
4. Identify a major strategic decision taken by a large company, and critically analyse its effectiveness with regard to the stages referred to in question 3 above.
5. Differentiate between the various forms of financial appraisal that may be used in deciding an appropriate return on investment.
6. Discuss the importance of having a strategic plan for an organisation.

PART FOUR

Implementation

Introduction to Strategy Implementation

The final part of the strategy process in any organisation is its implementation. It is arguably the most important part of the process. Up to this point, the organisation's strategic plan is merely a blueprint for action. The plan on its own will not achieve anything. The manner in which

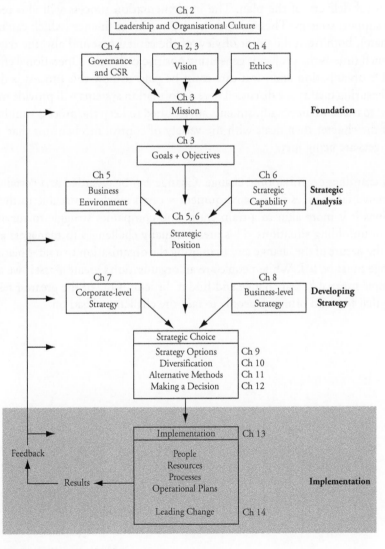

Figure 1.2 *The Strategic Planning Model*

it is implemented will have a direct result on the success or failure of the company, particularly in a competitive environment. Great consideration must therefore be given to how the strategic goals and objectives will be achieved. The Prussian General Von Moltke said that no plan survives contact with the enemy. Circumstances are constantly changing and the implementation process requires much flexibility as the organisation responds to new circumstances.

Part Four consists of two chapters. **Chapter 13** deals with the implementation of strategy. Throughout this textbook the importance of the role that people play in the strategy plan has been highlighted. Nowhere is this more evident than in the implementation process. Regardless of how automated processes are, those employed in the organisation, from the CEO down, are central to the successful delivery of the plan. The implementation process will also require significant resources to support strategy. These include having sufficient finance (which can be difficult in the current climate), both from the point of view of the capital cost and also the day-to-day running costs, until such time as the project is generating positive cash flow. Operational efficiency is central to a profitable organisation and great care must be paid to how this process is designed. Various methods of ensuring quality are discussed here. Information systems will provide managers with the data required to make whatever adjustments are required to keep the process running smoothly. The final part of the chapter then deals with the variety of control mechanisms that can be employed to ensure targets are being met.

Chapter 14 examines organisational change. Change can be regarded as a certainty. Sometimes it is small incremental changes in the environment – often barely noticeable in the short term. On other occasions it is more akin to a train crash, and companies struggle to survive as they try to make sense of unfolding situations. This presents many challenges to managers as they must first understand the nature of the change and then bring the organisation to a safer place. As John Kotter argues, change must be led. While people are an organisation's greatest asset, we are also creatures of habit. People invariably fear change and find it difficult. One of the greatest tests of leaderships is dispelling that fear and bringing people to face the challenges head on.

Strategy Implementation

LEARNING OBJECTIVES

On completion of this chapter, you will be able to:

- Critically examine the factors that must be considered when implementing a strategy
- Assess the style of leadership required to implement strategies in different organisations
- Evaluate each part of the organisation in terms of the impact that strategy implementation will have on that department
- Analyse the implementation process and assess the changes necessary to ensure that goals are achieved

"We are what we repeatedly do. Excellence, then, is not an act, but a habit."

Aristotle

INTRODUCTION

Part Three of this textbook examined the types of strategic options that are potentially available to an organisation. It examined the possible strategies at business and corporate level, as well as the various different methods with which those strategies could be achieved. The final chapter in that Part, **Chapter 12**, provided a decision-making process to enable managers to make a decision on the best way forward for their organisations.

The strategy implementation process – Part Four – is the final process required for an organisation to achieve its strategic and financial goals. There are two related chapters in this Part: this chapter dealing with the actual implementation, and **Chapter 14**, which deals with the change process that inevitably happens when strategy is being implemented. The implementation of strategy is concerned with the delivery of results and creating the environment where things happen. It requires a different set of managerial skills from the development of strategy. The development of strategy demands market-driven skills to analyse the environment and the organisation's ability to respond. Strategy implementation, on the other hand, depends on working with and motivating people, and building up competitive capability. It is operations-oriented.

Each section of this chapter deals with a different aspect of the implementation process. The first section concerns the people in the organisation as, without the right people, nothing can be achieved. It also deals with the leadership required to initiate the process and see it through to a successful conclusion. Leadership and management go hand-in-hand in this process, so it is vital that the organisation assembles the right management team and has the right employees.

Chapter 6 looked at analysing strategic capability to gain an understanding of the strengths and weaknesses of an organisation. This is referred to as strategic fit: creating a fit between the capability of the organisation and the opportunities that match that capability. In reality, it does not always fit that neatly, and organisations often have to 'stretch' themselves in terms of the strategies being developed. In light of this, the company will have to reappraise its resources and competences to ensure that they are sufficient to support the chosen strategy or, if not, take immediate steps to rectify the situation. In particular, IT systems need to support the business model and ensure that the company can use technology to develop a competitive advantage.

Following on from this, executives will have to fine-tune the structure so that it supports the strategies being pursued, and this process involves looking at factors such as the internal control processes, how the organisation relates internally and externally, where decisions are made within the organisation, and many more related issues. Policies and procedure will also have to be examined to enable the organisation to improve constantly and achieve best practice.

This chapter also examines strategies that will be required in different functional areas such as marketing, R&D and, in particular, finance. It has been stated before that strategies by their nature require considerable finance, and appropriate measures must be put in place to support the strategy. All of these elements of strategy implementation are separate but need to be woven together in one co-ordinated plan, and this comes back to the managerial skills required.

STRATEGIC CAPABILITY

The starting point of implementing strategy is having a clear understanding of the goals and objectives that need to be achieved. Each set of circumstances will require different resources, which will need to be carefully controlled for cost reasons. The use of these resources will need to be carefully planned, along with appropriate budgets. Kaplan and Norton (2008) suggest that the use of the Balanced Scorecard will greatly assist in providing clarity to the process of implementation, along with providing relevant dashboards to alert managers to any deviation from the plan.

In examining the resources needed to implement a chosen strategy, it should be recalled that resources must be coupled with core competences if the organisation is to develop strategic capability and gain a competitive advantage in the marketplace. For most organisations, building core competences is a slow and incremental process. In a competitive marketplace, it is these competences that will separate the company from others in the mind of the consumer. In each of the resource areas detailed below, it must therefore be remembered that it is ultimately strategic capability that will give an organisation that edge. The distinction between possessing resources and combining those resources with core competences to create strategic capability will become apparent in the first section below on people.

The organisation must have the capability to support the strategy it is endeavouring to implement. **Chapter 6** examined various ways in which an organisation can evaluate its strategic capability. The emphasis there was primarily on what is known as 'strategic fit' – fitting the strategy to the resources and competences of the organisation. There are often occasions when the company has to push itself out of its comfort zone and stretch its capability to reach strategic goals. The organisation must assess the situation and understand the difference between where it needs to be and where it is currently. This is known as '**gap-analysis**', and it highlights what the organisation must do to reach its targets. If there is a shortfall in terms of resources and competences, these can be made good in a variety of ways. It may be done by purchasing the resources and developing the skills in-house, or it can be achieved by acquiring companies that have those resources and skills or by forming strategic alliances. Once the deficit is understood, it can be rectified.

PEOPLE

The first part of the implementation process concerns the people working in the organisation, as without the energy and determination of those who make up the company nothing will happen. This applies to the top executives, middle management and all of the employees, as well as other relevant stakeholders, such as unions. 'Human Resources' (HR) is a standard term to describe the 'people' function in the organisation, and consequently it is used in this textbook.

However, from a strategic perspective, the term HR can be somewhat misleading in that people are a resource totally different to all of the other resources available to the firm, for three reasons. First, people can provide an organisation with a competitive capability different to all other resources. Secondly, the organisation does not own this resource. If people are not stimulated in their work and are not properly treated by the organisation, one of two things will happen: they will leave for a rival company, bringing their skills with them; or else they will sit back and do enough so as to not get fired, but not enough to deliver a competitive edge to the company. It therefore requires a different paradigm than just looking on employees as another resource. In many cases, particularly in the knowledge economy, they are *the* resource. Third, as discussed in **Chapter 4**, there is a moral dimension in how the organisation treats its employees.

For a company to be successful, everyone has to be working in unison to deliver on the vision. Collins (2001:41–2) argues that:

> "The executives who ignited the transformation from good to great did not figure out where to drive the bus and then get people to take it there. No, they *first* got the right people on the bus (and in the right seats) and the wrong people off the bus and then figured out where to drive it."

Collins further adds: "If you begin with 'who' rather than 'what', you can more easily adapt to a changing world". Collins has modified the adage that 'people are your most important asset'. He argues that "People are *not* your most important asset. The *right* people are" Collins (2001:13).

Leadership

Leadership forms an essential element in every aspect of running an organisation, from creating a vision and culture to laying down a proper ethical base on which staff at every level will make decisions. Making decisions, and seeing them through, are not the same thing. As the environment for most industries is changing at an ever-increasing rate, it becomes imperative that when decisions are made in the best interests of the organisation, that they are implemented quickly and decisively. Any discussion on managing the implementation process inevitably implies leadership to motivate all concerned to ensure the process is carried out efficiently and effectively.

There is an important distinction between efficiency and effectiveness. One can be carrying out a task with great efficiency, e.g. carrying two buckets from the well to fill a large tank of water. Or one could put the effort into connecting a pipe to the tank and have a constant flow of water thereafter – effectiveness. Leaders are able to see the big picture and decide where the effort goes to ensure the effective use of scarce resources. According to Collins (2001:86-7), it often involves operating under the 'Stockdale Paradox' (so called after an American admiral, who, as a young US Navy fighter pilot, was shot down during the Vietnam war by the North Vietnamese. He was held as a POW in Hanoi and survived years of torture by the North Vietnamese during his time in captivity). The Stockdale Paradox involves retaining faith that you will prevail in the end while confronting the most brutal facts of your current position. He added:

> "The good to great leaders were able to strip away so much noise and clutter and just focus on the few things that would have the greatest impact."

It requires clear thinking and the energy to make things happen quickly and effectively, as well as the ability to follow through. In an economic climate where organisations are facing extreme difficulties, it is vital that they maintain optimism that they will succeed in the end, while at the same time being realistic about the difficulties they face.

Management Team

Alongside visionary leaders, a strong management team forms an essential element of strategy execution. The two go hand-in-hand. Different managers will each bring their own set of skills and experience to the organisation, and it must be remembered that different strategies will require different managerial skills.

For a management consultancy organisation, the emphasis is on creating a learning organisation where knowledge is created and shared. For a low-cost airline, it is about reducing or eliminating costs at every juncture. With a lost-cost strategy, the emphasis is more on Taylor's 'scientific management', where there is one best way to do the job. It requires staff to follow these rules rather than act on their own initiative. In getting the 'right people on the bus', the organisation must pick managers with the right skills set. The company must also get 'the wrong people off the bus' as managers who do not have the appropriate skill or motivation will form a serious impediment to implementing the strategy. Creating the right team applies to management and to employees and how they both work together.

Depending on the size and scope of the strategic decision being implemented, the existing managerial team may or may not be sufficient to carry out the task. If not, the company will have to recruit additional managers with the appropriate skills. Alternatively, they can make an acquisition of a company with those capabilities or form some type of strategic alliance.

A corporate policy of promoting from within can have a positive motivational effect as people can see a career path within the company provided that they perform. There may, however, be occasions when the necessary managerial skills are not available in-house. An example could be a turnaround situation, where it may be that the existing managerial team did not take the necessary action to avoid the current situation. If the search to find suitable managers has been exhausted internally, the company will have to look elsewhere to appoint a suitable CEO and managerial team. While promoting from within often benefits an organisation, in the aftermath of the financial crisis, there was much criticism of some internal appointments at senior level in the bailed out banks. In this instance, the criticism centred on the fact that these appointees were in senior management positions when the banks ran aground. In situations such as these, there is often a requirement to recruit new executives from outside the organisation, or even the industry, who would bring fresh thinking with them and be unencumbered by the organisation's culture. There was some controversy in 2018, when the Irish Government appointed a former PSNI officer, Drew Harris, to take over as Commissioner of An Garda Síochána. However, it was considered desirable following a number of high-profile governance issues in the force.

More and more, companies are beginning to realise the importance of developing appropriate managerial skills. A core competence of GE, for example, is its ability to pick and develop outstanding managers with a wide range of problem-solving and leadership skills. These skills are honed at their corporate development centre at Crotonville, and promotion and incentives are closely tied to successful completion of these courses.

The importance of good management is obvious when we examine examples of bad management. It often happens that when things go wrong, management blame employees. However, Napoleon considered that 'there is no such thing as bad soldiers, only bad officers'. The fault often lies closer to home.

Every organisation, whether in the public or private sector, has an absolute requirement for effective (and not just efficient) management if it is to deliver on its purpose. In terms of strategy formulation and implementation, it should not be taken for granted that the presence of a management team is enough. It must be 'the right people on the bus'. However, an important qualification with regard to the discussion in this textbook about managers achieving results is that it is predicated on the basis that those results are achieved in an ethical and legal fashion. Unfortunately, this is not always the case.

Managers at every level play a central role in the implementation of strategy. While there is a general trend towards flatter organisations, it must be remembered that middle managers are particularly important in that they need to translate the overall corporate strategy into meaningful goals and objectives for each section (and individual) within their area of responsibility. Problems that are being encountered at local level, and that cannot be solved at that level, will need to be referred back up along the line. The implementation of strategy will often require several iterations and fine-tuning before it is right.

Employees

While good managers are essential, without good employees they cannot deliver on the strategy. In most organisations, the divide between managers and employees is blurring considerably in that progressive companies place much greater emphasis on teamwork. In many cases, in the knowledge economy, employees are often as well-educated as managers, and will be the source of many of the ideas that underpin strategy development and implementation.

There is a positive relationship between the ways in which organisations lead and manage their people, and the capacity of those organisations to drive performance. CIPD (the professional body for HR and people development), in collaboration with a number of professional bodies, has developed a model called 'Valuing your Talent' (Houghton, 2016). It is an holistic framework that enables organisations to realise the full potential of their workforce by understanding and measuring the contribution of people, and the impact of this contribution on the performance of the business. To achieve value creation, organisations must start with input measures and work through a series of stages, as shown in **Figure 13.1** below.

Input Measures The value creation process begins with the composition and diversity of the company's workforce, and having people with the right skills and aptitude who can play to their strengths. While employment costs are an issue for every organisation, they must be compared to the capability (and potential) of employees, and not as an absolute in itself. For example, a company following a differentiation strategy (see **Chapter 8**) will often require highly skilled staff that may well command top salaries (a 'cost factor'). However, the high-quality product or service that they are producing will be selling at a premium price that allows the company to pay high salaries and still make substantial profits. Thus, all costs are relative. Houghton (2016) considers regulatory compliance as another important input measure. Such compliance is becoming an essential element in corporate governance. However, well-trained and engaged staff members can play an essential role in ensuring regulatory compliance throughout the organisation.

Activity Measures People, of course, play a vital role in the operational processes of every organisation. In **Chapter 1** we saw how the US bank Wells Fargo focused on "injecting an endless stream of talent" into the company. Once recruited, how these employees share knowledge within the organisation, how they are developed, motivated, and rewarded are essential elements of any successful company. Retention goes hand-in-hand with recruitment, as a constant churn of employees is both extremely expensive and disruptive to organisational activities. Retention is achieved through a mixture of intrinsic and extrinsic rewards, as well as training and development.

In order to create a value system, numerous daily activities need to be tracked and monitored in regard to the work processes taking place in the organisation. Business intelligence systems, with real-time information, are a vital part of monitoring business processes and making informed decisions about these activities.

Training can be provided either in-house (usually in larger organisations) or externally through outside consultants. eLearning solutions are becoming a common way of standardising training in organisations, though they are not suitable for all training requirements. The ultimate purpose of training and development is to ensure that employees have the appropriate skills to underpin the strategic progress of the company, which in turn, can be developed into a competitive advantage.

While employee performance also needs to be monitored and measured, an essential element of an effective performance management system requires managers to create the right environment in which people are motivated, and where there is an emphasis on continuous learning and sharing of knowledge. Employee relations are central to this.

Outputs When the input and activity measures are right, this will lead to higher output and performance, and higher levels of employee engagement. In turn, this will create a more efficient operating model, while all the time developing the leadership capability at every level.

Outcomes Finally, there are the desired outcomes from whatever strategy the organisation is pursuing. In a VUCA business environment (volatile, uncertain, complex and ambiguous), it is necessary that the organisation must have an innovative, agile and resilient workforce. In **Chapter 2**, the importance of organisational culture was examined in detail. For an organisation to be successful, it is essential that it is supported by a high-performance culture. When all of these measures are in place, the organisation should achieve its strategic objectives that creates value for its customers. It must be remembered that the one common denominator to all four measures is the organisation's employees.

Such frameworks are valuable for engaging staff in strategy implementation, and there is one vital element that will determine whether the framework is useful or not: it all boils down to how the organisation is led, from the board and chief executive down to each manager and supervisor. As discussed in **Chapter 2**, leadership is an essential part of the foundation of strategy on which the entire strategy process depends. The reader will recall Napoleon's maxim that there are no bad soldiers; only bad officers. For many organisations, this requires a paradigm shift from dealing only with policies and procedures, to leading people. The prize, in the form of the outcomes listed above, will make the effort worthwhile.

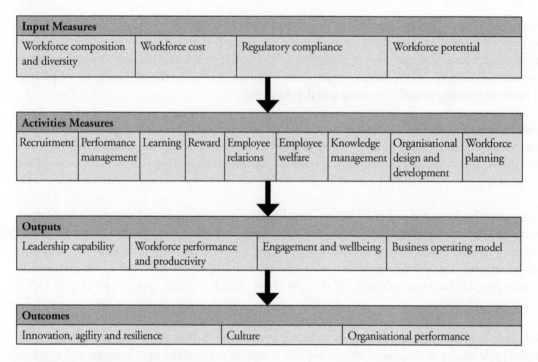

Input Measures			
Workforce composition and diversity	Workforce cost	Regulatory compliance	Workforce potential

Activities Measures								
Recruitment	Performance management	Learning	Reward	Employee relations	Employee welfare	Knowledge management	Organisational design and development	Workforce planning

Outputs			
Leadership capability	Workforce performance and productivity	Engagement and wellbeing	Business operating model

Outcomes		
Innovation, agility and resilience	Culture	Organisational performance

Source: Adapted from Houghton, 2016:21

Figure 13.1 *The 'Valuing your Talent' Framework*

The Human Resources Function

The HR function also plays an important strategic role in planning the long-term human resource requirements of a company. It monitors sociological and demographic trends (see PESTEL analysis in **Chapter 5**), along with the organisation's future plans and conducts a gap analysis in terms of its requirement for people.

For example, when companies like Intel in Leixlip, County Kildare, consider a major expansion of their facility, the company has to plan well in advance to ensure that it has the right number of managers and employees, with the appropriate skills. It also has to ensure that they are available at the time they are needed. This process entails identifying leadership development requirements as well as the immediate technical and operational skills needed, and making the appropriate arrangements to ensure the gap is bridged. This process is carried out against the backdrop of the corporate culture to see what cultural changes, if any, need to be effected to ensure the company can properly position itself in the future.

The HR strategy also has to be distilled into the day-to-day operational issues. In recent years, there has been a raft of legislation dealing with various aspects of employment. The specialised nature of such legislation, and the importance and relevance of the HR function, has increased significantly. In most organisations, the HR function is primarily an advisory one, with the direct responsibility for employees resting with their line manager. There should be close liaison between the HR manager and the various line managers to ensure that all aspects of employee rights are being upheld. Failure to do so could be costly for the organisation. The HR function maintains employee records and will normally co-ordinate training and development with the line managers.

OTHER RESOURCES

The people that make up an organisation are not just an essential resource, they can also become a competitive capability. However, there are numerous other resources required by organisations in order to succeed. In most instances considerable finance will be required, and this has to be sourced and planned. Operational facilities will also be required and there are many possibilities here as to whether they are conducted in-house or outsourced. Information technology underpins almost all strategy and this has to be tailored to suit the unique circumstances of each company. Research and development is not forgotten about at this implementation stage; it is an ongoing process, not just in terms of constantly improving and modifying existing products and services, but also in coming up with the next generation of products. Marketing resources will also be required to facilitate the sale of the product or service to the widest possible market. All of these will need to be considered in greater detail.

Finance

The finance required to support a strategy has to be carefully planned. There are two main aspects here: the capital cost required to finance the project and the current costs. There are two considerations that managers must plan for with regard to the financing of a project. First is the total amount of finance required for supporting a strategy; and second is the timing of cash payments.

Many of these aspects, such as funding strategies, have already been discussed in **Chapter 7**, which considered corporate-level strategy; and also **Chapter 12**, which examined the different financial appraisal systems as part of the decision-making process. In addition, **Chapter 6** examined the principle of cost competitiveness in an organisation. That cost perspective now needs to be examined in relation to each specific strategy to ensure that it is lower than rival companies offering a similar product or service or, if the cost is higher, that customers would be happy to pay a premium because they perceive the product or service to be of better quality. Costs are relative to what is being produced. The process, therefore, involves examining all of the cost drivers (those factors that create cost, both direct costs involved in production and overheads), and these must be compared to the value being created by the product and service. The latter is a function of the volume produced, multiplied by the sales price.

The cost of capital must also be taken into consideration and this applies to equity, bank and other borrowings, and retained earnings. Considerable amounts may well have been invested in capital costs involved in creating the necessary facilities (for large multinationals, this could amount to hundreds of millions of euro). There will also have to be adequate working capital pumped in to ensure that day-to-day costs can be met and the organisation does not become illiquid.

Once the total costs and the total revenues are known, profitability can then be calculated. Corporate finance can be complicated. However, in any business, in any industry, profitability boils down to a very simple equation:

- If a company is selling its products or services at a price greater than it costs to produce/provide them, it is making a profit.
- If a company is selling its products or services at a price lower than it costs to produce/provide them, it is making a loss.

The above equation may seem simplistic in a textbook about corporate strategy, yet it is amazing how often it seems to be forgotten. It is fundamental to the continued existence of any business.

Budgets form an integral part of the process of managing finance. Budgets are both a planning tool in setting out what the expenditures and revenues are likely to be, and a control device to compare actual with planned expenditure. There are situations where a particular strategy may be deliberately loss-making in the short term. This may be done for strategic reasons, such as wanting to gain a foothold in a particular market that would have good long-term potential. However, it is vital that managers monitor the situation and keep it under tight control so that the strategy does not haemorrhage funding. When things do go wrong, managers also need to be decisive when corrective action is required.

Marketing

Marketing is an essential element of an implementation plan. Every organisation must have customers for its products and services. The company needs to make as many people as possible aware of the range of products and services on offer before they will make a purchase decision. As with other activities, it will involve considerable resources and these resources must be used as effectively as possible. A marketing plan will assist in this process.

 A **marketing plan** is a document that sets out how an organisation will market its products and services.

A marketing plan has many functions:

- It helps in ensuring that the organisation is customer-focused and aware of the requirements of the marketplace.
- It is a guide for the organisation for implementing marketing strategies and assisting management in controlling and monitoring those strategies.
- It ensures efficient use of resources and specifies how those resources will be used.
- It assigns responsibilities and timeframes to individuals for specific tasks.

Each strategic business unit (SBU) has its own specific market separate from other SBUs. Consequently, there should be a separate marketing plan for each major strategy being pursued by the company. There will be an overall marketing plan that co-ordinates the activities of the entire organisation.

Kotler *et al.* (2016) suggest that marketing plans will generally conform to a similar outline, which includes: an executive summary of the plan; a statement of the goals and objectives to be achieved; the general background to the market; a general analysis of the market and an examination of realistic marketing opportunities; an examination of competitor activity; an outline of marketing strategy including target market priorities, differential advantage, as well as brand and product positioning; a statement of expected sales patterns; the detail of marketing mixes (price, product, place, promotion and people) required to implement the marketing plan; control mechanisms to monitor progress; financial requirements to implement the marketing plan and budgets; and, finally, any operational considerations that arise from the marketing plan.

Business Intelligence Systems

Business intelligence plays a vital role in supporting strategy and giving the company a competitive advantage in the marketplace. The term 'knowledge economy' has been used a number of times in this textbook to describe the evolution of the Irish economy away from basic manufacturing to more upmarket products and services. As companies develop, the importance of business intelligence grows substantially. Business intelligence has the ability to change the nature of the business in a strategic and operational manner. Business intelligence is primarily a strategic asset. In the context of this chapter, it impacts on the implementation of strategy in organisations in many ways, benefiting the company itself and the customer.

The flow of information and strategic capability go hand-in-hand. Organisations need accurate and timely information about customers' needs in order to develop products and services that meet those needs. Managers also need IT systems to provide them with information from all parts of the company, particularly financial information, in order to make sound decisions about the future. Financial statements can be compiled with much greater accuracy and in a fraction of the time compared to previously. This has also impacted on the structure of organisations and, as a general rule, organisations have become much flatter, cutting out layers of middle management and associated costs. Accurate and timely flows of information also has important implications in terms of leading change in an organisation, and this will be examined in the next chapter.

Business intelligence systems can transform how the company interacts with other businesses as part of the value system. In particular, it changes the nature of competition in the industry and how the level of competition is judged (using Porter's Five Forces Analysis). Some businesses have transformed from traditional-type companies into 'virtual' businesses. As technology improves and companies become more comfortable with technology, it is moving to centre stage in the structure of many business organisations.

Business models have changed considerably as a result of developments in business intelligence systems.

Definition   A **business model** describes the processes by which an organisation interacts with suppliers and customers to deliver its products or services.

The value chain explains how business models have changed. When discussing the supply chain, the importance of linkages was stressed, both internally in the organisation and with the wider value system. Information technology plays a vital part in such linkages. On the supply side, just-in-time manufacturing is dependent on integrated IT systems between the supplier of components and manufacturers. Dell, for example, holds on average a few days' supplies in order to minimise costs. As the components are used to assemble computers, suppliers are notified electronically and additional components are shipped to replace stocks. It also impacts on how customers interact with companies. Some organisations, such as airlines, have moved exclusively to online purchasing and others, such as banks, are attempting to move to online transactions as much as possible. These are all primarily strategic issues for IT systems, but they also have an enormous operational benefit with regard to the rollout of the strategy being followed.

While e-commerce benefits the customer in many ways, the main incentive for companies is that it reduces costs very significantly. When Ryanair first moved away from using travel agents, bookings were taken by call centres. This necessitated having people to take the calls, and in many cases perhaps deal with passengers who were indecisive about their arrangements, thus prolonging the transaction and increasing the costs. When an individual is browsing on an airline's website, the time spent on the site is not costing the airline as it is only the customer's time that is being taken up. When the customer makes a decision, the transaction is conducted immediately. In addition, information technology is a vital part of yield management whereby airlines attempt to maximise the revenue from each flight. IT systems allow this to happen in real time, and prices are adjusted according to the demand.

Another very important function for many industries is 'data mining'. **Data mining** allows companies to extract from their business intelligence systems information about customer demand, as well as trends and connections in that demand. Tesco is a prime example of a company that has exploited information technology to enormous effect.

Illustration 13.1: Data Mining at Tesco

An article in the *Financial Times* by Elizabeth Rigby illustrates the extent of the strategic capability contained in the Tesco Clubcard. In 1994, Tesco hired Dunnhumby, a firm that specialises in consumer data, to assist it with the development of 'Clubcard', its customer loyalty card. After an initial trial in a limited number of stores, Dunnhumby made a presentation to the Tesco board on the value the Clubcard could add to the company. At the end of the presentation, its chair Lord MacLaurin responded:

"What scares me about this is that you know more about my customers after three months than I know after 30 years."

Tesco is now a large multinational retailer with over 6,800 shops around the world and has over 450,000 employees. In 2017, the company had sales of £56.9 billion and profits of $2.2 billion.

Tesco bought a 53% stake in Dunnhumby in 2001 for a reported £30 million. Tesco increased its share to 84% in 2006, before later buying the entire company. Dunnhumby now employs over 2,000 people in over 30 countries around the globe selling marketing information to supplier companies.

With scanning machines at each checkout, every supermarket knows what items are sold and at what time. For the majority of companies, this resource provides them with just a basic competence. Tesco has turned this basic competence into a core competence. The application form for the Clubcard contains personal information about the applicant. The Clubcard matches information on purchases with an individual person and builds up a very detailed profile. What separates Tesco from other supermarkets that have similar loyalty cards is the ability to process the information that the card provides.

In the UK, two-thirds of households shop at Tesco. With such a large customer base and the ability to analyse individuals' shopping habits, it processes over 1 billion rows of data each week, providing insights from nearly 800 million shoppers globally in a 40-terabyte database (it probably has more frequently updated personal information about named individuals in the UK than any other organisation!). This information includes analysing 44 billion shopping baskets daily and 4.8 billion uniquely personalised offers. Its customer analytics allows it to analyse customer spending patterns and deliver offers that are targeted and timely. This has proven to be very successful in attracting customers into the stores where they are likely to make a lot of impulse purchases in addition to the products that were on offer.

This raw data is turned into useful information that allows Tesco to segment its customers into different categories and sub-categories giving it a competitive advantage across almost every aspect of its business. It has also informed strategic decision-making by the company to branch into other areas, such as mobile phones, insurance and Tesco Banking. With every purchase made, more information is added to the person's purchasing profile. This information is added to other data received from various sources, such as the statistics office, and it builds up socio-economic profiles of customers and areas. This allows the company to spot trends in shopping habits. Not only is this information of enormous value to Tesco in deciding what to stock in each individual store, and indeed where to locate stores, but the information is sold on to over 200 consumer goods companies, including giants like Unilever and Procter & Gamble, to assist them in product development that is tailored to suit customer demand. While data protection legislation has been in place since 1998, the implementation of the EU General Data Protection Regulation (GDPR) in May 2018 now places a considerable regulatory burden on how companies collect and use individuals' personal data. With fines of up to 4% of global turnover or £20 million (whichever is the greater), and potential severe reputational damage, companies cannot afford to get this wrong.

Sources: Rigby, 2006; Tesco, 2019; Dunnhumby, 2019

There are certain limitations and risks that must be taken into account with regard to IT systems. Ethical issues must be considered in relation to the use of information technology, especially in the use and distribution of confidential customer information. The organisation should prepare a detailed policy statement for all departments in relation to the use of information and monitor its adherence. It is important for executives to have a realistic expectation regarding what information technology can do for the company. No matter how sophisticated the system is, it is not a substitute for sound managerial judgement. In most instances, competitors will also be using similar technology and so competitive advantage is gained not so much by the technology itself, but by how it is used. In other words, the use of technology has gone from being a core competence to a basic, threshold one.

Costs involved in IT systems have come down considerably, making their use more universal. However, because of competitive pressures, IT systems must be regarded as an essential resource, rather than as a prohibitive cost. In addition, IT has raised the expectations of customers – company websites provide easy access to product information, allowing price/product comparison and informing their purchasing decisions.

There are many ways in which IT has changed and enhanced products to the benefit of the customer. As mentioned above, it provides quite an amount of pre-purchase information for the customer allowing them to make a better and more informed choice. As a result, there should be greater customer satisfaction. It also enables customers to tailor products to their own specific needs. This is done by Dell, for example, in that many of its computers are built to the customer's exact specification. It also allows significant savings that are passed on to the customer. When things go wrong, IT systems can assist in problem-solving. Car maintenance, for example, has become much more sophisticated; garages use computers to identify problems and they also make certain activities, such as fixing engine timing, much more accurate. Computers are also used in the National Car Test (NCT) to determine if vehicles are roadworthy. By correctly identifying a problem, it can be fixed in a shorter period of time and at less cost.

Finally, IT can improve customer service by sharing information between different parts of an organisation. There are many examples in the hotel industry where departments can share information on customers' requirements and this information can also be shared by hotel groups. Similarly in hospitals, departments can access information on a patient, thus improving the speed and accuracy of the treatment when collaboration between departments is required.

Operations

The operations element of strategy implementation will obviously differ significantly from one organisation to another, depending on the nature of the business. There are a number of general factors that must be considered. The importance of R&D was discussed in **Chapter 9**. There is an ever-increasing pressure on companies to constantly innovate by improving existing products and developing new ones. Such innovation is dependent on the people in the organisation having imaginative ideas and a system that fosters those ideas and brings them to fruition. This involves having a good understanding of customers and their requirements. In recent years, Ireland has been selected as the location for R&D facilities for many different reasons, not least being the ready availability of suitably qualified graduates. However, in **Chapter 5** it was seen that our ability as a country to produce graduates in sufficient quantity should not be taken for granted.

Operations systems must support strategy. Innovation refers not only to new products but also new systems. Being able to increase efficiency in operations will increase profitability. Decisions must be made about conducting operations in-house or outsourcing to third parties, e.g. Nike and Benetton. If companies are engaging in outsourcing, there are many ethical issues that need to be considered, particularly in relation to working conditions in the supply chain (Crane and Matten, 2016). If the company is to carry out operations in-house then a decision must be made as to whether the facilities are developed internally by the organisation or whether it acquires another company that has those facilities. Developing them in-house provides the opportunity to create state-of-the-art facilities that could have a very significant impact on efficiency, but is likely to take a number of years. Acquisition can provide the necessary facilities in a short period. The decision to opt for one or the other is dependent to a large extent on the industry and the nature of the technological changes taking place. The reader should refer back to **Chapter 11** for a fuller discussion of the relevant issues. Considerable financial resources will be required and these will have to be provided either at corporate level or by the division concerned.

BUILDING COMPETITIVE CAPABILITIES

The development of competitive capabilities is an integral element of the entire strategy development and implementation process. Organisations have no choice but to develop the competitive capabilities required to operate in their industry. **Chapter 6** examined the process by which strategic capability is identified as part of the development of strategy. In the implementation phase, the company needs to ensure the correct capabilities are in place and these must also be modified as conditions change in the marketplace. Building such capabilities takes a considerable amount of managerial time and effort. It requires identifying best practice, imitating it and eventually improving on it. This involves a number of stages. Companies must work on their basic skills and continually develop them. Over a period of time, and as the organisational experience grows, these activities can be performed more efficiently, ensuring acceptable quality at a competitive price. Further improvement should convert this activity into a core competence, giving the company a strong competitive advantage.

The Japanese sum up this incremental improvement in one word: *Kaizen.*

Definition   *Kaizen* is a philosophy that suggests that every aspect of our lives should be constantly improved.

In management terms, *Kaizen* underpins total quality control. Its key elements include quality, effort, involvement of all employees, willingness to change and good communication. The practical application of this concept is indeed difficult, but, in order to achieve excellence, it must be done.

This once again raises the issue as to whether these capabilities are developed in-house or whether they are outsourced to key employers.

The competitive capability of an organisation consists of the resources and the competences that it possesses and the knowledge that has been built up, often over a period of time. Porter (1985) stressed the importance of linkages between elements of the value chain and the wider value system. These linkages therefore are not only internal, but also involve working closely with suppliers and, in particular, customers in order to improve not just the products but all the process flows as well. Such linkages also make it very difficult for other companies to imitate these competences. Identifying these competences in a competitor is one thing; being able to replicate them is entirely different. The *Kaizen* approach is an holistic approach based on constant improvement over a sustained period of time. It involves examining all aspects of the organisation to identify areas that can be improved. In particular, it involves improving activities from the level of a basic competence to a core competence. This requires concentrating more effort and talent than rivals into strengthening that competence. This point highlights the importance of having talented people in the organisation. The business environment is constantly evolving and so too should the organisation in response to changing market demands. The process of *Kaizen* should therefore be viewed as a continuous process, rather than an end destination.

PROCEDURES FOR GOOD STRATEGY EXECUTION

The strategy implementation process must be supported by appropriate policies and procedures. While the organisation will have policies and procedures in place, these will have to be updated and adjusted for the strategies that are being implemented. Thompson *et al.* (2018) state that prescribing new policies and operating procedures will facilitate the process of execution in three ways:

- It provides top-down guidance on how the organisation does certain things. From that perspective, it helps align the actions and behaviour of company personnel with the strategy, and channels the energy of the organisation towards achieving its goals. It also provides parameters for employees on the types of decisions that they make.
- In larger organisations, it will help provide a certain consistency between the different geographical and product divisions of the company in terms of how the strategy is implemented and how the organisation interacts with its customers.
- It helps create an appropriate work climate that will enable the strategy to be implemented; such a work climate will also facilitate change.

In a competitive environment, managers must constantly identify opportunities for adopting best practices in all aspects of strategy implementation. Such practices are essential in reducing costs and improving quality. When the company has identified best practice for the relevant activities, it must then adopt and implement such practices. An important part of this process will be the development of metrics by which improvements can be measured. Best practice is something that is constantly evolving, so the organisation must keep up to date with the best performers around the world. Such excellence is only achieved over a period of time and with much effort. Indeed, identifying best practice can often be difficult: while it is easy to identify companies that are successful, it is another matter identifying what internal processes make them so successful. When this is identified, it then has to be translated into the specific circumstances surrounding the company wishing to adopt the practice. There are a number of different tools that managers can use to help achieve excellence. These include business process re-engineering, Six Sigma and total quality management.

Business Process Re-Engineering

Business process re-engineering (BPR) was made popular in the early 1990s by Michael Hammer and James Champy in their book *Re-engineering the Corporation* (1993). BPR is based on the premise that, in order to stay competitive, organisations have to redesign themselves using a clean sheet of paper if they are to survive. The purpose of BPR is to examine the processes rather than the products to see what efficiencies can be gained by aligning those processes across functional and divisional units in an organisation.

Supply chain management, for example, involves purchasing materials, storing them, manufacturing/ assembly, storing finished goods and distributing them. This involves several different departments and personnel, as well as countless procedures. It was believed that most of the time wasted on any particular process is wasted in moving from one department to another, particularly the flow of information. By reorganising these processes on the basis of work teams, enormous productivity gains can be made and it can cut costs significantly. By the mid-1990s, it was estimated that four out of five Fortune 500 companies were using some form of BPR, and not just in manufacturing but in services and the public sector.

Wooldridge (2011) believes that BPR is not without its critics. It is inextricably linked with 'downsizing' – getting rid of large numbers of employees and middle managers. It has been likened to Taylorism in that it treats employees like automatons rather than intelligent people, and this has a devastating impact on employee morale and a negative impact on innovation. Hammer and Champy (1993) consider that it is not the concept that is at fault, but the manner in which it is applied. It may well be that, in many cases, companies involved in cost-cutting and large scale lay-offs have termed it business process re-engineering without any realignment of their processes – just merely making people redundant.

Total Quality Management

It is ironic that while total quality management (TQM) is very much associated with the Japanese, it was two Americans, William Denning and Joseph Duran, who were the pioneers behind the concept. Denning developed a set of 14 points which he believed were essential for attaining quality in a company (Tiernan *et al.*, 2013). He believed that faults in manufacturing lay with the systems used rather than the people involved in the process. Duran believed that management could largely control quality defects. The two men worked with Japanese companies and their teaching gained widespread acceptance. This move towards quality led to the development of total quality management, which is essentially a customer-focused management philosophy aimed at achieving total quality at all levels of the organisation by all employees from the CEO down. It requires each and every employee to take responsibility for quality in their own work and for rectifying mistakes if they occur.

According to Stevenson (1989), TQM involves five stages: understanding what the customer is looking for; designing the product/service in a manner that exceeds the customers' needs; designing a production process that ensures everything is done correctly the first time; monitoring performance; and then working with suppliers and distributors to extend the process. It also emphasises continuous improvement – *Kaizen* – in every aspect of what the organisation does, including administrative functions as well as production and services. The process of TQM is an integral part of, and must be supported by, the corporate culture of the organisation. As a managerial tool, TQM has developed widespread appeal across the world.

Six Sigma Quality Control

Six Sigma Quality Control was originally designed by Motorola in the mid-1980s and has become an integral part of training in many top class companies such as Motorola, BMW, Nokia, Xerox, GE and many more Fortune 500 companies. In the section on training above, it was stated that GE sends employees on various training programmes, which includes all new employees completing a basic programme in Six Sigma. This is followed up with more advanced courses that are graded similarly to martial arts labels, such as green belt, brown belt or black belt and these qualifications are regarded as a prerequisite for promotion.

Six Sigma is a statistics-based system with the objective of having no more than 3.4 defects per million opportunities (DPMO) in the entire business process. It is the equivalent of 99.9997% efficiency. It was originally designed for manufacturing but it was later applied to other business processes and can also be used in non-profit organisations. In Six Sigma a defect is regarded as anything that would lead to customer dissatisfaction. It was inspired by previous studies on quality control methodologies such as TQM. Sigma (represented by the Greek letter: σ) is used to represent the standard deviation of a statistical population. Six Sigma operates on the premise that continual efforts to achieve top quality in business processes are vital for success. It considers that all business processes can be measured, analysed, improved and controlled, but this can only be achieved with commitment from the entire organisation, particularly top management.

Six Sigma Quality Control is aimed at improving various processes within an organisation. For new processes, the process involves five stages: define, measure, analyse, design and verify (DMADV). However, in most instances, existing processes are probably already in place and so a different Six Sigma process – DMAIC – is used. The five stages of DMAIC include:

- **Define** – team members must define what constitutes a defect from the customers' perspective.
- **Measure** – develop a process flow chart to enable the team to collect data on the defects, such as how and why they occur, and how often.

- **Analyse** – the data must be analysed to understand the process and where it is failing.
- **Improve** – develop and document best practice for the process.
- **Control** – the best practice must be used by all employees with regard to this process.

As with all such efforts to improve efficiency, it must have top managerial support and become embedded in the culture of the company. Many companies have championed the process, ensuring that it has become a central part of how they operate. While there are similarities between business process re-engineering, TQM and Six Sigma, the main difference between them is in the timeframe for improvements. Processes like TQM and Six Sigma emphasise continual improvements in quality and cost reduction over a long period of time, while business process re-engineering can achieve enormous gains in a very short period, although sustaining such improvement can be difficult.

Operational efficiency is important, but it is not a substitute for strategy. Porter (1996) suggests that while operational efficiency is needed, organisations must also keep a strategic focus. He believes that managers must respond quickly to competitive and market changes, but many fail to distinguish between operational effectiveness and strategy. They are both necessary but work in different ways. Cost advantages arise from performing activities more efficiently than competitors. Threats to strategy are often seen to emanate from outside the company because of changes in technology or competitors. Managers often start imitating everything about their competitors and chasing technology for its own sake. The pursuit of operational effectiveness is seductive because it is concrete, but it lacks a vision of the whole and the perspective to recognise trade-offs.

According to Porter (1996), organisations depend on leadership – "a clear intellectual framework to guide strategy". It is far broader than making operational improvements, defining and communicating the company's unique position, making trade-offs and forging fits among activities. The leader must decide what industry changes and customers' needs the company will respond to. This may mean saying no to certain courses of action in some instances. Porter suggests that improving operational efficiency is necessary but it is not strategy. "Both are essential, but the agendas are different." While operational efficiency requires constant change and flexibility for best practice, strategy demands a unique position, clear trade-offs, discipline and continuity.

Illustration 13.2 is a good example of how an Irish company, Shannon Aerospace, has responded to global pressures by introducing 'lean' techniques and, in the process, has radically transformed how the company operates. It demonstrates a strategic approach from corporate level to operational level with regard to issues facing the company. The illustration highlights the importance of senior managers realising that good ideas can come from anywhere in the organisation and that one of the most important functions of managers in an organisation is creating a forum and a climate whereby such ideas can filter through and be translated into a strategy that will work (see **Chapter 1**). It is also a good example of leading change (see **Chapter 14**).

Illustration 13.2: Lufthansa Technik Shannon Ltd – Lean Transformation

Lufthansa Technik Shannon Ltd (LTSL) is a company that specialises in the maintenance, repair and overhaul of commercial jet airframes. Operating in a global industry, it is based in Shannon, County Clare. The company is a wholly-owned subsidiary of Lufthansa Technik AG. Like many big companies, it has responded to challenges in the past that significantly changed its business environment, including the Gulf wars, 9/11, low-cost airlines changing the rules of the industry (and reducing maintenance business volume), deregulation and the collapse of former shareholder companies, GPA and Swissair. Perhaps one of the biggest challenges was the Celtic Tiger impact on costs and staff turnover. The company had to respond radically by growing business volume and transforming how they operated. Lean tool techniques were seen as essential in helping to reduce maintenance turn-around time, which in turn would reduce costs.

The company began the process by communicating the necessity for the programme to staff members. To bridge the gap between their lean strategy and actual implementation, value stream mapping (VSM) was used. The company mapped its end-to-end business processes with the specific goals of reducing aircraft turn-around time by 35% and its cost of production by 30%. The company brought together a team of 28 people from all levels and areas of the company, as well as the technical director of EasyJet to represent customers. The team received training in 'lean' principles, VSM and paradigm-shift training. The team applied their training by reviewing all practices within the organisation from the perspective of the customer. It was a very open approach to the problem and all company employees witnessed the executives spend a full week on the shop floor, questioning their own processes in terms of the value that each activity was adding. The process identified bottlenecks and inefficiencies, and the team learned to brainstorm for ideas to overcome these problems. From this, the team agreed an 'Ideal State Map' for the value stream analysis and developed realistic goals to enable the company to grow and transform the business.

The implementation plan involved a number of projects, with several process preparation and planning events, some 'just do it' tasks and many *Kaizen* events called rapid improvement events (RIEs). Using the implementation plan, the team then brought in all relevant employees and briefed them on the plan. Employees were given training in areas that impacted on their team's participation in the process. This process was not a one-off event but became part of the development of a continual improvement culture that persists in the organisation.

The implementation plan required new processes to be created, old processes to be made more efficient, safer or more reliable, and a relentless drive to identify and eliminate waste. It involved full engagement with staff members. RIEs involved the 'process owner' developing a plan that specified the purpose of the event, the specific deliverables, the benefits to be derived and the metrics used to verify results. The critical path of the project would be identified. Team members would then be selected, which also included people from outside the company to bring a fresh perspective. The process is tied in with a number of lean companies from around the world with which LTSL collaborates and shares information. The team is open to input from any source.

When an RIE is being planned, the team forms on a part-time basis three weeks prior to the event to start the planning process and define the scope and understand what success will look like. The team gets intensive training in the various tools, such as value stream mapping, etc., to plan the schedule effectively, with all the various manuals and other requirements available online. One of the biggest benefits of the RIE teams was the breaking down of barriers between different sections and the streamlining of the organisation. One innovation was the creation of a 'hub' on the hangar floor acting as a single point of contact between hundreds of various technicians as well as support teams.

Changes such as these have made enormous improvements, such as the time taken to strip and paint an aircraft, which has been reduced from 13 12-hour shifts to nine shifts, taking two days off each ground time and opening up new revenue slots for sale. Likewise, technicians contributed significantly to the success achieved in improving cash flow by reducing invoicing time from 78 days to 7 days. The company has benchmarked a number of different lean processes and adapted them to its own particular needs, such as its '6S' workplace organisation. Here, the workplace is laid out so that it is easy to operate following an agreed new process from which it is difficult to deviate. As improvements are made, both management and colleagues are briefed on those improvements, and the changes are then converted into new operating procedures.

There were many lessons learned by LTSL along the way. Initially, a lot of the change taking place was opposed. In response, the company realised that it was essential to create ownership of the process by all those involved and to include them in the problem-solving process. Some managers initially did not fully appreciate this, or carry out their role as 'facilitator of change and improvement'. As time went on, the quality of internal communications improved as this was seen to be an integral part of its overall success. Managers also underestimated how long the transformation would actually take. Some areas of excellence emerged, while other areas were initially left behind. This proved divisive, but created a positive demand and interest in these areas for improvement. However, LTSL learned from its mistakes and the company now has a culture of continual improvement. LTSL employees are rated by its customers as being among the best in the world. This is a source of genuine pride in the company, and, more importantly, it generates a lot of business in a globally competitive industry.

Source: Mr Tom Caffrey, Acting Chief Executive
Lufthansa Technik Shannon Ltd (LTSL)

PROJECT MANAGEMENT

Depending on the nature of the strategy, project management techniques are often used to implement major strategic initiatives. The Project Management Institute defines a project as a "temporary endeavour undertaken to create a unique product, service, or result" (Schwalbe, 2010:4). Projects can be large or small; they differ from normal operations in that projects end when their objectives have been reached or the project terminated. While every project is unique, they all share three common constraints:

- **Scope** – defining what will be covered by the project and how it will be verified.
- **Time** – what is the timeframe for completion?
- **Cost** – what will be the total cost and how can it be contained?

There is a natural tendency for these constraints to impact on the success of the project; people will want the scope to be expanded, and this will have an impact on time and inevitably on cost. As with all strategy implementation, the project manager plays a crucial role in ensuring its success and satisfying all stakeholders. According to Schwalbe (2010: 10), there are nine knowledge areas in project management. Four **core functions** include: scope management; time management; cost management; and quality management. In turn these are supported by four **facilitating functions**: human resource management; communications management; risk management; and procurement management. The four core functions and the four facilitating functions are all co-ordinated under **Project Integration Management**. Each of these functions is supported by various tools and

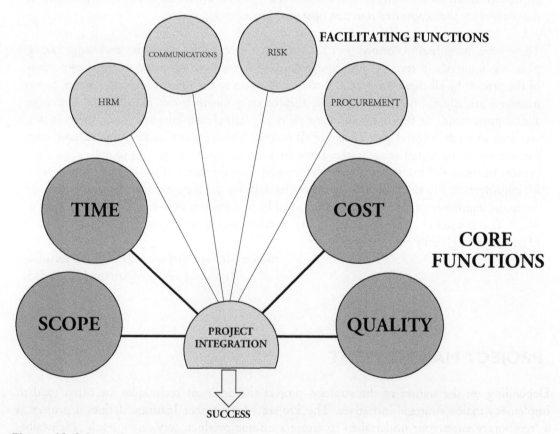

Figure 13. 2 *Project Integration Management*

techniques. While projects form a discrete body of work, they operate within a much broader context of operational strategy and, in some instances, such as strategic alliances, within the context of a number of organisations. The role of the project manager, therefore, is not just to co-ordinate all aspects of the project, but also to satisfy multiple stakeholders across organisations, bearing in mind each organisation will have its own culture and internal politics.

Project Life Cycle

A project was described above as a 'temporary endeavour' which implies that each project undergoes a number of stages. The first phase is the **concept**, where the business case for the project is discussed and the ideas teased out, along with an outline of the work involved and preliminary costs. If the initial idea seems worth pursuing, the second stage is development. The **development stage** involves expanding on the initial work to formalise the scope of the project, the timeframe and accurate costs. Stage three is its **implementation**, where the work is actually carried out. Most of the cost will be incurred during implementation. The fourth and final stage is the **close-out** when all the work is finally completed. The first two stages: concept and development are known as **project feasibility**. The last two stages: implementation and close-out are known as **project acquisition**.

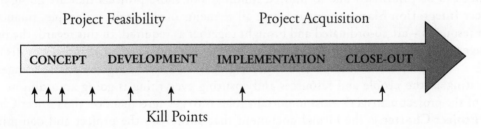

Figure 13. 3 *Project Life Cycle*

Not all projects go through all four stages. There should be a constant review as circumstances change and new information comes to light that might render the project no longer viable. As a result, a decision might be taken at any stage to terminate the project; such a decision is called a **kill point**.

Processes

There are a number of processes involved in project management, all of which are interlinked. The processes define the type of work managers do at each of the various stages of the project life cycle. In effect, these processes are superimposed on the four stages of the project life cycle outlined above. The processes involved in project management include:

- **Initiating** – initiating occurs primarily in defining the project itself and, to a lesser extent, at each stage of the project. Essentially, it gets the project team operating together for that particular phase.
- **Planning** – developing a plan that will ensure successful completion of each stage of the project taking into account the scope, time and cost.

411

- **Executing** – co-ordinating all of the resources (and people) to deliver on the project.
- **Monitoring and controlling** – every project needs systems in place to ensure it is running according to plan.
- **Closing** – bringing the project to a close and formal acceptance by stakeholders.

The balance between the various processes will vary considerably depending on the particular stage of the project life cycle. For example, the planning process will be very prominent during project feasibility, though each stage of project acquisition will also need to be planned. Planning is therefore a continual process throughout the project. Likewise, control will be required from start to finish, although it will be most prominent during the implementation phase.

Project Integration Management

As with all elements of strategy implementation, there must be clear strategic objectives to be achieved, and these objectives must be understood by all. Thus, the project must be an integral part of the company's strategic plan. It may be that there are a number of projects running simultaneously in the organisation, or that a number of projects have been identified, but need to be prioritised due to limited funding. For those projects that are going ahead, **Project Integration Management** is where all elements of the project – people, finance and other resources – are co-ordinated and brought together as required. In this regard, the project manager is like the conductor of an orchestra: they will utilise the five processes discussed above in order to deliver the project – getting it started, planning the various stages, co-ordinating all the people and resources and ensuring everything is going according to plan. One of the project manager's most important roles is to get agreement on the Project Charter. The **Project Charter** is the formal document that authorises the project and commits the necessary resources to it. This involves working with all the stakeholders to get agreement on what exactly the project will entail. If different stakeholders have differing expectations about the outcome, the project will be on a collision course from the very beginning. The charter also sets out the timeframe for the project: when it begins and ends, and key milestones. It also includes a budget for the project.

Project Scope Management

The **project scope** refers to the parameters of the project – defining exactly what it is going to achieve and, just as importantly, what will *not* be included. The project scope helps formulate the project charter at this stage and the work involved is examined in much greater detail in the form of a **work breakdown structure (WBS)**. A WBS examines the project in its entirety and breaks it down into specific modules that will be carried out by different people, perhaps at different times. The WBS is an important document because it forms the basis for the resources required, costs and the schedule of work. The use of Gantt charts assists in the process of 'decomposition' – subdividing the project into smaller elements, which in turn allows the project manager to estimate the time involved in each stage and thus schedule the entire project. While stakeholders will want to tie down the scope, it is important to build in flexibility as circumstances will change, in which case, agreement will have to be reached as to who has the authority to make changes to the scope, bearing in mind it will have implications for cost and time.

Project Time Management

Using the activities listed in the WBS, it will be possible to develop a schedule of work for the project. In turn, it will allow the project manager to estimate the resources required at each stage. This schedule will also include the sequencing of activities and the relationship between those activities. This is a very important process as some activities can be carried out at the same time, while other activities can only be carried out when another activity is completed. Using **network diagrams** (a schematic display of the relationship between the different elements of a project) and critical path analysis (see below) the shortest time for the completion of the project can then be estimated. There are different types of network diagrams, but the most common one is a precedence diagramming method (PDM) network. Cloud-based software such as Microsoft Project Online can construct these networks and show the various forms of dependencies.

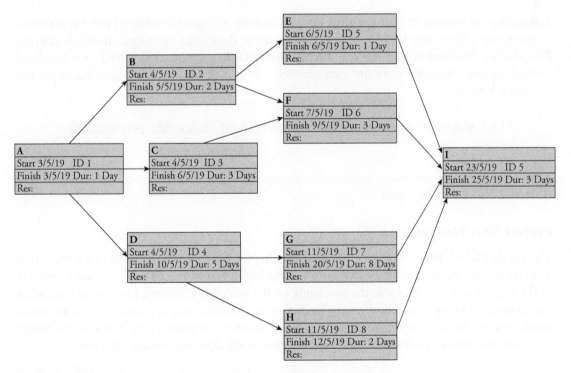

Figure 13.4 *Precedence Diagramming Method (PDM) Network Diagram*

In the diagram in **Figure 13.4** above, each particular activity is listed in a box and labelled with an ID number. The box shows: the start date and finish date of the activity; its duration (based on a five-day working week); and also lists the resources required. The diagram also displays the dependency between the different activities. The project starts with Activity A and goes simultaneously to Activities B, C, and D. In the case of Activity F, it cannot start until both Activity B and Activity C is finished (therefore its start date is the 7 of May).

The dependencies between the activities will show up the critical path. **Critical path analysis** is a network diagramming technique which is used to predict the total length of time a project will take. The critical path shows the series of activities that determine the **earliest** time that the project can be completed. It is the **longest** path (in terms of time) through the activities of the project, and has the least amount of slack time (the amount of time an activity can be held up without delaying the entire project). Understanding the critical path is important in preventing delays and in determining where resources are needed most urgently. In **Figure 13.4** above, the critical path is highlighted (A to D to G to I) and in this example is 17days long (1 + 5 + 8 + 3 days). There is slack time at various parts of the project, e.g. Activity H could be delayed by up to six days without adding to the overall length of the project. Knowing where there is slack time might present an opportunity to divert resources to the critical path and so speed up the project.

Estimating the amount of time required for each activity is largely a matter of prior experience. In some cases, there may be a lot of uncertainty about these time estimates, in which case the **Programme Evaluation and Review Technique (PERT)** may be used. PERT is a weighted average for the estimated time for each activity, taking risk into account. It is based on the following formula:

$$\text{PERT weighted average} = \frac{\text{optimistic time} + 4 \times \text{most likely time} + \text{pessimistic time}}{6}$$

As with all aspects of controlling strategy, the project manager needs to monitor progress and take corrective action when required.

Project Cost Management

The Garda PULSE system that was discussed in **Chapter 1** is a perfect example of a project that went far beyond the original timeframe for implementation and where the final cost was a multiple of the original estimate. (See also the case study on the National Children's Hospital at the end of the textbook.) In major projects, there can be enormous costs involved. Approval for such projects is based on a certain monetary cost. The project must, therefore, be managed in such a way to ensure that costs are contained within the approved budgets, while delivering on the objectives.

By constructing a detailed work breakdown structure listing all of the activities involved in the entire project, and examining the resources that will be required for these activities, it will be possible to come up with an accurate costing for the project. This will then determine the overall budget required. Importantly, the finance needed is unlikely to be required all at once, but will be staged over the lifetime of the project.

Project Quality Management

There are many definitions of 'quality', and, in many ways, it is a subjective term that means different things in different situations. When a project is commissioned there is, however, an expectation that it will be 'fit for purpose'. In other words, it will satisfy the needs of the end user. Those needs will have been clearly defined in the project charter, and the entire project then needs to be planned based on those expectations. Quality, therefore, has to be planned and built in to the project from the start, rather than an extra attached at the end. The project manager must then ensure that those quality requirements are being met as the project progresses, as rectifying mistakes later can be very expensive. There are a variety of quality assurance techniques that can be used to assist the process.

Project Human Resource Management

Throughout this textbook, the importance of having the right people on board has been constantly stressed. Managing projects is no exception, and, within projects, managing people is probably one of the most challenging tasks. In keeping costs under control, the project manager will have to make the most effective use of all team members. That requires planning the exact requirement for human resources in terms of numbers and skill sets, and the reporting relationship within the team. This will have to be formalised in a human resource plan. Team members will then have to be selected and their roles allocated. The requirement for people will vary considerably from one phase to the next, and so team members will be assigned and removed from the project as required. There may be many talented individuals on board, but they will be required to operate as a team, and creating such a team will require investment in time and effort. Motivating members to work hard and resolving personal conflict, should it arise, are all part of the challenges the project manager must face. A **responsibility assignment matrix** can be used to assign responsibility for specific tasks to different individuals. **Resource levelling** is a form of network analysis that may be used to ensure an even demand for personnel, and avoid staff shortages at critical times.

Project Communications Management

The project charter (see above) identifies all the stakeholders involved in a project. Each of these stakeholders will have different requirements in terms of the frequency and detail of progress reports. Ensuring effective communications can alleviate many problems. A communications management plan should be developed to provide people involved with the information they require, at the time they require it and in the form they require. For some it might be an oral briefing once a month, while others may require a detailed written report each morning. The project manager must understand the communication needs of different stakeholders and establish appropriate communication channels.

Project Risk Management

The importance of analysing risk was discussed in **Chapter 7**. Every project is going to entail some risk and the level of risk involved needs to be calculated and accepted. There are a whole variety of types of risk, not just financial. These include damage to the company's brand or image, technology risk, process risk and the risk of not having the right people on board. **A risk management plan** sets out the procedures for analysing and dealing with risk throughout the project. As with all risks, the probability of the risk occurring and the potential impact on the organisation should be assessed. Once risks are identified, contingency plans can then be drawn up to deal with those risks, and reserves built in to minimise the impact should they happen.

Project Procurement Management

Managing resources to contain the cost of the project is an important element of the project manager's role. Many of the resources required to complete the project may have to be sourced from outside the organisation. The most appropriate suppliers will have to be identified and contracts drawn up to ensure a just-in-time delivery of those components. They will then have to be issued to the different individuals as and when they are required, and their use will have to be accounted for. A **procurement management plan** will detail all the arrangements for procurement, including the planning of the resources that are needed, their ordering in a timely manner, authorisation for use and all the documentation required. There are various forms of eProcurement software packages that can assist in this process.

Successful Implementation

The successful implementation of any project requires leadership and a broad range of managerial and other skills (particularly soft skills) on the part of the project manager, including strong communication skills and the ability to build trust, team-building and conflict-resolution skills, critical thinking and the ability to set priorities. It also requires a detailed knowledge of all of the issues involved in the particular circumstances in which the project is being undertaken. The history of major infrastructural projects in this country paints a poor picture, with many projects, such as the rollout of the National Broadband Plan, delivered late and in some cases costing many times the original estimate.

Projects also need the support of all stakeholders. In the case of the Corrib Gas Project, it was originally planned that gas would come ashore in County Mayo in 2003. While other aspects of the project might have been meticulously planned, a narrow view of stakeholders was taken. Both Enterprise, the original exploration company, and Shell, who acquired the gas field in 2001, seemed to brush aside the environmental concerns of a wide number of groups as well as the health and safety concerns of residents in Erris, County Mayo. The approach by Shell E&P Ireland has set the project timeframe back significantly and added tens of millions of euro to the cost.

Notwithstanding these costly failures, project management techniques are an extremely effective way of implementing strategy. As with all aspects of strategy implementation, what matters is the efficiency with which the strategy is implemented.

INCENTIVES AND STRATEGY EXECUTION

In strategy execution, employees must be enthusiastic and committed to achieving the targets that have been set. To achieve good performance over a sustained period, the company must provide appropriate monetary and non-monetary incentives. In most cases it will be a combination of the two. Monetary incentives include pay increases, performance bonuses, profit-sharing and contributions to pension funds. Non-financial incentives include making the company an attractive place to work. This entails, in addition to suitable financial rewards, challenging job assignments, providing recognition for work well done, promoting from within and generally creating an atmosphere where employee's suggestions are valued and, where appropriate, adopted. In many larger organisations, greater emphasis is being placed on the physical surroundings of the business, and many include leisure and recreation facilities for staff members and their families. It requires a flexible approach by managers as people are motivated by different things and in different ways. The management of rewards, therefore, requires good people skills. It must also be transparent and be seen by all concerned to be fair.

The attainment of organisational results will inevitably bring a certain element of pressure with it. The pressure on employees must, however, be appropriate – undue pressure on achieving results will culminate in a demoralised workforce and work-related illnesses such as stress. Targets must be realistic and within the capability of staff to achieve them, and appropriate training and other resources must be put in place.

When targets are difficult but achievable, and employees see that attaining these targets is linked directly to generous rewards and recognition, it can have a powerful motivating effect that will generate commitment. These targets must be set for every level of the organisation. Within each area, they must be linked to both team and individual performance.

In a competitive environment, the emphasis needs to be on achieving results rather than just performing particular tasks. For senior executives this is usually tied in to overall sales growth, share performance, return on investment, etc. For others in the company it is usually linked more closely with their area of responsibility. In hotels, a service charge is paid to all staff, not just those who have direct contact with customers. The greater the level of sales in the hotel in terms of bed-nights, meals, bar sales, etc., the greater the financial reward will be. As a consequence, even those staff members who do not have direct contact with customers still have an incentive to maintain high standards.

There are a couple of important caveats in linking rewards with the attainment of results. First is the ethical foundation underpinning the achievement of those results. If there is a culture of achieving results at *any cost*, it may lead to managers and employees using unethical methods to attain targets. A study of the near-collapse of the banking industry around the world illustrates this point very clearly. There is an important ethical aspect to this. Incentives are linked to achieving objectives such as reaching specific sales targets. In recent years, the Central Bank of Ireland has had to deal with over

35,000 complaints by customers being denied their rights to tracker mortgages by the main banks. Variable rate mortgages were more profitable for the banks, but more expensive for customers, some of whom were forced on to these higher-rate mortgages – a clear conflict of interest by the banks. In many instances, either systems were not in place in the banks to detect such inappropriate behaviour or else such systems were ignored in order satisfy performance targets.

Secondly, there have to be measures in place to ensure that the underlying trend is one of sustained growth, rather than just focusing on the short-term (in the case of public limited companies on six months' results, or three months in the case of the US). In such cases, cutting back on costs in the short-term can increase sales, but have detrimental long-term effects in areas such as staff training or research and development.

STRUCTURAL DESIGNS

Chapter 7 introduced different structural designs for the corporation. It was introduced there to give the reader an understanding of what larger organisations look like from a structural perspective. However, structure must follow strategy and senior managers must make whatever changes are necessary to the structure of the organisation to ensure that it supports the chosen strategy. Flexibility is key and, for that reason, there will be much emphasis on cross-functional and cross-divisional teams. The use of strategy maps was discussed in **Chapter 3** (Kaplan and Norton (2008)). Strategy maps are very useful in overcoming structural difficulties in organisations and assisting executives in achieving strategic objectives. In other cases, it may be necessary to change the basic structure of the organisation.

In recent years, Kerry Group Plc has re-aligned its organisational structure to better support its strategy. It is important that companies ensure that the organisational structure is best suited for the type of strategy that is being pursued, and in particular, provides the appropriate level of control for the type of organisation. Depending on the type of industry in which they operate, some organisations will require tight control and procedures, and the type of structure chosen will assist in this process. Creative organisations, such as marketing companies, will need a much more flexible approach. Foreign expansion will often precipitate structural change. The domestic market for many Irish companies is very small, and they will look to foreign markets as a means of further growth. Such a move will often necessitate change in the type of structure in place. It will be recalled from **Chapter 6** that each company will develop a structure for their own needs, and there is no prescriptive formula. Goold and Campbell (2002) proposed nine 'tests' to facilitate the selection of an appropriate structure for the organisation.

In **Chapter 14** we will examine organisational change, and changing the organisational structure will often be a part of this change. In reality, such restructuring will only take place occasionally as it also causes a considerable amount of disruption and uncertainty within the organisation. It is also dependent on the nature of change taking place and, in particular, the speed by which it is taking place.

CONTROL PROCESSES

While every organisation will have an organisational structure in place, of equal importance is how all of the parts of the organisation are linked together. Each organisation will have to develop appropriate control processes that will provide managers with the means of implementing strategy and ensuring that the results are in line with expectations. A structure on its own will not achieve this. Just as the structure must be appropriate for the type of organisation, so too must the control processes as they can either help or hinder the implementation of strategy. There are many different types of control processes, both direct and indirect. Just as strategy is developed in many ways (see **Chapter 1**), likewise, an organisation will most probably employ a mixture of these control processes.

Direct Controls

Direct control processes include:

• Strategic planning process
• Performance targeting.

Strategic Planning Process This process is used to a greater or lesser extent by most organisations. It involves the setting of goals and objectives and detailing how these will be achieved. This is best illustrated by the use of budgets, which are a planning and a control device. It lays out the planned expenditure for the organisation as a whole (the master budget) and for each division and section within that organisation. For example, in the marketing plan described above, a budget for the proposed marketing activities is an integral part of that plan. Within the budget, each item of expenditure will be listed.

The benefit of planning will depend on the nature of the industry within which the company is operating. In stable conditions, planning can be very effective as any assumptions about the future are likely to remain valid for the duration of the plan. Most organisations involve a 'bottom-up' process in developing the plan rather than a prescriptive top-down approach. Each organisation will have different arrangements concerning the relationship between the corporate headquarters and each of the different divisions.

In addition to budgets, other forms of planning systems that control process include measures to standardise work practices, which include product and service features. Standard operating procedures (SOPs) ensure that each unit performs the service to a uniform standard across the organisation. Franchise operations use such standard operating procedures to ensure a uniform quality in each outlet that provides the customer with a standard of service that, if properly applied, will consistently meet or exceed their expectations. Such SOPs are internal to the organisation. External control measures include quality standards like ISO 9000 systems. These are externally validated quality programmes that certify a high level of product reliability and service delivery.

All of these processes require tight managerial control. In smaller organisations or family-run companies, this involves hands-on supervision by the owner/manager of the processes to ensure a high standard. In larger organisations, particularly those pursuing a cost-leadership strategy, it will involve each individual manager exercising stringent control within their area of responsibility.

Performance Targeting Setting targets and attaining them is a vital element of strategy. One of the big problems with many control measures, particularly financial control measures, is that they are lagging indicators, i.e. they reflect past performance, which is not necessarily a good indicator of future performance. Leading indicators of the company's future strategic position indicate whether the company will be in a stronger or weaker position in the marketplace. For example, by setting ambitious targets for the coming year and achieving those targets will, in all likelihood, result in strong end-of-year financial results. On the other hand, if the company sits on its laurels, it is unlikely that the results will be anything more than mediocre. The targets that are set for the organisation must reflect a balance between financial and strategic goals. **Chapter 3** examined the use of the Balanced Scorecard, which combines both qualitative and quantitative measures that reflect different aspects of the company. The four measures included are:

- Financial perspective
- Customer perspective
- Internal perspective
- Innovation and learning perspective.

The objectives should be based on the key success factors relevant to the market that the company is operating in. All four elements of the scorecard are linked together and what impacts on one will impact on the others, thus providing a forward-looking and holistic perspective on the performance of the organisation. Control is then exercised by ensuring that each element of the organisation is achieving the goals that have been set for it. Where these goals have not been met, appropriate action to rectify any problems needs to be taken. In taking such action, it is important that management has a clear understanding of the true nature of the problem and are not just tackling the symptoms (see the rational decision-making model in **Chapter 12**).

Indirect Controls

In addition to the direct controls, there are also indirect controls. Indirect control can be exercised by:

- The culture of the organisation, or
- Internal markets.

Organisational Culture The culture of the organisation was discussed in detail in **Chapter 2**. It was seen that the culture has an all-pervasive effect and so will impact on the effectiveness and control of the organisation. As organisations move up the value chain, the calibre of employees changes correspondingly. While tight control might be appropriate for a cost-leadership situation, it is inappropriate for a company in the knowledge economy that depends on bright, innovative employees. In such a situation, formal control would stifle creativity. While some form of control is of course appropriate, the emphasis here must be more on the internal motivation and self-control of the individuals concerned. For aid agencies operating in the developing world, the volunteer staff will, by necessity, have considerable latitude in how they do their work. The enormous impact they have in destitute parts of the world is driven by a common culture and work ethic, rather than by any traditional controls.

The culture can standardise control as it dictates 'the way things are done around here'. The pressure from colleagues can exert a powerful influence on the performance of others. The impact of peer pressure on workers' performance was first noted by Elton Mayo in the famous Hawthorne experiments carried out in the 1920s and 1930s at the Western Electric Company (Tiernan *et al.*, 2013). In the Bank Wiring Observation Room Experiments conducted in 1931–32, colleagues developed what they regarded as an acceptable rate of output. Those who produced more were known as 'rate busters' and those who produced below that rate were known as 'chisellers'. Pressure was put on both groups to conform to the group average (Tiernan *et al.*, 2006).

The workers in the Hawthorne experiments were doing relatively basic jobs in a very different work environment. In modern, high-performance companies such as Motorola and Microsoft, the culture is internalised and supports creativity and a strong work ethic. This ethic is pervasive within the organisation and exerts strong pressure on individuals to conform to the high standards expected by the company. In such situations, the culture exerts much more effective control than any traditional methods.

High-performance culture attracts a certain type of individual who will conform and fit in. It also dictates the type of person that is selected by the organisation in recruitment drives. Training courses and socialisation reinforce this culture, not just in the initial training but throughout the person's career. People who do not fit in with the culture will, generally speaking, leave after a short period of time.

Internal Markets When examining the value chain, it was seen that an organisation consists of primary and secondary activities. It is a useful tool for examining the organisation from the perspective of costs and value creation. This was then extended to the value system. In both the value chain and the wider value system, linkages between the different activities was said to be a vital element. Each of these elements is involved in providing services to one another. In many organisations, there is a 'contracting out' of the goods and services that each unit needs from other units. In addition, these different units are often treated as profit centres.

For example, many foreign companies operating in Ireland use transfer pricing within the company to avail of the lower rate of corporation tax. This raises a few issues. First, there has to be a price agreed by the corporate headquarters for the internal transfer of goods or the provision of services to another unit. Secondly, there has to be an agreement about the quality of service that one unit provides for another. If the price is too high, or the quality of service is poor, then it will reflect on the receiving profit centre. Therefore, if that profit centre were to obtain the necessary supplies or services from outside the organisation, they could do so at a more favourable rate or service level. By agreeing prices and service quality, it overcomes this dilemma, and effectively imposes a level of control on each of the units of the organisation. Mobil, the multinational oil company, implements the Balanced Scorecard for its different business units and applies it to all of its shared service units.

These units sell their services to the main business units and get agreement from them on price and service levels provided (Kaplan and Norton, 2001:46).

Johnson *et al.* (2017) highlight certain limitations to internal markets. First, they can increase bargaining between different units of the organisation, taking management attention away from critical issues. Secondly, in drafting regulations to cover such transfers, it adds to the bureaucracy of the organisation. Finally, it can lead to dysfunctional competition between the units, thus destroying a collaborative culture in the organisation.

In addition to the control processes mentioned above, the way the organisation, and all of the units within the organisation, relate to one another is central to the success of the company. These were discussed in dealing with corporate strategy in **Chapter 7**. However, in the context of implementing strategy, these will have to be revisited to ensure the smooth functioning of the organisation.

CONCLUSION

It is worth recalling the quote from Alice in Wonderland when Alice asked the Cheshire Cat in which direction she should go, and the Cat advised her:

> "That depends a good deal on where you want to get to."

Just as it is vital for organisations to have a clear picture of where they want to go, it is equally important that they have the energy and determination to see the plan through. Up to this point it is exactly that – just a plan. To deliver on the strategic goals and objectives that were developed, the organisation must implement the strategies that were designed to reach those targets. Everybody must have a clear understanding of the plan in so far as it impacts on their particular work and how that work fits in with the team around them.

In many cases, it is not so much the nature of the plan that ensures success in the marketplace, but the professionalism in seeing it implemented. This point is well illustrated by Ryanair. There is no rocket science in what the company does to deliver such consistently high profits. There are many other airline companies that pursue a low-fares strategy. What separates Ryanair from the rest is the absolute determination in examining every aspect of its operations and cutting costs at every opportunity. It is in the implementation of its strategy that it is different.

In a competitive world, successful implementation plays a central role in how companies perform, and central to the implementation process are the people within the organisation. Throughout the company, there has to be a determination by all concerned to achieve excellence in what they do. With a flexible and creative approach, all obstacles can be overcome. The best form of control for implementing strategy is a high-performance culture that creates a desire in each member to do their best. The following quotation from Darwin Smith (Collins, 2001:20) sums it up:

> "I never stop trying to become qualified for the job."

SUMMARY

Implementation is the final stage of the four-stage process of strategy formulation and implementation. To implement strategy, the organisation must have all of the necessary resources and a well-motivated team. It requires very different **managerial skills** than the previous stages. The resources must be coupled with the appropriate competences to have the capability to deliver on the strategy, and it requires **leadership** and strong management. Each of the different sections of the organisation will have to interpret the strategic plan and develop their own functional and divisional plans to achieve those objectives. While each of these relates primarily to its own area, they must all be co-ordinated to achieve synergy.

People are the most important resource in an organisation – without them, nothing will happen. There are three different elements to this. The first is **leadership** – providing the right direction for the entire organisation. It creates the vision and the culture and lays down the ethical parameters for all other decisions that are made. It also plays an important part in motivating staff to implement the chosen strategy effectively.

Secondly, a strong **management team** is essential. Different managers will each bring their own set of skills and experience to the organisation, and it must be remembered that different strategies will require different managerial skills. Creating the right team applies to management and to employees and to how they work together.

Thirdly, great care must be taken in picking **employees** with an appropriate mix of skill and enthusiasm that will fit in with the prevailing culture. Every person will have their own strengths and weaknesses and it is important that in picking a team each member can play in the position for which they are best suited. Their skills must be constantly updated.

In most instances, considerable **finance** will be required to support strategy execution, and this has to be sourced and planned to cover both capital and operating costs. **Budgets** are both a planning tool in setting out what the expenditures and revenues are likely to be, and a control device to compare actual with planned expenditure.

The company will need to create a **marketing plan** to support the strategy. In addition to the overall master plan, each division will have to have its marketing plan tailored for its own specific markets.

Business intelligence systems play an essential element in supporting strategy and providing linkages between all the various elements of the company. Information technology has the ability to change the nature of the business strategically as well as operationally. **Data mining** allows companies to extract from their IT systems information about customer demand, as well as trends and connections in that demand. **Business models** map out how companies interact with their customers. There are certain limitations and risks that must be taken into account with regard to IT systems and ethical issues must be considered.

The **operations** element of strategy implementation will differ significantly from one organisation to another. Innovation, both in systems and products is vital, and the strategic capability of the organisation must be constantly upgraded. This is a slow and incremental process. Decisions must be made concerning the location of operations and whether they are conducted in-house or outsourced.

Policies and procedures provide top-down guidance on how the organisation does certain things and help align the actions and behaviour of company personnel with the strategy. Managers can use a number of tools to achieve operational excellence, including: **business process re-engineering, Six Sigma** and **total quality management**.

Project management techniques are often used as a means of implementing strategy. It is based on four core functions which involve managing: scope, time, cost and quality. In turn, these are supported by managing: HR, communications, risk and procurement. The project manager integrates all of these functions to deliver the project on time and within budget.

Direct control processes include strategic planning and performance targeting. A strategic planning process involves the setting of goals and objectives and detailing how these will be achieved, and entails tight managerial control. Performance targeting is an interlinked and forward-looking control process that balances four separate perspectives – financial, customer, internal and innovation.

Indirect control can be exercised by the culture of the organisation and internal markets. The culture can have an important impact on the performance of an organisation, particularly where staff are well trained and motivated. Internal markets provide measurable standards for the exchange of goods and services.

DISCUSSION QUESTIONS

1. Critically evaluate the role that people play in the implementation of strategy.
2. With reference to question 1 above, to what extent does leadership play an important part in the implementation process?
3. Distinguish between the various functional strategies and their importance in the overall strategy.
4. Discuss the role of information technology systems in implementing strategy.
5. Critically evaluate the part that total quality management plays in ensuring sound strategy execution.
6. Discuss the role of culture in supporting the implementation of strategy.

Leading Organisational Change

LEARNING OBJECTIVES

On completion of this chapter, you will be able to:

- Analyse the various forces of change affecting an organisation
- Distinguish between the different types of change in an organisation
- Analyse the reasons underlying resistance to change
- Develop a model of change suitable to an organisation

"Change is not made without inconvenience, even from worse to better."

Samuel Johnson

INTRODUCTION

The implementation of strategy involves translating the strategic plan into meaningful goals and objectives throughout the organisation. It is an iterative process that will involve much adjustment before it is successfully completed. One of the biggest challenges in implementing the strategy is that everything does not stay still while the strategy is being rolled out (which could take many months, even years). The world around us is constantly changing. Most of the time, the business environment is probably changing at a reasonably slow, incremental rate. On occasion, it can happen quite quickly, such as the meltdown in global financial markets in 2008, when some of the biggest names in the financial world went out of business or were taken over.

Such change provides a great challenge for managers. In some cases it may mean that strategic plans, which were so long in the making, now have to be abandoned (see **Chapter 1**). In other cases it will involve substantial changes to the plan. In the previous chapter, it was seen that people play a central role in the implementation process. It is axiomatic that in implementing organisational change, the people that make up the organisation will be fearful and resistant to that change taking place. Such fear is not restricted to the lower levels of the organisation, but can exist right up to the top. In implementing change, it is therefore necessary to overcome that fear.

This chapter will examine organisational change from a number of different perspectives. First, it will examine the internal and external factors that are forcing change and the importance of the organisation being able to respond accordingly. Secondly, it will explore the different types of change and how these can be recognised. Each type will present its own difficulties in how the organisation deals with it. Some change may have only a small impact on the organisation as it is incremental; other forms of change can radically alter the way the company operates, and all of these will impact on its culture. A number of different models of change will also be examined. In leading change, the senior managers must be aware of the type of change and be able to respond, taking into account the particular circumstances facing the organisation. There is no universal prescription and each set of circumstances will impact on the approach taken by the company in dealing with change. Just as there are many factors driving change, there can also be a number of people using different styles involved in implementing the change process. Approaches to each situation may also differ, depending on timing.

In many respects, this chapter is a summation of the entire process in that it involves feedback into the strategic plan, while making any appropriate adjustments that may be required. In other cases, leading change involves using an entirely different paradigm than was used before, as the circumstances have now radically altered, and the old order no longer applies.

Illustration 14.1: Ernest Shackleton – Leading Change

The expedition led by Irishman Ernest Shackleton to cross the Antarctic in 1914 is an incredible account of leadership as the expedition changed from its original vision of being the first to cross the Antarctic continent (in 1911, Norwegian explorer Roald Amundsen beat Scott in the race to the South Pole), to one of survival under horrendous conditions. Shackleton's ship, the *Endurance* became trapped in the ice and was eventually crushed. Shackleton led his men over the ice floes, dragging three lifeboats, until they got to the open seas and eventually reached Elephant Island. However, this was away from the main shipping routes and so there would be little hope of rescue. Shackleton believed that their best chance of survival would be to reach the whaling station at South Georgia Island – some 800 nautical miles away. Leaving most of the crew on the shelter of Elephant Island, Shackleton picked five men and together they made the incredible journey in an open lifeboat in probably the world's roughest ocean to South Georgia Island. He then had to set about rescuing the remaining men on Elephant Island.

While the nature of this expedition is without parallel in the business world, it demonstrates extraordinary leadership and human insight. It also demonstrates that, with the right leadership, people are capable of achieving incredible results. Following the global financial crisis in 2008, many companies faced existential crisis. Brexit will bring similar challenges in some industries. In all such cases, people in the organisation must be led. The story of Shackleton is one of inspiring leadership that brought men through unimaginable hardship over an incredibly long period of time. The crew of the *Endurance* displayed all the normal characteristics of a group of individuals, and no doubt fear was a common emotion. When their original vision was no longer viable, Shackleton created a new vision – returning safely to England. His immediate mission changed to one of survival and he achieved this through character, resolution and personal courage, that held his crew together and got them to buy-in to that vision. He achieved it not by authoritarian rule but by creating an environment that brought out the best in each individual. It illustrates what Kotter (2002) suggests, that change must be led not managed. Lao Tsu defined a great leader as one "who the people say: 'we did it ourselves'". In Shackleton's case, his men would disagree. They would all say it was the "Boss" who brought them home.

(See also the case study about Ernest Shackleton at the back of this book.)

FORCES OF CHANGE

There are many factors driving change in the business environment. These forces are largely external but there are also some internal forces that must be considered. The external forces include rapidly changing technology, market changes, and changes in demographics and society. Some of these forces impact on organisations over a long period of time. In other cases, their effect is much more short term. Every organisation must accept change as a given and managers have to develop the necessary skills to understand the forces of change that are operating in their industry, and how they react to such changes.

Technology

Throughout this textbook, the importance of innovation in products and processes has been stressed. Some companies such as 3M are synonymous with innovation. When technology changes, it will diffuse down and impact on all companies in that industry. In turn, each one will be forced to develop new products or risk losing valuable market share or eventually going out of business. The pace of technological change is happening at an ever-increasing rate, and companies can no longer rely on long periods of unrivalled dominance after introducing new products, no matter how innovative they may be. For that reason, 3M has a corporate goal that 40% of its profits must come from products that are less than three years old. This is done to ensure the company does not become complacent in an ever-changing world.

In manufacturing, technology has impacted on the type of products on offer and how those products are made. In terms of products, technology can cause small modifications or fundamental changes. In some instances, changes to products that have been around for a long period of time are evolutionary, such as a car company bringing out a new model. In other cases, it can represent a major shift in the nature of the product and how it is produced, such as the move from traditional film-based photography to digital photography. Technology has also altered the way products are made. Car manufacturing used to be a very labour-intensive industry (Henry Ford pioneered assembly-line production using Fredrick Taylor's principles of 'scientific management'), now car manufacture is largely undertaken by robotic tools and computerised systems, including computer-aided design (CAD) and computer-aided manufacturing (CAM). In addition, it was seen in the last chapter that the integration of the different parts of the value chain are heavily dependent on computerised systems, particularly for just-in-time production.

It was also seen that managers are dependent on information and communications technology to provide them with accurate and up-to-date information on which to base decisions. Management information systems and financial information systems are essential tools in both manufacturing and service industries. The use of technology has radically changed the manner in which organisations interact with their customers and the nature of business models. Kenny's bookshop was a traditional store in Galway city for generations. Like many businesses, they established an internet site to sell books, aimed particularly at the Irish–American market. In 2007, the company decided to close their traditional city-centre shop and concentrate exclusively on online sales. The move has been hugely successful in a business environment that is changing rapidly. This textbook contains many examples of companies from other industries – from airlines to banks – that have used technology to change they way they operate. In most instances, change involves reducing the cost of doing business. The use of technology can greatly increase productivity, and hence it can have a positive impact on costs.

Market Changes

Globalisation has radically altered markets and how they operate. Ireland has witnessed many company closures as costs here are uncompetitive in many industries compared to Asian countries. Global competition has radically altered markets that existed for decades, if not centuries. Countries like Japan moved from manufacturing cheap products of relatively poor quality, to high-quality products that now dominate many industries from cars to electrical consumer goods. While many Irish businesses have not been able to compete on cost grounds in industries such as footwear and clothing, other industries have been transformed and are competing very successfully on the world stage. Such global pressures have also brought about many mergers and acquisitions as companies need to acquire scale and skill sets in order to survive. Even those companies that remain small and are competing here at home have also changed radically as a result of globalisation. For every large multinational company operating in Ireland such as those in the computing or pharmaceutical industries, there are hundreds of small, indigenous companies that are supplying them with vital services. The quality of the output of these small companies has to be equal to the standard of the larger multinationals with which they do business.

Governments often intervene in the markets. This is particularly the case in providing an environment in which there is open competition, such as in the EU's single market. It has long been recognised that restricted markets are bad for the consumer (see **Illustration 11.3** above). In times past, many companies in this country were effective monopolies and gave a very poor service or at a very high cost. Industries such as telecoms and airlines have changed radically as a result of open markets. As the nature of markets change, customers' demands also change and so managers need to be aware of the nature of these changes and respond accordingly. As with all aspects of strategy, this necessitates keeping in close touch with your customers – and listening to them. The challenge is then to respond to those needs. Such response might vary from new products to entirely new business models. In recent times there has been a strong and growing focus on the impact of climate change, which will have a significant impact not just on how we consume products and live our lives, but will also impact on businesses in how they respond to such challenges. It will inevitably bring a much greater focus for companies on corporate social responsibility and the ethical approach they take to doing business (see **Chapter 4**).

Demographic and Sociological Changes

For decades, Irish people emigrated to Great Britain or the United States as there was no work for them at home. The sociological impact of such emigration is outside the scope of this textbook, suffice to say it had a devastating impact on Irish society. From 2015 onwards, many Irish people began to return, especially those who might have left just a few short years before, having gained valuable experience in high-tech industries abroad. For those who emigrated many years ago, and only came back in recent times, they returned to see changes in Irish society that they could never have imagined.

The population of Ireland is now higher than at any time since the 1870s (CSO, 2019). Growing affluence and increasing numbers have led to the rise of many new industries and services that simply did not exist before, such as crèches. The nature of the workforce in Ireland has also been radically altered, and some 12% of the working population are now foreign nationals. They have brought with them a variety of new skills and knowledge, but it has also meant challenges for businesses in how they are integrated into the workforce. The rate of change in technology in the workplace will also have a major impact on not just how people work, but also the type of work they do.

While the main focus of the factors outlined above are primarily external, many of them also impact on the organisation from within. This is particularly so with changes in societal factors. While human resource legislation will dictate issues such as the entitlements of employees in areas like health and safety or maternity leave, the expectations of employees have also changed dramatically and work practices that may have been considered acceptable in the past are no longer so. In the knowledge economy, people expect interesting and stimulating jobs and a management style that supports, rather than just controls, their efforts. Legislation cannot dictate employee satisfaction, but if management cannot respond to the legitimate demands of a changing workforce, they cannot hope to remain competitive.

TYPES OF CHANGE

There are many different types of change impacting on organisations. To deal with changing circumstances, it is necessary to understand the nature or type of change facing the organisation. This section will examine three models for analysing the types of change taking place in organisations:

- Balogun and Hope Hailey's matrix
- Generic typology of change
- Theory 'E' and Theory 'O'.

Balogun and Hope Hailey

Some theorists, such as Balogun and Hope Hailey (2008), categorise the nature of the change taking place, and the extent of its cultural impact on the organisation, in terms of a matrix. The problem in using such matrices is the difficulty in correctly identifying the nature of the change and placing it categorically in one box as opposed to another. It is often difficult for a manager to make this call during the process of change, whatever about identifying it in retrospect. However, understanding the type of change, and its likely impact on the organisation, particularly on its culture, is a crucial part of the process of responding effectively. Balogun and Hope Hailey define change along two dimensions. First, the **impact of change** varies from *adjustment*, which can be a substantial change but does not impact on the organisation's beliefs and values, to *transformation* – where there is a fundamental change in the organisation. The second dimension is the **speed of the change** – how quickly it is implemented. This varies from *gradual* to *immediate*.

There are four positions resulting from these two dimensions:

- **Adaptation** – this occurs gradually and does not impact on the organisation's culture in any significant way. For example, aid agencies are adapting to new demands in a gradual way, but it is important that they maintain their fundamental culture.
- **Evolution** – transformational change implemented in a gradual way, probably using several different phases. Oil companies, for example, are adapting quite significantly to environmental concerns, and are diversifying into alternative fuels, though this is happening slowly.
- **Reconstruction** – where the organisation responds quickly to major changes, but it does not impact on the culture in any significant way. For example, though many exporting organisations had to respond very quickly to the most recent recession by cutting costs, there was no immediate demand for a more fundamental change.
- **Revolution** – this change is immediate and has a profound impact on the organisation and its culture. In the aftermath of the global financial crisis when the Government had to receive a €64 billion bailout from the 'Troika', fundamental change was required throughout the public service.

These four positions are represented in **Figure 14.1** below.

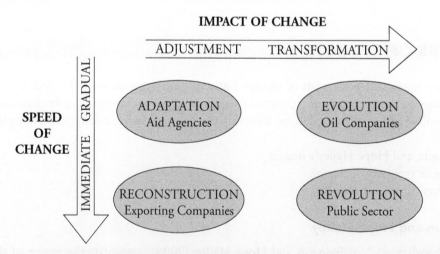

Source: Adapted from: Balogun, J. and Hope Hailey, U. (1999:21),
Exploring Strategic Change. Harlow, Prentice Hall

Figure 14.1 *Balogun and Hope Hailey Matrix*

Generic Typology of Change

In simple terms, a generic typology of change effectively describes parts of a continuum between minor, adaptive changes that happen very slowly, through the mid-way point of innovative change and on to radically innovative change that significantly alters the nature of the company (Nutt, 1986). As change moves along the continuum from adaptive to radically innovative, it will impact more and more on the degree of complexity, cost and uncertainty associated with that change. The potential for resistance to change will also move from low (for adaptive change), to high (for radically innovative change).

Theory 'E' and Theory 'O'

A third model, by Beer and Nohria (2000), examines how change is implemented in organisations. Theory E and Theory O are based on the context of change and use a range of assumptions. **Theory E** is based on the economic value of the change programme to the organisation and is a top-down approach. It is based on formal structures and systems being changed, and generally involves down-sizing and financial incentives. It is a planned approach to change and often involves outside consultants. Theory E is more suited when change needs to be focused in one direction. Business process re-engineering would fit this description.

Theory O on the other hand focuses on organisational capability and the development of culture through learning (both individual and organisational). This form of change is not planned and it is much more emergent. It is generally a slower process and involves considerable experimentation. It is more suited to situations that call for more sensitivity at local level as well as autonomy in how the process is handled.

Theory E and Theory O are different in their approach in terms of the goals being pursued, the leadership style, the focus of change, the actual process involved, the rewards system used to provide incentives, and the use of consultants in the process. Each one has its own advantages and disadvantages. Beer and Nohria suggest that the two theories should not be seen as dichotomous, but can be blended together to suit circumstances.

CHALLENGES TO UNDERSTANDING CHANGE

There are many challenges to understanding change. These challenges are complex and cannot be examined in isolation, as they are all interconnected. The factors affecting change examined at the beginning of this chapter act on an organisation in different ways. This happens at international, national and industry level. Against this background it has been suggested that it is vital for an organisation to carry out environmental analysis on a continual basis, and not as a once-off event before developing a new strategy (see **Chapter 5**). There are a number of issues that should be considered:

- Leadership
- Context
- Culture.

Leadership

In the previous section we examined the forces driving change. These forces are placing constant pressure on the organisation. The need for change must be recognised by those leading the organisation, and they must create a sense of realisation among staff for the need to adapt to new circumstances. Fitzroy and Hulbert (2005) suggest that the ability to lead the firm into new ways must become a core competence of the firm. Change must also be effected within an ethical framework.

The CEO must take a central role in both the design and implementation of the change process within the organisation, by either taking a lead in directing the change programme or indirectly through facilitating the process (Hayes, 2014). However, common to both will be the need for a clear vision as to the direction in which the organisation is going. There will be many factors driving change, but managers must ensure that the response to them is more strategic than operational. The vision, it must be remembered, is the long-term direction of the organisation and is underpinned by leadership, values and purpose. It is what guides the company through difficult times. From the vision, the mission evolves and then the goals and objectives. A company must keep a clear focus on what it is trying to achieve. As with all aspects of strategy, the CEO must lead by example, and personify the type of change being advocated.

While the vision remains constant, it may well be that the goals and objectives that were previously established are no longer relevant, particularly in the short term. Thus, new goals and objectives will therefore have to be set and communicated throughout the organisation. Leadership is particularly important in situations of post-acquisition integration, as there will inevitably be a large change programme in place. One of the big challenges in leading change is keeping that vision alive and giving people within the organisation a clear sense of direction – and hope.

Pettigrew and Whipp (1999) examined change in a variety of organisations in the UK on a longitudinal basis to see what constituted effective change in terms of organisational performance. They found that high performers led the change process. The managers in the companies that were examined conducted rigorous environmental analysis, linked strategic change and operational change, managed people in the organisation in terms of assets and liabilities (this is similar to the findings of Collins (2001)), and, finally, there was a coherence in the overall change process.

Miles (2010) suggests that change initiatives can often run into gridlock as different change projects are often launched with little or no strategic alignment. Senior executives need to select no more than three or four initiatives, each with just a couple of carefully selected areas of focus that are tied to clear outcome metrics. Fitzroy and Hulbert (2005) believe that a limited number of themes also make it easier to communicate the change process throughout the organisation. A Balanced Scorecard and, in particular, a strategy map (Kaplan and Norton, 2008), could be used for this purpose as it develops just a few specific themes, and then applies appropriate measures, targets, initiatives to achieve those targets, and necessary budgets to support those themes. This will allow the company to achieve more by concentrating resources where they are most needed.

In **Chapter 3**, the use of the Balance Scorecard was discussed in detail. **Figure 3.3** focused on three themes that were superimposed on the scorecard: operational excellence, customer service and customer relationship management (CRM). The third theme, CRM, was further developed in **Figure 3.4** and is reproduced here in **Figure 14.2**. It demonstrates how a particular theme that is driving change is supported by specific measures, targets, initiatives to achieve those targets, and the necessary budgeting allocation.

(Theme 3): Customer Relationship Management					
Perspective	**Strategy Map (Figure 3.3)**	**Measure**	**Target**	**Initiative**	**Budget**
Financial	Increase revenue and ROCE ↑	Revenue mix Revenue growth	New: + 10% Existing: + 25%		
Customer	Add and retain high value customers ↑	New customers Increase in repeat visits Longer stay	15% increase in new customers 10% increase in repeat visits (calendar year) 1 night extra per guest per visit	Marketing campaign Discount for extra night	€ __
Internal Processes	Create a comprehensive customer database to include detailed information about likes and dislikes ↑	Targeted marketing Improve process for customer feedback Develop integrated database	Complete database of all customers c/w personal preferences, interests, etc.	Data mining Social media Email/write to targeted customers	€ __ € __
Innovation and Learning	Develop a capable and efficient workforce Develop customer-focused competences	Staff training Staff development	Certification awards Top rating for customer feedback Staff incentive scheme	Internal training External training Secondment/ posting to other hotels and resorts Profit sharing	€ __ € __ € __ € __

Figure 14.2 *Customer Relationship Management*

Context

Every organisation is different and the nature of change in the environment will impact on each company in various ways. Consequently, the response of the company will also differ. The nature of the change taking place must be examined in its context. Balogun and Hope Hailey (2008) provide a framework for examining this context under eight headings. Each of these factors needs to be considered before formulating a response. The contextual features are:

- **Time** – as mentioned above, the business environment in Ireland has changed substantially over 20 years. In most cases, industries have been able to deal with this in a gradual response. On other occasions, such as with the financial crisis, the response of many organisations in both the public and private sectors had to be immediate.
- **Scope** – how much change is required in terms of the breadth of change across the entire organisation or one particular part? This would also include changing the culture of the company.
- **Preservation** – the company must decide what it needs to preserve in its culture and traditions and what must change.
- **Diversity** – how diverse is the organisation in terms of geographical location and business types?
- **Capability** – is the organisation under its present management capable of making the required changes?
- **Capacity** – does the organisation have the resources needed?
- **Readiness** – how ready is the workforce for change?
- **Power** – does the CEO have sufficient power to execute the change process?

The context will vary considerably, depending on a wide range of factors, from the type of organisation under consideration to the particular environmental circumstances. Understanding the nature of the above factors and their relevance to the circumstances within which the company is operating is of central importance in deciding how to deal with the situation. Each situation will be different and, therefore, there is no specific formula to guide the process. It is a matter of judgement and interpretation.

In addition to the contextual features listed above, Buelens *et al.* (2011) suggest that change in an organisation should also be studied on a longitudinal basis. This should examine previous instances of change, such as mergers and acquisitions, or other events where change would have taken place, as this will give some indication as to how future change might be handled.

Culture

The different aspects of the context discussed above must be considered in managing change. In addition, they must be understood in terms of the culture of the organisation, which forms a backdrop to the change process. Johnson *et al.* (2017:175) recommend the use of a 'cultural web' to analyse the nature of an organisation's culture. Evaluating the culture of an organisation will give managers or those attempting to effect change a better understanding of the type of change needed and how successful it is likely to be. The cultural web examines the organisation under a number of different headings, including symbols, power structures, operational structures, control systems, rituals, routines and stories. No one of these will give an accurate picture, but taken together they will provide a good appreciation of the type of prevailing culture.

It will be recalled from **Chapter 2** that the culture of an organisation has a profound impact on its strategy, and that changing a culture is a slow and difficult process. Nonetheless, there are times when cultural change is an imperative. Miles (2010) outlines a number of cultural challenges that may derail transformation processes. A cautious management culture may hold the organisation back when change is badly needed. All senior executives need to confront reality and agree on ground rules for tackling the problems they face. There may be other managers who are aware of the issues, but who do not want to come on board, or who are incapable of performing within the parameters of the change programme. Miles recommends that these executives are quickly confronted so that they do not undermine the transformation. Dealing with these individuals can send a powerful message to others in the organisation. It is equally important to confront disengaged employees. While employee training and development can play an important role in facilitating change, this must be preceded with a "rapid, high-engagement, all-employee cascade" where the importance of the change is defined with clear objectives, and a clear line of responsibility is established throughout the entire organisation. Then, when managers and employees are engaged, staff will be better motivated to adapt and take on board the necessary changes, and training will be more effective.

Throughout the change process, people play a central role. There are many different facets to change but yet most corporate turnaround situations focus on cutting costs – the 'bottom line'. Hassan (2006) believes that cost cutting is not always the answer and that change should be led from the 'top line'. This involves creating a motivated and respected sales force that will increase revenues from sales and develop the right kind of customer relationships. In turn, Hassan believes that focusing on people will have a quicker positive response for the company.

RESISTANCE TO CHANGE

In the discussion above, it was stated that there will be differing levels of resistance to change. An important element of the process of conducting change is to understand and manage this resistance.

> "To be worst, The lowest and most dejected thing of fortune, stands still in esperance, lives not in fear: The lamentable change is from the best; the worst returns to laughter."
>
> *King Lear*, Act 4, Sc.1

Why People are Resistant to Change

People are creatures of habit. Habit gives people a sense of security and confidence, and enables them to cope with life. Anything that will change everyday habits is going to be difficult for employees and managers as they attempt to get to grips with new circumstances. The organisational structure with which they are familiar gives them a sense of security that enables them to deal with the complexities of their job. This security can also lead to inertia when change is needed to cope with different market challenges. In most cases, people take comfort in the familiar, and there is a fear of the unknown. There are many reasons for resistance to change:

- Will their job still exist or will it be replaced by artificial intelligence? This has happened in many industries as more and more automation is introduced. Even if their jobs are secure, it could result in changes in work practices and substantial changes in productivity.
- Will they still be working with the same group of people? As people get older, they often find it more difficult to get to know new groups of people and there may be personality clashes. The Hawthorne experiments demonstrated the moderating effect of peer pressure, and while some individuals may be happy to go along with change, pressure from colleagues may prevent them from giving their support. Changing group structures will impact on the cultural dynamics at play in that group. When new members join, there can be a strong distrust of them.
- If new technology is being introduced, will employees be able to develop the necessary expertise to use it, particularly if adequate training is not provided? Many employees will have a fear of failure that they will not be able to make the transition.
- What is their perception of the change taking place and the reason for that change? There is often a mistrust of management's intentions and the rationale for making the changes. This is often accompanied by poor communication, and the grapevine takes over. The absence of accurate information will fuel employees' fears. It is imperative that managers take appropriate measures to keep people properly informed.
- Is the change affecting the entire organisation or just one part, and how will it affect how the different parts of the organisation link together? Understanding new systems will take time and effort. There may also be a fear that the necessary resources will not be provided to make the transition.
- When change is introduced, it is inevitably going to affect the power balances between different groups. This often impacts on the availability or call on resources by certain groups. These power structures may well prove a formidable force to implementing change.

There are many reasons for fear and these usually occur in various combinations. Managers must understand these reasons and the strength of these reasons before overcoming such resistance. **Forcefield analysis** (Lewin, 1951) is one method for understanding the forces operating in an organisation that support change and those resisting it.

Forcefield Analysis

In every situation, there will be factors pushing change and factors operating against it, and at any one point in time there will be a semi-permanent equilibrium between the opposing factors. The factors that impact in a positive way on change are obviously of great importance to managers. In all cases they must be recognised, and in some cases they may need to be strengthened. Likewise, managers need to be aware of the factors operating against change. Forewarned is forearmed, and managers can take appropriate measures to ensure that any resistance to change is either removed or at least lessened. Forcefield analysis is somewhat similar to stakeholder mapping, which was discussed in **Chapter 2**. The main difference between stakeholder mapping and forcefield analysis is that stakeholder mapping is looking at strategy in the context of people and the amount of power and interest they have in a particular strategy. Forcefield analysis involves listing all of the factors, not just people, that must be considered. It provides a list of these factors, but does not necessarily rank them or measure their impact.

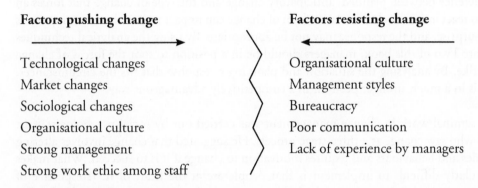

Factors pushing change

Technological changes
Market changes
Sociological changes
Organisational culture
Strong management
Strong work ethic among staff

Factors resisting change

Organisational culture
Management styles
Bureaucracy
Poor communication
Lack of experience by managers

Figure 14.3 *Forcefield Analysis*

Managers will have to form a judgement on each of the items listed above. Any one item could be a significant factor either supporting change or operating against it. In the above example, culture can either be pushing such change or resisting it. It is particularly important that managers understand each of these factors, as overcoming resistance is essential in the programme for change.

Manifestations of Resistance

Managers must be cognisant of the way resistance can manifest itself. Resistance to change can vary quite significantly, depending on the situation, the people involved, the organisation, industry and many other factors. A necessary part of the process of dealing with resistance is being able to judge its strength. Judson (1991) suggests resistance can be measured on a continuum, from acceptance, indifference, passive resistance, to active resistance. Each one of these divisions has several degrees, e.g. enthusiasm at the top of acceptance, to deliberate sabotage at the extreme of active resistance. The response by managers will obviously differ quite significantly, depending on the level of resistance encountered. Employees showing different forms of acceptance such as co-operation, or even passive resignation, will make the change process easier. On the other hand, those showing active resistance, such as doing as little as possible or deliberately working against the process, will make the task extremely difficult. There are a number of strategies for overcoming resistance to change, and these will be looked at below in the context of implementing a strategic change model.

It is important to note that while many people will be resistant to change, there are others who are quietly embracing change. Change is usually seen as a top-down process, but Pascale and Sternin (2005) remind us there are often people in organisations who are good at finding a way around problems and constantly looking at better ways of doing things. Managers must recognise that these employees can make a major contribution to the change process and their ideas should be infused into the corporate consciousness, and leveraged throughout the organisation.

Lewin's Change Model

There is a difference between planned, anticipatory change and the type of change that forces an organisation to react immediately. The latter form of change can impact negatively on a company as it is taken by surprise, and the response may not be appropriate. By using the analytical techniques outlined in Part Two of this book, managers should be in a position to spot the forces of change before they strike. By analysing the situation and planning a response that fits the circumstances, the company is in a much stronger position in a competitively advantageous way.

Much of the seminal work in change management was carried out by social psychologist Kurt Lewin (1951) who saw change as a three-stage process. He suggested that change involves altering current attitudes and behaviours and requires motivation to change if it is to succeed. What makes change particularly difficult to implement is that people are at the heart of it. Irrespective of whatever changes are made to structures and other factors, people have to change. Even when people recognise the need for change and perhaps welcome it, it is still a difficult process to overcome fear and natural resistance. The three stages are:

- **Unfreezing** – Managers need to create the motivation and urgency in staff to change their old behaviours and attitudes and embrace new ones.
- **Changing** – Having recognised the need for change, managers then need to move the organisation to the point where change begins to take place.
- **Refreezing** – Once all the necessary change has taken place, the final phase is refreezing. This is a critical part of the process and involves reinforcing the new behaviour so that it now becomes the accepted norm.

Lewin's model is criticised for not considering the range of factors that impact on the process from outside the organisation. However, like all seminal models, it forms the basis of other and more recent models of organisational change that take into consideration the relevant outside factors, as well as what the company actually needs to do in order to implement the change programme successfully.

STRATEGIC CHANGE MODEL: AN INTEGRATED APPROACH

Lewin's change model provides a basic linear framework for change, which views the process as being controlled entirely by the organisation's management, where the end state is always clear. However, clearly the change process is much more complex and iterative, and one that requires an integration of internal and external factors that are constantly evolving. The strategic change model presented here is a synthesis of a number of different theories of change, including those of

Kotter (2007), Hayes (2014) and Lynch (2018). This involves five main, interconnected **phases**, all of which are underpinned by leadership, communication and learning.

Leadership

The CEO plays a central role in the process of change and is ultimately responsible for the success of the organisation. He or she needs to provide a vision and the necessary clarity about how the organisation is going to achieve its goals. However, they may not be directly involved in the day-to-day implementation of the change. It should be remembered that the organisation must continue with the normal daily routines in meeting customers' needs as the change process is rolled out. For that reason, CEOs may well appoint senior executives as **change agents**, while they continue to run the company as normal. A change agent is either an individual or a group responsible for implementing change. As discussed below, middle managers also play a central role, but they must be empowered by senior managers to carry out their function. In turn, middle managers must accept responsibility for the decisions that they are enabled to make and not engage in 'upward delegation', where senior managers are then overburdened with routine decisions that should properly be dealt with at a lower level (Central Bank of Ireland, 2018).

Ultimately, the success of any change programme lies with the willingness of the staff to embrace change. If they resolutely refuse to support the change, the chances of success are greatly diminished. For that reason, it is imperative that change is led rather than managed (Kotter, 2007). Leadership is needed to kick-start the change process, but it must also be present throughout every phase. Leadership must ensure clear communication and also that appropriate learning takes place. In addition, when change has been implemented, leaders must ensure that the change that has already taken place is consolidated throughout the organisation and that it is embedded in the culture until such time further change is needed in the future, which inevitably will happen.

Communication

Irrespective of the type of change involved, clear and regular communication with all stakeholders is essential. Overcoming any resistance to change is an integral part of any change programme and without full information, stakeholders – employees in particular – are likely to react in a negative way. Bringing people on side will only happen when they have full, accurate and timely information. Communication is an essential component for building trust and, in turn, trust is a vital part of leading change (see **Chapter 2**). Even when the situation appears bleak, trust is built when managers are honest and upfront. People can accept tough decisions once managers keep them informed and give them the right information at the right time (CIPD, 2011). These lines of communication must be there from the beginning to the very end of the process.

Learning

The nature of change will vary from one situation to another, but change as a process will happen time and time again within an organisation. It is therefore imperative that leaders reflect on their experience and apply that learning to improve performance each time they are involved in change. If change occurs as a discreet project, e.g. implementing a major IT system, then there will be a major review at the end of the project as managers monitor the results (see Phase Five below). Learning must also take place during and at the end of each phase of the project.

At the start of the process it is vital to identify the need and type of change required. Obviously, any weaknesses here will need to be rectified immediately because if managers misdiagnose the need for change, and the type of change required, then it follows that the measures they will subsequently take in the change process will not be successful. Similarly, effective communication is an essential element of the process throughout, but quite often the communication plan may not be succeeding in its objectives. Again, that is something that needs to be rectified immediately, rather than waiting until the end. An analogy can be drawn to a cash business where the cash is reconciled each day: it is not left to the end of the year to discover there has been a continuous haemorrhage of funds.

A distinction needs to be drawn between what Argyris and Schön (1978) refer to as "single-loop" and "double-loop" learning. Single-loop learning is the detection and correction of mistakes in the existing system. If the system itself is properly designed but is not being implemented as intended, single-loop learning will work. Often, however, fresh thinking is required to recognise and deal with change and this is where double-loop learning comes in. Questioning the assumptions that guided the action in the first place is often required to develop a complete understanding of the situation.

"The significant problems we face cannot be solved at the same level of thinking we were at when we created them."

Albert Einstein

THE FIVE PHASES OF STRATEGIC CHANGE

Implementing major, strategic change is a long and complicated process, and one the organisation must get right. The following framework provides a comprehensive five-stage process that will assist managers in implementing organisational change. These headings will then be developed in detail below. It will be seen in **Figure 14.4** below that the five phases of change are supported by leadership, communication and learning.

Phase One – Identifying the Need for Change

- Identification of the forces of change impacting on the organisation
- Creating a readiness.

Phase Two – Diagnosing What Needs to Change

- Identifying the type of change required
- Assessing opportunities and barriers
- Understanding the levels of resistance.

Phase Three – Planning for Change

- Choice of strategy – 'push or pull'
- How the goals will be achieved – appropriate managerial styles
- A blueprint for change or an open-ended, iterative process
- Planning resources
- Planning the phases and timing.

Phase Four – Implementing the Change Programme

- Action
- Symbolic processes
- Change agents.

Phase Five – Monitoring Results and Sustaining the Change

- Monitoring the results of the change programme and making necessary changes
- Ensuring the process is sustained until the change is embedded.

These five phases are presented graphically in **Figure 14.4** below. Leadership (and communication) initiate the change process, as represented by the large arrow to the left, and they also support the entire change process right up to the end. Leadership and communication are a two-way process and not just top-down, as depicted by the two-way arrows. A lot of the learning from the change process will take place at the end, and must be fed back in to the organisation's overall learning, but in addition, each stage of the change process must be evaluated and lessons learned before proceeding to the next phase. This is also illustrated by the two-way arrows. The overall change process is not necessarily a neat sequential process, but iterative.

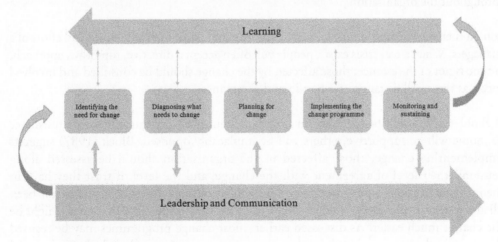

Source: Adapted from Hayes (2014:27)

Figure 14.4 *The Change Process*

Phase One – Identifying the Need for Change

Identification of the Forces of Change Impacting on the Organisation In any industry, there are many drivers of change. These are primarily external forces over which managers have little or no control (though, clearly, this does not mean that such forces may not have a significant impact on the business). This chapter has already examined how technology has radically changed many industries and the way companies interact with their customers and suppliers. Combined with changes in global markets and demographic changes, the nature of the business environment is constantly changing. Sometimes the nature of these environmental changes are easily identified; on other occasions, they fall into the category of what Donald Rumsted described as the 'unknown unknowns', where executives aren't even aware that change is taking place, let alone understand the exact nature of that change.

Chapter 5 dealt with the subject of monitoring the external environment. Such monitoring is not a one-off event. It is imperative that managers constantly examine the environment in which they operate and identify both the trends as well as the events that are taking place. Managers must also be mindful of the changes taking place within their organisations. For example, reductions in productivity or quality with corresponding drops in sales are indicators that all is not well.

Creating a Readiness for Change Leaders must create a readiness for change within the organisation and motivate people to work outside their comfort zones. If there is a crisis, the need for change can be clear to all. More often, however, it may not be so obvious and people will tend to be content with the status quo. In such situations it will require a great deal of effort to begin the change process as there is likely to be considerable resistance, ranging from passive resistance to outright opposition. Kotter (2007) suggests that senior executives create a sense of urgency within the organisation about starting the change process, and that they form what he termed a "powerful guiding coalition" of like-minded managers who will work together to drive the necessary change process throughout the organisation.

One person on their own is most unlikely to effect any change – it requires a co-ordinated effort of a team of managers. When a real crisis exists, people will often accept a directive, top-down approach, but when time is not of the essence, those affected by the change should be consulted and involved in the process as there will be far greater buy-in and acceptance.

Each stakeholder group will be different in terms of their level of commitment or resistance to change. Some will be supportive, others will be implacably opposed. Block (1987) suggests that in implementing change, those affected in the organisation should be assessed along two dimensions: their level of agreement with the change, and the level of trust they have in management. Trust is a long-term investment and will be difficult to create if it has not been present all along. If trust is present, it will make the process of winning over those who might be against the change much easier. As discussed earlier, most change programmes may be resisted initially by those in the organisation, but when the programme is properly led, the majority of employees will be won over in time. Not everyone will be convinced, but the change process is likely to succeed once the majority are on side (Olivier, 2013). Therefore, much effort could be wasted in targeting the wrong individuals who will be against the change no matter what is done. Such people may have to have the necessary change imposed upon them, or they may decide to leave the organisation.

According to Buelens *et al.* (2006) there are four factors that must be borne in mind when attempting to overcome resistance to change:

1. People's emotional evaluation of change is more important than their cognitive evaluation. This is why Kotter (2007) suggests that change must be led rather than managed.
2. Change is less successful when management fail to keep employees properly informed about the process.
3. People do not always resist change consciously. Managers should use a systems method of change which maps out the process and how it will impact on the organisation.
4. Employees' perceptions affect their resistance. They are less likely to oppose change if they perceive that the benefits outweigh the personal costs. Whatever benefits there are from the change process must be clearly communicated, early and often.

Any change programme is likely to disrupt the political power structures in an organisation. Management should use this opportunity to assess the situation and strengthen the official, formal structures that will support the change process, and will also weaken the informal power bases that may be opposing the change (power was discussed in detail in **Chapter 2**). This will reduce any negative influence on the rollout of strategy and may prevent similar situations arising in the future. The use of resources can assist senior managers in the re-alignment of power. Diverting necessary resources to a particular group will greatly strengthen their position, and likewise, removing resources can weaken their power base. Thompson *et al.* (2017) point out that there will often be 'casualties' and some people may leave the organisation because they are unhappy with the changes. Support should be provided for those who will be affected by change (Hayes, 2014).

Phase Two – Diagnosing What Needs to Change

Understanding the Type of Change As discussed above, the type of strategic change involved can vary quite significantly and, as a result, managers need to understand the nature of the change taking place. In some instances, change can be so incremental it can almost be imperceptible. Referred to in **Chapter 1** as 'strategic drift', this type of change is often very difficult to identify and companies tend to continue to operate as normal, seemingly oblivious of the gap that is appearing between their strategy and the environment in which they operate. Once strategic drift has been recognised by an organisation, it will require a significant change programme to realign its strategy with changes in the business environment (see **Chapter 1**). Occasionally, this realignment will be so significant that it will result in a major turnaround strategy being implemented. On the other hand, some companies make continual incremental adjustments, which keep them constantly aligned with market changes.

Current Assessment Throughout any strategic change process, senior managers must ensure that all objectives are in line with the values and purpose of the company. Along with the managerial tools used to evaluate the business environment (see **Chapter 5**), a focus on the organisation's values will enable managers to understand the current context and also to identify the main problems currently facing the organisation. In turn, this assessment will hopefully shed light on the direction the organisation needs to travel in order to overcome current problems, i.e. identifying the future state as discussed in **Chapter 3**. The assessment should be realistic and convincing in order to overcome likely levels of resistance within the organisation.

Phase Three – Planning for Change

'Push or Pull' Strategy Before embarking on change, managers must plan on how best to achieve their goals, and this will need to be communicated to all concerned. The first consideration here is whether to choose a 'push' strategy (top-down) or a 'pull' strategy where there is a high level of stakeholder involvement (see **Chapter 4**), or a blend of both. The type chosen will depend very much on the particular circumstances and the time frame involved.

Leadership Style It has been argued throughout this textbook that leadership is an essential requirement in developing and implementing strategy, and particularly so in leading organisational change. There are many different types of leadership styles that could potentially be used and each style will achieve a different result. **Figure 14.5** below is a summary of different leadership styles that may be used in the change process within the organisation.

	Style	Description
High	**Coercion**	Using power to force change through in the organisation. May be imperative in a crisis situation, but unlikely to get much support.
	Direction	Clear focus on what needs to be done. Change is still forced by senior management, but there may be some concessions with regard to the approach taken.
Degree of Control	**Participation**	There is some move towards involving staff in putting forward ideas, but managers still retain overall control of the direction that the change is taking. It is likely to build some element of support.
	Collaboration	Widespread involvement of employees throughout the organisation about the direction and methods of change. This takes much more time, however, and there is little control over the eventual outcome, though there is likely to be widespread acceptance by staff members.
Low	**Education**	Here the objective is to meet with small groups of people and convince them of the need to change, and gain their commitment. Staff members will then have the authority to effect change. Very time-consuming.

Source: Adapted from Balogun and Hope Hailey (1999)

Figure 14.5 *Styles of Leadership in Change Programmes*

The styles of leadership outlined above will often reflect the preferred leadership style of the CEO rather than what is necessarily the most suitable one. Different styles will also have more relevance at different stages of the change process. In the initial stage, clear direction might be needed to impress upon employees that change is required, and then it can switch to a more collaborative style in order to win support and engagement. Time is a critical issue in deciding. If the organisation is facing a crisis, there will not be time to engage in a long, consultative process when clear intervention is needed.

The staff profile in an organisation is another consideration that will have a bearing on the chosen leadership style. Highly trained professional staff will want to be central to the process and are likely to react strongly to any change being forced upon them. Likewise, if there is a strong union, a good deal of consultation and engagement will be required. Most organisations deal with a wide variety of stakeholders, and each group will require a different approach regarding any change. Therefore, the styles outlined above are not mutually exclusive and often a combination of styles will be used. The 2018 Central Bank of Ireland report, *Behaviour and Culture of the Irish Retail Banks,* is particularly critical of what it terms the banks' directive, "command and control" leadership style during the financial crisis and recommends placing an emphasis on "inclusive and collaborative leadership styles, aimed at integrating as many people and perspectives as possible" (Central Bank of Ireland, 2018:4).

Detailed Plan Where possible, managers should develop a detailed blueprint of the entire change process. This will guide all stakeholders in relation to all aspects of the plan and the timeframe involved. Such a blueprint is possible where there is a clear end-point to be reached and all the stages can be easily mapped, e.g. integration of an acquired company. However, the nature and complexity of the change involved may not facilitate such a planned approach of what needs to be done and how it should be achieved. In such cases, the process is evolving and iterative, and managers need to be flexible.

The timelines of the different phases of the process need to be defined. With planned change this will be relatively straightforward. Where there is greater uncertainty, the phases will not be as clear, but managers should still endeavour to map each of the phases involved, even if only rough timelines are available. One way or another, people need to have an understanding of how the process will unfold.

Resources Change will also require resources. In a turnaround situation, the main emphasis might be on reducing costs and saving resources. However, in many cases, an upfront investment may be needed in order to achieve the planned benefits. In particular, human resources need to be planned for in regard to expertise and number and people, particularly the main change agents. Middle managers are also central to the process. According to the CIPD (2011), middle managers are both transformers and translators who have an enormous value-adding capacity, but all too often senior management will by-pass middle management in times of change. Managers need to become comfortable with uncertainty and, through coaching, make staff comfortable also.

Phase Four – Implementing the Change Programme

Action The change process must be planned, but as with all aspects of strategy, success will only come when those plans are put into action. This requires leadership and effective communication. As the plan is rolled out, managers must ensure not only that the plan is still on track, but also that it makes sense. The assumptions on which the plan was based should be constantly challenged to ensure they still hold up to scrutiny.

Leading People The implementation of strategic change will inevitably cause significant operational changes in the organisation. In some cases, it may result in redundancies and this will have a negative effect on staff morale. Managers must be very clear about the importance of leading throughout the process, which requires the difficult task of motivating those that may not see the benefits of the change process.

Symbolism Symbolism, i.e. the use of symbols to represent ideas or qualities about an organisation, can play a significant part in changing an organisation, particularly where the culture of that organisation is also changing. Symbols such as company brands and logos can transmit important messages about the organisation and how it perceives the world around it. Any changes made to an organisation's symbols can help refocus the beliefs and expectations of its stakeholders, e.g. staff, customers, etc. For example, if as part of the implementation of a strategic change process the staff dress code is changed, while this will not in itself change work practices, and in isolation would be purely a cosmetic exercise, as part of a wider programme it would help signify the importance of the change taking place (see **Chapter 2**, **Illustration 2.3**).

One very powerful symbolic message that can be sent to employees is where certain staff members who are openly opposed to the change programme are transferred to other appointments or resign. Other staff members then see that the change is going to happen, one way or another. It is imperative, however, that senior managers lead by example, and are seen to share the impact of change.

Changing Routines Day-to-day organisational routines, along with policies and prodcedures, will also have to be changed to reflect the new circumstances. This should be a bottom-up as well as a top-down process, as staff will have constructive ideas as to how these work routines and processes can be made more efficient. There are many changes to organisational routines that can be made, starting with the recruitment and selection process, and also in requiring staff members to undergo certain training programmes, such as cultural awareness. Changes in the criteria used for promotion can also clearly communicate the model of behaviour that the organisation requires from staff.

Phase Five – Monitoring the Results and Sustaining Change

Monitoring In a change situation, it is likely that the environment will be turbulent and the change process will be iterative, rather than sequential and linear. As a result, management will need to be flexible in implementing change plans. This applies not only to achieving the goals and objectives that were set, but also requires managers to constantly assess whether they have analysed the situation correctly and whether those goals were realistic. In other situations there may be no clear path for the change process because of uncertainty in the markets. In all cases, results and performance must be constantly monitored throughout the change process and all necessary changes and adjustments made.

Leadership and Process Management Again, leadership is an essential part of the process. The plan may not be working properly because it was not properly developed, or it may be because there is little commitment by staff to implementing it. Managers need to ensure there is close alignment with incentives/rewards available to staff and the desired behaviour, and action needs to be taken if people are deliberately not conforming to the change process.

Managers must also listen to the feedback from staff, who are people 'at the coal face' and know what is working and what is not. There may be goodwill among staff members for making the necessary changes, but they may also be frustrated by a lack of communication from management or they may not have been given the resources necessary to carry out the required work. Implementing change will also require managers to choreograph the different phases and elements of each phase. If this co-ordination is found wanting, it will undermine the whole programme. Such frustration will not only impede progress, but it will also destroy trust – a vital ingredient in running any organisation whether undergoing change or not. In its report on banking culture, the Central Bank had an interesting observation:

> "The crisis has shown that one of its causes was not so much that governance structures were inadequate, but that board and management behaviour within those structures was below standard. After all, it is the people who determine a company's performance."
>
> Central Bank of Ireland (2018:14)

The change process must, in the first instance, be properly led and managed by those at the top. Employees must have confidence that those who are directing change have the competence to do so, as well as being committed to the best interests of the company.

Sustaining Change As we saw in the discussion above about Lewin's change model, the third stage was 're-freezing'. At first glance, this appears to suggest the need to cement the changes that have taken place, but Lewin was aware that change is never permanent and further change may be necessary after a short timeframe. That is why Kotter (2007) suggests that management should not declare victory too soon as it may be premature. However, Kotter also suggests that where important changes have been made, these must be embedded in the culture of the organisation. To support cultural change and keep the momentum, managers need to be able to demonstrate to employees the benefits that have accrued to date, while also maintaining the momentum for further changes. For that reason, continuity of management is important. New managers coming in to replace those who have moved on often bring their own agenda, which may well undermine work done to date (Hayes, 2014).

CONCLUSION

Nothing remains the same for very long. Every organisation will, over a period of time, adapt to changing circumstances, or else it will go out of business. Change is all around us and, as managers, we must learn to accept and deal with it.

The whole process of strategic management as outlined in this textbook is set against a background of changing circumstances. Managers must be aware of these changes and constantly assess their environment to examine what changes must be made. It was stated in the definition of corporate strategy that it was the long-term direction of a company. Therefore, there can be a time lag between the formulation of a strategic plan, and its rollout. During that time, events can impact on the validity of the plan which may cause it to be abandoned or altered significantly. That is ultimately a judgement call by management. Either way, adjustments to the original plan will have to be made.

Implementing change requires a broad range of management skills, and, most of all, it requires the ability to work with people and help them overcome their fears. By overcoming such fears, managers will remove many of the obstacles that might otherwise impede the successful implementation of the change strategy.

SUMMARY

One of the biggest challenges in implementing the strategy is that everything does not stay still while the strategy is being rolled out. Leading change is therefore an integral part of running any organisation. This chapter examined organisational change from a number of different perspectives.

There are many external and internal factors that drive change. External forces include rapidly changing technology, particularly information and communication technology; globalisation and the effect of market changes; and changes in demographics and society, both internationally and at home. In order to be able to deal with changing circumstances, it is necessary to understand the nature or type of change facing a company.

Three different models for analysing the types of change were examined:

- Balogun and Hope Hailey's matrix, which looks at the type of change and its impact on the culture of an organisation.
- Generic typology of change, which measures change along a continuum, from adaptive change to innovative change to radically innovative change. The level of complexity, risk and potential resistance increases as it moves along the scale to radically innovative change.

- Theory E is based on the economic value of the change programme to the organisation and is a top-down approach. Theory O focuses on organisational capability and development of culture through learning.

There are many challenges to understanding change which are complex and interconnected. These include the organisation's vision, creating a link between change and the outcomes, the context surrounding the change, including the timeframe, scope, preserving aspects of the organisation, the diversity of the organisation, its capacity and readiness for change, and the power of the change agents. The culture also needs to be understood.

An important element of the process of conducting change is to understand and manage the resistance to change. **Forcefield analysis** is one method for understanding the forces operating in an organisation that support change and those resisting it. **Resistance** to change can vary quite significantly, depending on the particular situation, the people involved, the organisation, the industry and many other factors. Resistance can be measured on a continuum, from acceptance, indifference, passive resistance, to active resistance. The response by managers will obviously differ quite significantly, depending on the level of resistance encountered.

Kurt Lewin saw change as a three-stage process: unfreezing – creating the motivation to change; changing the process; and refreezing – embedding the changes in the culture of the organisation.

A strategic change model is underpinned by leadership and communication and has the following elements:

Phase One – Identifying the need for change and creating a sense of readiness within the organisation for such change.
Phase Two – Diagnosing what needs to change and the level of possible resistance to that change.
Phase Three – Planning the change strategy – appropriate managerial styles, resources and timing.
Phase Four – Implementing the change process.
Phase Five – Monitoring results and sustaining the change.

Every change situation is different, so the response must be tailored to the exact circumstances. If the change is **adaptive**, the organisation has the time to assess the situation and experiment with different approaches. **Radically innovative** change presents very difficult challenges for managers. Time is of the essence in responding to a crisis situation. One major factor that will obviously differ in each situation is the likely level of resistance. There are different strategies for dealing with resistance, including education, collaboration, intervention, direction and coercion. Symbolism can play a significant part in changing an organisation, particularly where the culture of the organisation is also changing. The day-to-day routines will also have to be changed to reflect the new circumstances. There are often a number of people – change agents – involved in the process, each with their own role to play.

The change process is designed to realign the organisation in response to changing circumstances. The future of the company could well depend on the success of the process. However, while it provides a framework, change doesn't always follow such a logical process.

DISCUSSION QUESTIONS

1. Differentiate between leading change and managing change in organisations.
2. Taking an industry of your choice, critically analyse the various forces of change impacting upon it.
3. Explore the various challenges that managers face in attempting to understand the nature of change impacting upon their organisation.
4. Discuss the various reasons why employees in an organisation might be resistant to change.
5. Critically analyse the various elements required in a strategic change model.
6. Explore the different methods that managers might use in overcoming resistance to change.

Introduction: Case Study Analysis

Case studies are an important element in learning about corporate strategy. They illustrate the kind of problems that organisations actually face, and the strategic decisions that they make in the quest for survival and competitive advantage in the market place. The purpose of studying cases is to allow you to put yourself in the position of senior management and analyse all the factors that impact on the organisation in question and then consider or, in a class setting, debate the issues in order to come up with an appropriate response.

There is, of course, a marked difference between debating the issues raised in a case study and being in the position of a CEO having to make a decision in pressurised circumstances where full information may not always be available. While a poor answer in a case study might merit lower marks, poor decisions taken by managers can have enormous personal consequences, as well as shareholders who can lose life savings with plummeting share prices and staff members who may lose their jobs. This became very clear during the global financial crisis when so much wealth was destroyed by reckless decisions.

While case studies will not reproduce the same pressures of real-life situations, they can nevertheless provide you, as a student of corporate strategy, with the opportunity to develop your diagnostic and analytical skills. In analysing the case material and developing solutions, you can apply the range of strategic tools contained in this textbook. It is by applying these tools, and examining how they have been used that you can develop the managerial skills required to hold executive positions. You can also develop decision-making skills in honing your answer to specific questions about the cases within a limited timeframe, determining and then justifying an appropriate course of action or approach taken.

The case studies in this textbook involve a wide variety of companies and organisations, both large and small, and from different industries. In many situations, the problems or issues discussed might be on-going. When analysing a case, you should focus on the information provided in the case itself rather than trying to find the latest news about the company on the internet, etc.

Also, it is important to note that there is rarely a definitive answer to the problems presented in case studies. The decisions made by organisations can be examined in retrospect to see if they improved the situation or not. For some cases, the answer will be clear; for others, the answer may be open to debate. Strategy is not a precise science. What is important is that in the process of examining cases, you develop critical thinking skills and learn to articulate those views in writing and/or class debate. In reviewing your answer, you should seek to understand where your answer is strong and where it is weak. Gradually, your analytical skills will improve with each case studied. Eventually, you should be able to identify the issues in the case without being prompted by case questions provided by your lecturer.

As with other aspects of study, you will benefit most when you fully participate in the process. It will require a number of iterations before you fully understand the issues presented in the case. Each case is different, but a general approach can be applied to all. You may find the following useful:

- Briefly review the case to get a broad understanding of the problems facing the company. At this stage, do not concern yourself with the finer details.
- Now read the case in detail, reviewing any tables, graphs or financial information included. What are these telling you? Many students find using a highlighter useful to draw their attention to important detail. For maximum effect, use the highlighter sparingly.
- Re-read the case, analysing the strategic issues facing the organisation, making notes of the main points. In developing answers, you should be looking for information to be able to answer the following questions: who, what, where, when, why and how.
  Who are the main players?
  What are the problems facing the organisation, and what is their significance to the company?
  Where are they happening?
  When did these events happen – what was the time sequence?
  Why are they happening? Is it the result of previous action – or inaction?
  Finally, *how* is it happening?

There are a wide variety of strategic tools used throughout this textbook. Choose the appropriate tools and apply them to fully understand the implications of the situation for the company. Analyse the information in the tables, particularly the financial information. Use the financial ratios in **Table 6.1**, **Chapter 6** to analyse the figures and interpret their meaning. If it is a group case study, debate the issues among the group. Be able to justify your position, but be open to other opinions. Throughout this process you should be developing a clear understanding of the problems and their solutions.

When you receive questions relating to the case from your lecturer, you can begin preparing the answers based on the analysis that you have conducted. If the case is an in-class exam, care should be taken to answer all of the questions within the allotted time, paying particular attention to the breakdown of marks for the different questions. Support your answers with reference to the information contained in the case. Be objective in your analysis. Avoid using terms such as "In my opinion"; use statements such as: "the evidence in Figure 4 demonstrates…".

Develop recommendations for the company involved in the case. These recommendations should be based on your analysis of the information presented in the case and should be designed to improve the company's situation. These recommendations should be prioritised in terms of importance for the company and the timeframe involved. They should also be realistic in regard to the resources available to the company.

Finally, while case study analysis can be time consuming, the return for you in terms of your understanding of strategy is immense.

Case Study – Subject Matrix

The Case Study Subject Matrix provided on the following page illustrates the content of each of the various case studies. The column on the left lists the cases, and the row along the top identifies the various strategic themes as discussed in this textbook.

One asterix under a particular theme indicates that the case contains minor discussion on that point and two asterixes indicates that the case covers that theme in considerable detail.

The subject matrix will assist in choosing cases that demonstrate specific aspects of strategy.

There are 13 case studies, which are as follows:

- FenuHealth – Equine Health Products
- Glencore Plc
- The Move to Non-alcoholic Beer
- Fairfield Decom
- Primark
- Providence Resources
- Four Seasons Hotels and Resorts
- Information Technology in An Garda Síochána
- Independent News and Media
- Ryanair Holdings Plc
- CRH Plc
- The National Children's Hospital Project
- Ernest Shackleton – Leading Change

Case Study – Subject Matrix

Case Study	Strategy Formulation	Leadership	Culture Ethics	Business Environment	Capability	HRM	Corporate-level Strategy	Business-level Strategy	Product/Market Development	Strategy Methods	Implementation	Change
FenuHealth	*	**		**	*		*		**	*	*	
Glencore		**	**	**	*					**	*	
Non-alcoholic Beer				**	**		**	*	**		**	*
Fairfield Decom	*	**		**	*		**		**	**		**
Primark			**	*	**	**	**	**	**	**		
Providence Resources	*	*	*	**	*		**		**	**		
Four Seasons	*	**	**	**	**	**	**	**	**	**	**	
IT – Garda Síochána		**	**	*	*	**	**		*		*	**
INM		*		**	**	*	**	*	**	**		**
Ryanair	*	**	**	**	**	**	**		**	*	*	**
CRH	*	**	**	**	**	**	**		**	**	*	*
National Children's Hospital	*	*		*	**	**	**		*			
Ernest Shackleton	*	**	**	*	**	**					**	**

Legend: ** = Detailed discussion * = Minor discussion

FenuHealth – Equine Feed Products

The purpose of this short case study is to illustrate the challenges facing a new start-up company as it tries to get established and develop new products and markets. It also challenges stereotypes regarding the profiles of entrepreneurs.

FenuHealth was founded in 2015 by sisters Kate and Annie Madden from Summerhill, County Meath, who were then aged 14 and 13, respectively. The business was started as a result of a project they had entered in the BT Young Scientist Exhibition that year. The company makes eight variations of equine feed products in the form of powdered food supplements based on a blend of herbs, spices and various minerals, including calcium, magnesium, potassium and iron. The original recipe was first developed to help one of the sister's own horses to eat when it was sick, but soon discovered to have properties that could help deal with gastric ulcers in horses.[1] In order to substantiate the science behind their claims, the sisters have commissioned independent research, at a cost of €100,000.

The different variations of FenuHealth products are powdered food supplements that are sprinkled on horse feed and are designed to meet specific dietary equine needs. They are based on a range of natural ingredients to help reduce the acidity and quantity of gastric juices in a horse's digestive system. While humans produce stomach acid only when they eat, horses produce stomach acid all of the time. Unlike cows, the stomach of a horse is very small relative to its intestine, so it must eat small amounts, often. In the wild, horses are constantly grazing, and as they do so, they produce saliva which helps protect the lining of the stomach from the acid. However, the majority of horses are stabled, rather than grazing all day. As a result, these horses are constantly producing acid, but without the saliva to protect them. It is estimated that up to 50% of foals have stomach problems, while up to 90% of racehorses can suffer from the problem.

The products are 100% natural and are classified by the horseracing industry as feedstuff rather than as a medical product, which means they can be fed to horses just before races. Alternative products on the market may have to be withdrawn from feed up to five days before a race because they contain prohibited substances that would show up in equine drug tests. The disadvantage of taking a horse off these alternative products is that an ulcer can then reappear within two days.

---

[1] Keogh, O., 2017, "A prevention and cure for equine malady", *Irish Times*, Thursday, 21 September 2017

There are different gastric problems that can affect horses (and indeed camels*) and, consequently, FenuHealth manufactures eight products:[2]

- FenuSave – helps prevent stomach problems
- FenuCare – helps cure stomach problems
- FenuFeast – helps build appetite
- FenuCamel* – designed for camels[3]
- FenuJoint – suitable for older horses
- FenuCalm – helps horses relax
- FenuLyte – replaces electrolytes after exercise or travel
- FenuFoal – especially designed for young horses.

The Madden sisters received a lot of support from their parents in setting up the business. Their father is a teacher and their mother is a physiotherapist, but the family always had horses at home. Their grandfather bred National Hunt horses for over half a century. Balancing school and work has not been easy, and Kate is hoping to study at university, combining her interest in food and business. At present, Annie has no plans for a specific course, but has indicated she would like to study in the US.

The young sisters had a great idea for a business product but obviously no business experience. However, they have been very fortunate in the support they have received from established business people in the sector. One such mentor was Dr Owen Brennan of Devenish Nutrition in Belfast, a privately owned agri-tech company, with manufacturing plants also in the United States. Devenish Nutrition, originally established in 1952 and subject to a management buy-out in 1997, has been very successful. Dr Brennan, who sees the importance of helping new start-up companies, has provided FenuHealth with a lot of valuable advice on product manufacturing, markets and regulations.

Another important mentor for FenuHealth was the late Dr Pearse Lyons, founder of Alltech Inc, a global animal health and nutrition company established in 1980 and based in Kentucky in the US. Dr Lyons obtained a PhD in biochemistry in University College Dublin and worked for Harp Larger and Irish Distillers for a few years early in his career. Regarded as a great innovator in the animal nutrition industry, he also established a number of brewing and distilling companies. In 2012, he was named Irish Businessman of the year by *Business and Finance* magazine. The Madden sisters credit Dr Lyons with cutting their business costs in half by applying his immense experience from the industry.

Growth in the business has been substantial, running at 15% per the year to date; the salary bill rose from €250,000 in 2017 to €450,000 by the end of 2018, by which time FenuHealth was employing eight people. The sisters emphasise that everybody works closely as a team. Their

---

[2] See www.fenuhealth.com/products.php.

[3] Camels are particularly sensitive to the mineral content in water.

younger sister, Claire, is helping with their design work as they prepare to sell the products in retail outlets. The FenuHealth range of products is sold online, rather than through retail stores. At present there is no indication that the company will also use traditional sales channels in addition to online sales. Interestingly, the website's payment system, Stripe, was designed by the Limerick brothers, Patrick and John Collison, who also won the BT Young Scientist in 2005, and set up Stripe five years later. The Collison brothers are now reputed to be each worth $1 billion.

Kate and Annie have travelled to many well-known international equine centres, such as Kentucky and Dubai, to promote their products. The company currently sells the product to 14 countries, including Germany and Qatar, and has a 92% re-order rate. The sisters plan to sell their products in 150 countries within the next 10 years. FenuHealth sees the British market as being very important, not just because of its close geographical proximity, but also because of the size of the horse industry there. The plan is to establish a distribution base and an office outside of London by the end of 2019. Their product is manufactured in Britain, but the company is currently establishing another base in Europe.

On its website, FenuHealth mention that it has "5 Royal Families as customers". On a couple of occasions, the sisters have met Prince Charles and Camilla, Duchess of Cornwall. They have also met Prince Harry and Meghan, Duchess of Sussex. One of the topics the sisters discussed with Prince Harry was the establishment of a junior chamber of commerce as a forum where young business people could meet and exchange ideas.

As well as word-of-mouth, which is very important for the promotion of FenuHealth, the company uses Facebook to advertise its products, the cost of which is very low when compared to the return it gets on sales. The company has over 25,000 followers on Facebook and Twitter. Attendance at trade shows is also very important for sales. In 2015, when the company was in the process of being established, the young sisters went to Equitana, a major equine trade show in Germany, accompanied by their father. They received support from a number of organisations, including Enterprise Ireland, Horseracing Ireland, Meath County Council and the Local Enterprise Office. At the tradeshow, nobody came near the sisters on the first day because of their age, but by the third day, people were lining up to talk to them about their product. At that point, production was not even up and running, but the orders came in nonetheless. Within three months, production was ready and the company has grown constantly since then, with Qatar their biggest market. The young company has won many awards during its short existence and in 2017 they won the All-Ireland Business Summit Start-up of the year award. Looking to the future, the going is firm and the odds-on favourite FenuHealth is in the lead on the near side, with just half a furlong to go.

Glencore Plc

This case study illustrates a number of learning points on diversification, environmental and financial sustainability, international regulation and corporate governance. It is intended for class discussion and is not an indication of either good or bad management practice.

As electric cars are growing in popularity, there is an increasing demand for cobalt – a key material for the batteries required to run such vehicles. Such is the demand for cobalt that in 2019 it was selling for almost $100 a kilo on world markets. Cobalt, copper, zinc and nickel, along with other essential commodities are found in a few, often underdeveloped countries. The manufacturing companies that require these commodities to satisfy consumer demand for products are usually found in Europe, the United States and China. That is the nature of a lot of world trade – it requires Western commodity traders to move the necessary materials from the mines to the factory gate.

The world's largest commodity trader is the Swiss-based company, Glencore Plc. The company is diversified by geography, products and activities, which includes metals, energy and agricultural products. Such scope gives Glencore extensive global market knowledge. It produces and markets more than 90 commodities and has 146,000 employees based in over 50 countries.[1] It also deals in coal, oil and natural gas, as well as agricultural products such as grains, pulses, cotton and sugar. It is the world's second-largest independent oil trader, transporting 6.5 million barrels of crude and refined oil per day. These markets inevitably involve a good deal of risk, which can impact on financial performance, liquidity, asset values, growth potential, sustainable development and reputation. A considerable part of the Glencore annual financial report focuses on the types and levels of risk it faces. Risk can be mitigated in a number of ways, including measures such as credit insurance, letters of credit and company guarantees. Glencore's global size and scale reduces risk by allowing for timing differences in purchases and sales.

Glencore sources commodities from a myriad of different producers and then transports them around the world by sea, road and rail. It then stores the commodities and refines them to meet customer specifications. In addition to being an essential element in the supply chain, it also provides both short and long-term finance to its customers, as well as to the mining companies to facilitate varying supply and demand requirements.

The company began life as Marc Rich + Co AG in 1974 when it was established by the eponymous Marc Rich. He later had to flee the US to avoid Federal indictment charges relating to tax avoidance and trading with Iran, a country on which the US had imposed sanctions. He was subsequently pardoned by President Clinton in 2001.

---

[1] Glencore Plc. See www.glencore.com, Accessed 28 May 2019

In 1981, Marc Rich + Co AG acquired the Dutch company Granaria and over the next 20 years it made a number of other acquisitions. However, this created a financial strain and by 2015, the company (by then renamed Glencore) faced an existential debt crisis which required a major sell-off of its assets. In 2017, Glencore announced a joint venture with Mexican fuel group Network G500 to launch 500 G500-branded fuel stations. By this time, the company had achieved EBITDA of $14.8 billion.

The company was renamed Glencore in 2003 after a management buy-out with a new chief executive, South African-born Ivan Glasenberg. The company continued to acquire more businesses, including mines, throughout the world. In 2011, it was listed on the London and Hong Kong Stock Exchanges. The previous year, Glencore released its first sustainability report and, in 2013, it introduced a Code of Conduct across the entire Glencore group, along with its Safework programme, aimed at eliminating workplace deaths and accidents. It requires all staff to abide by the Code (which includes the company's values of safety, entrepreneurialism, simplicity, responsibility and openness) and to incorporate it into their work. In 2014, Glencore became a member of the International Council on Mining and Metals and rolled out a human rights policy for the company.

Glencore believes that it is the responsibility of its managers and supervisors to lead by example and to be seen by team members to work with integrity. The company's Code of Conduct stipulates that all suppliers and contractors maintain lawful business practices, along with safe, healthy and fair workplaces, with zero tolerance for human rights violations. The company is also committed to minimising any environmental impact on the communities in which it operates. Training for employees and communication with all stakeholders are seen as integral to making the Code of Conduct work. The company has a number of channels to enable workers to raise any concerns they have in relation to breaches of the Code of Conduct.

As a signatory of the Extractive Industries Transparency Initiative,[2] Glencore supports increased transparency around payments made to governments across the world and how they are redistributed and/or reinvested into the communities in which the company operates. It fosters public dialogue with governments in order to contribute to sound laws and regulations, and in dealing with governments it commits to working to the highest ethical standards.

The company's Code of Conduct, along with its anti-corruption policy, are quite detailed on compliance and expect everybody working for Glencore to take personal responsibility for ensuring that their conduct conforms to the Code's principles, particularly in relation to conflicts of interest, political contributions, bribery, sanctions, money laundering and insider information. The company's objective is to create a 'compliance culture' among all staff. It states that compliance will be rigorously pursued and that there are strong disciplinary measures in place, including dismissal

---

[2] Extractive Industry Transparency Initiative. See https://eiti.org, Accessed 28 May 2019

for serious breaches. In its 2017 annual report, Glencore stated that "we are committed to operating transparently, responsibly, and meeting or exceeding applicable laws or external requirements".

Glencore has set a high standard in terms of the governance of its operations. However, on 2 July 2018, the company announced on its website that Glencore Ltd,[3] a subsidiary of Glencore Plc, had received a subpoena from the US Department of Justice (USDOJ) to produce documents and other records with respect to Glencore Ltd's compliance with the Foreign Corrupt Practices Act and United States money laundering statutes. The requested documents relate to the Glencore Group's business in Nigeria, the Democratic Republic of Congo (DRC) and Venezuela from 2007 to present. The board of Glencore established a committee to oversee the company's response to the DOJ subpoena. On 11 July 2018, the company issued an update on its website. The chair Tony Hayward said: "Glencore takes ethics and compliance seriously throughout the group. The company will co-operate with the DOJ, while continuing to focus on our business and seeking to maximise the value we create for our diverse stakeholders in a responsible and transparent manner."

If the USDOJ decides to go ahead with a full investigation, it is likely to take a number of years, which is likely to have a negative impact on investor confidence in the company. Glencore could possibly be hit by large fines or criminal prosecutions. Either way, it will involve a considerable disruption to the company's operations as the USDOJ conducts its investigation.

Though the alleged malpractices relate to operations in Nigeria, Venezuela and the DRC, the USDOJ has jurisdiction under the US Foreign Corrupt Practices Act 1977 (FCPA),[4] which prohibits the payment of bribes to foreign officials to obtain business anywhere in the world. It applies to publicly traded companies, their directors, employees, shareholders and agents. The US Securities and Exchange Commission (SEC) and the USDOJ are jointly responsible for the enforcement of the FCPA. While Glencore is not a US company, it has many dealings with companies that are US-based. The company maintains that it always operates within the law. However, Glencore may have seen an opportunity to operate as an intermediary between sanctioned companies and international markets, and it seems that this is what brought it to the attention of the USDOJ.[5]

According to the *Financial Times*,[6] one such deal was buying a 20% stake in Rosneft (Russian petroleum company) in 2016, which was under Ukraine-related sanctions at the time. However, perhaps of most interest to the USDOJ is Glencore's involvement in the DRC, a resource-rich

---

[3] Glencore Plc. See https://www.glencore.com/media-and-insights/news/Subpoena-from-United-States-Department-of-Justice, Accessed 22 July 2019

[4] See https://www.justice.gov/criminal-fraud/foreign-corrupt-practices-act, Accessed 28 May 2019

[5] Zhdannikov, D. and Payne, J., 2018, "Exclusive: Justice Department demands details from Glencore on intermediary firms – sources". *Reuters* 23 October 2018, https://www.reuters.com/article/us-glencore-usa-subpoena-exclusive/exclusive-justice-department-demands-details-from-glencore-on-intermediary-firms-sources-idUSKCN1MX1JP

[6] Hume, N., Sheppard, D., Sanderson, H., 2018, "Glencore: an audacious business model in the dock". *Financial Times*, 6 June 2018

(particularly in copper and colbalt) but under-developed country, where the company has assets worth up to $10 billion. The company is alleged to have dealt with Dan Gertler, an Israeli businessman who was placed on a US sanctions list in December 2017 for his dealings with the DRC and its then-president Joseph Kabila. The company denies that Gertler was instrumental in securing its vast copper and cobalt mines there, saying its stake in the mines were acquired independently, alongside Gertler. In 2017, Glencore bought out Gertler's stake in two large mines in Katanga and Mutanda, but still owed royalties to him as part of his stake in Gecamines, the country's state-owned mining company. When Gertler was sanctioned by the US, Glencore stopped the royalty payments to him, but he then obtained a court order in the DRC freezing Glencore's assets in the country, as well as seeking almost $3 billion in payment. This proved quite a dilemma for Glencore, and to avoid the seizure of its assets in the DRC, the company agreed to pay Gertler in euros to avoid US sanctions.

On 25 April 2019, Glencore posted an announcement on its website that it had been informed by the United States Commodity Futures Trading Commission (CFTC) that the CFTC was investigating "whether Glencore and its subsidiaries may have violated certain provisions or the Commodities Exchange Act and/or CFTC Regulations through corrupt practices with the commodities".[7] This is in addition to the USDOJ investigation that is currently underway. This notice follows a separate announcement by Glencore of reaching a settlement with the Ontario Securities Commission in December 2018.[8] The settlement concerns the Katanga Mining company, a subsidiary of Glencore, and relates to Katanga's historic accounting practices, corporate governance and disclosures practices by the company and named company officers. Glencore stated that it had initiated a number of structural and managerial changes in light of the settlement.

At the time of writing, both the USDOJ and the CFTC investigations are at a very early stage, and the company has not been found by the various regulators to have done anything illegal. However, whatever the outcome of the investigations by the USDOJ and the CFTC, many analysts will no doubt be wondering what such investigations will uncover. According to the *Financial Times*, the share price of Glencore is down around 8% since the USDOJ subpeona was issued.[9] With the investigations continuing, it will be very difficult for the company to "focus on our business and seeking to maximise the value we create for our diverse stakeholders in a responsible and transparent manner".

---

[7] Glencore Plc, 2019, https://www.glencore.com/media-and-insights/news/announcement-re-the-commodity-futures-trading-commission, Accessed 22 July 2019

[8] Glencore Plc, 2018, https://www.glencore.com/media-and-insights/news/announcement-in-connection-with-katanga-mining-limited0, Accessed 22 July 2019

[9] Shuubber, K. and Hume, N, 2019, "Glencore under investigation by US commodities regulator", *Financial Times*, 25 April 2019

The Move to Non-alcoholic Beer

This case illustrates evolving consumer trends and how companies monitor these trends and adjust their product accordingly. The case is intended for class discussion and is not an example of either good or bad management.

Introduction

Drinking beer has been part of western society for many centuries. In the middle ages, the alcohol content in beer was seen as a way of overcoming the risk from drinking contaminated water. Gradually, it became part of people's social life: at celebrations or just 'going for a few beers' with friends. As in most countries, in Ireland the sale of beer and other alcoholic beverages is controlled, and may be purchased only in licenced premises such as hotels and bars, or in off-licence premises and licensed stores and supermarkets. The age at which alcoholic products can be sold to people varies among different countries; in this jurisdiction, the age is currently 18 years.

Alcohol Consumption in Ireland

Alcohol consumption in Ireland has dropped in recent years from a peak of over 14 litres of pure alcohol per person in the early 2000s. According to the Health Research Bureau, annual per capita alcohol consumption in Ireland is 11 litres of pure alcohol. However, these per capita figures do not give a totally accurate picture as they do not take into account that one in five people in Ireland does not drink any alcohol.[1] At least 75% of all alcohol is consumed in ways that are considered by medical professionals to be harmful. According to the World Health Organisation,[2] the harmful use of alcohol is a causal factor in a number of diseases such as cirrhosis, heart disease and cancer, and in Ireland approximately 500 people die from these diseases each year.

On the other hand, in Ireland there is a growing number of young people (16 to 24-year olds) who do not drink alcohol at all, and an even greater percentage of 25 to 44-year olds who do not consume alcohol.[3] Previously, a greater number of women did not consume alcohol than men, but this is changing. According to a report in the medical journal, *The Lancet*, the number of women who do not consume alcohol is falling, from 26% of women in 1990 to 13% in 2017.[4] It is not just health organisations and the Central Statistics Office who monitor these trends; so, too, does

---

[1] Mongon, D. and Long J, 2016, *Overview of Alcohol Consumption, alcohol-related harm and alcohol policy in Ireland*, Dublin Health Reasearch Board

[2] World Health Organisation, 2018, *Global status report on alcohol and health*, Geneva, World Health Organisation

[3] Taaffe-Maguire, S., 2019, "No booze, please, we're Irish", *Sunday Business Post*, 27 January 2019

[4] O'Regan, E., 2019, "Irish women among the world's heaviest drinkers, amid big fall in teetotallers", *Irish Independent*, 8 May 2019, p.4

the alcohol drinks industry and, in turn, these influence their product offerings and how those products are marketed.

Mature Market

The beer market is considered to be a mature market by brewing companies (see **Chapter 5**), although there has been a large increase in the number of new premium craft beers being produced in recent years and growth in this niche of the market. Non-alcoholic or low-alcohol beers have been around for decades, but their popularity was always low as it was perceived that not only did they lack the kick of full-strength beer, but also its flavour. However, in recent years, their popularity has grown significantly across Europe, with sales up by almost a fifth – and rising.[5] Supermarkets are reserving more and more shelf space for low- and non-alcoholic beers as people are becoming more health and lifestyle conscious.

The Process

In basic terms, beer consists of four main ingredients: grain (mostly malted barley), hops (of which there are many varieties), yeast and water. These can be combined in many different ways to produce a large variety of different types and flavours of beer. Alcohol is produced when the yeast and the grain ferment. Non-alcoholic and low-alcohol beers are made in much the same way as full-strength beer. Before the brewing process is finished, the un-carbonated beer is heated up to boiling point and, as the alcohol evaporates at approximately 70°C, the alcohol is removed from the beer'. An alternative method is to reduce the air pressure on the beer as it being brewed so that the alcohol evaporates at room temperature.[6] This is the preferred method as it has less impact on the taste. Once the alcohol has been removed, the final stage then involves carbonating the (alcohol-free) beer and bottling it. There have been significant improvements in the manufacturing process in recent years, which has dramatically increased the quality of the taste.

The alcohol level of these beers varies from country to country. In general terms, non-alcoholic beer contains a level below 0.5% alcohol by volume (ABV), although by law in the UK this figure is 0.05%, while low-alcohol beer has less than 3.5% ABV. In western markets, brewers are now viewing the full-strength beer market, and the low- or non-alcoholic beer market as complimentary rather than as competitors. In this regard, they are targeting new customers who do not drink alcohol at all, and also regular beer drinkers who are consuming less for health reasons or because of increased awareness of stricter drink-driving legislation. Non-alcoholic beer contains between one-third to half the amount of calories found in regular beer, thus appealing to people who are

---

[5] Abboud, L., 2019, "Brewers back consumer shift towards a taste for non-alcoholic beer", *Financial Times*, 20/21 April 2019, p.12

[6] The normal boiling point of a liquid is the temperature at which the vapour pressure is equal to atmospheric pressure (for water, this is 100°C at sea level – 100,000 Pa or 1 bar pressure). If the liquid is in a vacuum, the boiling point is lower than that at normal atmospheric pressure

weight conscious. There is also enormous potential in terms of future sales in Muslim countries where alcoholic drinks are restricted or prohibited.

New Image

From the brewers' perspective, the absence of alcohol means that no excise duty is payable on the beer, and therefore the margins are higher. Recognising the shift in consumer tastes, brewing companies such as Ab InBev (owners of brands including Budweiser and Beck's) have invested large amounts of cash into improving the taste and quality of non-alcoholic beers. In addition, unlike previous versions of non-alcoholic beers, brewers are now also investing heavily in the marketing of these new products. Heineken, for example, has allocated 25% of its marketing budget to its new product, 'Heineken 0.0', which was launched in 2017 in 14 markets. It has since been rolled out in over 50 markets worldwide.[7] Overall, total Heineken sales have increased 7.7% sales by volume – its best growth rate in over a decade. The holding company, Heineken NV, which owns Heineken, and several other brands, achieved strong overall growth in a number of markets including Vietnam and Mexico. The company's 2018 annual report notes the consumer trend towards low- and no-alcohol beverages, where company sales in this range increased from 12.5 million hectolitres in 2017 to 13.1 million hectolitres in 2018. In addition to Heineken 0.0, the company has 325 low- and no-alcohol products across 125 brands.[8] The nature of its advertising has also changed in an attempt to overcome previous stereotypes in relation to non-alcoholic beers. One such TV advertising campaign has the slogan "now you can", which shows people drinking beer while training in the gym, sitting in a parked car or at the office – with onlookers surprised until it is pointed out that it is alcohol-free and contains only 69 calories per 33cl bottle.

After two years of experimentation, another brewing giant, Guinness (owned by Diageo), launched its "Pure Brew" non-alcoholic lager in 2018, which is now available nationwide.[9] This was not the first time Guinness entered this market. In 1986, the company launched a non-alcoholic beer: Kalibur. Before that, it launched Guinness Light in 1979 (a low-alcohol version of the iconic Guinness stout). Despite extensive market research based on focus groups, however, and an enormous marketing campaign, the product was a failure and soon withdrawn from the market. Forty years later, with the market for low-and non-alcoholic beers growing, perhaps the product was right after all – just the timing was wrong.

---

[7] *Ibid*

[8] Heineken Holding NV Annual Report 2018, https://www.theheinekencompany.com/-/media/Websites/TheHEINEKENCompany/Downloads/PDF/Annual-Report-2018/Heineken-Holding-NV-2018-Annual-Report.ashx, Accessed 20 July 2019

[9] Taylor, C., 2018, "Guinness goes non-alcoholic with Pure Brew Larger", *Irish Times*, 17 January 2018, https://www.irishtimes.com/business/agribusiness-and-food/guinness-goes-non-alcoholic-with-pure-brew-lager-1.3358717, Accessed 9 May 2019

Fairfield Decom

This case illustrates the concept of a strategic inflection point whereby a company embarks on a very different strategic direction by capitalising on emerging opportunities. It also highlights strategic capability, regulatory oversight and corporate social responsibility. The case is intended for class discussion and is not an indication of either good or bad management.

Britain has been involved in North Sea oil exploration and drilling for over 50 years, which has involved drilling thousands of wells to satisfy the demand for oil, leaving thousands of wells that have to be plugged, the removal of thousands of kilometres of pipelines and hundreds of oil platforms. Oil platforms are moved from one location to another all the time, as new wells are drilled. However, like all structures, oil rigs have a limited useful life, and for many of the oil rigs in the North Sea, that useful life is now up. From a corporate social responsibility perspective, and in an era of close scrutiny by a number of regulatory stakeholders, that leaves a major problem for the oil companies: what to do with those rigs?

The British Oil and Gas Authority, the industry's regulator, estimates that it will cost up to £58 billion from 2018 onwards to decommission the oil infrastructure on the UK's continental shelf.[1] This could take another 50 years to achieve. This is against the background of a collapse of world oil prices in 2014, prices which still remain relatively low, which has huge implications for oil exploration companies and their cost structures. There is currently a good deal of research being undertaken by oil companies into reducing costs, specifically in relation to the plugging of wells and the disposal of old oil rigs in a manner that meet tough environmental standards. In this regard, protecting the reputation of the oil companies is essential.

The decommissioning issue may present a problem to the oil companies, but it presents an opportunity to Fairfield Decom, a subsidiary of Decom Energy Ltd.[2] As an operator-led decommissioning specialist company, Fairfield Energy was formed in 2005 and backed by a number of private investors to acquire North Sea assets that were being disposed of by the large oil companies, as they had reached the end of their useful exploration life. By 2008, the company had built up a number of assets in the Greater Dunlin area to the east of the Shetland Islands. In 2011, Fairfield decided not to proceed with an initial public offering as it was advised its portfolio was not sufficiently broad. Three years later, the price of oil crashed on world markets and this hit companies like Fairfield hard, putting pay to any plans of becoming a major player in the North Sea. In 2015, the company decided to change direction by reinventing itself as a decommissioning specialist.[3] According to its chief executive, Graeme Fergusson, Decom Energy's aim was to turn

---

[1] British Oil and Gas Authority. See https://www.ogauthority.co.uk/, Accessed 28 May 2019
[2] http://www.fairfield-decom.com/about-us/, Accessed July 2019
[3] Pfeifer, S., 2018, "Decom eyes £58bn market to plug North Sea Wells", *Financial Times*, 7 July 2018

decommissioning into a positive move. It is a small company with 75 highly specialised engineering staff.

Fairfield, now Fairfield Decom, began the process of dismantling oil rigs and the company is in talks with a number of other oil companies to do similar work on assets that are beyond the point of investment. The work is highly specialised, particularly in the rough waters of the North Sea. There are currently very strict guidelines regarding the environmental impact of such work. Rigs have been disposed of for many years, often in controversial circumstances. In 1995, Shell was permitted by the UK Government to dispose of *Brent Spar* rig by towing it from the North Sea to the Atlantic Ocean and sinking it. Greenpeace launched a successful world-wide campaign and forced Shell to tow the rig ashore to have it dismantled. In 2010, the Deepwater Horizon disaster in the Gulf of Mexico caused the deaths of 11 oil rig employees as well as enormous environmental damage. In the nine years since the explosion, the total cost to BP for cleaning up the damage to the sea and coastline, compensation to all those impacted by the disaster and federal and state fines amounted to $66 billion, which had a devastating impact on the company's reputation and its market capitalisation. Oil companies must realise that they need to guard their reputation carefully from any charges of environmental damage.

For Fairfield Decom, the need for extensive decommissioning presents a great opportunity, provided the company works within strict parameters and policies that reflect good governance and corporate social responsibility. This will require Fairfield Decom to earn and retain trust from a wide variety of stakeholders. To be successful, Fairfield Decom must be a company that others will want to partner with. It will also require considerable technical expertise to tackle significant decommissioning projects safely and efficiently. It is a steep learning curve. In 2017, Fairfield Decom was a winner in the Oil & Gas UK Awards for workforce engagement in the SME section. The award recognised significant steps taken by the company in involving its people, giving them a voice and developing an empowering culture. In 2018, Fairfield Decom was a finalist in the Excellence in Decommissioning category in the same awards, a category established in recognition of the (still emerging) requirement for end-of-life stage in the oil exploration life cycle.

Many of the existing North Sea oil fields are nearing the end of their productive capacity, although in 2018 there was an upturn in new drilling. In recent years, as a result of the decline in the oil industry off the coast of Scotland, cities largely dependent on the industry have been badly hit economically. However, with new drilling activity, and this emerging decommissioning industry, this situation could be turned around, as new opportunities present themselves. This would have important social and economic implications for the region.

Fairfield Decom hopes to lever its growing experience to access the global decommissioning market. While the North Sea itself poses significant challenges in dismantling the rigs, it is thought that this challenging experience will give Fairfield Decom a competitive edge in seeking business in other parts of the world.

Primark

This case illustrates a retail company pursuing a cost leadership strategy. It demonstrates the connections the company has with its supply chain and the ethical issues that these connections raise. With a general move away from a high street presence to online sales, this is one company that bucks that trend. The case is intended for class discussion and is not an indication of either good or bad management practice.

Introduction

The discount fashion chain Primark, or Penneys as it is known in Ireland, was established in Dublin in 1969, and now has 363 stores in over 11 countries worldwide, with more set to open in the future. The story began when Galen Weston bought a department store, Todd Burns, in Mary Street, Dublin. Weston is a British-Canadian businessman who owns numerous companies, including Selfridges in London and Brown Thomas in Dublin. Having been convinced by Arthur Ryan that there was a market for good value clothing in Dublin, Weston renamed the store Penneys, putting Ryan in charge of running it. Ryan had previously worked in London for the fashion wholesaler Carr & McDonald, and later returned to Dublin to work for another Irish company, Dunnes Stores. While working for Dunnes, Ryan was approached by Weston to work for him. Ryan was CEO of Primark until he retired in 2009 and was succeeded by Paul Marchant.

Expansion

In 1971, Penneys, as the company was then called, opened a second store in Cork, followed by one in Belfast. Two years later, in 1973, it opened a store in Derby in England. This required a different trading name to Penneys as there was another store with the same business name registered in the locality. The name 'Primark' was registered and all stores outside of Ireland trade under this name. Primark's expansion throughout Ireland and Britain continued throughout the 1980s and 1990s and the company opened its first store in Madrid in 2006 (see **Figure 1**). In 2008, stores were opened in the Netherlands, followed by Germany, Belgium, Portugal, Austria France, Italy and the United States. The company plans to open stores in Slovenia, Poland and the Czech Republic over the next few years, as well as expanding further in the US.

Country	First Established	Number of Stores
Ireland	1969	37
Britain	1973	182
Spain	2006	47
The Netherlands	2008	19

(Continued)

467

Figure 1 – *(Continued)*

Germany	2009	29
Belgium	2009	7
Portugal	2009	10
Austria	2012	5
France	2013	14
Italy	2014	4
United States	2015	9
Slovenia	2019	–
Poland	2020	–
Czech Republic	2020	–
Total		**363**

Figure 1 – *Store Expansion*[1]

Ownership

Primark is now owned by Associated British Foods Plc (ABF), a British-registered multinational food processing and retail company. Wittington Investments owns 54.5% of ABF shares. In turn, 80% of Wittington investments is owned by the Garfield Weston Foundation and the remaining 20% is owned by the Weston family. George Weston is CEO of ABF and Galen Weston is a non-executive director. According to its 2018 annual report, ABF had revenues of £15.6 billion and adjusted profits before tax of £1.37 billion, with Primark delivering its most significant profit growth in years.[2] This profit is expected to grow significantly in the coming years, which is bucking the trend. Many high street stores, such as Marks & Spencer and Debenhams,[3] have been performing poorly in recent years as more clothing is bought online, where prices are often cheaper and shoppers can readily compare prices. Shopping on smart phones is now making this process even easier. Younger consumers in particular have a strong preference for buying online. Indeed, Irish consumers are among the top spenders internationally for online purchases.[4]

---

[1] See www.primark.com, Accessed June 2019

[2] ABF Plc annual report 2018, https://www.abf.co.uk/investorrelations/annual_report_2018, Accessed 4 June 2019

[3] In April 2019, Debenhams Plc went into administration in the UK, but the company continues to trade. However, the company said it would close 22 stores. See "Debenhams to 'trade as normal' despite administration", *Irish Times*, 9 April 2019, https://www.irishtimes.com/business/retail-and-services/debenhams-to-trade-as-normal-despite-administration-1.3854434, Accessed 15 July 2019

[4] Taylor, C., 2018, "Irish are the biggest international online shoppers in the world", *Irish Times*, 30 August 2018, https://www.irishtimes.com/business/technology/irish-are-the-biggest-international-online-shoppers-in-the-world-1.3611205, Accessed 10 March 2019

primark.com

Primark has an extensive website showcasing its products and even has a section on its website – Primania – where shoppers (over the age of 18) can upload photos of themselves wearing Primark products. This is closely monitored by Primark to ensure there is no inappropriate material posted. The company also has a strong social media presence, using Facebook, Instagram and Twitter to show shoppers its latest offerings. Primark also uses online influencers to create awareness and raise the profile of its products. However, unlike almost all other major 'bricks and mortar' retail businesses, Primark does not sell its products online. Shoppers can view all the products online, but to purchase them, they must go in-person to a Primark store. This is contrary to the main trend in retailing where online sales have been the major growth in the last number of years.

Product Range and Shopping Experience

Primark has a wide range of clothing items for women, men, and children, as well as home items and beauty products. The stores are bright and spacious, which allows it to display a vast array of colourful fashion items aimed at the younger market. Primark's product range offers great value for money for customers, with many attractive fashion products costing less than €10, and many accessories selling for under €5. The average total spend in store by customers is €30.[5] When Primark's flagship Bank Building store in Belfast was damaged by a fire in August 2018, other retailers in the vicinity of the store reported a 60% drop in their footfall until it reopened after renovations were carried out.[6] In 2019, Primark is due to open a new store in Birmingham, which will embrace another trend of retail shopping – the 'shopping experience'. The new store will include a beauty studio for make-up and hair, a barber shop, three cafés and free Wi-Fi.

Code of Conduct

Primark has been a member of the independent Ethical Trading Initiative (ETI) since 2006. The ETI was established in Britain to support ethical trading in supply chains. As a member, Primark has a Code of Conduct in place which is based on the ETI's code, which, in turn, is based on the standards of the International Labour Organisation (ILO), which is a UN agency. The Primark Code of Conduct forms the basis of the terms and conditions in its supplier contracts, and every supplier must commit to meeting these standards. Suppliers' factories are audited annually to ensure compliance. The Code has 12 core principles covering areas such as child labour, bribery, the living wage, general working conditions, workers' rights and trade union membership. It also encompasses sustainable environmental practices. Primark has an 'Ethical

---

[5] Marchand, R., 2019, "Can Primark stay off the Internet for much longer", *Sunday Business Post*, 24 February 2019

[6] RTÉ, 2018, "Primark store reopens after Belfast city centre fire", 8 December 2018, https://www.rte.ie/news/ulster/2018/1208/1015994-belfast-primark/, Accessed 20 July 2019

Trade and Environmental Sustainability Team', which works with suppliers to help them get their standards right.

Ranza Plaza, a commercial building in Dhaka, the capital of Bangladesh, collapsed in 2013, killing 1,134 people and injuring another 2,400. The building housed a number of separate garment factories that supplied a number of major international companies, including Primark, Benetton and Monsoon, among others. Primark received a great deal of negative publicity in the aftermath of the tragedy for dealing with such suppliers.[7] Following the disaster, there was widespread criticism of Bangladeshi labour conditions from within the country, and many international companies that source products there have placed considerable pressure on their suppliers to improve working conditions.[8] However, Primark was one of the few companies involved in sourcing supplies in the Ranza Plaza building to pay compensation to the families of the victims in the immediate aftermath of the disaster.[9]

In July 2018, Primark, announced a three-year partnership with UNICEF whereby the company would contribute to the UN agency's work in education and emergency response aimed at improving the lives of vulnerable children. The company will invest over €4 million in the project. In Europe, Primark also has a partnership with the children's charity, Newlife. All unsold clothes items from its stores, along with samples from factories, are donated to the charity to help it raise funds. This also prevents such items ending up in landfill, which in turn reduces its impact on the environment. In the US, the company has partnered with a not-for-profit organisation, Delivering Good (formally known as K.I.D.S/Fashion Delivers), which distributes unsold clothing to areas around the world affected by natural disasters.

According to the ethics section of its website, Primark also works with its suppliers on their manufacturing processes, guiding them on how to reduce environmental impact and make supply chains more sustainable. Particular emphasis is placed on minimising the impact of dyes and chemicals in the production of clothing and to eliminate the discharge of hazardous chemicals. Primark is a member of the Sustainable Apparel Coalition, which has over 190 member companies and works to improving supply-chain sustainability. Rather than sourcing materials directly, Primark's approved factories are responsible for sourcing these materials. Primark works with the Sustainable Clothing Action Plan to reduce waste scrap material in manufacturing and to identify the origin of cotton and other materials used in the garments. In 2019, Primark launched a new range of jeans that are made from 100% sustainable cotton. The

---

[7] *Irish Examiner*, 19 December 2014

[8] Safi, M. and Rushe, D., 2018, "Ranza Plaza, five years on: safety of workers hangs in balance in Bangladesh", *The Guardian*, 24 April 2014, https://www.theguardian.com/global-development/2018/apr/24/bangladeshi-police-target-garment-workers-union-rana-plaza-five-years-on, Accessed 15 July 2019

[9] Butler, S., 2014, "Primark to pay £6m more to victims of Ranza Plaza factory in Bangladesh", *The Guardian*, https://www.theguardian.com/world/2014/mar/16/primark-payout-victims-rana-plaza-bangladesh, Accessed: 20 July 2019

company considers that it is a first step towards ensuring that all the cotton garments it sells are made from sustainable cotton.

While the company does not use Fairtrade material, it teamed up in 2013 with cotton agronomy experts, CottonConnect, and the Self-Employed Women's Association (SEWA) in India to create the Primark Sustainable Cotton Programme. The programme trains cotton growers in sustainable methods so they can improve their livelihoods through increased income. The programme launched with 1,251 female farmers in Gujarat, India, and has seen substantial improvements in their income. This programme is now being rolled out in conjunction with NGOs to train a further 10,000 female farmers in India and 20,000 in Pakistan.

According to Primark, animal testing is not permitted for any of the company's products. Primark stipulates that any of its supplier companies must adhere to industry recognised standards of animal welfare throughout the entire supply chain.

Costs

In order to be able to sell clothing items at highly competitive prices, costs throughout the organisation need to be minimised. One way this is achieved is by not advertising on television. Primark also works with suppliers to minimise the amount of packaging used in shipping goods. For example, instead of garments being individually wrapped in plastic, an entire bundle of garments is packaged together, which means that when garments arrive in a store they are ready to be placed directly onto the shelves. When garments are sold to customers, they carry them away in recyclable, Primark-branded paper bags. Trucks delivering garments to stores also remove all waste packaging and return it to their depots, reducing the amount of onsite waste collection in-store. This material is then processed for further recycling at the company's resource recovery units in its UK and German depots.

The company's Energy Reduction Group (ERG) identifies and implements a number of energy-saving initiatives in Primark stores, e.g. the use of smart energy systems to minimise the amount of energy required to keep stores heated and lit. This is reinforced with behavioural changes in energy management through training, advice and the introduction of standard operating procedures. Part of the ERG programme has been the development of a bespoke software system, the Energy Reduction Information and Control Console (ERICC), which provides real-time information on how each store is consuming and using energy, and advice on how the store should be performing in terms of energy management. So far, the system has been rolled out in over 100 stores.[10]

Given the scale of Primark as a business, ordering is conducted on a bulk basis allowing for large economies of scale in purchasing and distribution in both shipping and road transport. Workers' wages is one area that the company does not seek to minimise costs, both with directly employed staff

---

[10] See www.primark.com, Accessed 4 June 2019

and in source suppliers. The company was a founding member of the ACT (Action, Collaboration, Transformation) initiative for living wages right throughout the supply chain.

In July 2019 the company's founder, Arthur Ryan, died in Dublin at the age of 83. Primark has come a long way from a single store in Dublin to several hundred across Europe and the US, particularly when one considers how many big name retailers are struggling to maintain high street sales. Its slogan 'Amazing Fashion, Amazing Prices' seems to resonate well with its target markets.

Providence Resources

This case illustrates a number of different aspects of the oil exploration industry, including capital costs, various forms of risk and return, scientific appraisals, environmental issues, regulation and state oversight, and strategic alliances. It is intended for class discussion and is not an indication of either good or bad management practice.

Introduction

Providence Resources (Providence) is a Dublin-based oil and gas exploration company with a market valuation of €75 million; it has a number of exploration assets off the Irish coast.[1] The company is headed up by Tony O'Reilly Jr, son of former Heinz CEO, Dr A.J.F. O'Reilly. A graduate of Brown University in Providence, Rhode Island, and the London School of Economics, Tony O'Reilly Jr spent a number of years working in investment banking in New York, specialising in the mining industry. From there he went to work in Ireland for his father in the mining company, Arcon, and later at Wedgewood, part of the Waterford Wedgewood company, which was also owned at the time by Dr O'Reilly. Arcon was sold in the mid-2000s and Providence was established, which also had links to Atlantic Resources, a company established by O'Reilly Sr in the early 1980s. The company explored for oil in the Helvic area off the coast of County Wexford, but no commercial find was made. Despite many attempts by Providence to find oil off the Irish coast, none has been successful to date, though commercially viable finds of gas were made by other companies off Kinsale Head in County Cork a couple of decades ago and, more recently, in the Corrib gas field off the coast of County Mayo.

The Oil Industry

The oil and gas exploration industry requires enormous capital investment to sink wells and, because of the cost involved with no guaranteed return, there is a high commensurate level of risk. Oil and gas commodities are price-takers on world markets, i.e. the market dictates what the price will be, not the producer. This differs from most manufacturing companies in that the producer calculates the cost of production and adds on a percentage profit, which is the price the consumer pays. In March 2018, Providence negotiated a deal with APEC Consortium Ltd, to help develop Ireland's first ever commercial oilfield at Barryroe, 50 km off the south coast of Ireland, within a five-year period. The deal with APEC, which has the project and operations capacity, as well as financial backing from Chinese state funds, did not require Providence to put money into the project up front. Previous appraisal studies were conducted there in 2011 and 2012, which gave some valuable though incomplete reservoir information on the potential of the site. With the enormous capital costs needed, it would be necessary to farm-out further exploration activity. The collapse of oil

---

[1] Providence Resources Plc. See www.providenceresources.com, Accessed 6 June 2019

prices on world markets in 2014 made this extremely difficult. Leaving aside systemic oil price considerations, there was also considerable project risk relating to the uneconomic uncertainty of the Ballyroe field being developed as a viable project. Providence also has a stake in a field off the coast at Dunquin South in west Kerry, and is currently conducting survey work in deeper water (300 m) at Newgrange, some 250 km off the south-west coast. In addition, Providence has stakes in other fields off the west coast of Ireland and also off the Dublin coast.

Business Model

The Providence oil exploration business model is to secure licences from the State and then seek multinational exploration companies as partners, which have included Exxon Mobil, Eni, Repsol, Cairn and Total. The cost of drilling activity in the seven wells at the Ballyroe field (at a depth of 100 m) is estimated to be between $200 to $300 million. Ballyroe is thought to have a potential yield of up to 311 million barrels of 2C recoverable oil in the target area, between the vertical and horizontal wells. It is estimated that the break-even point for Ballyroe will be between $20–$30 per barrel based on 2018 industry costs.[2] The oil will then need to be refined, which will necessitate it to be landed via offshore pipeline or ship-based transport. There is only one oil refinery in Ireland, at Whitegate in Cork harbour, where the jetty facilities and deep-water access can accommodate ships of up to 100,000 tonnes.

Development of Oil Fields

There are two features of the Barryroe field that are likely to impact on costs. First, it consists of a series of large fault blocks, a factor that impacts on the number of wells required. Secondly, the oil is waxy in quality, which requires additional measures for its efficient extraction from the sea-bed. Providence believes that Barryroe contains up to 300 million barrels of oil, provided it flows fast enough to be commercially viable. At present, it is hoped that the oil will be flowing by 2023, though the field still needs more appraisal to get it to the production phase. Providence believes that APEC is the company to do this, as it has both the finance and the technical expertise required. APEC will fund the drilling programme and provide $19.5 million as a cash advance in working capital for Providence to fully participate in the project. Providence knows the Irish regulatory framework and licencing process. The new company will comprise three partners: APEC with 50% ownership, Providence with 40%, and a third company, Lansdowne Oil & Gas, will hold the remaining 10%.

In 2013, a significant development was a major find in the Bay du Nord region off the coast of Newfoundland, Canada, by Husky and Equinor.[3] While this might seem a long way from Ireland, the geological conditions are similar to the west coast of Ireland. There are many instances of oil being found in geological conditions on one side of the Atlantic Ocean which are mirrored on the

---

[2] Davy Research, 2018, "Ex-Oriente Lucrum – Ballyroe gets the deal it deserves", Dublin, Davy Research Department

[3] Equinor Plc. See www.equinor.com, Accessed 6 June 2019

other side. For example, oil finds in Ghana, West Africa, were reflected in similar finds in Guyana in South America. This is referred to as the 'Atlantic Jurassic Superhighway'.[4]

There have also been important technological developments in recent years. For example, 3D seismic technology allows exploration companies to take detailed analytical pictures of what lies beneath the sea bed. According to O'Reilly, this new technology is like the difference between an X-ray and an MRI scan.

In recent years, in addition to Providence, a number of other companies including Exxon, Equinor (formally known as Statoil), BP ENI and some other companies have begun oil and gas exploration in various locations in Irish waters. The giant Chinese state-owned company CNOOC (not to be confused with APEC, which is a privately owned company) was getting ready to drill in summer 2019, which indicates that a significant oil find is likely. Given the nature of the industry, there is inevitably a long time lag between the issuing of exploration licences and actual drilling taking place. These current exploration drilling operations date back to 2015 with the issuing of the Irish State's 'Atlantic margin licensing round'. The issuing of these licences coincided with gas coming ashore for the first time in the Corrib Gas Field.

In 2013, Exxon drilled a single exploration well in the Dunquin North field, but abandoned it after the oil there was deemed not to be commercially viable. Further exploration by Providence found a 1 km wide gap in the bedrock, which was allowing water to seep into it, thus contaminating the oil underneath. A seismic 3D image of Dunquin South has revealed that there is no such gap, as well as a 700 km^2 sedimentary ridge, which means that the prospects for the area are highly encouraging, therefore reducing the risks involved. As a result of the positive exploration developments in this area, Providence announced in July 2018 that a 25,000 km^2 area to the west of Barryroe in Dunquin South was back on its exploration radar. Providence holds 26.85% of an exploration licence in Dunquin South, along with ENI, Repsol and the British company Sosina Exploration.

Irish Government Involvement

The Irish Government has been quite active in marketing Ireland as an exploration destination for the major oil companies, which are, as a result, are taking a renewed interest in licencing options here. There has been much contentious debate over the past few decades as to whether the Irish State is getting a sufficient price for selling the licences when compared to the enormous potential return for the exploration companies if they strike oil or gas in commercially viable quantities. One defence of this policy is that the Irish State does not have the expertise to get directly involved in oil and gas exploration, and needs to involve companies with expertise and a proven track record in the field. According to Davy (2018), the estimated long-term price of oil is $70 per barrel, though this price would need to be discounted at a rate of 10% to reflect the time value of money and the cost of capital.[5] The tax rates that apply to oil exploration in Ireland are at the higher rate of

---

[4] Providence Resources Plc. See www.providenceresources.com, Accessed 6 June 2019
[5] Davy Research, 2018

corporation tax of 25% and an additional profit resource rent tax (PRRT) of between 5% and 15% applies, with the actual level being linked to project profitability. If the Barryroe field is successful, the estimated tax take by the State over a 16-year project life would be $2.9 billion.

When significant oil finds were first made off the Norwegian coast in the early 1970s, the Norwegian state had no direct experience of oil exploration at that stage, similar to the position Ireland is currently in. Norway, however, established the state-owned company Statoil in 1972, which became a Plc in 2001, then changed its name to Equinor in May 2018. The Norwegian Government is still the largest shareholder of Equinor, owning 67% of the shares. The development of the Norwegian oil industry has made it one of the richest countries in the world on a per capita basis. Ironically, the Norwegian oil fund, the world's largest sovereign investor, is set to sell some $7.5 billion of its oil and gas shares. The fund owns about $623 billion in its equities portfolio, of which $37 billion are in oil and gas shares.[6]

The Irish Government has chosen not to go down the route of direct state involvement, consistently arguing that oil exploration is very risky and expensive. Instead, under the licensing model, the oil exploration companies will absorb the risk, while the Irish exchequer will benefit from royalties from any finds.

Licensing

The Department of Communications, Climate Action and Environment (DCCAE) is the government department that currently controls the issuing of licences for the Republic of Ireland and its territorial waters.[7] The principal pieces of legislation governing the area are the Petroleum and Other Minerals Development Act 1960 and the Continental Shelf Act 1968. A foreign exploration company is required by the licensing conditions to have a permanent commercial presence in Ireland, which is fully authorised to act in its name and enter into contracts. Licensing options are generally granted for a three-year period. There are longer licence periods for the development of the oil or gas field itself, but with various provisions attached. If a commercial find is made, a separate licence – a petroleum lease – is required by the company to extract the oil, along with an environmental impact assessment. Royalties and tax will be levied by the Government on any finds, and all companies must agree to be bound by relevant Irish law and the jurisdiction of the Irish courts.

As of November 2016, there were 66 Irish exploration licences in existence: an all-time-high figure. In addition to Providence, other companies have bought up licences, including Europa Oil and Gas (Holdings) Plc, a UK AIM-listed exploration company, which has six licences off the west and south-west coasts of Ireland. These licences cover 4,986 km², an estimated 5 billion barrels of oil and 2.5 trillion cubic metres of gas. The company is currently in negotiation with potential partners to

---

[6] Milne, R. and Sheppard, D., 2019, "Norway's wealth fund to divest $7.5bn of oil shares", *The Financial Times*, 9 March 2019, p.13

[7] Department of Communications, Climate Action and Environment. See www.dccae.gov.ie, Accessed 6 June 2019

develop the South Porcupine field, some 200 kms of the south-west coast and in 1,500 m of water. An oil discovery there would necessitate an investment of up to $10 billion, which would create hundreds of highly skilled and highly paid jobs in the west of Ireland, as well as employment in the ports and heliports that would be needed to service these rigs. The development of the Corrib field generated $3 billion in investment – one of the biggest single inward investments made in Ireland.

From the perspective of the oil companies, the cost of exploration has dropped considerably in recent years as a result of development in exploration technology and a surplus of oil and gas exploration equipment available worldwide. In addition, the price of oil on world markets has risen again quite significantly over the last number of years from a low of around $30 a barrel in 2014 to over $80 a barrel in 2018. These two factors provide a strong incentive for oil companies to accelerate the development of existing projects.

Energy Security

Natural gas accounts for around 30% of the energy Ireland uses to generate approximately half of the electricity used domestically and to heat around 650,000 homes. The Kinsale field is due to run dry in early 2021 and the Corrib field a few years later. Corrib currently supplies 60% of Ireland's natural gas needs, Kinsale supplies 5%, and the remainder comes from Britain through three natural gas pipeline connectors. The demand for natural gas is expected to rise as coal- and peat-burning electricity generating stations are closed down due to their greenhouse gas emissions. Britain's North Sea gas supply, on which Ireland is highly dependent, will end by 2030. Gas will then come from Norway, Russia, Qatar and other countries outside Europe, clearly with greater risk of supply disruption.

In 2018, US company NextDecade signed a deal with the Port of Cork to develop a liquefied natural gas (LNG) terminal in Cork harbour, Ireland's biggest natural harbour. A report by Engineers Ireland[8] has stated that Ireland needs to build a terminal for importing LNG to ensure energy security and provide access to the competitive global gas network. This should be done in parallel with promoting offshore exploration.

New Beginnings?

In an interview with the *Irish Times*,[9] Tony O'Reilly Jr stated that the board of Providence Resources is examining whether it may enter the green energy market, possibly in partnership with larger multinational energy groups. This could include wind farms or geothermal projects. "That's the way the industry is going," said O'Reilly Jr, adding, however, that it would only happen if it creates shareholder value, not because "other people think it is the right space". He also warned against the Government's proposals to bring in climate change laws that could limit oil and gas

---

[8] Engineers Ireland, 2010, *Infrastructure for an island population of 8 million*, Dublin, Engineers Ireland

[9] Paul, M., 2018, "Oil explorer Providence may get into renewables", *Irish Times*, 13 July 2018, Business This Week, p.1

exploration in Ireland, as the required oil and gas will have to be transported to Ireland from abroad and increased importation of fossil fuels would lead to increased prices, trade imbalances, loss of potential exchequer revenue and a rise in CO^2 emissions. O'Reilly considers that the attempt to de-carbonise the world will have to be done over time rather than through revolutionary change.

About to Drill?

In the meantime, Providence expects that the long-awaited drilling programme in the Barryroe field will start in the third quarter of 2019. It issued this statement a month after An Taisce (an independent, non-profit environmental group) sought a High Court judge review of the decision by the DCCAE to permit a survey of the area around Barryroe. In January 2019, the High Court quashed the licence granted officially to Providence's subsidiary, Exola, for sonar testing and seabed clearance at Barryroe. In the hearing, An Taisce raised issues with the environmental screening process that had been conducted in July 2018. The environmental group argued that the DCCAE had failed to comply with several EU Directives concerning environmental impact assessments when it had granted permission to survey the site. While the review was in progress, Providence reapplied for permission and it is now hoping that the drilling programme will not be materially delayed.

Also in January 2019, the State granted Providence a frontier exploration licence (FEL) for a site in the southern Porcupine basin. The licence, 2/19, is operated by TOTAL E&P Ireland (50%) on behalf of its partners, Providence (40%) and Sosina Exploration Ltd (10%), known collectively as the JV Partners. FEL 2/19 contains the undrilled Paleocene 'Avalon' exploration prospect. Providence stated that new 3D seismic data should greatly enhance exploration potential and reduce the cycle time to the drill decision.[10]

When Providence struck its deal with APEC on the Barryroe Field, private bank Mirabuad upgraded its share price target for Providence by more than 50%. Assuming a discovery is made, it places a value on Providence's stake in the joint venture at over €1.2 billion.[11] Under the deal, Providence was due to receive $10 million in the first tranche of funding from APEC by 14 June 2019. However, APEC missed this deadline on a number of occasions: 14 June, 3 July, 10 July and 12 July, and 19 July, when a new deadline of 2 August was set by Providence. As a result of the delays, Providence had to issue an update to the Irish Stock Exchange (Euronext Dublin) and this had an impact on its share price, which dropped by 10%.[12] Looking ahead, Providence considers that it has the portfolio, the necessary financial resources as well as the right partners and people in place to develop its exploration assets that will provide a solid return for its shareholders.

---

[10] Donnelly, E., 2019, "Providence Resources receives approval to convert Avalon prospect into full exploration licence", *Irish Independent*, 18 January 2019

[11] Hamilton, P., 2018, "Providence Resources' target price upgraded by 50% by private bank", *Irish Times*, 2 October 2018, p.18

[12] Providence Resources, 2019, Update on Ballyroe Farm-Out Transaction, http://www.providenceresources.com/sites/default/files/UPDATE%20TO%20BARRYROE%20FARM-OUT%20-%20EXTENSION%20TO%20BACKSTOP%20DATE%20TO%20AUGUST%202%202019.pdf, Accessed 30 August 2019

Four Seasons Hotels and Resorts

Gerry Gallagher

This case illustrates the role of leadership in forming corporate culture and values, and in running a major international hotel company. It highlights the importance of people in a service industry and how value is created by developing people to their full potential. It also illustrates product and market development. This case is intended for class discussion and is not an indication of either good or bad management practice.

> "So much of long-term success is based on intangibles. Beliefs and ideas. Invisible concepts."
>
> Isadore Sharp

Background

The son of Polish immigrants, Isadore Sharp was born in Toronto, Canada, in 1931. He qualified as an architect in 1952 from Ryerson Polytechnical Institute in Toronto and followed his father, Max, into the family construction business. In his youth, he was a keen sportsman, which influenced his thinking on the importance of teamwork. In sport, winning is the result of team effort rather than any talented individual. The role of the coach is getting the best out of people.

At first, Max Sharp & Son built houses, later expanding to begin constructing apartment buildings. Sharp's first introduction to the hotel business was when he built a hotel in the mid-1950s for a friend, Jack Gould. Seeing the hotel do well, he secured funding and built his own hotel in 1961.[1] He consulted widely with professionals on the design, interior décor and other aspects of the hotel finish, and in so doing began many partnerships that would last for decades. He also negotiated with suppliers and many others to hold off on payment until the hotel was built.

Sharp's brother-in-law, Eddie, was just back from Germany where he had stayed at a hotel called *VierJahrzeiten*, which translated as 'Four Seasons'. It was the finest hotel he knew. That was the limit of their market research on the name, and so it stuck. Sharp hired an experienced hotelier, Ian Munro, to manage the new hotel and the two became friends as well as colleagues.

The Golden Rule

Initially, there was no grand vision for the company. Although Sharp, did not know anything about the hotel business, he always approached it from the perspective of the customer. As the company

---

[1] Sharp, I., 2009, *Four Seasons: The Story of a Business Philosophy*, New York, Penguin Group

grew, the new Four Seasons hotel defined the concept of the luxury hotel in terms of service excellence and top-class facilities and operations. It focused on the affluent, frequent traveller and built a worldwide reputation and brand. Central to its definition of luxury are the people who work for Four Seasons and its unique culture. The guiding philosophy that rules how the company treats all its stakeholders, including its employees, is the 'Golden Rule' – treat others as you would like them to treat you. This particular value is the cornerstone of its corporate culture.

Expansion

The first hotel was a success and a second hotel followed, also in Toronto. The hotel – the Inn on the Park – was also the location for a new fitness institute for guests (a first for the industry) as well as a cabaret club. Sharp's third hotel venture was in London, where he linked up with the McAlpine Group, a large construction company and owner of the Dorchester Hotel. The London Inn on the Park opened in January 1970. Ian Munro was now overseeing three hotels. The new hotel quickly established itself and was awarded European Hotel of the Year in its first year.

Around the same time, Sharp became involved in a bid to build a massive, 1,600-room hotel in Toronto. The project was way out of the league of his original backers. Instead, he approached the conglomerate ITT, which was in the process of taking over Sheraton Hotels. Sharp convinced them that he could build a flagship hotel for them, and invested $3.5 million for a 49% partnership with ITT to develop the hotel. Sheraton, now controlled by ITT, kept making changes to the new hotel that did not meet with Sharp's approval, and which he believed were not in keeping with five-star standards. He decided to exercise his right to sell his share in the ITT partnership at the then market price, making an $18 million profit on his $3.5 million investment. This meant that he was able to clear his debts on his other hotels; it also taught him many lessons about dealing with large corporations. Along with some other deals that potentially could have ruined the company, Sharp decided to limit its financial liability in any future deals.[2] From that point on, Sharp began developing a vision of specialising in medium-sized hotels (200–400 bedrooms) of exceptional quality and with the aim of being the best.

Four Seasons now manages over 100 hotels in 40 countries worldwide, and the company continues to expand its portfolio. Three-quarters of its hotels are built by developers and then managed by Four Seasons. When Canada appeared to have no more potential for expansion for the company, Four Seasons looked to the US where the level of competition was a great deal stronger. The company landed some big deals, taking over the Clift in San Francisco and the Ritz-Carlton in Chicago. The Four Seasons in Washington was the first hotel it acquired in the US to bear the Four Seasons name. Perhaps its biggest coup was in 1981, when it secured The Pierre in New York. In the early 1980s, the company experienced a lot of demand from other hotel owners to take on the management of its hotels on a contract basis. Finding enough staff of the right calibre for rapid expansion was going to be a problem, and Four Seasons declined most of the offers.

---

[2] Sharp, I. (2009).

The hotel industry is cyclical and the company grew at varying levels over the years as they expanded into other countries. The 1990s saw further expansion in the US and Japan. Doing business in Japan proved to be a challenge initially as the company found the business culture very different. Opportunities in Europe were harder to find as so many of the main cities had well-established luxury hotels. The company's biggest deal to date was when it bought the troubled Regent hotel chain in August 1992, giving Four Seasons control of 15 hotels in choice Asian locations. In one move, the size of the group greatly increased at a knock-down price. Unfortunately, the acquisition happened at the time of the slump following the first Gulf War, and the group's earnings dropped substantially. Four Seasons tried to enter the Indian market on a number of occasions and protracted and costly negotiations proved fruitless as different investors pulled out at the last minute. However, in 2008 the Four Seasons Mumbai opened. The company also ran into difficulty in Caracas, Venezuela, in the mid-1990s when they partnered with a developer but the deal turned sour and Four Seasons lost $10 million.

Competition

There are numerous luxury hotels in every country. What makes the Four Seasons different from its competitors and what makes people want to pay a premium for this product? A necessary part of creating a difference is preserving the elements that separate a business from its rivals and ensuring that competitors do not imitate the very aspects of that business that made it different in the first place. Worldwide competition for Four Seasons comes from other luxury chains like Ritz-Carlton, Marriott, Westin, and Sheraton.

The 'Four Pillars'

Four Seasons differentiates itself based on what the company terms the 'Four Pillars', which were developed at different stages over its history.[3] Isadore Sharp describes the four pillars thus:

- **Quality:** "We will only operate medium-sized hotels of exceptional quality with an objective to be the best." (1972)
- **Service:** "True luxury will be defined not by architecture or décor, but by service. So we must make the quality of our service our distinguishing feature and a competitive advantage." (1976)
- **Culture:** "We will create a work ethic based on the Golden Rule to give our people a framework to pursue a superior service culture." (1980)
- **Brand:** "We will grow as a management company and build a brand synonymous with quality." (1986)

Four Seasons has recently added another strand, or fifth pillar:

"To become our industry's undisputed leader, known globally as number one."

---

[3] Higley, J., 2007:26, "The Man Behind the Brand", *Luxury Hotelier*, September 2007

Over the years, Sharp has spent much time travelling around the group, talking to managers and staff in the different hotels, preaching the Four Seasons 'gospel' and encouraging everyone to understand the importance of service and trust. As new managers replaced the ones who left, they were hired first and foremost for their compatibility with the Four Seasons' corporate culture, excellent communication skills and strong leadership and coaching skills.

The Product

'Luxury' is a relative concept and it can be easily imitated. While sumptuous facilities at Four Seasons hotels must be taken for granted, other aspects of the (now) five pillars can help separate the company from its competitors. Brands represent a sense of promise to the guest in terms of what to expect. It is then up to the hotel to exceed that promise, and in so doing, generate loyalty and repeat custom.

Each Four Seasons hotel is designed and furnished to reflect its locality, and this is intended to give it a sense of place. Many aspects of five-star luxury that are taken for granted today by travellers were first developed by Four Seasons, such as big bedrooms, sound-proofing from external noise, large bespoke beds, luxurious bathrooms with telephones, 24-hour room service, overnight laundry, non-smoking floors, twice-daily housekeeping service and valet parking. While all of these factors could now be considered to be standard industry practice, the Four Seasons maintains its differential in the quality of its service.

Service is the product of people, systems and culture. These factors are built up over a period of time. In a globalised world, while comfort levels are constantly increasing, the one factor people value most of all is time. In that regard, good service can make the guests' time more productive and enjoyable. Service in the Four service standards are developed for all aspects of guest interaction. These are not prescriptive, but act as a general guide that allows the individual staff member to tailor the service to the needs of the customer, and is based on the 'Golden Rule'. In turn, it places a large degree of trust on the employee: on their character and their competence to do the job impeccably.

Mission Statement

Four Seasons created a corporate mission statement that would guide the actions of everyone in the organisation. It is designed to underpin their goals and beliefs, and how they interact with their guests.[4]

---

[4] See https://www.fourseasons.com/about_four_seasons/service_culture/, Accessed 30 July 2019

Four Seasons' Mission Statement

Who we are

We have chosen to specialise within the hospitality industry by offering only experiences of exceptional quality. Our objective is to be recognised as the company that manages the finest hotels, resorts and residence clubs wherever we locate.

We create properties of enduring value using superior design and finishes, and support them with a deeply instilled ethic of personal service. Doing so allows Four Seasons to satisfy the needs and tastes of our discriminating customers, and to maintain our position as the world's premier luxury hospitality company.

What we believe

Our greatest asset, and the key to our success, is our people.

We believe that each of us needs a sense of dignity, pride and satisfaction in what we do. Because satisfying our guests depends on the united efforts of many, and we are most effective when we work together co-operatively, respecting each other's contribution and importance.

How we succeed

We succeed when every decision is based on a clear understanding of and belief in what we do, and we couple this conviction with sound financial planning. We expect to achieve a fair and reasonable profit to ensure the prosperity of the company and to offer long-term benefits to our hotel owners, our customers and our employees.

How we behave

We demonstrate our beliefs most meaningfully in the way we treat each other and by the example we set for one another. In all our interactions with our guests, customers, business associates and colleagues, we seek to deal with others as we would have them deal with us.

Competing on service has allowed Four Seasons to achieve and maintain Rev PAR (revenue per available room) leadership.[5] It is not just about staff numbers but more about the quality of those people delivering that service. Four Seasons has, over the years, developed a deep understanding of

---

[5] Talbott, B., 2006, "The Power of Personal Service: Why it Matters. What Makes it Possible. How it Creates Competitive Advantage", *CHR Industry Perspectives*, No. 1, September 2006 (Cornell University)

what its guests expect and a culture that facilitates meeting and exceeding those expectations. The company is also constantly innovating.

Hotel Divisions

Depending on their location, Four Seasons hotels are normally operated on the following lines, all of which are designed to provide a seamless service to the guest:

Operational hotel divisions:
- Rooms
- Food and beverage
- Spa and fitness facilities
- Four Seasons Residences.

Administrative hotel divisions:
- Sales and marketing
- Engineering
- Administrative and general.

Four Seasons' head office is in Toronto and is the base for a number of senior management positions including HR and Administration, Marketing, Finance, Worldwide Development, Business Administration and General Counsel. Each hotel has a general manager responsible for all that happens in that hotel.

People

People play a central role in service delivery. In every country that Four Seasons operates, it has been able to find the exceptional employees which makes the company what it is and where teamwork is the norm. The quality of its outcome is therefore solely dependent on its frontline employees, such as porters, receptionists and restaurant staff – in most instances, these are not highly paid jobs. Managers cannot be everywhere at the same time, so trust plays a large part in daily operations. It is estimated that in a 200-room hotel, there can be as many as 5,000 interactions between guests and staff each day.[6] This provides a lot of opportunities to excel or to fall short of expectations. Four Seasons aims to have no mistakes in interacting with its guests; however, human nature being what it is, this will not always be achieved. While guests can therefore be disappointed, such situations can also provide new service opportunities and what guests usually remember is not the original problem, but how it was handled. Employees are encouraged to think for themselves and empowered to make decisions to solve the problem immediately.

---

[6] *Ibid*

The role of managers therefore is to act as mentors and develop their staff. Good communication is vital as all employees must always know precisely what is expected from them. Managers should also be visible – and accessible – and are expected to lead by example and to live up to company values.[7]

Four Seasons believes in treating every employee with dignity and respect. Individual employees are recognised for their contribution. As a result, it has consistently ranked high in *Fortune* magazine's '100 Best Companies to Work For'.

Many companies focus on remuneration as a means of attracting and retaining employees. While pay is important, Four Seasons also believes that other factors are even more important. Research among *Fortune* 100 companies[8] indicates that the three main things employees consider most important in choosing employers are:

- To work for leaders who inspire the best in individuals
- A physical environment that makes work more enjoyable
- A sense of purpose – a feeling that one is working for more than just a pay cheque, but that they are helping to build a company in which they can take pride.

It is this common sense of purpose that helps build teamwork and shared values that inspires commitment to the company's success. While the 'Golden Rule' which mandates everyone to treat others as they would want to be treated is not a unique philosophy, in Four Seasons it is strictly enforced. The company treats staff complaints as seriously as it deals with guest complaints. Whenever hotel renovations are taking place, staff facilities are also upgraded. There is a clear career path developed for them and all promotions are internal. Training plays an essential part in ensuring that Four Seasons personnel deliver a high level of service on a consistent basis. It is a learning environment designed to assist managers to get the best from their employees. Training managers, or 'learning managers' as they are termed, are available to assess training needs and advise on appropriate solutions. People are seen as an asset, and not as a cost. Training is thus made easier by the quality of the employees that the company hires.

In recruiting staff, most hotels will usually look for experience. Four Seasons looks primarily for attitude. Isadore sharp believes that anyone can be trained to be a waiter, but attitude is ingrained. The company aims to have 90% of the staff in any hotel coming from the local area. Irrespective of the position for which they are applying, each employee is interviewed normally around four or five times, the final time by the general manager. When Four Seasons opened in New York, it had 15,000 applicants for 400 places. Such a rigorous recruitment and

---

[7] Sharp, I., 2010, Conference on Entrepreneurship at the Graduate school of Business, Stanford University, www.videosurf.com/video/2010-conference-on-entrepreneurship-keynote-speaker-1237262530, Accessed 6 May 2010

[8] *Ibid*

selection procedure is inevitably very time-consuming and costly, but the company believes that it is not expensive in the long run as it does not have to deal with employees who are clearly unsuited to their jobs. Staff turnover at Four Seasons is less than half the industry average. Four Seasons personnel qualify for benefits such as free meals, medical care, pension arrangements and complimentary holidays at Four Seasons hotels.

Whenever a staff member leaves the company, HR conducts an exit interview and the information obtained is discussed by managers with a view to lessons learned. The company's overall philosophy for treating its staff is that in a service environment, staff members cannot properly look after guests if they themselves are dissatisfied.

Implementation

Four Seasons ensures that its values are enacted on a daily basis with its guests. It begins with the morning briefing meeting, which includes the hotel manager, all departmental heads, and the guest relationship manager (departmental head level). The guest relationship manager goes through the guest list for the hotel, and everyone who will be arriving and checking out that day. The purpose is to identify the guests and their individual needs. The daily briefings also include the 'glitch report' – a review of anything that went wrong in the previous 24 hours, and what was done to rectify the matter. The policy is that if something is not up to standard, it must be rectified straight away, beginning with a sincere apology, and then whatever additional steps are required to ensure that the guest is satisfied. The third part of the meeting is a review of the coming day – the events that might be happening and the relevant times, as well as a staff review and any other matters that the hotel staff may need to know about. Good service can only come through teamwork and that requires co-ordination.

Ownership

Though Four Seasons went public in 1985, launching on the New York stock exchange, it went private again in 2006 in a deal worth $3.4 billion.[9] Four Seasons needed an equity injection, but the primary reason was to secure its future free from such demands that would place short-term profitability above long-term success. It was funding, without the pressure. The investors, Cascade Investment, controlled by Microsoft's Bill Gates, and Kingdom Hotels, controlled by Saudi Prince Al-Waleed bin Talal, were viewed by Sharp as long-term investors who considered the hotel industry worldwide to be a major growth industry. Sharp still retains a 5% interest and remains as CEO.

Four Seasons currently has 50 new hotels at various stages of development around the globe, and it is planned to have up to 150 new hotels over the next eight to 10 years. In particular, Europe is

---

[9] Higley, J., 2007:26, "The Man Behind the Brand", *Luxury Hotelier*, September 2007

providing the company with some of its best opportunities. Now that the company has grown, it can provide considerable support at corporate level to each individual hotel, and so help build the reputation of the brand. In terms of goals, the focus for Four Seasons is on the three Ps: people, product and profit. Given the size of the investment by Bill Gates and Prince Al-Waleed, it would appear that the prioritising people and product before profit is still providing adequate return on investment.

Information Technology in An Garda Síochána

This case illustrates the necessity for modern information technology (IT) systems in organisations to enable managers to make the type of strategic decisions required to run that organisation effectively. It also illustrates how decisions about technology are long-term in nature. Finally, it demonstrates how the use of such IT both enables organisational change to take place and also requires organisational change to fully exploit its potential. This case is compiled from a number of official reports in the public domain, including, inter alia, *the Garda Inspectorate. Intended for class discussion, the case is a snap-shot in time and is not intended as an example of either good or bad management.*

Introduction

An Garda Síochána (the Irish police force), like all other public and private sector organisations, must ensure it has good governance procedures in place in order to achieve its strategic goals. An essential element of this process is to have appropriate levels and quality of information available to decision-makers when it is required. This, in turn, requires the strategic use of IT throughout the force to enable Garda managers to use resources effectively and to minimise risk. Effective management of IT requires a strategic, whole-of-organisation approach, aligning technology with corporate goals and priorities. As organisations evolve, so do their IT requirements.

Information and Communications Technology Branch

Each organisation will differ in its use of IT depending on the sector within which it operates. Technology enhances the ability of police services to capture, analyse and share information. Such technology is more than the sum of hardware, software and systems. It means a better return on investment in human capital and enables the establishment of a more efficient and effective police force. It also has the potential to deliver cost savings. Within An Garda Síochána, the Information and Communications Technology (ICT) Branch is responsible for providing all ICT services to the organisation, including radio, voice and data communications infrastructure, information systems and ICT security on a 24/7/365 basis. An Garda Síochána is different from most police forces around the globe in that it has a dual role: policing and security (intelligence services).

An internal Garda review in 2014[1] established a new ICT Branch structure based on five sections:

- An ICT Programme Office (co-ordinating all ICT programmes, projects, financial management and administration)

---

[1] Garda Síochána Inspectorate, 2015, *Changing Policing in Ireland: Delivering a Visible, Accessible and Responsive Service*, Dublin, Garda Síochána Inspectorate

- An ICT Service Delivery Section (day-to-day delivery of all ICT services)
- A Technical Infrastructure Section (technical support)
- Information Systems and Future Policing (communications, IT infrastructure and security)
- Digital and Innovation Section (future digital policing solutions).

The current IT governance structure of An Garda Síochána is project-based rather than focusing on organisational goals. Within the five sections outlined above, the first section, the ICT Programme Office, referred to in the *An Garda Síochána Information and Communications Strategy 2013–2015* as the Project and Programme Office, is the unit responsible for developing new ICT projects. The Project and Programme Office is aligned to the Garda Response to a Changing Environment (GRACE) Programme Board. In turn, the GRACE Programme Board oversees a number of project boards, each one of which deals with individual ICT projects across the organisation. The GRACE Board is supported by an ICT Senior Management Team. This is illustrated in **Figure 1** below.

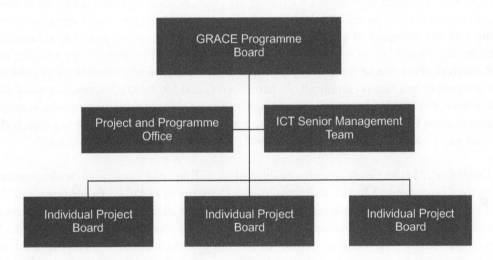

Figure 1 *ICT Governance Structure in An Garda Síochána*

The GRACE Programme Board is jointly chaired by the Chief Administrative Office, the Deputy Commissioner Operations, and the Deputy Commissioner Strategy and Management. It provides overall direction on the various IT initiatives in the organisation and prioritises them in order of importance. Each of the individual project boards is chaired by an assistant commissioner or the Executive Director of IT, while the ICT Management Team provides the necessary co-ordination between the projects and also any support that may be required. The Project Boards report back to the GRACE Programme Board on the progress being made. The chairpersons of the GRACE Programme Board and all of the individual project boards have full-time responsibilities in other areas, and a background in technology or project management is not a requirement to chair these boards.

Stand-alone Systems

An Garda Síochána uses a number of stand-alone IT systems, which provide a range of types of information. These systems were originally designed to meet whatever specific organisational need existed at that time and were built up incrementally. Consequently, there is little connectivity across the systems. In that regard, they lag behind systems in other police forces. One such system is 'PULSE' – Police Using Leading Systems Effectively, which was introduced in November 1999 (see **Chapter 1**). PULSE is a database system used for the recording of crime. Twenty years later, not all Garda stations have PULSE system terminals available for Gardaí to input data or access information, and the system has a number of significant limitations.

Another example is the Property Exhibits Management System (PEMS) which, though it manages property inventory records, operates independently of a system developed subsequently for the Garda Technical Bureau (GTB) that tracks the intake of evidence at the GTB, and also independently of the Forensic Science Laboratory tracking system, to which most exhibit items are sent to be forensically processed. ('Exhibits' are physical items that may form part of evidence, e.g. a crowbar may be an exhibit; the burglar's fingerprints on the bar would constitute evidence, along with the testimony of a witness.) An integrated inventory system would be able to track all exhibits from reception to evidentiary processing, provide information on the specific location and status of the evidence item at any point, and generate reminders for the proper disposal of the property once a case is completed. As part of An Garda Síochána's *Modernisation and Renewal Programme 2016–2021*, the organisation recognises the need for an enterprise content management system to allow Gardaí investigating a crime to search all Garda content relative to a case, including documents, photos, CCTV, videos and audio. This process is currently done manually.[2]

In December 2014, An Garda Síochána established an ICT Steering Committee, with representatives from the Department of Justice and Equality, the Department of Public Expenditure and Reform and the Garda Inspectorate, to develop a five-year strategy for technology implementation to support the corporate goals of the organisation and ensure value for money.[3] In a 2015 review, the Garda Inspectorate found that though a number of software systems had recently been updated, as they would no longer be supported by the vendor, there were still significant restrictions limiting the ability of the force to provide crime investigation support remotely.[4] In its *Capital Investment Plan 2016–2021*,[5] the Government announced an additional allocation of €205 million for the development of Garda technology and ICT systems. This five-year investment plan was the result of the 2014 ICT Interdepartmental Steering Committee that was established with the intention of achieving

---

[2] An Garda Síochána, 2016, *Modernisation and Renewal Programme 2016–2021*, Dublin, An Garda Síochána

[3] Garda Síochána Inspectorate, 2015, *Changing Policing in Ireland: Delivering a Visible, Accessible and Responsive Service*, Dublin, Garda Síochána Inspectorate

[4] An Garda Síochána, 2016, *Modernisation and Renewal Programme 2016–2021*, Dublin, An Garda Síochána

[5] *Ibid*

greater integration between public bodies, and improving ICT governance in An Garda Síochána. It also reflects the 2015 *Public Service IT Strategy* (below). The developments under the five-year strategy will have to consider not just current needs but also any future requirements. The Inspectorate's review of An Garda Síochána's *Information Communications and Technology Strategy 2013–2015* found that the organisation had a primary focus on maintaining the existing systems but little focus on the future. Developing new systems under the five-year strategy, while maintaining and supporting existing ICT infrastructure and services, will pose quite a challenge for the organisation. This entails supporting over 100 information systems, 9,000 devices and 15,000 end-users across 570 locations.

The International Experience

Internationally, police services have faced similar challenges in implementing technology changes, including: identifying the real costs and benefits; determining the actual effects of implementing various technologies (including unintended consequences); and exploring the best way for technology to be evaluated, acquired, maintained and managed. Large-scale technology projects require strong management and oversight to achieve the benefits required. Many international police forces, including Police Scotland and the Police Service of Northern Ireland (PSNI) have had integrated systems in place for years and this experience can be of benefit to An Garda Síochána. The PSNI has an IT governance structure which oversees all technology acquisitions and ensures alignment to its strategic plan. Oversight by senior Garda management of IT systems and processes is critical to ensure their effective use. In its 2015 report, the Garda Inspectorate cites a number of examples of project delays and cost overruns in IT programmes in police forces in the US and Canada. From the perspective of exchequer funding and operational efficiency, it is imperative that mistakes previously made by other police forces are not replicated in Ireland.

Financing IT Programmes

All large organisations require significant and ongoing investment in IT. In the period 2009–2013, IT accounted for approximately 5% of the overall budget of An Garda Síochána. Against a background of government cuts in spending in the public sector following the collapse of the Irish banking sector, the Garda budget was reduced. This had implications throughout the organisation and the IT budget saw significant year-on-year cuts, dropping from €74.6 million in 2009 to €68.3 million in 2013. In 2014, the IT budget rose for the first time in five years to €71.8 million – still 3.8% below the 2009 figure (not including inflation). This had a serious cumulative effect on the ability of the organisation to fulfil its purpose, an issue highlighted in various reports by the Garda Inspectorate over a number of years. Speaking on RTÉ Radio in 2014, then Minister for Justice, Frances Fitzgerald, stated:

> "The systems are completely out of date. It's very clear that during the years of the Celtic Tiger and in the recession that the Gardaí did not get the investment in IT that a modern police force needs in order to keep up with the sophistication of current crime.[6]"

---

[6] Fitzgerald, J., 2014 cited in An Garda Síochána (2016) *Modernisation and Renewal Programme 2016–2021*, Dublin, An Garda Síochána

Effective planning of strategic ICT projects requires a multi-year framework to allow for the development and integration of systems in a flexible cost-effective manner and for adaptation to organisational needs. However, as with many public sector organisations, An Garda Síochána is restricted to an annual planning and expenditure planning process.[7] The Garda Inspectorate has recommended that An Garda Síochána should seek sanction from the Department of Public Expenditure and Reform (DPER) to plan and budget for its IT needs on a multi-year basis. For its part, DPER has identified large potential savings to be achieved by integrating the Garda procurement system with the Office of Government Procurement.[8]

Integrated Public Service Systems

Until relatively recently, many public sector organisations operated in isolation, certainly in terms of ICT. There is now an increasing need and drive for shared services, and for co-ordination and integration of systems. The 2015 *Public Service IT Strategy*[9] recommended five key strategic objectives for innovation and excellence in ICT within the Irish public sector:

- Creating ICT shared services to support integration across the wider public service to drive efficiency, standardisation, consolidation, reduction duplication and cost control.
- Digitisation of key transactional services and the increased use of ICT to deliver improved efficiency within public bodies and provide new digital services to citizens, businesses and public servants.
- In line with statutory obligations and data protection guidelines, facilitate increased data sharing and innovative use of data across all public bodies to enable the delivery of integrated services, improve decision-making and improve openness and transparency between government bodies and the public.
- Ensure that the ICT strategy is aligned, directed and monitored across public bodies to support the specific goals and objectives at a whole-of-government level with an emphasis on shared commitment.
- Ensure the necessary ICT skills and resources are available to meet the current and future ICT needs of the public service.

In addition to its own internal requirements, An Garda Síochána also needs to have integrated systems with a wide variety of stakeholders including, *inter alia*, the Department of Justice and Equality, the Road Safety Authority, the Prison Service, the Irish Naturalisation and Immigration Service, etc., as well as international policing bodies and other police forces, for example the Police Service of Northern Ireland (PSNI), sharing a broad range of data in different formats, from videos to biometrics.

---

[7] Garda Síochána Inspectorate, 2015, *Changing Policing in Ireland. Report of the Garda Síochána Inspectorate*, Dublin, Garda Inspectorate

[8] *Ibid*

[9] Department of Public Expenditure and Reform, 2015, *Public Service ICT Strategy. Delivering better outcomes and efficiency through innovation and excellence in ICT*, Dublin, Department of Public Expenditure and Reform

New Governance Structures

In its 2015 report, the Garda Inspectorate recommended the establishment of a new, organisation-wide Governance Board for An Garda Síochána chaired by the Deputy Commissioner Governance and Strategy.[10] The purpose of this board would be to develop a single command for governance units and all governance processes, ensuring a more consistent approach to oversight and accountability. The Inspectorate also recommended the establishment of a strategic, organisation-wide ICT Governance Committee to facilitate joined-up technology planning and oversight of an integrated IT strategy that would support corporate goals and priorities, and be aligned with DPER's public sector ICT strategy. This committee would provide a single decision source for a structured review of all IT projects and implementation plans, and have the authority to implement plans and oversee the governance of IT projects. The Inspectorate further recommended that the executive director of the Garda ICT Unit would be an integral member of the ICT Governance Committee. This committee, along with a Risk Committee and a Training Committee, would all report to the Governance Board (see above).

Five year ICT Strategy 2016–2021

An Garda Síochána's five-year strategic plan for ICT[11] covers areas such as computer-aided dispatch (CAD), enterprise content management, property management, investigations management, in-car technology, custody management, HR management, rostering and duty management, learning management (for training) and a custom-built intelligence management system. Integration between existing systems and future requirements will be a key aspect of the implementation of this strategy. There are a number of different projects that are currently in various stages of development.

Computer-aided Dispatch Systems A CAD system is essential technology for any modern police force, providing a management information resource that drives resource allocation and deployment as well as forecasting crime trends. It can deal with personnel information and rosters, connecting with other record systems, crime analysis reports and mapping features. As with any system, the first step is to determine the specific needs of the organisation, both current and future. The existing CAD system used by An Garda Síochána needs considerable modernisation. Business process mapping and activity analysis are two tools that can assist in such a project. Business process mapping defines what a business area does, who is responsible and by what standard a business process should be completed, thereby improving efficiency and effectiveness. Activity analysis provides a comprehensive understanding and measurement of demand for a particular service regarding the needs of particular end users. It involves capturing all activities that are conducted in the organisation, the time spent on them and by whom.

---

[10] Garda Inspectorate, 2015, *Changing Policing in Ireland. Report of the Garda Síochána Inspectorate*, Dublin, Garda Inspectorate

[11] An Garda Síochána, 2016, *Modernisation and Renewal Programme 2016–2021*, Dublin, An Garda Síochána

When informed in 2018 that a new CAD system was being rolled out, the Garda Inspectorate noted that the capabilities of the existing system are not fully understood throughout the organisation and not used to best effect.[12] In addition, the existing system is incomplete as it only operates in the Dublin Metropolitan Region and in a limited number of divisions, and not nationwide. Furthermore, the PULSE system does not provide a complete picture as not all calls for service are crime- or incident-related.

HR Systems Another IT system of key importance to any police force is an integrated HR system. Police forces face three types of service demand:

- Responding to the public notifying crime
- Proactive work aimed at preventing crime (using an intelligence-led policing model allows the most effective identification of both time and location where policing will have the greatest impact)
- Self-generated service demand, such as internal processes and administrative tasks.

An Garda Síochána currently has over 16,000 members and over 84% of the annual Garda budget is spent on personnel costs.[13] It is essential that senior managers have a workforce plan regarding the optimum number of personnel and the mix of skills required to police the country, and how these should be allocated to Headquarters and across the different policing regions and divisions. Abstractions (where Gardaí are not available for rosters due to being required for court work, etc.) are currently a big drain on resources and need to be better managed. The 2018 Garda Inspectorate report found that "the 'one-size-fits-all' garda roster is not making the best use of finite resources" and "while popular with members, it does not effectively support the delivery of local policing services".[14] It recommended that An Garda Síochána needs to develop multiple rosters that are more closely aligned to a unit's core policing function.

The organisation is currently undergoing a structural change, with the emphasis shifting from the old police districts (there are 96 in operation) to making the 28 divisions the basic unit of policing. This is in response to changing demographics and significant rises in population over the past two decades, particularly in the larger urban centres. The nature of crime is also changing rapidly; criminal activity is increasingly becoming more international in scope, and there is also a growing use of sophisticated technology by criminal gangs. These changes will have significant implications for how Gardaí are deployed, as well as the level of technology at their disposal to fight crime.

Technology can support the work of the force and the productivity of Gardaí, for example by increasing the amount of time individual members can spend on patrol. In 2018, An Garda

---

[12] Garda Inspectorate, 2018, *Policing with Local Communities*, Dublin, Garda Inspectorate

[13] Garda Inspectorate, 2015, *Changing Policing in Ireland. Report of the Garda Síochána Inspectorate*, Dublin, Garda Inspectorate

[14] Garda Inspectorate, 2018, *Policing with Local Communities*, Dublin, Garda Inspectorate

Síochána began the process of issuing new mobile systems that allow Gardaí on patrol to check instantly if vehicles are taxed, etc. (and without the necessity to stop them) or if the driver has a valid licence. Previously, a lot of this work was done back at the Garda station, thus reducing the amount of time spent on active patrol.

An Garda Síochána has a Human Resource Management System (HRMS) which records all staff duties, leave, attendance, training, performance and all aspects of personnel management. Much of the system is paper-based, however, which severely limits the ability of senior management to make effective decisions on resource allocation. In addition, there is a Human Resource Information System (HRIS) which records the personal details of staff such as addresses, payroll information and tax reference/PPS numbers. In reports previous to its 2018 report, the Garda Inspectorate recommended the replacement of legacy systems with one core integrated Human Resources Information Management System (HRIMS) for effective HR management within the organisation. This would have the capacity to produce analytical HR reports covering a wide variety of areas, such as personnel data, resource management and rosters (including the most effective use of overtime), performance management, sick leave management, training records, payroll, discipline records, HR recruitment projections and CAD. There is an important relationship between a resource management system and deployment of those resources through a CAD system. Having only one data entry point to feed multiple systems will assist in reducing unnecessary bureaucracy.

Crime Recording and Case Management Another area for development that has been prioritised by the Garda Inspectorate is an electronic Crime Recording and Case Management System (CRMS). This would cover the entire life-span of crime record development, from start to final use in court and closure of the case, and would supersede the modernisation of the PULSE system. In addition, the Garda Inspectorate have also recommended the development of a technology-based custody system to ensure appropriate oversight and management of persons in Garda custody.

Implementation

The Garda Inspectorate considers that the implementation of their recommendations will result in a number of benefits to An Garda Síochána, including:
- Increased clarity in authority and decision-making on IT projects
- Improved alignment of IT project development with organisational goals
- Improved management data to support more effective deployment of people and other resources
- Delivery of an IT platform that facilitates integration and single entry of data
- Reduced redundant or duplicated data
- Reduced operational and administrative costs.

In its 2018 report, the Garda Inspectorate state that while some progress is being made, An Garda Síochána is well behind comparable police services in terms of its use of technology, and still does not have "an updated strategy that integrates with and supports the Garda Síochána's vision for policing".[15] The 2018 *Policing Plan*[16] issued by An Garda Síochána does, however, contain a number strategic objectives, including:

- Improving data quality within the organisation
- Developing a strategic planning framework to include the introduction of an IT solution to promote compliance with the inspection process
- Developing a cyber-crime and security strategy to enhance the organisation's ability to respond to cybercrime and security incidents.

Whether these will address all of the concerns of the Garda Inspectorate in relation to An Garda Síochána's governance of IT remains to be seen.

---

[15] Garda Inspectorate, 2018, *Policing with Local Communities*, Dublin, Garda Inspectorate
[16] An Garda Síochána, 2018, *2018 Policing Plan*, Dublin, An Garda Síochána

Independent News and Media

This case illustrates how a company can become an acquisition target and how the takeover process, including due diligence, is conducted. It also illustrates how technology is changing the face of the media industry. It is intended for class discussion and is not an indication of either good or bad management practice.

Introduction

Independent News and Media Plc (INM)[1] is the leading newspaper and online publisher on the island of Ireland. The company is vertically integrated with print, digital and distribution assets, and is the largest wholesale distributor of newspapers and magazines on the island. INM is headquartered in Dublin and its shares are quoted on the Dublin and London stock exchanges. The company was formed in 1904 as Independent Newspapers Ltd by William Martin Murphy. Twenty years later, the *Irish Independent* merged with the *Freeman's Journal*. In recent decades, the company expanded by acquiring a number of Irish regional newspaper titles including, among others, the *Drogheda Independent*, the *Wexford People*, *The Kerryman*, *The Corkman* and the *Sligo Champion*.

In 1973, Dr A.J.F. O'Reilly (former CEO of the US multinational Heinz Corporation) acquired a significant shareholding in the paper and the company was floated on the Dublin and London stock exchanges. The company expanded internationally under O'Reilly, acquiring newspaper titles in Australia, New Zealand, South Africa and the UK. In 1999, the company became known as Independent News and Media Plc. At this stage, INM was valued in excess of €2 billion.[2] In 2004, INM moved from its original offices in Middle Abbey Street, Dublin 1 to Independent House in nearby Talbot Street. The company had previously moved its printing operations to Citywest in West Dublin. By 2007, INM's revenues were €1.67 billion, with profits of €350 million and total assets of €2.88 billion.[3] While involved in a range of very different businesses, Dr O'Reilly took great interest in the development of INM.

Circulation of INM's titles were badly hit in the recession that began in 2008. Advertising revenue dropped significantly, putting the company under severe strain financially, particularly for the *Sunday Independent* newspaper, which was heavily dependent on advertising revenue. This coincided with a huge structural shift to digital advertising on platforms such as Facebook and Google. At this stage, the company had amassed considerable debt (in 2007, it had borrowings of

---

[1] INM Plc, 2019, Group Overview, https://www.inmplc.com, Accessed 7 May 2019

[2] Guider, I., 2019, "War of Attrition." *Sunday Business Post*, 5 May 2019, p.10

[3] INM Plc, 2007, Annual Report, https://www.inmplc.com/~/media/Files/I/INM/investor-docs/reports-and-presentations/INM_Annual_Report_07_-_FINAL.pdf, Accessed 8 May 2019

€1.462 billion), which led to the sale of its foreign-owned assets and inevitably left it vulnerable to takeover. Such a move eventually came in 2019 from the Belgian newspaper group, Mediahuis.

Mediahuis

Mediahuis was formed in 2013, following the merger of two Belgium newspapers, *Corelio* and *Concentra*.[4] It grew rapidly over the next few years by acquiring a number of newspapers in the Netherlands, including *De Telegraaf.* The company sells 1.4 million newspapers every day and also owns radio stations, classified ad websites and television channels. The newspaper group was intent on further expansion, particularly with English language titles. Flemish industrialist Thomas Leysen, chair of Mediahuis, has many years of experience in the newspaper business. In 1976, his father André was one of a number of businessmen who rescued the bankrupt De Standaard group of newspapers in Belgium, which then became part of the Corelio group. In 1996, Thomas Leysen became chair of Corelio and in 2013 he led the merger with Concentrata to form Mediauis.

The interest by Mediahuis in INM began in 2017 when it appointed an Irish advisor with experience in the media industry to begin gathering information on INM as a possible takeover target. No doubt the Belgian company carefully followed events at INM and a series of governance issues faced by the company that resulted in the appointment of High Court inspectors in 2018 at the request of the Office of the Director of Corporate Enforcement.[5]

By February 2019, Mediahuis believed they had enough information regarding INM and Leysen contacted Murdoch MacLennan, chair of INM, about a possible bid for the company. The initial response was favourable and Mediahuis then appointed JP Morgan as advisors in the takeover bid, while INM appointed the UK investment bank Lazard as its advisors. Detailed talks then began behind-the-scenes.

The Takeover

On 4 April 2019, a few days after the publication of INM's annual report and financial results, the chief executive of INM, Michael Doorly suggested to investors that the company was open to offers.[6] The Irish Takeover Panel directed INM to make an announcement, and the company confirmed it had received offers for a takeover, but did not name Mediahuis. The INM share price, which had been hovering around 7 cent per share for some time, immediately rose by 30%

---

[4] Mediahuis, 2019, https://www.mediahuis.be, Accessed 7 May 2019

[5] Phelan, S. "High Court agrees to appointment of inspectors to INM", *Irish Independent*, 5 September 2018, https://www.independent.ie/irish-news/courts/high-court-agrees-to-appointment-of-inspectors-to-inm-37284189.html, Accessed 19 July 2019

[6] Brennan, J. Paul, M., 2019, "INM chief raises prospect of sale of media group", *Irish Times*, 4 April 2019, https://www.irishtimes.com/business/media-and-marketing/inm-chief-raises-prospect-of-sale-of-media-group-1.3848704, Accessed 19 July 2019

in response. It is believed that INM had received other tentative offers at this time, but Mediahuis made a formal offer for INM, conditional on the irrevocable support of INM's two largest shareholders, Denis O'Brien and Dermot Desmond, who also became involved in the negotiation process. Mediahuis brought in Cian McCourt, a partner with Arthur Cox Solicitors, to advise on the process.

Leysen, along with Mediahuis CEO Gert Ysebaert, met executives from INM on 30 April 2019 to finalise a deal to buy the biggest Irish-based newspaper group for a price of €145.6 million or 10.5 cents per share.[7] The meeting was followed up by a stock exchange announcement on the price agreed and that the deal had the Denis O'Brien, who held 29.8% of the shares, and Dermot Desmond, with 15%.[8] The two irrevocably agreed to sell 26% of their shares in INM to Mediahuis, effectively blocking any rival takeover bid from succeeding. The sale price included the €81.7 million in cash reserves on INM's balance sheet, meaning that the net price of the purchase by Mediahuis was €64 million, representing just a little more than three-times earnings, which by any standards is a bargain price.

Shareholder Reaction

Following the deal with Mediahuis, there was a shareholders' meeting to discuss the takeover. Those shareholders present were informed that Mr O'Brien and Mr Desmond had sold a blocking stake, which effectively made any other potential bid futile. However, the price paid by Mediahuis undoubtedly factored in a number of legacy issues currently under investigation[9] by the High Court, the Office of the Director of Corporate Enforcement and the Data Protection Commissioner, as well as a number of possible private actions being taken by individuals whose data had allegedly been leaked by INM to third parties. On 12 April, an interim report of the progress of the investigation by the two High Court Inspectors was submitted to the High Court. At the time of writing, the contents have not been made public, but the various parties involved in the inspection have received a copy from the High Court. It is expected that the cost of the High Court inspection may run to tens of millions of euro and there may well be implications at both a corporate level and at individual level in terms of corporate governance.[10] While many of the shareholders present would have lost significant money on their shares, Denis O'Brien has seen the value of his shares drop from over half a billion euro to €43 million.

---

[7] Paul, M. and Brennan, J., 2019, "How Belgian publisher Mediahuis chose INM as its next takeover target", *Irish Times*, 3 May 2019, Business Agenda, p.5

[8] Denis O'Brien had begun building up his shareholding in INM in 2006, with a 3% stake and he continued to build this up over the next number of years, acquiring his 29.8% shareholding by 2012, having spent some €500 million in the process

[9] Curran, R., 2019, "Mediahuis had the INM takeover nailed before breakfast", *Sunday Independent*, 5 May 2019, Business News, p.2

[10] Carey, B. and Dayly, G., 2019, "Paper Losses", *Sunday Times*, 5 May 2019, Business, p.5

Despite such issues, INM is quite a profitable business. At the 2019 AGM, INM's chief executive gave a very positive presentation on the company's performance. It is selling 1 million newspapers a week and has a weekly readership of 2.5 million. It is expected that its 2019 profits will be approximately €19 million, meaning a profit margin of almost 10%, compared to Mediahuis's margin of 3%.[11] The revenue generated by each employees in INM averages €230,000 – just slightly lower than Mediahuis, where the average is €260,000 per employee. Such figures indicate that the extensive cost-cutting at INM in the number of years prior to the takeover has paid off, but also indicates there is not much room for further cost savings, though savings might be achieved by creating economies of scale. There remains, however, a large hole in the company's occupational pension fund, which will have to be funded.

The Future

INM is operating in an industry that is very competitive and undergoing significant structural change due to technology and changes in audience and consumer behaviour. Mediahuis has a strong track record of developing digital content and successful online services, and it has boosted the number of paying subscribers at the group's titles in Belgium and the Netherlands. While Mediahuis has yet to announce any plans for INM, it is thought that it sees digital media services as an avenue for further growth. INM already publishes digital content, but it is currently free to view. Mediahuis may decide to put such content news behind a paywall. A move to increase online presence would be seen as an opportunity to target some of the estimated 70 million Irish diaspora around the world. In turn, entry into the English-speaking Irish market could also provide Mediahuis with a base for further print expansion into the larger UK and US markets by using shared content. However, a move to charge for online content may alienate Irish readers who are used to free online access.

Mediahuis has stated that it will keep investing in quality independent journalism to secure the future of all its titles, and the company has indicated it is willing to invest in INM. Indirect savings can be made through synergies and economies of scale, but cultural issues will present a challenge, particularly in relation to the sharing of editorial content. Mediahuis is not a publically owned company, meaning that INM, once purchased, will no longer be quoted on the stock exchange and therefore not subject to the pressures of quarterly or half-yearly reporting cycles and the short-term focus such pressures bring with them.

As at 8 May 2019, Mediahuis had acquired 29.91% of the shares and, under stock exchange rules, anything above 29.9% ownership means it must make a bid for the entire company.[12] Mediahuis made this bid and it was approved by INM's board of directors. On 27 June 2019,

---

[11] Oliver, E., 2019, "It's all about the numbers in media land", *Sunday Business Post*, 5 May 2019, p.11

[12] O'Donovan, D., 2019, "Mediahuis lifts its INM stake to 29.91 pc", *Irish Independent*, 8 May 2018, https://www.independent.ie/business/media/mediahuis-lifts-its-inm-stake-to-29-91pc-38089848.html, Accessed 8 May 2019

INM's shareholders formally approved the sale of the company to Mediahuis for €145.6 million, or 10.5 cents per share. The approval came despite widespread criticism by small shareholders of the low price for the shares being offered in the deal. Mediahuis now acquired the remaining shares of the company that it did not previously own. The takeover was approved by the Competition and Consumer Protection Commission and also the Minister for Communications, Climate Action and Environment. On 30 July 2019, the takeover received formal court approval from the High Court in Dublin. This was necessary because the inspectors appointed by the High Court were still conducting their investigation. With the purchase price so favourable, and its experience in digital content, it should be well within the scope of Mediahuis to build a profitable media business in Ireland and secure a healthy return on its investment.

Ryanair Holdings Plc

Catherine Moylan[1] and Gerry Gallagher

This case illustrates how a company has developed a core competence in how it exercises very tight controls over its operational cost base, and the implementation of its strategy, including how it maximises publicity at little or no cost to the organisation. It also examines a number of corporate-level issues, from funding to how the company interacts with different stakeholders. This case is intended as a basis for class discussion and not as an illustration of good or bad managerial practice.

In the early 1980s Aer Lingus and British Airways offered cross-channel flights, but the cost for most people was prohibitive. At that time there were international rules governing air travel which gave national flag carriers (such as Aer Lingus) considerable control over landing rights at airports. As a result of such restrictions, competition was severely curtailed. The European Union recognised that a lack of competition was damaging to the consumer and deregulated the industry in Europe in the mid-1980s. On 28 November 1985, Tony Ryan, a former Aer Lingus employee and chair of Guinness Peat Aviation (GPA), established Ryanair. It flew initially from Waterford to London Gatwick and then from Dublin to Luton charging IR£99 – half the rate charged by Aer Lingus at the time.[2]

Ryanair immediately met with strong opposition from Aer Lingus, which matched its lower fares, believing that the new airline would not be able to sustain that level of pricing. Over the next couple of years, Ryanair expanded its routes, taking in other cities in Ireland and the UK. However, it was losing a considerable amount of money and by 1988 had accumulated debts of €20 million. Tony Ryan's personal assistant, Michael O'Leary, advised his boss to close the airline and cut his losses. Ryan refused and put a case to the Minister for Transport, Seamus Brennan, to be given exclusive rights to fly into Stansted airport, situated to the north east of London. The Minister agreed and in September 1989 Aer Lingus was restricted to flying to Gatwick and Heathrow, while Ryanair would fly to Luton and Stansted. In 1993, the EU Commission issued the 'Open Skies' Directive, which fully deregulated European air routes, allowing non-state airlines to fly wherever they wanted in the EU without any state interference in regard to landing rights. That year, 57 new airlines were created in Europe, though the majority of these closed within two years. However, it provided the basis for massive expansion in Europe for Ryanair.

---

[1] Catherine Moylan, FCA, is a senior lecturer at the Institute of Technology, Tralee
[2] Creaton, S., 2004, *Ryanair: How a Small Irish Airline Conquered Europe*, Aurum, 2004

In 1989, PJ McGoldrick became CEO, though by this stage O'Leary was controlling the finances at the airline, and he began cutting costs. The Gulf crisis in 1991 hit the airline industry badly and passenger numbers worldwide were down. In December 1991, Conor Hayes took over as CEO. Tony Ryan called an old contact, Herb Kelleher, founder of Southwest Airlines in Texas, and asked if they could study Southwest's operations. O'Leary was duly dispatched to learn from America's most successful low-cost operator.[3] On 1 January 1994, Michael O'Leary took over as CEO of Ryanair.

Today, what separates Ryanair from all the other European low-cost operators is its ability to successfully and consistently cut costs down to the bare minimum. How did the small airline that was once just an annoying blip on the radar of Aer Lingus come to dwarf the former national carrier and redefine air travel? The answer lies with Ryanair's CEO Michael O'Leary and the strategies he developed over the last few decades that have changed the way the industry operates. Even before he became CEO, O'Leary had a strong personal incentive to reduce costs. He had struck a private deal with Tony Ryan whereby he would be paid 25% of all Ryanair profits above IR£2 million.[4]

Operating Costs

Achieving a fast turnaround is central to keeping operating costs low. This is particularly important on the Dublin–London route, where Ryanair can achieve a 25-minute turnaround at Stansted compared to 60 minutes for Aer Lingus at Heathrow. From the very beginning, Ryanair flew only point to point – any connecting flight by Ryanair would be treated as a totally separate journey. This had implications for passengers in terms of check-in and baggage transfer. Flying on specific routes to and from the base airport also facilitates crew rosters and ensures that crew will be back in their home station at the end of their shift.

Ryanair often fly to secondary airports where landing charges are much lower than the main airports. The drawback for passengers is that some of these airports are a considerable distance from the intended destination. The flight from Dublin to Frankfurt Hahn, for example, will leave the passenger over 120 km from the city. While Ryanair has been able to negotiate good deals from some of these airports, this has not always been a smooth process. In 2004, the European Commission ruled that Ryanair had received illegal state subsidies from Charleroi airport in Belgium. The airline seems to be in constant battle with airport authorities over landing charges, not least of all with the Dublin Airport Authority (DAA). Michael O'Leary has consistently criticised the DAA over what he sees as excessive charges to pay for the building of Terminal 2 – which he describes as a "white elephant" project. O'Leary believes that Ryanair could have built and operated the new terminal for a fraction of the cost incurred by the State.

Unlike most other airlines, Ryanair has a *common fleet*, i.e. all of its aircraft are Boeing 737-800s. Having a common fleet has many advantages in terms of flight-deck and cabin-crew training

[3] *Ibid*
[4] Cooper, M., 2018, *Michael O'Leary: Turbulent Times for the Man Who Made Ryanair*, London, Portfolio Penguin

(crew have to be 'rated' separately for different models of aircraft). Given that fuel costs represent the single biggest expense as a percentage of operating costs, these newer jets are significantly more fuel efficient than their older counterparts. Newer aircraft also save considerable money on maintenance compared to older models.

In the aftermath of the 11 September 2001 terrorist attacks, Ryanair reduced its prices to boost demand. The response was a significant increase in demand, so much so that Ryanair needed more jets. It bargained hard with Boeing, and given that worldwide demand for flights and therefore aircraft had fallen significantly, O'Leary got a reputed 50% price reduction on 100 new 737–800s, with options on another 50 aircraft. It was a brilliant deal for Ryanair. Speaking about the deal, Michael O'Leary said that being a farmer's son gave him an advantage:

> "I grew up in Mullingar and farmers know that the time to buy is when everybody else is selling and the time to sell is when everybody else is buying. It was quite simple. We had money. Boeing and Airbus couldn't give away planes. So we went and bought up about two years' worth of production."[5]

When Ryanair purchased the aircraft in 2001, the latest version of the Boeing 737–800 had a bigger capacity, carrying 189 passengers, but without the need for extra flight or cabin crew.

There are no free meals on Ryanair flights which, as well as being a saving on food costs, also allows cabin crew the time to sell drinks, sandwiches, scratch cards and other items that generate money for the airline. They also work on a commission basis for in-flight sales, which helps boost their take-home pay. Cabin crew ensure the plane is clean by the time the aircraft has landed. The company made a decision in the early 1990s not to carry cargo as the revenue generated would easily be offset by delays in unloading and thus missing take-off slots. Ryanair was the first airline to take on the travel agents industry, by reducing their 12% commission and by taking direct telephone bookings, which allowed other sales opportunities, such as car hire and hotel bookings, yielding commissions for Ryanair. In 2000, Ryanair developed a very basic website on a low budget which took online bookings. Online booking facilitates yield management, thus maximising revenue from each flight.

Heavy passenger luggage means extra weight on the aircraft and the airline introduced hefty fees for checked-in luggage, encouraging passengers to carry their own luggage on board as this saves on baggage handlers, check-in staff and fuel (fewer people bringing extra luggage means a lighter load and less fuel burn). Other optional fees include priority boarding, SMS confirmation and travel insurance. If passengers turn up without their printed ticket, the company will charge them €30 for printing another boarding card. Combined fees quickly add a considerable amount to the initial fare charged and, from the airline's perspective, firmly switches the emphasis from 'low fares' to low cost.

---

[5] Creaton, S., 2004:212

Ryanair generates considerable revenue from its ancillary services. In 2018, according to the company's annual report, non-operating income amounted to €2.1 billion. This figure includes revenue from services such as advertising on its website, selling hotel accommodation and car rental, as well as in-flight sales, priority bookings, etc. The average booked passenger fare in 2018 was €39.40, while the ancillary revenue per booked passenger was €15.48.[6]

Publicity

Traditionally, Ryanair did not use an advertising agency. Instead, staff members would come up with advertising ideas to form the basis of newspaper advertising, much of which could be controversial and sometimes lead to litigation. On numerous occasions Michael O'Leary has appeared in Dublin Airport in various costumes ranging from Santa Claus to the Pope in order to launch a particular promotion. When interviewed, his turn of phrase is usually quite colourful, particularly when people or organisations are criticising Ryanair's customer service. He tends to get particularly exercised when discussing the DAA or the European Commission. While many may find these incidents amusing, the airline has frequently gone beyond what most find acceptable. However, in recent years, the CEO has toned down the nature of his publicity stunts. In 2014, Ryanair changed its policy of not using advertising agencies and engaged the advertising company Dare to run a TV, print, radio and outdoor advertising campaign for the airline.[7] The international advertising agency Oliver has since taken over the contract for Ryanair's advertising.[8]

Throughout its history, Ryanair has been involved in numerous High Court cases, often defending actions taken against the company. One example was in 2008 when the former President of France Nicholas Sarkozy and his wife Carla Bruni, sued the airline over the unauthorised use of their image in a Ryanair newspaper ad. Sometimes these court cases have generated positive publicity for the airline; in other cases, the airline's image has been tarnished by the publicity. In 2010, in a dispute over landing charges in Dublin Airport, Ryanair managers gave evidence in the High Court in Dublin which did not find favour with the judge. Mr Justice Peter Kelly stated that "the truth and Ryanair are uncomfortable bedfellows".[9] Legal cases take up a lot of management time in Ryanair, and must amount to a considerable cost to the airline, although this cost is not broken down in its annual accounts.

[6] Ryanair, 2018, Annual Report 2018, https://investor.ryanair.com/wp-content/uploads/2018/07/Ryanair-FY-2018-Annual-Report.pdf, Accessed 20 July 2019

[7] McCabe S., 2014, "Ryanair's daring new ad strategy", *Irish Independent*, 17 April 2014, https://www.independent.ie/business/media/ryanairs-daring-new-ad-strategy-30193127.html

[8] See https://www.oliver.agency/ryanair/

[9] Irish Examiner, 2010, "Truth and Ryanair uncomfortable bedfellows". *Irish Examiner*, 5 June 2010, https://www.irishexaminer.com/business/truth-and-ryanair-uncomfortable-bedfellows-121637.html, Accessed 20 July 2019

Industrial Relations

While Ryanair has modelled itself very successfully on Southwest Airlines, until relatively recently there have been two major differences between them: customer service and union recognition. In establishing Southwest Airlines, Herb Kelleher wanted the company to be a fun place to work for all its employees, and in turn, employees would be motivated to offer good customer service to passengers. Over the years, Ryanair considered that customer service did not matter once people could get good value on what they were paying to travel. A number of events began to challenge that belief and caused the airline to reconsider its approach to customer service.

For the first 30-plus years, Ryanair did not recognise trade unions, while Southwest had excellent union relations – and was extremely profitable. In December 1998, baggage handlers in Dublin Airport sought union recognition and when this was not forthcoming, they began a series of strikes. The dispute did not cause much disruption, as senior managers, along with a number of volunteer staff from the airline, loaded and unloaded baggage. After a number of weeks, the dispute fizzled out. O'Leary told the workers that he would close the airline rather than negotiate with a trade union. Under the Irish Constitution, workers have the right to free association, including the right to join unions. However, there is no commensurate law to compel companies to recognise unions, unlike in many other EU Member States. There have been a number of attempts over the years by Ryanair pilots to be represented by groups such as the Irish Airline Pilots Association and similar bodies across Europe. There have been claims by the pilots, who have accused the airline of intimidation relating to what the pilots believed was the unilateral imposition of terms and conditions.

Corporate-level Strategy

Ryanair Ltd was originally set up as a private company owned by the Ryan family trust: CDS (named after Ryan's sons: Cathal, Declan and Shane). In 1996, a new company, Ryanair Holdings, was set up by the Ryans, Michael O'Leary and David Bonderman, an American investor, to buy the airline from the trust for IR£56.7 million. In order to relinquish the deal whereby O'Leary would receive 25% of the profits above IR£2 million, he was given a 22% share of the new company for a personal investment of IR£900,000. His investment was now worth IR£29 million.

Ryanair became a plc in 1997, floating on the Dublin and London stock exchanges and later on the NASDAQ exchange in New York. The shares were 20-times oversubscribed. Ryanair employees received some free shares and O'Leary's stake now rose to IR£71 million.[10] That year the airline carried 3.7 million passengers and the UK Civil Aviation Authority said it had the best record for punctuality on the Dublin–London route.[11]

---

[10] Cooper, M., 2018, *Michael O'Leary: Turbulent Times for the Man Who Made Ryanair*, London, Portfolio Penguin

[11] Ryanair, 2019, About Us, https://www.ryanair.com/ie/en/useful-info/about-ryanair/about_us, Accessed 6 June 2019

Most of Ryanair's expansion over the years has been by organic growth. In 2003, Ryanair purchased Buzz, the Dutch low-cost airline from KLM. Buzz, with a staff of 570 people, was losing €1 million a week and Ryanair moved quickly, saying it would make one-quarter of its pilots and 80% of its cabin crew redundant, and discontinue the brand. The real attraction for Ryanair were the valuable slots that Buzz held at Stansted, which would give it considerable latitude for further growth. Ryanair set up a subsidiary company called Buzz Stansted Limited in order to get around legislation protecting employees in redundancy situations. The unions representing the workers put pressure on the parent company KLM and a new deal was struck, which saw Ryanair acquire Buzz for €20.1 million, along with 130 staff members out of the original compliment of 530 staff in the Dutch airline. KLM would retain the other 400 staff. Ryanair also assumed responsibility for outstanding leases and other costs, bringing the total payment to €46.7 million.[12]

Shortly after Aer Lingus was privatised in 2007, Ryanair purchased a 25% stake in the rival airline. It was a move that caught the markets by surprise. The stake in Aer Lingus was increased later to 29.8%. Anything above 29.9% would trigger a bid for the entire company. There was strong opposition to the move by Aer Lingus employees (its pilots controversially used their pension fund to buy Aer Lingus shares in a bid to prevent the takeover). The Irish Government was also against the move, believing that it would give Ryanair a dominant position on the Dublin—London route. The European Commission took a similar view and blocked the takeover on several occasions.

An airline has two options when it comes to obtaining aircraft: either to lease them (from a leasing company such as GE Capital Aviation Services) or purchase them outright, which Ryanair has done. To grow the airline, therefore, requires large sums of money which can be obtained from borrowings and retained profits. Throughout its history, Ryanair has issued dividends to shareholders on only a few occasions. On other occasions, the company has bought its own shares in the open market. This is an alternative method of giving investors back some money, as with fewer shares on issue, the value of each share rises. Financial ratios are also boosted. Because of the constant and high level of profitability of Ryanair over the years, the company has reinvested the bulk of its profits back into purchasing new aircraft in order to drive further expansion. The company considers that in the long run, shareholders will get a better return on their investment.

Fuel costs have always been the largest cost factor for the airline, and they fluctuate considerably on world markets. Airlines the world over are subject to these variations, as oil prices are beyond the control of countries let alone individual companies. A common practice to overcome these peaks and troughs in oil prices is to hedge the cost – enter into a contract that will fix the price for a certain period, normally 12 months. In 2008, Ryanair had not hedged fuel costs, when oil reached $147 a barrel on international markets which resulted in a huge increase in fuel costs (they subsequently hedged the following year). Rising fuel costs, along with a major depreciation of the value of its Aer Lingus investment on its balance sheet, saw the airline making a loss of €169 million in its financial year ending 31 March 2009. This was the first time the company lost money since

---

[12] Creaton, S., 2004

its early years. Oil prices have fluctuated considerably since the peak of 2008. As the recession took hold across the globe, oil prices fell considerably to $40 per barrel on world markets, rising again in 2011 following the Arab Spring. In 2014, oil prices started falling dramatically, reaching a low of $27 a barrel in 2016. By July 2019, prices had risen again to $64 a barrel.[13]

Ryanair is named after its founder Tony Ryan, but for a variety of reasons it is associated throughout Europe with its CEO, Michael O'Leary, who has very much driven the company's strategy. By 2013, things began to change. The airline received a lot of bad publicity regarding its customer service, and it was affecting its bottom line. Perhaps the most damaging event concerned Dr Muhammad Taufiq Al-Sattar, a neurosurgeon working in Dublin but living in Leicester, England. On the morning of Friday, 13 September 2013, Dr Al-Sattar was informed by West Midlands police that his family had been burned to death in an arson attack on his house in the early hours. He rushed to Dublin Airport and explained to Ryanair staff his devastating situation and asked them to change his ticket from that evening to that morning. Ryanair staff duly obliged, but charged him €188 for the new ticket.[14] The public response was one of outrage, and Ryanair had to issue an acute apology. The company's AGM was held immediately after this incident and it issued a profit warning (at a time when its rival airline, EasyJet, was increasing passenger numbers and passenger revenue). A second profit warning was issued two months later in November 2013.

"Always Getting Better"

The company realised that it was time to change and in March 2014, it initiated its 'be nice' campaign: *Always Getting Better*. It was to be headed by a new manager, Kenny Jacobs, who had responsibility for marketing, communications and sales, with particular emphasis on digital technology. This was done as part of a major management reshuffle which also saw Eddie Wilson, the personnel director, being re-designated as Chief People Officer.

There were immediate changes to three key areas:

- On the company's website, the number of clicks needed to make a booking was drastically reduced (a major source of consumer irritation)
- At the airport check-in excess baggage costs were reduced)
- On flights, where a 'Business Plus' offering was introduced to attract business travellers.

With the business traveller in mind, Ryanair decided to introduce new routes to primary airports in order to reduce travel time to the final city destination. Traditionally, this would have increased landing charges and slowed down turnaround times. However, Ryanair stated it would only do this when it got a good deal from the airports in regard to landing charges and other expenses.

---

[13] Bolton, P., 2019, "Oil Prices". *House of Commons Library Briefing Paper*, Number 2106, 2 January 2019

[14] Cooper, M., 2018, *Michael O'Leary: Turbulent Times for the Man Who Made Ryanair*, London, Portfolio Penguin

In another surprising move, the company began to re-engage with travel agents, as many of the business travel bookings with other airlines were being done using this channel. It also signed up to global distribution systems, such as Amadeus, which was seen as necessary to grow the business beyond the 100 million passengers per annum mark. In yet another change with tradition, Ryanair believed the time had come to vacate the basic prefabricated offices used in the cargo area of Dublin airport for its head office and move to a plush building in a retail park in Swords, County Dublin, which contained a state-of-the-art operations room showing every Ryanair flight in the air at any point in time.

There was a major investment in technology, which was seen as essential in catching up with technological developments that had passed Ryanair by in the previous decade and a half. This involved a large increase in the number of 'techies' employed by the company and a complete rebuilding of the website from the ground up. This was seen as vital in improving customer relations and maximising revenue from bookings. Technology would now become central to its operations – not just the website, but also through mobile apps. Digital media would also be a rich source of raw material for data mining purposes and for maximising opportunities for ancillary sales.

By 2015, Ryanair's average load factor[15] had increased from 80% to just over 92% and it announced that its profits for the financial year ending March 2016 would be circa 25% higher than stock market expectations.[16] *Always Getting Better* was having a positive impact on profits: between 2013 and 2017, the company's market capitalisation increased from €9 billion to almost €19 billion, with €1.35 billion in profits. In June 2017, O'Leary sold 4 million shares at €18 each, though he still retained 4.1% of Ryanair, making him the third biggest shareholder. By 2018, the average load factor had increased to 95%.

Ancillary sales now comprised 27% of total sales and the target was to drive this above 30%. The German market was seen as providing good potential for further growth – by 2015 Ryanair had only 4% market share there. Not everything was rosy, however. The company received a lot of negative publicity over its allocation of seating that was not pre-booked, which meant that families were often split up on flights. O'Leary rejected the claim that this was done intentionally, responding that people should pay the charge for seat selection if they wanted to sit together.[17] The second 'free bag' on board was also withdrawn for passengers who did not have priority booking, although the price for check-in baggage was reduced from €35 to €25 per bag, as were some of the other ancillary costs.

---

[15] Load factor is the percentage of available seating capacity that is filled by passengers on a flight. The average load factor over a year is a measure of an airline's efficiency

[16] Cooper, M., 2018, *Michael O'Leary: Turbulent Times for the Man Who Made Ryanair*, London, Portfolio Penguin

[17] Pope, C., 2017, "Turbulent winds blow through Ryanair", *Irish Times*, 27 December 2017, p.18

Trouble Brewing

Over half of Ryanair's pilots are not employed directly by the company but instead work on a contract basis, which means that they are paid only for the hours that they are actually flying. Thus, these contract pilots do not get paid for home stand-by time or flight preparation time, both of which are part of a normal working week for a pilot. In addition, they have no entitlements to sick pay or corporate pension schemes. These pilots are effectively treated as self-employed people who offer their services to companies established specifically to provide Ryanair with pilots.[18] This was causing concern with the authorities in many EU Member States as it was being interpreted as a means to circumvent employment legislation and protection. The industrial relations issue was generating a lot of negative publicity for Ryanair. In October 2016, the company issued a profit warning.

On 13 September 2017, Michael O'Leary was informed by his operations director that there was a major problem with staff rosters. The working hours of pilots and cabin crew are tightly controlled by the Irish Aviation Authority (IAA) and other European regulators to prevent fatigue and therefore accidents. Pilots can fly a maximum of 900 hours per year (with pro-rata limits for each day and each week). Ryanair was told by the IAA it would have to adjust its 'roster year' from 1 April to the calendar year, i.e. starting 1 January. O'Leary had been aware of this, but believed the situation was under control. However, many pilots were due annual leave and were unwilling to give up leave to meet the demands of the roster, despite being offered significant financial incentives. The only consolation from Ryanair's perspective was it would only happen in 2017, as 1 January 2018 would be a fresh leave year for pilots and Ryanair managers could plan the year-long roster accordingly.

During the next couple of months, hundreds of Ryanair flights had to be cancelled due to the unavailability of pilots and cabin crew. The big issue for Ryanair passengers was that it was unknown in advance which flights would be affected. While over 300,000 passengers would be affected – a very small percentage of total passengers – it left 18 million passengers unsure whether it would be their flight or not. There were also complaints from passengers about experiencing difficulty in getting the compensation for cancelled flights, as is their entitlement under EU law. It turned into a complete mess from a company communications perspective. The reaction in the media was negative; the reaction on social media was disastrous. In a matter of days, the company lost almost €2 billion in market capitalisation, which would impact on growth.[19]

At the same time, the Court of Justice of the European Union (CJEU) issued a significant ruling that Ryanair staff based outside of Ireland have the option of bringing court proceedings in the country where they conduct the main element of their work (prior to this, Ryanair staff from all over Europe had to bring proceedings before an Irish court as the company is registered in Ireland).

---

[18] O'Halloran, B., 2017, "Ryanair's problem foreseen by pilots", *Irish Times*, 23 December 2017, p.14

[19] Cooper, M., 2018, *Michael O'Leary: Turbulent Times for the Man Who Made Ryanair*, London, Portfolio Penguin

The move was welcomed by the International Transport Workers' Federation, which represents over 700 transport unions across 150 countries. This would strengthen the hand of staff in negotiations.

If the rostering problem and CJEU ruling was not enough, at a press conference following the September (2017) AGM of the company, Michael O'Leary used the opportunity to apologise for the mess up but then proceeded to state that pilots were extremely well paid to do an easy job, and that the planes were essentially flown by computers. He restated that his long-held contention that 'hell would freeze over' before Ryanair would recognise trade unions. The pilots were outraged by O'Leary's press conference tirade, which is likely to have damaged whatever goodwill was left.

Union Recognition

Airlines across the globe currently face a shortage of qualified pilots. Ryanair is no exception and it also faces a retention problem,[20] which affects not just existing schedules but also the ability to introduce additional routes. While O'Leary was offering incentives to pilots to give up their leave, he was also issuing threats about pay freezes or base transfers in relation to other issues, particularly in response to any demands for union recognition and the use of contract staff.

The pilots started using social media channels such as WhatsApp to keep in touch and co-ordinate their responses to the airline. They wanted union officials to negotiate on their behalf and, in a number of locations, balloted for industrial action. Ryanair could not afford further flight cancellations in addition to the cancellations due to the rostering debacle. With the Christmas rush about to begin, Ryanair finally capitulated on 15 December 2017 and agreed to negotiate with pilots' trade unions, and unions representing cabin crew, who also demanded recognition. Negotiations now began on the issues of which unions Ryanair would recognise. Many thought the announcement to deal with unions was a tactic to buy time and as negotiations dragged out, a number of short strikes were initiated in various bases across Europe in 2018.

In March 2018, Ryanair made its second acquisition when it purchased 75% of the Austrian airline Laudamotion for €50 million and agreed to put another €50 million into the company as operating capital. Profits to the end of May 2017 were €1.45 billion, up 10%, while revenues were €7.15 billion, up 7%. However, in October 2018, the company issued a profit warning, which saw its market capitalisation drop from €14.85 billion to €12.86 billion.[21] By 31 July 2019, its shares were trading at €9.48, down considerably from its 12-month high of €16.98.

In June 2019, Ryanair launched a new Malta-based subsidiary airline, Malta Air (not to be confused with the State-run airline, Air Malta). This followed on from Ryanair Sun, which was established in

---

[20] O'Connor, F., 2017, "After a terrible year, what next for Ryanair supremo O'Leary", *Sunday Independent*, 31 December 2017, p.20

[21] O'Halloran, B., 2018, "More turbulent times ahead for Ryanair and its shareholders", *Irish Times*, 5 October 2018, Business Agenda, p.5

Poland in 2018. Malta Air will take over a number of existing Ryanair routes in the Mediterranean area and will also create new routes. In turn, these two new additions to the company will require extra pilots and cabin crew.[22] In summer 2019, there were threats of further strikes by Ryanair pilots, who remained unhappy with the rate of progress in relation to negotiations regarding their working terms and conditions. Ryanair profits for the three months ending 30 June 2019 were €240 million, down 21% on the same period in 2018.[23]

There was also a major restructuring in 2019 of Ryanair as a holding company, similar to IAG. The new company, Ryanair Holdings Plc, will be run by Michael O'Leary, and the four subsidiary companies will each have their own CEO: Ryanair DAC; Ryanair UK; Ryanair Sun (to be rebranded as Buzz); and Laudamotion. This restructuring will see Michael O'Leary at a further remove from the day-to-day issues facing the airlines and will allow Ryanair Holdings to concentrate on fleet purchases and acquisition of smaller rivals.[24] Now that 'hell has frozen over', it remains to be seen whether Ryanair can regain its previous highs.

---

[22] Smith, O., 2019, "Ryanair to launch new Malta-based airline", *The Telegraph*, 11 June 2019, https://www.telegraph.co.uk/travel/news/ryanair-to-launch-new-malta-based-airline/, Accessed 21 July 2019

[23] O'Halloran, B. and O'Brien, C., 2019, "Ryanair profits fall 21% due to costs and lower fares", *Irish Times*, 30 July 2019

[24] O'Halloran, B., 2019, "O'Leary's move is succession planning by another name", *Irish Times*, 5 February 2019, https://www.irishtimes.com/business/transport-and-tourism/ryanair-o-leary-s-move-is-succession-planning-by-another-name-1.3782085, Accessed 22 July 2019

CRH Plc

Catherine Moylan[1] and Gerry Gallagher

The purpose of this case study is to illustrate a number of aspects of corporate strategy. In particular, it examines various aspects of corporate governance, the type of decisions taken at the corporate headquarters of a large multi-national company (MNC), mergers and acquisitions, and market development. It is intended for class discussion and is not an indication of either good or bad management practice.

With its headquarters in Ireland, CRH is a leading globally diversified building materials group that employs over 90,000 people at 3,700 locations in 32 countries. CRH (Cement Roadstone Holdings) was formed in 1970 through a merger of Cement Ltd (established in 1936) and Roadstone Ltd (established in 1949). The company reached a market capitalisation of €20.8 billion in early 2019. CRH is the largest building materials company in North America and the second largest worldwide. It has a primary listing on the London Stock Exchange, with a secondary listing on the Irish Stock Exchange (Euronext Dublin).

Company Structure and Business Model

The buildings materials industry produces commodities in which there is little differentiation and as a result, such products are price-sensitive to competition. The industry is notoriously cyclical, depending on economic cycles. An extreme example of this was in Ireland in 2007 when in the region of 93,000 houses were built; two years later, as a result of the financial crisis, this dropped to about 24,000, resulting in the redundancy of thousands of construction workers.

Growth in the industry is also dependent on the type or profile of the market involved. In general, growth will be slower in mature markets as there are fewer new builds taking place and these markets are more dependent on building upgrades. In developing markets there will be a greater proportion of new building taking place, offering more potential for producers. Furthermore, markets will differ in terms of building specifications. In 2018, 'New Build' accounted for 55% of CRH's global sales, with repair, maintenance and improvement (RMI) representing the other 45% of sales. In terms of end-use, 35% is residential, 30% of non-residential and 35% infrastructure.

Building materials are bulky, heavy and expensive to transport long distances. As a result, a wide network of production sites is required. There are high fixed costs involved in production, which require economies of scale. Production, particularly cement manufacture, is also an energy intensive process.

---

[1] Catherine Moylan, FCA, is a senior lecturer at the Institute of Technology Tralee

The structure of CRH has changed over time as its product range and markets have developed. With effect from 1 January 2019, the group has simplified its organisational structure, and it is now based on three main divisions:

- Americas Materials
- Europe Materials
- Global Building Products.

CRH considers that the new structure will provide the company with more focused business units, driven by a lean corporate centre focusing on leveraging its strengths to create growth in key markets and businesses. The company's businesses are diversified across a range of products, geographical regions and end uses (residential, non-residential and infrastructure – see above). With a strong emphasis on sustainability, the board established a new Safety, Environmental and Social Responsibility (SESR) Committee. However, Cevian Capital, Europe's largest shareholder activist (which owns 3% of CRH's shares), believes CRH is still too complex both from an operational and structural perspective.[2]

The Europe and North American markets proved very successful for CRH in 2018 across all end-user markets, with the company benefiting from the post-recession increase in spending by governments, companies and households. In addition to acquiring companies, CRH has invested in greenfield projects with the intention of achieving vertical integration. CRH aims to be in either the No. 1 or No. 2 market position in the manufacture and supply of building materials, from heavy products such as cement to sanitary, heating and plumbing products. In Europe alone, CRH employs 43,000 people in 1,870 locations across 24 countries.

CRH first entered the US market in 1978 when it purchased Amcor, a concrete products group in Utah. A number of other purchases of companies across the US, from California to the East Coast, followed over the next couple of decades. The company is now the number one producer of asphalt and aggregates in the US and the third largest producer of ready-mixed concrete. CRH now has a presence in 46 US states. In 2018, the company divided its US operations into five divisions: North, South, Central, West and Cement. CRH also has a presence in seven Canadian provinces, and in South America it operates in the southeast region of Brazil. In the Americas Division, there are 45,100 people employed by CRH in 1,820 operating locations. In 2018, sales in the region were €13.4 billion – up 9% from the previous year. Poor weather impacted on like-for-like sales for many of the products, but turnover still increased as a result of acquisitions. A focus on cost control resulted in increased margins. The Americas have grown in importance for CRH and in terms of operating profits. The Americas now account for 66% of the company's geographic portfolio, Europe represents 33% and Asia the remaining 1%.

---

[2] "Activist shareholder wants more focused CRH, says stock could double", *Irish Times*, 28 June 2019, https://www.irishtimes.com/business/construction/activist-shareholder-wants-more-focused-crh-says-stock-could-double-1.3940578, Accessed 26 July 2019

In 1990, the company expanded into France with a number of purchases, including Raboni SA, a builders' merchants company. In 1995, CRH entered the Polish market when it bought Holding Cement Polski, and by the end of the decade, it had over a dozen operations there. In 1999 it also bought Finnsementti Oy, the only cement producer in Finland, along with a leading producer of aggregates, Lohja Rudus Oy.

This was followed in 2000 by the purchase of the Jura Group in Switzerland for €425 million, which gave CRH a regional distribution channel for cement, concrete and aggregates. In 2001 the company acquired a stake in the only Israeli company producing cement when it took a 25% stake in the holding company, Mahav. In 2003, CRH paid €693 million to acquire Cementbouw, a building materials producer and DIY store chain in the Netherlands. The following year, it paid €429 million for a 49% holding in Secil, a Portuguese cement producer. Nearer to home, CRH acquired the UK building materials producer, Lafarge Tarmac, in 2015. In 2017, the company made 95 acquisitions in its Europe Heavyside division, and made 110 divestments. The division is divided into three geographical areas: Europe North, Europe West and Europe East. Sales revenue for the division was €6.9 billion in 2017, down 1% from the previous year, but operating profits were up 24%.

In 2006, CRH moved further afield when it invested in a Chinese cement factory based in the Heilongjiang region of the country. It also bought a 26% stake in the Jilin Yatai Group in China. In 2008, CRH bought a 50% stake in the Indian cement company, My Home Industries Ltd, for €290 million. The company formed an Asia Division in 2015 when, in addition to its other acquisitions in Asia, it bought the number-two cement producer in the Philippines, Republic Cement. In Asia, the main entry point tends to be in cement. The extent of the industrialisation and urbanisation happening in these countries is enormous, and population growth in the region is a key driver for growth.

The new Global Buildings Platform division operates across North America, Europe and Asia. It covers a wide range of manufactured products that are used in the construction industry. The main categories include:

- Infrastructure – a range of precast concrete and polymer-based products, such as pipes
- Network Access Products and Perimeter Protection – fences and gates
- Construction Accessories – a wide variety of products used in construction
- Building Envelope – a variety of windows and doors
- Architectural Products – concrete masonry products for homes and gardens (bought primarily through DIY stores)
- Shutters and Awnings – roller shutters and awnings for outdoor protection.

These products are marketed at three different sectors: residential, non-residential and infrastructure, and cover both new and RMI (renovation, maintenance, improvement) use.

Over the decades, CRH has developed a proven model of continuous business improvement which, together with its acquisitions strategy, has made it a leader in the global building materials industry. The value created by its strategic approach has led to a cumulative total shareholder return (TSR) of

14.8% since it was formed in 1970. To put this in perspective, if an investor bought €100 worth of shares in 1970 and held on to them (reinvesting the dividends), that investment would now be worth €97,000. To achieve this level of growth, CRH has had to identify businesses suitable for takeover and then acquire them at a price that allowed for future growth. (The main challenge for companies when making acquisitions in terms of a return on investment is the integration of those acquisitions into the parent company.) In its 2018 annual report, CRH stated that it spent a total of €3.6 billion on 46 transactions. Included in this was the acquisition of Ash Grove cement factory in Texas for €2.9 billion. In 2018, CRH also made €3 billion on disposals. In 2017, CRH spent €1.9 billion on acquisitions.

CRH now has a global reach, which is important in an industry where the products are heavy, bulky and costly to transport. The company's global reach and network allows it to shorten the supply chain for its customers and provide them with a wide range of products. The global reach also allows CRH to be close to its customers and to keep focused on their changing needs.

	2018 €m	2017 €m	2016 €m	2015 €m
EBITDA	3,365	3,146	2,980	2,079
Net finance costs	305	289	317	295
Average net assets	22,763	21,017	20,871	16,707
Total group operating profit	2,177	2,238	2,027	1,277

Figure 1 – *CRH: Key Financial Information*[3]

Strategy

The company's strategy is focused on three objectives:

- Maximising returns on its businesses
- Conducting those businesses responsibly and sustainably
- Expanding its balanced portfolio of diversified products and geographic regions.

According to CRH's 2018 annual report, the company is guided by a number of strategic imperatives:

- **Continuous business improvement** – constantly making the business better by achieving operational, commercial and financial excellence
- **Disciplined and focused growth** – maintaining financial discipline, a strong balance sheet, cash-flow generation and focused allocation of capital to achieve optimum growth

---

[3] Summary of key financial information from CRH financial statements/annual reports 2015 to 2018

- **Leadership development** – being able to attract and empower the next generation of leaders
- **Benefits of scale** – being able to lever group scale to fund acquisitions and build leadership positions in local markets.[4]

Corporate Governance

CRH's vision is to be the leading building materials business in the world and in so doing, create value and superior returns for its shareholders. There are two executive directors on the board of CRH: Albert Manifold, the CEO, and Senan Murphy, the Group Finance Director, as well as 11 non-executive directors. The board is led by non-executive chair, Nicky Hartery (Ireland). The other directors are: Patrick Kennedy (Ireland), Richie Boucher (Ireland), Heather Ann McSharry (Ireland), Siobhan Talbot (Ireland), Gillian Platt (Canada), Lucinda Riches (UK), Henk Rottinghuis (Netherlands), William Tueber (US), Mary K. Rhinehart (US) and Donald A. McGovern (US). Mr McGovern retired in 2019, as he completed a second three-year term as director. In July 2018, Ms Platt succeeded Mr McGovern as Senior Independent Director.

In the CRH 2018 Annual Report, the board stated that it is committed to gender diversity at board level and throughout the organisation, while also acknowledging that achieving gender diversity below board level is proving to be a challenge.[5] At board level, the number of female directors has increased each year from 15% in 2013 to 42% in 2019. The number of females in senior management roles has risen from 8% in 2016, to 9% in 2017, and to 10% in 2018. The board considers that 80% of its directors could be deemed independent. Twenty-nine per cent of CRH directors had served three years or less on its board, and 71% have served between three and six years.

In its 2018 annual report, CRH stated that the company was following and adhering to the 2018 *UK Corporate Governance Code*. According to the report, the board is responsible for the leadership, oversight, control, development and long-term success of the group. It is also responsible for instilling the appropriate culture, values and behaviour throughout the organisation. The main areas of focus for the board include risk management, IT and cyber security, talent management, succession planning and strategy.

There are six permanent board committees to assist the board in its work, including:

- Acquisitions
- Audit
- Finance
- Nomination and Corporate Governance
- Remuneration
- Safety, Environmental and Social Responsibility.

---

[4] CRH 2018 Annual Report
[5] CRH 2018 Annual Report

The new Safety, Environmental and Social Responsibility committee has additional responsibility for inclusion and diversity. The board now considers sustainability and safety to be key risk areas that need to be actively managed. Sustainable manufacturing processes that will lessen the impact on environmental damage has to be of concern to any company in the broader construction industry. In many cases, this will be demand-led. This will have to take into account the full life-cycle of the company's products.

Each board committee has its own terms of reference. A number of matters are reserved for consideration solely by the board: appointment of directors; strategic plans for the group; annual budgets; major acquisitions and disposals; significant capital expenditure; approvals of full-year and interim results.[6] In 2018, an independent external audit of the effectiveness of the board and its committees was conducted. This audit included observation of the board meetings, and reviewed the content and structure of board papers. The audit also consisted of one-to-one interviews with board members and senior managers.

The audit committee of CRH comprises three non-executive director board members, considered by the board to be independent. The audit committee, on behalf of the board, is responsible for liaising with the company's auditors. The audit committee is also responsible for monitoring the effectiveness and quality of the external audit process and ensuring it adheres to the agreed audit plan. To ensure auditor independence, CRH has changed its policy on the amount of non-audit work, such as consultancy, that can be supplied by the auditors. The level of non-audit fees as a percentage of total fees paid to the company's auditors dropped from 27% in 2015 to 11% in 2017, and in 2018 it was down to 6%.

CRH is committed to ongoing communication with its shareholders and recognises the importance of effective dialogue. The Investor Relations team meets with institutional shareholders each year to inform them of the organisation's activities. Equally, the company is committed to internal communication, using a variety of methods to achieve this objective.

Alfred Manifold, the Group CEO, was an internal appointment. He joined the company as Finance Director for Eastern Europe in 1988. In 2004, he became Group Development Director and in 2007 he was appointed Managing Director, CRH Europe Materials. During this time, he played a lead role in the company's expansion into Asia. In 2009, Mr Manifold was made Group Chief Operating Officer and he also joined the board of directors. This was a difficult time for CRH with the impact of the global financial crisis and its fallout.

At its AGM in Dublin in April 2017, 17% of the shareholders voted against a proposed executive pay structure. The total remuneration for the CEO was €10 million (in 2016, 40% of the shareholders voted against the pay package). The board pointed out that the share price of the company had increased by 80% since 2014. In its 2018 annual report, CRH acknowledged

---

[6] CRH 2018 Annual Report

the shareholder reaction in relation to the vote on executive pay, and this prompted a review of executive remuneration and engagement with shareholders. The review resulted in a number of new detailed policy measures in relation to remuneration being implemented by the board.

The company states that it is committed to high ethical standards. On its website, CRH has published a detailed *Code of Business Conduct*[7] which covers a number of areas including: business ethics; workplace health & safety; employment policies; the company's commitment to its customers; suppliers and business partners; IT and data security; bribery and corruption; fraud; conflicts of interest; environmental sustainability; and political contributions. The company has a 24/7 multi-lingual confidential 'hotline' facility called 'Speak Up'. This is available to all employees to report issues of concern to them regarding unethical behaviour or misconduct.

At the beginning of 2019, CRH reviewed its operations and the challenges it faces. In general, while the company's prospects for at least the medium-term looks good, with Brexit looming, there should be no room for complacency.

---

[7] See https://www.crh.com/our-group/our-people/corporate-governance/codes-of-conduct, Accessed 28 May 2019

The National Children's Hospital Project

This case illustrates a number of issues arising from the construction of the National Children's Hospital in Dublin, including project management, stakeholder management, corporate governance and human resource management. The case was written in April 2019, and the project was still ongoing, and its issues evolving. Nevertheless, the case is sufficiently developed for class discussion. It does not necessarily illustrate effective or ineffective management of a project; nor is it intended to be a commentary on any particular political party.

Background to the Project

At the beginning of this century, the Irish Government planned to build a state-of-the-art national children's hospital (NCH) in Dublin. The chief executive of the Health Services Executive (HSE), Professor Brendan Drumm, stated the site should be located next to the Mater Hospital in Dublin's north inner city, and this view was supported by Government. It was considered to be essential to build the children's hospital co-located with an adult teaching hospital so that there would be a sharing of equipment and medical expertise between the children's and the adult hospital, and it would also facilitate the training of junior doctors. Co-location is considered particularly important in situations where newborn babies and/or their mothers require urgent specialist care that would not be available in maternity hospitals to the same level, e.g. cardiac or respiratory emergencies. The Mater proposal proved controversial, particularly as it was believed that access to the hospital would be severely restricted by city-centre traffic grid-lock.

Then, in 2003, solicitor-turned-developer, Noel Smyth, offered to build a children's hospital on a not-for-profit basis, offering a large site free-of-charge to the Government at Newlands Cross, Naas Road, on the outskirts of Dublin.[1] The proposal was backed by philanthropists and European Investment Bank funding. Leading firms of architects and accountants offered their services at cost price to support the project. The plan included co-locating a maternity hospital with 1,000 beds at a cost of €600 million. The offer was turned down by the Government in favour of the Mater Hospital site. Development plans for the Mater Hospital site were drafted and submitted to Dublin City Council, which subsequently granted planning permission. There were a number of objections to this decision, and it was appealed to An Bord Pleanála (the national planning appeals board), which rejected the proposal in 2011. The €40 million spent so far in development costs was now written off as a 'sunk cost'. The Government went back to the drawing board.

In 2012, the Government approved an 8.7 acre site at St James's Hospital, to the west of Dublin's city centre, as the location for the new national children's hospital. Though there was

---

[1] Sheehan, M., 2019, "Powerless Board and Red Tape Saw Costs Spiral", *Sunday Independent*, 3 February 2019, p.4

a lot of opposition to the St James's Hospital site, with many believing it was too small and had restricted traffic access,[2] the then-Minister for Health, Dr James Reilly TD, said the site would bring together three Dublin-based children's hospitals under one roof: Our Lady's Children's Hospital, Crumlin; Temple Street Children's University Hospital; and the National Children's Hospital, Tallaght. The new building would have 473 in-patient beds and 22 operating theatres (with 6,000 rooms in total) and it would be completed by 2018, at an estimated cost of €650 million.[3] There would be two out-patient and urgent-care centres at Connolly and Tallaght hospitals, both in west Dublin. Speaking at the appointment of Eilísh Hardiman as Chief Executive Officer of the Children's Health Ireland (formally known as the Children's Hospital Group) in July 2013, Dr O'Reilly said the board running the project would ensure that the country would have the best hospital in the "quickest fashion". However, the project was beset by delays and cost escalations.

The planning for the new hospital had begun in 2012, and the Chair of the National Paediatric Hospital Development Board (NPHDB),[4] Tom Costello,[5] appointed a design team in August 2014,[6] which consisted of the civil and structural engineering firm, O'Connor Sutton Cronin; the international multidisciplinary engineering company, ARUP; quantity surveyors, Linesight; and architects, BDP/OCMA. A planning application was lodged with Dublin City Council in August 2015 and planning was granted in 2016. The then-Minister for Health, Dr Leo Varadkar TD, said at the time that the hospital could be completed by 2020. The project team decided on a single-contract, two-stage planning process.[7] After the initial enabling works to clear the site were competed, Phase 1 consisted of the laying of foundations and other subterranean work. This allowed the NPHDB and BAM to jointly establish an agreed 'guaranteed maximum price' (GMP) for the construction project (the GMP was finalised in November 2018). Phase 2 consisted of the building of the seven-story hospital and other above-ground works. The main construction work of Phase 2 commenced in January 2019.

---

2 Cullen, P., 2019, "Timeline of National Children's Hospital Development", *Irish Times*, 5 February 2019

3 This was an estimated cost of the new hospital given by the Minister in 2012, but was not based on any detailed costings. The first detailed 'official' project budget was completed in 2013 and the estimated cost at that point was €790 million, the majority of which related to construction costs.

4 The function of the NPHDB is to plan, design, build and equip the National Children's Hospital.

5 Tom Costello is a Chartered Engineer, whose career was in the construction industry. He was formerly managing director of John Sisk and Son (Irl) Ltd., where he oversaw the development of major infrastructural projects.

6 Mitchell, S., 2019, "National Children's Hospital: The neverending story", *Sunday Business Post*, 20 January 2019, p.8

7 This two-phase approach was decided as a means of speeding up the project timeline. Phase 1 could be proceeding while the detail of Phase 2 was still being worked on. This method is in line with international practice for unique projects, but had not been used previously in any major infrastructural project in Ireland.

According to PwC's report from April 2019 (see below), the tender documents for the competition for the main construction contract (Phase 2) were completed by the NPHDB in October 2016 and submitted for tender.[8] After evaluation by the NPHDB, the contract was awarded in January 2017. The *construction* budget at that time was €570 million and there were four companies that submitted bids, all of which were over the budget figure. BAM Ireland Ltd, a wholly owned subsidiary of the Dutch building company Royal BAM Group, submitted a bid for €631 million. This was €61 million above the construction budget but was €131 million, or 20%, lower than the second lowest bid, which came in at €767 million (€192 million above the budget). The highest bid received was €239 million above the budget. The criteria for judging submissions was heavily weighted in favour of price. By the time the Government signed off on Phase 2 of the project – the Definitive Business Case – in April 2017, Dr Varadkar said the total costs (construction and other costs) had risen and would now be €983 million. In October 2017, works on the hospital foundations (Phase 1) commenced.

By December 2018, the Government was advised by the NPHDB that the projected cost had risen once again, this time to €1.43 billion. This was a rise of almost €450 million more than the €983 million as stated in the Definitive Business Case a year and a half earlier in April 2017. This figure, however, did not capture the full amount, as IT services and other fit-out costs were not included. This is planned to be the first fully digital hospital in Ireland, where all patient records will be accessed online anywhere in the hospital. In turn, it will be linked to the wider electronic health record (EHR) programme, which is being developed by eHealth Ireland for the HSE. To protect against computer crashes and power outages, extensive back-up systems would be required. By January 2019, the projected cost was being estimated at €1.7 billion (and rising) with a completion date set for 2022. This would be followed by a period of commissioning and staff familiarisation before services would transfer. Eilísh Hardiman sent an email to staff working in the three existing children's hospitals in January 2019 advising them that they would transfer to the new hospital in 2023 – some 11 years after the project began.

These cost increases and time delays worried stakeholders. Dr Andrew Jordan, Chair of the National Association of General Practitioners, questioned why, given that it would be the most expensive children's hospital anywhere in the world, there would not be any extra bed capacity over the three existing children's hospitals. To put this projected total cost in perspective, the entire multi-annual capital budget for the health service for the four-year period from 2019 to 2022 was set at €3 billion. Cost over-runs for the NCH project will inevitably take from other major capital programmes in communities around the country, either causing them to be postponed or cancelled.

---

[8] PwC, 2019, *New Children's Hospital: Independent review of escalation of costs*, Dublin, PwC, https://merrionstreet.ie/MerrionStreet/en/News-Room/Releases/20190409_NCH_Report.pdf, Accessed 23 July 2019

Comparable Projects

When compared to similar projects in the private sector, the timeline for the NCH project bears no comparison.[9] In 1984, the Blackrock Clinic in Dublin was developed by retired surgeon Jimmy Sheehan. The hospital was built and equipped within a 10-month period. Mr Sheehan also developed the Hermitage Clinic and the Galway Clinic, which were each constructed within a 15-month period. Sheehan had been introduced to Gerrits Construction in Florida in the early 1980s, who were involved in the building of a number of hospitals around the world. Gerrits places a one-year time-limit on all its projects and the size of the building does not impact on this time-frame – it merely dictates the level of resources put into the project. The contract is for a fixed price, including the design cost, but allowing for construction-cost inflation. All plans are frozen before the construction begins and the entire project team, consisting of the client, the design team and the construction contractor meet every week to address any issues and change requests there and then. All medical equipment is ordered at the time construction begins and is stored until needed, ensuring no delays in the fitting-out phase.

Reasons for Cost Increases

When questioned about the hospital project (and its rising costs) at the Oireachtas Committee on Health in January 2019,[10] Tom Costello, Chair of the NPHDB, told committee members, including chair Dr Michael Harty TD, that the project team had gone about the process in a competent and professional manner and would not do anything different if they "were starting the project today". When asked about the cost overruns, Mr Costello, and project director, John Pollock, provided various reasons, including:

- Construction cost increases and extended timelines for completion (€320 million)
- Other construction works on the two satellite facilities in west Dublin and decanting the St. James's Hospital site (€13 million)[11]
- Extra project costs (€36 million)
- Providing the two satellite facilities with extra equipment (€16 million)
- 'Risk' (€16 million)
- Additional VAT of €50 million.

Costello and Pollock further explained that the complexity of some of the services was not initially realised and they had under-estimated the quantity of some of the materials. For example, while they were given an initial cost per metre for cables to wire the hospital, they did not know what

---

[9] Sheehan, J., 2019, "How to build a world-class hospital in just one year", *Sunday Business Post*, 20 January 2019, p.19

[10] Oireachtas, 2019, Joint Committee on Health, https://www.oireachtas.ie/en/committees/32/committee-on-health/debates, Accessed 12 February 2019

[11] 'Decanting' involves demolishing buildings and clearing out an existing site, as opposed to starting on a new green-field site, and in the process, moving existing offices and staff to facilitate the building process.

quantity of cables would be required. In addition, subsequent to the Grenfell Tower disaster in London in 2017, Dublin's Chief Fire Officer directed that extra fire sprinklers be added, which entailed a cost of €27 million. The project leaders were also asked to what extent the brown-field location of the new hospital had an effect on the complexity of the building project in a congested site, along with its impact on the cost and timeframe for completion, but the answer was not known by the Development Board.

Human Resource Management

Building a state-of-the-art hospital is one thing; staffing it is another. Such an advanced hospital will require world-class nurses, doctors and a wide range of other healthcare professionals and medical specialists, as well as support staff. However, it was reported early in 2019 that hospitals across Ireland were finding it difficult to recruit and retain nursing staff due to what nurses perceive as poor pay and working conditions[12] In January 2019, nurses began a series of strikes to fight for better pay and conditions, claiming that recruitment and retention of nurses is a serious problem for the HSE. On graduating, many nurses trained in Ireland are recruited by hospitals in the Middle East, where large salaries are available, or by the NHS in Britain, where working conditions and career prospects are deemed to be much more favourable than working in the Irish health system. According to the OECD, Ireland has 11.6 nurses per 1,000 population, in comparison to an EU average of 8.4 per 1,000.[13] The Irish figure does not take account of job-sharing posts which, given the high cost of childcare in Ireland, is quite common among the predominantly female nursing workforce, i.e two nurses working half-time is considered one nursing job or 'whole-time equivalent', but accounts for two nurses on the register.[14] The Irish figure also includes nurses working as managers and educators. Having statistics that reflect the reality on the ground is a prerequisite for planning staffing requirements, and the ability to recruit and *retain* sufficient numbers.

The same issue holds true for doctors. The joint medical board of the Children's Hospital Group wrote to the Minister for Health, Simon Harris TD, in late 2018 expressing the board's concern about its ability to "adequately staff both the main hospital and the satellite units for urgent and ambulatory care". At the time of writing (2019), there are over 3,000 full-time equivalent consultant doctors working in the Irish health service and 455 hospital consultant posts filled by locum, temporary and agency staff. Not only are locum staff more expensive to hire, but many have not completed specialist training in their respective areas. In 2018, the President of the

---

[12] Mitchel, S., 2019, "National Children's Hospital board is worried about the shortage of consultants", *Sunday Business Post*, 27 January 2019, p.9

[13] OECD, 2018, *Health at a Glance. Europe 2018. State of Health in the EU Cycle*, Paris, OECD, https://ec.europa.eu/health/sites/health/files/state/docs/2018_healthatglance_rep_en.pdf, Accessed 23 July 2019

[14] O'Malley, C., 2019, "Statistics skew nurse numbers and mask real shortage in hospitals." *Irish Times*, 30 January 2019, https://www.irishtimes.com/opinion/statistics-skew-nurse-numbers-and-mask-real-shortage-in-hospitals-1.3775004, Accessed 23 July 2019

High Court, Mr Justice Peter Kelly, expressed alarm when it emerged that a locum (temporary) consultant radiologist was not on the specialist register. The Medical Council had stated in court that this doctor was responsible for a "litany of failures". Cases of medical negligence can result in grievous damage to patients and enormous compensation payments. According to the HSE, there were 161 doctors working in Irish hospitals in early 2019 who were not on the specialist register. Many vacancies exist around the country for hospital consultants. According to the Public Appointments Service, 128 consultant posts were advertised in 2018. Twenty-one of those were not filled. In many cases, either no one with sufficient experience applied or, in other cases, there were no applications at all.

In 2013, Minister O'Reilly initiated a 30% cut to the starting salary of newly appointed medical consultants, resulting in a starting salary of €150,000 – much lower than that paid to their more experienced colleagues who joined the system in previous years. Many Irish doctors travel to Britain, the US, Canada and Australia to undergo specialist training when they graduate. Consultants tend to receive much higher salaries and enjoy better working conditions in these countries and, as a result, many consultants are reluctant to return to work in the Irish health system. In terms of percentage of GDP, Ireland's expenditure on health is one of the highest comparatively among developed countries. Though it trains more doctors than other Member States, Ireland has the lowest number of hospital consultants *per capita* in the EU. While clearly this affects the entire Irish health service, it is of particular concern when it comes to resource-planning for the new national children's hospital. Talks are ongoing between Irish Hospital Consultants' Association and the Department of Health to address this anomaly. In July 2019, the NCH Outpatient Centre in Connolly Hospital was opened on a restricted-hours basis only, after concern was expressed about the lack of sufficient hospital consultants.[15]

Corporate Governance

From a governance perspective, there are a number of different organisations involved in overseeing the development of the national children's hospital:

- **The National Paediatric Hospital Development Board (NPHDB)**, chaired by Fred Barry, and includes Paul Quinn, Head of Procurement at the Department of Public Expenditure and Reform, i.e. the Irish Government's Chief Procurement Officer.
- **Children's Health Ireland**, the board of which is chaired by Professor James Brown, which oversees the running of the three existing children's hospitals in Ireland and will take over the new children's hospital when it is completed. (As mentioned above, the CEO of Children's Health Ireland is Eilish Hardiman.)
- **The Children's Hospital Project and Programme Board**, chaired by the Secretary General of the Department of Health, Jim Breslin. This board oversees the whole process from the perspective of the Department of Health.

---

[15] Wall, M., 2019, "New children's facilities 'unsafe', say top doctors", *Irish Times*, 26 July 2019

- **The Children's Hospital Project and Programme Steering Group**, chaired by Dean Sullivan, Deputy Director, Strategy, at HSE.
- The Oireachtas Committee on Health.
- The Oireachtas Public Accounts Committee.
- The Office of the Comptroller and Auditor General.

According to project director, John Pollock, in his account to the Oireachtas Committee on Health in January,[16] the Department of Health was informed of massive cost overruns on the NCH project in August 2018. Mr Pollock told the Committee that the Department of Health had been alerted to a cost escalation of €200 million in August, but it would appear that the Minister for Health, Simon Harris (or the public), was not informed of the cost over-runs until December 2018. This is in despite of the fact there was a senior civil servant on the board of the NPHDB. While board confidentiality is a normal requirement for board directors, under a 2010 circular, civil servants appointed to state boards are obliged to report to the relevant Minister when a serious concern arises.

In September 2018, in response to a parliamentary question, Simon Harris had stated that the hospital would cost €1.07 billion, which included €983 million for all aspects of construction and equipping, plus €88.3 million for ICT. It would appear that this statement was made in spite of the Department of Health being made aware of the much higher costs. As we have seen, it has since emerged that the overall cost of the project will be €1.7 billion, with €1.43 billion being the capital cost.

In January 2019, Robert Watt, Secretary General of the Department of Public Expenditure and Reform was invited by the Chair of the Oireachtas Committee on Health, Dr Michael Harty, to attend the hearing into the cost overrun.[17] However, Mr Watt declined the invitation, saying it was a matter for the Department of Health. Harty responded by informing him that he was responsible for "ensuring proper use of resources and the provision of cost-effective public services". The Secretary General of the Department of Health, Jim Breslin, had previously told the Committee that he would be unable to attend due to a prior commitment. While the Oireachtas Committee on Health does not have compellability powers, the Public Accounts Committee does. In February 2019, Tom Costello resigned as chair of the NPHDB, stating that he was concerned about the reputational damage that the on-going commentary on increasing costs was having on "this critically important project". He was the third chair to resign from the post. He was replaced by Fred Barry, former chair of the National Roads Authority.

---

[16] Oireachtas, 2019, Joint Committee on Health, https://www.oireachtas.ie/en/committees/32/committee-on-health/debates/, Accessed 12 February 2019

[17] Oireachtas, 2019, Joint Committee on Health, https://www.oireachtas.ie/en/committees/32/committee-on-health/debates/, Accessed 12 February 2019

In summing up the work of the Oireachtas Health Committee's January 2019 inquiry into the cost over-runs on the NCH project, Dr Michael Harty explained that though he had concerns about the procurement process, he was not getting complete answers. As a result of the Health Committee inquiry, the Government asked PwC to conduct a full review of the project. The terms of reference of the 2019 PwC report did not include findings of culpability in relation to the building project. Chris Fitzpatrick, former Master of the Coombe Women and Infants University Hospital in Dublin, argued that the scope of the review should be widened to look at why it was decided to locate the NCH at the St James's Hospital campus, rather than the much bigger campus at the Coombe, which has green-field space in its grounds.[18]

Despite the fact that the Dáil voted to include the possibility of a change of site for the hospital, this was not included in the terms of reference of PwC's review. PwC's report, *New Children's Hospital: Independent review of escalation in costs*, was published in April 2019.[19] It found that only €16 million of the overrun could have been controlled, that there were numerous changes in the design, as well as delays, and that the initial projected cost had been vastly under-estimated, The impact and probability of risks had also been significantly unforeseen or unplanned for, and the project was "driven by an imperative for timely completion, within a cost envelope that was never adequate to deliver the envisaged outcome, and from a design that was continually evolving".

The PwC report questioned the ability of the NPHDB to be completely objective because it was performing both a management and an oversight role before the appointment of a full hospital executive team. It also criticised the lack of industry experience on the board necessary to challenge the construction companies, as well as the level of communication between the various oversight bodies. From a management perspective, one of the big issues was that a number of red flags were missed at various stages of the project, particularly when the first phase of the process was completing. In particular, the responses to tender received from prospective suppliers for the second phase should have alerted the project team that the budgeted cost was too low – they were all considerably higher than the budget. Some 750 points of the 1,000 points included in the tender documents criteria were for cost-related, thus "encouraging lean pricing" in suppliers' bids. The fact that the building contractor for Phase 1 was already on site made it less likely that another contractor would make a competitive bid for Phase 2 as there would be significant costs involved in taking over the project.

In December 2018, the Minister for Health signed the contract for the building of a new maternity hospital at the campus of St Vincent's University Hospital in South Dublin, at an estimated cost of €300 million. Will there be parallels in the project management of this new maternity hospital project? That remains to be seen.

---

[18] Cullen, P., 2019, "Calls for PwC to expand review into location of hospital", *Irish Times*, 5 February 2019, p.3

[19] PwC, 2019, *New Children's Hospital: Independent review of escalation in costs*, Dublin, PwC

Ernest Shackleton – Leading Change

This case is an example of incredible human resilience and survival under extraordinary conditions and how the leadership of Ernest Shackleton brought his men through changing circumstances that could never have been originally envisaged. It demonstrates that while aspects of change may be managed, primarily change must be led.

The race to the South Pole had ended when the Norwegian explorer Roald Amundsen reached it in 1911. In 1913, Sir Ernest Shackleton, a polar veteran who had accompanied Captain Robert Falcon Scott on earlier expeditions, came up with an ambitious plan: to be the first person to walk 3,000 km across the Antarctic continent from the Weddell Sea to the Ross Sea. He planned the trip meticulously and chose the expedition members. Shackleton understood the necessity of selecting the main trans-Antarctic team (as opposed to support teams) from the outset, and also the resources required – especially the use of skis and dogs. To the crew he was always 'The Boss', though his authority derived from his well-developed leadership skills and his understanding of human nature rather than through any hierarchy. In short, his approach to the expedition showed that there was a clear, consistent line running from his vision through to his goals.

Though he failed in his bid to cross the continent and the expedition became a two year-quest for survival, Shackleton succeeded in the greater task of leading his men to safety in unimaginable conditions. Sixty years after the expedition, Lionel Greenstreet, the first officer of the *Endurance,* was asked how they survived when so many other expeditions had perished. The 82-year-old answered in one word: "Shackleton".[1]

Early Life

Ernest Shackleton was born on 15 February 1874 in Kilkea, County Kildare. His parents were Quakers and this seemed to influence many of his values later in life and gave him a strong moral compass. The family later moved to Dublin and then to London, where he attended Dulwich College. He did not like student life and decided to join the Merchant Marine, where he completed a four-year apprenticeship, later taking exams to secure promotion. He served on a number of ships and learned much from their captains about what constituted good and bad leadership. He was an avid reader and began developing an interest in exploration. In 1901, Robert Falcon Scott, a Royal Navy captain, led an Antarctic expedition and Shackleton was selected as a junior officer on the *Discovery*. On his return from the first Scott expedition, Shackleton worked at a variety of jobs,

---

[1] Morrell, M. and Capparell, S., 2001, *Shackleton's* Way, London, Nicholas Brealey Publishing

including journalism, and in April 1904 married his long-time sweetheart Emily Dorman, who was six years his senior.

The Nimrod

In 1907, Shackleton launched his own expedition on board the *Nimrod*, with the aim of reaching the South Pole. He had learned a great deal from the mistakes that Scott had made about food and clothing and, in particular, leadership. He quickly earned the respect of his men who called him 'the Boss', a name that stuck. In fact, the contrast in leadership styles between Scott and Shackleton could not have been more pronounced. Scott had been brought up in the tradition of the Royal Navy. He was controlling, strict and believed in tough discipline, putting the mission above everything else. In contrast, Shackleton, though physically tough, was kind and considerate. He had a strong, clear focus on his goal, but was never foolish or obstinate. He always put his men's safety before personal glory. There would be other opportunities: "better a live donkey than a dead lion".[2]

In November 1908, Shackleton, with Dr Eric Marshall, Lt Jameson Boyd Adams and Frank Wild, set out for the South Pole. By 9 January 1909, however, they were forced to turn back or face certain starvation. They reached 88 degrees, 23 minutes south – just 155 km from the Pole. Shackleton had beaten Scott's previous record by 570 km. On the way back, they were desperately short of food. One of the men, Frank Wild was feeling particularly weak. Shackleton gave Wild his limited rations so that he could continue. They made it back safely to the ship.[3] On their return to England, Shackleton was knighted.

The Race to the South Pole

At this time, though there were many countries planning polar expeditions, the two main contenders were Scott and Norwegian Roald Amundsen. In 1910, Scott embarked in the *Terra Nova* for the Antarctic. The intention was to reach the South Pole from the Ross Sea. A group of Norwegians was also making for the South Pole across the Ross Sea but, using skis and dogs, they made much quicker progress. Scott's group (which included Irishman Tom Crean), reached the pole on 17 January 1912, only to find a Norwegian flag planted in the snow (Amundsen had reached it on 14 December 1911). On the way back to his ship, Scott, along with Wilson, Oates, Bowers and Taff Evans, perished.[4]

The Vision

Shackleton was clearly bitten by the exploration bug. The race for the South Pole was over, but in 1913, he came up with a new vision: to be the first to lead a trans-Atlantic expedition 3,000 km across the continent from the Weddell Sea to the Ross Sea. He wrote to *The Times* to announce the

---

[2] *Ibid*, see above, n.1
[3] Alexander, C., 1999, *The Endurance: Shackleton's Legendary Antarctic Expedition*, New York, Alfred Knopf
[4] Smith, M., 2000, *An Unsung Hero*, Cork, The Collins Press

"Imperial Trans-Antarctic Expedition" and in January 1914 set up an office to plan for the men, supplies, scientific team (necessary to get official backing) and considerable financial support that would be required.

In the windiest, coldest place on earth, the success of the expedition would depend on the personnel chosen. Despite the danger involved, there was no shortage of applicants (over 5,000 in total). Shackleton began by picking the key players. Frank Wild, a veteran of previous Antarctic trips, was a natural choice as Shackleton's second in command. Captain Frank Worsley, who had excellent navigational skills, was chosen to command the main ship, *Endurance*, named after Shackleton's family motto: *FortitudineVincimus* (by endurance we conquer). The intrepid Antarctic explorer from Kerry, Tom Crean, was made second officer. All personnel were chosen first and foremost for their temperament; then their proven ability. While each in his own right was talented, Shackleton also wanted positive, optimistic people who would work together as a team. The group included biologists, geologists, physicists and other scientific personnel that would be required to attract funding from the Royal Geographical Society.

Shackleton's exploits had caught the public imagination and he was able to raise the enormous sum of £50,000 (the equivalent of £10 million today) needed to finance the trip. He sent an individualised fund-raising prospectus for the voyage to numerous wealthy people. He also pre-sold the rights to all photographs and books that would arise from the trip.

Shackleton's plan was for the *Endurance* to drop off the main shore party at the Weddell Sea side of Antarctica and the *Aurora* would sail around to the opposite side to Cape Evans at the Ross Sea where a second shore party would be dropped off. Their role was to lay food depots at intervals along the second part of the route that would sustain Shackleton and his group as they made their way towards their pick-up point at the Ross Sea. Shackleton paid great attention to the selection of the equipment required for the journey. Experience had taught him that poor equipment can cost a great deal of time and destroy morale. He had also learned first-hand the limitations of poor clothing. He chose the best materials available (made then by Burberry) and used the latest scientific information on nutrition and food packaging, ensuring that they would have a balanced diet sufficient to match the demanding needs of the rough climate.

The Journey

Endurance left England on 4 August 1914, and sailed for the Antarctic via South America and South Georgia island. Shackleton was now 40 years old. Shackleton was a decisive leader and he had built a cohesive team. Some of the crew, however, did not shape up well on the voyage south, and when they reached Buenos Aires, four of them were sent back to England. He demanded total commitment.

Shackleton had established a strict schedule that ensured everyone participated in the ship's daily routine, regardless of rank. Such routine, balanced by periods of recreation, lessened the social division among the crew members and helped forge deep friendships. Any breach of discipline was dealt with immediately and fairly. It was then forgotten about. *Endurance* left South Georgia for Antarctica on 5 December 1914.[5]

The Weddell Sea

As *Endurance* approached the Weddell Sea, it made very slow progress, encountering a considerable amount of pack ice. They eventually sighted land on 12 January 1915. Days later, they were caught in a storm which surrounded *Endurance* with ice, trapping the ship and its crew of 28. Though they were only one day's sailing from their landing base, they would have to wait for the ice to break up before continuing. The crew settled in to wait until conditions improved. However, the summer months of the southern hemisphere passed and the ice did not free the ship. During that time, the dogs that would pull the sledges had to be exercised each day and trained to work together in harness.

On 24 February 1915, with the Antarctic summer drawing to a close, and no let-up in sight, Shackleton designated the ship a winter station. According to surgeon Alexander Macklin, Shackleton never showed any outward sign of frustration and never lost his optimism.[6] During this time, the ice, and with it the *Endurance,* was drifting further north from their landing point. Winter clothing, intended for the shore party, was issued to all. Adjustments were made to the interior of the ship to make it better suited for winter conditions. Shackleton spent a considerable amount of time talking individually to each crew member, getting to know all about their background and aspirations. This was balanced by ensuring they stayed together as a group. He had extraordinary skill in communication and earned their trust and respect. He ensured they all kept fit, and regularly practised emergency drills should the situation worsen. For relaxation, they would read, play games of charades, listen to the gramophone or have sing-songs with Hussey playing the banjo. Despite living in such confined quarters for such a long period, the men's diaries show no sign of anguish.

The Sinking

The ice around *Endurance* became more solid, putting pressure on the sides of the ship. Eventually, on 27 October 1915, *Endurance* began taking in water and Shackleton gave the order to abandon ship and move onto the ice. They salvaged essential supplies along with three small life boats and camped on the ice. Shackleton was the last to leave. *Endurance* had drifted 1,950 km from its original point of entrapment, and was 1,600 km from the nearest human settlement. The ship finally sank on 21 November 1915. Shackleton's vision of the Imperial trans-Antarctic Expedition was at an end. No one outside the expedition knew where they were or even that they were in trouble. His mission now became one of survival for his crew and getting them home safely. Shackleton wrote: "The task was likely to be long and strenuous, and an ordered mind and a clear programme

---

[5] Morrell, M. and Capparell, S., 2001, *Shackleton's Way*, London, Nicholas Brealey Publishing
[6] Alexander, C., 1999, *The Endurance: Shackleton's Legendary Antarctic Expedition*, New York, Alfred Knopf

were essential if we were to come through without loss of life."[7] He had, however, considered this eventuality many times during their entrapment and thought about different contingencies.

Situation: Desperate

Shackleton called the group together and explained the situation in matter-of-fact, realistic terms. He offered a number of options, putting forward his preferred one, and asked for their support. His plan was that that they would march across the ice, hopefully making five miles per day, pulling the lifeboats, until they got to open water. His proposal seemed logical and no one argued. Macklin wrote:

> "As always with him, what had happened had happened. It was in the past and he looked to the future … without emotion, melodrama, or excitement he said the ship and stores have gone – so now we'll go home."[8]

From the beginning, Shackleton took control, leading by example. He ordered the crew to jettison anything that was not essential. He made a point of being the first to throw away personal items. He allowed Hussey to keep his banjo ("vital mental medicine"), the surgeon was allowed to keep his medical instruments and Frank Hurley was allowed to salvage some of his photographic plates which survive to this day (in the possession of the Royal Geographical Society). Trapped on an ice-floe, "Ocean Camp" was established. Between them, they had five tents and Shackleton assigned each man to a particular tent, mindful of the personalities involved, and appointed a team leader for each group. He assigned the most difficult to his own tent, including the photographer Hurley, who was a potential rival for group leader.

Over the next few days, they made very poor progress and the Boss called a halt to the march. He held frequent emergency drills to pack up camp if the ice split and each man was assigned a specific duty. The weeks passed and fresh supplies began to diminish. Their diet was supplemented with fresh seal meat, which would provide vitamin C, vital to prevent scurvy. From his own first-hand experience with Scott, Shackleton saw that it was imperative that everyone should take it. Knowing there would be resistance to its strong flavour, he announced that it would be available only for the officers. After a while, a delegation came to him demanding that the rest of the men have their fair share. After brief consideration, he agreed to their request!

Even in blizzards, the Boss went to each tent every day to talk to the men and inquire as to their welfare. It was an opportunity to listen to their concerns. It also allowed him to plant ideas about what needed to be done and give people time to come to terms with the proposition. Shackleton decided to make another attempt to march across the ice to Paulet Island in order to give the men a sense of control over their destiny. After many days of very hard work and very little progress, he once again called a halt to the effort. Dragging the boats was just too much work and outweighed any mental

---

[7] Morrell, M. and Capparell, S., 2001, *Shackleton's Way*, London, Nicholas Brealey Publishing

[8] Alexander, C., 1999, *The Endurance: Shackleton's Legendary Antarctic Expedition*, New York, Alfred Knopf

benefit. He decided to set up a new camp – "Camp Patience" – and drift on the two-metre thick ice until they reached the open sea.

Trouble Brewing

Morale was beginning to sag as any hope of survival diminished and one member of the group, the carpenter McNeish, was became mutinous. He was refusing to do certain work when ordered by Captain Worsley. Shackleton pulled McNeish aside and made it clear that he would have to obey orders. Later that evening, he called together the crew and told the men that they were still under the command of the ship's officers until they reached safe port and that, unlike the situation under normal ships' articles, they would also be paid during this time. It was enough to diffuse the situation. McNeish backed down and Shackleton's action held the group together at a vital time.

The ice on which they were camped was drifting northward. Elephant Island was now the nearest landfall, but it was uninhabited. The pack ice was slowly breaking up and eventually, on 9 April 1916, they were able to launch the three lifeboats. Again, the Boss picked the crew for each boat, putting the best men in the worst boat, knowing their sea-faring skills could handle it. During the day they rowed and at night they tied up alongside the ice floes. Shackleton had to change the plan on a few occasions. Days later, they hit the open sea and made a run for Elephant Island. Whenever he felt morale sagging, the Boss ordered extra rations to be distributed. After 170 days adrift and seven days in open boats, they finally found a landing spot between the 600-metre high cliffs on the island. It was 497 days since they last set foot on solid land. Many in the group were at the point of mental and physical exhaustion.

Elephant Island

Uninhabited and inhospitable Elephant Island was 1,000 km from the tip of South America and some distance away from any known shipping routes. While the island provided plenty of fresh water from glaciers as well as seal and penguin meat, it could only ever be a staging post. Shackleton quickly set up a routine and designated different tasks to the men. He decided that the best hope for rescue was to take six men in the biggest and most stable boat – the *James Caird* – and try to reach civilisation and return with a rescue ship for the remaining men. There were three options open to them. The two nearest options were South America (1,000 km) and the Falkland Islands (885 km), but both would have entailed crossing Drake Passage, probably the most treacherous piece of ocean on the planet. Shackleton believed that the best option was to make for the whaling station on South Georgia Island, some 1,300 km away but with prevailing winds to help them.

Shackleton would lead the attempt and asked his second in command, Frank Wild, to stay on the island and maintain discipline and morale among the 22 men remaining behind. Shackleton had implicit trust that Wild would hold the group together in his absence. He called for volunteers for the trip, but he knew precisely who he was going to bring. The five men who travelled with Shackleton were: Captain Frank Worsley, captain of *Endurance* and chosen for his navigational skills – an essential requirement on the trip; Irishman Tom Crean for his mental and physical strength, all-round ability and good humour; another Irishman, Timothy McCarthy, a strong and experienced seaman; "Chips" McNeish who had already caused trouble – Shackleton wanted to keep a close eye on him and not leave him behind where he could destroy morale; and, finally, Jack Vincent, another man who needed to be watched. To his credit, McNeish proved very resourceful and did a splendid job preparing the *James Caird* for the journey, taking pieces from the other two boats to build up the sides and create a canvas deck cover that would prove vital in keeping out the Antarctic swell. They packed the boat with supplies and ballast and on 24 April 1916 (Easter Monday – the same day that Patrick Pearse led the Easter Rising in Dublin) they set out on the 1,300 km journey for South Georgia.

Journey to South Georgia

The *James Caird* experienced some dreadful conditions on the journey and the crew was continuously pumping water out of the boat. The crew split into two groups, taking four-hour shifts. Worsley was incredibly skilled at navigation. Determining their position required using a sextant to calculate the angle of the sun on the horizon. In appalling weather conditions, most of the time no opportunities presented themselves. In total, they had only four sightings of the sun during their entire voyage to South Georgia. When those opportunities arose, it took two men to hold Worsley steady as he stood up in the mountainous swell to use the sextant, while Shackleton did the calculations. A tiny margin of error would mean that they would miss South Georgia and perish. Conditions were deteriorating rapidly with waves running 20 metres high. Salt water then contaminated their fresh-water supply. It was imperative that they reach South Georgia soon. Again, Shackleton kept a close eye on each member's health, and ability to cope.

At midday on 8 May they spotted the island. It was an incredible feat of navigation and seamanship. They wanted to land on the north eastern side of the island near the harbours, but 90 km winds were blowing them to the south side and preventing them from landing. Finally on 10 May, with the sail broken, the men rowed the remaining few miles to shore. They had spent 17 days at sea, were exhausted and were out of fresh water. It was 522 days since they last set foot on South Georgia. They had completed the most extraordinary sea journey ever taken, but their problems were still far from over.

They now had to cross the island to the whaling station at Stromness, a distance of 48 km as the crow flies, but over alpine-like peaks – the Allardyce mountains. McNeish and Vincent were physically unable to make the journey and Shackleton asked McCarthy to look after them while Crean, Worsley and Shackleton would attempt to cross the mountains and get help. Once again, the weather had deteriorated and it was the evening of 19 May before the three could set out. McNeish demonstrated great ingenuity by taking brass screws out of the *James Caird* and fixing them to the soles of their boots to give them traction on the ice.

Crossing the Allardyce Mountains

They made many attempts to cross the mountains and had to retrace their steps on numerous occasions and try a different route as their way was blocked by sheer cliffs. Exhausted and dehydrated, they continued. The Boss knew the lives of all the other men depended on his keeping them moving. As dawn broke, they heard the steam whistle at Stromness. Thirty hours after they had set off, they knew they were almost there. But the terrain was still extremely difficult, and dangerous. When they finally arrived at the station, the station manager looked at them and asked "who the hell are you?" and the Boss addressed the startled men inside: "My name is Shackleton". The men were bathed, fed and given fresh clothes. A rescue party set out immediately by sea to collect NcNeish, Vincent and McCarthy from the west coast of the island.

Rounding up the Crew

Shackleton then organised a steamer, the *Southern Sky*, to rescue the remaining 22 men from Elephant Island, but the ship ran into heavy ice and was unsuited for the task. Shackleton then headed for the Falkland Islands to get another ship. With the First World War still raging, it proved impossible, but he then appealed to the Uruguayan Government who sent a steamer, the *Instituto do Pesca No 1*, to Port Stanley in the Falkland Islands where it picked up Shackleton, Worsley and Crean (the other three had already returned to Britain). The second attempt also failed to get through the ice to Elephant Island and they sailed to Punta Areanas in Chile where they chartered a schooner, *Emma*. That attempt also failed, and once again they returned to Port Stanley. Shackleton appealed to the Chilean Government for help and they dispatched a steel-hulled steamer, the *Yelco*. This time they succeeded, and on 30 August 1916, Shackleton led the rescue party ashore – 128 days after they had originally set out for South Georgia Island. His first words to the astonished men were: "Are you all well?" All 22 men on Elephant Island were still alive, although some were in bad condition after their ordeal. With all the men on board the Yelco, the ship returned to Punta Arenas in Chile on 20 September 1916. From there, the crew made their way to Buenos Aires and back to Britain. Shackleton then set about rescuing the remaining men from the *Aurora,* who had been stranded on the Ross Sea side of the Antarctic. He finally arrived back in Britain in May 1917.

Shackleton had not succeeded in the difficult task of crossing the Antarctic. He did succeed, however, in leading the most amazing turnaround situation ever imagined. The 28 men of the *Endurance* arrived safely home to their families. To paraphrase the words of the BBC journalist Brian Hanrahan during the Falklands War in 1982 – he counted them all out, and he counted them home again.

References

Aer Lingus, 2019, www.aerlingus.com, Accessed 10 March 2019

AccountAbility, 2011, *AA1000 Stakeholder Engagement Standard 2011. Final Draft Exposure*, London, AccountAbility

Adair, J., 1983, *Effective Leadership*, Aldershot, Gower

Aiello, R. and Watkins, D., 2000, "The Fine Art of Friendly Acquisitions", *Harvard Business Review*, November/December 2000, Vol. 78, Issue 6, pp.100–107

Alexandre, C., 1998, *The Endurance: Shackleton's Legendary Antarctic Voyage*, New York, Alfred A. Knopf

Amabile, T. and Kramer, S., 2010, "What really motivates employees?", *Harvard Business Review*, January/February 2010, Vol. 88, Issue 1, pp.43–44

Ambrose, S., 2003, *Eisenhower: Soldier and President*, London, Pocket Books

Argyris, C. and Schon, D., 1978, *Organisational Learning: A Theory of Action Perspective*, Wokingham, Addison-Wesley

Aristotle, Translated by Thomson, J., 1976, *Ethics*, Harmondsworth, Penguin

Armstrong, R., 2019, "Wall St. reacts to a dressed-down Goldman", *Financial Times*, 9 March 2019, p.15

Arnaud, S. and Wasieleski, D., 2014, "Corporate Humanistic Responsibility: Social Performance Through Managerial Discretion of HRM", *Journal of Business Ethics*, Vol. 120, No. 3, pp.313–334

ASAI (Advertising Standards Association of Ireland), 2019, *Manual of Advertising Self-Regulation*, Dublin, Advertising Standards Association of Ireland, www.asai.ie/code.asp, Accessed 10 March 2019

Aschoff, N., 2017, "Whole Foods represent the failure of Conscious Capitalism", *The Guardian*, 29 May 2017, www.theguardian.com/commentisfree/2017/may/29/whole-foods-failures-conscious-capitalism, Accessed 24 May 2019

Ashkenas, R. and Francis, S., 2000, "Integration Managers, Special Leaders for Our Times", *Harvard Business Review*, November/December 2000, Vol. 78, Issue 6, pp.108–116

Balboni, F. *et al.*, 2010, "Analytics: The New Path to Value", *IBM Institute for Business Value and MIT Sloan Management Review*, Fall 2010

Balogun, J. and Hope Hailey, V., 2008, *Exploring Strategic Change* 3rd Ed., Harlow, Essex, Prentice Hall, Financial Times

Barney, J., 1991, "Firm Resources and Sustained Competitive Advantage", *Journal of Management*. Vol. 17, No 1. pp.99–120

Barney, J., 2002, *Gaining and Sustaining Competitive Advantage*, 2nd Ed., Upper Saddle River, NJ, Prentice Hall

Barney, J.B., 1986, "Organisational Culture: Can it be a source of sustained competitive advantage?", *Academy of Management Review*, 1986, Vol. 11, No. 3

Barrington, K., 2010, "Truth-seekers are left to whistle down the wind for real protection", *Sunday Business Post*, 23 May 2010, p.5

Barry, F., 2010, "Politics and Economic Policy Making in Ireland" in J. Hogan *et al.* (Eds), *Irish Business & Society*, pp.28–43, Dublin, Gill & Macmillan

Bartlett, C. and Ghoshal, S., 1990, "Matrix Management: Not a Structure, a Frame of Mind", *Harvard Business Review*, July/August 1990, Vol. 68, Issue 4, pp.138–145

Bass, B., 1990, "From Transactional to Transformational Leadership: Learning to Share the Vision", *Organizational Dynamics*, Winter 1990, p.22

Baum, T., 2008, "Implications of hospitality and tourism labour markets for talent management strategies", *International Journal of Contemporary Hospitality Management*. Vol. 20, No, 7, pp.720–729

BBC, 1998, http://news.bbc.co.uk/2/hi/europe/221508.stm, Accessed 24 May 2019.

Beasley, A., 2010, "McCreevy quits over 'privileged' position", *Irish Times*, 9 October 2010, p.17

Benavides-Valasco, C., Quintana-García, C., and Marchante-Lara, M., 2014. "Total quality management, corporate social responsibility and performance in the hotel industry", *International Journal of Hospitality Management*, Vol. 41 pp.77–87

Beer, M. and Nohria, N., 2000, *Breaking the Code of Change*, Boston, Harvard Business School Press

Benis, W. and Nanus, B., 1985, *Leaders: The Strategies for Taking Charge*, New York, Harper & Row

Berton, E., 2010, "Dress to impress, UBS tells staff", *The Wall Street Journal*, 14 December 2010, http://online.wsj.com/article/SB10001424052748704694004576019783931381042.html?mod=djemTMB_t, Accessed 24 May 2019

Bettis, R. and Prahalad, C., 1995, "The Dominant Logic: Retrospective and Extension", *Strategic Management Journal*, Vol. 16, Issue 1, pp.5–15

Bhopal, 2019, The Bhopal Medical Appeal, https://www.bhopal.org/. Accessed 22 March 2019

Bloom, M., 1999, "The Performance Effects of Pay Dispersion on Individuals and Organisations", *Academy of Management Journal*, February 1999, pp.25–40

Bohan, H., 2009, "A new kind of leadership now required", *Irish Times*, 6 October 2009, p.14

Bower, J., 2001, "Not All M&As Are Alike – and That Matters", *Harvard Business Review*, March 2001, Vol. 79, Issue 3, pp.92–101

Bower, J. and Gilbert, C., 2007, "How everyday decisions create or destroy your company's strategy", *Harvard Business Review*, February 2007, Vol. 85, Issue 2, pp.72–79

Bowie, N., 2012, "Corporate Social Responsibility in Business", A commissioned background paper about CSR in business as it relates to the creation of public value, June 2012, Centre of Integrative Leadership, University of Minnesota, https://www.academia.edu/37786979/Corporate_Social_Responsibility_in_the_Business, Accessed 1 August 2019

Boxall, P. and Purcell, J., 2011, *Strategy and Human Resource Management*, 3rd Ed., Basingstoke, Palgrave Macmillan

Bray, A., 2019, "Whistleblower Maurice McCabe settles claims against the state for undisclosed sum", *Irish Independent*, 30 April 2019, https://www.independent.ie/irish-news/news/whistleblower-maurice-mccabe-settles-claims-against-the-state-for-undisclosed-sum-38066939.html, Accessed 4 July 2019

Breen, J., 2008, *Interview with the Author*, September 2008

Brousseau, K. *et al.*, 2006, "The seasoned executive's decision-making style", *Harvard Business Review*, February 2006, Vol. 84, Issue 2, pp.110–121

Brown, A., 1994, "Transformational Leadership in Tackling Technical Change", *Journal of General Management*, Vol. 19, Issue 4, pp.1–10

Bruntland, G.H., 1987, https://sustainabledevelopment.un.org/content/documents/5987our-common-future.pdf, Accessed 1 August 2019

Buelens, M. *et al.*, 2006, *Organisational Behaviour*, Maidenhead, McGraw-Hill

Burke-Kennedy, E., 2019, "Workers may be only half as productive as thought", *Irish Times*, 8 February 2019, Business This Week, p.1

Business and Finance, 2018, "Merger and acquisition activity in Ireland valued at over €70 billion for first half of 2018", *Business and Finance*, 10 August 2018

Byrne, E., 2012, *Political Corruption in Ireland 1922–2010. A Crooked Harp?* Manchester, Manchester University Press

Callanan, G., 2015, *An Introduction to Irish Company Law*, 4th Ed., Dublin, Gill

Campbell, A. *et al.*, 1995, "Corporate Strategy: The Quest for Parenting Advantage", *Harvard Business Review*, March/April 1995, Vol. 73, Issue 2, pp.120–132

Carey, B., 2008, "Fund boss wants DCC broken up", *Sunday Times*, 29 June 2008

Carey, D., 2000, "Making mergers succeed", *Harvard Business Review*, May/June 2000, Vol. 79, Issue 3, pp.145–154

Carroll, A., 1979, "A Three-Dimensional Conceptual Model of Corporate Performance", *Academy of Management Review*, Vol. 4, No. 4, pp.497–505

Carroll, L., 1989, *Alice's Adventures in Wonderland*, London, Hutchinson

Carswell, S., 2006, *Something Rotten: Irish Banking Scandals*, Dublin, Gill & Macmillan

Carswell, S., 2009, "Bankers must create Climate of Responsibility says Archbishop", *Irish Times*, 29 January 2009, p.21

Cassells, P., 2016, *Investing in National Ambition. A Strategy for Funding Higher Education*, Dublin, Department of Education and Skills

Central Bank, 2015, *Corporate Governance Requirements for Credit Institutions 2015*, Dublin, Central Bank of Ireland, https://www.centralbank.ie/regulation/how-we-regulate/codes, Accessed 1 August 2019

Central Bank, 2018, *Behaviour and Culture of the Irish Retail Banks*, Dublin, Central Bank of Ireland, https://www.centralbank.ie/publication/behaviour-and-culture-report, Accessed 1 August 2019

Central Bank, 2018, *Gender Pay Gap Report 2018*, Dublin, Central Bank of Ireland, https://www.centralbank.ie/docs/default-source/careers/policies/gender-pay-gap-report-2018.pdf, Accessed 1 August 2019

Central Bank, 2019, *Tracker Mortgage Investigation*, Dublin, Central Bank of Ireland, https://www.centralbank.ie/consumer-hub/tracker-mortgage-examination, Accessed 21 March 2019

Chandler, A., 1962, *Strategy and Structure*, Cambridge, MA, MIT Press

Chapman, B., 2018, "'I wish I had acted sooner,'" Carillion ex-boss tells MPs", *Independent* [UK] 7 February 2018, p.17

Charities Regulator, 2019, *Information for the Public*, https://www.charitiesregulator.ie/en/information-for-the-public/search-the-charities-register, Accessed 1 February 2019

Charities Regulator, 2019, https://www.charitiesregulator.ie/en/who-we-are/what-we-do, Accessed 15 February 2019

Charleton, Mr Justice Peter, 2018, *Third interim report of the tribunal of inquiry into protected disclosures made under the Protected Disclosures Act 2014 and certain other matters*, http://www.disclosuretribunal.ie/en/DIS/Third%20Interim%20Report.pdf/Files/Third%20 Interim%20Report.pdf, Accessed 22 May 2019

CIPD, 2011, *Shaping the Future*, London, Chartered Institute of Personnel and Development

CIPD, 2012, *Where has all the trust gone?* London, Chartered Institute of Personnel and Development

CIPD, 2014, *Keeping culture, purpose and values at the heart of your SME*, London, Chartered Institute of Personnel and Development

CIPD, 2016, *A Duty to Care? Evidence of the importance of organisational culture to effective governance and leadership*, London, Chartered Institute of Personnel and Development

Chesborough, H. and Garman, A., 2008, "How Open Innovation Can Help You Cope in Lean Times", *Harvard Business Review*, December 2009, Vol. 87, Issue 12, pp.68–76

Clancy, P. and Murphy, G., 2006, *Outsourcing Government: Public Bodies and Accountability*, Dublin, TASC

Clancy, P. *et al.*, 2010, *Mapping the Golden Circle*, Dublin, TASC

CLRG, 2007, *Report of the Company Law Reform Group 2007*, Dublin, Company Law Reform Group

Cohen, E., 2010, *CSR for HR. A necessary partnership for advancing responsible business practice*, Sheffield, Greenleaf Publishing Ltd

Collins, J. and Porras, J., 1996, "Building your company's vision", *Harvard Business Review*, September/October 1996, Vol. 74, Issue 5, pp.65–77

Collins, J., 2001, *Good to Great*, London, Random House Business Books

Collins, L., 2007, *Irish Family Feuds*, Dublin, Mentor Books

Committee on Standards in Public Life, 2010, *Review and Annual Report 2008-2009*, London, Committee on Standards in Public Life

Connolly, T., 2017, *Brexit & Ireland: The Dangers, the Opportunities, and the Inside Story of the Irish Response*, Dublin, Penguin Ireland

Cooke, N., 2008, "Irish firms must look to foreign markets for growth", *Sunday Business Post*, 29 June 2008

Cooke, N., 2011, "Plane Talker", *The Sunday Business Post*, 30 January 2011, p.17

Cooper, M., 2009, *Who really runs Ireland?*, Dublin, Penguin Ireland

Covey, S., 1994, *The Seven Habits of Highly Effective People*, London, Simon & Schuster

Crane, A. and Matten, D., 2016, *Business Ethics*, 4th Ed., Oxford, Oxford University Press

Creaton, S., 2004, *Ryanair*, London Aurum

Creaton, S. and O'Cleary, C., 2002, *Panic at the Bank*, Dublin, Gill & Macmillan

CRU, 2019, *Commission for Regulation of Utilities, Water, and Energy*, https://www.cru.ie, Accessed 1 August 2019

Csikszentmihalyi, M., 1990, *The Psychology of Optimal Experience*, New York, Harper Collins

CSO, 2019, *Goods Exports and Imports*, https://www.cso.ie/en/statistics/externaltrade/goods exportsandimports, Accessed 12 February 2019

Czeisler, C., 2006, "Sleep Deficit: The Performance Killer", *Harvard Business Review*, October 2006, Vol. 84, Issue 10, pp.53–59

Dalkey, N.C. *et al.*, 1972, *Studies in the Quality of Life: Delphi and Decision-making*, Lexington, Lexington Books

Darwin, J. *et al.*, 2002, *Developing Strategies for Change*, Harlow, Essex, Prentice Hall, Financial Times

Davis, K., 1973, "The Case for and against Business Assumption of Social Responsibilities", *Academy of Management Journal*, Vol. 16, No. 2, pp.312–322

Davis, K., 1960, "Can Business afford to Ignore Social Responsibilities?" *California Management Review*, Spring 1960, Vol 2, Issue 3, pp.70–76

De Bono, E., 1985, *Six Thinking Hats*, London, Penguin

Deegan, G., 2019, "McDonald's appeals EU decision to cancel trademark on Big Mac", *The Irish Times*, 20 March 2019, Business + Commercial Property, p.1

Department of Enterprise and Innovation, 2017, *Towards Responsible Business: Ireland's national plan on CSR 2017–2020*, Dublin, Department of Enterprise and Innovation

Dess, G. *et al.*, 2004, *Strategic Management*, Boston, McGraw-Hill

Devine, J., 2008, "Mergers and Acquisitions Surge 32%, Mainly in First Half of Year", *Irish Times*, 5 January 2008

Dibb, S. *et al.*, 2006, *Marketing Concepts and Strategies*, Houghton Mifflin

Digby, D. and Vishwanath, V., 2006, "Localisation: The Revolution in Consumer Markets", Boston, *Harvard Business Review*, April 2006, Vol. 84, Issue 4, pp.82–92

Donaldson, T. and Dunfee, T., 1994, "Towards a Unified Conception of Business Ethics: Integrative Social Contracts Theory", *Academy of Management Review*, Vol. 19, Issue 2, April 1994, pp.252–84

Donaldson, T. and Preston, L., 1995, "The Stakeholder Theory of the Corporation: Concepts, Evidence and Implications", *Academy of Management Review*, Vol. 20, No. 1. pp.65–91

Donovan, D., 2011, "Loss of fiscal sovereignty inevitable if euro is to survive", *The Irish Times*, 13 January 2011, p.16

Donnelly, E. (2018) "Irish Firms seal deals worth €50m in China", *Irish Independent*, 7 November 2018, p.18

Dose, J.J., 1997, "Work Values: An Integrative Framework and Illustrative Application to Organisational Socialisation", *Journal of Occupational and Organisational Psychology*, September 1997, pp.219–40

DPER, 2016, *Code of Practice for the Governance of State Bodies*, Dublin, Department of Public Enterprise and Reform

Drucker, P., 1954, *The Practice of Management*, New York, Harper & Row

Dublin Docklands Development Authority, 2008, *6th Annual Social Regeneration Conference*, Dublin, DDDA

Duff, D., 2014, *Managing Professionals and Other Smart People*, Dublin, Chartered Accountants Ireland

Duffy, D., 2017, *A Practical Guide for Company Directors*, Dublin, Chartered Accountants Ireland

Duffy, S., 2017, "Former Bank of Ireland Investor Wilbur Ross slams China's Free Trade claims", *Irish Independent*, 19 January 2017

Dunhumby, 2019, https://www.dunnhumby.com/clients/case-studies/tesco, Accessed 19 January 2019

Dyck, K., Lins, K., Roth, L., and Wagner, H., 2019, "Do institutional Investors Drive Corporate Social Responsibility? International Evidence", *Journal of Financial Economics*, Vol. 131, No. 3, pp.693–714

Dyer, J. *et al*, 2004, "When to Ally and When to Acquire", *Harvard Business Review*, July/August 2004, Vol. 82, Issue 7/8, pp.108–115

Earley, P.C., and Mosakowski, E., 2004, "Cultural Intelligence", *Harvard Business Review*, October 2004, Vol. 82, Issue 10, pp.139–146

Elkington, J., 1997, "Cannibals with Forks", *The Triple Bottom Line of 21st Century Business*, Oxford, Capstone Publishing Ltd

Enterprise Ireland, 2010, *Chief Executive Officer's Report*, http://www.enterprise-ireland.com/annualreport2009/ceo_report_2.html, Accessed 28 March 2011

Enterprise Ireland, 2019, Researchers in Higher Education Institutes, https://www.enterprise-ireland.com/en/researchers/eu-programmes-and-networks/horizon-2020.html, Accessed 15 February 2019

Enterprise Ireland, 2019, SME Definition, http://www.enterprise-ireland.com/en/about-us/our-clients/sme-definition.html, Accessed 3 March 2019

Europa, 2011, http://europa.eu/index_en.htm, Accessed 22 March 2011

European Commission, 2011, *Communication from the Commission to the European Parliament, The Council, the European Economic and Social committee and the Committee of the Regions. A renewed EU strategy 2011–2014 for Corporate Social Responsibility.* Com (2011) 681 Final. Brussels, EU Commission, http://eur-lex.europa.eu/LexUriServ/LexUriServ.do?uri=COM:2011:0681:FIN:EN:PDF, Accessed 24 May 2019

European Commission, 2016, *Gender balance on corporate boards. Europe is cracking the ceiling*, Brussels, Directorate-General for Justice and Consumers

European Commission, 2018, https://europa.eu/rapid/press-release_IP-18-4581_en.htm. Accessed 1 August 2019

Fáilte Ireland, 2018, *Tourism Facts 2017*, http://www.failteireland.ie/FailteIreland/media/WebsiteStructure/Documents/3_Research_Insights/5_International_Tourism_Trends/Tourism-Facts-2017_1.pdf, Accessed 24 May 2019

Fallon, J., 2010, "Outsmart and outthink them: ex Intel chief gives his vision", *The Irish Times*, 17 November 2010, Business Today, p.19

Feldman, D., 1981, "The Multiple Socialisation of Organisation Members", *Academy of Management Review*, April 1981, pp.309–18

Financial Times, 2018, Lex Column, p.22. 28/29 July 2018

Finlay, P., 2000, *Strategic Management*, Harlow, Essex, Prentice Hall, Financial Times

Fitzgerald, J., 2014, cited in An Garda Síochána, 2016, *Modernisation and Renewal Programme 2016–2021*, Dublin, An Garda Síochána

Fitzroy, P. and Hulbert, J., 2005, *Strategic Management: Creating value in Turbulent Times*, London, Wiley

Fisher, C., Lovell, A. and Valero-Silva, N., 2013, *Business Ethics and Values*, 4th Ed., Harlow, Pearson Education Ltd

Flemming, L., 2010, "Whistleblowing and White Collar Crime, Why Ireland needs Legislative Change", *Accountancy Ireland*, December 2010, Vol. 42, Issue 6

Floriday, R. and Goodnight, J., 2005, "Managing for Creativity", *Harvard Business Review*, July/August 2008, Vol. 83, Issue 7/8, pp.124–131

Forbes, 2019, "The World's Most Valuable Brands", https://www.forbes.com/powerful-brands/list/#tab:rank, Accessed 25 March 2019.

Forfás, 2005, *Making Technological Knowledge Work*, Dublin, Technopolis/Forfás

Franklin, D. *et al.*, 2008, "Just Good Business" Special Report, London, *The Economist*, 19 January 2008

FRC, 2016, *Corporate Culture and the Role of Boards*, London, Financial Reporting Council

FRC, 2018, *Guidance on Board Effectiveness*, London, Financial Reporting Council

Freeman, R. E., 2010, *Strategic Management. A Stakeholder Approach*, Cambridge, Cambridge University Press

Freeman, R.E., Harrison, J., Wicks, A., Palmar, B. and de Colle, S., 2010, *Stakeholder Theory, The State of the Art*, Cambridge, Cambridge University Press

French, J. and Raven, B., 1959, "The Basis of Social Power" in *Studies in Social Power*, Ed. Cartwright, D., Michigan, University of Michigan Press

Friedman, M., 2002, *Capitalism and Freedom*, 40th Anniversary Edition, Chicago, The University of Chicago Press

G20/OECD, 2015, *Principles of Corporate Governance*, Paris, Organisation for Economic Co-operation and Development

Garay, L. and Font, X., 2012, "Doing good to do well? Corporate social responsibility reasons, practices and impacts in small and medium accommodation enterprises", *International Journal of Hospitality Management*, Vol. 31, pp.329–337

Garrahan, M. and Marriage, M., 2018, "WPP shareholders revolt over executive pay", *The Financial Times*, 13 June 2018, https://www.ft.com/content/9beec208-6efc-11e8-852d-d8b934ff5ffa, Accessed 23 February 2019

Garratt, B., 2003, *The Fish Rots from the Head. The Crisis in Boardrooms: developing the crucial skills of a competent director*, London, Profile Books

Garda Inspectorate, 2015, *Changing Policing in Ireland. Report of the Garda Síochána Inspectorate*, Dublin, Garda Inspectorate

Gerstner, L., 2002, *Who Says Elephants Can't Dance*, London, Harper Collins

Ghemawat, P., 2001, "Distance Still Matters", *Harvard Business Review*, September 2001, Vol. 79, Issue 8, pp.137–147

Ghemawat, P., 2003, "The Forgotten Strategy", *Harvard Business Review*, November 2003, Vol. 81, Issue 11, pp.76–84

Ghemawat, P., 2010, "Finding your strategy in the new landscape", *Harvard Business Review*, March 2010, Vol. 88, Issue 2, pp.54–60

Gibson, K., 2000, "The Moral Basis of Stakeholder Theory", *Journal of Business Ethics*, Vol. 26, pp.245–257

Giuliani, R., 2002, *Leadership*, London, Time Warner

Glavas, A. and Kelley K., 2014, "The Effects of Perceived Corporate Social Responsibility on Employee Attitudes", *Business Ethics Quarterly*, Vol. 24, No. 2, pp.165–202.

Goleman, D., 1995, *Emotional Intelligence*, London, Bloomsbury

Goleman, D. *et al.*, 2002, *The New Leaders*, London, Little Brown

Goold, M. and Campbell, A., 2002, "Do You Have a Well-designed Organisation?", *Harvard Business Review*, March 2002, Vol. 80, Issue 3, pp.117–224

Goold, M. and Campbell, A., 1987, *Strategies and Styles*, Oxford, Blackwell

Goold, M. and Campbell, A., 1998, "Desperately Seeking Synergy", *Harvard Business Review*, September/October 98, Vol. 76, Issue 2, pp.131–45

Goold, M. *et al.*, 1994, *Corporate Level Strategy: Creating Value in the Multibusiness Company*, Chichester, Wiley

Government of Ireland, 2019, *Project Ireland 2040*, https://www.gov.ie/en/campaigns/09022006-project-ireland-2040, Accessed 15 February 2019

Grant, P., 2011, "An Aristotelian approach to sustainable business", *Corporate Governance*, Vol. 11, No. 1, pp.4–14

Grant, R., 2010, *Contemporary Strategic Analysis: Text and Cases*, 7th Ed., Chichester, John Wiley & Sons Ltd

Grant Thornton, 2010, *Corporate Governance Review 2010*, Dublin, Grant Thornton

Green, S., 2009, *Good Value. Reflections on money, morality and an uncertain world*, London, Allen Lane

Griffeth, R. and Horn, P., 2001, *Retaining Valued Employees*, Thousand Oaks, CA, Sage Publications

Griffin, R., 2005, *Management*, Boston, Houghton Mifflin

Guerrera, F., 2009, "Welsh Condemns Share Price Focus", *The Financial Times*, 12 March 2009

Gunnigle, P. *et al.*, 2017, *Human Resource Management in Ireland*, 5th Ed., Dublin, Institute of Public Administration

Halford, T., 2018, "How a radical agency changed the world", *The Financial Times*, 28/29 July 2018, p. 11

Hamilton, P., 2019, "Supermac's wins bumper battle with McDonald's", *Irish Times*, 16 January 2019, Business News, p. 3

Handcock, C., 2008, "Kerry to Appeal Competition Authority Ruling On Breo", *Irish Times*, 30 September 2008, p.23

Handcock, T. and Woodhouse, A., 2018, "BMW to raise stake in China joint venture to 75% in €3.6 billion deal", *The Financial Times*, 11 October 2018

Handy, C., 2002, "What's a Business For?" *Harvard Business Review*, Vol. 80, Issue 12, pp.49–56

Hamel, G. and Prahalad, C., 2005, "Strategic Intent", *Harvard Business Review*, July/August 2005, Vol. 83, Issue 7/8, pp.148–161

Hamm, J., 2006, "The Five Messages Leaders Must Manage", *Harvard Business Review*, May 2006, Vol. 84, Issue 5, pp.115–123

Hammer, M. and Champy, J., 1993, *Reengineering the Corporation*, New York, Harper Business

Handcock, C., 2010, "Elderfield says level of mortgage arrears likely to get worse but should not destabilise banks", *The Times*, 9 November 2010, p.18

Harding Clark, S.C., M., 2006, *The Lourdes Hospital Inquiry: An Inquiry into Peripartum Hysterectomy at our Lady of Lourdes Hospital, Drogheda*, Dublin, Stationery office

Handy, C., 1999, *Understanding Organisations*, London, Penguin

Harper, N. and Viguerie, P., 2002, "Are You Too Focused?", *The McKinsey Quarterly*, 2002 Special Edition: Risk and Resilience

Harrison, R., 1972, "Understanding your Organisation's Character", *Harvard Business Review*, May/June 1972, Vol. 50, Issue 3, pp.119–128

Hartman, L., 2002, *Perspective in Business Ethics*, New York, McGraw-Hill

Hassan, F., 2006, "Leading Change from the Top Line", *Harvard Business Review*, July/August, 2006, Vol. 84, Issue 7/8, pp.90–97

Hayes, D., 2010, *Revenue Management for the Hospitality Industry*, Chichester, Wiley

Hayes, R. and Wheelwright, S., 1979, "The Dynamics of Process-Product Life Cycles", *Harvard Business Review*, March/April 1979, Vol. 57, Issue 2

Hesselbein, F. and Cohen, P. (Eds.), 1999, *Leader to Leader: Enduring Insights on Leadership*, New York, Jossey-Bass

Higgs, D., 2003, *Review of the role and effectiveness of non-executive directors*, London, The Stationery Office

Hill, C. and Jones, G., 2004, *Strategic Management: An Integrated Approach*, Boston, Houghton Mifflin

Hill, C. and Jones, G., 2009, *Theory of Strategic Management with Cases*, New York, South-Western Cengage Learning

Hines, P., 1993, "Integrated Material Management: The Value Chain Redefined", *The International Journal of Logistics Management*, Vol. 4, Issue 1, pp.13–21

Honohan, P., 2010, *The Irish Banking Crisis: Regulatory and Financial Stability Policy 2003–2008*, Dublin, Central Bank of Ireland

Hope Hailey, V. and Gustafsson, S., 2014, *Cultivating trustworthy leaders*, London, Chartered Institute of Personnel and Development

Houghton, E., 2016, *A duty to care? Evidence of the importance of organisational culture to effective governance and leadership*, London, Chartered Institute of Personnel and Development

House, R., 1971, "A Path-goal Theory of Leader Effectiveness", *Administrative Science Quarterly*, 16 September 1971, Vol. 16, Issue 3, pp.321–338

Huff, A. *et al.*, 2009, *Strategic Management: Logic and Action*, Hoboken, NJ, Wiley

Humphries, J., 2004, "Women hold 5 per cent of seats on Irish Boards", *The Irish Times*, 23 January 2004

Hunt, C., 2010, *National Strategy for Higher Education*, Dublin, Strategy Group for Higher Education

Hurley, F., 2001, *South With Endurance: Shackleton's Antarctic Expedition 1914–1917. The Photographs of Frank Hurley*, London, Bloomsbury

Huselid, M., 1995, "The impact of human resource management practices on turnover, productivity and corporate financial performance", *Academy of Management Journal*, Vol. 39, Issue 3, pp.635–672

Institute of Chartered Secretaries and Administrators (ICSA), 2017, *The Stakeholder Voice in Board Decision Making*, London, ICSA: The Governance Institute

IDA Ireland, 2019, *Research & Development in Ireland*, https://www.idaireland.com/doing-business-here/activities/research-development-and-innovation, Accessed 15 February 2019

IPCC, 2014, *Climate Change 2014 Fifth Assessment Synthesis Report*, Copenhagen, United Nations Intergovernmental Panel on Climate Change

Irish Franchise Association, 2019, https://irishfranchiseassociation.com/about/, Accessed 24 July 2019

Irish Management Institute, 2010, *Closing the Gap*, Dublin, IMI

Irish Times, 2018, "Chinese companies in Ireland – a win-win story", *Irish Times*, 31 October 2018, https://www.irishtimes.com/sponsored/gateway-to-china/chinese-companies-in-ireland-a-win-win-story-1.3676834, Accessed 24 May 2019

ISE, 2010, *Irish Stock Exchange Adopts New Rules in relation to Corporate Governance*, Dublin, Irish Stock Exchange

Jamali, D., 2008, "A Stakeholder Approach to Corporate Social Responsibility: A Fresh Perspective into Theory and Practice", *Journal of Business Ethics*, Vol. 82, pp.213–231

Janis, I., 1982, *Groupthink*, 2nd Ed., Boston, Houghton Mifflin

Jensen, M, 2002, "Value Maximization, Stakeholder Theory, and the Corporate Objective Function", *Business Ethics Quarterly*, Volume 12, Issue 2, pp.235–256

Johnson, G. *et al.*, 2008, *Exploring Corporate Strategy*, 8th Ed., Harlow, Pearson Education Limited, Financial Times

Johnson, G. *et al.*, 2017, *Exploring Strategy: Text and Cases*, 11th Ed., Harlow, Pearson Education Limited, Financial Times

Jolly, J., 2018, "Once an American Powerhouse, can General Electric regain its spark", *The Guardian*, 1 December 2018

Jones, L., Jennings, B., Goelz, R., Haythorn, K., Zivot, J., and de Waal, F., 2016, "An Ethogram to Quality Operating Room Behaviour", *Annals of Behavioural Medicine*, Vol 50, No. 4, pp.487–496

Judson, A., 1991, *Changing Behaviour in Organisations: Minimising Resistance to Change*, Cambridge, MA, Basil Blackwell

Kanter, R.M., 1987, "Managing Traumatic Change: Avoiding the 'Unlucky 13'", *Management Review*, May 1987, pp.23–24

Kanter, R.M., 1989, *When Giants Learn to Dance*, London, Simon & Schuster

Kanter, R.M., 1994, "Collaborate Advantage: The Art of Alliances", *Harvard Business Review*, July/August 1994, Vol. 72, Issue 4, pp.96–108

Kanter, R.M., 1999, "From Spare Change to Real Change", *Harvard Business Review*, May/June 1999, Vol. 77, Issue 3, pp.122–132

Kanter, R.M., 2003, "Thriving Locally in the Global Economy", *Harvard Business Review*, August 2003, Vol. 81, Issue 8, pp.119–127

Kanter, R.M., 2004, "The Middle Manager as Innovator", *Harvard Business Review*, July/August 2004, Vol. 82, Issue 7/8, pp.156–161

Kanter, R.M., 2008, "Transforming Giants", *Harvard Business Review*, January 2008, Vol. 86, Issue 1, pp.43–52

Kaplan, R. and Norton, D., 1993, "Putting the Balanced Scorecard to Work", *Harvard Business Review*, September/October 1993, Vol. 71, Issue 5, pp.134–147

Kaplan, R. and Norton, D., 2001, *The Strategy Focused Organisation: How Balanced Scorecard Companies Thrive in the New Business Environment*, Boston, Harvard Business School Press

Kaplan, R. and Norton, D., 2005, "The Balanced Scorecard: Measures that Drive Performance", *Harvard Business Review*, July/August 2005, Vol. 87, Issue 7/8, pp.172–180

Kaplan, R. and Norton, D., 2006, "How to Implement a Strategy Without Disrupting your Organisation", *Harvard Business Review*, March 2005, Vol. 84, Issue 3, pp.100–109

Kaplan, R. and Norton, D., 2008, "Mastering the Management System", *Harvard Business Review*, January 2008, Vol. 86, Issue 1, pp.62–77

Kaplan, R. *et al.*, 2010, "Managing Alliances with the Balanced Scorecard", *Harvard Business Review*, January/February 2010, Vol. 88, Issue 1, pp.114–120

Katzenbach, J. and Smith, D., 1993, *The Wisdom of Teams: Creating the High-Performance Organisation*, New York, Harper Business

Keogh, O., 2017, "A prevention and cure for equine malady", *Irish Times*, 21 September 2017

Kerry Group Plc, 2019, https://www.kerrygroup.com/our-company/group-structure, Accessed 1 August 2019

Ket de Vries, M., 2001, *The Leadership Mystique*, London, Financial Times, Prentice Hall

Kim, C. and Maubourgne, R., 2002, Charting your company's future, *Harvard Business Review*, Vol. 80, Issue 6, pp.76–82

King, A., 2007, "Disentangling interfirm and intrafirm causal ambiguity: a conceptual model of causal ambiguity and sustainable competitive advantage", *Academy of Management Review*, Vol. 32, No. 1, pp.156–178

Knights, D. and Willmott, H., 2007, *Introducing Organisational Behaviour and Management*, London, Thomson Learning

Kotler, P. *et al.*, 2007, *Principles of Marketing*, 4th European Ed., Upper Saddle River, NJ, Prentice Hall Europe

Kotler, P., Keller, K., Brady, M., Goodman, M., and Hansen, T., 2016, *Marketing Management* 3rd Ed., Harlow, Pearson

Kotter, J., 1996, *Leading Change*, Boston, Harvard Business School Press

Kotter, J., 2007, "Leading Change: Why Transformation Efforts Fail", *Harvard Business Review*, January 2007, Vol. 85, Issue 1, pp.96–103

Kotter J. and Cohen D., 2002, *The Heart of Change*, Boston, Harvard Business School Press

Kouzes, J. and Posner, B., 1995, *The Leadership Challenge*, San Francisco, Jossey-Bass

Kreitner, R., 1998, *Management* 7th Ed., Boston, Houghton Mifflin

Lane, B., 2008, *Jacked Up: The Inside Story of how Jack Welch Talked GE into Becoming the World's Greatest Company*, New York, McGraw-Hill

Lavery, B. and O'Brien, T., 2005, "Insurers' trails lead to Dublin", *The New York Times*, http://query.nytimes.com/gst/fullpage.html?res=9805EED9103FF932A35757C0A9639C8B63, Accessed 30 January 2011

Lawrence, A., 2010, "Managing Disputes with Nonmarket Stakeholders", *California Management Review*, Fall 2010, Vol. 53, No.1

Leahy, P., 2009, *Showtime: The Inside Story of Fianna Fáil in Power*, Dublin, Penguin Ireland

Lencioni, P., 2002, "Make Your Values Mean Something", *Harvard Business Review*, July 2002, Vol. 80, Issue 7, p.113–117

Levitt, T., 1958, "The Dangers of Social Responsibility", *Harvard Business Review*, Sept/Oct 1958, Vol 36, Issue 5, pp.41–50

Levitt, T., 2002, "Creativity is not enough", *Harvard Business Review*, August 2002, Vol. 80, Issue 8, pp.137–14

Levitt, T., 1983, "The Globalisation of Markets", *Harvard Business Review*, May/June1983, Vol. 61, Issue 3

Lewin, K., 1951, *Field Theory in Social Science*, New York, Harper & Row

Likert, R., 1961, *New Patterns of Management*, New York, McGraw-Hill

Liu, Y., 2007, "The Value of Human Resource Management for Organisational Performance", *Business Horizons*, November/December 2007, Vol. 50, Issue 6, pp.503–511

Locke, E. and Latham, G., 1990, *A Theory of Goal Setting and Task Performance*, Upper Saddle River, NJ, Prentice Hall

Lonergan, J., 2006, *Address to Social Care Conference*, Institute of Technology, Tralee

Lunn, P., 2008, "Economic Uncertainty Takes Revenge on Hubris of Traders", *Irish Times*, 24 September 2008, p.14

Lynch, R., 2003, *Corporate Strategy* 3rd Ed., Harlow, Essex, Prentice Hall. Financial Times

Lynch, R. 2018, *Strategic Management* 8th Ed., Harlow, Essex, Prentice Hall, Financial Times

Lynch, S., 2010, "AIB to Pay up to €10m in Backdated Employee Bonuses", *The Irish Times*, 10 November 2010, p.18

Lynch, S., 2010, "Irish Management Skills Weak", *The Irish Times*, 21 December 2010, p.17

Lyons, T., 2008, "Dublin Port in Mekong Move", London, *Sunday Times*, 17 August 2008, Business and Money, p.1

Lyons, T., 2008, "Irish IT blow as Dell boss quits", London, *Sunday Times*, 11 August 2008, Business and Money, p.1

Lyons, T. and Carey, B., 2011, *The Fitzpatrick Tapes: The Rise and Fall of One Man, One Bank and One Country*, Dublin, Penguin Ireland

Macaro, A. and Baggini, J., 2010, "The Shrink and the Sage", *Financial Times Magazine*, 27 November 2010, p.51

MacConnell, S., 2011, "Bord Bia Says 70% of Exporters are Confident About Outlook", *Irish Times*, 13 January 2011, p.18

Mac Donnell, V., 2015, *An Introduction to Business Law* 2nd Ed., Dublin, Chartered Accountants Ireland

Mackey, J. and Risodia, R., 2014, *Conscious Capitalism. Liberating the Heroic Spirit of Business.* Boston, Harvard Business Press

Maclear, M., 1981, *The Ten Thousand Day War*, London, Thames Mandarin

Magee, B., 1998, *The Story of Philosophy*, London, Dorling Kindersley

Mandl, I and Dorr, A., 2007, *CSR and Competitiveness – European SMEs' Good Practice – Consolidating European Report*. Vienna, KMU Forschung Austria (Austrian Institute for SME Research), http://www.bsocial.gva.es/documents/610767/716777/CSR_competitiveness_european.pdf/64db87c9-3062-4e76-bcbf-bc1bcace91b3, Accessed 10 June 2014

Mankins, M. and Steele, R., 2005, "Turning Great Strategy into Great Performance", *Harvard Business Review*, July/August 2005, Vol. 83, Issue 7/8, pp.64–72

March, J. and Simon, H., 1958, *Organisation*, New York, John Wiley & Son

Margolis, J. and Stoltz, P., 2010, "How to Bounce Back from Adversity", *Harvard Business Review*, January/February 2010, Vol. 88, Issue 1, pp.86–92

Markides, C., 1997, "To diversify or not to diversify", *Harvard Business Review*, November/December 1997, Vol. 75, Issue 6, pp.93–99

Marriage, M. and Beioley, K., 2019, "Fake invoices resulted in Café's collapse", *Financial Times*, 26/27 January 2019, p.1

Martin, J., 2005, *Organisational Behaviour and Management* 3rd Ed., London, Thomson Learning Ltd

Martin, J. and Schmidt, C., 2010, "How to Keep Your Top Talent", *Harvard Business Review*, May 2010, Vol. 88, Issue 5, pp.51–61

Martin, R., 2010, "The Age of Customer Capitalism", *Harvard Business Review*, January 2010, Vol. 88, Issue 1, pp.58–65

Mason, C. and Simmons, J., 2014, "Embedding Corporate Social Responsibility in Corporate Governance: A Stakeholder Systems Approach", *Journal of Business Ethics*, Vol. 119, pp.77–86.

McCall, B., 2010, "Are We Ready to Wean Off FDI?", *Irish Times*, 26 November 2010, Innovation, p.45

McCaughran, S., 2008, "Investors Looking for Blue Gold", *Sunday Business Post*, 20 July 2008

McClelland, D., 1961, *The Achieving Society*, New York, Free Press

McElhaney, K.A., 2008, *Just Good Business: The Strategic Guide to Aligning Corporate Responsibility and Brand*, Williston, Barrett-Koehler

McGreevy, R., 2008, "Hibernian Insurance to Outsource Jobs", Dublin, *Irish Times*, 3 July 2008

McKay, S., 2009, "The Kindness of Strangers", *Irish Times*, 14 March 2009, Magazine, p.17

McKinsey & Co., 2009, *Management Matters in Northern Ireland and Republic of Ireland*, Dublin, Forfás

McKinsey & Co., 2012, False Summit. The State of Human Capital 2012, McKinsey & Co and The Conference Board

McNamara, R., 1995, *The Tragedy and Lessons of the Vietnam War*, New York, Times Books

McShane, S. and Von Glinow, M., 2009, *Organisational Behaviour*, 2nd Ed., New York, McGraw-Hill

Melé, D., 2014, "Human Quality Treatment: Five Organisational Levels", *Journal of Business Ethics*, Vol. 120, pp.457–471

Miles, R., 2010, "Accelerating Corporate Transformations (Don't Lose Your Nerve)", *Harvard Business Review*, January/February 2010, Vol. 88, Issue 1, pp.68–75

Miles, R. and Snow, C., 1978, *Organisational Strategy, Structure and Process*, New York, McGraw-Hill

Mintzberg, H., 1979, *The Structuring of Organisations: A Synthesis of Research*, New Jersey, Prentice Hall

Mintzberg, H., 1994, "The Rise and Fall of Strategic Planning", *Harvard Business Review*, January/February 1994, Vol. 72, Issue 1, pp.101–114

Mintzberg, H. and Waters, J., 1985, "Of Strategies: Deliberate and Emergent", *Management Journal*, Vol. 6, Issue 3, pp.257–272

Monks, R. and Minow, N., 2011, *Corporate Governance* 5th Ed, Chichester, John Wiley & Sons Ltd

Moore, G., 2005, "Strategy and Your Stronger Hand", *Harvard Business Review*, December 2005, Vol. 83, Issue 2, pp.62–72

Morley, M. and Heraty, N. (Eds), 2000, *Strategic Management in Ireland*, Dublin, Gill & Macmillan

Morris, R., 1956, "A Typology of Norms", *American Sociological Review*, October, Vol. 21, No. 5, pp.610–613

Motta, E. and Uchida, K., 2018, "Institutional investors, corporate social responsibility and stock price performance", *Journal of the Japanese and International Economies*, Vol 97. No. 3, pp.91–102

Mourkogiannis, N., 2006, *Purpose – The Starting Point of Great Companies*, New York Palgrave Macmillan

Murphy, D. and Devlin, M., 2009, *Banksters: How a powerful elite squandered Ireland's wealth*, Dublin, Hachette Books Ireland

Murphy, Y. *et al.*, 2009, *Report into the Catholic Archdiocese of Dublin*, Dublin, The Stationery Office

Neilson, G. *et al.*, 2008, "The Secrets to Successful Strategy Execution", *Harvard Business Review*, June 2008, Vol. 86, Issue 6, pp.60–70

New, S., 2010, "The Transparent Supply Chain", *Harvard Business Review*, October 2010, Vol. 88, Issue 10, pp.76–82

Nichols, J. and Roslow, S., "The S Curve: An Aid to Strategic Marketing", *Journal of Consumer Marketing*, 1986, Vol. 3, Issue 2, pp.53–64

Nickson, D., 2007, *Human Resource Management for the Tourism and Hospitality Industries*, Oxford, Elsevier Ltd

Nidumolu, R. *et al.*, 2009, "Why Sustainability is the Key Driver of Innovation", *Harvard Business Review*, September 2009, Vol. 87, Issue 9, pp.57–64

Nonaka, I. and Takeuchi, H., 1995, *The Knowledge Creating Company*, Oxford, Oxford University Press

Nugent, F., 2003, *Seek the Frozen Lands: Irish Explorers 1940–1922*, Cork, The Collins Press

Nutt, P., 1986, "Tactics of Implementation", *Academy of Management Journal*, June 1986, pp.230–261

Nyberg, P., 2011, "Misjudging Risk: Causes of the systemic banking crisis in Ireland", *Report of the Commission of Investigation into the Banking Sector in Ireland*, Dublin, The Stationery Office

O'Brien, J. and Marakas, G., 2008, *Management Information Systems* 8th Ed., New York, McGraw-Hill

O'Cleary, C., 2013, *The Billionaire Who Wasn't: How Chuck Feeney Made and Gave Away a Fortune*, New York, Public Affairs (Perseus Books Group)

O'Donovan, H., 2009, "CRAIC – A Model Suitable for Irish Coaching Psychology", *The Coaching Psychologist*, Vol. 5, Issue 2, December 2009

OECD, 2004, *OECD Principles of Corporate Governance*, Paris, OECD

OECD, 2009, *Corporate Governance and the Financial Crisis: Key Findings and Messages*, OECD, https://www.oecd.org/corporate/ca/corporategovernanceprinciples/43056196.pdf, Accessed 27 May 2019

OECD, 2010, *Better Regulation in Europe – Ireland*, Paris, OECD

OECD, 2018, *OECD Economic Surveys, Ireland 2018*, Paris, OECD

O'Halloran, B., 2008, "Bord na Móna to Invest €1.4bn over Five Years", Dublin, *Irish Times*, 22 July 2008

O'Halloran, B. and Lynch, S., 2011, "Exports to exceed €170bn, predicts trade body", *Irish Times*, 6 January 2011, p.16

O'Higgins, E., 2010, "Corporations, Civil Society, and Stakeholders: An Organisation Conceptualisation", *Journal of Business Ethics*, Vol. 94, Issue 2, pp.157–176

O'Higgins, E., 2012, "Executive Remuneration. The Myth of Pay-For Performance", *Accountancy Ireland*, Vol. 44, No. 4, pp.26–28

Ohmae, K., 1982, *The Mind of the Strategist*, New York, McGraw-Hill

Ohmae, K., 1989, "The Global Logic of Strategic Alliances", *Harvard Business Review*, March/April 1989, Vol. 67, Issue 2, pp.143–152

Ohmae, K., 1989, "Managing in a Borderless World", *Harvard Business Review*, May/June 1989, Vol. 67, Issue 3, pp.151–161

Oireachtas Reports, 2018, www.oireachtas.ie, Accessed 13 June 2019

O'Leary, J., 2010, "I should have been more pushy in opposing risk-taking at bank", *Irish Times*, 24 July 2010, p.11

O'Leary, K., 2010, "Partnership in Enterprise Level in Ireland", in Hogan, J. *et al.* (Eds), *Irish Business and Society*, Dublin, Gill & Macmillan

O'Toole, F., 2017, Fintan O'Toole: McCabe also a victim of Irish Hunger for toxic gossip, *Irish Times*, 14 February 2017, https://www.irishtimes.com/opinion/fintan-o-toole-mccabe-also-a-victim-of-irish-hunger-for-toxic-gossip-1.2974162, Accessed 2 July 2019

Olivier, R., 2013, *Inspirational Leadership: Richard V and the Muse of Fire*, London, Siro Press.

Osborn, A.F., 1979, *Applied Imagination: Principles and Procedures of Creative Thinking* 3rd Ed., New York, Scribners

O'Sullivan, K., 2019, "Kingspan targets recycling rate of 1bn bottles per year", *Irish Times*, 22 March 2019, https://www.irishtimes.com/news/environment/kingspan-targets-plastic-recycling-rate-of-1bn-bottles-per-year-1.3835335, Accessed 22 March 2019

O'Toole, F., 2009, *Ship of Fools: How Stupidity and Corruption Sank the Celtic Tiger*, London, Faber and Faber Ltd

O'Toole, F., 2010, "Balancing profit and loss, ups and downs, right and wrong", *Irish Times*, 6 March 2010, Weekend Review, p.7

Papasolomou-Doukakis, I., Krambia-Kapardis, M., and Katsioloudes, M., 2005, "Corporate social responsibility: the way forward? Maybe not!" *European Business Review*, Vol. 17, No. 3, pp.263–279

Park, S. and Levy, S., 2014, "Corporate social responsibility: perspectives of hotel frontline employees", *International Journal of Contemporary Hospitality Management*, Vol. 26, No. 3, pp.332–348

Parker, C., 2009, "Meta-Regulation", in D. McBarnet, A. Voiculescu and T. Campbell (Eds.), *The New Corporate Accountability. Corporate Social Responsibility and the Law*, pp.207–237, Cambridge, Cambridge University Press

Parker, C., 2010, *The Open Corporation: Effective Self-regulation and Democracy*, Cambridge, Cambridge University Press

Parker, G.M., 1990, *Team Players and Teamwork: the New Competitive Business Strategy*, San Francisco, Jossey-Bass

Pascale, R., 1984, "Perspectives on Strategy: the Real Story behind Honda's Success", *California Management Review*, Vol. 26, Issue 3, pp.47–72

Pascale, R. and Sternin, J., 2005, "Your Company's Secret Change Agents", *Harvard Business Review*, May 2005, Vol. 83, Issue 5, pp.73–81

Paul, M., 2008, "Ireland Misses Out on New Google jobs", *Sunday Times*, 21 December 2008, Business and Money, p.1

Peters, T.J. and Waterman, R.H., 1982, *In Search of Excellence: Lessons from America's Best-run Companies*, New York, Harper Collins

Pettigrew, A. and Whipp, R., 1999, *Managing Change for Competitive Success*, Oxford, Blackwell Publishing

Pfeffer, J., 1995, "Producing sustainable competitive advantage through the effective management of people", *Academy of Management Executive*, Vol. 9, No. 1, pp.55–69

Pfeifer, S., 2019, "Under the hood. Move to scrap white elephant A380 surprises few in the industry", *Financial Times*, 16 February 2019, p.16

Pfeifer, S., Pooler, M., and McGee, P., 2019, "Forced into the slow lane", *Financial Times*, 23 February 2019, FT Weekend, p.9

Picciotto, S., 2011, *Regulating Global Corporate Capitalism*, Cambridge, Cambridge University Press

Plato, Translated by Lee, D., 1974, *The Republic,* Harmondsworth, Penguin

Pocock, T., 1987, *Horatio Nelson*, London, Brockhampton Press

Porter, M., 1980, *Competitive Strategy: Techniques of Analysing Industries and Competitors*, New York, The Free Press

Porter, M., 1985, *Competitive Advantage*, New York, The Free Press

Porter, M., 1996, "What is Strategy?", *Harvard Business Review*, November/December 1996, Vol. 74, Issue 6, pp.61–78

Porter, M. and Kramer, M., 2006, "Strategy and Society", Boston, *Harvard Business Review*, December 2006, Vol. 84, Issue 12, pp.79–92

Porter, M. and Kramer, M., 2006, "Strategy and Society", *Harvard Business Review*, Vol. 84, Issue 12, pp.79–92

Porter, M. and Krammer, M., 2011, "Creating Shared Value", *Harvard Business Review*, Vol. 89, No. 1/2, pp.62–77

Prahalad, C.K., 2010, "The Responsible Manager", *Harvard Business Review*, January/February 2010, Vol. 88, Issue 1, p.36

Prahalad, C.K. and Hamel, G., 1990, "The Core Competence of the Organisation", *Harvard Business Review*, May/June 1990, Vol. 68, No. 3, pp.79–91

Press, G., 1990, "Assessing Competitors' Business Philosophies", *Long Range Planning*, October 1990, Vol. 23, Issue 5, pp.71–75

Public Appointments Service, 2018, https://www.publicjobs.ie/en/, Accessed 22 November 2018

Purcell, J., 2004, "The HRM-performance link: why, how and when does people management impact on organisational performance?" Paper presented at the Twelfth Annual John Lovett memorial Lecture, University of Limerick

PwC, 2017, *Sizing the Prize. What's the real value of AI for your business and how you can capitalise*, London, PwC

Quinn, J., 1980, *Strategies for Change*, Homewood, Ill, Irwin

Regling, C. and Watson, M., 2010, *A Preliminary Report on the Sources of Ireland's Banking Crisis*, Dublin, The Stationery Office

Reich, R., 2008, *Supercapitalism: The Battle for Democracy in an Age of Big Business*, Cambridge, Icon

Ricks, T., 2006, *Fiasco: The American Military Involvement in Iraq*, London, Penguin

Rigby, D. and Vishwanath, V., 2006, "Localisation: The Revolution in Consumer Markets", *Harvard Business Review*, April 2006, Vol. 84, Issue 4, pp.82–92

Rigby, D. *et al.*, 2009, "Innovation in Turbulent Times", *Harvard Business Review*, June 2009, Vol. 87, Issue 6, pp.79–86

Rigby, E., 2006, "Eyes in the Till", London, *Financial Times Magazine*, 11/12 November 2006, pp.16–22

Robins, F., 2006, "Corporate governance after Sarbanes-Oxley: an Australian perspective", *Corporate Governance*, Vol. 6, No. 1, pp.34–48.

Rokeach, M., 1973, *The Nature of Human Values*, New York, The Free Press

Ross, J. and Straw, B., 1993, "Organisational Escalation and Exit: Lessons from the Shoreham Nuclear Power Plant", *Academy of Management Journal*, August 1993, pp.701–32

Ross, M. *et al*, 1999, "Basic Individual Values and the meaning of Work", *Applied Psychology: An International Review*, January 1999, pp.49–71

Ross, S., 2009, *The Bankers: How the Banks Brought Ireland to its Knees*, Dublin, Penguin Ireland

Ross, S. and Webb, N., 2010, *Wasters*, Dublin, Penguin Ireland

RSA, 2018, https://www.rsa.ie/RSA/Road-Safety/Campaigns/Current-road-safety-campaigns/Drunk-With-Tiredness/, Accessed 30 July 2019

RTÉ, 2018, "McCabe says report is 'hard to take', but he is happy with its publication", https://www.rte.ie/news/politics/2018/1011/1002457-disclosures-tribunal-report/, Accessed 22 March 2019

RTÉ, 2018, "Whistle-blower: McCabe family to tell their extraordinary story", https://www.rte.ie/news/2018/1108/1009623-whistleblower-mccabe-family-to-tell-their-extraordinary-story/, Accessed 22 March 2019

Russell, H., Maître, B., Watson, D., and Fahey, É., 2018, *Job Stress and Working Conditions: Ireland in Comparative Perspective*, Dublin, Health and Safety Authority

Rust, T. *et al.*, 2010, "Rethinking Marketing", *Harvard Business Review*, January/February 2010, Vol. 88, Issue 1, pp.94–101

Ryan, S.*et al.*, 2009, *The Commission to Inquire into Child Abuse*, Dublin, Government Publications Office

Schein, E., 2010, *Organisational Culture and Leadership*, 4th Ed., San Francisco, Jossey-Bass

Science Foundation Ireland, 2019, Funding. http://www.sfi.ie/funding/, Accessed 15 February 2019

Schwalbe, K., 2010, *Managing Information Technology Projects*, Augsburg, Cengage Learning

Schwartz, S. and Sagie, G., 2000, "Value Consensus and Importance: A Cross-National Study", *Journal of Cross-Cultural Psychology*, July 2000, p.468

Scott, C. and Brown, C., 2012, "W(h)ither Better Regulation?" UCD RegGov Policy Brief, http://www.ucd.ie/t4cms/Whither%20BR%20Policy%20Brief%20May%202012.pdf, Accessed 18 March 2019

Senge, P., 1990, *The Fifth Discipline: The Art and Practice of the Learning Organisation*, London, Doubleday

Sethi, P., 1975, "Dimensions of Corporate Social Performance: An Analytical Framework", *California Management Review*, Vol. XVII, No. 3, pp.58–64

Sharda, R., Delen, D., and Turban, E., 2018, *Business Intelligence, Analytics and Data Science: A Managerial Perspective*, New York, Pearson Education, Inc

Simmons, J., 2011, "Mergers & Acquisitions hit €10.3bn in 2010", *The Irish Times*, 7 January 2011, Business This Week, p.5

Simmons, J., 2004, "Managing in the post-managerialist era. Towards socially responsible corporate governance", *Management Decision*, Vol. 42, No.3/4, pp.601–611

Simon, A.H., 1979, "Rational Decision-making in Business Organisations", *American Economics Review*, September 1979

Simon, H., 1956, "Rational choice and the structures of the environment", *Psychological Review*. Vol 63, No.2, pp.129–139

Smith, D., 2006, *Exploring Innovation*, Maidenhead, McGraw-Hill

Smith, M., 2000, *An Unsung Hero*, Cork, Collins Press

Smyth, P., 2018, "Google fined €4.3bn over Android abuse", *Irish Times*, 19 July 2018, Business, Technology & Innovation, p.1

Sprinke, G. and Maines, L., 2010, "The benefits and costs of corporate social responsibility", *Business Horizons*, Vol. 53, No. 5, pp.445–453

Staunton, D., 2009, "US Combat Troops to Leave Iraq Next Year", *The Irish Times*, 28 February 2009, p.11

Stevenson, W., 1989, *Production/Operations Management*, Illinois, Irwin

Stewart, J. and Rigg, C., 2011, *Learning and Talent Development*, London, CIPD

Stewart, T.A., 1999, "The Conquest for Welch's Throne Begins: Who will Run GE?", *Fortune*, 11 January 1999, p.27

Stogdill, R.M., 1948, "Personal Factors Associated With Leadership: A Survey of the Literature", *Journal of Psychology*, 1948, pp.35–71

Stogdill, R. and Coons, A., 1957, *Leader Behaviour: Its Description and Measurement*, Columbus, Ohio, Ohio State University Press, Bureau of Business Research

Suarez, F. and Lanzolla, G., 2005, "The Half-Truth of First Mover Advantages", Boston, *Harvard Business Review*

Sweeney, L., 2009, *A Study of Current Practice of Corporate Social Responsibility (CSR) and an Examination of the Relationship between CSR and Financial Performance using Structural Equation Modelling*, Doctoral Thesis, Dublin Institute of Technology, 2009

Tansey, P., 2007, "Public Sector Reform Would Aid Productivity", *Irish Times*, 23 November 2007, p.34

Tansey, P., 2008, "Innovate or Stagnate", Dublin, *Irish Times*, 29 February 2008

Taylor, C., 2010, "The Four Year Challenge", *Sunday Business Post*, 10 October 2010, p.10

Taylor, C., 2018, "Irish are the biggest international online shoppers in the world", *The Irish Times*, 30 August 2018, https://www.irishtimes.com/business/technology/irish-are-the-biggest-international-online-shoppers-in-the-world-1.3611205, Accessed 10 March 2019

Tesco, 2019, https://www.tescoplc.com/about/our-businesses, Accessed 19 January 2019

The Economist, 2011, "Irish Mist", *The Economist*, 19 February 2011, p.14

The Guardian, 2019, "Google fined record £44m by French data protection watchdog", 21 January 2019, https://www.theguardian.com/technology/2019/jan/21/google-fined-record-44m-by-french-data-protection-watchdog, Accessed 3 July 2019

Thomas, M., 2008, *Belching out the Devil*, London, Ebury Press

Thomas, T. *et al.,* 2004, "Strategic Leadership in Ethical Behaviour", *Academy of Management Review*, Vol. 18, Issue 2, May 2004, p.58

Thompson, A. *et al.*, 2008, *Crafting and Executing Strategy: The Quest for Competitive Advantage*, New York, McGraw-Hill

Thompson, J., Martin, F., and Scott J., 2017, *Strategic Management: Awareness and Change*, 8th Ed., London, Cengage Learning

Tian, X., 2018, *Managing International Business in China*, 2nd Ed., Cambridge, Cambridge University Press

Tiernan, S., Morley, M. and Foley E., 2013, *Modern Management: Theory and Practice for Irish Students*, 4th Ed., Dublin, Gill

Towers Watson, 2012, *Global Workforce Study. Engagement at Risk: Driving Strong Performance in a Volatile Global Environment*, http://www.towerswatson.com/assets/pdf/2012-Towers-Watson-Global-Workforce-Study.pdf, 29 August 2012.

Tricker, B., 2015, *Corporate Governance. Principles, Policies, and Practices*, 3rd Ed., Oxford, Oxford University Press

Trompenaars, F. and Hampden-Turner, C., 1998, *Riding the Waves of Culture: Understanding Cultural Diversity in Global Business*, 2nd Ed., New York, McGraw-Hill

Tsai, H., Tsang, N. and Cheng, S., 2012 "Hotel employees' perception on corporate social responsibility: the case of Hong Kong", *International Journal of Hospitality Management*, Vol. 31, pp.1143–1154

Uhlaner, R. and West, A., 2008, "Running a Winning M&A Shop", *McKinsey Quarterly*, Spring 2008

Vroom, V., 1964, *Work and Motivation*, New York, John Wiley & Sons

Wagner, S. and Dittmar, L., 2006, "The Unexpected Benefits of Sarbanes-Oxley", *Harvard Business Review*, April 2006, Vol. 84, Issue 4, pp.133–140

Walker, D., 2009, *A Review of Corporate Governance in UK Banks and Other Financial Institutions*, London, The Walker Review Secretariat

Walker, M., 2018, *Why we sleep: the new science of sleep and dreams*, London, Penguin Books

Walker Review, 2009, *A Review of Corporate Governance in UK Banks and Other Financial Industry Entities*, London, The Walker Review Secretariat

Wall, M., 2006, "Inefficiency and High Labour Costs Blamed for Expensive Electricity", *Irish Times*, 2 October 2006, p.5

Walsh, K., 2010, "The world's not big enough for Louis Vuitton", *Sunday Times*, 21 November 2010, Business, p.10

Ward, A.M., 2014, *Finance, Theory and Practice*, 3rd Ed., Dublin, Chartered Accountants Ireland

Ward A.M. and Wylie, J., 2014, "Word of Mouse. Using Social Media to Inform your Corporate Social Responsibility Strategy", *Accountancy Ireland*, Vol. 46, No. 6, pp.58–60

Weckler, A., 2008, "The evolution of invention", Dublin, *Sunday Business Post*

Weilrich, H. and Koontz, H., 1993, *Management*, New York, McGraw-Hill

Welch, J., 2001, *Jack: What I've Learned Leading a Great Company and Great People*, London, Headline

Wernerfelt, B., 1984, "A resource-based view of the firm", *Strategic Management Journal*, Vol. 5, No. 2, pp.171–180

Whole Foods Market, 2019, https://www.wholefoodsmarket.com/company-info. Accessed 1 August 2019

Wind, J. and Main, J., 1999, *Driving Change*, London, Kogan Page

Wood, D., 1991, "Social Issues in Management: Theory and Research in Corporate Social Performance", *Journal of Management*, Vol. 17, No. 2, pp.383–406

Woodall, P., 2003, "House of Cards", *The Economist*, 31 May 2003, pp.3–16

Yarlagadda, R., Zheltoukhova, K., Bailey, C., Shantz, A. and Brione, P., 2017, *Purposeful Leadership: what it is, what causes it and does it matter?* London, CIPD.

Yip, G., 2003, *Total Global Strategy II*, London, Financial Times, Prentice Hall

Young, S. and Thyil, V., 2008, "A holistic model of corporate governance: a new research framework", *Corporate Governance*, Vol. 8, No. 1, pp.94–108

Zhang, M., Fan, D., and Zhu, C., 2014, "High-Performance Work Systems, Corporate Social Performance and Employee Outcomes: Exploring the Missing Links", *Journal of Business Ethics*, Vol. 120, pp.423–435

Zheltoukhova, K., 2014, *Leadership. Easier said than done*, London, CIPD

Vroom, V., 1964, Work and Motivation, New York, John Wiley & Sons.

Warner, S. and Ditzian, T., 2006, "The Unexpected Benefits of Sarbanes-Oxley", Harvard Business Review, April 2006, Vol. 84, Issue 4, pp.133-140

Walker, D., 2009, "A Review of Corporate Governance in UK Banks and Other Financial Entities", London, The Walker Review Secretariat

Wallace, M., 2014, Why we buy: the psychology of ideas and dreams, London, Penguin Books

Walker Review, 2009, A Review of Corporate Governance in UK Banks and Other Financial Entities, London, The Walker Review Secretariat

Walsh, M., 2006, "Reflections and High Labour Costs blamed for Expensive Electricity", Irish Times, 2 October 2006 p.9

Walsh, K., 2010, "The world's not big enough for Louis Vuitton", Sunday Times, 7 and 14 November 2010, Business, p.10

Ward, A.M., 2014, Finance, Theory and Practice, 3rd Ed, Dublin, Chartered Accountants Ireland

Ward, A.M. and Welch, J., 2014, "Word of Mouth: Using Social Media to Inform your Corporate Social Responsibility Strategy", Accountancy Ireland, Vol. 46, No. 6, pp.38-40

Wechler, A., 2006, "The evolution of invention", Dublin, Rouge Review, Per

Weihrich, H. and Koontz, H., 1995, Management, New York, McGraw-Hill

Welch, J., 2001, Jack: What I've learned leading a great company and great people, London, Headline

Wernerfelt, B., 1984, "A resource-based view of the firm", Strategic Management Journal, Vol. 5, No. 2, pp.171-180

Whole Foods Market, 2019, https://www.wholefoodsmarket.com/company-info, Accessed 1 August 2019

Wind, J. and Main, R., 1995, Driving Change, London, Kogan Page

Wood, D., 1991, "Social Issues in Management: Theory and Research in Corporate Social Performance", Journal of Management, Vol. 17, No. 2, pp.383-406

Woodall, P., 2003, "House of cards", The Economist, 31 May 2003, pp.3-16

Yaqub, R., Abdoulkarim, K., Billey, C., Shantu, V., and Suren, P., 2017, "Proposed C-suite as seen in solar power at one stage in reality", London, CIPD.

Yip, G., 2003, Total Global Strategy II, London, Financial Times, Prentice Hall

Young, S. and Thyil, V., 2008, "A holistic model of corporate governance: a new research framework", Corporate Governance, Vol. 8, No. 1, pp.94-108

Zhang, M., Fan, D., and Zhu, C., 2014, "High Performance Work Systems, Corporate Social Performance and Employee Outcomes: Exploring the Missing Links", Journal of Business Ethics, Vol. 120, pp.423-435

Zuchowiova, K., 2014, Fundamentals of human resources, London, CIPD.

Glossary

Acquisition – One company purchases a controlling interest in another company.

Architecture – The network of relationships both within the organisation and between the organisation and other groups.

Artificial intelligence – A collective term for computer systems that can sense their environment, think, learn and take action from what they are sensing.

Authority – Where an individual has legitimate power within the organisation to give work-related orders.

Autonomy – The extent to which employees have freedom to take the initiative with regard to their work.

Backward integration – The development of activities into areas concerned with the supply of inputs into the organisation.

Balanced Scorecard – Performance measurement that combines qualitative and quantitative measures in a balanced manner across the organisation.

Barriers to entry – Factors that prevent an organisation entering a market.

Benchmarking – The comparison of performance between an organisation and other organisations, regardless of which industry they might be in.

Big data – Refers to very large data sets that can be used to reveal patterns, trends and associations, especially relating to human behaviour and interactions.

Boston Consulting Group Matrix – A matrix used to place business units according to the level of market share and market growth.

Bounded rationality – The mental limitations of managers which makes them choose a course of action that may not be the optimum course.

Brands – A name, term, design, symbol or any other feature that differentiates one seller's products or services from another.

Break-even – The point where total costs equal total revenue.

Break-even analysis – A method of examining the relationship between costs, revenue and the volume produced.

Budget – A statement of plans and expected outcomes for various activities within the organisation. It is normally expressed in financial terms.

Bureaucracy – A form of management or organisational structure which is hierarchical and based on detailed rules and procedures.

Business ethics – The ethical conduct of people within organisations and the impact it has on decisions they make at corporate and individual level.

Business intelligence – Comprises the strategies and technologies used by enterprises for the data analysis of business information.

557

Business-level strategies – Strategies that relate to a single business unit.

Business model – How an organisation produces products and services and interacts with customers.

Business process re-engineering – Carrying out a substantial and radical redesign of business processes within an organisation in order to improve efficiency.

Business risk – The risk of loss or failure due to pursuing a particular strategy.

Cash cows – Products or companies that have high market share in a low-growth industry, and generate substantial profits.

Change agent – A person or group of people tasked with leading change within an organisation.

Cognitive dissonance – Where an individual has conflicting attitudes with regard to a decision that they made.

Competences – The skills and abilities by which resources are used in an organisation. They can be basic or core competences.

Competitive advantage – The significant advantages that one company possesses over its competitors.

Competitive strategy – The basis by which an organisation competes in a competitive environment.

Computer-aided design (CAD) – The use of computer technology in designing products.

Computer-aided manufacturing (CAM) – The use of computer technology in manufacturing products.

Computer-integrated manufacturing – The use of CAD and CAM to sequence the production process efficiently.

Consistency – Where the strategy being pursued by an organisation is consistent with its goals and objectives.

Consolidation – When an organisation concentrates its efforts on maintaining its current market share.

Context – The circumstances in which a company is operating and how it impacts on its strategy.

Contingency theory – Applying a management style to suit the particular circumstances.

Control – A management function that compares actual performance with planned performance. If there is a deviance, corrective action should be taken.

Core competences – The distinctive set of skills that an organisation possess that bring significant benefit to the customer.

Core values – The values and principles considered fundamental to an organisation.

Corporate governance – The control mechanism by which senior executives are held accountable to stakeholders for the legal and ethical operations of a company.

Corporate-level strategies – Strategies pursued by the headquarters of an organisation that impact on all divisions of the company.

Corporate social responsibility (CSR) – A strategy that is integrated with (1) core business objectives and (2) core competences to create financial and social/environmental returns and is embedded in corporate culture and day-to-day business operations.

Corporate strategy – Charting the future direction of a company by developing long-term goals which reflect stakeholders' interests and achieves competitive advantage.

Cost–benefit analysis – The examination of a strategy that takes in broader criteria in addition to the main financial benefits.

Cost leadership – A competitive generic strategy which aims to minimise costs.

Cultural web – Shows the behavioural, physical and symbolic manifestations of a culture within an organisation.

Culture – See organisational culture.

Data mining – The interrogation of information systems for trends and insights into customers' buying habits or preferences.

Delegation – The process by which a manager assigns responsibilities to a member of staff.

Deliberate strategy – Strategy that has been planned in a formal manner.

Devolution – The extent to which the corporate headquarters empowers business units to make strategic decisions.

Differentiation – A competitive generic strategy aimed at developing goods and services that are viewed as being of superior quality.

Direct supervision – The direct control of work in an organisation.

Discounted cash flow – The sum of projected future cash flows from a strategy converted into present day values. It takes account of the time value of money.

Diversification – A strategy whereby a company expands from being a single business operation into different businesses of varying relatedness.

Divestment – When a company sells a business or division.

Division – A separate and self-contained part of a company, usually with responsibility for profits.

Dogs – Business units in low-growth markets with low market share.

Driving forces – Those changes taking place that are altering the fundamental nature and competition of that industry.

E-commerce – The conduct of business transaction through electronic media.

Economies of scale – When the unit cost of production decreases as the volume increases.

Economies of scope – The cost savings derived from the internal sharing of competences.

Effectiveness – The degree to which a company achieves its objectives.

Efficiency – Using the minimum amount of resources to achieve results.

Emergent strategy – A strategy that develops through the everyday routines of an organisation that become part of the long-term direction.

Employment citizenship – Concerns an organisation's standing as an employer and its employment practices.

Empowerment – The devolution of power and decision-making to members lower down in the organisation.

Entrepreneurship – The process of starting a new business venture, and undertaking risk.

Environment – All of the factors that impact on an organisation, both internal and external.

Environmental complexity – The number of environmental factors impacting on an organisation and the difficulty in understanding them.

Environmental scanning – The process of collecting information about the forces in the business environment.

Expectancy theory – A model of motivation (Vroom) which considers the level of effort required to do work and the subsequent level of performance.

First-mover advantage – The competitive benefits that accrue by being first into the market with a product or service.

Five Forces Analysis – A framework for understanding the competitive forces at play in an industry.

Flexibility – The ability to change organisational direction when required.

Focus – A generic competitive strategy aimed at a niche market.

Forcefield analysis – Identifies the factors forcing and blocking change in an organisation.

Foreign direct investment – Investment of manufacturing or other facilities by a foreign company in another country.

Foreign trade – The exporting and importing of goods and services to and from foreign countries.

Franchise – A form of licensing whereby the franchisor grants the franchisee the right to use certain intellectual property rights such as brand names, copyrights, patents, etc., in return for various fees.

Functional departmentalisation – The division of a company along functional lines, e.g. marketing.

General Data Protection Regulations (GDPR) – EU-wide regulations covering the collection, storage and use of personal data.

Gearing ratio – The ratio of debt to equity in a company.

Generic strategies – Originally developed by Michael Porter, they are general strategies that can be used by companies to compete in a particular market. They consist of cost leadership, differentiation, niche markets and best cost provider strategies.

Goals – Goals are broad statements of intent in line with the mission and focusing on a specific outcome. They are generally qualitative in nature.

Groupthink – A form of thinking that people engage in when making decisions that is so pervasive it clouds clear thinking.

Human capital – The human skills, knowledge and experience possessed by an individual or group and its value to the organisation.

Human resource management – The management of employees of the organisation. It is a strategic approach that recognises people as the company's most important asset.

Hybrid strategy – A competitive strategy that combines high quality with good value.

Implementation – The final part of strategy generation, whereby the plan is put into effect, and results are monitored.

Industrial relations – The rules, practices and conventions governing the relationship between employees and their managers. It often includes collective employee representation and bargaining.

Industry – A group of firms in a sector that produce goods and services that are very similar.

Industry driving forces – Those changes taking place that are altering the fundamental nature and competition of that industry.

Innovation – The application of new knowledge and approaches to developing products or services that have application in the market place. It is different from invention, which is the creation of an entirely new product.

Intangible resource – Non-physical assets including brand name, goodwill, reputation and knowledge.

Intellectual capital – The future earnings of a company that are derived from the calibre of people working in the organisation.

Intended strategy – The desired strategy that an organisation had planned to achieve.

Intrapreneurship – The development of new enterprise within an organisation, along with the necessary support.

Joint venture – When two companies come together and create an alliance in the form of a third company that is jointly owned and managed by the two parents who remain separate entities.

Just-in-time – Management processes which ensure that stock is delivered just as it is needed for production, thus keeping stock costs at a minimum.

Kaizen – The Japanese concept of continual improvement in an organisation.

Key success factors (KSFs) – The resources and competences required by an organisation to be successful in a competitive industry.

Key value and cost drivers – The factors that most influence the generation of profits as well as the costs associated with them.

Leadership – The ability to inspire and motivate others to work willingly towards achieving organisational goals.

Learning organisation – An organisation that has a culture that supports knowledge generation, continuing learning and the development of staff skills.

Leasing – A type of debt where an organisation hires a particular asset for a defined period, often with an option of purchase at the end of the lease.

Legitimacy – Concerns the rights and expectations by society on a firm. It confers a 'licence to operate'.

Leverage – The exploitation of assets by a company.

Life cycle – The evolution of a product or industry from its introduction to its eventual decline.

Logical incrementalism – The development of strategy by experimentation and learning from partial commitment rather than through global formulations of total strategies.

Logistics – The management of the sourcing of materials right through to the delivery of goods to customers.

Market – A group of customers that will buy products or services from a firm. The market will have certain characteristics in common, such as the type of demand, geographical area, etc.

Market development – The development of new markets by creating new segments for products, new uses for existing products or geographical spread.

Market positioning – The selection of a strategy that allows a company to compete at a particular level in the marketplace.

Market segment – Dividing the market into distinct groups based on different variables such as age, gender, etc.

Marketing concept – A philosophy that an organisation should try to provide products that satisfy customers' needs through a co-ordinated set of activities that also allows the organisation to achieve its goals.

Matrix structure – A form of multi-divisional structure which combines two overlapping structures, e.g. product line and geographical area.

Merger – Where two companies, generally of roughly equal size, decide to join operations and form a new company.

Mission – A mission guides the members of an organisation in making decisions that will achieve strategic goals and objectives.

Mission statement – A mission statement is the articulation of a company's mission to employees. It describes the company's current business – 'who we are; what we do and why we are here'.

Multidivisional structure – An organisational structure that divides the company into different divisions based on product lines or geographical areas.

Multinational company (MNC) – A company that operates in many countries around the world.

Net cash flow – The sum of pre-tax profits arising from a strategy.

Niche market – A small market segment with its own distinctive characteristics.

Objectives – Statements of specific outcomes that the organisation intends to achieve.

Oligopoly – A market that is dominated by a small number of companies.

Operational strategies – Strategies concerned with how the organisation will convert corporate- and business-level strategies into day-to-day routines in the various parts of the company.

Opportunity costs – The cost of not taking a particular course of action in terms of benefits foregone.

Organic development – Development of the organisation through its own capabilities.

Organisational culture – The basic assumptions and beliefs that are shared by members of an organisation.

Organisational knowledge – The knowledge, values, understanding and experience that have been built up throughout an organisation over a period of time.

Organisational politics – The power relationships within an organisation.

Outsourcing – Contracting out certain parts of the organisation's value chain to companies who specialise in that work.

Paradigm – The manner in which an organisation views the world around it.

Parenting – How a corporate headquarters guides and assists divisions within the group.

Payback period – The time it takes a company to recover the cost of a strategy.

Performance targets – Targets that the organisation sets based on output. It is based on quality, products, etc.

PESTEL framework – A framework for examining the environment from six related perspectives: political, economic, sociological, technological, environmental and legal.

Porter's Diamond – A framework for examining the competitiveness of industry clusters within a country. It has four inter-related factors.

Portfolio – A collection of businesses owned by a company.

Positioning – Involves creating an image of the product or service in the minds of the customer that will form a central part of a company's promotional strategy.

Primary activities – The parts of a value chain directly concerned with the production of goods or services.

Product – Anything that is offered to a market for attention, acquisition, use or consumption and that might satisfy a want or need and consists of a set of attributes, including physical goods, services, experiences, events, persons, places, properties, organisations, information or ideas.

Product development – The development of new products in an organisation.

Product life cycle – The cycle that a product undergoes from introduction, growth, maturing and eventual decline.

Product mix – The variety of different products that a company has on offer.

Production management – The management of the process of transforming materials into finished products.

Quality – The test of whether a product is fit for its intended purpose.

Realised strategy – The strategy that an organisation is actually following.

Related diversification – Corporate development into different areas but within the same value chain.

Resource allocation – The allocation of resources to support strategy.

Retained profits – Previous profits that have been retained by a company.

Risk – Concerns the probability and consequences of a strategy failing.

Scenario planning – An outline of alternative future developments and their impact on an organisation.

Segmentation – The process by which diverse customers in a large market are divided into smaller groups that have similar needs.

Short-term debt – A short-term loan that is normally repayable within one year.

Stakeholder mapping – It plots different stakeholders' likely position regarding a proposed strategy according to their interest and the likely commercial impact on the stakeholders.

Stakeholders – People, both groups and individuals, who have a direct or indirect interest in the organisation and its goals, including shareholders, directors, managers, employees, trade unions, government and the wider community.

Star – A business unit which has a high market share in a growing market.

Strategic alliance – When two or more separate companies agree to collaborate on a strategic basis and share resources, risk and control for their mutual benefit.

Strategic business unit (SBU) – A part of an organisation for which there is a distinct external market for its goods and services.

Strategic capability – The combination of resources and competences needed to support strategy and succeed.

Strategic choices – Analysing the various strategic options that are open to an organisation.

Strategic drift – When the strategies of an organisation diverge from the demands of the market.

Strategic fit – The matching of a company's strategy and its resources.

Strategic gap – An opportunity to exploit a gap in a market segment that is not being served by competitors.

Strategic group map – A graphical depiction of the positioning of various companies competing within an industry.

Strategic intent – Envisions a desired leadership position and establishes the criteria the organisation will use to chart its progress.

Strategic planning – The systematic planning required to develop and implement strategy.

Strategy – The direction and scope of an organisation over the long term, which achieves advantage in a changing environment though its configuration of resources and competences with the aim of fulfilling stakeholder expectations.

Suppliers – People or organisations who supply the company with the necessary materials and components for production or support activities.

Supply chain management – The development of partnerships with suppliers and distributors to facilitate the movement of goods or services.

Support activities – The parts of a value chain directly concerned with supporting the primary activities in the production of goods or services.

Sustainable development – Development that meets the needs of the present without compromising the ability of future generations to meet their needs.

SWOT analysis – An analysis of the internal strengths and weaknesses and the external opportunities and threats of an organisation.

Synergy – The benefits gained by the creation of a whole that is greater than the sum of the parts.

Tangible resources – The physical resources of the organisation such as plant and machinery.

Targeting – The decision about which market segment(s) a company will focus on.

Technology transfer – An agreement which involves the transfer of technology or use of technology between organisations.

Tipping point – A tipping point is reached when the demand for a product or service takes off exponentially.

Total costs – The combination of fixed and variable costs.

Total quality management – A systematic approach to improving quality in the production of goods and services.

Turnaround strategy – A strategy aimed at turning a company around in a crisis situation and bringing it back to viability.

Uncertainty – Factors that impact on the organisation, but are difficult to quantify.

Unrelated diversification – Diversification into products or services that have no connection with the current value chain.

Value chain – Developed by Michael Porter to examine the elements of a company where costs and value are created.

Values – Standards or criteria for choosing goals or guiding actions.

Value system – The expansion of the value chain to include all of the suppliers and distributors involved in delivering a product to the end customers.

Venture capital – Capital provided by individuals and organisations to support the creation of new enterprise.

Vision – The desired end-state of an organisation, which consists of its values and purpose, underpinned by leadership and expressed in motivating terms to inspire its members.

Vision statement – Articulation of the long-term vision of the organisation – what it aspires to be.

VRIO analysis – A method for examining an organisation's resources and capabilities that are valuable, rare, inimitable and supported by the organisation.

Whistleblowers – People who report unethical or illegal behaviour being conducted in organisations to outside bodies.

Yield management – The application of information systems and pricing strategies to maximise revenue from resources of a relatively fixed but perishable capacity by anticipating and directing consumer behaviour.

Index

3M 84, 268, 285, 427

abandoned strategies 25
accounting rate of return 377, 378–9
acquisitions 16, 62, 69, 225, 300, 318–9,
    343–53, 374, 403, 497–501, 513–19
Action-Centred Leadership model 48
activity-based costing 211, 212
activity maps 215–16
actual products 281
adaptive change (organisational) 431, 449
adaptive culture 61
adaptive systems *see* artificial intelligence
Aer Lingus 24, 59, 113, 181, 217, 343, 502–7
Aer Rianta International 336
Allied Irish Banks (AIB) 46, 101, 119, 124–5,
    347–8, 363
Alpyra 343
Amazon 65, 144, 212
American Airlines 219
Amundsen, Roald 41–2, 426, 528, 529
Anaeko 22
An Post 20
Anglo Irish Bank 363
Ansbacher affair 119
Ansoff's Matrix 275, 330
Antarctic expeditions 41–2, 426–7, 528–35
Apollo space programme 86–7
Apple 144, 281
Aquinas, Thomas 116
Aristotle 23, 114–15
artefacts (organisational culture) 56–7, 71
artificial intelligence (AI) 5–7, 184, 208, 283,
    304, 436
Arthur Andersen 83

Atlantic Philanthropies 146
audit committee 109, 517, 518
augmented products 281

Babcock & Brown 344
backward vertical integration 314
bailouts 54, 160, 363, *see also* banking crisis
Balanced Scorecard 86, 91–5, 96, 98, 99, 132,
    216, 249, 343, 349, 390, 420, 421, 432
Balogun and Hope Hailey's
    matrix 429–30, 434
Bank of Ireland 314, 363, 505
Bank of Scotland Ireland 279
'Bank Wiring Observation Room
    experiments' 62, 421
banking crisis 54, 254, 259, 347–8, 366–7
banking sector
    automation/technology 208, 282, 400
    board structures 112
    collapse 14, 54, 84, 118, 147, 175, 363,
      366, 417
    corporate governance 108, 109, 110, 147,
      364, 447
    ethical behaviour 118–20, 417–18
    and funding 253, 286, 322, 331, 335, 397
    and leadership 45–6, 101–2, 109, 445, 447
    management of 393, 447
    mergers/acquisitions 345, 347–8
    and rewards/incentives 254, 276
    and risk 256, 259, 279, 366
bargaining power (Porter's Five Forces) 179,
    181, 182
basic assumptions (Schein) 56–8, 67–8
basic competences 200, 227, 401, 404
behavioural theories (leadership) 37, 40–2

565

CORPORATE STRATEGY FOR IRISH COMPANIES

CRH plc 315, 513–19
critical path analysis 413, 414
critical success factors *see* key success factors
cultural beliefs 56–8, 62, 65
cultural differences 62, 69, 345
cultural intelligence 39–40, 249, 294
cultural strength (Thompson *et al*) 61
cultural web 25, 67–8, 201, 434–5
currency considerations 159–60, 167, 296, 376
currency risk 297
current ratio 218
customer equity 204
customer perspective/service 92, 94, 95, 420
customer relationship management 96–7, 433
customer service 96, 189, 268–9, 271, 402, 433

Dairymaster 332–3
damage control approach (ethics) 126
data analytics 5, 303, 371; *see also* big data; data mining
data mining 206, 207, 370, 371, 400–1
data protection *see* General Data Protection Regulation (GDPR)
data warehousing 371
DCC plc 280, 315–18
debt (as funding) 202, 227, 376
debt (risk) 252–3, 297
decentralised decision-making 250, 261
decision-making 52, 53, 117–18, 246, 250, 261–2, 309, 358–84
decision support systems 206, 370
decisive decision-making style 369–70
decline (industry life cycle) 183, 353, 354–5
decline (product life cycle) 286–7, 294
Decom Energy Ltd 465–6
Deepwater Horizon 111, 144–5, 335, 466
Dell, Michael 87, 242
Dell Computers 87, 203, 205, 210, 265, 266–7, 400, 402
Delphi technique 368
demographics 40, 225, 429, 442, 494

deontological ethical systems 115–16
detachment, fallacy of 18
development stage (projects) 411
Diageo 80–81
differentiation strategy 68, 264–5, 268–70, 271
direct controls 419–20
Directional Policy Matrix 321, 322–5, 327
directors *see* company directors
DIRT inquiry 111, 119
discounted cash flow analysis 202, 379–80
disruptive technology 172
distribution channels 180, 210, 219, 354
distributive justice 115
diversification 16, 275, 293, 308–29, 334, 458–61
dividend policies 253
dominant logic 313
dominant market position, abuse of 351
Dongfeng Motors 335
dress codes 58–9, 446
Dublin Docklands Development Authority 19–20
due diligence 344, 347–8, 497–501
Dunnes Stores 23, 60, 267
Dyson vacuum cleaners 286

e-commerce 182, 224, 237, 400
earnings per share (ratio) 218
Eastman Kodak 86, 184, 283
economic risk 297
economic structure (industry) 176–8
economies of scale 176, 180, 185, 208, 224, 266, 270, 289, 294, 299, 300, 302
education 146, 164–5, 170, 171, 285
efficiency *see* operational efficiency
Eir 311, 344
Electricity Supply Board (ESB) 20–21
ESB International 336
electronic data interchange 209, 212
emergent strategy development 17, 21–5, 76
emerging markets 294, 296
emigration 54, 170, 429

568